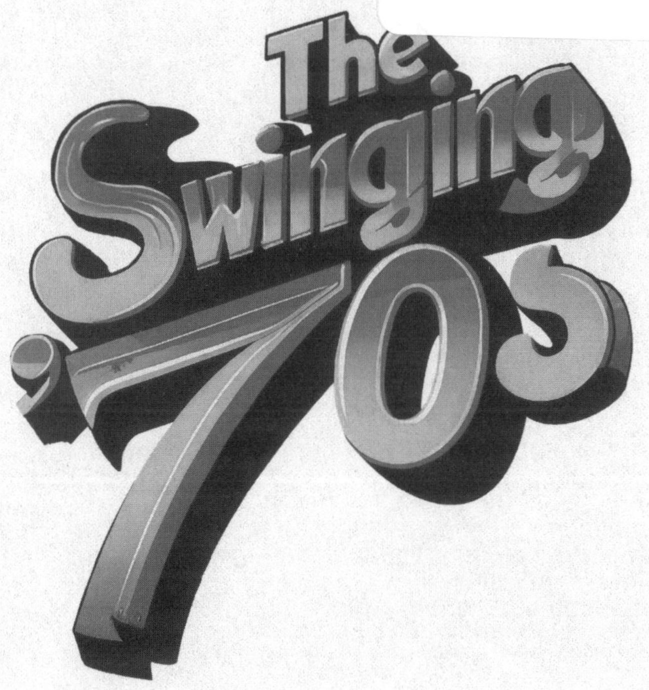

Stars, Style and Substance in Hindi Cinema

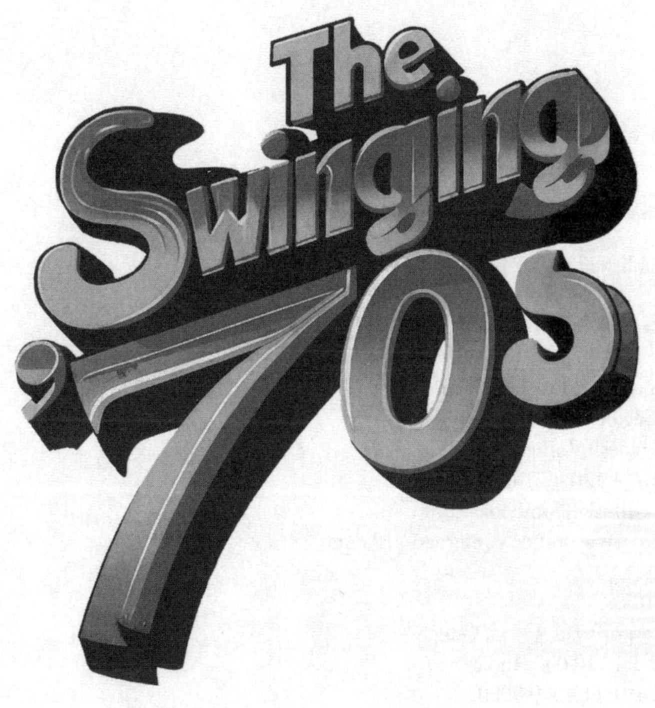

Stars, Style and Substance in Hindi Cinema

Edited by
Nirupama Kotru
Shantanu Ray Chaudhuri

Om Books International

First published in 2024 by

Om Books International

Corporate & Editorial Office
A-12, Sector 64, Noida 201 301
Uttar Pradesh, India
Phone: +91 120 477 4100
Email: editorial@ombooks.com
Website: www.ombooksinternational.com

Sales Office
107, Ansari Road, Darya Ganj,
New Delhi 110 002, India
Phone: +91 11 4000 9000
Email: sales@ombooks.com
Website: www.ombooks.com

ISBN: 978-81-19750-47-4

Printed in India

10 9 8 7 6 5 4 3 2 1

In loving memory of my mother, Mrs Rama Kotru....
And also for my kids Tanya and Neil – this book is for you.
You inspire me.

– Nirupama Kotru

For Shashwata, who has introduced me to the films he grew up on – MCU and Harry Potter – and to whom I hope to introduce the cinema that I watched growing up; to Panchali and my parents, with whom I have watched many of these films; and to my brother Atanu, for hours of discussions on these films and their music

– Shantanu Ray Chaudhuri

Contents

Preface: Nirupama Kotru xiii
Introduction: Shantanu Ray Chaudhuri xxiii

Trivia Quiz: Harini Srinivasan and Vinod Krishnan

SECTION I
Moods and Memories

Nishant: '*A Very Negative Film*' 3
Amitava Kumar

Bachchanpur to Ghataknagar: *A Family Trip through the 1970s* 12
Shamya Dasgupta

North by South-East: *How We Found Bombay in Madras* 21
Krishna Shastri Devulapalli

How to Listen to Films before Watching Them: *Memories of a Prakash Mehra–Amitabh Bachchan Audiocassette* 30
Jai Arjun Singh

First Day, First Show: *The Big-Screen Movie-Watching Experience of the 1970s* 39
Diptakirti Chaudhuri

How My Grandmother Came to Love Hindi Cinema and Amitabh Bachchan: *Memories of Another Day* 50
Shantanu Ray Chaudhuri

The Cassettes Revolution in India: *How the Seventies Changed the Way We Listened to Music* 64
Bobby Sing

The Broken Melody: *A Personal Nostalgia of the Seventies Lyrics* 75
Varun Grover

SECTION II
Icons and Idols

Shyam Benegal: *The Reason I Write on Cinema* 87
Aseem Chhabra

Sanjeev Kumar: *Jisey Dil Dhoondta Hai* 96
Gajra Kottary

Zeenat Aman: *More than the Body* 105
Kaveree Bamzai

Hrishikesh Mukherjee: *The Man Who Made the Stars Brighter* 116
Raja Sen

From Bharat Kumar to *Beimaan* and Back: *Manoj Kumar's Fabulous Box Office Run in the 1970s* 124
Nirupama Kotru

Amol Palekar: *Hindi Cinema's Extraordinarily Ordinary Common Man* 136
Amitava Nag

The Cinema of the Big Four: *Manmohan Desai, Prakash Mehra, Yash Chopra, Ramesh Sippy* 144
Alaka Sahani

The Amar Akbar Anthony of Writers: *Kader Khan, K.K. Shukla and Prayag Raaj, and the Seventies Blockbuster* 154
S.M.M. Ausaja

The King of Melody: *R.D. Burman and the Transitional Early 1970s* 161
Anirudha Bhattacharjee

Rajesh Khanna: *A Star Like No Other* 171
Deepa Gahlot

Dharmendra: *He-Man and Master of the Universe* 181
Roshmila Bhattacharya

R.D. Burman, 1970s: *The Master of Masala Excess as Global Musician* 191
Kaushik Bhaumik

Gulzar: *A Poet in Cinema* 208
Shantanu Ray Chaudhuri

Raakhee: *Beauty Unparalleled, Actor Nonpareil* 252
Shantanu Ray Chaudhuri

The Girl Next Door and Other Divas: *Women in Hindi Cinema of the Seventies* 258
Ratnottama Sengupta

Anand Bakshi: *The Common Man's Poet and Philosopher* 278
Shantanu Ray Chaudhuri

Laxmikant–Pyarelal: *Mass Music, Class Act* 287
Deepa Buty

'Kahaan Hai Re Doosra?': *Amitabh's Jodidaars in Films of the Seventies and Eighties* 296
Nirupama Kotru

SECTION III
Themes and Tropes

A Tale of Two Vijays: *Violence in Hindi Cinema of the 1970s – From Salim–Javed to Vijay Tendulkar* 307
Amborish Roychoudhury

You Sharrup! Sharrup You!: *The Missus, The Moll and Everyone In-between* 319
Nandini Ramnath

Twinkle Twinkle Little Stars: *Flirting with Stardom* 329
Avijit Ghosh

Well Begun: *Opening Credits in Seventies Hindi Cinema* 345
Uday Bhatia

Good Flops, Bad Flops and *Shalimar*: *The Anatomy of the Box Office* 352
Nirupama Kotru

Looking Through the Keyhole!: *Film Journalism in the 1970s* 365
Sathya Saran

'Kya Khoob Lagti Ho': *The Costumes and Style Statement of Seventies Hindi Cinema* 376
Niyati Bhat

The Seventies: Hindi Cinema's Defining Decade: *Eloquence of Extremes, Rigour of Fresher Forms* 390
Amrit Gangar

Looking the Star in the Eye: *The Everyman Avatar of Superstars* 403
Gautam Chintamani

The Bards of Bombay: *Songwriters of the Seventies* 410
Mira Hashmi

Fat Lady: *Feminism and Desire in Hindi Cinema of the Seventies* 423
Maitreyee B. Chowdhury

A Few Bad Men: *Villains in Hindi Cinema of the Seventies* 430
Balaji Vittal

Conjuring a Different Beat: *Parallel Cinema's High Noon* 441
Maithili Rao

From Gungi Gudiya to Maa Durga: *The Evolution of Indian Cinema in the 1970s – A Cultural Tapestry of Revolution and Renaissance* 450
Vinta Nanda

SECTION IV

Insiders' Insights

Languages, Learning, Theatre and Films: *A Conversation* 463
Dr Mohan Agashe

Storyteller Extraordinaire: *A Conversation* 478
Subhash Ghai

'I Came to the Industry Because of Gulzar Sa'ab': *Memories of Cinema of the Seventies* 494
Vishal Bhardwaj

Duvidha: *Mani's Dilemma* 505
Rajat Kapoor

Guilty Pleasures: *The Masala Entertainers of the Seventies* 513
Sriram Raghavan

A Turning Point: *The Beginning of a New Wave* 522
Ketan Mehta

SECTION V
End-credits

Twenty-Twenty: *The Ones that Made It* 533
Nirupama Kotru

Notes on Contributors 551

Acknowledgements: Nirupama Kotru 566

In Gratitude: Shantanu Ray Chaudhuri 569

Preface

Nirupama Kotru

Serendipity and passion. These are the two factors responsible for bringing Shantanu and me together for this book. Shantanu found me through Facebook, invited me to an event in April 2022, the release of film-maker Suman Ghosh's book on Soumitra Chatterjee, and boom! A week later we were discussing this book. Who says social media is a waste of time? Those days I was obsessed with a project on Balraj Sahni which I mentioned to Shantanu in the hope that he would help me trace the copyrights of the original books. After exchanging umpteen notes about the Balraj Sahni project, during the course of one of our chats Shantanu asked me, 'Hey, would you like to co-edit an anthology with me? I've been thinking about writing one on the cinema of the seventies, because if we don't document this period, it will vanish.'

My reaction was 'My God! *Neki aur pooch pooch*!'(That expression cannot be translated into Queen's English, so let's go with the American: 'You're kidding me, right?'). The brainstorming started immediately thereafter, despite both of us having very hectic schedules – our full-time jobs, Shantanu's professional writing commitments, work-related travel, packed weekends, etc. And both of us had some domestic crisis or the other – somebody falling ill, somebody leaving the country, a death in the family, and so on and so forth. Luckily we pulled through.

As for passion, Shantanu has amply demonstrated his, through his writings on cinema, and through all the film books by other authors that he has commissioned, some of which have won National Awards. My film writing is more recent. I started writing on cinema in 2015, after leaving the Ministry of Information and Broadcasting, where I was Director (Films) for three years, in charge of the film production units, viz., the NFDC, Films Division of India and Children's Film Society of India, the film training institutes (FTII and SRFTI), censorship and film policy matters, promotion of films through festivals in India and abroad, and other exciting stuff. But my passion for films goes back to my childhood.

My earliest memory of myself is from LKG (Lower Kindergarten) in Mount Carmel School, Lucknow. My father had been transferred to the city shortly after my birth. My teacher had noticed me keeping my head down and singing '*Inhi yodon ne*' (lispy version of '*Inhi logon ne*') while dangling my short legs from the tiny, colourful wooden chairs that were typically found in our schools in the 1970s, and mentioned this to my father. That's how I found my voice. Like many other kids of my generation, I started singing before I could speak complete sentences. *Pakeezah* (1972) had come home to the city in which it had been set, and Lucknow had gone crazy. My parents would ask me to keep quiet in the hall and I meekly complied. For three hours in the darkness of that theatre, I was mesmerized. Mayfair cinema hall in Hazratganj wore a festive air for months on end. Watching *Pakeezah* in Lucknow, followed by having a Tutty-Fruity ice cream sundae in Kwality restaurant next door was a treat to beat all treats.

Sholay (1975) was the next memorable film that my family watched – twice in Lucknow and twice in Delhi. My father was transferred back to Delhi midway through the film's run, perhaps the longest ever in the history of cinema. And then the magical dual LP record came home. I played the red-coloured record which contained only the dialogues (perhaps the highest selling LP record of dialogues ever) so many times that to date I can rattle off Basanti's dialogues verbatim. Or those of Gabbar Singh, Jai, Veeru, Thakur, Jailor, Soorma Bhopali, Imam sa'ab and even Ramu Kaka.

Kashmir has had a rather intimate connection with Hindi cinema right from the time Raj Kapoor shot the song '*Hawa men udhta jaye*' from *Barsaat* (1949) on location. Saira Banu made her debut here opposite Shammi Kapoor in *Junglee* (1961). While Sharmila Tagore played a *Kashmir Ki Kali* in Shakti Samanta's 1964 film by the same name, Shashi Kapoor playing a shikarawallah in *Jab Jab Phool Khile* (1965). Notable films starring Rajesh Khanna and Mumtaz shot here in the seventies include *Aap Ki Kasam* (1974) and *Roti* (1974). Shankaracharya temple of Srinagar and the meadows of Gulmarg are instantly recognizable in the song '*Jai Jai Shiv Shankar*' from *Aap Ki Kasam*. A number of Amitabh Bachchan starrers were shot in Kashmir, including Yash Chopra's *Kabhi Kabhie* (1976) which was filmed on location at the iconic Oberoi Palace Hotel now run by Lalit group that overlooks the Dal Lake. Parts of *Mr Natwarlal* (1979) were shot in Pahalgam. The superstar returned to Kashmir to shoot *Laawaris* in 1981 (the Oberoi Palace and Shalimar/Nishat Gardens were used in key scenes and songs) and *Satte Pe Satta* the next year, for which a set was created in Sonmarg. You also had the actor extolling the virtues of the valley with co-star Raakhee in the song '*Yeh Kashmir hai*' (*Bemisaal*, 1982). The honeymoon continued till the late eighties when the sudden spurt of terrorist attacks on civilians made shooting too risky.

The Kashmiri Pandit (KP) community that I was born into had a largely conservative attitude towards cinema until recently, notwithstanding the odd export we sent to Bombay in the seventies like our Srinagar acquaintances Onkar Nath Aima (*Zanjeer*, 1973). His son Alok Aima and nephew Satish Kaul followed him soon thereafter. The Rainas, MK and KK, took the theatre route to enter films, following *pravasi* KP pioneers of theatre A.K. Hangal and

Om Shivpuri. Omkar Nath Dhar, aka Jeevan, and Kulbhushan Pandit, aka Raaj Kumar, had already established themselves as actors of repute much before. Auteur Mani Kaul made a mark as a director in the seventies, as did the talented Awtar Krishna Kaul whose life was cut tragically short in a drowning accident, hours before the announcement of the National Film Awards for the year 1974. His brilliant debut feature film *27 Down* won Best Feature Film in Hindi as well as Best Cinematography for A.K. Bir's work.

My extended family were avid film buffs, though. My sisters and I would visit Srinagar every summer vacation, which was when stars from Bombay would also descend upon the valley. I remember an amusing incident from the seventies, which has become part of family folklore. We were on a day trip to Pahalgam when we learnt that Manmohan Desai's *Roti* (1974) was being shot nearby. The song being picturized was '*Yeh jo public hai*', and there was a lady standing with her back to us, who was part of the shot. My uncle, in response to his wife's query about who the lady was, said, 'She's an "extra" (as junior artists were then called).' Quick came the retort from the lady in question: '*Extra hogi teri maa*!'

'On another occasion, Raaj Kumar, an avid horse rider, was enjoying some quiet time on a horse in Pahalgam, possibly during an extended shooting break. As he dismounted, my teenaged cousin approached him for an autograph, with trepidation. His response, delivered in that perfect *Pakeezah* baritone, reinforced my poor cousin's fear: 'Jaao, chane khao!' (Run along, young lad. Don't bother me.)

It was quite unthinkable in my growing years for a KP girl to consider acting as a profession, but the community seemed to briefly relax its rigid norms for the great showman Raj Kapoor. A pretty, light-eyed cousin of mine was chosen for a brief appearance in a scene of *Bobby* along with some of her friends. When it was finally released in 1973, *Bobby* went on to become a huge hit in Kashmir. There was a poor man who went quite mad after watching *Bobby* a record twenty times or more. One could find him muttering, 'I'm Bobby, *mujhse dosti karoge*?' outside Palladium cinema hall in Srinagar for months.

My favourite memory of a shoot in Srinagar is at the turn of the decade, when we kids were taken to Oberoi (Lalit) Palace by my father as a special treat, to watch Hrishikesh Mukherjee shoot his film *Bemisaal* (released in 1982). The scene was set in a restaurant. Some tables and chairs were set around the famous Chinar tree in Oberoi gardens, the very same one under which Mahatma Gandhi once sat, and under which the hotel now runs a restaurant-cum-bar. The director offered my dad (and us) an opportunity to join the set as customers in the restaurant, an offer my father refused politely. We were so excited that I remember us cousins fanning out in the garden to collect autographs. The boldest one approached the superstar: Amitabh Bachchan.

That was the day I experienced up close the magic of make-up. The superstar appeared rather dark when we first saw him emerge from this room in a bright yellow pullover. A short break later, he looked all fair and red-lipped, and ready for the camera. Vinod Mehra came out from another room wearing a rather healthy shade of pink, with his doting wife Bindiya Goswami fussing over him with a '*Mere sona, sona*'. I was given the task of approaching Raakhee. Hesitating, I did so with my autograph book. She looked through me and turned her head away. My feelings were hurt, but I felt better later when someone mentioned that she was running a high fever on the day of the shoot.

The superstar was in his elements that day. Perhaps it was the great weather; after all, Srinagar in summers used to be delightful those days, one didn't even need a fan. Or perhaps he was putting on a show for the benefit of his young admirers who were close enough to hear every single word he said. When Raakhee walked into the designated area, he said, 'Here comes the Bengal tigress!'

Suddenly it started drizzling. Hrishi-da said, in a typical Bengali accent, 'This place is zinxed!'

Pat came the retort from Amitabh, 'It is not zin-xed as in zinc oxide, it is jinxed!'

If Hrishi-da was offended, he didn't show any signs of the same. I honestly believe that what we had witnessed was something special – a great director who had an excellent rapport with one of his favourite actors, enjoying some light-hearted banter while preparing for an intense scene. It is believed that Hrishi-da once told Amitabh, 'Omit (Amit), acting *karna ho toh mere paas aa jana.*'

The scene was completed after a brief interruption. It's a scene where a customer passes a lewd comment about Raakhee, suggesting that she is in a relationship with two men at the same time. Amitabh, who is about to eat a pakora, summons a waiter, makes him hang on to the snack, and proceeds to bash the hell out of the rude customer. He nonchalantly picks up the pakora after the fight, takes a bite and says, '*Achha hai, naram hai.*' Did that dialogue have a layered meaning? You tell me. All I know is that *Bemisaal* is one of my favourite films of Amitabh Bachchan for reasons more than one.

But I digress. Let me go back to telling you about how the book happened.

Getting the writers on board was good fun. My connection with film writers actually goes back to my Information and Broadcasting days, 2012 to 2015. I reached out to all my friends. Some of them had other commitments and some weren't sure what they should write about. But the ones who came on board are great fun; I hope you enjoy their writing as much as I do. There are film critics who are also authors of well-received books, like Jai Arjun Singh (*Jaane Bhi Do Yaaro*, *The World of Hrishikesh Mukherjee*), Uday Bhatia (*Bullets over Bombay*) and Raja Sen (*The Best Baker in the World*). The remarkable thing is although these three writers are almost a decade younger than Shantanu and me, they are really passionate about films of that decade and their love for that cinema shines through their writing. The next lot is the power ladies – again, people I love chatting about cinema with. Nandini Ramnath, editor of *Scroll*, sharp and incisive, for whom I been writing articles for many years now. Ratnottama Sengupta, or Ratna-di, a friend since my I&B days and a respected name in art and film writing. Kaveree Bamzai, a fellow Kashmiri Pandit, whose writing is always great fun. There's Aseem Chhabra, whose books on Shashi Kapoor and Irrfan are notable. Then of course Shantanu and my common acquaintances like Anirudha Bhattacharjee and Balaji Vittal, both of whom have day jobs which have nothing to do with films, and yet produced a National Award–winning book. Others acclaimed authors and writers joined along, like Shamya Dasgupta, Amborish Roychoudhury, Krishna Shastri, Gautam Chintamani, Avijit Ghosh and Gajra Kottary, among others. As Majrooh said:

Main akela hi chala tha janib-e-manzil magar,
Log saath aate gaye, aur karwan banta gaya

(I had set out alone for my destination
But people kept joining me, and the caravan kept growing)

But the coup d'état, the feather in my cap as far as getting eminent authors on board, was commissioning Amitava Kumar to write for us. How it happened was truly exciting.

I first met Amitava at an event in April 2022 in Delhi. We got along immediately and parted with a promise to meet in Poughkeepsie soon after, where he teaches in a renowned liberal arts college (Vassar). Coincidently, my daughter was finishing her bachelor's degree from the same college and my son was about to join it. As luck would have it, not only was Amitava in town when I visited Poughkeepsie a month later for my daughter's convocation, but he graciously played local host for a day. He took me around to see the mighty Hudson river. As we were walking along the windy walkway on the Hudson, he told me about the history of the place, whaling on the Hudson, and about his sundry artist friends who had visited Poughkeepsie. He showed me all the vantage points. We started chatting about what I was preoccupied with, and I told him about this book on cinema of the seventies that I was planning to co-edit. Suddenly he pulled this picture out of his phone and asked me, 'Have you seen this pic?' It was a black-

and-white pic someone had shared on Twitter (now X), which had a young Shyam Benegal posing on the *Côte d'Azur* with Shabana Azmi and Smita Patil, a promo for his film *Nishant* (1975),which was in competition for the Palme d'Or at the Cannes film Festival, 1976.

I replied, 'Yes, of course I have seen it.'

We discussed Vijay Tendulkar's Hindi film screenplays and he finally said, 'So, what do you think?'

And I said, 'Yes, please! Write about *Nishant*!'

And that was that. One month later, I sent him a book on Vijay Tendulkar, a special NSD publication and in return he delivered a beautiful essay in my email on *Nishant*, well within the impossible deadline we gave him, because that's what professional writers do!

There was so much to write. We kept coming up with ideas and rejecting them. There was a very funny take on income tax in films. Jai had told me about this hilarious albeit brief scene in Basu Chatterjee's *Chhoti Si Baat* (1976), where Amitabh Bachchan asks Colonel Julius Nagendranath Wilfred Singh (Ashok Kumar) about some income tax advice. The scene was a good starting point for an essay, but I soon realized I had gone off track, and had started dwelling upon actual investigations by the Income Tax Department into the film industry because I had worked in Bombay in the nineties, and had been part of some of those searches ('raids' as they are called in popular parlance). That track would have distracted from our theme, so I abandoned it. I did want to talk about one of my favourite films, which is unfortunately branded as a flop: *Shalimar*.

Shantanu and I were conscious of the fact that there is a certain arrogance that creeps into the writing of most film critics and reviewers who tend to look down upon directors and actors with a mass appeal, including Manoj Kumar and Subhash Ghai. Having both of them in the book was therefore important to us to fix this bias. We have also included music director duo Laxmikant–Pyarelal, whose contribution to music has been dismissed perfunctorily by some venerable film writers.

Discovering that Shantanu was a fanboy of Amitabh Bachchan, like my husband, was fun. He said, '*Main toh likhoonga*,' and I said, '*Likhiye na*!'

I can't thank my friends from the film industry enough for sparing time from their crazy-busy shooting, pre- and post-production schedules for this book. These uber-talented film-makers are also affectionate and caring. Rajat Kapoor and I had a fun chat about films of seventies. I told him about a film I had watched on TV when the book was in the making, *Hawas* (1974), which was directed, as per the credits, by one Saawan Kumar. He said, 'Do you know who that is? It is Sawan Kumar Tak!' (Less than a week later, Sawan Kumar Tak passed away. Uncanny.) Rajat added, 'Give me time, I will write about a film I like.' I asked him which one, and he said, '*Duvidha*.' I jumped! '*Duvidha*! I love that film! It's so unlike Mani Kaul's other films. So stunning and so beautiful. The leading lady Raisa was Alyque Padamsee's niece!' Enthused by my response, Rajat grinned and agreed. (Nandini had watched *Hawas* for her piece and agreed that it was a pulp classic.)

Vishal Bhardwaj, who is a dear friend and a fellow foodie, agreed to write. And since Vishal and I are Gulzar sahab's *mureeds*, Vishal decided to write about a Gulzar film he loves (*Aandhi*, 1975). Gulzar sahab himself was reluctant to do so and said, 'Vishal *keh denge jo bhi kehna hoga*.' Eventually, Vishal spoke about more than *Aandhi*. Sriram Raghavan was very kind to agree to write for our book, even as he was burning the candle on both ends, working on his film *Merry Christmas* (2024) and simultaneously writing another script. I reached out to the redoubtable Ketan Mehta rather late, in February 2023, and his response was an affectionate, '*Haq se mango*.' Varun Grover contributed a personal nostalgia piece about a time before he was born. (We are all suffering from *sehnsucht*, Varun.) I am grateful to Subhash Ghai and his daughter Meghna for their warmth and generosity. I interviewed Ghai in his institute, Whistling Woods, perhaps the only credible institute of film-making in the country which is not funded by the government. Dr Mohan Agashe shared his own perspective of how Marathi theatre and literature contributed to parallel cinema of that decade. Being neck deep in professional commitments, Vidhu Vinod Chopra and Raju Hirani couldn't make the time, but have sweetly endorsed the book.

We bring to you all these different perspectives about this wonderful decade – some are thematic, some are mood pieces, and some try to decode the art and craft of a particular film. Whether you agree with us or not about this decade being a good one for Hindi cinema, we hope that by the end of this book, you will agree with us that it was a remarkable decade. As Saeed Mirza sa'ab, who was the first person I brainstormed with as soon as I said 'Yes' to Shantanu, put it, 'The period 1973 to 1983 was one of the best in Hindi cinema because it was a unique time when three kinds of cinema happily co-existed and flourished – commercial cinema, parallel cinema, and middle-of-the-road-cinema.' Unfortunately, Saeed sa'ab was busy with his own writing commitments, but he conveyed his blessings and wrote a touching blurb.

This book is about the decade of the seventies – the music, the stars, the directors, the scripts. And stories. Storytelling, as you will realize when you read these essays, was the mainstay of this decade. Which is why you remember these stories; why you end up watching them again and again. Every time a retro film plays on television, chances are that if it is a seventies film, you will watch it till the end. Every time a retro song plays on the radio, chances are it will be an R.D. Burman song from the era. So we bring to you this labour of love. I hope you enjoy reading as much enjoyed putting it together. Thank you.

Introduction

Shantanu Ray Chaudhuri

Anemoia. Nostalgia for a time or place one has never known. That is what this book is all about. As I write in my essay on Amitabh Bachchan and my grandmother, it has been an abiding regret that I was not old enough in the 1970s to experience its cinema first-hand. I lived it in the 1980s. Which is true for a lot of contributors in this volume – who have seen these films primarily on the television in the decades that followed. I was fortunate enough to watch a lot of the films of the decade in the theatres when they released in a particularly lean phase for Hindi cinema in the mid-eighties. However, one of my favourite pastimes is to imagine the crowds who might have thronged to films like *Rajnigandha* or *Amar Prem* or the electric excitement that Amitabh Bachchan's many films might have generated.

I watched *Sholay* in 1977 in a hall in Dimapur, Nagaland (I remember my mother asking my brother and me to cover our eyes as Gabbar Singh is about to chop off Thakur's hands). Or watching *Hera Pheri* in a hall in what turned out to be an exercise in surrealism. Even as a ten-year-old, I knew there was something wrong. I knew that Hindi film heroes and heroines danced. But there was something not quite right in the way Vinod Khanna and Amitabh Bachchan were going about it. For one, there was no song accompanying the sequence. It was in fact a rather dramatic scene they were putting across. I hadn't heard of Luis Bunuel, and so wasn't sure whether a perfectly normal commercial film had suddenly taken a turn for the surreal (not that I was aware of the terms 'commercial cinema' and 'surreal', either, at the time). I did not know of 'break dance' (in fact, Michael Jackson would perform it for the first time only five years later, in 1983). Neither had I seen a 'Nagin' film yet that could provide context to the way the two stars were swaying onscreen. It is only after three minutes of this 'dance' that it dawned on me that Vinod Khanna and Amitabh Bachchan were shifting shape to the rivulets of water running down the screen. It was raining outside. Right through the 1980s and '90s, I spent considerable time at some rather rundown and ramshackle theatres, but this one in Bokajan, Assam, 1978, is right up there.

However, these gave me no idea of the craze that Bachchan's films generated. I would of course witness it live with *Shahenshah* in 1988 or wistfully partake of it when the Big B shared a photo, on X, of the serpentine queue waiting to book tickets for *Don* (which we reproduce in this anthology in Diptakirti's essay). But apart from these, I lived the seventies largely in my imagination. This anthology gives me an opportunity to live the era on page, pay my debt to what the films and the music meant to me growing up in the eighties.

It was fun putting the anthology together with Nirupama Kotru. Deciding on the contributors to approach, going back and forth on the aspects to cover. She brought in her considerable network of contacts – in the industry and in the writing community – that have enriched the book immeasurably. It is with some pride that I look at the contributors here, many of whom have published a number of times with me during my career as an editor. I was fortunate to commission and/or edit the first books of a quite a few of them here, including Krishna Shastri, Balaji Vittal, Anirudha Bhattacharjee, Gautam Chintamani, Jai Arjun Singh, Uday Bhatia, Mira Hashmi, Maithili Rao, Roshmila Bhattacharya, Amitava Nag, among others. And to have had the pleasure of working with writers like Sathya Saran, Avijit Ghosh, Shamya Dasgupta and others on their books. The anthology gave me the opportunity of engaging with a number of writers on my bucket list of authors to work with – Amborish Roychoudhury, Amrit Gangar, Ratnottama Sengupta, Deepa Gahlot, Alaka Sahani (with whom my efforts to do a book have come unstuck a couple of times), Diptakirti Chaudhuri, Gajra Kottary (though I have published her fiction, this is one of her few explorations in the non-fiction format), and many others.

It is impossible to do justice to a decade like the seventies. As Vinta Ninda writes: 'Over the decade, a staggering 4,945 full-length films, averaging 494.5 films annually, graced the screens of the nation's 10,000 cinema halls, captivating millions of viewers. Film production surged from 398 films in 1970 to a staggering 680 in 1979, representing nearly two films completed every single day.' Imagine those numbers. Which other decade offers you this contrast: Shyam Benegal and Manmohan Desai making their best works at the same time. It's the decade that had both *Sholay* and *Shatranj Ke Khilari*. And of course *Jai Santoshi Maa*. It's a decade whose flops too – clangers like *Shalimar* – have a place in the memories of viewers even today (see Nirupama's brilliantly researched essay in this volume). It's the decade that R.D. Burman rewrote musically (Kaushik Bhaumik has an absolute stunner on this, classifying RDB as a global musician); it's also the decade when Kanu Roy and Vanraj Bhatia created some of our most beloved melodies. It's the era when Anand Bakshi made '*Achha toh hum chalte hain*' a catchphrase; it's also the decade that Yogesh wrote the seminal '*Kai baar yunhi dekha hai*'. (See Mira Hashmi's essay on the lyricists and Varun Grover's nostalgic exploration of songs of the seventies.) It's the decade that Shabana Azmi owned with Indian cinema's finest performances; it's also an era that swung to Zeenat Aman's '*Dum maro dum*' (Kaveree Bamzai gives us a wonderful account of this star). The 1970s belonged as much to Amitabh Bachchan as it did to Naseeruddin Shah and Sanjeev Kumar (Gajra Kottary's '*Jisey dil dhundta hai*' is quite an enjoyable take on an young adolescent falling in love with the 'elderly' avatars that this actor essayed, often worrying if he has died), as much to Salim–Javed as to Vijay Tendulkar (see Amborish's fascinating essay here).

We have tried to cover as many aspects of the era as we possibly could. And we let the contributors more or select what they wanted to write on within the themes we had decided we needed to cover. If Jai Arjun waxes eloquent about the audiocassette as his introduction to the cinema of the era, Bobby Sing discusses how the cassette was influential in popularizing the films of the decade. Uday Bhatia does an interesting take on opening credits of films. While Sathya Saran gives us an entertaining take on film journalism in the seventies, Niyati Bhat's is an informative account of the fashion that informed the films. And for those who think that Salim–Javed is all there is to the screenplays and dialogues of the films of the seventies, S.M.M. Ausaja provides an eye-opener with his essay on the criminally neglected trio of Kader Khan, Prayag Raaj and K.K. Shukla, who wrote more films for Amitabh Bachchan than Salim–Javed.

If Krishna Shastri does a, what else, laugh-out-loud take on Hindi films of the era remade in Tamil and Telugu, Nandini Ramnath's is a delightful account of the era's 'dishonourable' filmy women, while Amrit Gangar is characteristically scholarly in his take on the cinema of Mani Kaul and a new aesthetic. Then there are the tributes to the many stalwarts and classics of the era – Dharmendra, Zeenat Aman, Rajesh Khanna, Hrishikesh Mukherjee, Amol Palekar, Sanjeev Kumar, Shyam Benegal and his films, including *Nishant*, and others. A special word of thanks for Harini and Vinod for the 51 trivia quiz questions that are scattered throughout the book. We have divided the book into five segments, keeping with the general direction of the content of the essays in each, though it is possible that the odd essay could easily belong to another section.

We are aware that there are aspects of the cinema of the decade that we have not been able to address. The contribution of Mangesh Desai, for example. Or K.K. Mahajan. We look forward to your inputs that will enable us to add to the volume when we reprint.

It's taken me some time to get this to the finishing line. As much because of my other engagements as also because often one would realize that we had missed out on a star contributor to the decade (like we did Laxmikant-Pyarelal, and literally steamrolled Deepa Buty to submit her insightful essay at the last minute even as the book was being typeset). I would like to thank all the contributors here for their patience and understanding. And for the faith.

Waheeda Rehman was the first choice for the role of Chand, the female protagonist of which 1970 movie starring Sanjeev Kumar? This role was later essayed by Mumtaz who won her first Filmfare Award for Best Actress.

Answer: Khilona

Since Meena Kumari was very ill during the shooting of the long-delayed classic Pakeezah (1972), another actress was brought in as her body double in all the dance sequences. Name the actress.

Answer: Padma Khanna

Section I

Moods and Memories

He starred in a cult Hindi spy action film which released in 1977; he has been credited in movies with three different variations of his name. After seventeen movies as an actor and one movie as a director in the early 1980s, his fledgling career in the movies ended and he began his next phase as a real estate agent. Who is he?

Answer: Mahendra Sandhu

Asha Bhosle won the Best Playback Singer Award in 1975 for this song which did not make it to the final cut of the movie. Evocative and poignant, this signalled the end of a fruitful personal and professional partnership for Bhosle. Identify the song and movie.

Answer: *Chain se humko kabhi* (*Praan Jaaye par Vachan na jaaye*, 1974)

Nishant

'A Very Negative Film'

Amitava Kumar

This cannot have been my experience alone.

You too could have watched a film, say, forty or fifty years ago. You remember only two or three scenes from it, but those scenes are deeply etched in your memory.

I was in the audience each afternoon for a few days in the early 1980s at Pragati Maidan for a retrospective of Shyam Benegal's films. Sitting in the dark in Hamsadhwani Theatre, I remember watching *Ankur* first, then *Nishant*, followed by *Manthan*, and then *Bhumika*.

This piece is about *Nishant*.

I never forgot Shabana Azmi's walk when she steps out to shop. This is fairly early in the film. In that scene, only a few seconds long, that manner of walking conveyed a sense of abandon. It made its own kind of music. Nothing terrible had yet happened to this character. I can imagine the director telling the actor that because soon she would be kidnapped, and be forced to spend most of the film in bondage, this walk would be her last chance to show the viewer that she was once free.

I never forgot the zamindar played by Amrish Puri, in particular the physical way in which he imposed his presence on the screen. When he spoke, his tone was harsh and yet there was a lot of control. It was as if there was so much power in his words that he didn't need to waste any energy on a wild display of aggressiveness.

How often in the decades that followed I would recall a single statement of the zamindar delivered to his younger brother as a homily about keeping women and emotions separate. '*Aurat and jazbaat … Yeh dono alag-alag cheezan hain.*' (Woman and emotions … they are two separate entities.) This line had been delivered from patriarchy's pulpit; I would tell myself that this was the sermon that one had to sin against.

A third scene I didn't forget was one that showed the Girish Karnad character, a schoolteacher, reading a book in bed. Karnad wore a white vest and dhoti; that is how my father dressed at home. His little son is asleep next to him. The schoolteacher's handsome looks, not to mention the pencil moustache and the short, wavy hair, were like my father's in his younger days. Even the plainness of the room, a few family pictures on the wall, a nail from which the wristwatch hung when not in use, the cheap whitewash, resembled what was familiar to us from our visits to our family's homestead in Champaran.

However, there was no joy in this recognition because it seemed to me that my father, with his faith in institutions of government, would also, just like the Karnad character, make futile rounds of offices in an attempt to save his kidnapped wife and would be met everywhere with indifference and contempt. I wasn't thinking so much of my father and his imagined impotence; instead, whether in a sentimental way or not, I was thinking of my mother and my sisters, whom I had seen subjected to catcalls and harassment on Patna's streets.

The script for *Nishant* was written by the very talented Vijay Tendulkar. Women in his powerful plays are often only victims. I didn't know this then but it didn't matter because my own sense of the world at that time, ignorant of any real, meaningful interactions with women, didn't go beyond that of a frightened, bookish youth.

Before going any further, I suppose I should offer here a synopsis of the film.

The setting for *Nishant* is a village in Telangana in pre-independence India; the milieu is feudal and the brutality of this setting is brought alive through the men in the landlord's family. The poor are their property and women are treated like chattel. In this feudal scenario arrives a schoolteacher with his wife and child. (The late novelist John Gardner once said that there are only two kinds of stories: a man goes on a journey, or a stranger comes to town.) The schoolteacher's pretty wife attracts the youngest brother and, to please him, and maybe also to tease him, his older brothers abduct the schoolteacher's wife. The film portrays the kidnapped woman's terrible trials. And then, in a slow but climactic build-up, the violent uprising of the villagers against the oppressive feudals.

That is the skeletal outline of the story. At the time that I first watched *Nishant* I hadn't become a writer. I very badly wanted to be one. My heart was hungry for realism in art. Benegal and Tendulkar offered exactly that in *Nishant*; Shama Zaidi's art direction meant that there were several details, in the décor we saw in the landlord's house and even his car, that were true to the period in which the film was set. Early in the film, Susheela, the schoolteacher's wife, washes her little son's bum while pouring water from a copper pot. My grandmother would do the same when I visited our village home as boy of four or five. This was embarrassing to recall, yes, but the scene was familiar to me. No Hindi film, escapist to the core, would have ever shown such a thing.

Nishant also has a more sophisticated kind of realism. Anna (Amrish Puri) is the oldest in the zamindar's family; he has younger brothers, two debauched rogues, Prasad (Mohan Agashe) and Anjaiya (Anant Nag), and also the youngest, Vishwam (Naseeruddin Shah) who, bringing nuance to the story, is inhibited and even shy. The creation of the Vishwam character is a stroke of genius. His older brothers are plainly evil but Vishwam presents a complication. Crucially, he is married. His young wife, Rukmini, played with great confidence by Smita Patil in her debut role in cinema, is critical of the animality displayed by the older brothers. Vishwam and Rukmini are complicit in what happens in the landlord's haveli, of course, but they also stand apart as witnesses and because of this the story is able to breathe. We are not locked in a strict binary; instead, we are caught in a rich human drama.

I'm trying to remember the short poems or stories I was beginning to write then. Did I understand what Tendulkar had done in *Nishant*? The film didn't just present a portrayal of barbaric men and oppressed women; it was also an account of a tussle between men of different kinds. Any viewer would have responded to it, I believe.

Even all women aren't the same. There is an extraordinary sequence of scenes in which we meet a young peasant woman who doesn't utter a word. At first, we watch Prasad and Anjaiya telling a shareholder who is toiling in the field to send his wife to the haveli in the evening. The wife occupies the frame too, saying nothing. We see the young woman later, putting on her clothes in Anna's room. Then she appears, a trapped animal in the flickering light, in that part of the house where Prasad and Anjaiya are drinking. We have just learned that Anjaiya's wife has left him and Prasad's wife died after she threw herself into a well. All of this is striking and brutal but what is truly remarkable is that the young peasant woman before them hasn't spoken a word. And despite this, how eloquent is her presence, her face! A valuable lesson there about making silence speak.

The two principal female characters, however oppressed, shone because they were not silent. Even in the opening scene, Rukmini begins with a complaint. She asks her husband Vishvam, 'Where were you all night?' She is unable to sleep well. (Her husband was out with his brothers, stealing the jewels from the village temple.) It is the same with Susheela. She is full of complaints about her circumstances. The pitiful village, the condition of the house, the door that needs repair, her husband's forgetfulness. How charming is her reprimand to her husband – why does he keep telling her to stop eating paan, when, instead, he ought to remember to tell the carpenter to repair the damn door?

Susheela is still unaware of the terrible fate that awaits her. We are too. For the moment, we are caught up in her charm and the drama of her desires. In bed, she tells her husband that for a long time she has been asking for a big mirror. Their conversation takes a flirtatious tone. The schoolteacher gives in and agrees to the mirror the next time he goes to Warangal. Now, Susheela adds to her demands. She wants a sari too. The husband can't say no. He also wants something from her, right then, in bed. It is a seductive dance. Things are soon going to go wrong. Susheela will be forcibly carried away by men whom she will call beasts. Her husband will go from pillar to post, trying to find a way to rescue his wife. Nothing will work. One day, he will be at the temple, sleeping, when his wife will be brought there by the car belonging to her kidnapper. Here, once again, the outraged female doesn't remain silent when asked by her timid husband the simple question, 'How are you?' She has a few questions of her own. 'How does it matter to you? I was abducted in front of you and you didn't say one word … You are asking me how I am?'

When the schoolteacher protests, saying that he did everything in his power, Susheela lashes out with even greater fury. It is a stunning rebuttal. I'm going to quote her words in full, partly because they are so powerful, but partly also because they overturn the theory that all the women in Tendulkar's work are victims. The truth is that Susheela's words act as the pivot of change. They act as an incendiary provocation and spark the revolution that follows in the film. Here is what she says to her husband after he asserts that he has done his best:

> You did your best? Like hell you did! Did you try to find out what my condition is? I'm a kept woman of those scoundrels in the haveli. I am being treated like an animal.

> Every time they were hungry they came. But I sat there thinking you would free me some day. But you seem to not care. And then you claim you did your best. You should have set the haveli on fire. You should have axed them all. You need to be a man to do that. You seem to have no shame. You coward!

Everything in the film follows such a wonderful arc. We are introduced to the villainy of the landlords, the way in which Susheela becomes an object of desire for Vishwam, the abduction and rape, and then, the negotiations through which Susheela fights for a few rights in the house where she is being held. There is a complexity at every turn. Nothing is reductive or too simplistic. Even the radicalization of the illiterate peasantry follows a classical leftist line. I had forgotten this bit but recently, when I watched *Nishant* again, I discovered it contained a bit of Brechtian theatre. The village priest, played by Satyadev Dubey, erupts in anger during a performance of an epic play: he does this in response to the laughter of the villagers after the villain in the play lies down on the ground and dies. The priest asks what is funny in the situation and then adds, 'You forget if it is a crime to do injustice, it is an even bigger crime to endure injustice.' It isn't difficult at that point to anticipate the revolt of the masses.

A couple of years before his death, I went to meet Vijay Tendulkar in his home in Mumbai. In my mind, I was going to pay tribute to a writer I admired and from whom I had learned a few things. When I asked him about his making as a writer and artist, Tendulkar told me that when he was forty, he had been awarded a two-year Nehru Fellowship to research what he had titled 'Emerging Patterns of Violence and Its Impact on Literature'. This was in 1972–73. He went everywhere in India, especially Bihar, my home state. Equipped with a tape recorder and two cameras, Tendulkar tried to get a sense of ordinary life. He spent time with tribals. He roamed in rural areas as well as mofussil towns. He travelled to the border. He visited jails and attended trials. He didn't write a single word towards his thesis. But, he said, every bit of creative writing that he did afterward had 'a genuine complexity of experienced reality'.

At some point in our conversation, we started talking about *Nishant*. I told Tendulkar some of what I have described above, the elements I admired in the film. There was a degree of irritability in his response. Even annoyance. He began by saying that his career in scriptwriting 'wasn't a happy one. It was a trying one.' He felt Benegal had softened the blow that Tendulkar had wanted the film to deliver. He had wanted more blood at the end.

When Vishwam and Susheela are killed by the villagers, Tendulkar said he wanted the audience to know that Susheela was carrying Vishwam's child. There was a bit of history there. Tendulkar said that he had heard the story of abduction in Telangana. A schoolteacher's wife had been kidnapped and this had lit the spark of an uprising against feudal rule there. A man was narrating the story from the past to Tendulkar, and this man had said that 'when the youngest brother and the teacher's wife were killed, it was sunset'. This impressed Tendulkar. He told me, 'That single visual stayed with me. All the time, I could see a gory climax to the film. It had to be that way. It couldn't be bloodless.'

There was no occasion for me to return to that particular part of the conversation with Tendulkar till I began to write this piece. I decided to call Shyam Benegal himself and talk about the making of *Nishant*. Benegal said that the germ of the idea for the film had come from an incident that had taken place during his childhood in Andhra. When Benegal told him about the idea, Tendulkar traveled to Telangana. Tendulkar was 'such a wonderful researcher' that he found some of the people who had been witnesses to the incident – the kidnapping of the schoolteacher's wife and the insurrection that followed. I asked Benegal about the process of writing the script. The film-maker said that Tendulkar was a master of structure. Benegal said that when he explained what he wanted, Tendulkar would listen 'very quietly, without ever making notes' and then he would come a back with a dramatic narrative that had 'a beginning, a middle, and an end. It was extraordinary.'

When the film was being shot, in the early months of 1975, both Tendulkar and Satyadev Dubey, who worked on the dialogue, were there on the sets with Benegal. I brought up the criticism that Tendulkar had levelled against him. Benegal said in response that Tendulkar had 'tremendous skills as a playwright' and he knew 'how to create drama' but he also had a 'tendency towards melodrama'. This is something that Benegal said he didn't want. Of course, melodrama was the standard fare in Hindi cinema and Benegal also recognized that Tendulkar had his roots in Marathi theatre where melodrama flourished. Benegal said, 'It became a matter of friction between him and me. Eventually he felt that I hadn't done justice to his work.'

Even as Benegal and I were talking about this issue, my mind went back to Vishwam as a character. I said to Benegal that Vishwam, played by Naseeruddin Shah, is the opposite of melodrama. In fact, he is a rarity in Hindi cinema. And even sometimes in literature. It is easier for writers to adopt the mantle of moralizers and present their characters as good or bad when the truth is that life is messy. How did Vishwam's character emerge? Benegal said that Tendulkar had seen Vishwam as a cowardly character but for the film-maker himself he was much more complex. The audience could on occasion sympathize with him and on other occasions turn away from him. Benegal was careful to make him neither a hero, nor the villain. The role of Vishwam's was Shah's first major role in films and Benegal said that it was 'a very difficult character for him to play'. Shah was never sure whether he was doing it right or not, and it was only later that he felt he had done it right.

Benegal said that when he made *Nishant*, 'nobody liked the film too much'. Many people thought that it was 'a very negative film'. It was only later that the film got traction when a British distributor acquired *Nishant* and the film opened in London and received appreciative critical notices. The same happened in France. It was also chosen for the Cannes Film Festival.

I reminded Benegal that just the previous month, when the 2022 Cannes Film Festival was under way, Shabana Azmi had shared a beautiful black-and-white photo on Instagram. The photo had been taken in Cannes in 1976. It showed Azmi and Smita Patil wearing saris and, behind them, a laughing Shyam Benegal. Azmi had shared the story that because they had no publicity material and no funds, Benegal had asked them to dress up in saris and then persuade the people who stopped to talk to them to come to their film screening. Azmi had written on Instagram that they had ended with a full house. When I recounted this story, Benegal said, 'We were like church mice. We had no money. The only way to publicize was to ask these two beautiful girls to dress up in their Sunday best.'

The next year, *Nishant* won the National Film Award for the best feature film in Hindi.

Chhote Sarkar (1974) was his last film in a leading role. In his next film, the following year, he graduated to supporting roles – playing the role of the leading lady's father. The leading lady had incidentally made her debut opposite him in another movie. Identify the actor and the actress.

Answer: Shammi Kapoor. Saira Banu debuted opposite him in *Junglee* (1961) and played his daughter in *Zameer* (1975)

Bachchanpur to Ghataknagar

A Family Trip through the 1970s

Shamya Dasgupta

My first memory of Amitabh Bachchan is not from a film at all. On the inside of the door of my father's almirah – a beautiful old wood-carved thing – in Calcutta was a photograph of the star (sorry, megastar). A close-up. Possibly from a magazine. In colour. It might have been scissored into a cut-out, I don't remember anymore. Bachchan staring into the distance.

Nothing remarkable about the photograph, really, except that it was there, in Baba's almirah.

I don't think Baba ever watched a Bachchan film. Or had an opinion of him as an actor. All I ever heard him say on the matter was, 'He has bovine eyes.' The revolution had passed Baba by.

The photograph got where it had as a joke. My sister, nineteen years my senior and a very committed mischief-maker, had glued it in there at some point. A photograph of Lenin, maybe, would have been more appropriate for the red card–carrying old man. But he, presumably amused, didn't take it down. It stayed there for years. When I opened the almirah after Baba's death, I saw that it had been removed. When, or by whom, I can't say. Ma, by then struggling with her memory, which would only get worse in the next few years till she died, couldn't tell.

The 1970s, and the decades before that, came to me in the 1980s, as it did for all of us born in the '70s. (I've always wished I was born fifteen years earlier!) But when the '70s did come, for me, it was like a juggernaut; there was space for little else.

Calcutta then, as now, was a strange place. There was the heaving, breathing intellectual elite that attended film festivals, spoke about de Sica and Godard and Kurosawa, and the Ray–Sen–Ghatak triumvirate, went to art exhibitions and the theatre and wrote – or at least read – a lot of poetry. Happily, that set continues to exist; perhaps not heaving like before, but breathing fine. The rest watched the mainstream Hindi and Bangla films, went to the football, swore either by East Bengal or by Mohun Bagan (or Mohammedan Sporting, but that's a separate story), spoke in colloquial lingo, organized (not just Durga) pujos. They called Uttam Kumar 'Guru'. In the 1970s and the 1980s, they had haircuts styled like Bachchan's (also 'Guru') and wore Bachchan jeans (Mithun Chakraborty, 'Guru' too, took over later). The anti-intellectual, in a way. Both lots were rebels in their own way, to my mind.

The twain met in our home, with a mother and a father whose interests varied (and were various).

When I think back, Baba is easier to describe in this context, so let me start there. A scholar, he had spent a lot of the 1950s and 1960s in America and Canada, first studying and then teaching economics, and had come back home with thousands of books and hundreds of records (LPs/vinyls), not a lot of money, well-formed ideas about the world and its politics, a strong communist core, and, I like to think, hope. Hope went away over time. Before that happened, though, he became part of the various film societies in the city, worked as a journalist, made friends with the movers and shakers of the city's art world, and wrote prolifically, in English and in Bangla.

Ma is trickier to box. She had grown up in a home of stalwarts, exposed to the most radical thoughts and ideas, and literature. But it was also a family steeped in tradition, in Brahminical values, for all the non-conformism and anarchism it was known for.

She counted among her closest relatives Mahasweta Devi and Ritwik Ghatak, Sachin Chaudhuri and Hiten Choudhury, and had the most memorable time of her life while in Bombay in the 1960s. She got to meet Madhubala and Dev Anand, and Dada, my brother, fifteen years my senior, brought home Kutu from Pran's collection of dogs. Kutu, my sister tells me, travelled to Calcutta, but had to be given away afterwards. She can't remember why.

In the home Ma and Baba built together, in Calcutta, after they had both faltered with their first marriages, there was room for *Psycho* and *The Sound of Music*, for *Belle de Jour* and *Rashomon*, for *Pyaasa* and *Half Ticket*, for *Nayak* and *Subarnarekha*, for *Saptapadi* and *Haatey Bajaarey*, and for *Kodiyettam* and *Ankur*. And a lot of music. Baba's LPs were of the more classical kind, Western and Indian, with some Dylans and Seegers and Baezs there too, relics of 1960s America. Ma was more Rabindrasangeet and film songs. She had a filmy bent. In Bangla, in Hindi. She even did a spot of modelling for Pond's while in Bombay. I loved, and still love, the Baba stuff. I lived for the films, and the music, the Ma things. Ma was happy to partake of Baba's world. Baba didn't often go the Ma way, except with Rabindrasangeet – he was Bangali after all.

*

So, as I was saying, when the 1970s did hit me, it knocked me out. Which '70s, though?

First, the '70s of Parveen Babi and Bachchan, Rajesh Khanna and Dharmendra, Yash Chopra and Manmohan Desai, Kishore Kumar and Asha Bhosle. Naseeruddin Shah and Smita Patil, with Shyam Benegal and Shabana Azmi and Om Puri in tow, would follow.

But, for a brief while before that, there was Uttam. In large part because he died in 1980. At the end of a career of incredible highs, by the time he died – of a heart attack at just fifty-three years of age – he was also acknowledged as a fine actor. Ray's *Nayak* had ensured that, the sort of legitimacy a mainstream actor, or star, could only dream of. He was also kosher at home. Ma swore by his *bhubonbholano haashi* (the smile that mesmerizes the world), and the general bhadralok feel of that brand of cinema. Baba accepted him after *Nayak*, though Uttam's trademark 'erm' before answering a question left Baba speaking in grunts.

After Uttam died, the local Doordarshan telecast his films endlessly, for days and weeks and months, like it did in 1987 for Kishore or in 1992 for Ray. Uttam had started in the early 1950s, and his best work was pre-1970s, but we got such excellent films as *Mouchak*, *Baghbondi Khela*, *Dhanraj Tamang*, and *Agnishwar* (perhaps his best after *Nayak*) in the years leading up to his death.

There was a family consensus that we had arrived at, although I'm not sure how those negotiations were conducted. Suchitra Sen, none of us liked much. Too affected. As was her playback voice, Sandhya Mukherjee. Soumitra Chattopadhyay we liked. Or, I think, we liked his films but not him so much. He refused to sign in my autograph book when ten-year-old me met him at a function. But Aparna Sen was astoundingly good, as was Sabitri Chatterjee. And a few other women who wouldn't be on too many lists, possibly: Anjana Bhowmick, Subrata Chattopadhyay, Anubha Gupta. And Bangla cinema's assembly line of outstanding (all male, if I remember correctly) actors who made a name in comic roles, they were massive favourites.

On the whole, though, I was merrily going with the Bachchan flow. We didn't have a videocassette player at home. But there were the travelling video shows I could go to – like in *Swades*, you know? Sita-di, who worked in our home, lived in a slum not far from our apartment. Her daughter, my age, and son, slightly younger, were my friends. Some enterprising sorts organized video shows in a field near their home every other week with really low-priced tickets – even for the time, even for Sita-di. I would be invited. And I was allowed to attend. That's where I first saw – the memories are vivid – *Trishul* and *Muqaddar Ka Sikandar*, as well as *Veerana* and *Purana Mandir* and many other films. Some Bangla films too. On a big screen! Plus the occasional visit to the theatre, though mainly for English films. And good old Doordarshan.

*

But our home was haunted by the Ghatak ghost.

Ray was fine. Especially his films for children. But to a youngster, not yet a teen, Ghatak and Sen films were unwatchable. Why was I made to sit through black-and-white films that I could make no sense of? I was not completely insensitive to the troubles of others – or our country's, and region's, chequered past – I'd like to think. But two-and-some hours of funk, with some words and music floating out of the haze, was not for me. In some cases, Ghatak's *Titas Ekti Nodir Naam* especially, I couldn't even make out the words, it was all in Bangaal. My wife once told me how moved she was by Prakash Jha's *Damul* when it was telecast on Doordarshan back then. All I recall is a black screen. And perhaps an oil lamp. I can't be sure. Were we married by then, when this conversation took place? It could have been a dealbreaker.

Sure, things change, and Ghatak – Sen, too, more recently – has opened more doors than I had thought to knock on in that Bachchan mist back in the day. But, at the time, it was torture. And a lot of it. As you can imagine, in Calcutta, with the communists in power, the state-run four-screen Nandan found enough excuses to show these films. As also *good cinema* from around the world. And Baba wanted me to grow up educated and enlightened, even if it seemed something of a lost cause.

I do remember that silent tussle, between the old man and the old lady, to give me a bit more of themselves. There was no outward show of disappointment at my rejection of one (Baba), or happiness at my embracing of the other (Ma). Let the boy figure his way out was their parenting plan, I think. A good plan it was, too, I'd say.

At some stage, though, and it's tough to say when this was, perhaps the early 1990s, it all started to come together. The Angry Young Man of Bachchan, and the Angry Young Men and Women of the parallel world. Were they not the same at their core? Disillusionment, the promise of independence gone wrong, Nehruvian socialism having run its course, a point where it was time for a new 'ism'? Communism? Perhaps. Perhaps not. But these films were about the corrupt and the powerful and the oppressors, and hitting back at the corrupt, at the powerful, at the oppressors. They made visible the powerless and the oppressed. It was a time when you had to take sides. To quote Brazilian educator and philosopher Paulo Freire [*Pedagogy of the Oppressed*], 'Washing one's hands off the conflict between the powerful and the powerless means to side with the powerful, not to be neutral.' In the worlds of mainstream and parallel cinema, most people did take sides. The right side. A far cry from where we stand in 2024.

Hindi cinema has traditionally had a sympathetic ear for the plight of the common man – I say 'man' because the main protagonists have usually been the men. 'Common' in terms of class position; caste – what did I know back then? This empathy quickened in the 1970s. India was in turmoil. Emergency, certainly, but also the events leading up to it. *Deewaar* released twenty-seven years after independence. Hope and optimism had all but withered away. India's role in Bangladesh's war of liberation had done no harm to the country's, and Indira Gandhi's, image. But the refugee crisis that followed, adding to widespread food shortage, unemployment, the rise of the underworld – primarily in Bombay but also in other urban centres – and mass corruption were realities in those years. It was a time when labour unions mushroomed with power across the country, Jayaprakash Narayan's Total Revolution took shape and flight, a number of student agitations – the Naxalite movement prime among them – gathered force and ferocity.

An awareness of, and engagement with, political issues was a natural outcome of this churn, the unrest. The cinema of the 1970s reflected the society it was bred in.

Take 1976. If *Manthan* was about the White Revolution, also the first crowdfunded film, the same year, we had *Dus Numbri*, *Hera Pheri*, *Kalicharan*, *Fakira*, *Charas*, *Ek Se Badhkar Ek*, *Shankar Dada*, *Ginny Aur Johnny*, all about criminals, some good and some bad, about Robin Hoods and honest police officers and corrupt politicians. Between 1973 and 1976, Bachchan made *Zanjeer*, *Namak Haraam*, *Deewaar* … the outstanding *Trishul*, *Kala Patthar* and *Parvarish* were on their way. (*Sholay* too, of course, but I was hoping to get to the end without mentioning it, as a test.) Parallelly, we had *Nishant* and *Ankur* from the Benegal stable, and Ray turned more political than before with *Pratidwandi*, *Jana Aranya*, *Seemabadhdha* and *Ashani Sanket*.

Sure, the form, the treatment, were not the same, kind of like the gulf – in every way possible – between Shah and Bachchan, Benegal and Desai. But back then, there was a thread of social consciousness that stretched between these towering figures of Hindi cinema.

I chose 1976 here because that was the year Ghatak died. In penury and misery. I was born some months after his passing, but he – Chhotokaka to Ma and Ritwikbabu to Baba – was a frequent topic of conversation at home in my earliest years. Between my parents, and when their friends visited. It's possible that the release of *Nagarik* – his first film, made in 1952, but released posthumously in 1977 – was the trigger. Not that you needed a reason to discuss Ghatak. Aren't we still figuring him out?

Much like me, I suppose, the world took its time acknowledging and appreciating his genius. Perhaps you need to grow up to *see* Ghatak. The original rebel, the maker of unabashedly political films, the great despairist ... He must have watched *Garam Hawa* with affection of some sort when it released in 1974. If he watched it. If he watched *Ankur*, the year before, in 1973, he must have felt some kinship. Maybe even hope, that the world was opening up to his kind of cinema. It might have been misplaced optimism, though, because Ghatak was, more than anything else, a misfit, too much of an outlier, to ever *make it*. In a country that was equal parts feudal (the class he belonged to, it has to be acknowledged) and capitalist under its socialist sheen, and yet to rid itself of its colonial baggage, he would always be seen as a kook. An unstoppable hellraiser.

But, again, my generation grew up in the 1970s, right through the '80s, and then grew up some more after 6 December 1992. For me in Calcutta, and for my wife, in Delhi, the trajectory was largely the same. This, though, we discovered after the turn of the millennium, which is when we met. A couple of years before Godhra and its immediate aftermath, February–March 2002.

At some point, amid all of this cinema-watching, I began to understand and appreciate Baba's world. A world that, I have discovered, my wife naturally inhabited, but one that I took time to get into. It was a world where there was little space for mundanity. Not that Baba didn't have a sense of humour, or a lighter side to him, but there were too many important things to worry about, whether anyone (let alone he) could do anything about those or not. And he didn't have the bandwidth for frivolity. My wife is, in some ways, cut from the same cloth. Not entirely, thankfully.

But Baba never did know the world Ma and I lived in.

Do you know if you've made the right choice if you have no idea what you are staying away from? So, while Ma and I opened ourselves to a gamut of possibilities, Baba didn't, and Bachchan and *Deewaar*, among many other things, remained alien concepts to him. His loss, clearly.

Because, really, there was the tale of a changing India in the mainstream of the 1970s too, exactly as it was in the cinema he watched and the conversations he had. All it did was tell the tale in a way palatable to a bigger group of people, warts – and tears and songs and dances and dhishoom-dhishoom – and all.

Who am I to judge, though? For someone born in the 1930s, someone who had lived through the last stages of the independence struggle and Partition and the Famine and the Bangladesh war and everything else, perhaps palatable truth was irrelevant, even indigestible? Ma had lived through all of it too, but processed it differently, I think. As for me, born in the 1970s, the journey had to start with Bachchan before I could get to Ghatak. Fortunately, I got there in the end.

Oh, and did Baba remove that Bachchan picture from his almirah and throw it away? Or did he keep it safely tucked away, like he did everything else, in one of his numerous Files of Old and Useless Things? That I'll never know, will I?

When Padmini Kapila was signed for the Ravi Chopra directorial, *Tumhari Kasam* (1978), little did she know that she was to star opposite her ex-boyfriend. Her ex-boyfriend was an actor who showed much promise in the 1970s but could not live up to it. Who was he?

Answer: Navin Nischol

Which 1976 movie, based on an Odia short story named 'Shikaar', marked the debut of a popular hero?

Answer: *Mrigayaa*; Mithun Chakraborty

North by South-East

How We Found Bombay in Madras

Krishna Shastri Devulapalli

My first memory of a Hindi film involves *Ek Phool Do Maali*. Come to think of it, it is not so much a memory as its suppression. Story was I cried so much while watching the film that Mother had to request my nanny to take me out of the theatre, prompting me to promise the sexagenarian that I would marry her when I grew up. Such, apparently, was my relief and gratitude at being freed of this Sanjay Khan–Sadhana tearjerker. (I was too young then, I suppose, to recognize the greatness of Balraj Sahni.) It was a story Mother would repeat whenever there was a lull in the conversation.

An actual memory of a Hindi film, a pleasant one – while there must have been other, sporadic viewings in the 6–7 years between *Ek Phool* and this one – involved the movie *Barood*, the Rishi Kapoor–Shoma Anand revenge drama. It was a noon show. I was with Mother. Eating a softie. With my sisters nowhere in the picture (on or offscreen). And it was a school day. What more could a boy ask for? (*Barood*, apparently no great shakes back home then,

I recently found out, was the top-grossing Hindi film of 1978 in Russia. So, in retrospect, my bunking school on that summer day in 1976 I feel was entirely justified.)

Film watching was a highly political affair in my family. And the ruling party and opposition were Dad and Granddad, constantly interchanging positions. Granddad wrote songs for Telugu films. So watching them at preview theatres, sitting in the privileged last row, slurping 'cool drinks' served by the producer's obsequious flunkeys, was a given. But there was a catch. Telugu movies were okay (that was the subliminal message I got from Dad) but *only* the ones my granddad wrote for. More often than not, Dad himself managed to skip these movies (despite his much-hyped closeness to his father) because most previews were matinées on weekends. And for him weekends meant one thing and one thing only: the races.

And why were Telugu – or for that matter, Hindi or Tamil movies – bad? Because they were *not* Hollywood movies, silly, Dad had dinned into me from birth. And that, too, ones made in the '40s–'50s. Which were all things elegant, classy and aspirational. And everything else was junk. (I knew he secretly liked Vidya Sinha though. And not for her Nylex saris and eyeliner, I'm guessing.)

Mother, on the other hand, saw movies. Period. It didn't matter whether they were Telugu, Tamil, Odia or Iranian dubbed into Swahili. If there was a movie to be seen, it would be seen. Sometimes she would go see a movie she disliked a second time just to see how much she had disliked it the first time. She would have bought tickets in black for a Films Division newsreel if it gave her a chance to get away from us all.

But as films went, Mother had a soft corner for Hindi ones. Perhaps because she was the only one among us who could speak fluent Hindi, having grown up in Nagpur, among other places, when her grandfather, Pattabhi Seetaramayya, was governor of Madhya Pradesh. Hindi was the one thing she had that the all-erasing Devulapallis didn't have. And sharpening this weapon and waving it about at us southies made her feel good. As I said, movies were political at home.

My own love for cinema – and by that I mean Hollywood fare exclusively – stemmed from the fact that, in the vein of idiot sons from time immemorial, I was a Dad groupie. How could I not love what Dad loved? When all he spoke about was the perfect arch of Tyrone Power's brows and the translucence of Gene Tierney's green, green eyes (except on the weekends when he ignored me and spoke to his other chamchas of handicaps, trebles and tanalas). And like a typical fanboy, how could I not hate every other kind of film, for what better way to display love than by hating the opposite?

So in a family where the fight was between Telugu films and English films, thanks to the two warring patriarchs, and the opinions of mothers and other women didn't count for much, where did Hindi films even come in? And how did I begin watching them?

Two reasons: school and girls.

Barood had taught me that if there was a way to bunk school and get away with it, the best way to do it was to make Mother a partner-in-crime. So it came to be that I watched, among others, *Sabse Bada Rupaiya*, *Pati, Patni Aur Woh* and *Dulhan Wahi Jo Piya Man Bhaye*, completely guilt-, punishment- and sister-free, thanks to this magic trick I had learnt that could get me out of school. So, in a sense, like all passionate pursuits, my Hindi-movie journey, too, was fuelled by hate – hate of school. I was harbouring a lot of hate those days, as you can see. I hated Hindi movies because I loved Hollywood films. But I hated school so much that I could two-time my first love by cosying up to a subservient 'hate', Hindi films.

If hate had set me off on my shaky Hindi movie journey, love gave me the staying power. It was a time when posh girls liked Hindi movies. (The '70s and the early '80s was still a time when convent-educated Madras maidens, who shampooed their hair and waxed their legs, would rarely be caught dead watching a Tamil film.) And I loved posh girls.

So if one wanted to sit next to this kind of a girl, tentatively hold a hand even, one had to go to watch Hindi movies. It was solely to achieve this end that, in my busy schedule of being obsessed with Hollywood fare, bunking school (and college later), and endeavouring to be a career bum, I enthusiastically squeezed in anything celluloid that Bombay had to offer. Ranging from Amol Palekar's 'homely' vehicles to Mithun-da's early Nagaich outings, from Rishi–Neetu popcorn entertainers to Prakash Mehra–Manmohan Desai three-hour epics, nothing was spared, as long as there was a girl in there somewhere.

As Dad's influence on me weakened, and a one-man tornado called Amitabh Bachchan ravaged all of India, like tumbleweed, I, too, succumbed. I watched everything he was in. At the time, thanks to my small stature, short-fuse, and forever hangry state, my friends then – all older, hairier guys whose fists had come into intimate contact with my face at least once – christened me Amitabh 'Bachcha'. When the name made me angrier than I already was, ironically, I proved the sobriquet true.

But despite the name, despite what the entire nation was telling you, my heart belonged to someone else.

I got sucked into this magnetic field called Vinod Khanna when Doordarshan telecast the movie *Imtihan*. Thanks to my old man, I had already seen *To Sir, With Love*, the movie this one was a rip-off of. But I couldn't take my eyes off this quiet man with the long sideburns, oversized glasses, and striped suits with their giant lapels and flared trousers. Hard to believe that he was barely thirty then. (Or that Bindu was a student.)

Vinod Khanna was my first bona fide boy crush.

My completely agenda-free, wilful watching of Hindi films – unaided by my infatuation of yet another girl, or the profound need to skip school or college – I owe entirely to this man.

So, in *Amar Akbar Anthony*, when Khanna beat the crap out of Amitabh Bachchan, the crowd favourite, I was the only one in the audience who cheered. I also wrote a letter to Manmohan Desai that the unjust snipping of Vinod Khanna's role hadn't gone unnoticed, and that I would be taking it up with the proper authorities. I may have addressed it to Morarji Desai because I didn't get a reply.

I loved it when Khanna got the better of Bachchan yet again in *Parvarish*, with that neat leakproof-stocking-that-can-cover-a-bullet-wound trick.

In *Muqaddar Ka Sikandar*, when 'Memsaab' preferred him to Bachchan, I went 'No shit, Sherlock' or whatever the '70s Indian equivalent of that phrase was. I also thought he deserved better than that big crybaby Raakhee. Or Rekha, for that matter, in her annoyingly husky *Pakeezah*-mode.

I saw atrocious movies like *Maha Badmaash* twice for him.

I loved the famous picture of him in saffron sleeveless vest and folded-up trousers, giving the 'Number 1' sign with his forefinger. I had a poster of it. Whether his resting on bamboo sticks was to aid and abet the theme of giving the finger to everyone or whether it was pure coincidence, we will never be able to tell.

I loved his pairing with Dharmendra in *The Burning Train*. Parveen Babi, Hema Malini and Vinod Khanna valiantly trying to misstep during '*Pehli nazar mein*' to coordinate with Bollywood's foremost layashoonyam, Dharam-paaji, is the stuff of legend.

In *Qurbani*, it was obvious that that idiot Feroz Khan should have been the one who died. And Zeenat Aman be taken immediately to a good optometrist. When Vinod Khanna took off to Oregon, I stopped watching Hindi films. For an entire month.

Funny that almost every memory I have of Vinod Khanna seems to be of him pitted against another actor. That's probably because of how much suaver and cooler than the other guy (whoever he may have been, with a much bigger, better role, in some cases) he came off in almost all these films. Without even trying.

Soon, confident of the fact that I wasn't going to amount to much in life (aided in no small way by reassurances from family and friends), I found my movie-watching rhythm. I realized by then that my mind, completely free of all clutter academic, had enough and more non-judgemental space for films of all kind.

Then, not that I needed any further impetus, a curious phenomenon gave my manic film-watching career a double dose of nandrolone: a new wave of Hindi to Telugu (and Tamil) remakes.

Without doubt smoking hallucinogens that have been banned since, a bunch of Telugu film-makers led by Messrs K. Raghavendra Rao and K. Bapayya, thought it fit to remake popular Hindi films of the time – mostly Bachchan's angry young man vehicles – with 'Visvavikhyata' 'Nata Sarwabhowma' Nandamuri Taraka Rama Rao (NTR) in the lead. For the unversed, NTR was a Raj–Dilip–Dev contemporary. And in the late '70s, he was in his late fifties. And, mind you, it wasn't the kind of fifties SRK, Salman or Aamir inhabit today. It was a no-gym, no-diet, no-botox, no-hair-transplant, no-Photoshop, no-holds-barred, let-it-all-hang-out, as-is-where-is fifty-going-on-seventy.

Sporting a wig doing a twisted imitation of Bachchan's distinct hairstyle, insanely large bell-bottoms in primary colours, and clog heels, NTR played the angry young man in remakes of *Don*, *Deewaar*, *Hera Pheri*, *Suhaag* and *Khoon Pasina*, to name a few. Playing Vinod Khanna or Shashi Kapoor in these vehicles sometimes was NTR's contemporary, an equally bewigged, lipsticked, orange-tongued 'Nata Samrat' Akkineni Nageswara Rao (ANR) who, one had to admit though, was in slightly better physical condition than his compatriot.

For me, the one scene that stands out among these badly transplanted, insanely miscast epics was the post-coital cigarette scene from *Deewaar*'s demented Telugu twin, *Magaadu*. Watching a bare-chested NTR lying next to Manjula (filling in for Bachchan and Babi respectively), sharing a cigarette after a bout of passionate offscreen lovemaking was a reward in itself. But the surprise twist added to this scene by director K.S.R. Das (the man who brought cowboys to Andhra) – NTR's casual inhalation, using a reverse shot, of the exhaled cloud of smoke from Manjula's cigarette – is the kind of thing one takes to the afterlife.

Given below, a sample from *Satyam Shivam*, the official remake of *Suhaag*, which I rewatched (with no dilution of pleasure whatsoever) as research for this piece:

To escape from Akkineni Nageswara Rao, Kaikala Satyanarayana is holding Pushpalata hostage with a gun to her head. Satyanarayana and Pushpalata are husband and wife. And ANR, a good five–ten years older than either, is their son. He also happens to be gloriously blind. This is evident not only by his stumbling around looking at the ceiling and grabbing a hapless Rati Agnihotri for support but also by his choice of costume and wig.

Now why would a man with a gun need a hostage if all he has to do is escape a blind man, you may ask. ANR, you see, is a crack shot. And he can hit his target by mere sound. He is like an old bat in that sense. A few minutes earlier, he proves his marksmanship by tossing a vase into the air and shooting it to a million bits. So wily old Satyanarayana is not taking any chances, and grabs his wife by the neck just as soon as she has returned from the temple after performing an archana in his name.

Well, Satyanarayana, and a fairly cooperative Pushpalata (she has been estranged from her husband for many years, after all, and probably wants alone-time without a creepy, blind son who is older than her peering over their canoodling) make good their escape from their family home in a conveniently parked outdoor unit van. Probably the same one that brought lunch for the cast and crew in the giant tiffin carriers that no movie shoot could without in the '70s. The couple heads off at high speed in the direction of the docks. It is the climax, and it is mandatory for cast and crew of those times to head off to the docks, an abandoned factory or the villain's den in an array of vehicles.

But ANR has other plans.

Blind though he may be, a rope that has been tied to the luggage carrier on the van's roof snakes past him as the vehicle zooms off. ANR, still looking at the ceiling, grabs hold of it. And off he goes with the van. Dragged along the road horizontally, kicking and bleeding, you say? No. Why?

Because ANR has roller-skates on his feet. When did he put them on? Maybe when his mother was being strangled by his father a minute earlier? Maybe he was born with them like Karna with his kavacha and kundalas? Maybe, unbeknownst to viewer, Pushpalata bought them at Burma Bazaar and had slyly passed them on to her blind son while Satyanarayana was inappropriately distracted by his overaged son's underaged love interest, Rati Agnihotri? Who knows? Who cares?

Now we have a van zig-zagging across the bewildered roads of Vizag with a blind ANR on skates attached to it. Multi-tasker Satyanarayana juggles driving and kidnapping duties with firing intermittently at his son who is holding on like a blind barnacle. There is some hardcore back-projection with ANR doing an equally hardcore impersonation of a vision-impaired man on skates powered by a runaway van.

Finally, one of the bullets gets the rope – *dichukiyaan!* – and ANR is disengaged from the vehicle.

Or is he?

From a conveniently situated hill, the till-now absent other hero, Nandamuri Taraka Ramarao, espies this, and makes an entry like only he can. By diving on top of the van, grabbing the broken rope and keeping the chase alive...

Not to be outdone by his Telugu brothers of the same vintage, Tamil Nadu's own 'Nadigar Thilagam' Sivaji Ganesan did his share of Bachchan remakes, too. His *Amara Kaviyam*, *Muqaddar Ka Sikandar*'s Tamil interpretation, needs special mention. If you asked anyone what defined *Muqaddar Ka Sikandar*, nine out of ten would say it's the title song. Bachchan mouthing '*Rote hue aate hai sab*', his lustrous hair slicked back into a silken cap by the wind, as he zooms about Bombay city on his scrambler bike philosophizing in Kishore Kumar's inimitable voice, is the signature moment of the film.

Well, Sivaji Ganesan, too old then for scrambler bikes unlike certain bearded philosophers today, sings the Tamil version of this song, wearing a suit, a wig, in T.M. Soundararajan's voice, sitting hands-free on the backseat of an Impala convertible. Comedian Nagesh doing chauffeur duty somehow doesn't add much to the purported rebelliousness of the protagonist.

You'd think that was the end of it, right?

No.

The North by South-East saga had another chapter. The same Raghavendra Rao, Bapayya and Co, having perpetrated this Hindi-to-Telugu carpet bombing, figured there was still some residual sanity and good taste in the country that needed to be addressed. And this they achieved by reversing the formula: a slew of Telugu-to-Hindi remakes, in which a toupéed (despite possessing a perfectly good head of hair) Jeetendra, sporting a dead millipede on his upper lip, filled in for Telugu stars Krishna, Sobhan Babu, Krishnam Raju, et al, in *Himmatwala*, *Tohfa*, *Maqsad*, *Kaamyab*, etc. Rajesh Khanna, Dharam-paaji, Raj Babbar and everyone's uncle, all equally bewigged and moustachioed, dived in enthusiastically when Jeetu had no more dates to spare.

For anyone lamenting the state of the country today, and lying sleepless wondering about the legacy our children are going to inherit, I suggest they watch these Hindi-to-Telugu and Telugu-to-Hindi remakes of the '70s and early '80s alternately. Contact me for a curated list.

Nasir Hussain named a character after his close friend in all his movies. The close friend was also a film-maker of repute. Among the movies he produced and directed was a popular 1970 film which explores the marriage between a scientist and an actress. Identify the producer/director and the 1970 film.

Answer: Subodh Mukherjee; *Abhinetri*

How To Listen To Films Before Watching Them

Memories of a Prakash Mehra–Amitabh Bachchan Audiocassette

Jai Arjun Singh

One afternoon in the mid-1980s, during a summer vacation spent in Bombay with my mother and nani, I took out a double-deck audiocassette player-cum-recorder and made my first – to date, my only – attempt at recording my singing voice.

We were staying in Nani's flat on the ground floor of a building in a muddy nook of (then-unfashionable and suburban) Andheri, I was eight or nine years old, and just recovering from one of the seasonal illnesses that marred many of my holidays. Chickenpox. Measles. Mumps. Looking back now, my summer breaks seem made up of a litany of these sadistic pronouncements, followed by days spent in bed with food I didn't want to eat. (There were probably also some regular but persistent flus that kept me bedridden for a few days, which can seem like eternity to a child on vacation.)

Anyway, I was feeling well enough this afternoon to take out my favourite cassette, put it in one deck of the recorder, and rewind it to the start of my favourite song. In the other deck I placed an empty tape. After figuring out, as best as I could, how the player-recorder worked, I began the experiment: first playing part of the song in the left deck so I could remember the lyrics and the tune, and then singing that bit for the recorder. Rinse and repeat. It must have taken six or seven attempts to get through the song.

Full of trepidation, I checked the results. '*O saathi re*,' I heard in an unfamiliar, reedy, definitely-not-Kishore-Kumar voice, '*tere bina bhi kya jeena. Tere bina bhi kya jeena*.'

To put it mildly, I wasn't impressed with my trilling. Though I don't remember every detail of this afternoon, I know my mother and grandmother were out of the flat at the time – probably shopping nearby, or visiting one of the building's other residents – which is why I had made bold to try this in the first place. By the time it was over, I was assured that the doors to a potential career were closed to me. I would be a listener forevermore, not a crooner.

*

And I did spend a lot of time in my childhood listening to this particular cassette. So much so that I felt a great sense of loss a few months ago when I realized that of all the possessions I have held on to from the deep past, this one item no longer seems to be around.

The tape would have been bought for me sometime between 1982 and '84. The cover had two people on it, one of whom – Amitabh Bachchan – was the cynosure of my young eyes, while the other was someone I didn't even recognize at the time. On the right was the superstar, looking haunted and melancholy, probably in a still from *Muqaddar ka Sikandar* (the film that contained the song I would try to record in my voice). On the left was a pudgy man whose name I could guess only because of the cassette's title – *A Musical Decade: Prakash Mehra and Amitabh Bachchan*.

Most of my favourite audiotapes of the early '80s, including a cherished *Naseeb/Amar Akbar Anthony* combination (bought by my mother out of one of her first salaries as a doctor's receptionist), had busy, colourful covers featuring the most popular stars in as many images as could be fitted onto the small rectangular paper cover: here, occupying a space of barely one inch, is a tiny Rishi Kapoor imploring Amitabh to '*Chal mere bhai*'; there, in an equally compressed space, are Bachchan and Vinod Khanna wrestling in their undershirts. So it was strange to see a spare, uncluttered cover with just two people on it – and Bachchan alongside someone who was unfamiliar to a casual movie viewer. I had no idea who Prakash Mehra was, or what he did, when I first saw the tape – I may have thought he was a playback singer like Mohammed Rafi or Kishore Kumar, or a musician like R.D. Burman. It was only when my mother told me he was a movie director that the penny dropped. With analytical literature about the auteur theory and other such critical exegeses still in my distant future, this might have been the first time I ever thought consciously about the person who *directed* a film.

The tape was a collection of dialogues and songs from the films the two men had done together starting with the 1973 *Zanjeer* – famously Bachchan's star-making role – and continuing till *Namak Halaal* in 1982. The films in between were *Hera Pheri*, *Khoon Pasina* (which was produced by Mehra, not directed by him), *Muqaddar ka Sikandar*, and *Laawaris*.

The key word in that last paragraph is 'dialogues', and it's what marked this cassette as very special – almost in the league of the other iconic dialogue tape I owned (more on that in a bit). Because here's the thing: the first few times I listened to *A Musical Decade*, I hadn't yet watched any of these films (or may have seen fragments of them on TV when I was very small, without remembering anything about them). Of course, I *intended* to watch them all – I had a two-page pull-out of Bachchan's filmography up to the year 1984 from one of the movie magazines my mother read – but for a long time it were the prose sections on the Prakash Mehra cassette that gave me ideas about what those films may contain.

It was exciting, but could also be a vessel for confusion. I would try to piece together the stories of the films from the dialogues, and would sometimes end up lost. Much conjecturing was required, some detective work too. Imagine Hercule Poirot twirling his moustache and going 'Monsieur, this "*Raat baaki baat baaki*" *seems* to be a romantic song – but, mon dieu, it's really a song that heralds danger!'

Or take '*O saathi re*'. It is a beautiful track, still one of my favourite Hindi film songs – and yet, not having watched *Muqaddar ka Sikandar*, I was every bit as fascinated by the dialogue segments that preceded the song on the tape. Bachchan's pain-soaked voice, the repeated references to Raakhee as 'memsahib', which seemed to be a motif in the film (in the same way that the more sarcastically uttered 'sakhi' would later be a running thread between the same two actors in *Bemisaal*). I remember being both intrigued and irritated by that word – why 'memsahib' if this was a romantic relationship? And I had to wait to watch *Muqaddar ka Sikandar* – maybe a year or two later – to make sense of it. (Though even then, it would take another few years before I recognized, as a more experienced viewer, that this film was one of our cinema's most interesting variations on the Devdas trope – and perhaps the only one where the self-absorbed male lead doesn't place a heavy guilt trip on the woman who doesn't return his love; instead he makes a heartfelt speech about how she was a guardian angel for him when they were children, and how indebted he will forever remain to her. That Bachchan speech before '*O saathi re*' was, as it turned out, the beating heart of the film – and it remains one of my favourite Hindi-movie sequences all these decades after I first heard, rather than watched, it.)

Most movie nerds and obsessives know the process of *anticipating* the viewing of a film: collecting information on it beforehand, imagining what it will be like, thinking one already knows the film intimately, maybe even 'making' a version of it in one's head. In today's information-saturated times, this often takes the form of watching teasers and trailers: Teaser 1 followed by Teaser 2, then Trailer 1, Trailer 2 and so on – all of this perhaps punctuated by reading online reviews or analyses of each of these snippets! But even in the pre-Internet, pre-media-explosion age, there were other avenues for this sort of thing. During a long trip to London in 1988 (one of those school summer breaks that *wasn't* marred by illness), I got my hands on a promotional scrapbook about the upcoming live-action He Man film *Masters of the Universe*; the pages had small blank spaces where circular stickers – 'reveals' of the individual characters – could be collected and pasted. (The book also had larger images showing action sequences, in which some of the characters could be glimpsed – but these were hazy black-and-white backgrounds on the pages, and you couldn't see the faces clearly. This brought a special excitement to the process of collecting new stickers from the local Tescos upon the purchase of candies.) It wasn't until months later, back in Delhi, that I got a videocassette of the film and watched it – the experience being inevitably disappointing given how many weeks I had already spent thinking about it, playing out its action sequences in my mind, based on the images in the scrapbook.

Later, in the early 1990s, reading about countless old Hollywood classics in my thick Leonard Maltin film guide and a few other books, I felt like I knew the films long before I watched them. (Today, well into my forties, I STILL haven't watched many of them!) Or later still, there was a 'Cinemania 1997' CD-ROM, containing two-minute clips of films that one could watch on the computer – before I got an Internet connection for the first time or could imagine online streaming videos.

But long, long before all this, my aural-sensory experience of unwatched films came from the Mehra-Bachchan cassette. And, to a lesser degree, from the famous double-cassette of *Sholay*'s dialogues, which I also owned (like every Hindi-movie buff of the 1970s and '80s). Strangely, I don't have vivid memories of the *Sholay* cassette; it might be that I deliberately refrained from listening to it too closely because I didn't want to spoil the film in advance. The one clear memory I have is of being stunned, and then giggling, when I heard the line '*Thakur ne hijron ki fauj banayi hai*' – Thakur has raised an army of eunuchs. I somehow hadn't expected to hear the sudden, savage use of a word like 'hijra' in a Hindi film.

The Prakash Mehra cassette was another matter: I probably spent more time listening to the fragments of dialogue than the songs. Having read in magazines about the 1970s rivalry between Bachchan and Vinod Khanna, I was curious about the storylines of *Hera Pheri* and *Khoon Pasina*, but from the few dialogues on the tape I couldn't for the life of me tell whether their characters were friends or enemies in these films. And was *Hera Pheri* a serious drama, a goofy comedy or a thriller? (Pointless speculation, as it happened, since most of these films were all of the above, and many other things besides at the same time.) I had probably only watched *Amar Akbar Antho*ny of the films they made together, and I still felt sore about Khanna getting to 'defeat' my hero in their fight scene in that one – so I was hoping for the reverse in these other films. All this added to the intrigue, and hastened the process of seeking the movies out to watch.

Then there was the famous comic scene in *Namak Halaal*, with Bachchan in a monologue about Wasim Bari and Wasim Raja and Vijay Merchant and Vijay Hazare, and English being a very phunny language. Phunny as the dialogue was, I also loved the idea of AB playing an 'Arjun Singh' just a few years after he was 'Jai' in *Sholay*; it felt like my favourite hero had authenticated or notarized my full name in between all those Vijays he played onscreen.

And speaking of Vijays, there was *Zanjeer*.

This was one of those mainstream Amitabh films that I would watch in its entirety quite late in life – as a *dhishoom-dhishoom*-obsessed child I had little appetite for the early-1970s Bachchan without the sidelocks (I think I associated this look with the 'boring' films that played on TV, such as *Anand* or *Sanjog* or *Saudagar*), and so I stayed away from *Zanjeer* for very long, despite knowing of its importance.

But I enjoyed listening to the song '*Yaari hai imaan mera*', and I didn't know what to make of it for a while. It felt out of place because surely a solid track like this should be given to the film's male lead – and yet Manna Dey's playback singing didn't sound like it could be for Amitabh. It was only after I heard part of the dialogue track on the cassette – the fiery confrontation between Bachchan's Vijay and the Pathan Sher Khan, played by Pran – that I realized Sher Khan must be doing the onscreen singing.

I was riveted by the sounds of that confrontation, which played out in full on the tape's dialogue track. It begins with Pran's memorable line '*Sher Khan kaale ka dhanda karta hai, par imaandaari se*' (Sher Khan may run an illegal gambling den, but he does it with honour and honesty). This was an intriguing moment for a naïve listener: unlike most of the other films included on the tape, *Zanjeer* was a one-hero story, and this Sher Khan didn't sound like a typical villain – so what was going on here? Why was the *antagonist* speaking of *imaandaari*?

I would learn years later that *Muqaddar ka Sikandar* had a similar 'honourable villain' part for Amjad Khan (and that the film would, with apologies to Vinod Khanna, have been better if it had recognized that Khan was its second male lead). But back to *Zanjeer*, and to the sound of the meeting that haunted me for months: the first encounter between Vijay and Sher Khan, after the former has summoned the latter to the police station. Here is Bachchan's voice – even-keeled at first, then a little more cutting, then rising slowly but unmistakably to rage in that way that so thrilled those of us who were his biggest fans. '*Tumhara naam Sher Khan hai?*' he asks; followed, shortly after, by a shouted '*Jab tak baithne ko na kaha jaaye, sharafat se khade raho! Yeh police station hai, tumhare baap ka ghar nahin*!'

Oh, the *frisson* of that moment! Especially since Sher Khan wasn't replying in a similar vein. Vijay the cop, the hero, is screaming 'Shut up, you bloody…' but his adversary, the presumed 'bad guy', maintains a relatively calm tone. As the minatory background music builds and builds and builds, Sher Khan quietly observes that Vijay feels free to bully him around only because he is wearing a uniform and is on his own turf, protected by his cop privileges.

To which Vijay responds by showing up in regular clothes at Sher Khan's den. ('*Sher Khan. Ab na toh vardi hai na kursi, aur na hee main duty par hoon. Ilaaka tumhara hai aur main akela hoon.*') The inevitable fist-fight takes place (I don't remember how much of this was played on the audio-tape – they probably condensed it to a few dhishooms), it ends in an honourable draw, and Sher Khan, pledging to give up his illegal activities, says: '*Aaj zindagi mein pehli baar Sher Khan ki Sher se takkar hui hai.*' They end up friends. What a strange trajectory for a cop and a black-marketer in a mainstream Hindi movie. And stranger yet, I heard it all without seeing any of it.

Time passed, as it does, and *A Musical Decade* drifted off my personal radar. It had offshoots, of course: having processed the general idea of Mehra as an important director, I rushed to get an audiocassette of his next film *Sharaabi*, and spent many a fascinated hour listening to the 'chooha billi' segments – in Bachchan's voice – from the song '*Jahaan chaar yaar*'. *One o'clock / In my house/ There was a cat / There was a mouse.* I pictured an animated interlude featuring guest stars Tom and Jerry dashing around a drunk Amitabh as he balanced a bottle of Vat 69 on his head. The reality of the sequence would turn out to be less exciting, despite Bachchan's enjoyably over-the-top comic performance, and a nifty pantomime between him and Smita Patil.

Before wrapping up this tribute, I should mention that another song I loved – the very first one on the cassette – was a source of mystery to me because it *wasn't* from a Bachchan film: this was '*Chale thay saath milke*' from *Haseeena Maan Jaayegi*, which Mehra had directed in 1968. At first I thought its inclusion was a mistake. Then I saw that the track listing described this song as the album's 'mukhda'. I had no idea what that meant – it was only later that I figured the lyrics were meant as a refrain, a tribute to the Mehra-Bachchan relationship, their '*chalenge saath milkar*' which had spanned a decade's worth of very popular films. (The collaboration would eventually last till *Jaadugar* in the late 1980s, a messy film that thankfully fell way outside the ambit of this collection: I doubt I would have felt the same affection for this audiocassette if it had included dialogue from *Jaadugar*, or its salacious double-entendre song which went '*Padosan apni murgi ko rakhna sambhaal/ Mera murga ho gaya hai deewaana*'.)

Years later, I finally got down to watching *Zanjeer*. I wasn't thinking about the audiocassette of my childhood, I may even have forgotten about it. But there was an immediate, visceral thrill of recognition – a trunk-call from the past – when the moment of the Vijay–Sher Khan meeting arrived: Pran, hair and beard heavily henna-ed, sauntering into the police station, looking and behaving like every Hindi-movie stereotype of the Honourable Pathan; Bachchan's explosive anger as he kicks the chair out from under him. I rewound the scene on my DVD, closed my eyes, and listened – only *listened* – to the scene; I was transported back, through time and space, to dusty Andheri with its buzzing flies and long hot days spent in bed and smiling aunts dropping in to ask how I was, the sustaining dialogue-baazi of Arjun Singh and Sikandar and Shiva and Vijay Khanna, and the plaintive beauty of '*O saathi re*' which could never be replicated by a child with a croaky voice.

Sometimes a time machine can be as small as a four-inch-by-three-inch box.

First Day, First Show

The Big-Screen Movie-Watching Experience of the 1970s

Diptakirti Chaudhuri

First day, first show. For generations of Indians, these four words have held such allure, such glamour, such crazy attraction that they've bunked school, shirked work, lied at home, and given up many meaningful things in life, only to be able to have the bragging rights of having seen Amitabh Bachchan before anyone else. For some, this was a refuge from the daily humdrum of life. For some, it may even have been an inspiration – to get on to a screen and a poster on any given Friday.

In her autobiography, *A Country Called Childhood*, Deepti Naval lovingly describes growing up in Amritsar and watching films. On 30 January 1971 – first day, first show – she went to watch the reigning heartthrob Rajesh Khanna's *Kati Patang*, braving the crushing crowds that Khanna commanded those days. And remembers Bindu's magnetic presence during the cabaret song '*Mera naam hai Shabnam*' when she taunts Asha Parekh with '*Tumhara naam kya hai? Neena, Meena, Anju, Manju...*' and the entire theatre chorused, '*YAAAA... MADHUUUU!*'

Only '70s Kids Know This

The adrenaline thump of responding to onscreen magic in unison with a theatre full of people is something we have lost in the plush interiors and the caramel popcorn counters of the modern-day multiplex. Suresh Kumar, a movie buff who grew up in Ahmedabad, remembers the entire theatre standing up with folded hands when the goddess first appeared on the screen in *Jai Santoshi Maa* (1975), a film he thinks was the true precursor of *Ramayana* and *Mahabharata* on Doordarshan. Apparently, devotees came with flowers and offerings to watch the movie and performed a makeshift pooja at opportune moments during the movie.

This thing – audience reaction – was something the film-makers were also extremely sensitive about and planned around. The simple logic was that if at least a couple of highlights elicited a big reaction, it would create word-of-mouth publicity, drawing audiences from the friends and families of the first set of viewers. (Yes, this is now called micro-influencer marketing.) Sometimes, they knew what to expect, and a few times, the audience reaction – or the lack of it – was entirely out of the blue. Like when Javed Akhtar went for a show of *Zanjeer* (1973) and realized the audience hadn't seen anything like this. When Amitabh Bachchan's angry young policeman character kicked the chair away from Pran,

> Released in 1975, along with box-office behemoths like *Sholay* and *Deewaar*, *Jai Santoshi Maa* was a bigger hit than *Deewaar* in industry jargon because it cost a pittance to make. Beyond the collections, *Jai Santoshi Maa* became a cultural phenomenon with the *vrat* of sixteen Fridays – the prescribed manner of worshipping the goddess – kicking off nationwide. Not to mention the sixteen (yes, that number again!) films on religious themes that were released or announced in the seven months after the release of the superhit.

one man went, '*Arre baap re baap*' – a reaction never seen before in a Hindi cinema screening, a mixture of surprise and admiration that heralded Bachchan's stardom. The lack of audience reaction and the resultant insecurity plagued the makers of *Sholay* (1975) during the film's early run. But the theatre owners had a different take. One of them assured Ramesh Sippy that the film was so good that the audience was stunned. In fact, to such an extent that they were not coming out for soft drinks and samosas during the interval.

During the initial stages of *Deewaar*'s (1975) production, Salim–Javed narrated the entire script to Yash Chopra and critical members of his crew. When they came to the scene of tattooing '*Mera baap chor hai*' on young Vijay's arm, Chopra's assistant director Ramesh Talwar started clapping. He says, 'I was thrilled as a cine-goer. I was the youngest in the group and closest to the emotions portrayed in the script.' This spontaneous reaction gave Yash Chopra the confidence to pick up a script that was quite radical for the times, was supposed to feature a relatively untested actor, and initially had no songs.

Manish Rathore, a film fan growing up in Lucknow, had no idea what the film *Don* (1978) would be about. Few knew the meaning of the title, and many thought it was an English film. Helen's song, '*Yeh mera dil yaar ka deewana*', got a great response (as did Don's smart escape immediately afterwards), and word of mouth kicked in for the film to become a massive hit.

Going Viral (a.k.a. Word of Mouth)

Those who follow him on social media might remember Amitabh Bachchan posting a picture of a serpentine queue for buying tickets for *Don*. This picture is as unusual in the 2020s of online booking as it was before the film's release. *Don*'s producer, Nariman Irani, passed away during the last stages of the film's production, and there was no plan for publicity and promotion. The promotion was run on funds borrowed by the director and on the goodwill of the actors. And on the phenomenal run that Bachchan was having at the box office in 1978.

Movie buff Anand Parasuram remembers watching the trailer of *Don* when he was watching *Kasme Vaade* (1978) at Bombay's Sahakar theatre. As a kid, he loved the stunt of Don spraying petrol at his pursuers and escaping, deciding immediately to watch the film. (In between, he also caught *Trishul* [1978] at Natraj theatre.)[1] Acclaimed author and film fan Balaji Vittal was studying *Don Quixote* at school in Calcutta when he watched *Don* and promptly dropped Quixote from his mind! *Don*, released somewhat later in Calcutta, had gained popularity by tremendous word of mouth – on the back of the thrill-a-minute plot and the '*Khaike paan Banaras wala*' song – and had drawn massive opening-day crowds in south Calcutta's Priya theatre, where Vittal watched the film.

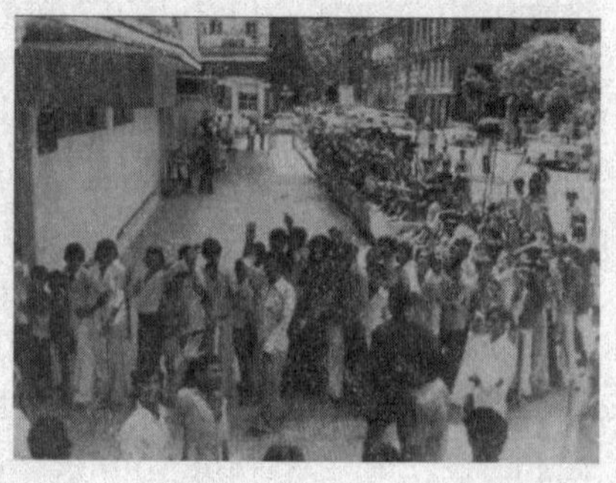

Massive queues were the ultimate hallmark of 1970s' movie successes, queues that would make passers-by wonder what great spectacle they were missing out on. These queues around Bombay's Minerva theatre became so regular between 1975 and 1980 that BEST bus conductors started calling it '*Sholay* stop'. Minerva was where *Sholay* ran, and the world stopped to watch.

Word of mouth often made the fortunes of smaller-budget films. Hrishikesh Mukherjee and Basu Chatterjee's middle-of-the-road cinema spread through praise and recommendations and stood a good chance at the box office, slowly building an audience through fewer theatres and limited shows to start with

[1] Amitabh Bachchan's dream run in 1978 is one of the greatest commercial runs in Indian cinema, maybe even world cinema. His *Kasme Vaade*, *Trishul*, and *Don* were released in a space of just three weeks over April and May, apart from *Ganga ki Saugandh* in January and *Muqaddar ka Sikandar* in October.

and then expanding to more theatres and more shows. Word of mouth wasn't without pitfalls. Balaji Vittal remembers newcomer Amol Palekar being called 'Amal Palit' – a Bengali surname – in the Chinese whispers between Bombay and Calcutta! A different kind of regionalism played out among the south Indians living in Bombay. Anand Parasuram remembers Yesudas singing for Amol Palekar was a big draw for his family, friends, and neighbours.

In these days of orchestrated movie releases on special weekends (often planned months, if not years, in advance), it is difficult to comprehend the staggered release of movies. Due to the high cost of publicity and even making prints,[2] producers made a few prints of the film and released them in a few theatres to test the waters.

Films were usually released in the Bombay (distribution) territory first and then expanded to other territories, often crafting the pan-India marketing strategy based on initial response, and sometimes even modifying the film. The most famous example of the latter is, obviously, *Sholay*. After bad reviews and dire predictions by the industry journals, Ramesh Sippy went into panic mode and decided to reshoot the ending. After *Deewaar*, Amitabh Bachchan was too big a star to die, they said. So he will live, Sippy thought. A core team even met at Bachchan's residence to plan a weekend shoot in which Jai lives and is united with Radha. Writers Salim–Javed opposed this plan vehemently and managed to convince Sippy to hold on for a week more, to see if the collections picked up. By another week (or two), the collections had picked up, the snack sales had dropped, and *Sholay* continued to disrupt the neat 12-3-6-9 show timings for months (years?) to come. (One of the many complaints against *Sholay* was that it was too long, and the 3.5-hour runtime messed up theatre schedules.)

---

[2] Because prints were quite expensive to make, distributors often saved money by making fewer prints and having two nearby theatres share them. So in Calcutta's Priya theatre, films sometimes paused midway because the subsequent reel hadn't arrived from the nearby Menoka.

Performance + Marketing

Sholay was one of the few films with a sustained advertising campaign – in trade magazines, in prominent hoardings across Bombay, and later, a radio campaign. Every member of the cast got a separate creative, as did some of the main members of the crew like Salim–Javed and R.D. Burman. But this was an exception.

For fans, word of mouth was supplemented only by scraps of information gleaned from the radio, newspapers, film magazines, and posters. Movie buffs collected each scrap dutifully and pieced them together to form a jigsaw of decision-making that would take them to the movie. Or not.

Balaji Vittal remembers listening to *Chitralok* on the radio every morning at 8.30 to get a sense of the forthcoming movies from their songs. Across the country, in Ahmedabad, Suresh Kumar was doing the same and remembers being absolutely elated when the *Mr Natwarlal*'s (1979) '*Pardesiya*' song came on screen. Film-maker Sriram Raghavan recalls the radio spots for *Zanjeer* – '*Yaadon ki zanjeer mein lipta hua inteqam ka shola*' – and getting totally excited by it. He managed to swing his family away from *Anamika* (1973) (also starring Jaya Bhaduri, a bigger star then) when they were deciding what films to watch that week.

Songs on the radio were such a critical part of a film's promotion that films without songs were actively discouraged, if not for anything else but to get into *Binaca Geetmala*. Manmohan Desai's *Dharam Veer* (1977) brought out a music disc as a trailer, which had all the songs, and Ameen Sayani compered the material. (According to Deepti Naval's memoir, the audience could chorus with Bindu only because the song was already a superhit on radio's *filmi geet* programmes.)

It is interesting that newspapers were the source of information only for their show listings and movie ads. Most of the filmgoers of the 1970s (whom I spoke to) couldn't recall any reviews that informed their movie watching. This may have a reason. The reviewers of leading newspapers and even film magazines were

Hindustan Times panned *Sholay* for having 'uncensored violence', *Deewaar* for portraying '[Haji] Mastan on celluloid', and wondered about *Don*, 'Could it be that the stunt director conceived his action scenes in this film first and then asked Salim–Javed to weave a story around them?' *Filmfare* gave *Deewaar* a rating of one star, under the title, 'They're hijacking the matron'. *Haathi Mere Saathi* also got one star and was called 'Drawing room safari'. *Sholay* got an extra star and was called a 'Tonga-riding Western'.

often guilty of being completely at odds with public taste and writing terrible reviews of films we now hail as classics.

Film magazines of the 1960s were typical fan mags with beautiful photo features of the stars. Advertising man Nari Hira realized the goody-two-shoes coverage could be quite tiresome and started *Stardust* which was run by people who rarely saw Hindi films but bitched the hell out of the stars. Their racy copy about the gossip of the times found many takers and *Stardust* was a runaway success but didn't offer much to filmgoers to decide what film they wanted to watch.

The final piece of the jigsaw was, of course, the film posters. Manish Rathore says that large cutouts of Dimple Kapadia in a bikini towered over Lucknow's Mayfair theatre, and they drew him to *Bobby*. (Though it's a different matter that he developed a crush on Aruna Irani after watching the movie.) The posters were such a critical piece of the movie-watching experience that top poster artists were always in demand. Legendary artist Diwakar Karkare commanded up to Rs 50,000 per film and was often tasked with completing artworks for multiple films in a given week. His signature technique of 'over-painting' (i.e., painting using oil colour with a knife over photographs of actors) made several of his works – *Kaala Patthar*, *Deewaar*, *Sholay*, *Amar Akbar Anthony*, *Suhaag* – classics then and collectors' items now.

The film poster was supplemented by another artwork of the bygone era – lobby cards. About A4-sized in size, each of these cards focused on one character or scene from the movie, piquing interest and providing just enough fodder for people to guess the drift of the plot or the general disposition of the character, or – if one was lucky – both! The walk from the theatre entrance to the darkened hall was made exciting by these lobby cards, now no longer part of promotional material but still in demand among old-movie aficionados.

Aakhir Queue...

'*Jabalpur ki advance ki line mein chaku chal gaye...*' says debutant director Ranjit Rolly (played by Sanjay Kapoor), gleefully describing the response to his film in the film, *Luck By Chance* (2009). This wasn't fiction. Journalist and editor Sandipan Deb recounted in an article about buying tickets in advance for Amitabh Bachchan-starrer *Besharam* (1978).

> As soon as the counter opened, everyone abandoned the queue and got into serious hand-to-hand combat. My cousin waded into the melee, fists and feet flailing. Then a couple of young men ran up from a distance and launched themselves into the air, landing on the heads of the mob, and started literally swimming through the crowd, five feet above the ground, towards the counter, where the man behind the grill sat watching the mayhem with studied boredom. All this was clearly business as usual. So I too joined the skirmish with full rabidity. Then some young men took off their belts and started whipping random people with total abandon. At this point, my cousin and I quit the action, bought tickets in black and went home.

The operative phrase in this passage is 'this was clearly business as usual'. Like the scooter, like the telephone, like so many other things in the 1970s, cinema tickets were in short supply. They were not unaffordable yet, and hence cinema was the entertainment of choice for millions of middle-class families. But the intersection of good occasions, good films, and good theatres was a difficult spot to hit. Manish Rathore recounts that he stood in the queue for four hours for *Qurbani* (1980), a record of sorts since the queueing time was higher than the showtime.

Anand Parasuram was the designated ticket-buyer of his family, going to the theatres well in advance. Since he grew up in Bombay's Tilak Nagar – then ruled by Chhota Rajan – even buying the tickets had a frisson of excitement. Balaji Vittal remembers going with his father to buy advance tickets for Manmohan Desai's *Chacha Bhatija* (1977) and getting caught in the rain on the way back. He was most concerned if his father would be able to save the precious tickets – printed on very thin paper – from getting wet. Another time, his father had to take leave from work to buy tickets for the Rajesh Khanna-starrer *Mehbooba* (1976). This set of adventures gave credence to the rumour that theatre owners colluded with black marketers and gave away tickets to the 'blackers'. This rumour was certainly not unfounded because the industry journal *Trade Guide* reported that the police had found theatres where the owners had kept aside tickets for black marketing.

Life Itself…

'*Sau saal pehle mujhe tumse pyar tha, aaj bhi hai aur kal bhi rahega…*' Hasrat Jaipuri's words, Shankar–Jaikishen's tune, and Lata–Rafi's voices remind us about our affair with cinema. Writing about the 1970s makes you realize that the era is now half a century away. The decade has now gone past the bounds of good ol' days, is unlikely to be captured by merely oral history, and probably needs serious research by serious scholars. Given the shuttering of so many theatres and cultural hotspots, the services of an archaeologist might not be out of place. As a film fan, however, I have avoided the historical underpinnings of the decade. The angry revolutions eliciting governmental crackdowns before the victory of democracy and the slow onset of cynicism – the 1970s were a momentous set of years, and tomes have been written on how the films mirrored the zeitgeist.

Before multiplexes removed the constraints of show timings, the life of a cinemagoer was neatly divided into four blocks, 12-3-6-9 – whether they liked it or not – which cost them 90 paise, Rs 2.10, Rs 3.70, Rs 4.65, or Rs 5.60. Balaji Vittal remembers stature in life was also broken up into ticket prices from the front row (avoidable) to dress circle (unaffordable). The rickety (sometimes bug-infested) seats, the whirring fans, the soggy carpet, the dodgy sound system, the cranky projector – all seemed hell-bent on reducing the enjoyment of the movie-going experience.

And yet, when I spoke to these movie buffs, what struck me was the casual steadfastness with which they went about their job of watching films. Did you identify with the 'Angry Young Man'? Identify? Was censorship a big issue? What censorship? Did the violence in films turn off women and family audiences? What violence? Were the facilities at theatres good enough? Why? It was as if – as Suresh Kumar said – the 'whole country's life mission was to watch Amitabh in the first week, if not the first day itself'. It was indeed the worst of times, it was the best of times. If getting tickets was difficult, taking a day off from work to stand in the queue was still possible. Information was scarce, but time wasn't to look for those scraps. If entertainment was limited, the passion to experience it was unbounded.

I will try to explain the 1970s through the defining movie of the decade, *Sholay*. Of the thousands of memorabilia associated with the film, one of my favourite *Sholay* artefacts is a nondescript listing of weekly collections for the first fifty weeks at Rajkot's Galaxy cinema. The first few months of houseful breathlessness gave way to a substantial audience week after week, filling up multiple shows even during weekdays, till the shows reduced after a couple of quarters and finally, *Sholay* made way for another film. This is a good metaphor for the times when you grew up;

you grew older as stars became superstars. Bit-part players became household names. Dialogues became lingua franca. And cinema became our culture. People talked about the art, not collections. People mimicked their favourite stars, and children often unwillingly entertained guests with those acts. People bought the records and went deep into the music. They went back to see the film again and again, often buying tickets in black, for many times the actual price. For years.

It is said that years dull the pain, and only happy memories survive. Movie-watching in the 1970s had the anxiety of not having enough information, the discomfort of queueing, the disappointment of missing shows, and the often-exorbitant ticket prices. But all that paled into insignificance when you did manage to get the tickets, picked up popcorn and cream rolls from the snack counter, and went through the ads of Wills Filter and the trailers of forthcoming attractions. Finally, the movie started, and the magic made up for all the pain. Indeed, it made up for life itself.

SHOLAY

At

Galaxy Cinema

RAJKOT

Week	Net Collections
1st	27,307.14
2nd	27,602.00
3rd	28,982.10
4th	27,602.00
5th	28,982.10
6th	28,982.10
7th	28,716.90
8th	28,556.30
9th	28,775.40
10th	28,303.15
11th	27,913.00
12th	28,708.00
13th	27,074.50
14th	27,981.95
15th	24,000.50
16th	25,833.90
17th	25,348.65
18th	24,844.25
19th	24,373.40
20th	25,418.40
21st	24,942.40
22nd	24,121.65
23rd	22,497.90
24th	18,456.20
25th	19,201.83
26th	15,438.80
27th	16,227.17
28th	15,331.21
29th	16,075.40
30th	16,184.26
31st	18,347.76
32nd	16,859.28
33rd	16,532.81
34th	13,424.50
35th	11,833.49
36th	13,895.35
37th	12,425.23
38th	12,287.11
39th	11,184.08
40th	13,779.02
41st	8,279.97
42nd	10,395.92
43rd	9,316.99
44th	9,558.20
45th	15,578.68
46th	12,818.01
47th	7,092.28
48th	8,851.22
49th	9,813.87
50th	17,041.97
TOTAL	Rs. 9,83,398.64

How My Grandmother Came to Love Hindi Cinema and Amitabh Bachchan

Memories of Another Day

Shantanu Ray Chaudhuri

It has been an abiding regret with me that I was not old enough in the 1970s – the decade Amitabh Bachchan ruled the world of Hindi cinema – to understand the magnitude of the Big B phenomenon, to be part of the crowd that thronged his films. In 1979, when *India Today* termed him the 'one man industry', I was barely ten years old and having recently arrived in New Delhi from a small township in Assam, I hadn't even heard of *India Today*.

Again in 1982-83, when he hit a purple patch with the success of *Khuddaar*, *Namak Halaal* and *Coolie*, I was in Shillong, where films came a long time after their release all over the country. I had just an inkling of the kind of hysteria he could generate during his battle for life after the accident on the sets of *Coolie*. An elderly lady who lived next door came over to our place every day on her way back from the temple and, with tears in her eyes, would tell my mother about having offered prayers for Bachchan's recovery.

I discovered Bachchan in 1984, the year the Big B took a sabbatical from films to join politics at the behest of Rajiv Gandhi.

Cable TV was still unheard of and Doordarshan was the only avenue for films on television. Bachchan's films were few and far between, often limited to only one film in the entire year. So when *Faraar* was shown on TV it was celebration time as was the rare Bachchan song aired on *Chitrahaar*.

During this period, Bachchan's absence from tinsel town, the video boom and a string of big budget multi-starrers which bombed at the box office made a host of theatres opt for rereleasing old Bachchan films from the seventies. And most of these films – *Mr Natwarlal*, *Shaan* – went on to do better business than the new releases. Theatre owners opted for a strategy of releasing his well-known films in the main shows while the morning shows were generally reserved for his smaller, relatively untalked-of films.

At sixteen, I was probably just the right age to appreciate the angst of *Deewaar*, *Trishul* and *Zanjeer* and I often returned home with an anger directed at all forms of authority, carefully cultivating an image of a wronged loner. Even as a lonesome Vijay kicked a can around on the beach in *Shakti*, I did that on my solitary wanderings. My poor father must have wondered how he had wronged me when my attitude towards him changed after I watched *Trishul*. I just could not get '*Main uss Shanti ka beta hoon, Mr R.K. Gupta … aur aap mere naajayaz baap hai*' out of my head (though my mother was very much alive and had not been wronged by my father in any way). I might have even considered having '*Mera baap chor hain*' tattooed on my arm! And my maternal grandmother could never get me to visit a temple. For the longest time I could not walk past one without muttering, '*Aaj khush toh bahot hogey tum*'. Till one day my grandmother declared, '*Chhamra tar maatha khachhe ei lokta.*' (There's no way I can translate that to get the exasperated essence of that, but roughly: This man [Amitabh Bachchan] will be the ruin of the boy.) How she, by the time she passed away years later, had become a die-hard Bachchan fan is a story worth narrating.

Over the years, a change came over her. As she stayed on with us, she began watching Hindi films on television. Then, when we acquired a VCR, and then when cable TV arrived, her love for cinema became more pronounced. And she would spend hours watching films. In the afternoons, when he cajoled her to take her forty winks, she would pretend to be folding the clothes from the clothesline, spending the entire duration of the film standing next to the sofa, arranging and rearranging the stack of clothes, shaking her head and shedding tears at what the film's hero, often Amitabh Bachchan had to go through. My maternal uncle, her son, resembled Bachchan from certain angles – at least he did so to our childhood imaginations and we often discussed that at home – and I wonder if she too saw in Bachchan her son. Towards the end of her life, she not only watched teenybopper romances like *Qayamat Se Qayamat Tak* with me in the theatres, but was also among the eager, almost delirious crowds that thronged blockbusters like *Shahenshah* and *Hum*. It must have been a strange sight – a seventy-year-old in a crowd going crazy with '*Jumma chumma*'. And though Dad's verdict for both films were unprintable, and my own feelings were not very charitable either, nothing could shake Didima's conviction in how great the films and Bachchan were. I had converted her to the cause of Hindi films and Amitabh Bachchan.

But I digress. In the 1980s, when I discovered the Bachchan of the seventies, if the main shows screened most of his angry young man and popular films, the morning shows screening films like *Manzil*, *Do Anjaane*, *Mili*, *Benaam*, *Bandhe Haath*, and *Saudagar* revealed a different facet to the actor. His everyman roles in these films made him seem like a close relative, a benevolent young uncle rather than the superstar he was.

A little older and in the throes of life's first crush I watched *Muqaddar Ka Sikandar* and my starry eyes, on the verge of tears, discerned in his unrequited longing for his beloved 'memsaab' my own story of floundering amorous yearnings. Or for that matter as he called out 'sakhi' to Raakhee in *Bemisaal* (1982) in an unforgettable intonation, he launched my own adolescent search for someone I could call by the name. People who swear by films like *Deewaar* and *Zanjeer* as his finest performances and generally run down his ability as a romantic lead do him a great injustice.

Bemisaal is undoubtedly his most accomplished performance for the sheer complexity of the role, with its shades of the lover, the loner, the gregarious flirt and yes, probably the most subtle representation (along with *Alaap*) of his ubiquitous 'angry young man'. I watched *Alaap* in 2023 on the TV with my author–friend Gajra Kottary – she hadn't watched it yet – and cried without a thought that I was over fifty years old and was sitting next to an author I had just published!

Conventional Hindi film wisdom credits Salim–Javed with the creation of Amitabh Bachchan's angry young man image, with directors like Prakash Mehra, Yash Chopra and Ramesh Sippy, to name just a few, helming some of the most iconic 'angry young man' films. However, even though *Zanjeer* is credited with birthing the image, and films like *Deewaar*, *Trishul* and *Shakti* popularizing it, the real credit for it should go to Hrishikesh Mukherjee.

More than two years before *Zanjeer*, Hrishikesh Mukherjee – and his regular team of writers like Gulzar, Bimal Dutta and D.N. Mukherjee – gave us Dr Bhaskar Banerjee or Babumoshai in *Anand*. And the one thing that makes the film work, apart from the music, is the despair and angst that Amitabh Bachchan imbued Babumoshai with. Frankly, I never quite bought into Anand's philosophy of life. Rajesh Khanna looks too in the pink of health to work as a cancer patient. And the joy he radiates becomes a tad too overbearing after a point. There's little consideration for the travails of a cancer patient, and the lack of a family takes away one huge aspect of dealing with cancer – the effect it has on a family. I am aware that the film is more about a certain philosophy than anything else, but these are lacunae I could never get over. The one true persona in the film is Babumoshai and it's the first of Bachchan's angry characters.

Following soon after *Zanjeer* (which means they were very much in production simultaneously with *Zanjeer*), we have *Abhimaan* and *Namak Haraam*, the latter largely instrumental in Bachchan's superstardom in the wake of *Zanjeer*. Directed by Hrishikesh Mukherjee, both films cast Bachchan in roles with bitter overtones. It was a template he would resort to for all his films starring Amitabh Bachchan, barring *Chupke Chupke*: *Mili*, *Alaap*, *Jurmana* and *Bemisaal*. Of course, Mukherjee's angry young man was vastly different from Salim–Javed's. For one, he never raised a fist, there were no dishum-dishum, no explosive dialogues and no final catharsis in a fight to the finish. The anger simmered at a subterranean level, as a subtext.

Of these films, *Alaap* stands out for a number of reasons. For one, in an era when the superstar could not deliver a flop even if he tried to – just look at his roster of films in the years 1976-79 – *Alaap* came a cropper at the box office (the only other Bachchan film of the time that failed miserably was *Imman Dharam*, ironically, scripted by Salim-Javed). But while *Imman Dharam* was a rank bad film, *Alaap* has come to be regarded as one of Bachchan's best, just that it broke away too much from the star's popular image, with an outlook that is relentlessly bleak.

Second, it cast Amitabh as a trained classical singer – another first (in fact, there are no other films in his career which had him play a classical singer). For an Amitabh film of the era, it might come as a surprise that the film begins with a dedication to Mukesh and K.L. Saigal and the title credits play out against a visual of Amitabh Bachchan singing the Saraswati Vandana! Though I never bought the argument made by many during the era that his films sounded the death knell for good music, *Alaap* remains a true outlier among Amitabh's films – the one with a truly classical score and arguably his finest musical. And though by this time, Kishore Kumar was the recognized and acknowledged voice of the star, *Alaap* made a change here too with Yesudas providing the playback for the star for the first time, and how!

So, *Alaap* took one risk too many for a mainstream Hindi film of the era. As the film-maker himself observed, it was almost blasphemous to have Amitabh play the sitar and harmonium when audiences wanted him to be firing guns. In an interview to *Filmfare*, he said: 'The film had Amitabh Bachchan holding a tanpura – which was too much for the audience to take. Amit's image of the angry man, always fighting, was becoming very strong then. Besides, the film was depressing, the characters were faced with far too many problems. The classical music base for the songs didn't go down well either.'

But for the viewer looking for a different take on the angry young man, *Alaap*, based on a story idea by the irrepressible Harindranath Chattopadhyay, developed by the director, with scintillating dialogues by Rahi Masoom Raza and Biren Tripathy – offers a richly rewarding experience. It begins with Alok (Amitabh Bachchan) returning home after training in classical music. That his father Triloki Prasad (Om Prakash) – whom he refers to as 'Herr Hitler' – does not approve of his passion is evident at their first meeting when he peremptorily asks Alok what he intends to do with life now that he has had his little diversion in music. He fails to recognize Alok's dedication to music, and above all, his sense of fair play and justice, that will cast asunder all familial ties.

Back home, Alok meets his old friend Ganeshi (Asrani, who also gets to sing two songs) who drives a tonga. It is through Ganeshi that Alok makes the acquaintance of Sarjubai (Chhaya Devi), a retired courtesan of Banaras in whose home Ganeshi and his sister Radhiya (Rekha) are tenants, and who imparts music lessons to Radhiya. After a tetchy first meeting with Sarjubai, who initially comes across as cantankerous and dismissive of Alok's musical credentials, Alok eventually manages to win her heart and confidence and becomes her pupil too.

In the course of his interactions with Sarjubai, Alok also meets her long-time companion, 'Maharaj' (Manmohan Krishna), who, we learn, left his privileged upbringing and family to devote his life to Sarjubai (a theme that is echoed in Alok's relationship with Sarju too), accompanying her as a tabla player. It is here that he also hears of Raja Bahadur (Sanjeev Kumar), a connoisseur of music who shares a special relationship with Sarjubai.

Triloki Prasad, a 'respected' member of the town who prides himself on his family honour and who is looking to contest local elections, discovers his son's association with people he categorizes as 'no-account riffraff'. To teach his son a lesson and put an end to his relationship with his newfound friends, he uses his skills as a lawyer to evict Sarjubai from her home, eventually forcing her to go back to Benares. But he has not reckoned with his son's determination and strength of character, and the stage is set for a classic father-son conflict, the staple of quite a few of Bachchan's angry young man films.

It begins with Triloki giving Alok money to purchase a second-hand car, which the latter uses to acquire a tonga. In a fitting riposte to his father, Alok decides to make his living by driving a tonga, thus demonstrating his solidarity with the 'humble' people his father seeks to destroy given his false pride in his lineage and family honour. But Triloki is not one to take this lying down. He introduces a bus service in the town, thus rendering Ganeshi and other tongawalas out of work. A distraught Ganeshi sets a bus on fire and is imprisoned.

Nothing, however, can dampen Alok's resolve to fight it out. He marries Radhiya at Sarju's request and they have a son. But conditions are tough and with neither party willing to give in, Alok contracts tuberculosis, an affliction common to rickshaw pullers. Finally, it takes Raja Bahadur's intervention for Triloki Prasad to see the error of his ways. But it may already be too late. The song that Alok sings at the memorial service for Sarjubai is as much an ode to her as it is an elegy for him.

Though the conflict between father and son is the staple of many a Hindi film, including many of Bachchan's, what sets *Alaap* apart is its approach to the conflict. You can see the understated fire in Alok, in the way he chides Radhiya for suggesting that he make it up with his father, in the way he dares his father by deciding to make a living as a tongawala. Above all, in the way he reasons that as an artist he would amount to nothing if he cannot stand up to the injustice meted out to his fellow human beings. These are all aspects that feed off his angry man image, but rendered anew, with none of the fire and brimstone of his other films in this avatar. Above all, where *Alaap* scores is in the way it makes a point about the egalitarian nature of music, one that transcends caste and class. No other Bachchan film has ever done this.

The film is also notable for the way it addresses social and political issues. In one brilliant sequence, more effective for the unobtrusive way in which it plays out, Triloki hails a tonga, realizing that his son is the driver only when he proffers him money for the ride. It says a lot about the way we approach a certain class of people. Triloki does not even look at the face of the rickshawallah till he reaches out to make the payment. Or consider Sulakshana (Farida Jalal), a trader's daughter with whom Triloki contemplates Alok's marriage, who tells Alok, 'Enough is enough, you can't go on being a tongawalla' to which Alok's response reveals our inherent biases against work that involves manual labour. There's also an offhand comment on the changing face of electoral practices as Triloki Prasad asks his campaign manager to make a bloc-wise break-up of the electorate by caste and religion to ensure that the right canvasser goes to the right region. A practice that has reached its full flowering in many states of contemporary India.

Another beautifully done aspect pertains to the way the film paints the picture of a surrogate family and its strong ties over biological ones. In one of the film's most telling sequences, as Sarjubai lies dying, the three men around her are Maharaj, Raja Bahadur and Alok, none of whom are related to her by blood. It is a common love for music that has bound them together for a lifetime. That extends to every other relationship that Alok has – with Ganeshi, with his sister-in-law (played with great feeling and charm by Lily Chakraborty), with Sulakshana. In contrast, the one blood relationship, with his father, is fraught with discord and discontent.

What makes this aspect come across so strongly is also Chhaya Devi's performance. Though in many ways, Sarju is the mother figure we see in countless Bachchan films, and though she stands in as a surrogate for his deceased mother, there's none of the stereotypical melodramatic overtones we normally associate with the mother figure in Hindi films of the era. And that also holds for her portrayal of the courtesan which flies against the conventional portrayal of baijis in Hindi films. It is ultimately the relationship between Alok and Sarju, and between Sarju and the rest that gives the film its narrative strength.

A palpable sense of loss pervades the film, which is as much a lament for a lost way of life, a new more aggressive world replacing a genteel one of adab and tehzeeb and leisure, an era of classical music and its practice coming to an end (as the guru at Alok's music school says, '*Ab toh sadhana ka lamba raasta hai, jo jeevan ki tarah saral bhi aur kathin bhi hai*'). Music calling for a lifetime of commitment and dedication, and thus rendered irrelevant in a world changing by the day. This is also manifest in the way automobiles replace the hand-driven rickshaw, leading Ganeshi to say, '*Bus mein tel jalta hai, par tange mein janawar ka khoon*.' (A bus runs on fuel, but a tonga runs on the animal's blood.)

Towering above all is the film's music by Jaidev, that outstanding and criminally neglected and overlooked composer. I have already mentioned the film's classical music credentials and this being the Amitabh Bachchan film with the finest music. Rahi Masoom Raza too never scaled the highs as a lyricist that he did with *Alaap*. But what makes the music really stand out is the way it is integrated with the narrative and underlines its many relationships, with some of its most memorable vignettes woven into the songs.

Consider, Yesudas's mellifluous '*Chand akela jaaye sakhi ri*', for example, in which Alok pleads the moon's case as a plaintiff, with Amitabh's mock courtroom dialogues punctuating the song. Not only does it provide the narrative with some lively moments, it also establishes the deep bonding between Alok and his sister-in-law, one of the driving forces behind his passion for music. Then there's '*Ayi rut sawan ki*', impeccably rendered by Bhupinder and Kumari Faiyyaz, which provides a delectable short-hand to Sarjubai's relationship with Raja Bahadur, and is bound to bring a lump to every throat. In '*Nai ri lagan*' (Yesudas, Madhurani and Faiyyaz), you have the film's most heart-warming scene as Alok bends down to touch Sarju's feet during a Holi celebration – in a typically, for the film, low-key commentary on music's ability to upend social and caste rigidities, a moment that moves you beyond words. And the pièce de resistance: Harivansh Rai Bachchan's '*Koi gaata, main so jaata*'. Both a lullaby and an elegy, I wonder if there's another song in Hindi cinema that brings these two forms together with as much feeling as this. In three-and-a-half minutes of exquisite poetry, flawless composition and heartfelt rendition (by Yesudas), the song provides a snapshot of the film and the journeys its characters have undertaken.

For me, *Alaap* epitomizes a lost world in Hindi cinema, when technique and technology had not yet overshadowed content. All Hrishikesh Mukherjee films for that matter are basic when it comes to the technique, he was never breaking new ground with style, but there's something about the telling that make the films resonate even today. And as a fan of Amitabh Bachchan, others may swear by *Deewaar* and *Sholay*, *Agneepath* and *Zanjeer*, but for me nothing beats the charming everydayness he imbued his characters with in films like *Saudagar* and *Manzil*, *Bemisaal* and *Alaap*.

One only needs to look closely at his 'smaller' films to get an idea of the range he is capable of. The repentant playboy of *Jurmana*, the husband in *Do Anjaane* and the tumour-afflicted fugitive in *Majboor* are veritable showcases of his range as an actor. Not that any actor who delivers films as diverse as *Deewaar*, *Kabhi Kabhie* and *Amar Akbar Anthony* in three consecutive years needed any proof. Ask anyone about his memorable drunk sequences, and chances are that people will mention *Amar Akbar Anthony*, *Satte Pe Satta* or even *Hum* – there was of course *Sharaabi* too – but if you ask me, the sequence in *Do Anjaane* stands heads and shoulders above these.

What endeared me most to Bachchan of these films was the fact that he so eloquently conveyed emotions without ever seeming to try. He did not have to rave and rant to convey his anger. His eyes sufficed and his baritone would do the rest. A case in point is the scene in *Kala Patthar* where he confronts a thug (Sharat

Saxena) who brandishes a knife. Bachchan simply looks at him and intones deadpan, '*Tu to gaya, Dhanna.*' (You are a goner, Dhanna). And you knew the man has had it. And if he was the larger-than-life entertainer in the Manmohan Desai films, he punctuated these with the man-next-door roles in the films by Hrishikesh Mukherjee. The star and the actor working in tandem well enough not to encroach into each other's territories.

Those were the days when Bachchan was relatively inaccessible to the media. Information on the man and the star was not forthcoming. But all this was to change, and I am yet to understand if the change was for the better. As he began to feel the heat following the suspicions of his involvement in the Bofors tangle, he opened up to the media. To my delight, film magazines fell over each other in coming out with 'specials' on the man and the star.

For the first time, I had access to the fact that in the eleven years since 1973, when *Zanjeer* was released, only three of his films (*Alaap*, *Imaan Dharam* and *Faraar*) had failed to recover their investments. Films like *Shaan* and *The Great Gambler* which were written off as flops at the time of their initial release, went on to become successful when re-released. In fact, some of his films made more money on re-releases than many a hit film starring other actors.

It delighted me to learn that of the fifteen top grossers in the history (at that time) of Hindi films, as many as six starred Bachchan in the lead. And it seemed a matter of personal pride to know that in a particularly golden streak in 1978, five of his films – *Muqaddar Ka Sikandar, Trishul, Don, Kasme Vaade* and *Ganga Ki Saugandh* – were released in the span of two months and each went on to become a jubilee hit.

Armed with the facts and figures of the box-office performances of his films, the stories of his legendary professionalism, I would slug it out with any friend and acquaintance who dared cast an aspersion on the man or his stardom. The mid-1980s were a period when stars like Mithun Chakraborty, Sunny Deol and Anil Kapoor had started to make their presence felt. A number of my friends were shifting allegiance to these stars, and would needle me with stories of the successes of their films. However, as far as I was concerned, they were merely pretenders.

With the data I had on me I inevitably came out trumps. When they talked about the poor quality of some of his films (*Mard*) I only had to point out his rare charisma which catapulted some real clangers to box-office glory. It helped that *Geraftaar*, which released at the time, smashed the box office despite his billing as a 'special appearance'. And when people carped about his financial duds like *Alaap*, I always had the trump card of his performance which no one could argue about.

That invariably brought people to talk about his involvement in Bofors which I pooh-poohed with the comment that character assassination is a favourite Indian pastime. I lost a few friends in the bargain. I took any slight on Bachchan personally, and would fight and sever ties with anyone who dared to question his stature or compare any of the wannabe newbies with him. But as long as I had Bachchan and his films, everything else was dispensable.

Shahenshah marked his return to films post-politics. It also marked the first chink in my blind devotion. The media had gone to town with the impending release. The hype was overwhelming with reports of Bachchan himself being so impressed with the film that he had seen it close to seventy times. The radio promos with Kishore Kumar belting out '*Andheri raaton mein*' sent a chill down my spine. The advance bookings – with mile-long lines – were threatening to turn film theatres into veritable war zones. I would visit theatres simply to partake of the thrill of seeing lines of ticket seekers snaking a mile and more long.

So when I saw the film, my first taste of the Bachchan draw in live (I had seen *Kaalia*, *Satte Pe Satta* and *Desh Premee* in the theatres when they had released in 1981-82, but it was my father who had purchased the tickets), I was filled with a disappointment I could not account for. His next films did nothing to assuage the sense of being let down. In fact there was probably no sight more tragic (discounting the abominable '*Mere angne mein*' in *Laawaris*) than Bachchan on screen with a crocodile on his back in *Ganga Jamuna Saraswati*, as though saddled with déjà vu. For the first time I could not come up with arguments to counter those who were beginning to write him off. I felt betrayed, as though Bachchan owed me a better deal personally.

I wonder whether I had grown up or whether his films had become smaller. Because none of his films in this phase came remotely close to my expectations and the hype they generated. There were the odd sparks in *Agneepath* and *Main Azaad Hoon* but something had gone missing. His return after another five-year break following his misadventures with ABCL and beauty contests was even more disappointing.

Somewhere down the line he seemed to have lost that endearing connectivity. The entertainer had overtaken the actor. In his post brand-entity image, he may have become more accessible to the media, with interviews and promotions dime a dozen, but paradoxically for me he seemed to have become inaccessible and distant.

His performances, particularly the anger, seemed forced and in contrast to the subtlety of the past, was loud and jarring. *Major Saab* is a major case in point where he simply barked out a one-note performance devoid of any vocal nuances. Or *Khuda Gawah* for that matter, the first Bachchan film I left midway through because I simply could not take the loudness (there was this pronounced 'hainn' that had entered his dialogue delivery which grated), let alone the loopholes in the script through which entire battalions could pass. And what could have been sadder than watching him try to outpace Govinda in *Bade Mian Chote Mian*. Or being a pale shadow of himself trying to match Daler Mahendi in '*Na na na na na re*' in *Mrityudaata*. But my falling out of Bachchan fandom is a piece for another day.

In his avataar as a TV game show host, he rediscovered his touch, his ability to connect with the masses. He reinvented himself. Unlike those who made rather uncharitable comments about his fling with television and his endorsement of every conceivable product, I had nothing against that. He was a performer and it was a job that paid him well. If we as individuals are free to take up work we like, there was no reason why Bachchan should be judged any differently.

For me what counted was the kind of films he delivered and that is what disappointed with unfailing regularity. To say that he is the strong point or the only good thing in mediocrities like *Mohabbatein* or the puerile *Kabhi Khushi Kabhi Gham* and *Kabhi Alvida Na Kehna* is a hoary cliché. He is the strong point of any film he acts in. Period.

Yes, he was brilliant in *Khakee* and *Dev*, *Nishabd* and *Eklavya*, but there was something about him in films like *Cheeni Kum* and *Paa*, *Pink* and *102 Not Out* (just watch Rishi Kapoor closely in this and you would know what I am saying), all rather celebrated, that I found jarring, that did not quite seem organic. I am not sure if the younger directors are too much in awe of him to rein him in, or that he had bought into his legend as the greatest of actors, but there is in these films a subtle playing to the gallery that takes away from his performances.

Watching *Mili*, again with Gajra Kottary, in the theatres, as part of Amitabh Bachchan's eightieth birthday celebrations, 'Bachchan: Back to the Beginning', with Jaya Bhaduri attending the screening, took me down a road I have not visited in ages. It's almost four decades now since Amitabh Bachchan first held me spellbound and I realize that the spell is a lot weaker than it was then. I know it will never be the same again. That is the price one pays for growing up, I guess. The last line of Rainer Rilke's poem 'Fears' – 'growing older has served no purpose at all' – could well have been written for what I experienced watching *Mili*. Though I know that it will never be, I would give anything to have restored in my heart what once was. That ultimately I think is the magic called Amitabh Bachchan.[1]

---

[1] I would like to thank Sumit Dasgupta for permission to reproduce parts of the essay which were published in *The Telegraph*, 11 October 2022, and Vinta Nanda, for the part pertaining to *Alaap*, which was published in *The Daily Eye*, 13 April 2022.

The Cassettes Revolution in India

How the Seventies Changed the Way We Listened to Music

Bobby Sing

The 1970s is largely known and discussed for social and political unrest within the country, the Emergency, and the rise of dissatisfied, angry youth revolting against the authorities. In the world of Hindi cinema, it is mostly remembered, or rather celebrated, for the emergence of the angry young man on the screen (Amitabh Bachchan), the success of writers (Salim–Javed), the fashion inspired by the West, and the change of sound in film music led by R.D. Burman.

However, what always remains missing in these mentions and celebrations is the way our country and its citizens gradually shifted to a new mode of playing music, which was independent of the restricted nature of the official medium or budget constraints.

The audio recording and music publishing industry in India virtually functioned as a monopoly right from its initial decades of the early twentieth century. Despite the presence of a few smaller labels, the industry manufacturing and releasing 78 rpm (revolutions per minute) records was largely represented by HMV (His Master's Voice), and film music was the genre that captured the major production for the market.

With the introduction of sound in movies in the 1930s, followed by playback recordings, film music grew further, reaching out to the remote areas of the nation. But another monopoly continued in the pattern of consumption, depending upon only one public broadcasting medium, the radio.

There were only three ways the general public could establish direct contact with their onscreen icons: theatre, radio, and gramophone records. Film magazines were there, but they had a narration given by a third party, thus devoid of the desired direct connect, and Doordarshan (television) reached the masses much later in the 1980s. Out of these three, while an occasional visit to the theatre was affordable, the radio was within the reach of the common man, allowing collective consumption, even if not personally owned by an individual. Gramophone records were never the medium of general public consumption due to their high price, limited production, and other technical requirements, including an electricity connection. That is the reason a gramophone record player and records remained confined to urban areas and the rich, elite class, who could afford to spend on them.

Thus, for a substantial majority of our population, radio was the only affordable option for listening to music (airing from either India or Sri Lanka), but that too had a limitation. The radio never gave the liberty to listen to what one wished to hear at any point in time. Through radio, one could only hear what was being aired, and that is where the 'out of reach' gramophone record players enjoyed the upper hand. This gap between what listeners wanted and the medium of playing music continued for almost three decades post-Independence, till the West made a breakthrough in the audio industry.

The Arrival of Cassettes: The Biggest Game-Changer in the Music Market

Introduced around 1966, audiocassettes arrived in major parts of the world during the late 1960s. But since India was a developing country, it took almost a decade for the medium to get established here because of various technical and political reasons.

The arrival of cassettes, tape recorders, and players proved to be the biggest game-changer in the music market world over. It was nothing short of a revolution that soon started overtaking LP (Long-Play) records production and sales, winning over enthusiastic music lovers. Apart from the low cost of production and distribution, the major reason for their success among the masses was the ease of operation. Having the option of being battery operated, they were not dependent on electricity, allowing the owners to take along their music on their travels out of home (just like a radio/transistor). A few years later, cassette decks in cars and small Walkmans became a key attraction, and then the availability of blank cassettes on which one's choice of songs could be recorded did the rest.

In short, cassettes made everyone – ranging from a daily wage labourer and driver to a school-going teenager – the owner of their music, as they could easily listen to their kind of songs in their cassette players at will.

The Delay in India

As the decade began with the Indo-Pak war in 1971 that resulted in the creation of Bangladesh, it took a long time for cassettes and affordable players to reach the common man in India. Surprisingly, even the market leader HMV was not quick enough to switch over to the production of cassettes during the early 1970s. Film magazines and print publications continued with the advertisements of new radios and record players in these years. In fact, the two leading music companies of that era, HMV and Polydor kept writing 'Records Now Available On' on the posters of their film soundtracks and other advertisements instead of 'Cassettes and Records Now Available On'. The change, including the mention of cassettes, began during the late 1970s and early 1980s.

The production and availability of cassettes and tape recorders/players got delayed because of various reasons, the key being the import restrictions imposed upon the new technology and related goods and raw materials by the government. The Emergency during the mid-1970s also became one of the causes behind the delay. But that is exactly how and when piracy or unauthorized cassettes and foreign-brand tape recorders, manufactured abroad, started coming into the market.

Imported Cassettes and Players: The Trending Two-in-Ones

One of the popular characteristics of the 1970s was the craze for imported products brought in by the affluent 'foreign-returned' friends and relatives. The most awaited and precious gift among those used to be the imported two-in-one radio-cassette players made in Japan, namely, Bush, Sony, National Panasonic, Akai, Aiwa, and Sharp. With these imported two-in-ones also came the unauthorized cassettes of our Hindi film soundtracks and hit compilations, recorded and manufactured abroad, not by HMV but by local labels mainly operating in the UK and the Middle East. Exploiting the technological advancement of that era, these labels smartly used the official LP records released in India as the original masters for their cassette-replicating units. It is an irony that the cassette revolution came to India through imported sets and piracy that continued to be a substantial part of the trade until the next decade.

Interestingly, this also got documented in the Hindi films made in the 1970s and period dramas depicting the era conceived in the later decades. The villains depicted as smugglers in these films can be seen dealing in gold, imported watches, and electronic equipment manufactured abroad. These goods escaped heavy import duty as they were smuggled into the country through different routes to be sold in the illegal, grey market.

The Widespread Cassette Mania and *Sholay*

The growing popularity of the medium in the unauthorized market alarmed the leading manufacturers in India and they gradually started the production of twin radio-cassette players and recorders, importing their major components like motors, belts, heads, ribbons, etc.

Incidentally, Ramesh Sippy's *Sholay* (1975) and its gradual box office success made an important contribution to this movement, providing a wake-up call to the Indian music industry. While the film was gaining momentum at the box office, its music was not selling. Polydor, the music company holding the rights, worked on the reason and found that instead of the songs, the dialogues of the movie were making a solid impact on the viewers. The audiences mouthed the dialogues in their repeated visits to the theatres and that gave an innovative idea to the company.

Catering to the public response, Polydor released different dialogues' EP records (extended play records, shorter than an album), with titles based upon the famous scenes of *Sholay*, for the first time in the audio industry. These short-duration EPs, with titles such as 'Veeru ki Sagai', 'Soorma Bhopali', 'Hamein Jail Jaana Hai', 'Gabbar Singh', and more, became an instant success. These EPs carried interesting quotes like 'The merry marriage proposal leading to the "Sooside" act'.

As the sales of these dialogue EPs soared, the company went ahead and released a three-LP set of complete dialogues and songs from the film, with a duration of almost three hours, with an inviting three-fold artwork. A first for the Hindi film industry. However, that 'never before 3LP set' was not within the reach of the common man thanks to its steep price. And that is again where piracy quickly came in with an unofficial triple- and double-cassette set of *Sholay*'s dialogues and songs, a format which later became a norm of the audio industry in the 1980s. The official 3LP set served, yet again, as the original master for these unauthorized duplications in the form of cassettes.

This pirated double-cassette set could soon be found playing in every retail outlet both in metros and smaller centres, which forced the music company to release the original cassette set serving popular demand. One of these pirated sets was the first to reach our home too, along with a National Panasonic tape recorder, and I am sure most of the readers would fondly remember having the same in their personal collection of those exciting times.

Such was the popularity of these dialogue cassettes that when played in shops, they would often result in people gathering in front of the display windows, simply listening for hours, exactly as we see people congregating for a cricket match in front of TV showrooms.

The Ease of Playing and Prices

Being battery operated, the two-in-one tape recorders became a preferred substitute for the immensely popular radio/transistor. Besides, the prices of the cassettes (mostly pirated) were a big attraction, available at less than half the price of an LP record. This price structure reduced further with more competition in the market, and the Indian household shifted to tape recorders and cassettes once they became affordable towards the late 1970s and early 1980s. However, radio still remained the most commonly available medium among the masses.

The shift was also evident when the print advertisements of leading music companies started mentioning 'Records and Cassettes Now Available On…' by 1980. Gradually, the cassette completely won over the market with LP record sales rapidly shrinking, giving way to a massive cassette-mania. In no time, these small-sized musical treasures and their market reached the lower-income group, slums, and remote areas of the country, existing without an electricity connection. The unprecedented popularity of the medium could be seen in the corner paan–beedi shops. They also became an economical medium for pre-recorded publicity (played in rickshaws) in times of elections campaigns and new film releases in villages and smaller towns.

Lajpat Rai Market in Old Delhi: The Cassettes Market Hub

With more players coming into the fast-progressing trade, a centralized market in a metro city was the need of the hour. The already existing radio-parts/electronics market known as Lajpat Rai Market in Old Delhi became the hub for the wholesale trade in cassettes in the country for the next three decades. Situated right in front of the Red Fort (Lal Qila), next to Moti Cinema building in Chandni Chowk, Lajpat Rai Market (one of the oldest markets in Delhi) was now the trending place for traders from the capital as well as other states of north India. Incidentally, another market next to Moti Cinema, known as Bhagirath Palace, was also the hub of film distributors' offices, who kept a sharp eye on the music business of their respective films.

Within a few years, small-sized authorized shops and roadside *khokhas* dealing in tape recorder parts and cassettes mushroomed in Lajpat Rai Market. The radio-parts/electronics market existed but the place was never the same once it became the famous cassette hub of the country. It turned into one of the most visited places in the next decades with traders taking trains in the morning and returning the same day or the next, ordering or getting their desired goods in bulk for their local supply in various cities. Coolies carrying heavy loads on their heads or carts could be seen moving throughout the day within the premises, and big trucks used to arrive with the cassette-lots in the morning, a fact many will find hard to believe in the present digital world, unaware as it is of the physical form of music.

One of my uncles owned a radio / tape recorder spare parts shop in the market, and I spent countless days and evenings sitting on the counter, looking for my free cassette of the day. It was in the course of these visits that I also saw Gulshan Kumar and his team briskly moving around in the market, from where he rose to become the undisputed king of the trade towards the late 1980s.

Crushing the Prevailing Monopolies

The cassette revolution conquered the era and, importantly, crushed three kinds of monopolies exploiting the people, the music, and its exponents since Independence. It first ended the domination of HMV in the music industry, making way for many other prominent players such as Polydor (Music India), T-Series (Super Cassettes), Weston, Venus, Tips, and hundreds of other local labels joining in the 1980s.

Second, it killed the monopoly of singers in film music, led by Lata Mangeshkar, Mukesh, Mohammed Rafi, Kishore Kumar, and Asha Bhosle. The arrival of other music companies brought more names into the limelight, widening the horizon in terms of voices. HMV, as the leading company with a strong hold over the industry proceedings, was always reluctant to give opportunities to new deserving singers, and it had its commercial reasons for the same. With new entrants in the music industry, fresh, talented voices found good support as they reached the masses, offering them a variety.

Third and most importantly, the cassette-mania gave a new lease of life to various musical genres in the country, which were otherwise not receiving any attention from either the music companies (led by HMV) or the public. Pop music and ghazal, independent of films, began to flourish, providing strong competition to film soundtracks. The change finally brought an end to the monopoly of film music ruling over the market for the last three decades.

The Rise of Various Musical Genres and Regional Markets

As cassette sales surged, HMV came up with a few albums of devotional and regional folk genres that were initially released as LPs but in limited numbers. These albums reaching the masses in the form of cassettes turned out to be a huge success. Hindi devotional tracks sung by names such as Lata Mangeshkar and Mukesh, and Punjabi folk songs sung by Surinder Kaur and Parkash Kaur were key examples of these bestsellers.

'Non-filmi' music such as traditional folk, classical renditions, ghazals, devotional, and pop music (which ruled the market in the 1990s) flowered. The music companies now had a new target audience to make music for, ranging from regional-language listeners to mature music connoisseurs, young teenagers, and kids. There was even music especially made or compiled for certain events and professions such as Holi, Diwali, Eid, Raksha Bandhan, shaadi/bidaai ke geet (wedding songs), and brass band/shehnai/dhol instrumental.

While other genres found a new audience through the arrival of cassettes, the real treasure for the music companies was the regional and devotional music genre. With a country blessed with such diversity of religions, languages, and cultures, these were the two genres that soon became as big as film music in the next two decades. For instance, HMV rediscovered the goldmine of Punjabi traditional folk and Shabad Gurbani lying in their vaults waiting to reach the masses in the form of cassettes. T-Series became the biggest player of both Hindi and Punjabi devotional music beginning in the late 1980s, going on to rule the market in northern India.

T-Series also introduced albums of qawwalis, ghazals, and stage plays (of Umar Sharif) by Pakistani artists in India; these were well received by the masses. In a nutshell, it will not be an exaggeration to claim that the introduction of cassettes was the reason behind the popularity of folk music, devotional music, ghazals, and cross-border content among the masses from the late 1970s.

The success of these genres further resulted in the development of the regional cassette market in India. Many more small-scale production units installed by local cassette companies were seen throughout the country mainly recording and selling region-based content that offered a plethora of musical options to the consumers.

The skyrocketing sales of such local albums resulted in the establishment of dedicated shops in Lajpat Rai Market which dealt in only regional-language albums in wholesale. On a personal note, I still recall smiling at a board close to our shop that read, '*Nepali Cyassette Yahan Payeench*' (Nepali cassettes are available here).

Since it wasn't the era of digital communication, the mega success of one regional-language album was not immediately known to the makers and sellers of other regions. But similar success stories were regularly reported from south India as well as other parts of the country in these particular genres, along with film music.

Piracy, Versions, Copyright Laws and Gulshan Kumar's Rise in the 1980s

The cassette business flourished, scaling new heights when the much-awaited tax rebates and liberal laws related to imports and local manufacturing were announced by the government around the late 1970s and early 1980s. It resulted in India becoming one of the biggest cassette markets all over the globe, selling both official and pirated products together with an unbelievable range of regions, languages, cultures, and genres – a feat unparalleled in the world market.

But with over 200 production companies operating in various states, the next decade grappled with bigger issues along with many notable successes. Continuing with the menace of piracy, this was the decade of the rise of cover versions, which created a big debate both within the industry among artists and among lawmakers in the government. Gulshan Kumar and T-Series were accused of being the pioneer of piracy, but the visionary knew how to deal with it all by finding the loopholes nobody could think about.

In the language of films, the 1980s were like the extravagant second half of a hugely entertaining musical movie. It had new amendments in copyrights laws, police raids, corporate rivalry, court cases, murders, and a lot more. But since we are here to recall the 1970s, I will conclude the essay with '*Picture abhi baaki hai, dost*'.

This hit 1977 musical production starred Rameshwari as the heroine and the son of Premnath and Bina Rai as the hero. Ravindra Jain composed the music and it won the Filmfare Awards for Best Dialogue and Screenplay. The success of this movie is said to have revived the flagging fortunes of Rajshri films. Identify the movie and its hero.

Answer: *Dulhan Wahi Jo Piya Man Bhaaye*; Prem Krishen

The Broken Melody

A Personal Nostalgia of the Seventies Lyrics

Varun Grover

There surely exists a German word for 'nostalgia for a time before our birth'. In fact, it's so common an emotion that every language in the world could have a word for it. Maybe the Urdu word *sadaa* (pronounced with a soft d) – echoes from a distant, invisible place – comes close to capturing the idea. But sadaa is too plain, too direct. Maybe no word exists because no word could capture this deep and complex emotion. How do you explain the taste of gulaab-jaamun to an alien who has accidentally landed on this planet?

It probably needs an art installation – something huge and momentous Anish Kapoor or Ai Wei Wei could make. Or an orchestral masterpiece – a complete album by Philip Glass perhaps. Or maybe a mix of science, art, and music – like a golden braid of Gödel, Escher, and Bach.

I have lived with this emotion all my life. The nostalgia of a time before me. Not to sound too dramatic but I remember a ten-year-old me crying alone in a room, hugging an audiocassette of Raj Kapoor's *Mera Naam Joker* (1970) while playing songs from the film on a small, elegant tape recorder with beautiful, industrial perforations on its body, acting as its speaker. I was probably overwhelmed by the kinetic violins in '*Jeena yahaan marna yahaan*' (lyrics by Shaily Shailendra) but I distinctly remember that some portion of sadness was from the fact that this music came into this world ten years before my birth. In a way, I had fallen in love with an older person. The impossibility of this love was making me sad.

Kal khel meim
Hum hon na hon,
Gardish mein taare rahenge sada.

This trend of falling in love with older persons continued in my life. Not just older, but in some cases dead also. Shiv Kumar Batalvi, Nazia Hassan, Begum Akhtar, Jaidev – all have given me the sadness of love.

I was born in the year 1980, just twenty-six days into the new decade, and hence the first images and music I consumed were from the decade just gone by, the 1970s. As many culture historians have theorized, the 1970s were like the age of post-puberty adolescence for our young nation. A decade of anger, confusion, and disillusionment for India on many fronts. Satyajit Ray's Calcutta Trilogy and Salim-Javed's Angry Young Man films depicted this social-political decline in its various dimensions.

In a way, I was born into this age of disillusionment. Everything 'great' was already behind me and only disappointment lay ahead. The moon landing and the theory of relativity had already happened; Ghalib, Dushyant Kumar, and Manto were dead; Nehru, Gandhi, and Patel were portraits on school walls; Dilip Kumar, Dev Anand, and Raj Kapoor were into their overacting phase; Lata, Kishore, and Rafi were *considered* past their prime; and the abstract, powerful idea of humanity itself felt like a cracked bathroom mirror with little of value to reflect back.

What made things even worse was that the '80s arrived not with introspection or even guilt but like an arrogant, blindfolded rhino running into a china shop – a rhino with huge, colourful speakers fitted on its back, blasting ribald derivative rhymes from them.

The quality of music degraded, cinema turned into a three-act circus, politics turned violent with multiple insurgencies rising, and barring a cricket World Cup victory in 1983, life in general felt listless. It's in times like these that my sinking heart started claiming the '70s as my own decade – a post-golden but pre-rotten period when poetry, music, and cinema were still full of joy and insights.

Initially it was an instinctive, need-based clinging to something, anything that could define me and my growing-up years. The strangeness of '*Acha unhein dekha hai, beemaar huyi aankhein*' (*Shankar Hussain*, 1977, lyrics by Kaifi Azmi, music by Khayyam, and the raspy vocals by Aziz Nazan and Babban Khan) or the insomniac restlessness of '*Raat bhar, aapki yaad aati rahi*' (*Gaman*, 1978, lyrics by Shahryar, music by Jaidev, and sung by Chhaya Ganguli) initially felt like a substitute for something greater that could have been. The memories of the '70s had that feel of insufficiency even for people who had lived through that decade.

But now when I look back, with the advantage of perspective, I can see that the '70s were not just the transitory, lost years but had a strong character of their own. They were full of prophesies and birthmarks unique – a sadaa of its own making.

The song that opened the doors for me to re-examine my relationship with the '70s was '*Main na bhoolunga*' from *Roti, Kapada, aur Makaan* (1974). Santosh Anand, a genius who didn't get his due, pens some of our deepest existential fears in words so *sahaj* that Shailendra sa'ab would have been proud. *Samay ki dhaara mein, umar beh jaani hai* is as good a phrase for the fleeting nature of life and memories as ever written. *Do ghadi jee lenge, wahi rah jaani hai*, he continues with a mix of hope and assurance.

Santosh Anand's other equally magical works are in *Shor* (1972) where he writes three versions of '*Ik pyaar ka naghma hai*' for three different situations in the film. *Zindagi aur kuchh bhi nahin, teri meri kahaani hai* – the chorus line of the song in itself is one of the most effortless encapsulations of this complex beast called life. *Kis baat ka rona hai, har cheez toh faani hai*, sings Mukesh's voice near the climax of the film and the sinking heart soars.

Much like Santosh Anand, another lyricist who made the '70s his own and still remained lesser-known was Yogesh sa'ab. I still meet people who are surprised to find that '*Zindagi kaisi hai paheli*' and '*Kahin door jab din dhal jaaye*' from Hrishikesh Mukherjee's *Anand* (1971) are *not* written by Gulzar sa'ab but by Yogesh. The tinge of sadness at being unable to crack the great puzzle of life captured in just one sigh, a '*haaye*' at the end of '*Zindagi kaisi hai paheli*' line is a work of true genius.

In 1972, Yogesh wrote lyrics for a stunning multi-mood album by Salil Chowdhury, Asit Sen's *Annadata*. Complex compositions like '*O meri praan sajani champawati aaja*' and '*Raaton ke saaye ghane*' were nailed with great precision by Yogesh sa'ab. The range of dialect-registers employed is also huge here, while retaining the playfulness in songs like '*Nis din nis din mera julmi sajan*'.

Later in *Rajnigandha* (1974) he broke new ground with the use of scholarly-Hindi phrases like *Mann ki seema-rekha* and *Anuraagi mann* in a meditative album composed by Salil Chowdhury. And again, the very next year he stamped his authority over philosophical-songs with the S.D. Burman-composed *Mili* (1975).

Jab main raaton mein taare ginta hoon
Aur tere qadmon ki aahat sunta hoon
Lage mujhe har taara, tera darpan
Aaye tum yaad mujhe, gaane lagi har dhadkan.

The way these lyrics flit between almost-tatsam-Hindi (*darpan*), tadbhav-Hindi (*taara, dhadkan*), and spoken-Urdu (*qadam*) while painting a picture of loneliness so vivid – my heart skips a beat every time.

Yogesh sa'ab's works even in lesser-known films like *Priyatama* (1977) shined. I don't think many people would know on which actor's face the famous Kishore Kumar song '*Koi roko na deewaane ko*' has been filmed. But the real tragedy is that even lesser number of people would know that the annual monsoon anthem even now – '*Rimjhim gire saawan, sulag sulag jaaye mann*' (from *Manzil*, 1979) has been penned by Yogesh – a criminally underrated grandmaster.

Jab ghunghron si, bajti hai boondein
Armaan humaare, palke na moondein.

But perhaps that was the real tragedy of the '70s – the minds and moods were shrouded in a fog of sorts, leaving many deserving names forgotten. Nothing stuck, so to say. It was also a decade of many poets dabbling in Hindi film lyrics and probably (just my assumption) going back disillusioned.

Kaif Bhopali was one such name who wrote gems like '*Chalo dildaar chalo*' (Kamal Amrohi's magnum-opus *Pakeezah*, 1972). It is a much-celebrated song with words that read like they just broke free of a cage:

Zindagi khatm bhi ho jaaye agar
Na kabhi khatm ho ulfat ka safar
Ulfat ka safar
Chalo dildaar chalo
Chaand ke paar chalo

But Kaif Bhopali's true masterpiece is a gentle song from *Shankar Hussain* (1977) sung by Lata Mangeshkar: '*Apne aap raaton mein*'.

Apne aap raaton mein
Chilmanein sarakti hain
Chaunkte hain darwaaze

Seedhiyaan dhadakti hain
Apne aap.

A whisper of a song with words that evoke anticipation and sensuousness through the use of simple objects like *chilman* and *darwaaza.*

Koi pahle din jaise
Ghar kisi ke jaata ho
Jaise khud musaafir ko
Raasta bulaata ho

So many images of nervousness, doubt, and still a sense of magnetic compulsion appear in front of our eyes with these four short lines. True mastery.

Another underrated, nearly forgotten name from the decade is Naqsh Lyallpuri. In spite of his fairly long list of popular songs – '*Tumhein ho na ho*' (*Gharonda*, 1978, another song often mistakenly credited to Gulzar; '*Rasm-e-ulfat ko* nibhaayen' (*Dil Ki Rahein*, 1973), '*Ye mulaaqaat ik bahaana hai*' (*Khandan*, 1979), '*Pyar ka dard hai*' (*Dard*, 1981) – he could never hit the big league. It's the skewed effect Hindi cinema's 'star system' has had on every creative soul since its advent in the '70s. A lot of Naqsh sa'ab's great songs (like '*Ye wahi geet hai*' from *Man Jaiye*, 1972 – one of Kishore Kumar's all-time-great songs) were filmed on bad or unsuccessful actors, resulting in way lesser acclaim than they deserved.

Another much-loved Kishore Kumar song written by Naqsh Lyallpuri was '*Ulfat mein zamaane ki*' from *Call Girl* (1974), filmed on Vijay and Zaheera, the two actors with more wooden-expressions between them than Pinocchio.

The Lata Mangeshkar version of the song has this truth-bomb-laced call-to-hearts unlike anything else written before or after.

Duniya se bahot aage
Jis raah pe hum honge

Ye soch lo pahle se
Har mod pe gham honge
Hai khauf ghamon se toh
Ruk jaao, thehar jaao

The pain never leaves, even if we decide to brave the world and unite in love, says Naqsh sa'ab. Rarely has a Hindi love song tried to alert the lovers to this very real possibility of failure ahead. Derek Cianfrance's 2010 masterpiece *Blue Valentine* comes to mind. The song, and especially the lyricist, have been forgotten though.

It could still be me theorizing, but I believe it's exactly this characteristic – a did-it-even-exist-in-the-first-place kind of feeling that made the '70s unique. As if an entire decade fell and disappeared between the cracks of the decades before and after – and now we can only reconstruct it partially through names and words that echo faintly.

If I listen closely, I can hear Lata Mangeshkar's haunting voice, set to Jaidev's Escher-staircase-like composition wafting over a desert in *Reshma aur Shera* (1972). Lyricist Balkavi Bairagi, a much-respected literary poet, wrote for just a few Hindi film albums but the poetic weight of '*Tu chanda main chandni*' alone is enough to counter the entire filmographies of many others.

Na sarvar, na baavdi, na koi thandi chhanv
Na koyal, na papeehara, aisa mera gaanv
Kahaan bujhe tann ki tapan, o saiyaan sirmor
Chandra-kiran ko chhod kar, jaaye kahaan chakor

Could there ever be a more elegant, matter-of-fact expression of desire in a film song? Waheeda Rahman's character Reshma sings in Balkavi Bairagi's words – 'My village has no lakes, no trees, not even koyals whose sweet singing could at least make one forget their thirst. So tell me, o lover, how do I quench it?' It's ecology, romance, and biology all combined in some of the most delicate folk-Hindi poetry tradition. A high point of a decade that floated by like sand in this song.

Again in *Reshma aur Shera* (1972) – there was lyricist Udhav Kumar writing another sensory experience of a poetry with '*Ek meethi si chubhan*'.

Ae mere bhagwaan, itna kar ehsaan
Ye raswanti hawa kahin na, bann jaaye toofaan

Udhav Kumar uses such beautiful metaphors of *raswanti hawa* and *toofan* for a woman expressing her desire freely while also requesting fate to temper the feelings, lest she should lose control over her passions.

Jaidev sa'ab, as is well known, always remained open to working with new lyricists and singers, resulting in a body of work that has sustained the test of time and memory. In *Prem Parbat* (1973), Jaidev worked with Jan Nisar Akhtar ('*Ye dil aur unki nigaahon ke saaye*') as well as a rare female lyricist in the '70s, Padma Sachdev ('*Ye neer kahaan se barse*').

There are many more names to remember – an entire decade to reconstruct and hold up to the sun like a film-roll strip found on the roadside. Kavi Neeraj's rousing, breathless '*Dil aaj shaayar hai*' (*Gambler*, 1971) started the decade on a note of hurt but in the same year he gave us another rousing, breathless song of hope and togetherness in '*Ae maine kasam li*' (*Tere Mere Sapne*, 1971). Just a year ago, he had elevated the love-poetry genre to the skies with '*Phoolon ke rang se*', yet again for a Dev Anand film, *Prem Pujari*.

Saanson ki sargam
Dhadkan ki veena
Sapnon ki geetanjali tu

What could a boy born in 1980, pretending to be a memory-offspring of the decade before, write about this weaving of music metaphors in a musical. Nothing actually.

Kamal Amrohi also dabbled in lyrics writing for films not directed by himself – and one particular song that still resonates is '*Kahin ek maasoom, naazuk si ladki*' from *Shankar Husain* (1975). Rafi sa'ab's rendition of this Khayyam melody is exquisite but what stands out for me is the poetry. The minimal use of instruments and the alliterative use of words (*kasmasa-kasmasa kar, kapkapaati, gungunaati, jhanjhanaati*) creates an aura of spoken-word genre.

Another perspective time has given us is that the initial few decades of Hindi film music, even when labelled as 'Golden Era', are highly male-centric with more than 99 per cent of composers and lyricists being cishet men. We are covered in an entire sheet of blindspots, when looking back. Even Amrita Pritam, one of the most acclaimed poets of those times, would barely write a couple of songs for Hindi cinema ('*Ambar ki ek paak suraahi*' from *Kadambari*, 1975, is masterful). The voices silenced or lost, the words erased or never written robbed an entire era of diverse points of view, making the poetry and music poorer.

But who said nostalgia can only be guilt-free? The times and people that gave rise to this nostalgia must share the blame too. To extend the theory of the 1970s being post-pubescence years of our nation, we can now say they were the post-pubescence years of a typical Indian male. Full of possibilities and still trying to hold onto the old customs.

Inn rasmon ko, inn qasmon ko,
Inn rishte naaton ko – main na bhoolunga!

I would like to believe that in the recent years, and especially the last two decades, we have moved to a more equitable, more diverse nostalgia-making in the space of arts and sciences. This nostalgia of the 1970s, flawed and broken and poetic and sad and truly, truly hummable, we still have to own. And I own it, even if I was born in 1980.

Harindranath Chattopadhyay played the role of the patriarch, referred to as Daduji, in the Hrishikesh Mukherjee comedy, *Bawarchi* (1972) that starred Rajesh Khanna in the title role. What is his name in the movie?

Answer: Shivnath Sharma

Section II

Icons and Idols

Utpal Dutt's character in *Gol Maal* (1979) gets mistaken by Om Prakash for a smuggler in the penultimate scene. What is the name of the smuggler?

Answer: Pascal D'Costa

Dev Anand's *Ishk Ishk Ishk* (1974) starred three actresses – Shabana Azmi, Zeenat Aman and an actress who made her debut in this film in a supporting role. Identify the actress.

Answer: Zarina Wahab

Shyam Benegal

The Reason I Write on Cinema

Aseem Chhabra

Early 1974. A school friend told me about a film that was playing in theatres in Bombay. The film was *Ankur*, starring a young actress Shabana Azmi, who knew my friend's cousin. The director of the film was a man named Shyam Benegal.

Decades before social media and the Internet we would hear about films from word of mouth, articles in publications or advertisements on All India Radio. Even then there was little written about *Ankur* and I had not heard of Shabana Azmi or Shyam Benegal.

I was raised on a healthy diet of popular Hindi cinema. Film music was everywhere – playing at home, on the streets, blaring out of the corner paan shops, on transistor radios people would sometimes carry in buses. There was *Chitrahaar* (renamed *Chhayageet* for the Bombay market) – the half-hour-long weekly programme of Hindi film songs that I eagerly looked forward to on Doordarshan, where the stars would appear in black-and-white, lip-synching old classics.

Eventually, *Ankur* did play in a theatre in Delhi. In the pre-social media days Hindi films would often open first in Bombay and then slowly roll out in the rest of the country. I watched *Ankur* at Regal Cinema – a prime single-screen theatre located in Connaught Place. Basu Chatterjee's *Rajanigadha* also opened the same year – first in Bombay and later in Delhi.

A few years earlier I was charmed by the eccentricity of *Bhuvan Shome* – considered the first film in what was eventually referred to as the New Wave (a term inspired by the French New Wave) or parallel cinema movement – when it was broadcast on Doordarshan, after it won the National Film Award in 1969.

But *Ankur* blew my mind. The teenager in me had never seen or imagined a world in rural Telangana (the film was set in feudal India in 1945), where class and caste politics played out in a story of lust, a liaison between a young landlord (Anant Nag) and the wife (Azmi) of a farm-hire (a superb Sadhu Meher) and its consequences – the beating of the deaf-mute farm-hire, the outburst by his wife and the last shot of the smashing of the window that shocked me out on my privileged comfort zone.

There has been other Hindi films that dealt with discrimination and poverty in rural India – from *Dharti Ke Lal* (1950) to *Do Bigha Zamin* (1953) and *Mother India* (1957). But there was a specific authenticity in the world Benegal and his co-writer Satyadev Dubey created that impressed me – the colours of Azmi's saris, the way Govind Nihalani's camera captures her tying her hair as she wakes up from the landlord's bed, the dialogues spoken in Dakhni Urdu, the background sounds and the random characters populating the village. One could smell, feel the texture of this world, believable, with flawed characters who were no heroes.

Ankur won three National Film Awards including best actor and actress for Meher and Azmi. Her quiet, yet explosive performance made me a lifelong fan. In his collection of essays *Our Films, Their Films*, Satyajit Ray referred to Azmi as 'one of our finest dramatic actresses'.

A year later Benegal was back with an even more powerful film – *Nishant*, a bleak portrayal of a repressive feudal system which leaves no room for hope for humanity. Again set in the mid-1940s, *Nishant* was a tale of a village in Telangana terrorized by four landlord brothers; the kidnapping of a schoolteacher's wife and his desperation since no government agency was willing to help him by challenging the landlord brothers.

Based on a script by Dubey and Vijay Tendulkar, *Nishant* was populated with a large ensemble cast of actors – many from the Film and Television Institute of India and the National School of Drama. Yash Chopra introduced Hindi cinema to the first multi-starrer *Waqt* (1965). In 1975 two iconic mainstream films in Hindi were released – Chopra's *Deewaar* and Ramesh Sippy's *Sholay*, with all the top stars of the industry. In *Nishant*, Benegal matched the casts of these box-office chartbusters with what would become his repertory company of parallel cinema actors. These actors would appear again and again in his films and also of other film-makers working within the same framework of socially relevant New Wave films.

In addition to Azmi and Nag, *Nishant*'s cast also included Girish Karnad (his first Hindi film role), Amrish Puri, Mohan Agashe, Kulbhushan Kharbanda and two actors who would change my life, how I would view cinema and my perception of what talented performers were capable of doing in front of the camera. I am talking about Naseeruddin Shah and Smita Patil.

What a magical and a special time it was. The only equivalent of that in the current times would be when Anurag Kashyap's two-part *Gangs of Wasseypur* (2012) exploded on the screen with a number of talented relatively new actors – Nawazuddin Siddiqui, Huma Qureshi, Richa Chadha, Rajkummar Rao, Pankaj Tripathi, along with veterans like Manoj Bajpayee and Tigmanshu Dhulia.

But *Gangs of Wasseypur* was a one-time phenomenon. Benegal was now on a roll.

Ankur and *Nishant* were funded by Blaze Film Enterprises, India's biggest advertising-film company at that time. But for his third film in three years, *Manthan*, also referred to as part of his trilogy, Benegal found a unique way to of raise finances. For a story inspired by the work of Verghese Kurien, the pioneer of the milk cooperative movement in India, Benegal crowdfunded the film. Half a million farmers donated Rs 2 each to finance the film. *Manthan* opens with a title card that reads '500,000 FARMERS OF GUJARAT present'.

Manthan was a dramatic story written by Kurien and Benegal, and based on Tendulkar's screenplay. A well-meaning group of people – a veterinary doctor and his team – arrive in a village to develop a milk cooperative society, but their plans are hampered with caste politics and other rural complexities that city dwellers can never fully understand. The film was bookended with the catchy song '*Mero gaam katha parey*' sung by Preeti Sagar and composed by Vanraj Bhatia. In an acknowledgement of the parallel film movement, *Filmfare* recognized '*Mero gaam katha parey*' as the best song by a female playback singer.

Manthan also won the National Film Awards for best Hindi film and for Tendulkar's screenplay. All National Film Award winners would be assured at least one screening at Delhi's Vigyan Bhavan and that is where I saw the film. I still remember the sense of exhilaration when I went to Vigyan Bhavan for what was becoming an annual event of the year, a new Benegal film with the same group of actors: Karnad, Nag, Shah, Patil, Meher, Kharbanda among others.

By the mid-1970s a few more unique voices had emerged within the parallel film movement. Basu Bhattacharya explored middle-class marriages in *Anubhav* (1971), with Sanjeev Kumar and Tanuja. Three years later (the same year that *Ankur* was released) he cast two of the biggest Hindi film stars – Rajesh Khanna and Sharmila Tagore – in a slightly less successful *Aavishkar*. And the other Basu, as in Chatterjee, was dealing with lighter romantic comedies – *Rajnigandha* (1974), *Chhoti Si Baat* and *Chitchor* (both 1976).

Also in 1974, M.S. Sathyu, after a lot of struggle, managed to release what could be the best Hindi-language film of all time –

Garm Hawa. Sathyu worked behind the scenes with some of Shyam Benegal's regular contributors, namely, Kaifi Azmi and Shama Zaidi (Sathyu's wife, who wore many hats including production designer and later scriptwriter as well). And later in 1978 Muzaffar Ali, made *Gaman*, a heart-wrenching ode to migrant workers in big cities who can never save enough money to return home.

In a parallel universe – what seemed like a far-off galaxy – Amitabh Bachchan ruled the box office and the hearts of the masses, having acted in a string of popular films: *Kabhi Kabhie* (1976), *Amar Akbar Anthony* (Azmi played a supporting role in it, 1977), *Parvarish* (Azmi was in this too, 1977), *Trishul*, *Muqaddar Ka Sikandar* (both 1978), *Mr. Natwarlal* (1979), among others.

But with Benegal's cinema the viewer was assured of films laced with intense performances, rural settings far removed from the worlds of Amitabh Bachchan or what the two Basus were recreating, and a strong dose of caste and class politics that would make me sit up. All my political and social education in the 1970s came from Benegal's films. This was until Saeed Akhtar Mirza also began to explore the idea of class warfare in films such as *Arvind Desai Ki Ajeeb Dastan* (1978) and *Albert Pinto Ko Gussa Kyon Ata Hai* (1980).

The year 1977 had a few firsts. Satyajit Ray released his first Hindi/Urdu-language film, *Shatranj Ke Khilari*, a tale of two friends obsessed with the game of chess, while the British connivingly usurped Awadh. Ray cast Shabana Azmi (whom he noticed in *Ankur*) in a supporting role of a frustrated housewife, whose husband (Sanjeev Kumar) cannot get his mind off chess. Ray roped in Amitabh Bachchan to do the opening voiceover. The dialogues were written by Zaidi, who also designed the film's costumes. Around the same time Mrinal Sen was back with a Hindi film *Mrigayaa*, the struggles of a tribal community, where he introduced Mithun Chakraborty and Mamata Shankar.

But for his fourth feature film – in the same number of years (in between he had also made a children's film *Charandas Chor*) – Benegal changed the pace and the mood of his film-making.

Inspired by the autobiography of the Marathi stage and film actress Hansa Wadkar, he directed *Bhumika* and he cast Patil in the lead, giving her the best role of her short career. And once again he dipped into the pool of his regular actors – Shah, Nag, Puri, Agashe, Kharbanda. To the mix Benegal added two new faces – the renowned Marathi actress Sulabha Deshpande and Amol Palekar, who until recently was playing the charming boy-next-door kind of roles in Basu Chatterjee's films. In *Bhumika*, Palekar played a negative role of Usha's (Hansa's name is changed for the film) husband.

One Sunday afternoon a friend called to inform me about a small private screening of *Bhumika* at Delhi's Lady Shri Ram College. This was long before I became a film journalist and would be invited to press screenings and film festivals. So an invitation to the latest Shyam Benegal film was the best gift someone would give me.

Bhumika stunned me. By now I had seen enough social dramas exploring marital challenges, but mostly within the popular cinema framework. The level of reality, the period details in *Bhumika* were of another standard, with a very different aesthetic sensibility. The details of Usha's childhood home, the costumes, the furniture in the home of Vinayak Kale (Puri), where Usha is brought after she walks out of her marriage to Keshav Dalvi (Palekar), opened up another world, another India for me. Having grown up in Delhi, it was a world I knew little about since I had not been exposed to Marathi cinema or theatre.

Since it covered the career of a movie actress, *Bhumika* was the first Benegal film to feature a number of songs, all set to Vanraj Bhatia's music. He would not use so many songs in another film until 2001 when he made his most Bollywood film *Zubeidaa* with compositions by A.R. Rahman. For the title role of Zubeidaa, Benegal cast the leading actress of the Hindi film industry at the time, Karishma Kapoor, along with Rekha, who had already appeared in one more of his films – *Kalyug* (1981).

But *Bhumika* was a solid star-making vehicle for Smita Patil, much like what *Ankur* had done for Shabana Azmi. The challenging role covered Usha's life from childhood to a middle-aged woman. Patil was only twenty-two when the film was released. For *Bhumika*, Patil won the first of her two National Film Awards in the best actress category. Until *Bhumika*, she had been a reluctant actress. That film finally convinced her to pursue acting as a career and like Azmi she also began to seek work in the mainstream industry.

After what is considered a minor film *Kondura* (1978), also shot simultaneously in Telugu as *Anugraham*, Benegal was back in 1979 with a bang. *Junoon*, his most expensive film to date, was produced by Shashi Kapoor's Film-Valas production house.

Kapoor had never intended to become a film star. He essentially wanted to work in films to support his family. His heart was always into theatre, and smaller films such as those produced by Merchant Ivory Productions. But now that he had become a solid star, albeit reluctantly, he decided to give back to the industry by producing quality arthouse films. To pursue this goal, Kapoor produced six films – all artistic and critical success (except for the last one *Ajooba* which Kapoor himself directed). But baring *Junoon*, the other films lost money, putting Kapoor and his family in a dire financial situation.

That Kapoor chose to work first with Benegal, was an indication of how well the director had established his credentials as the leader of the parallel film movement.

Junoon was based on a novella by Ruskin Bond, *A Flight of Pigeons*. Bond's story about the romance between a young Anglo-Indian woman and an older married Muslim man, in the midst of the 1857 Mutiny, was set in Shahjahanpur, Uttar Pradesh.

Junoon again turned out to be a project where Benegal brought together his group of actors – some who had worked with him before: Azmi, Shah and Kharbanda. But this time it was a larger team including Shashi and Jennifer Kapoor, Nafisa Ali, Sushma Seth, Benjamin Gilani, Deepti Naval, Jalal Agha, Tom Alter, Pearl Padamsee and novelist Ismat Chughtai, in her only film role, while she also wrote the dialogues of the film.

Junoon holds a special place in my heart. The performances – especially some key scenes between Shashi and Jennifer – were among the best I had seen in my adult life, where I was beginning to understand the idea of good art in cinema. It was only the second time that Shashi and Jennifer had shared screen time. Prior to this they played lovers in James Ivory's *Bombay Talkie* (1970). But in *Junoon* they argued fiercely over the young Anglo-Indian woman Ruth Labadoor (Ali). Shashi's Javed Khan wanted to marry Ruth, while Jennifer's Mariam (Ruth's mother) stood between them, placing one condition after another. Meanwhile, Javed's frustrated first wife Firdaus (a terrific Azmi) helplessly watched the drama unfold in her house. And outside, the world was burning as Indian soldiers were giving up their lives fighting the British.

I have seen *Junoon* a number of times since the first viewing at Delhi's Archana Cinema. And in recent years I have attended two screenings of the restored print of the film courtesy Shashi's older son Kunal. He has meticulously restored all the films his father produced, preserving them for future generation of filmgoers. The print is in pristine condition with digital soundtrack. Had it not been for the sad fact that many of the actors in the film have passed on, it would seem as if *Junoon* had been made recently.

Junoon was a wonderful marriage, a perfect example of different strands of the Hindi film industry coming together – with a director committed to pursuing cinema as an art form, getting the backing of a producer who had the vision to finance projects that on paper appeared risky. Kapoor and Benegal would work together again in *Kalyug* (1981), a modern-day retelling of the Mahabharata where instead of the Pandavas and Kauravas we had two related business families in Bombay at war with each other.

Benegal kept busy through the next three decades and more, continuing with his quest to bring to screen stories of empowered women (*Mandi*, 1983 and *Hari-Bhari*, 2000), less fortunate citizens of India (*Susman*, 1987 and *Samar*, 1998). He also transitioned to biopics of leaders of modern India (Mahatma Gandhi, Subhash Chandra Bose) and a trilogy based on the life of film critic Khalid Mohamad (*Mammo*, 1994, *Sardari Begum*, 1996 and *Zubeidaa*, 2001). When the parallel film movement started to slow down and eventually died due to lack of financing and distribution options, Benegal turned to television and undertook a massive project *Bharat Ek Khoj* (1988–89), the retelling of the history of India based on Jawaharlal Nehru's *Discovery of India*. As late as 2023, Benegal directed *Mujib*, a biopic based on the life of the late Bangladeshi leader Sheikh Mujibur Rahman.

It has been a well-lived, rewarding life, and for his work he has been recognized by the Indian government with a Padma Shri in 1976, Padma Bhushan in 1991 and the Dadasaheb Phalke Award in 2005.

When I look back at my life, why I chose to become a writer on cinema, Benegal's influence is immense. His cinema of compassion inspired me, gave me tools to develop empathy for others. But it also made me understand that serious, socially committed cinema with deeply engaging narratives and great performances is an art form to admire, appreciate and explore.

This legendary actor was writer Salim's (of Salim–Javed fame) first choice for the role of Thakur in *Sholay* (1975). But the actor turned the role down saying it was a limiting one. Who was he?

Answer: Dilip Kumar

Which 1972 movie was directed by Ram Mukherjee and starred brothers Joy and Deb Mukherjee?

Answer: *Ek Baar Muskura Do*

Sanjeev Kumar

Jisey Dil Dhoondta Hai

Gajra Kottary

It was in the year 1973, when I was barely eight years old, that I first experienced the magic of the darkened cinema hall with *The Sound of Music* (1965). The film was considered a must-see for all children in the convent schools of Delhi.

From *The Sound of Music* to my infatuation with Sanjeev Kumar makes for an unusual story rooted in the traditional and discerning family values instilled in us by our father, a revered classical Indian musician. At an early age, I recall him being of the opinion that the golden era of Hindi cinema was the 1950s and '60s when socially relevant films were made. Such films told relevant stories and had fantastic actors and good music, but they were not being made any more. It's probably what every new generation of art and culture has to go through – a belief in the golden past and the sullied present.

Being a purist steeped in the art and the craft of classical music, my father naturally abhorred most film music. But he had heard the songs of the Sanjeev Kumar-starrer *Parichay* (1972), especially '*Beeti na bitayi raina*', and the music of this film had passed muster with him. Incidentally, Bhupinder had been one of my father's favourite playback singers, one who sang his few non-classical compositions. Soon he became my favourite singer too and over the years, he was associated with Sanjeev Kumar's best songs in films.

It was primarily because of its music that my father had approved of his children watching the movie. More importantly, my father had heard that *Parichay* was inspired by the acknowledged classic *The Sound of Music*. Little did he know the forces he was unleashing in me, with this small decision to allow us to watch *Parichay*.

So the three of us kids, including my brother and sister who were more than a decade older than me, went to the movie hall with our parents on this somewhat momentous occasion. As the movie unspooled, we watched agog, absorbing every moment, saving and filing it in our memories, to be able to relive it later, as avid viewers did those days.

And then 'he' appeared on screen. Even close to fifty years later, I get goosebumps recalling that moment, so clearly etched it is in my mind, being mesmerized by the man who 'sang' that iconic song in the film in Bhupinder's haunting, distinctive voice. He reminded me so much of my father, in his white kurta-pyjama and shawl. Like my father, his character spoke little as he went about wrapped in music and want, his eyes shining with love for his children. Incidentally, after seeing how realistically classical music had been portrayed here, my father too grudgingly accepted that *Parichay* might be an exception to the 'bakwaas' films of the '70s.

Unable to clearly demarcate reel from real, I came back possessed from the screening. So powerfully and perfectly did Sanjeev Kumar emote the role of the introvert musician that for many days after, in a case of convoluted logic, I imagined and feared that like Sanjeev Kumar, my father too would die soon. I froze with fear every time my father coughed, my mind conjuring up images of the dying Sanjeev Kumar.

It was a fear that I found tough to articulate even to my siblings, who, in those days, engaged in many discussions on

Jeetendra, Dharmendra, and Rajesh Khanna and their films which they, unlike me, could see with their peers from college as they were old enough, while I wasn't. While hearing these discussions, I tried hard and sometimes succeeded in pretending to be as grown up as they were. But truly speaking, I often did not understand the context in which they spoke as I had not seen any of the movies they were talking about.

My ears pricked up at the occasional mention of the 'also-ran' Sanjeev Kumar. But I was still confused. For me, the actor who sang '*Beeti na bitayi raina*' was now dead, wasn't he, as shown in the movie? I once remarked this to them, remembering *Parichay*. My siblings laughed at my naïveté and resumed discussions on the triumvirate of heroes of their time, while kindly reassuring me that the man who played the musician in *Parichay* had only been acting; he was not really dead. I wasn't entirely convinced about that. While I privately relived the scenes of Sanjeev Kumar from the only movie of his that I had seen until then, I still remained confused and hoped that neither he nor my father would ever die. This went on for many years. Time moved much slower then than it does now.

It was only after a few years when I watched *Koshish* (1972) and *Anamika* (1973) – both on television, and well after their official release – that my burdens finally lifted. I was relieved to realize that Sanjeev Kumar really was just an actor who had been playing only a role in *Parichay*. And that Jaya Bhaduri, my other childhood crush, was not his daughter, but an actor playing the woman he loved, in both these more recent celluloid viewings.

I wept watching *Koshish* and of course felt sheepish about that when my father 'caught' me. He then commented with an equal measure of pride and fear that I was too mature for my years, a phenomenon they describe in Hindi as '*payt mein daadhi hona*'. Little did he realize that this display of EQ was only due to the phenomenon called Sanjeev Kumar, an actor who had the capacity to make me cry and feel emotions that I did not even fully comprehend at that age.

If *Koshish* made me cry, *Anamika* made me smile, while I crushed even stronger on Sanjeev Kumar. In the absence of YouTube, where one can revisit scenes from movies as many times as one desires, I kept reliving the scenes from these movies in my mind. I recalled his dialogues that had stayed with me, sounding comic even to myself as I did so. Not even a teen yet, but with a '*daadhi* in my *payt*' (for the longest time I also agonized about the wrongness of a *daadhi* in my *payt* as I was a girl and not a boy), I felt strangely protective about this vulnerable young hero, every bit wanting to believe that that sunshine smile of his was actually meant for me. I wondered why the world was so difficult on him, why he was so innocent to the wiles of the world, and why he was this wonderful person that the world misunderstood.

And so, ever so slowly and surreptitiously, I began to perceive Sanjeev Kumar as my secret classic hero. The box-office triumvirate could be happy with my siblings and their friends. Or was it the other way round? But for me, it was only Sanjeev Kumar whom I loved.

My crush remained a secret for a long time. I was like a young girl embarrassed at being in love with a much older man, not someone from her generation. In those days, when it wasn't acceptable to even admit to a crush, to acknowledge one who was not from one's generation would be inviting ridicule from even one's closest friends.

To top it all, there now came Rishi Kapoor with his chocolate-boy good looks, in addition to the rugged Vinod Khanna. Dharmendra, Jeetendra, and above all, the poster boy of romance, the seductive head-tilting Rajesh Khanna were still ruling filmdom, and the hearts of us, young dying-to-have-a-crush-on-a-hero girls. In this scenario, I knew that I would be the butt of jokes if I admitted to a crush on the unstylish and pot-bellied Sanjeev Kumar. So I sealed my lips tight. What's that they say about love being truly blind? Well, it can also make one dumb by choice!

Frankly, I was too young and did not understand acting at all, so my liking for Sanjeev Kumar was not a matter of distinguishing a great actor from just a good-looking one. At least not till this point in time. For me, it was just a mysterious pull of the unique ordinariness of Sanjeev Kumar's charisma. He had this way of making everyone feel warm about him. And all his imperfections made him even more endearing and likeable to people like me.

So the fear of being politically, or should I say 'peer-ically', incorrect made me never admit to my crush on Sanjeev Kumar. I continued to like the films of Rajesh Khanna, Dharmendra, Jeetendra, and most of all, Rishi Kapoor, and discuss them with my siblings and friends. But each time as I retreated to myself, I would secretly imagine Sanjeev Kumar in those roles, even unrealistically finding him infinitely better than how each one of the original actors had essayed the characters. *Kya yahi pyaar tha? Haan yahi pyaar tha...* (Was it love? Yes, it was.)

In the second half of the 1970s, there was a bonanza of Sanjeev Kumar films – three films, virtually back-to-back releases, happening at a time when the tables were turning in my relationship with my father. I could finally, and a little bossily, convince my father to see some films with me, especially as by now his curiosity about Sanjeev Kumar's great performances too had been piqued by the actor's roles in *Koshish* and *Anamika*. And this cause had been helped by our together-watch of *Naya Din Nayi Raat* (1974) and a timely repeat of one of Sanjeev Kumar's oldest hits, *Khilona* (1970), on Doordarshan during the Sunday evening Hindi film telecasts. By the time we had seen all these films – only because they had been available and freely accessible on TV – my father had to change his mind about Hindi films of the era being 'trashy'.

In fact, so complete had the turnaround been that I was able to bully my father to become my partner in crime in watching a film on most Fridays at the theatre. So there was *Aandhi*, followed by *Sholay*, and topped by *Mausam* (all in 1975). The common factor among these was of course sterling performances by Sanjeev Kumar – the same dazzling smile, his trademark calm, and reassuring demeanour that warmed my heart.

But this time there was one big change. Now he had so much grey in his hair that it seemed completely wrong for me to crush on him. It felt more right to respect and admire him instead. It was a dilemma initially, but I graduated to it. In fact, I gradually started having long discussions with my father on his performances and the characters he played in these three films, though when I tried to do the same with my friends, they teased me about going on and on about this 'uncle-ji' actor.

The multi-starrers now started coming up and *Trishul* (1978) sealed the old-man image of Sanjeev Kumar. Even when he played characters who abandoned their women when he should have stood by them, as in *Mausam* and *Trishul*, I just could not bring myself to dislike him. So even when his characters from these films were being discussed academically, I found myself speaking on their behalf and justifying their flaws. Until my father smiled one day as I argued vociferously, reminding me that these were only characters played by Sanjeev Kumar, they were not Sanjeev Kumar himself.

By now, my love for Sanjeev Kumar had metamorphosed, but it still remained steadfast. I didn't miss seeing a single one of his films at the cinema. By this time, my father's conversion to Hindi cinema too was complete. Also, he related more and more to the age of the characters portrayed by Sanjeev Kumar in almost all of the actor's outings of the late 1970s. I was happy, but somewhere, since I knew that Sanjeev Kumar was actually not so old, I kept hoping that he would play his real age sometime.

My prayers were answered soon enough. Just as I had given up hope of him 'being young again', there came *Swarg Narak* (1978), followed by the intense extramarital affair stories *Silsila* (1981) and *Griha Pravesh* (1979), and a little later, *Angoor* and *Namkeen* (both 1982). Each time I saw these films, I fell in love all over again as I admired this actor's ability to make me understand complex situations or believe in the unbelievable, by the sheer power of his performances.

My curiosity about what he really was all about peaked, and I wondered how I could know more about the real Sanjeev

Kumar, *jise dil bahut dhoondta tha* (whom the heart yearned for). The absence of the Internet might have added to the mystique of Sanjeev Kumar. I desperately wanted to know more about what made this actor tick with perfect emotions, no matter whom he played. I had to find some other resource to help my cause, stalk my beloved in the only way possible at the time.

Now around this time, fortunately, I was 'allowed' to read film magazines and through them the layers to Sanjeev Kumar's persona began to peel for me. Yes, there was a whole lot of chaff too, but if you dug deep enough, a picture did emerge that resembled what he was all about.

To begin with, Sanjeev Kumar was actually Haribhai Jariwala, I discovered as I devoured the film magazines that wrote ever so much about him – from him putting his head on his mother's lap every evening as he got back from 'work' to the fact that he still bathed with a bucket and mug and didn't have any fancy showers in his spartan bathroom. This, incidentally, echoed the delightful '*Thande thande paani se nahana chahiye*' track from *Pati Patni Aur Woh*, of course minus the warmth of the wife and child to goof around with. But more often than not, film magazines wrote about his affairs, being slapped by Nutan, rejected by Hema Malini, and later, him belittling Sulakshana Pandit. But even while devouring all this, I was also sure that I didn't want to believe that Sanjeev Kumar was just what the magazines wrote about him. After all, how could this serene-looking man with soulful eyes and a kind demeanour be a miser or a chauvinist?

Of course, he did have some vices; he was a latecomer – a bad habit that he never denied even in public – but that was a minor character aberration. Was he not the same guy who was all set to marry Nutan, who was in a troubled marriage but loved him equally, if not more? And not just that, he 'agreed' to be publicly slapped by her for effect, when she decided not to leave her abusive husband. Was he not the one who on many occasions patched up the squabbles between Shatrughan Sinha and his wife Poonam, and Amitabh Bachchan and his wife Jaya, since he truly believed in the sanctity of a trusting long-term marriage?

I wondered whether he would not have yearned for the same long-term happiness of a marriage in his own life. Was he not the same person who resisted marriage with a woman he cared for as he feared that his family's hereditary heart ailment could prematurely claim his life too and leave her a widow? Was he not the one who ensured that all his brothers and sisters and their families were well provided for, even as he was losing the will to live and the faith to be happy?

The more I dug, the more enigmatic he seemed, *aur mera dil abhi bhi dhoondta hi tha* (and yet my heart yearned for more). But despite the nature of the information available to me, I did realize at the end of this phase that he was more human than ever before. He missed his mother, like most of us do. He indulged in the wrong food and drink, like many of us do. He was full of insecurities and fears about those he loved, like all of us are. I realized that he was human beyond the powerful celluloid characters that he brought to life. And it was precisely because he was so human that he was such a great actor. So I concluded, much like the magazines did, that for us fans, to enjoy seeing him perform for as long as God willed was the only way to understand and continue to love him.

Sanjeev Kumar, it was reported, began to do fewer films after his first heart attack at the age of thirty-seven, in the year 1975, and his erratic health began to show in his appearance if not in his performances in the early 1980s. Film magazines said that he had been depressed, moody, neglectful of his health, etc. But ironically, this was also the phase when he delighted everyone with his comic timing in *Angoor*. '*Kis mitti ka bana hai ye banda?*' (What is this man made of?), commented my father as he tried to correlate what I told him about Sanjeev Kumar with the characters he played during that period.

For Haribhai Jariwala, his role ended on 6 November 1985. Thereafter, the only way I could keep him alive was by watching his films on Doordarshan. As I journeyed from a girl to a woman and understood more about the enigmas of life, I related even more to his nuanced portrayals.

A few years later, my father too passed away. Finally, my childhood fears after watching *Parichay* had come true. *Magar dil toh abhi bhi kuchh dhoondta hai.*

Which leading lady of the 1950s and 1960s had been offered the role of Amitabh Bachchan's mother in *Deewaar* (1975)? The role went to Nirupa Roy after this actress rejected it saying she would never play the role of a mother.

Answer: Vyjayanthimala

Asha Parekh called this 1972 movie, 'her worst movie ever that sank like the *Titanic*'. She not only starred in a dual role in this movie but also backed and distributed it. Opposite her were two new heroes – Vijay Arora and Danny Denzongpa. Name the movie.

Answer: Rakhi aur Hathkadi

Zeenat Aman

More than the Body

Kaveree Bamzai

He was looking for someone like her. She knew she could be the one. When she introduced herself to him at a party, she was smoking a little pipe and offered him a light for his cigarette, he knew she was the one. He asked her to audition the next day, and voila, Jasbir/Janice in *Hare Rama Hare Krishna* (1971) was born, a woman lost to the world in the haze of drugs and free love in Nepal. She was nineteen, he was forty-seven. She was Zeenat Aman and he was Dev Anand.

She was a neophyte, barely two films old, and he was a megastar who came to regard her as his 'prized possession'. As he wrote in his autobiography, *Romancing With Life* (2007): 'While she as a person was God's creation, her image was of my making, and together we became inseparable in the public eye.' And that was the Pygmalion-like trap, ever since she stepped into the movies with *Hulchul* (1971), where she played second lead to Helen, who was cast opposite the actor-director O.P. Ralhan, and three young men. One of them was Kabir Bedi, who had just wrapped up a Cinthol ad with Zeenat Aman, then a top model and former second runners-up in the Miss India contest. As Bedi writes in his autobiography, *Stories I Must Tell: The Emotional Life of An Actor* (2021): '*Hulchul* flopped at the box office but neither Zeenat nor I got the blame.'

But with her first shot in *Hare Rama Hare Krishna* – shot from the back, in a short orange dress, with every bit of her fabulous figure clearly outlined – Zeenat Aman was a star. Ironically, she was playing Anand's sister in the movie, a product of a broken home of an Indian couple living in Canada, who abandons herself to the counterculture of the times.

It was to set the template for her career. Her accented Hindi, her flirtation with aspects of life that good Hindi film stars could never imagine, and her lack of inhibition about her body marked her out as a woman who redefined what the Hindi film heroine could do. And though she was considered a prisoner, both of her body and the men who designed movies around it, she came to symbolize much more than that. Contrary to the image grafted of her in film magazines which ran stories such as 'Rich, Famous, Beautiful, 50 Films Old and A Monster', 'The Centre of a Hate Campaign' (*Cine Blitz*, 1981), and 'It's a Curse to be a Single Girl' (*Super*, 1978), she was a professional to the core, who rode a wave of change in the industry, heralding a modern, Indian woman.

Building on the swell of transformation indicated in the 1960s by smart young women such as Sharmila Tagore and Sadhana, her influence transcended the big screen. She and Parveen Babi, from Junaghad, Gujarat, breathed new life into the heroine/vamp binary then quite fashionable in Hindi cinema. From the first role that brought her instant fame, with its song sung with abandon, '*Dum maaro dum*', in *Hare Rame Hare Krishna*, she played a variety of good bad girls or bad good girls. And she was breathtaking, whether she was Roma, the martial arts specialist out to avenge her sister and brother-in-law in *Don* (1978), or a model who murders a rapist in *Insaf ka Tarazu* (1980), whether she was a woman who chose money over struggle in *Roti Kapada aur Makaan* (1974) or a club dancer in *The Great Gambler* (1979), whether she was the girl who falls in love with her mother's one-time lover in *Prem Shastra* (1974) or a woman married to a cripple but involved in an extramarital relationship in the atmospheric *Dhund* (1973).

Zeenat didn't always stick to the straight and narrow. She also showed that women could be beautiful and flawed, they could be intelligent and human, they could be haughty and naughty. How many of our contemporary female actors can pull off a dialogue like she did in *The Great Gambler*, by the poolside, dressed in a bikini, and lighting a cigarette from her male friend's lit cigarette: '*Agar sulgana hai to hothon ki chingari se sulgao.*' (If you have to light it, do it with the spark of your lips). All of this with a smile and a sashay, even as her hero, Amitabh Bachchan, says: '*Jo khud shola hai usse sulgane ki kya zaroorat*?' (Why does fire needs a spark?)

Or who could say these lines and be happy about sounding materialistic? As she says to her jobless boyfriend, Bharat (played by Manoj Kumar, also the director of *Roti Kapada aur Makaan*): '*Mera ek sapna tha ki buson ki line main nahin khada hona padega, apni ek car hogi, aakash ko chhoota hua sundar sa ghar hoga, rang birange kapdo se bhari almari hogi, badhiya se badhiya gehne pehnoongi, aur phir hawai jahaz main baith kar aakash main udenge.*' (I had a dream, I won't have to stand in line for a bus, I will have a car of my own, we will live in a skyscraper, have an almirah full of colourful clothes, have the best jewellery, and then fly off in an aircraft high above.) And just in case we didn't get the point that Zeenat (playing Sheetal) is not a Sita Savitri, she says it for us in the movie: '*Main aur Sita? Nahin. Sita to vanvas main bhi saath deti hai. Maine to dukh main uska saath chhod diya tha.*' (I am not Sita. Sita supported Ram even in exile. I left him when he was in trouble).

Zeenat was no Sita, but she was also not the vamp of earlier times. Even if she died for her 'sins' as in *Roti Kapada Aur Makaan*, it was a good death, with a touch of nationalism attached to it. When a police officer asks her where is Bharat, in her dying moments, with Bharat's blood as her sindoor, she says: '*Kashmir se Kanyakumari tak*' (from Kashmir to Kanyakumari).

She was insulted for her body. Raj Kapoor infamously said of her, 'Let them (the audience) come for her tits, they will go out loving the movie (*Satyam Shivam Sundaram*).' She acknowledged the role her body played in her stardom. Read this interview with her in *India Today*, 1985, 'When the Bouquets Run Out': 'There was just a little bit of the real Zeenat Aman in all that. The rest was a lot of hype, the cameraman, the film director and the costume designer. They created a persona that had little to do with my reality; I was projected in a glossy, superficial, posturing way. It was what sold. My body. All of them (the directors) did it to me, every single one of them. There was nothing I could do about it. It was part of the game. I don't blame them. I don't blame myself. It was business.'

So Bachchan, playing Vijay, a police officer in *Dostana* (1980), tells her, while looking at her bikini top and sarong-clad body: '*Kuch farz ladkiyon ka bhi hai. Zara dekhiye apne aap ko. Is tarah ke kapde pehen kar agar aap sadak par niklengi, to gundon ki seetiyan nahi bajengi to kya mandir ki ghantiyan bajengi?*' (Girls have a duty to society. if you walk on the streets clad in so little do you expect whistles or the ringing of temple bells?). When Zeenat asks: 'What do you mean? *Kya kharabi hai in kapdon mein*?' (What's wrong in these clothes?), Bachchan answers, almost insolently: '*Bahut kam hai*' (They are not enough). Or when she is playing a model in *Insaf ka Tarazu*, and the photographer at a Madh Island exhorts her: '*Har movement main sex chahiye*' (I want sex in every move), which clearly excites the future rapist, played by Raj Babbar, and is used as testimony against her because '*Yeh jism ki numaish kar rahi thi*' (she was exhibiting her body).

Perhaps the film that best established Zeenat Aman's insouciance towards sex and sexuality was *Manoranjan* (1974), the Indian adaptation of Marguerite Monnot's 1956 French play (remade as a 1963 Billy Wilder comedy) *Irma la Douce*, directed by Shammi Kapoor. '*Sab dhandhe barabar hai, rozi kamane ke liye aur pet bharne ke liye*' (All businesses are alike. One has to do everything one can to make a living and fill one's stomach). *Manoranjan* was most unusual for its time, with its complete lack of judgement about sex and sex work. Zeenat played a sex worker, who rues the day her mother, a courtesan in Lucknow, married and came to Mumbai. A criminal, he left his wife to carry the conviction, with Zeenat's character being born in prison. Yet Zeenat is the embodiment of good cheer, shrugging her shoulders every time anyone says she has had a hard life. She spends most of the movie clad in underpants and a short kurta, and has no inhibitions being shot in the shower, in the tub and astride her hero, Sanjeev Kumar.

Even the most vicious articles about her in film magazines would acknowledge that she was a thorough professional, who did what the director demanded of her. As she says in the *India Today* article in 1985, in response to a question on how she survived: 'I was on top of them all. I was a good businesswoman too. I may have had the body and emotions of a woman, but I've always had the head of a man. I've lived my life like a man.'

If that meant she was ambitious and driven, she showed it in spades when she pursued Raj Kapoor so he could cast her in his magnum opus about a disfigured village woman and her love affair with a city engineer (played by Shashi Kapoor). It meant the end of her relationship with her mentor Dev Anand, but it was worth the price. When Zeenat's familiarity with Raj Kapoor at a party confirmed rumours he had heard about her being cast in *Satyam Shivam Sundaram*, Anand writes in his autobiography: 'My heart was bleeding. Zeenat was not the same Zeenat for me anymore. My heart broke into a million pieces and I wanted to leave the party immediately.'

But as *India Today* wrote in 1977: 'To Zeenat Aman, *Satyam Shivam Sundaram* (SSS) represented an opportunity of a lifetime. While producers continued to line up outside her door with offers of roles, Aman was getting tired of playing the glamour girl in film after film. A new trend for action films had begun and in such films, heroines ended up getting short shrift, a love scene or two was the most they could hope for. Additionally, even her most ardent fans did not dare to claim that she was a good actress, and her critics were convinced that she was no more than a pretty face, useful for filling the background, but hardly enough to hang an entire film on. Zeenat decided to win the *SSS* role for herself. She saw *Barsaat* (1949), *Awaara* (1951) and other old Raj Kapoor films and arrived at Kapoor's doorstep to claim the part. By this time, Kapoor had decided to launch a search for an actress because he felt that none of the current crop of heroines could do justice to his conception of the character. Zeenat was probably the last person he would have thought suitable. The girl he had in mind had to be plain looking and willing to be made up to look scarred and burnt in the film. Aman was attractive, no great shakes as an actress and spoke Hindi with an accent. However, Zeenat refused to give up. She had herself made up to look scarred, dressed in a costume from the film, and burst into his cottage one day. Flabbergasted, Kapoor rang his wife and said, "Come and see what this girl has done." Mrs Kapoor arrived with a gold coin to bless Zeenat, and Raj knew that he had found his heroine.'

If Zeenat thought *Satyam Shivam Sundaram* would make her immortal, she was convinced Krishna Shah's *Shalimar* (1978), co-starring Rex Harrison and Sylvia Miles, was her ticket to Hollywood. Her clipped English accent was on point as were her gowns, but the film did not set the box office on fire. Its mahurat shot though, graced by Italian bombshell Gina Lollobrigida, was billed by cheeky film magazines as the 'War of the cleavages', with Zeenat's gown vying for attention with Lollobrigida's.

Zeenat's contribution to a new 1970s femininity cannot be underestimated. As film scholar Ajay Gehlawat has written in a paper for *South Asian Popular Culture*: 'Along with redefining the rules of a screen heroine's identity, Aman also created a range of grey characters, such as Sheetal in Manoj Kumar's *Roti Kapada Aur Makaan* and Sheela in Feroz Khan's *Qurbani*.' And she is usually made to suffer for it with death, in *Hare Rama Hare Krishna* and *Roti Kapada Aur Makaan*. In *Qurbani*, the 'other man' has to sacrifice himself so the new woman's liberation cannot be challenged.

Zeenat and Parveen were regrettably seen as interchangeable by most Bollywood film-makers and would often end up playing roles that had been intended for the other. Shabana Azmi and Smita Patil were their contemporaries in the more independent movies of the 1970s, though the former managed more than a foothold in commercial cinema. *Ashanti* (1982), where Azmi stars with Aman and Babi as desi Charlie's Angels, is still worth a watch. Smita Patil, ironically, took on the role of Babi in Prakash Mehra's *Namak Halaal* (1982), opposite Amitabh Bachchan. It was a role she despised and the rain dance performed with Amitabh Bachchan made her so uncomfortable that she wept copiously.[1]

Azmi and Patil were almost as unconventional in their personal lives as Zeenat and Parveen Babi. Azmi's relationships with Benjamin Gilani and Shekhar Kapur were well known, as was her eventual marriage in 1984 to Javed Akhtar, then already married to Honey Irani. Patil was also involved with Raj Babbar, who too was already married to Nadira Babbar. Both chose love over convention. Azmi battled on, expanding her range, working in different genres and different cultures. Patil died due to childbirth complications, putting a sudden end to a career that had seen smouldering performances, ranging from *Bhumika* (1977) to *Mirch Masala* (1987). Both starred in *Nishant* (1975) and Mahesh Bhatt's *Arth*, with Patil playing a version of Babi with chilling authenticity.

Both Azmi and Patil were vocal about their politics, and indeed came from politically inclined families. But Aman and Babi were championing a different kind of politics, one where the woman had agency over herself and her sexuality. They may not have fully articulated their views, but they were very young at the time. Aman was nineteen when *Hare Rama Hare Krishna* was made and objectification by the camera became her gilded cage. Babi was

---

[1] https://openthemagazine.com/cinema/tragedy-queens/

nineteen when she was cast by the maverick director Babu Ram Ishara as a pregnant, unmarried woman in *Charitra* (1973).

The two embodied the confusion of that era, where sexual liberation and cultural freedom went hand in hand with more conservative family ideals and straitlaced women. Hindi cinema, after briefly celebrating their sexuality and totally exploiting it, decided to reduce the actresses to song and dance routines in the mid-1980s. But make no mistake, Zeenat Aman and Parveen Babi, with their sensuous disco movies, figure-hugging gowns and often kickass action, were there first.

It would take another awesome twosome, Sridevi and Madhuri Dixit, to restore women to their rightful place at the top with an unselfconscious and uninhibited interpretation of Saroj Khan's sensuality that would bring crowds back to the theatres and set the stage for a more equal representation.[2]

But the irony of Zeenat's life is that she tried her best to be the traditional Indian wife to both the men she married. Her marriage to actor–producer Sanjay Khan lasted about a year and is referred to only elliptically by Khan in his memoir, *The Best Mistakes of My Life* (2018). Khan is said to have assaulted her infamously in the Neptune suite of Taj Mahal Hotel in Mumbai. She chose unremarkable domesticity with second husband, actor Mazhar Khan, whom she has accused of depriving her of her career.

Sanjay Khan met Zeenat for the first time in 1973 on the sets of B.R. Chopra's *Dhund*, and quickly became friends with her. While shooting for the film in Mahabaleshwar, the two often sneaked out for walks and long drives to Panchgani, he says. It was on the sets of *Abdullah* in 1978, though, that something more serious blossomed between them. But, in his book, Khan only makes oblique references to his love affair with the actress, referring to himself and her by their respective characters in the movie. He writes, '...The setting, the costumes, the music worked their charm (in the movie), bringing the intense passion of the

---

2 https://openthemagazine.com/cinema/tragedy-queens/

Sheikh (played by Khan) and Zainab (played by Zeenat) to life on the screen. How could the Arabian prince and princess not fall in love? She was not only stunningly beautiful but filled the room with her presence and her intelligent, scintillating conversation. The Sheikh was totally smitten … But there was another element to the Arabian prince's infatuation – the princess's vulnerability, her lack of self-confidence which seemed at odds with her other, confident side. The princess was in constant need of love, and the prince wanted nothing more than to save her.'

Her second marriage to actor Mazhar Khan in 1985 was not happy either. In her interview with Simi Garewal in 1999, she admits as much, saying: 'My biological clock was ticking and I wanted to be a mother. I wanted to raise a family and now I think Mazhar just happened to be there at the right time … Mazhar never wanted me to grow as an individual or as an artist. He always wanted me to be with the kids and be at home. During the very first year of marriage I realized I had made a huge mistake, but I decided to live by it and make it work. I tried to make it work for another twelve years. There was no light at the end of the tunnel for me. There was not a single moment of happiness or joy during those twelve years. But I still tried making it work.'[3]

She stayed not only for her two boys but also because Mazhar fell grievously ill, and Zeenat says she tried everything humanly possible to get Mazhar the best treatment possible for his pancreatic cancer. It was a 'lone battle' she says in the interview, adding, 'You give, give, give and you give, until you're completely depleted … 1993 to1997 was a continuous battle for me. I literally lived with him in the hospital all these years. From learning how to give injections to how to do the dressing, I did everything in my capacity single-handedly. I looked after my children, I looked after my husband but there was no one to look after me. I am sure no other woman would have lasted in my situation for too long. But I held onto Mazhar. When the doctors in India gave up I took him

[3] https://www.youtube.com/watch?v=2-iQPpeX7nA

to the best doctors abroad, and finally in 1997 he was allowed to go home. These five years I did not see day and night.' In 1998, Mazhar Khan passed away due to kidney failure.

In movies though she was often the wife who was less than perfect. In *Ajnabee* (1974), she was the rich girl who didn't know how to cook and decided to become a model to earn extra income to complement her husband's salary. In *Yaadon ki Baaraat*, she confessed she didn't know how to pray, as she buttoned her top and declared to God that she had never been in a temple. In *Aashiq Hoon Baharon Ka* (1977), her character, of an Indian who lives abroad, didn't even know how to wear a sari.

She was always the woman about town, driving a car down twisted hill roads, sailing boats, swimming, or even doing martial arts in *Don*. 'I feel fortunate as an actor, especially for commercial Hindi cinema where music is such an integral part of the things that you do, that I had the songs that I did whether it was '*Dum maaro dum*' or '*Chura liya*' (from *Yaadon Ki Baaraat*) or Nazia Hassan's '*Aap jaisa koi*' (from *Qurbani*). There was some memorable music which brings back a wave of nostalgia.'[4] The songs have been remixed and reshot several times, right up until 2022, with Malaika Arora and Ayushmann Khurrana singing '*Aap jaisa koi*' in *An Action Hero*.

Her style was distinct. She wore what was comfortable. Whether that involved ditching the pink churidar kurta that had been designed for '*Chura liya*', which she exchanged for the iconic white, wide-legged jumpsuit, or whether it was carrying off the blouse-less, half-sari created for her by Oscar-winning designer Bhanu Athaiya in *SSS*, she carried it off with élan. Who doesn't recall co-star Tariq calling out to her in *Yaadon Ki Baaraat* as the '*Lal kapron wali memsahab*'?

Zeenat Aman's appearance on Instagram in 2023 became a social media sensation, as she posted old photos from her films from the 1970s with cheeky captions, supported worthy causes,

[4] https://www.easterneye.biz/a-walk-down-memory-lane-with-zeenat-aman/

and occasionally spoke up for ageing gracefully by allowing her hair to go grey. Whether it was laughing at herself or gently recalling her parents, Amanullah Khan and Vardhini Scindia, she showed everyone what class is.

There is a scene in a 2010 movie *Dunno Y Na Jaane Kyun…*, where Zeenat tells a female admirer, 'These girls today can't compete with us. We rock. So let's drink to that.'

Indeed.

The story of this blockbuster came to the director while reading the newspaper. The main plot was lifted from an interesting news item that caught the director's fancy. Name the film and the director.

Answer: *Amar Akbar Anthony* (1977), Manmohan Desai

What is the name of Raakhee's character with whom Dev Anand is in love with and who passes away in the 1973 Navketan movie, *Heera Panna*?

Answer: Reema

Hrishikesh Mukherjee

The Man Who Made the Stars Brighter

Raja Sen

One of the most remarkable scenes across Amitabh Bachchan's long and storied filmography is one where the actor, entering a film as late as an afterthought, answers the door to his best friend, notices that the friend is wearing a waistcoat that is of a pair with one in his wardrobe, and – excusing himself politely from the friend's wife – dutifully goes off to change into his own matching jacket. Once suitably twinned, the friends break into a song ('*Sa re ga ma*', voiced by Kishore Kumar and Mohammed Rafi, composed by S.D. Burman) about the nature of songs themselves, a song in which Bachchan's character, visibly carried away by fraternal fervour, sings a touch too loudly, much to the amusement (and momentary discomfort) of his friend's wife.

Hrishikesh Mukherjee's 1975 classic *Chupke Chupke* gives us Bachchan at his most guileless, a kurta-pyjama-wearing academic thrilled to see a fellow professor he visibly idolizes, all too eager to win the approval of his friend's wife. The performance ranks among the actor's finest, one entirely free of self-consciousness and stardom, mercifully unencumbered by any need to be heroic, and – incredibly rarely, in the Bachchan oeuvre – one where he appears tail-waggingly happy to play second fiddle. Applause for the acting aside, it feels astounding that the actor would even take up a role like this, a simple supporting part, two years after his breakout *Zanjeer* and in the same year he did *Deewaar*.

Though it was Prakash Mehra who birthed Bachchan's 'Angry Young Man' image with *Zanjeer*, Yash Chopra's *Deewaar* is the film where Bachchan draws himself up to his full larger-than-life stature, defiant and fiery-eyed and proud, unwilling to bend down to pick up money thrown his way, towering higher than the skyscrapers reflected in his sunglasses. To contrast this with the soft-spoken literature professor he plays in *Chupke Chupke* – forever pushing golden-rimmed spectacles up his nose – feels utterly absurd.

Bachchan, of course, did *Chupke Chupke* because of director Hrishikesh Mukherjee, who gave him his big, superstar-toppling break in *Anand* a few years earlier. This, however, was de rigueur for Mukherjee. The prolific director routinely cast megastars in his movies, but always made them park their pedestals outside his set. There was no room for the larger-than-life in Mukherjee's genteel, relatable films, and – somehow seduced by his modest masterpieces – the biggest actors flocked to the director, eager to balance out their increasingly loud blockbusters with something less showy, but invariably heartier.

I remember speaking with Raza Murad at Mukherjee's funeral in 2006, where the actor was understandably choked up. Murad, with his legendary baritone, first broke through in Mukherjee's *Namak Haraam*, where he played Alam, a politically aware poet who was profound yet playful of phrase. 'This death has orphaned the film industry,' he told me. 'Yes, we are aware that Dadasaheb Phalke is regarded as the father of Indian cinema, but he was a father we never saw. Hrishikesh Mukherjee was the father we not only saw, but also worked with and loved deeply.'

It was not as if actors were venturing down a particularly brave arthouse alley by working in Mukherjee's slice-of-life films. His cinema, while acutely observed, was eminently accessible and wholly engaging, cinema that eschewed pretension even when dealing with lofty themes. Mukherjee's films would not commonly be described as radical – even when the subjects were bold, or the storytelling was novel – and, because the film-maker was essentially a great humanist, his films would attract all manner of audiences. The stars, therefore, were not losing out on box office by working in Mukherjee's films. Some rank among their biggest successes.

They were, however, taking a pay-cut. Actors ruling the roost in the 1970s like Dharmendra, Rajesh Khanna and Bachchan reportedly slashed their fees by half in order to keep working with Mukherjee, who shot several of his unforgettable films right in his own Bandra bungalow. Sharmila Tagore, when working with Mukherjee, would forsake her iconic winged eyeliner, the otherwise flamboyant Rekha would be clad in cotton, and every single one of them feared the director. Looking back, they appeared admirably eager to be shaped by a film-maker who had little patience for their stardom.

In the 1970s, popular actors would often shoot two or three films at the same time. While Ramesh Sippy's *Sholay* was being shot near Bangalore, Bachchan was intimidated by Dharmendra regularly polishing off the most alcohol in the evenings – and then also being the first one up at dawn, doing push-ups to look suitably sculpted for a sword-and-sandal film (Manmohan Desai's *Dharam-Veer*) he was shooting at the same time. Bachchan himself was shuttling between Ballard Estate and Bangalore, shooting the climax to Yash Chopra's *Deewaar* by night, before catching an early-morning flight to the *Sholay* sets. Unlike their other directors, however, Mukherjee would not suffer tardiness.

In *Chupke Chupke* (also shot in the same year), Dharmendra is strikingly smooth and charming as a botany professor pretending, on a lark, to be a garrulous chauffeur. The actor has often recalled how, when he arrived late for the shooting of the film's climax, a peeved Mukherjee didn't allow him to rush to the rescue of heroine Sharmila Tagore. Instead, the unrelenting director ordered him to enter the frame while adjusting his trousers, running past a 'Toilet' sign. A nonplussed Dharmendra complied, and the film's denouement is now – and forever – coloured by this punishment, spelling it out that Dharmendra's botanist-chauffeur hero Dr Parimal Tripathi was late to the climax of his own film.

Perhaps the only director to have worked with Raj Kapoor, Balraj Sahni, Kishore Kumar, Dev Anand and Dilip Kumar, Mukherjee always held actors in his thrall. This may be one reason that coming generations of superstars, like Rajesh Khanna, Dharmendra and Amitabh Bachchan, were so keen to be moulded – and scolded – by Mukherjee. Otherwise warm and affable, the director was exacting and implacable on his sets. When Deepti Naval pleaded with him for another take of a scene during the shooting of *Rang Birangi*, an irked Mukherjee brushed her off. Being a trained and exceptional editor – who had cut *Madhumati* and *Do Bigha Zameen* for Bimal Roy – Mukherjee was never one to indulge an unnecessary shot. He knew he already had what he needed, and told Naval that she would have to pay for the extra footage used in the retake. The actress, instantly embarrassed, moved promptly on to the next shot.

This frugality found its way to the costume department. On more than one occasion, Bachchan was asked to shoot in clothes he showed up in, Jaya Bhaduri had to break out the stylish saris from her wedding trousseau for *Abhimaan*, and a distinctive, even unforgettable silk dressing-gown – beige, with a chocolate brown lapel and cuffs – is worn by many a Mukherjee film elder: Ashok Kumar in *Guddi*, Om Prakash in *Chupke Chupke,* and Utpal Dutt in *Gol Maal*. This idea of costuming in the style of a theatre repertory shows up in *Gol Maal*, where the protagonist Ramprasad Sharma (Amol Palekar), a modern youngster suddenly in dire need of a kurta, is taken by his friend to a movie studio. This is where he is compelled to choose between Sanjeev Kumar's oversized kurta and Asrani's undersized one. These repetitions create an intimate cinematic world, with varied characters being connected by the same garments and the same gardens.

Unlike most 'entertainers' then or now, these films were also politically aware. In *Gol Maal*, made after the Emergency, characters arguing over tickets to a football game shout, 'Down with Personality Cult.' In *Namak Haraam*, Simi Garewal lectures a privileged (and practically yawning) Amitabh Bachchan about socialism. In the unsparing and heart-breaking *Satyakam*, we see bright engineering students on the brink of the country's Independence, brimming with hope and expecting all the evils – starvation, unemployment, black marketing – to end. Yet nothing actually ends except the idealistic hero Satyavir (Dharmendra, in a career-best performance) who goes down fighting and disillusioned.

What sets Mukherjee's films apart – from both the mainstream where his stars came from, and from the parallel cinema that was simmering alongside – is their simplicity. There is very little showiness in his craft. One would, for instance, be hard-pressed to speak about the cinematography of his celebrated films, even compared to his immediate peers like Basu Bhattacharya. Mukherjee's priorities appeared to lie elsewhere. The master director's greatest triumph may have been in the way he evoked a casual air. Mukherjee's films, like his characters, revelled in never trying too hard.

As was said in his *Bawarchi*, 'It is so simple to be happy but so difficult to be simple.' The films, punctuated by endless servings of tea, are marvellously relatable – and continue, miraculously, to feel just as familiar decades after they were made. He made actors serve up their most naturalistic performances, and we enthusiastically befriended his characters. Characters who were both memorable and commonplace. We not only got to know them, but felt like we had shared cake with them and accompanied them on job interviews.

As I previously mentioned, Mukherjee – due to dwindling budgets, as well as health issues with gout that got more severe and restrictive over the years – shot several of his movies in his own Carter Road bungalow, named Anupama. 'For five years at a stretch,' wrote critic Sadanand Menon, 'every time you visited the house you could lose your way. I remember rushing in through a door where I was sure a toilet existed, and stopping, petrified, at the sight of Utpal Dutt sitting in an easy-chair, rehearsing his lines for a shot. He looked up, understood the situation in a jiffy, and returned to his reading with a bemused shrug.' Mukherjee's bungalow, with over a dozen rescue dogs in residence – not to mention innumerable playwrights, poets and performers – sounds like an artistic utopia.

For a movie star, this must have felt revolutionary. To leave behind their hangers-on and yes-men and step into this creative wonderland in order to rediscover – or, in some cases, to finally discover – their own artistic potential. Look, for instance, at Shatrughan Sinha, the bombastic tough guy, a frequently amoral character cast by Mukherjee as a feminist radical in *Naram Garam*, leading to one of his tenderest performances. The director made it a habit of unchaining popular actors from the images that had enshrined them in the popular imagination. He gave screen seductress Rekha the most innocently wholesome parts, turned the brawny Dharmendra into an articulate, even academic figure, and removed the heroic camera angles typical to matinee idol Rajesh Khanna while casting him as a helpful cook or a talkative patient.

'I will have to admit that most of the interesting characters that I played have been in films that were made by him,' said Bachchan to the BBC in 2006 after the director's passing. 'Be it *Anand* or *Mili* or *Chupke Chupke* or *Bemisaal* or *Namak Haraam* or *Jurmana*. They were all exceptionally well-etched and, of course, the greatest opportunity to perform for me has been in his films. His characters were close to reality, and certainly the scenes that were written and the situations that we were put in were so genuine and real, and realistic, that they gave great opportunities to actors.'

After casting a star in atypical light, the director surrounded them with an ensemble of fantastic actors. The 'Hrishikesh Mukherjee Repertory Company' included Utpal Dutt, Deven

Varma, Amol Palekar, Jaya Bachchan, Asrani, Ashok Kumar, Dina Pathak, Om Prakash – and these superb actors (many with a background in the stage) would strip the varnish off the stars merely by showing them how to do it right. One problem with success in the movies is that once stars begin to gleam brightly enough, their films start revolving around them, and, because they are being made in service of their already-beloved personas, they are less of a challenge and more of an affirmation. Mukherjee, forever casting performers against type, compelled the stars to up their game as they had to match emotional or comic beats versus the finest, most natural actors out there.

Mukherjee's nuanced and believable characters, so far removed from their existing screen 'image', liberated the stars and enabled them to forget about convention and expectation and really *act*. This was where they learnt to be subtle, to be casual, to be unhurried. Working with Mukherjee added to their stardom by adding to their toolkit as performers: they discovered a sense of ease, and a lightness of touch. Not only did this sculpt some of their most memorable and most enduring performances, but they took these learnings forward into their commercial cinema.

Look at Bachchan, possibly Mukherjee's most iconic graduate, and one who worked with the director even more than he did with blockbuster-makers Prakash Mehra or Manmohan Desai. It was in Mukherjee's films that he found and honed his comic timing, his sarcasm, his deadpan deliveries, even – it could be argued – the sly pauses that characterize his most crowd-pleasing one-liners. These may not have been the most commercial of Bachchan's projects, but they certainly made him a brighter star. The director was a one-man school of naturalism and simplicity, and it is to the credit of the stars who worked with him that they relished this gruff, genius headmaster.

Contrast that with today, where a handful of so-called stars not only decide which Hindi films will be bankrolled, but sign off on everything, from co-stars to script. It is harder to imagine these stars being as eager to submit to a storyteller. Their social media following, along with the hype of their own headlines, has them convinced that they (and their publicists) know best. Most films they headline are – entirely without irony – referred to as 'star vehicles', films built on already-proven success, films that exist not only to flatter the star but to cash in on their greatest hits. Maybe the unwillingness to learn is the reason that many of this generation's top performers hit a creative plateau and seem unable to grow beyond a point. They remain doomed to repeat their own tricks, film after film, with diminishing returns.

During the shoot of *Chupke Chupke*, when Dharmendra and Bachchan were confused about a certain scene, they asked Mukherjee to explain it to them. Dharmendra, in a recent interview, laughed about the way the director put them in their place: 'If you had a story sense, would you be playing heroes in films?' he had chastised, and the two actors had meekly gone back to their positions. It is rather easy – even, dare I say, pleasurable – to imagine Hrishikesh Mukherjee growling at the stars of today, twisting their ears and setting them straight. He was not one for entourages, tantrums, public relations exercises or posing for photographs with prime ministers. 'Down with Personality Cult.' All that matters is the story, and the sense.

In which 1974 movie did Rajesh Khanna play a decadent prince, Karan, who idles his time away and is reformed only through love?

Answer: *Prem Nagar*

From Bharat Kumar to *Beimaan* and Back

Manoj Kumar's Fabulous Box Office Run in the 1970s

Nirupama Kotru

Na izzat ki chinta, na fiqr kisi apmaan ki,
Jai bolo beimaan ki, Jai bolo…

(Neither is he worried about his image
Nor does he care about being insulted
All hail the unscrupulous man)

The above lines sung by Mukesh are from the title song of the film *Beimaan* (1972). This film, a hotchpotch of ideas floating around in Hindi cinema of the 1970s – a simpleton rising against the system, a common man exposing the hypocrisy of the powerful, etc. – was one of the biggest hits of the year, leaving behind superstar Rajesh Khanna's *Apna Desh and Amar Prem.*[1] The film won an incredible seven Filmfare awards including best film, best director for Sohanlal Kanwar, best actor for Manoj Kumar, best music for Shankar-Jaikishan, best lyricist (Verma Malik), best playback singer Mukesh for the title song and best supporting actor (Pran). Veteran actor Pran turned down his award to protest against *Pakeezah* being denied the best music award; a rare instance of a big name from the Bombay film industry turning down an award and clearly indicating his reason for doing so. The success of the film inspired master satirist Kaka Hathrasi to compose a poem, which lent its name to a poetry collection titled, *Jai Bolo Beimaan Ki.*[2]

The question that has been bothering me ever since I recently attempted watching *Beimaan* during my research on Hindi films of 1970s was this: Why did audiences flock to the theatres in droves to watch this film? That the film won seven *Filmfare* awards can be easily explained; one can speculate that the jury had been compromised, the awards had been bought, and so on and so forth. But what about the popularity of the film? By all objective standards such as the quality of acting, story and screenplay, direction, editing, music, set design, costumes, etc., other films of the year like Hrishikesh Mukherjee's *Bawarchi* and Gulzar's *Parichay* were far better. So how did *Beimaan* pip them to the post?

The answer, by all accounts, seems to be: It was the leading man of *Beimaan* who made it the crazy hit it was. The man who loomed large over Bombay filmdom in the 1970s in spite of the presence of existing stars like Shashi Kapoor, Dharmendra, as well as two rising superstars Amitabh Bachchan and Rajesh Khanna; the one and only Manoj 'Bharat' Kumar.

Before tracing Manoj Kumar's first steps into filmdom, let us quickly recollect was happening in Hindi cinema in the 1970s.

---

1 https://www.koimoi.com/box-office/highest-grossers/from-seeta-aur-geeta-to-pakeezah-top-10-bollywood-box-office-grossers-of-1972/

2 Kaka Hathrasi, Diamond Pocket Books 2004

The decade was a very interesting one. For one, you had parallel cinema spreading its wings during the time, with Shyam Benegal taking the baton from Mani Kaul, Basu Chatterjee and Mrinal Sen, all of whom made what are considered the first neo-realist Hindi films, in 1969 – *Uski Roti*, *Sara Akash* and *Bhuvan Shome* respectively. All these films were low-budget and what they lacked in terms of technology and expensive production design, they made up in technique.

Then there were the blockbusters helmed by directors who were peaking during the 1970s – Prakash Mehra, Manmohan Desai, Ramesh Sippy, Yash Chopra and others – all of whom were making films with great music, great performances and more importantly, great scripts, usually written by Salim-Javed. The huge budgets available for some of these films meant that they could experiment with the latest technologies and hire the best talent, sometimes from abroad, as Ramesh Sippy did with *Sholay* (1975).

There were many interesting experiments happening within the commercial set-up as well. Middle-of-the-road cinema started flourishing at this time. So you had these film-makers who were essentially from the Bimal Roy school of film-making, like Hrishikesh Mukherjee, Basu Chatterjee, Basu Bhattacharya and Gulzar, who made some really good films during this time. A remarkable aspect of this cinema was that these directors managed to get big stars to act in their small-budget films. For example, *Chupke Chupke* (1975) had four major stars of the time – Dharmendra, Amitabh, Sharmila Tagore and Jaya Bhaduri. Story, screenplay, dialogues and music were the greatest strengths of these films.

Then there were bold experiments in content being made by people like B.R. Ishara, who made standout films like *Chetna* (1970). The posters of the film, the story of a sex worker played by Rehana Sultan, focused on her bare legs, sending shockwaves among audiences. There were films like *Hawas* (1974), too, about a nymphomaniac played by Bindu. These films would probably struggle to get a censor certificate today. There were umpteen spy stories (*Barood*, 1976, and *Agent Vinod*, 1977) and fantasies like shape-shifting snakes (*Nagin*, 1976). There were low-budget films like *Dil Ki Rahein* (1973) and *Shankar Hussain* (1977) which promoted communal harmony. There were curry Westerns too, like *Khote Sikkay* (1974) and *Kaala Sona* (1975), and the Godfather-inspired *Dharmatma* (1975).

There was a great churning happening in society during the 1970s which was reflected in our films. The old Nehruvian order had given way to the new. Corruption had slowly started eating the vitals of the country. Smuggling, black-marketing and profiteering were rampant, and the disenchantment of the common man with the establishment was reflected in Hindi films. Different kind of films were being made and they were finding audiences, whether these were massy or classy. Actually this was a healthy trend, if you think about what it means for the industry. For a film industry to flourish, you needed audiences to watch more and more films, and that is exactly what was happening. To add to the heady mix being served to hungry audiences, there were films directed by directors like Sohanlal Kanwar which may not have pleased critics, but had a fabulous run at the box office. The stories of such films were written by writers such as Sachin Bhowmick who seems to have an unerring sense of the pulse of the people. Manoj Kumar rode this wave of diverse films, particularly those which told stories of the common man fighting the establishment.

Harikrishen Giri Goswami, born in Abbottabad, Pakistan, spent his childhood in a refugee camp of Delhi following the partition of India. During those days, he watched the thespian Dilip Kumar in the films *Jugnu*[3] and *Shaheed* and started dreaming of a better life as an actor in Bombay.

Starting with bit roles in *Fashion* (1957), *Sahara* (1958) and *Chand* (1959), Manoj moved to a lead role in H.S. Rawail's *Kaanch ki Gudiya* (1960). Inspired by the name of the character played by his idol Dilip Kumar in Filmistan's *Shabnam* (1949), Harikrishen

---

3 *Guftagoo*, Rajya Sabha TV, 9 September 2014

gave himself the screen name 'Manoj Kumar' when he started acting in films.

Slowly but surely, he made a place for himself as an actor in the 1960s with hit films such as *Woh Kaun Thi* (1961), *Hariyali aur Rasta* (1964) and *Do Badan* (1966). But his moment in the sun came with *Upkar* (1967), after which he started being identified as 'Bharat' Kumar.

So how did Manoj make this successful turn from the squeak-clean image of Bharat Kumar of *Upkar* to the lawless scoundrel of *Beimaan* and *Dus Numbri* (1976), both of which were wildly successful at the box office? And how did he smoothly transition to playing Bharat again in *Kranti* (1981)?

Before we move on to the 1970s, I want you to cast your mind back to the 1950s and to one of the biggest superstars of that era – Raj Kapoor. The character of The Tramp as played by Charles Chaplin found an Indian avatar when Raj Kapoor adopted it for his films in the 1950s. Raju/Raj was the Little Man, the simpleton with the golden heart. His eyes shone bright and were full of dreams; dreams of a new India where no one would be poor, where every man, woman and child could lead a life of dignity. The films of Raj Kapoor and that of his seniors in the industry such as Bimal Roy (*Do Bigha Zamin*, 1953) and Mehboob Khan (*Mother India*, 1957), represented the idealistic stream in Hindi cinema.

Was Raju/Raj a patriot? If patriotism means loving your fellow Indians, he was definitely one. Raju's values were intrinsic human values. He was a Gandhian who turned the other cheek in *Jis Desh Mein Ganga Behti Hain* (1960). He placed great emphasis on universal human values such as honesty and spoke the universal language of love. His world view is best exemplified by this song from *Shree 420* (1955), which, along with '*Awara hoon*', the title song of his own film *Awara* (1951), made him the darling of the masses in Russia, China and many other countries (Not only did Raj Kapoor produce and direct both these films, he substantially contributed to their music which was composed/written by his close associates Shankar-Jaikishen and Shailendra).

Mera joota hai Japani, Yeh patloon Englistani,
Sar pe laal topi Roosi, phir bhi dil hai Hindustani

(My shoes are from Japan, my trousers are English-made,
On my head I wear a red Russian cap, yet at heart I am an Indian)

The song was a diplomatic masterstroke. It was a brilliant affirmation of India's non-aligned stance. Raju the tramp was comfortable sporting goods from other countries, yet he remained first and foremost an Indian. He was a global citizen, but at heart a local Indian boy. He embraced the worldview of both Rabindranath Tagore and Mahatma Gandhi, and was proud to do his best work when the nation was taking baby steps under the leadership of its first Prime Minister Pt. Jawaharlal Nehru. A worldview that he shared with the other two superstars of the time who were also good friends of his, Dilip Kumar and Dev Anand.

Post *Bobby* (1973), Raj Kapoor's cinematic language changed. Sensing the public mood, Raju had moved on after the last hurrah in *Mera Naam Joker* (1970), which flopped badly. Raju had now become a patriarchal figure, a relic of the Nehruvian past. His acting roles were now few and far between. For a while it seemed as if younger son Randhir Kapoor would step into his father's shoes and play the lovable simpleton. He had a brief, albeit good run with *Rampur Ka Lakshman* (1972) and *Ponga Pandit* (1975). But there was someone who had been waiting in the wings to take over the baton of the good-Samaritan-cum-patriot from Raj Kapoor. He started by appropriating the very soul of Raj Kapoor – his voice, Mukesh. He was Manoj Kumar.

Manoj Kumar's first brush with patriotism came in the film *Shaheed* (1964) where he played the role of Bhagat Singh. However, it was with *Upkar* – which invoked Lal Bahadur Shastri's slogan *Jai Jawaan, Jai Kisaan* and which Manoj Kumar directed himself in the lead role of the righteous son-of-the-soil Bharat – that he started being identified as 'Bharat Kumar'. In fact it was Shastri-ji himself who asked Manoj to make the film, at the premiere of *Shaheed*. This nickname stuck with the actor. As the actor explained,[4] farmers reside in Bharat, the villages of India. Manoj's directorial debut was a smash hit and the biggest film at the box office in 1967. It extolled the contributions of the farmer and the soldier to the nation, in the backdrop of the Indo-Pakistan war of 1965.

Bharat Kumar never looked back. He directed three more highly successful films which were unabashedly patriotic: *Purab aur Paschim* (1970), *Roti Kapada aur Makaan* (1974) and finally, *Kranti* (1981). He broke away from the formula to make *Shor* (1972). In all these films, Manoj Kumar showed his mastery over content and form. Story writing was his forte. He knew that Indians were an emotional people, so he wrote stories which had an easy connect with the audiences. All his stories gave audiences an emotional peg to cling to. There was something in there for everybody.

Shor is a small and beautiful film about a family of three – a tragic story of father, mother and son. Happiness eludes the family when they are struck by one tragedy after another. The film established Manoj as a director to be reckoned with, and one with an ear for music, like Raj Kapoor. The soundtrack was highly popular with '*Ik pyaar ka naghma hai*' ruling the airwaves for a long time. '*Jeevan chalne ka naam*', '*Paani re paani*', '*Shehnai baje na baje*', '*Macha diya shor*' were on everybody's lips. The picturization of '*Ik pyaar ka naghma hai*' used Manoj's favorite mirror technique to great effect.

Purab aur Paschim, released in 1970, was a huge hit. Manoj Kumar's second major film on a patriotic theme after *Upkar* had him play a patriotic young man who woos a blonde NRI in London and convinces her to return to her Indian roots. Take a look at the song '*Bharat ka rahnewala*'. The setting is a party in a club run by Indians to which Bharat is invited. He finds the reception cold, and says this to Madan Puri. Pran, who has cut off all ties with India in his eagerness to be accepted in London, insults Bharat by

---

4 *Lehren Retro*, 24 July 2022

mocking Indians and calls the contribution of India, a big zero. Bharat responds by singing about India's contribution of 'zero' to the world. Madan Puri coaxes Bharat to tell the gathering more about India, which he does by way of a catchy song (composed by Kalyanji-Anandji, lyrics by Indeevar):

Jeete hon kisi ne desh toh kya hamne to dilon ko jeeta hai
Jahan Ram abhi tak hai nar me, nari me abhi tak Sita hai
Itne paawan hon log jahan
Main nit-nit sheesh jhukaata hoon
Bharat ka rahnewala hoon,
Bharat ki baat sunata hoon

(Others may have won territories, we conquer hearts,
Ram resides in every man here and Sita in every woman,
People are so virtuous here, I bow my head in respect
I am an Indian and I sing of the glory of my land.)

This song remains a master class in picturization, as do many other songs of Manoj Kumar. The visuals of a lone patriotic Indian surrounded by indifferent, even hostile NRIs, made this *Purab aur Paschim* song special. A blonde Saira Banu blowing smoke into the camera as Manoj 'Bharat' Kumar talks about virtuous Indian women is a stark imagery that is hard to forget. The camera moving round and round continuously, mimicking the motion of the revolving restaurant in the club, the snapping of fingers by Rajendra Nath and company to encourage Bharat, the waitress and her dancing tray, all these directorial touches make for a delightful, enjoyable song.

Four years after *Purab aur Paschim* came *Roti, Kapada aur Makaan*, Manoj's biggest hit, which focused on the burning issues of the 1970s such as inflation and unemployment. The title is said to have been inspired by one of the slogans popularized by the then Prime Minister Indira Gandhi during the late 1960s, suggesting that her government was committed to providing Indians with the bare necessities of life. *Roti, Kapada aur Makaan* had a highly popular soundtrack, with '*Hai hai yeh majboori*' being one of the most imaginatively picturized rain songs in Hindi cinema. Zeenat Aman dancing with gay abandon in a Bombay Dyeing sari is a memory that is firmly etched in the minds of her fans. The song uses her natural charm and pizzazz to stunning effect. '*Main na bhooloonga*' (happy and sad versions), '*Aur nahin bas aur nahin*', '*Mehngayi maar gayi*' and '*Panditji mere marne ke baad*' (Aruna Irani doing a drunken act), added to the appeal of this multi-starrer, which was the biggest box-office hit of 1974. Shashi Kapoor as Zeenat Aman's boss and Amitabh Bachchan in the role of Bharat's younger brother Vijay, Moushumi Chatterjee as Tulsi and Prem Nath as Sardar Harnam Singh added heft to the film.

Kranti came seven years later, and was the biggest hit of 1981. The film was a period drama set in the British era and starred Dilip Kumar in the title role. It was Manoj's only collaboration with Salim-Javed, who wrote the story and screenplay.

Although Manoj Kumar may have started out by imitating his idol Dilip Kumar in films of the 1950s and '60s, picking up some mannerisms of Dev Anand on the way, by the '70s he had actually stepped into Raj Kapoor's shoes. Besides their films successfully focusing on the common man, hit tunes accompanied by innovative song picturization was a huge common factor between them. Incidentally, Raju and Bharat did meet on screen, in Raj Kapoor's ambitious multi-starrer *Mera Naam Joker*. Manoj played David, the fiancé of the young teacher Mary (Simi Garewal), whom the teenaged Raju (played by Rishi Kapoor) has a crush on. It was a sensitive part, and he did full justice to it.

There was one huge difference between the films of Raju and Bharat though; one which becomes obvious when their films are viewed from a feminist lens.

In all his films post *Upkar*, Manoj Kumar played an innocent soul trapped in a corrupt world. And more often than not, women in his films symbolized the corrupting effect of the West. It was a problematic depiction in one film after another, whether it was the westernized Saira Banu who is portrayed as a wayward lass in *Purab aur Paschim* or the gold digger Zeenat Aman who chooses her rich boss Shashi Kapoor over Bharat in *Roti Kapada aur Makaan*. In both these films, the leading ladies come to their senses in the end, and accept Bharat as their Pati Parmeshwar/soulmate. In *Purab aur Paschim*, the wayward daughter of the East comes home, drops her vices, changes into a sari, and becomes a good Indian girl. In the climax of *Roti, Kapada aur Makaan*, a repentant Zeenat Aman is overwhelmed when Manoj Kumar's blood drips onto her forehead as Mukesh sings '*Aa main teri maang sanwaroon, tu dulhan bann ja*' in the background. She dies in Bharat's arms, handing him over to the care of the virtuous Tulsi (Moushumi Chatterjee).

In Sohanlal Kanwar's *Sanyasi* (1975), the nymph-like Hema Malini fails to seduce the celibate youth in the title song '*Chal sanyasi mandir mein*' as well as '*Sun bal brahmachari, main hoon kanya kunwari*'. In *Pehchan* (1970), also directed by Sohanlal Kanwar, as the simpleton Gangaram, Manoj Kumar rejects every single girl paraded before him by leading lady Babita in the song '*Woh pari kahaan se laaon, teri dulhan jise banaoon*' (Where do I get a fair damsel fit to be your bride); he finds the girls either too forward-looking, or having short hair (considered a vice among conservatives), or being too strong-headed. By the late 80s, his portrayal of women had hit rock bottom in his home production *Kalyug aur Ramayan* (1987), in which he depicted leading lady Madhavi as a fallen modern woman with no redeeming features whatsoever, who harasses the poor man by the poolside in the cringe-worthy '*Chal bhaag chalen poorab ki ore*' (Come let's run towards the East, the West is corrupt).

In a stark contrast to Manoj's films, women characters play an important role in guiding Raju/Raj Kapoor's moral campus and keeping him on the straight and narrow path, and also lifting him up when he is in danger of falling. Vidya in *Shree 420*, true to her name, was the guiding beacon in Raju's life, as was Rita (Nargis) in *Awara*. The appearance of Nargis in the last scene of *Jagte Raho*, singing a lovely bhajan, '*Jaago Mohan pyare*', is an affirmation of his views about women being pure, noble creatures who guide men who have wandered off the path of truth.

One could argue that depiction of women as equal citizens is an issue with most commercial film-makers. Raj Kapoor turned his voyeuristic gaze on women in *Satyam Shivam Sundaram* (1978) and *Ram Teri Ganga Maili* (1985), even if the women were depicted as noble. However, the problematic depiction becomes more noticeable when the (fallen) women are pitted against the patriotic and/or celibate male protagonist, making them appear as selfish, irresponsible beings, unconcerned with the nation or the world.

Notwithstanding this problematic aspect of his films, Manoj Kumar had a loyal fan following among men and women. There were thousands, if not millions of Indians, who adored his screen presence, his looks, his mannerisms, his on-screen and off-screen persona. It is a fact is that unlike other superstars of the 1970s, Manoj was completely controversy-free where his private life was concerned. Judging by an interview of his given to ITMB[5] channel, at times the image of the virtuous Bharat Kumar became a millstone around his neck. Manoj Kumar revealed how, during his early days as a hero, a young girl once chided him for smoking openly in a restaurant during dinner. Since that day, he became very conscious of his public image.

To his credit, Manoj Kumar remained committed to cinema till his very last film. Good, bad or ugly, his owned his films. Like Dev Anand, who had gone from making thoroughly entertaining films like *Hare Rama Hare Krishna* in 1971 to the trite *Chargesheet* in 2011 (his last film), Manoj Kumar had a slow and steady decline. It is difficult to believe that the director of *Upkar* and *Shor* also made *Clerk* (1989), which was his last leading role as Bharat Kumar. *Clerk*, which starred two leading Pakistani actors Zeba and Mohammad Ali, along with Rekha, Ashok Kumar and Shashi Kapoor, was rejected by critics as well as audiences. It was in the

[5] ITMB Shows, 15 February 1984

same year that another director who was tipped to be called the next 'showman' after Raj Kapoor, Subhash Ghai, had a smash hit called *Ram Lakhan*. By then, Subhash Ghai had already taken over the mantle of making patriotic films with *Karma* (1986). *Pardes* (1997) followed. '*Har karam apna karenge*' (*Karma*) and '*I love my India*' (*Pardes*) are played on TV channels and radio stations along with '*Mere desh ki dharti*' from Manoj Kumar's *Upkar*, on every Republic and Independence Day.

The 1970s were Manoj Kumar's golden years. His innocent face and earnest manner endeared him so much to audiences that they were willing to accept him as a crook, because they believed that a crook with a good heart is better than a powerful, heartless and corrupt person. He was the eternal underdog and a patriot. Viewed from that prism, it becomes crystal clear as to why the audiences loved him regardless of the quality of the films.Even if the films were bad, he was always good.

Manoj Kumar said in an interview[6] that when he started making meaningful and entertaining films for his audience, he often introspected about his choices. And then he thought to himself: 'Give them (the audience) a sugar-coated pill or don't try at all. Some actors say, if you want a message, go to the post office. Why come to the movies? That's ok, that's their outlook. I am always answerable to my annadata, my audience.'

His messaging was consistently clear. He was a patriot who spoke directly to the audience, reminding them of the greatness of this noble nation which has survived many setbacks and has always emerged stronger. He didn't care what critics thought about his worldview. No wonder his audience stayed loyal to him.

Jai bolo Bharat Kumar ki, jai bolo.

---

[6] *Guftagoo*, Rajya Sabha TV, 9 September 2014

Amol Palekar

Hindi Cinema's Extraordinarily Ordinary Common Man

Amitava Nag

On 1 May 1960, Bombay State was divided into two based on linguistic criteria. Two new states were born: Maharashtra, a Marathi-speaking one, and Gujarat, the Gujarati-speaking other. The city of Bombay became the capital of Maharashtra. Six years later, a new political party was born in Maharashtra which held the reins of the state's politics (and more so of Bombay's, later known as Mumbai) to a large extent in the following decades. In 1966, the Shiv Sena was formed with a definite majoritarian principle – 'Bombay for the Marathi *manoos*.'

In his essay, 'The Popular Hindi Film: Ideology and First Principles', Ashis Nandy emphasizes that the Hindi film hero

> … will simply be Mr. Rakesh or Mr. Raj or Mr. Ashok – surnameless and, thus, regionless, casteless, ethnically non-identifiable and ultimately ahistorical. He is in this sense an archetype, a representation of cultural concerns

> which, if given a specific historical setting, would become less forceful, less black-and-white, and thus less communicative.
>
> There is one other important reason why the hero and the heroine have to be abstracted from everyday social reality. Unlike modern literature and the modern cinema, the average Hindi movie does not choose for detailed treatment a few cultural themes or personality-types from a universe of themes and types. Instead, it seeks to provide, like a Puranic epic, an alternative universe.

However, equally important is the fact that Bombay's Hindi film industry had been a cinematic melting pot for decades prior to the attempted homogenization of the city's cultural and linguistic strands. Most of the leading actors, the Khannas, the Deols and the Kapoors, to name a few, came from Punjab or the North-Western provinces of undivided India, now Pakistan. Their generally broad, well-built physiques were aligned with the traditional delineation of 'masculinity'. Directors and singers thronged from all over the country but mostly from Calcutta and Madras. This cosmopolitanism, which was a hallmark of Bombay city in general, was also a trait of its film industry.

But, the abstraction of realism as mentioned by Nandy happens equally on a spatial scale as well. Post-independence, like in major metropolitan cities, there was an influx of population from the rural spaces to the urban conurbations. By design a city is always intimidating, its extents would unnerve any newcomer. While Raj Kapoor's vagabond would come to the city (Bombay) and be forced to adopt immoral means for livelihood, Bimal Roy's Sambhu Mahato of *Do Bigha Zamin* would run away from the city (Calcutta), unable to cope up with it. The intricate spaces within the city, its magnitude of non-negotiable terrain, its warmthless crude brutality all compound the problems of the migrant. More importantly, a city of the enormity of Bombay also extends vertically – a double blow for the stranger. In the commercial

Hindi cinema it became increasingly important, hence, not only to obliterate the ethnic, racial identities of the heroes but also to balance out the spatial exclusivities wherever possible by setting the film in nondescript locales without an identifiable address. In short, a Hindi film made in Bombay was not cynical about its linguistic, racial, or even spatial identities the way a Bengali film or a Tamil film used to and continue to be.

It is in this context of Bombay as a city of dreams, a city of films and the temporality of the decade of the 1960s that we will look at the early films of Amol Palekar and his profile of the commoner in Hindi cinema.

'Moustache is the mirror of human soul and mind'

In 1979, Palekar acted in *Gol Maal*, a Hrishikesh Mukherjee film. In it he played the character of Ramprasad Dasrathprasad Sharma. Sporting a pencil-thin moustache, Sharma told Bhavani Shankar in a job interview: '*Moonch to mann ka darpan hai*', to which Shankar concluded, '*Jis ka moonch nahi uska mann nahin.*' But Palekar's tryst with such a pencil-thin moustache started with his very first film *Shantata! Court Chalu Ahe*. He sported the same in his subsequent films as well – *Rajnigandha* (1974), *Chhoti Si Baat* and *Chitchor* (both in 1976), then in *Gharonda* and *Bhumika* (both in 1977).

It is to be noted that none of the prominent heroes of Hindi cinema apart from Raj Kapoor and Guru Dutt sported a moustache. Kapoor was shaping up his profile as the Indian Charlie Chaplin and he couldn't afford to let go his moustache. On the other hand, Dutt, with a cultural lineage of southern and eastern India started off with comic/dramatic entertainers in films like *Baazi*, *Jaal*, *Mr and Mrs 55* before solemnly shifting to personal tragedies in the form of *Pyaasa* and *Kaagaz ke Phool*. And he was never a megastar.

The commercial Hindi cinema's idea of masculinity approved of a clean-shaven hero most of the times and occasionally a fully-bearded one. There are exceptions in Shatrughan Sinha, but Sinha emerged more as a villain in his early films. There was Rakesh Roshan as well, a hero with a wig and a moustache who was never a match for Palekar in importance or success. Different shades and shapes of moustache were more at home on the faces of Hindi cinema's iconic villains – from Pran to Ajit, from Amrish to Madan Puri. Palekar's moustache, commonplace and nonpartisan, doesn't have the virile phantasms of a super-human, be a hero or a villain. His was that of a common Indian.

In 1969, the Indian New Wave lapped on the Marine Drive with three films made in Hindi that had nothing to do with Bombay as a city or Maharashtra as a state. All three were located in western and northern India – Mrinal Sen's *Bhuvan Shome*, Mani Kaul's *Uski Roti* and Basu Chatterjee's *Saara Akash*. The artistic success of these films opened up avenues of experimentation in other parts of India, notably in the south and also in Marathi cinema with Satyadev Dubey-Govind Nihalani's *Shantata! Court Chalu Ahe*. In parallel, the 1970s Marathi cinema also witnessed the advent of an innocent buffoon revelling in Tamasha-based bawdy comedy. Dada Kondke took Marathi cinema by storm with *Songadya*. His success lay in his characterization of a halfwit in shabbily outrageous costumes. His bodily gestures, at times loaded with sexual innuendos, were an antithesis of popular heroism. His dialogue delivery was racy, fast, comical, and he ruled the decade and well into the next with a series of silver-jubilee hits.

Turning to Hindi cinema we find a widening rift between the commercial mainstream films and the more serious artistic endeavours. Hindi cinema by the mid '70s had already moved on to its delicately fashioned profile of the 'angry young man'. Violence ruled the screen – from *Zanjeer*, *Deewaar* to *Amar Akbar Anthony* or *Muqaddar Ka Sikander* with *Sholay* topping the chart. The likes of *Haathi Mere Saathi*, *Pakeezah* and *Bobby*, although hits at the box office, would be considered as exceptions to the gun-throttling reality of Hindi commercial cinema of the time.

Amol Palekar's advent can be understood in observing these developments in Hindi and Marathi cinema, this junction of an aggressively, tumultuous industrial man (Amitabh Bachchan) speaking the official language of the country and a loquacious simpleton (Dada Kondke) cracking jokes in the local language. In a cinema where the heroes had marked handsome traits bearing their geographic identities, Palekar's rather mediocre frame is decidedly unheroic. He is, indeed, the Marathi 'manoos' in Hindi cinema (as opposed to Dada Kondke, the Marathi 'manoos' in Marathi cinema) who would incorporate comedy and humour in his acting style to stay clear of the violence popular in the films of his more gangly and/or muscled compatriots.

To his persona, Palekar's moustache also lent its bit. It was not a Handlebar, a Chevron or a manly English. Rather its frugal presence elevated Palekar's profile just enough to that of a man from a boy. Palekar perfected this in his very second Hindi film, *Chhoti si Baat* – neither an adult, nor a child, one who is an intermediary. He remained such – distant from both Hindi and Marathi cinema, and halfway between cinema and his first love theatre.

Even before venturing into Hindi cinema with Basu Chatterjee's *Rajnigandha* (1974), Palekar was a regular in theatre. In a discussion at Natya Shodh Sansthan, Calcutta, on 1 July 1982 Palekar elaborated:

> I did *Suno Janmejaya*, after that I did *Aadhe Adhure*. Till then I was just there doing theatre as I was doing my bank job. No more interest than that ... At that time, (Satyadev) Dubey asked me, 'Why don't you direct a play?'... And that is how I directed my first play in 1969 – *Ballabhpur* ... now looking back I can clearly say that this was the point when I became interested in theatre.

Palekar continues that while doing Hindi theatre for Dubey he

> ... realized that the audience which comes to see the play is totally non-Hindi in any case. People who come are Maharashtrians and a few Gujaratis. Now, in any case, if I am going to communicate to this audience, I think I can communicate to them much better in Marathi than I can do in Hindi which is not my language in any case.

Forming his own theatre group Aniket in 1972, Palekar engaged in staging Marathi theatre. Aniket performed all over Maharashtra in cities other than Bombay as well as several interior towns of Maharashtra. Breaking the proscenium arch, the group would perform at office canteens, garages and even on terraces of housing complexes. People from different walks of life would come to watch the plays and the audience base expanded over time.

All these were happening at a time when Marathi theatre was generally appreciated by the middle-class Maharashtrians and not by the urban sophisticates of Bombay. To Palekar's credit he would experiment in theatre and take it to the masses of his native state in their own vernacular while working in Hindi films to cater to his urbane Bombay audience and the larger pan-Indian one. In this regard he resembles Utpal Dutt with whom he forms one of the finest comedy dyads in Hindi cinema. A lifelong theatre activist, Dutt would pursue his aspirations on the Bengali stage while simultaneously working in Bengali and Hindi commercial films.

'Ek akela is shahar mein'

Palekar acted in Bhimsain's *Gharaonda* in 1977. It was a film about a young couple's desperate attempts to find a house in Bombay. Sandwiched between the big-budget Amitabh Bachchan starrers *Amar Akbar Anthony* and *Parvarish*, this was Palekar's second film of the year along with Shyam Benegal's poignantly crafted *Bhumika*. There had been quite a few Hindi films that depicted the crisis of a living space in the city of Bombay. Basu Chatterjee's *Piya ka Ghar* comes to mind immediately. Where *Gharaonda* scores is in its depiction of shared accommodation spaces in Bombay for working professionals, akin to similar representations on the Bengali screen of the 1950s.

The film holds the city in two aspects – the high rises and the construction sites with forlorn overhead bridges acting as connections between these two worlds. It sheds light on the lives of all who come from the rural spaces with a dream to relocate one day in the harsh city. As per the article 'Mumbai City Résumé', in 1971 slum population in Bombay was 10,00,000 out of a total population of 59,70,575, at 16.7 per cent. Ten years later, in 1981, it was 36,76,000 out of 82,43,405 – a sharp increase to 44.6 per cent. Through the decade, as immigrants thronged the city from rural Maharashtra and also from outside, the dream of the middle / lower-middle class to own a house fizzled out gradually. It is in this sense as well that Palekar represents the hopelessness of the non-Bombayite Marathi – a man who is dispossessed in his own native state. He is the drifting hero without roots, without home, longing for love. That is why we find him walking on the streets of Bombay, boarding the iconic BEST buses, a man who can't afford a vehicle of his own. It is in this insufficiency of purpose that Palekar resonates with the other immigrants of the city in particular and with the pathos of all migrants in any part of the country.

Early in the film we find Sudip (Palekar) taking Chhaya (Zarina Wahab) to his hostel of sorts with an intention to be intimate with her. It irks Chhaya who feels insulted and runs away only to be placated by Sudip eventually. This sequence is important not only in the context of this film alone but also when we look back at *Chhoti Si Baat* made just a year prior. In Chatterjee's film, the protagonist Arun Pradip (Palekar) also invites his ladylove Prabha (Vidya Sinha) to his residence at the very end of it. Both Arun and Sudip seem to be ahistorical with no significant familial or genealogical background being furnished. But Arun, unlike Sudeep, is more traditional, hence he drops the plan feeling it may insult Prabha as a woman. In the lack of courage, in the endeavour not to impose his physicality on the woman, Palekar could carve out a mould of a common man with suppressed desires and unspoken emotions grappling to survive in the big city.

In his modest way, Amol Palekar could deliver hits in his first three Hindi films – *Rajnigandha*, *Chhoti Si Baat* and *Chitchor*, all three directed by Basu Chatterjee. In the first, Sanjay (Palekar) carries a bouquet of tuberose to Deepa as mark of his love for her. It is such a bouquet which at the end of the film finally sways Deepa towards him. In *Chitchor*, it is Geeta (Zarina Wahab) who brings Vinod (Palekar) a bouquet of homegrown flowers daily. Instead of wielding guns or flexing muscles, the shy sober chap prefers flowers as a currency of exchange. His persona, earnest yet trifling, distant yet comely stays on with a soft luminance.

Using wit and humour as his armour, mostly dressed in full-sleeve untucked shirts, Palekar perfected the image of the urban, ordinary, may be a sobered version of the quintessential Chaplinesque 'tramp'. Indeed, Palekar is no Chaplin, though, he probably never wished to be as well. Neither is he R.K. Laxman's The Common Man, a silent observer of life in a checked coat and a dhoti. In the urban fables of Bombay, Amol Palekar's characterization of the common denominations of life shine bright like the shadows caressing the ripples of the sea that engulfs the seven islands and a metropolis.

He did the voiceover for two Hindi films by arthouse giants from Bengal. Who was he and for which films?

Answer: Amitabh Bachchan in Mrinal Sen's *Bhuvan Shome* and Satyajit Ray's *Shatranj Ke Khilari*

The Shyam Benegal movie, *Bhumika* (1977) was based on the real life of which 1940s Marathi actress?

Answer: Hansa Wadkar

The Cinema of the Big Four

Manmohan Desai, Prakash Mehra, Yash Chopra, Ramesh Sippy

Alaka Sahani

If there was a period in Hindi cinema that resolutely lived by the mantra 'entertainment, entertainment, entertainment', it was the seventies. In all likelihood, the film-makers at the forefront of mainstream cinema at the time realized that telling a story on the big screen without a generous dose of 'entertainment' and dramatic effects was akin to serving paratha without aachar or idli without sambar. So, a bunch of movie mavericks not only redefined Indian commercial movies (colloquially referred to as 'masala' movies) with unparalleled swag and sass, but also informally created the template for crowd-pullers. Nearly, half a century later that remains unchanged.

The seventies saw the nation's mood undergoing a major upheaval: optimism was waning as poverty, joblessness and public angst were on the rise. The new generation of storytellers that emerged in the film industry grasped the prevalent mood. Most successful in feeling the public pulse were Manmohan Desai and Prakash Mehra. Giving them company were Ramesh Sippy and

Yash Chopra. They deftly translated their understanding of the public mood and aspirations on the big screen. This was the era of maximalist cinema and these directors believed in an overwhelming display of emotions.

Small wonder there was a profusion of good-triumphing-over-bad stories. Even when the movies focussed on public disillusion and disappointment against the system, the eternal clash of good versus bad or moral dilemma was at the heart of their narratives. Concurrently, the industry witnessed the phenomenal rise of superstar Amitabh Bachchan, who came to be known as 'the angry young man'. Yet, the film-makers were quite aware that the public needed to keep faith. Escapist fare became de rigueur as concoctions of romance, action, comedy and unbridled melodrama that pivot around larger-than-life characters were churned out. This resulted in an unprecedented mass hysteria and hero-worshipping, as evident from the serpentine queues outside single-screen theatres (remember the photo of ticket-seekers queued up outside a single screen theatre to watch *Don* [1978] shared by Bachchan on social media?).

Notwithstanding the dominance of stalwarts such as Raj Kapoor, Hrishikesh Mukherjee and Dev Anand – who carried forward their already popular storytelling from the preceding decade – this quartet of directors infused fresh vigour and aesthetics in Hindi cinema. Interestingly, all four of them dabbled with different genres and narratives. Yet, what stands out in their filmography of that decade are the massy blockbusters they made. In the following decades, this kind of mass connection became the parameter to judge a movie's impact and success. Though Desai and Mehra – who shared similar sensibilities – started their career in the sixties, it is in the seventies that they found their mojo and emerged as the masters of formulaic movies. Interestingly, they both worked extensively with Bachchan, delivering multiple super hits over a span of fifteen years. Sippy and Chopra too collaborated with Bachchan in more than one movie.

Son of Kikubhai Desai, who produced a number of stunt movies, Manmohan was a second-generation film-maker. His brother Subhash Desai too was a producer and helped Manmohan make his directorial debut with *Chhalia* (1960). Manmohan used the lost-and-found formula for the first time in *Chhalia*. This, he went on to replicate, albeit with some tweaking, in a number of his films. Though Manmohan directed several entertainers such as *Bluff Master* (1963) and *Kismat* (1968), it was post the success of *Sachaa Jhutha* (1970) that he perfected his winning formula. He stepped into the seventies with a bang as *Sachaa Jhutha*, headlined by Rajesh Khanna who was then at the peak of his superstardom after the astounding success of *Aradhana* (1969), became a super hit. The director followed it up with back-to-back successes like *Aa Gale Lag Jaa* (1973) and *Roti* (1974).

In 1977, Manmohan consolidated his status as a hit maker with four major releases: *Parvarish*, *Dharam Veer*, *Chacha Bhatija* and *Amar Akbar Anthony* (*AAA*). In fact, all the signature tropes of Manmohan's movies converged in *AAA* to create a kind of potboiler that came to represent a typical Indian entertainer; the kind of cinema that the overused term 'Bollywood' signifies. Speaking to Channel 4 in 1987, Manmohan deconstructed his success. Insisting that he continued to lead a regular middle-class life in Mumbai's Girgaon neighbourhood, he said: 'You have to think from a layman's point of view and think what they would like. So far, they have liked what I have made. That's what counts.'

With the fatal accident during the shooting of *Coolie* (1983) that had the entire nation praying for Bachchan's recovery, Desai's cinema strengthened its mass connect. Even though Desai-Bachchan continued to work together, five years later *Gangaa Jamunaa Saraswathi* (1988), a box-office dud, marked their last theatrical outing as director-actor team.

Unlike Desai, Prakash Mehra came to Mumbai from outside but unbeknownst to them their career was going to run parallel. Though this native of Uttar Pradesh's Bijnor made his directorial debut with *Purnima* (1965) and had several notable outings such as *Haseena Maan Jayegi* (1968) and *Samadhi* (1972), it is *Zanjeer* (1973) that's regarded as his breakthrough movie. That also showcased Bachchan's breakout performance. With Bachchan cast in it as an upright cop harbouring the childhood trauma of watching his parents being murdered, *Zanjeer* contributed majorly to building Bachchan's Angry Young Man persona. After *Zanjeer*, they collaborated on seven more films including *Hera Pheri* (1976), *Khoon Pasina* (1977, which he produced), *Muqaddar Ka Sikandar* (1978), *Lawaaris* (1981), *Namak Halaal* (1982) and *Sharaabi* (1984). In a 2015 interview with *Bollywood Hungama*, Bachchan said: 'Prakash-ji had a great sense of the story and music. He was quite the opposite of Manji, who used to dress up his sets and make them larger than life … Prakash-ji's strength was his writing.' They worked together for the last time on *Jaadugar* (1989), which was a flop. Mehra, who had promised the superstar earlier that they won't work together again if a film of theirs flopped, stuck to his word and didn't direct Bachchan again.

During those pre-multiplex days, the mainstream film-makers aimed for crowd-pleasers by combining high-decibel performance, gravity-defying stunts, improbable action sequences, applause-worthy dialogue-baazi, and plotlines that were filled with twists-and-turns to keep the audience glued to the screen. They made sure the viewers were emotionally invested in the characters and their journey. To make them all-round entertainers, romantic tracks, comedy, dance sequences and catchy music were incorporated. All these efforts were meant to earn the tag of 'paisa vasool' for the new releases. Desai and Mehra, unabashedly, used these cinematic devices to entice and entertain moviegoers. Desai, however, was more flamboyant in his approach to film-making and believed in extravaganza. His biggest trick: seemingly ludicrous scenarios that made suspension of disbelief absolutely essential.

Son of G.P. Sippy, the founder of Sippy Films, Ramesh stepped into the film world as a child artiste. G.P. Sippy, a lawyer-turned-film producer, who migrated from Karachi to Mumbai during the partition was drawn to the world of cinema after moving to Mumbai, produced *Sazaa* (1951) and, two years later, *Shahenshah* (1953) in which then nine-year-old Ramesh acted. After working for seven years as an assistant, Ramesh debuted with *Andaz* (1971) which captures the romance between two single parents. This is a subject that's considered 'unusual' even today. His next was the delightful *Seeta Aur Geeta* (1972) which had nation's heartthrob Hema Malini in a double role. But it's his third movie, *Sholay* (1975), that was going to become an all-time great while his fourth *Shaan* (1980), a Bond-like thriller, would see his grand ambition flounder. The story of *Sholay*'s super success – which remains unmatched in terms of the reach it had, the reaction it generated and the way it impacted the next generation of film-making – contributes to the uniqueness of seventies cinema. Though this movie, revolving around two adorable petty criminals, opened to a lukewarm response and was dismissed by many, it went on to enjoy a record-run at theatres.

Like Sippy, Chopra oscillated between relationship dramas and action sagas with ease. Chopra's family migrated from Lahore. The biggest influence on Chopra, during his initial years as a director, was his elder brother B.R. Chopra, a film-maker known for infusing socially conscious themes in movies. Backed by his elder brother's production, Yash's directorial debut was *Dhool Ka Phool* (1959) in which a child born out of wedlock is brought up by a Muslim man. Reflecting the secular mood of the time, the movie features the landmark song '*Tu Hindu banega na Musalman banega, insaan ki aulaad hai, insaan banega*'. After directing some more films under the BR Films banner, including *Dharmputra* (1961), *Waqt* (1965), *Aadmi Aur Insaan* (1969) and *Ittefaq* (1969), Yash decided to come out from the shadows of his big brother.

In the year 1970, he founded Yash Raj Films and three years later he released the first film under the banner, *Daag: A Poem of Love* (1973), a relationship and moral drama. As he tried to establish himself and Yash Raj Films in the years that followed, he delivered several intense social dramas – *Deewaar* (1975), *Trishul* (1978) and *Kaala Patthar* (1979). These movies reinforced Bachchan's Angry Young Man image, though Chopra's romantic sensibilities, which eventually became more pronounced in the

1980s, were evident in these movies. Referring to certain scenes in *Deewaar*, Bachchan recounts in the Netflix documentary *The Romantics* that one could sense the aesthetics of Chopra in the way the director used to find a way to zoom the camera on flowers or something beautiful even in a hard-hitting film. It is hardly surprising that in between making these films, he delivered *Kabhi Kabhie* (1976), an examination of modern relationships that features a number of evergreen songs, which were composed by Khayyam and written by Sahir Ludhianvi.

Even though the cinematic sensibilities and influences of this quartet varied, they were all excellent storytellers. As they created a new chapter in Hindi cinema, albeit unwittingly, that celebrated emotionally charged dramas, they had the advantage of having a very receptive audience. The viewers lapped up even the most incredulous storyline as well as in-your-face social messages. They embraced tearjerkers, mushy love stories or action dramas as long as they were engaging. Though they made massy entertainers, which a lot of times bordered on being emotionally manipulative, they didn't take their audience for granted. Rather, these directors tried their best to tell stories of the moment – something the single-screen audience could relate to. *Zanjeer* highlighted bootlegging and corruption; *Deewaar* condemned unscrupulous businessmen; and designed as a historical epic, *Dharam Veer* (1977) showed class conflict. Some movies cast a wide net and took up more than one issue. For example, *Muqaddar Ka Sikandar* (1978), one of the highest-grossing movies of the decade, combined class conflict with unrequited love, friendship and empathy. It also showed that a family can be found as long as there is love and concern for each other.

Even as improbable twists in the tale turned out to be the secret sauce that boosted a movie's commercial prospect, what also worked surprisingly well are tried-and-tested formulas. So, the tropes of mistaken identity; family members separated under tragic circumstances and reunited in the climax; mother as the moral compass; and an upright protagonist speaking up for the poor and vulnerable were used ad nauseam. Yet, they managed to captivate the audience. Possibly because they were heavily influenced by traditional Indian storytelling, including mythologies. There were traces of Shakespearean elements, especially in dramas that explored the lost-and-found or mistaken-identity formula. Decades later, it still remains a mystery how the audience was overwhelmed by *AAA*'s opening credit scene that shows its three lead characters, lying on three different beds in a hospital and donating blood. Their blood is collected in a single tube and is simultaneously given to an injured elderly woman (essayed by Nirupa Roy). Like many others in the team, Bachchan was wary of this scene. But Desai stuck to his conviction and created a pop culture landmark.

All the four directors worked with talented screenwriters. Salim Khan and Javed Akhtar (known as Salim-Javed) established themselves as a formidable writing duo with the success of *Zanjeer*. They worked with all the top directors of the time including Mehra (*Zanjeer* and *Haath Ki Safai*), Chopra (*Deewaar*, *Trishul* and *Kaala Patthar*) and Sippy (*Seeta Aur Geeta* and *Sholay*). Desai too collaborated with them for *Chacha Bhatija* (1977) even though his frequent writing collaborators were Prayag Raaj, K.K. Shukla and Kader Khan. It's Khan's writing that gave Bachchan's character Anthony in AAA its tapori lingo. Take, for example, the famous dialogue: '*Apun bahut famous aadmi … bada bada paper mein apun ka chota chota photo chapta hai.*' This helped Bachchan show his talent as a comedian.

These film-makers dreamt big – with multi-star casting; overachieving protagonists; over-the-top villains; and elaborate song-dance sequences. For instance, *Sholay*, *Parvarish* (1974), *Dharam Veer*, *Suhaag* (1979), *Trishul*, *Kaala Patthar*, *Kabhi Kabhie*, *Khoon Pasina*, *Muqaddar Ka Sikandar* – these movies brought several top stars of the time together. These movies also featured the much-loved supporting actors such as Pran, Nirupa Roy, Ajit and Iftekhar. Villains, who seemed to be fashioned after comic-book baddies, remained one of the star attractions. While Sholay's Gabbar Singh occupies the top ranking among Indian villains for his swag and dialogues, Ajit's screen persona and dialogues in *Zanjeer* – such as *Kutta jab pagal ho jaata hai toh usse goli maar dete hai* – became quite popular too.

Most of these star-studded movies aimed for grand scale with spectacular action sequences. In Manmohan's *Dharam Veer* two new-born babies were swapped by the baddie and then swapped back without his knowledge. More outlandish is the fate of another baby. When flung outside a palace, it is saved by a falcon and carried off safely to his comatose father. The influences of epic tales were evident in *Dharam Veer*, as Dharam (Dharmendra) dresses up like ancient Greek heroes, claims to have a chest that's as tough as steel while Prince Veer (Jeetendra) could often be seen doing a flip to ride his horse or to get off it. The film features a fight with a tiger; epic clash of brothers who don't know that they are related; and a lengthy climax that takes place on a ship.

The persona of male protagonists mostly matched the idea of the righteous macho man that drove the popular narrative. In fact, after Bachchan burst into the scene, the portrayal of such male characters became larger than life. Desai and Mehra became primary architects of this. These male characters were brooding, sensitive, upright, kind, and nothing short of a messiah for the needy. Vijay in *Zanjeer* can't be lured with hefty bribes. His namesake in *Deewaar* won't just pick up the money that's thrown at him while his brother Ravi being an honest cop would make it a mission to stop his brother's wrongdoing. In *Sholay*, once Jai and Veeru learn about the magnitude of the tragedy that Thakur had suffered, they won't stop till they ensure Gabbar's downfall. Considering the prominence that the male protagonists enjoyed, it is probably not surprising that male bonding has played such a key role in most of these entertainers.

Barring a handful of movies, female leads were never given the prominence that the 'heroes' enjoyed, especially in those made by Desai and Mehra. While 'mother' was put on a pedestal, the love interests of male leads made routine appearances to mainly facilitate romantic tracks and song-and-dance sequences. In

Muqaddar Ka Sikandar, the eponymous protagonist Sikandar (essayed by Bachchan), though an orphan, finds two mother figures – Roy and later Sulochana Latkar – who dote on him at different stages of his life. As the mother, Roy's character in *Deewaar* is the epitome of morality and has some of the best dialogues. In *Muqaddar Ka Sikandar*, she would rather give up her job than let go of her adopted son. In *Amar Akbar Anthony* too, Roy has some of the best scenes compared to those featuring the three heroines – Neetu Singh, Shabana Azmi and Parveen Babi.

Compared to Desai and Mehra, heroines in movies made by Sippy and Chopra had well etched-out characters and even had agency. Ramesh cast Hema Malini as a young working mother in *Andaz*. In *Seeta Aur Geeta*, Hema Malini as Geeta not only teaches her evil relatives some lessons but also does some daring stunts such as hanging from a ceiling fan. However, it's probably her portrayal as chatterbox Basanti in *Sholay* that created a lasting impact. In Chopra's movies too women enjoyed more screen space. Employed as a secretary in *Trishul*, Raakhee is shown as an efficient and honest worker. In *Doosra Aadmi* (1977), produced by Chopra, she is a sought-after professional who ends up having an affair with her young boss. In *Kabhi Kabhie* (1976), she is the muse of a shayar.

Though, looking back, these entertaining movies seem like dominant celluloid narratives of the decade, let's not forget it was in the seventies that Shyam Benegal made a powerful debut with *Ankur* (1974) and followed in up with *Nishant* (1975), *Bhumika* (1977) and *Junoon* (1978) – all four were celebrated for their powerful stories and performance. This is also the period when Hrishikesh Mukherjee made classics like *Anand* (1971) and *Abhimaan* (1973). Raj Kapoor shifted gears to deliver *Bobby* (1973) and present two young heartthrobs. Kamal Amrohi finally released the aesthetically rich *Pakeezah* (1972), Gulzar brought in his unique sensibilities with his directorial outings *Koshish* (1972) and *Aandhi* (1975). There was also Basu Chatterjee with his feel-good stories, such as *Chhoti Si Baat* (1976) and *Baton Baton Mein* (1979).

The audience undoubtedly embraced all kinds of movies. But they expressed a special love for cheesy and sappy stories playing out on the big screen. They wanted to have a good time. They loved the movies that made them cry and laugh. Manmohan Desai, Prakash Mehra, Ramesh Sippy and Yash Chopra pandered to the popular demands with panache. They packed their movies to the brim with emotion, drama, action and romance. Most of these movies worked. Some didn't. Yet, film-makers never lost their faith in the magic of this formula. In the '80s and '90s, many fell back on these formulas even though the unique touch of Desai and Mehra was missing. Today, storytelling might have evolved but formulaic fare is still very much in circulation. How else will you explain *Jawan* repackaging of some of these tropes, although with the help of technology and contemporary approach, as Shah Rukh Khan positions himself as a mass entertainer?

Which actor made his debut as Surya, the landlord's son in the film *Ankur* (1974)?

Answer: Anant Nag

The soundtrack of the television commercial for Amul was the title track of which Shyam Benegal National Award-winning movie?

Answer: *Manthan* (1976)

The Amar Akbar Anthony of Writers

Kader Khan, K.K. Shukla and Prayag Raaj, and the Seventies Blockbuster

S.M.M. Ausaja

If one sets aside the discerning cinema connoisseurs' perception of films and delves into the most impactful films made in India in terms of success and prominence within the 'popular-culture' framework, few scriptwriters stand out for not just being consistently successful, but also for the impact their work has left on a generation. Besides Salim–Javed (the celebrated writer-duo credited for the advent and the subsequent sway of the 'Angry Young Man' at the box office), three writers who deserve to be celebrated are without a doubt Prayag Raaj, K.K. Shukla and Kader Khan. Not many cinema fans know that they, individually and collectively, have delivered more hits featuring megastar Amitabh Bachchan than Salim–Javed! And yet very little is known about these stalwarts as scriptwriters.

Kader Khan did his early education in Mumbai, completed a degree in civil engineering, and became a professor in a South Mumbai engineering college, but concurrently he was always into theatre. His talent was noticed by actor Agha in one such play, who recommended his talent to Dilip Kumar so that he could assist on Tapan Sinha's *Sagina*. But it was Narinder Bedi who gave Khan his first break with Rose Movies' *Jawani Diwani* – his debut hit which he co-scripted with Inder Raj Anand. This was followed by Bedi's *Benaam* (where he also provided the voiceover for the villain played by Prem Chopra, lending his 'yaani ke' on the phone a chilling resonance) as well as Manmohan Desai's *Roti* (where he was recommended to Desai by Rajesh Khanna) – two back-to-back hits in 1974 establishing him as a dependable writer. *Roti* began his long and hugely successful association with Manmohan Desai and writer Prayag Raaj (who also did a memorable cameo in the film).

His association with Prakash Mehra began with Rakesh Kumar's *Khoon Pasina* (which was produced by Mehra) in 1977 – the year in which he delivered three gigantic hits for Manmohan Desai, namely, *Parvarish, Dharam-Veer* and *Amar Akbar Anthony* – all co-scripted with Prayag Raaj. K.K. Shukla was also the co-scriptwriter for *Parvarish* and *Amar Akbar Anthony*. Bachchan's iconic dialogue to actor Jeevan – '*Aise to aadmi life mein doich time bhagta hai, Olympic ka race ho ya police ka case ho*' – is part of Hindi cinema folklore and was the product of Kader Khan's brilliance with the language of the streets. The very next year, Khan delivered the monster hit for Prakash Mehra – *Muqaddar ka Sikandar*, in which he also essayed a memorable cameo as a fakir. This film emerged as the biggest success of 1978 despite a stiff competition from Chandra Barot's *Don*, Yash Chopra's *Trishul* and Sultan Ahmed's *Ganga Ki Saugand*.

Backed by Manmohan Desai and Prakash Mehra, Kader Khan's repertoire expanded to other prominent directors of the era as he delivered successive hits right up to the nineties, contributing hugely to the sustained success of Amitabh Bachchan. The jubilee hits with Amitabh stretched well into the nineties with *Agneepath* and *Hum*. *Mr Natwarlal, Suhaag, Naseeb, Laawaris, Yaarana, Satte Pe Satta, Desh Premee, Namak Halaal,*

Khuddaar (one of his two films for which story, screenplay and dialogue are credited solely to him, the other being *Shama*), *Coolie, Sharaabi, Geraftaar* – it is almost an endless list of hits that he delivered as a writer with Amitabh Bachchan. The cricket commentary in *Namak Halaal* – Vijay Merchant and Vijay Hazare, Wasim Raja and Wasim Bari – rendered brilliantly by Bachchan is Kader Khan at his best.

Concurrently in the eighties, Khan prodded Jeetendra's career with a string of hits for south Indian producers. The Jeetendra–Kadar Khan combination won the box office across the decade beginning with *Meri Awaz Suno* (1981) and including *Farz aur Kaanoon, Himmatwala, Jaani Dost, Justice Chaudhury, Mawaali, Tohfa, Maqsad, Akalmand, Sarfarosh, Pataal Bhairavi* and *Singhasan*. In the 1990s Kader Khan was primarily responsible for the rise of Govinda as a dependable star with big hits like *Coolie No.1, Saajan Chale Sasural* and other hits of the era.

It's commendable that since 1974, his journey as a successful dialogue writer continued alongside his journey as an actor, with the man exuding brilliance on both fronts. He first caught the eye as the sympathetic police officer in *Adalat* (1976). And right through the seventies he was a bankable villain in a host of Manmohan Desai films too, often playing second fiddle to Amjad Khan.

Unlike Kader Khan and Prayag Raaj, K.K. Shukla was an industry child. His father Laxmikant Shukla was into film production. Shukla did his schooling at Don Bosco and graduated from St Xavier's, Bombay. As a young man, Shukla had no interest in the film industry, yet gradually he was drawn to the world, beginning as an assistant to Tarachand Barjatya of Rajshri Productions. He married actress Daisy Irani in 1971, and was signed by Sunil Dutt for *Nehla Pe Dehla* the next year, his first assignment as a screenplay writer. But technically he was launched by director Ravi Tandon with *Anhonee* (1973) since the film released first, following it up with Kundan Kumar's *Anokhi Ada* the same year.

He teamed up with Kader Khan for the first time with Narendra Bedi's *Rafoo Chakkar* (1975), and then in Rakesh Kumar's *Khoon Pasina* (1977). It was with *Amar Akbar Anthony* that the three stalwarts – Prayag Raaj, K.K. Shukla and Kader Khan – worked together for the first time and hit the jackpot, making history thereafter. Shukla reached his zenith as a writer with Feroz Khan's stylish racy musical *Qurbani* (1980) – the suave characterization of Amjad Khan as the gum-chewing cop in the film is widely regarded as one of the best roles created for the talented actor. Shukla co-scripted hits like *Parvarish, Suhaag, Naseeb, Taqdeer, Shakka, Baghavat, Coolie, Geraftaar, Mard, Janbaaz, Insaaf,* and *Hifazat.*

Prayag Raaj had creativity in his genes. He is the son of a well-known poet Ram Das 'Azad'. Azad belonged to Lahore, worked in the Indian Army, and was posted in Allahabad when his son was born and named after his celebrated birthplace (Allahabad was traditionally called Prayag Raj). Azad's interest in theatre and cinema, and his association with Prithviraj Kapoor and K.L. Saigal led him to give up his job and migrate to Bombay in 1941 where he wrote plays for Prithvi Theatre and even directed a couple of films. Prayag Raaj entered films as early as 1948 as a child artist with RK's *Aag* where he played a tramp. RK's *Awara* (1951) followed, where he was once again a child artist.

In 1961, Shammi Kapoor's rebellious on-screen 'Yahoo!' refrain in Subodh Mukherjee's *Junglee* was actually Prayag Raaj's voice at the studio while recording the song '*Chahe mujhe koi junglee kahe*' with Mohammed Rafi. The song in Saira Banu's debut film took the nation's youth by storm. Groomed at RK Studios and Prithvi Theatres, and being Shashi Kapoor's best friend, Raaj eventually turned to direction in 1962, assisting Lekh Tandon in *Professor*.

He got a high-profile launch as a writer when James Ivory and Ismail Merchant penciled him for the Hindi dialogues of *Householder* (1963) – besides working as an assistant in direction. In *Shakespearewallah* (1965), Prayag Raaj assisted in direction, did a cameo, and wrote his first song composed under the baton of Satyajit Ray and rendered by Mubarak Begum. This song was listed among Ray's best songs in a commemorative collection record released later by HMV where the celebrated director acknowledged the young lyricist.

In 1968, Prayag Raaj wrote his first Hindi film, *Juari*, and followed it up with his first hit as a writer, *Jhuk Gaya Aasmaan*. For Merchant–Ivory's *Guru* (1969), besides acting, he was promoted as a second-unit director. His association as an actor with Merchant Ivory Productions lasted till *Cotton Mary* (1999).

The seventies belonged to Prayag Raaj. Impressed with the success of *Jhuk Gaya Aasmaan*, Manmohan Desai signed him for *Sachaa Jhutha* (1970) starring the reigning superstar, Rajesh Khanna. Prayag Raaj delivered a golden jubilee for the director resulting in the now-famous writer–director association. Prayag Raaj scripted all Manmohan Desai films in collaboration with (mostly) K.K. Shukla and Kader Khan. With a grooming of almost two decades, Prayag Raaj finally wielded the megaphone as an independent director for *Kundan* in 1972, and wrote his second huge hit for Desai – *Rampur Ka Laxman*. His stock as a scriptwriter rose under Desai with *Aa Gale Lag Jaa* in 1973 and *Roti* in 1974. In 1975, he directed the hit comedy *Ponga Pandit* and the following year wrote Raj Kapoor's *Dharam Karam*. His meteoric success reached its zenith in 1977. Prayag Raaj directed the successful *Chor Sipahee* and delivered the year's four biggest hits for Manmohan Desai – *Parvarish, Dharam Veer* and *Amar Akbar Anthony* in collaboration with K.K. Shukla and Kader Khan, while *Chacha Bhatija* had the legendary writer working with the high-profile duo of Salim-Javed.

In 1977, began the association of Amitabh Bachchan and Prayag Raaj with two smash hits back to back – *Parvarish* and *Amar Akbar Anthony.* The latter has the distinction of being the first film to celebrate a silver jubilee in eleven theatres in Bombay! If Salim–Javed crafted the Angry Young Man persona for Amitabh, Prayag Raaj, K.K. Shukla and Kader Khan made him multifaceted, and thereby diluted the argument that the actor was typecast in anger-oriented roles. For the audience, Anthony was a welcome change after the vendetta-driven Vijays, giving Amitabh an opportunity for comedy and coming up trumps in that as well. These writers actually made Amitabh Bachchan the complete entertainer. *Suhaag* released in 1979, brought Kolhapuri chappals in vogue, and went on to triumph at the box office. *Naseeb* in 1981 remains Desai's most flamboyant film. It was one of the biggest hits of the year, and included a number of unforgettable highlights – Amitabh's drunken act in the song '*Chal mere bhai*', the revolving restaurant climax, and the song '*John Jani Janardhan*' which brought together a galaxy of stars.

By the time Desai's next film – *Desh Premee* (1982) – hit the theatres, it was time for the celebrated director to honour his consistently successful writer by giving him a film to direct under the MKD production house. Prayag Raaj directed Amitabh Bachchan for *Coolie* (1983) – a film that almost cost the actor his life! Desai had to add his name after Prayag Raaj in credits for commercial reasons. The film towered above all releases that year, zooming to the platinum jubilee! Buoyed by the spectacular success, Prayag Raaj stormed the box office once again in 1985 with Desai's *Mard*, a film where his hero took on the might of the British Empire – a character reportedly inspired by The Phantom comic strip – a favourite of Desai! (The horse and the dog as constant companions of the invincible protagonist.)

But the element of crudity in the film earned it substantial flak from discerning critics. Desai remained unfazed, having complete support from Bachchan who, being an MP, ensured the double entendre in the song '*Tambu mein bamboo*' (penned by Prayag Raaj) went past the the censors! The song became a hit, and the film the second biggest hit of the year after Raj Kapoor's *Ram Teri Ganga Maili*. The same year, Prayag Raaj pulled off a coup of sorts by bringing together and directing Amitabh Bachchan, Kamal Haasan and Rajinikanth in *Geraftaar*. Coming at a time of relative drought of new films, in the wake of Bachchan's tryst with politics, the film witnessed hysterical advance bookings, roared to a silver jubilee, and its star cast has gone down in the history of Hindi cinema – being the only time the three superstars were seen in a film. The hit *Toofan* song sung by Amitabh and Manhar Udhas, '*Don't worry be happy*', was penned by Prayag Raaj.

The last MKD film with Prayag Raaj was *Deewana Mastana* in 1997 – a breezy comedy starring Anil Kapoor and Govinda, made years after the death of Manmohan Desai. This film is also the last hit from the prestigious banner. In his brief stint with television, Prayag Raaj scripted the most successful costume drama of its time for Doordarshan – Sunil Agnihotri's *Chandrakanta*. And Doordarshan's weekly comedy countdown show *Truck Dhina Dhin* – co-scripted by Prayag Raaj and featuring Jaaved Jaffrey and Jagdeep – was the highest TRP fetching countdown show in the country.

Manmohan Desai's *Amar Akbar Anthony* changed the landscape of entertainment in Hindi cinema of the seventies. And behind the scene it was another trio – Prayag Raaj, Kader Khan and K.K. Shukla – who transformed the grammar of writing in mainstream cinema with their stories, screenplays and dialogues for some of the biggest hits of the era.

Who played the role of Mrs Braganza in *Bobby* (1973)?
Answer: Durga Khote

Which famous 1973 movie was inspired by the failed marriage of Kishore Kumar and Ruma Guha Thakurta?
Answer: *Abhimaan*

The King of Melody

R.D. Burman and the Transitional Early 1970s

Anirudha Bhattacharjee

I have never managed to lose the conviction that music for cinema is a team effort. Hindi films have been validating the point for almost a hundred years. Apart from having composers who operated in pairs, and a few phenomenally successful ones at that like Shankar–Jaikishan, Laxmikant–Pyarelal, and Kalyanji–Anandji, Hindi or Hindustani cine music would comprise the collective effort of a sixty-piece orchestra. Or more. Sometimes the numbers could be in three figures, with many musicians, especially fiddlers, being forced to stand outside the recording room, and thus being branded as 'outstanding musicians.' Hence, it is much more than just a morbid curiosity that the Burmans – Sachin Dev (SD) and Rahul Dev (RD, aka Pancham) – remained to me two sides of the same coin, whatever the cognoscenti and their moral policing stands are about music rights being attributed to only the official composer.

While the hardcore supporters of the rival camps are completely entitled to hold on to their point of view, the musician and rationalist in me refuses to swallow the thought that papa and son did not discuss music over breakfast, lunch, or dinner. Or over multiple cups of tea, though papa was strictly economical with the budget allocated for niceties like teatime. To cut a long joke short, tea in the Burman household, then at 'The Jet' on Linking Road, Khar, would be served with lots of milk and in large cups made of the finest bone china that the senior Burman had received from the royal family of Tripura, of which he too was a member. SD was reluctant to share tea with anyone outside the family. It could upset his wife Meera, as she would supervise the making of tea and would get overworked.

Incidentally, Pancham's first job as a team member was to bring tea during sittings and rehearsals. Apart from serving and tasting the finest of tea, the son surely gained a lot in the fifteen-something years he was an assistant. One of his major musical tasks would be to write antaras for mukhras already composed by his father. SD had the habit of assigning this part to his assistants – Jaidev, Suhrid Kar, and Pancham.[1] By the end of the 1960s, Pancham must have composed a few hundred antaras, of which most were discarded by his father, while some made it to the final cut. He was also accorded the honour of composing and arranging full songs, as in the case of '*Gaata rahe mera dil*' (*Guide*, 1965),[2] and a few more in *Teen Devian* (1965),[3] *Jewel Thief* (1967), and *Gambler* (1971), among others. The task of sitting on the recording console at times had become a given. Probir Mukherjea, a lawyer-cum-musician who was close to the Burmans, recalls Pancham doing the honours with the recordist during a song recording of Jaidev for the film *Mujhe Jeene Do* (1963).[4] He was not acknowledged.

But the act of experimenting with knobs would have a major impact on his music. Sound, and its myriad frequencies, became a

---

[1] R.D. Burman, 'My God, That's My Tune,' *Filmfare*, June 16-30, 1984

[2] Nilu N. Gavankar, *The Desai Trio and The Movie Industry of India* (Bloomington: Author House, 2011)

[3] Interview with Probir Mukherjea in Calcutta, December 2012

[4] Ibid.

subject of deep interest. Musicians would go ahead and acknowledge that nobody understood sound balancing like Pancham, especially his 1970s music which was a blend of the acoustic and the electric. He was the driver of ideas which were essentially his own.

The driving act he extended to his father's car as well. SD had abandoned driving after suffering an accident leading to the detachment of one retina.[5] Pancham, in the meantime, started driving SD's ash-coloured Austin. In the 1960s, Pancham, accompanied by Sachin Bhowmick (story and screenplay writer), Bhisham Kohli (film producer and actor), Ravinder Kapoor (actor), et al., would drive to places like Khandala and Lonavala, streaking as a group fully naked in the evening. They bought cigarettes on credit, as none of them carried wallets. It is interesting to note that Pancham survived such shenanigans.[6] Not everyone in the industry, including his father, was approving of Pancham's approach to life. But then, that was Pancham.

He followed his father's advice on music though. 'Whatever you compose sounds like a composition by Roshan or Madan Mohan. Try to create your own style.' And thus, was born the brass-driven music of *Teesri Manzil* (1966). Though *Teesri Manzil* was pulled out of theatres in Bombay (now Mumbai) after twenty-four weeks by distributors, Pancham did not have to look behind thereafter.[7]

Incidentally, Pancham's first stepping stone to the 1970s had him going against his father. Probably the first time he disagreed on music with his old man.

❖

The Naxalite movement in the late 1960s and early 1970s led to many film personalities leaving Calcutta (now Kolkata). This included Uttam Kumar, who took temporary refuge in producer

---

[5] Interview with Sachin Ganguly, SD's Calcutta-based secretary, December 2012

[6] Interview with Sachin Bhowmick in April 2010

[7] Anitaa Padhye, *Ek Hota Goldie* (Bhopal: Manjul Publishing House, 2005)

Debesh Ghosh's Waterfield Road flat in Bandra West. Ghosh had shifted to Bombay on account of political disturbances in his city of work as well. R.D. Burman, whom Ghosh knew through his filmi circle, was looking for a toehold in Calcutta too. He was eager to do music for *Rajkumari* (1970), a film Ghosh had in mind, the proposal of which was floated by Uttam in 1968. The deal was set with Salil Sen as the director; Pancham settled for a low remuneration, promising exemplary music. The shoot started in January 1970. It was Pancham's first film of the decade.

S.D. Burman was hesitant of his son scouting for opportunities in Bengal. His own attempt at a comeback in Bengali cinema after a gap of twenty-something years with *Chaitali* (1971) was met with apprehension as the film was held up for several years.[8] Father promptly advised son to avoid Bengali cinema. True to SD's forebodings, *Rajkumari* failed, and Pancham summarily stopped signing Bengali films. But the film played a leading role in defining his musical style.

Rajkumari has a scene where Tanuja, who, under her regimental mother (played by Chhaya Debi), sings a *tarana* during a party organized to find her a suitor. Groomed strictly to avoid anything not sombre and solemn, her kitty of songs is limited to Hindustani classical music. Slowly but steadily, the population in the room thins down. Greater attraction lies in the dining room. Till the camera zooms to a solitary person, the hero, played by Uttam Kumar, who, overwhelmed by the singing (after all, it is Asha Bhosle), showers unabashed appreciation. It is later revealed that he too had learnt Hindustani classical, but is currently proficient in a form which is ostensibly removed from what he was trained in. Light music. Rhythmic, sans the clutter.

In a way, this was the story of Pancham. Though he had a background in Hindustani music – he trained under many, including Ustad Ali Akbar Khan – his exploration of world music

---

[8] *Chaitali* was signed in the mid-1960s. The exact year is not known. It was delayed for five or six years. SD's last Bengali film was released in 1945.

and the jazz of Dave Brubeck had instilled in him the belief that music was beyond boundaries. Also, any form of sound could be musical. And it was there for him to take and use the same in his own inimitable style. The ability to connect to various sources of music – Blues, Latino, Cuban big band, Japanese, along with Hindustani classical – helped in creating forms hitherto unexplored or less explored in Hindi cinema.

No wonder, '*Aaj gun gungun kunje amar*', the song Uttam Kumar (only the first line was used, sung by Kishore Kumar) is seen teaching Tanuja during a subsequent interaction, and later sung by Asha Bhosle, was extremely pleasing to the ear. Pan India, the Hindi counterpart was more famous. Kishore Kumar's '*Pyar diwana hota hai*' from *Kati Patang* (1970). Bubbling with youthful energy, the songs highlighted the different facets in Pancham. The Bengali song had the 4/4 rhythm with a cadence-like waltz (3/4), something exceedingly difficult to achieve as the two patterns are different. The Hindi version, where each antara began in a slightly offbeat manner, had the piano acting like a melody-cum-rhythm instrument. While the fillers were more or less the same, the characters of the songs were different. If stripped of the main melody and the interim fillers, it could be difficult to tell that the two songs were the same. This was remarkable as both the songs were recorded at the same studio (Film Centre), and within weeks of each other, and with approximately the same basic set of musicians. Mike Machado playing the piano in the Hindi version was additional, as were a few supplementary fiddlers. But both the songs had Basu Chakraborty, Manohari Singh, Maruti Rao Keer, Devichand, Bhupinder, Bhanu Gupta, Homi Mullan, Chandrakanth, and Amrut Rao playing the main parts. Pancham's *navratna*.

This was a partnership at another level. Maruti Rao would add syncopated beats, Manohari's fillers would play a prominent part during antaras, Basu's string section would avoid being screechy, and Bhupinder's guitar obligatos made their presence felt even when the riff lasted a few seconds. Joining the group in 1971 was

Ranjit Gazmer aka Kancha. Tony Vaz followed soon, and the bass guitar in Pancham's music would never be the same again. Pancham would place full confidence in his musicians, and they would reciprocate the respect given to them.

In all, the musicians understood the mind of the genial and welcoming music director and would augment his tunes with their interpretations, often playing the melodies with embellishments as part of the background score too. Probably his love for Hollywood and Western music had instilled in Pancham a fascination for background scores, and he would occasionally use his own tunes as part of the same.

Going back to the 1960s, we hear the duo of Pandit Shiv Kumar Sharma and Pandit Hariprasad Chaurasia playing an instrumental version of '*Aja piya tohe pyar doon*' in *Teen Devian* (1965), which was later sung in *Baharon ke Sapne* (1967). The thought surely arises: Was this an RD composition or a tune by SD? One would never know, but the inflexions in the mukhra seem to have influences of the father. The antara, mostly comprising straight notes, can safely be accorded to the son.

There is hardly any doubt about the origin of '*Aaj unse peheli mulaqaat hogi*' (*Paraya Dhan*, 1971) though. Played on the santoor by Pandit Shiv Kumar Sharma, Pancham uses the tune liberally in the background in *Pyar ka Mausam* (1969) and *Caravan* (1971), both Nasir Husain films. In *Caravan* we also get to hear not once, but twice, the strains of '*Bahon mein chale aao*' (*Anamika*, 1973) on the flute. Pandit Chaurasia is in action, playing a melody which producer Tahir Husain would use in his next production. The interlude of '*Jiya mein toofan*' (*Kahtey Hain Mujhko Raja*, 1975) is also heard twice, this time on Bhupinder's twelve-string guitar.

Testing his tunes before they made it as songs? Could be. One never knows.

'*Jiya mein toofan*' also takes us to the title of *Goldfinger* (1964). The long play of the film was among Pancham's prized possessions, and the title song served as an inspiration for more than one composition. Apart from '*Jiya mein toofan*', you had the first phrase inspiring a tune Pancham had composed in 1970. Thirty-four minutes into *Kati Patang*, you would get to hear the tune of '*O hansini*' (*Zehreela Insaan*, 1974) played on the electronic synthesizer by Kersi Lord. No, *Summer of'42* (1971), as mentioned in itwofs.com,[9] was not the inspiration behind '*O hansini*'. *Kati Patang* was censored in late 1970, months before *Summer of '42* made it to the theatres in the US. Point to note is that Pancham took only the opening note of *Goldfinger* and composed a song that was radically different from the original. His happiness stemmed from the fact that he could use melodies and sounds from around the world and impart to them a feel which was unique.

This brings us to the 'Pancham sound.' It was his gift to Hindustani film music. He thought on his feet, and circumvented traditional and time-tested chord progressions, often going by the ear, and sticking to an adage he believed in: what sounds good to the ear is grammar. Hence you might find experiments like the essential seventh chord getting replaced by something more conventional, though not fitting into the circle of fifths – the framework used by composers for music arrangement.

The protocol for rhythm arrangement was completely his own. Though he had excellent rhythm players in Maruti Rao, Devichand, and Chandrakanth, rhythm never intruded into his music. It held his tunes elegantly through layers that were delicate, with instruments making an appearance only when the need was there. The tabla or the dholak was not a constant feature playing alongside the melody. Use of the bongo, the conga, or the tumba depended entirely on the mood of the situation. In fact, they could also be used as just fillers, like in the song '*Kisise dosti karlo*' (*Dil Diwana*, 1974), where it is the flamenco-style guitar and castanets sharing the honours till the first antara comes into play. Without Pancham, Hindustani film music might have never heard the prolonged used of side percussion like the reso reso, the duggi, or the madal. Especially the reso, which found its application in all categories of songs, from

9 https://www.itwofs.com/coincidence.html

the club number '*Matwali ankhon wale*' (*Chhote Nawab*, 1961), the comic '*Mere saamne wali khidki mein*' (*Padosan*, 1968), the seductive '*Hum tum gumsum*' (*Humshakal*, 1974) to the deeply introspective '*Chingari koi bhadke*' (*Amar Prem*, 1971).

Apart from being a major contender for the best music score of Pancham, *Amar Prem* is one of the finest examples of the Burman brand of music at work. In a rare instance of singing under his son's baton, SD moulded his '*Kalo sape donshilo amaye*' into '*Doli mein bithaike kahar*.' This remains one of the two songs SD sang for a composer other than himself post his move to Bombay in 1944.[10] His inputs to '*Bada natkhat hai re*' has been acknowledged by none other than Pancham himself, in a feature published ten years after SD's death.[11] This, in turn, brings us to the use of raga Khamaj, something that once was almost classified as a Burman monopoly. '*Bada natkhat*' was composed on Khamaj, as was '*Kuch toh log kahenge*.' Deeply insightful yet relaxed in the manner in which the hero reacts to hurt, the song is perceptive and heart-wrenching at the same time. Pancham plays with feelings as he juggles with the mixing of ragas, the import of raga Kalavati during the phrase '*Beet na jaye raina*' giving vent to a vortex of emotions. The palette of raga mixing plays a key role in '*Raina beeti jaye*' too. Depending on the 'Sa' you choose, the mukhra can be on Todi or Lalit,[12] while the antara moves back to his favourite – Khamaj.

If these songs are mostly about ragas and how the same are used to create the emotional impact befitting the varied situations, '*Chingari koi bhadke*' is largely about the voice of Kishore Kumar and the various orchestra sections. Basu Chakraborty, who conducted

---

[10] The second song SD sang was composed by Tapan Sinha for *Sagina* (1974)

[11] R.D. Burman, 'My Father SD Burman,' The Illustrated Weekly of India, 10 February 1985

[12] Information courtesy Archisman Mozumder, music aficionado and expert

the string section, remained an underappreciated genius. '*Chingari koi bhadke*' is one of the few songs in the history of music which can be identified by the first note. The jazz chord F-sharp minor flat second, played on the twelve-string guitar by Bhupinder, runs like a motif throughout the song. Its hypnotic quotient rises, and its resonance intensifies as the song progresses and reaches a crescendo, slowly fading with the reassuring humming of Kishore Kumar. Created by sheer accident when Bhanu Gupta's hand slipped over the strings, it was Pancham's finely honed sense of music which led to the genesis of one of the most famous obligatos in Hindustani cine music.[13] Basu Chakraborty and Bhupinder did the rest.

Playing second fiddle but an extremely significant role is the woodwind section. Arranged by Manohari Singh, whose alto sax pieces have been one of the mainstays of Pancham's music, the song has Pandit Hariprasad Chaurasia playing the flute almost continuously, complementing the melody with fillers and obligatos.

At another level, '*Chingari koi bhadke*' is a visual song. The lyrics could fit in a mushaira, as envisaged by Anand Bakshi. But on screen, with the Howrah Bridge acting as the backdrop to the waterbody created at Natraj Studios,[14] it creates an impression which is fragile.

As does '*Yeh kya hua*,' another song which has a *Rajkumari* connection. It is a Hindi version of '*E ki holo*' with the mukhra being almost a word-for-word translation of the original, also sung by Kishore Kumar. There is a basic difference though. If the essence of '*E ki holo*' is in the muted pain, '*Yeh kya hua*' has a positive spin. While the emotion is raw and the lament agonizing, unlike the heroes of the 1950s and the 1960s, Rajesh Khanna does not languish in love. Or drown his sorrows in raw country liquor at the nearby gutter. Doing a balancing act, he tries to conquer his sorrow by consoling himself with the lines, '*O chhoro, yeh na socho*' (Come on, let it be).

---

[13] Interview with Bhanu Gupta in Calcutta in January 2007

[14] Interview with Ashim Samanta in August 2020

This is a song which grows on you. Initially buried under the greatness of heavyweights like '*Chingari*,' '*Kuch toh log*,' and '*Raina beeti jaye*,' '*Yeh kya hua*' has finally come of age. You smile with it. You cry with it.

Fifty-something years later, *Amar Prem*, released in 1972, is counted among the best scores in Hindustani cine music ever. It is interesting to note that it did not even find a nomination at the annual *Filmfare* Awards for the year 1972 (the nominations were *Beimaan*, *Pakeezah*, and *Shor*). To add insult to injury, the jury comprising Justice S.P. Kotwal (chairman), Mohan Wadhwani, Helen (actress), Dr R.S. Tarneja, and Burjor Karanjia (ex-officio) gave all the music awards to *Beimaan*. This happened in April 1973. Wonder how many from today's generation know the name, forget recalling the film and its music.

Sometime later, at a Sur Singar Samsad's (an organization for the support of classical music and dance in cinema) function, Shatrughan Sinha, who had singing aspirations too, sang '*Jai bolo beimaan ki*.'[15] Poetic justice or plain mockery? Something nobody will ever know.

Which Indian cricketer had an important role in Parveen Babi's debut movie, *Charitra* (1973)?
Answer: Salim Durani

What is the name of Shreeram Lagoo's character in the 1977 Bhimsain-directed drama *Gharaonda* also starring Amol Palekar and Zarina Wahab?
Answer: Mr Modi

[15] A news report of Sur Singar Samsad published in 1973

Rajesh Khanna

A Star Like No Other

Deepa Gahlot

An office in a nondescript part of the Mumbai suburbs. A man comes in most days and makes his way to an inner cabin. A factotum waits outside to get the boss whatever he wants. It is his job to answer the phone and he has one response to all callers, 'He is in a meeting.' Once in a while a visitor drops in without an appointment because of the stonewalling on the phone. The factotum stoically says, 'He is in a meeting.' A faint silhouette visible through the one-way glass shows a man sitting alone, almost motionless.

In the film industry, they say, be nice to people on your way up, because you will meet the same people on the way down. But who thinks of this when they are zooming up so fast the world is a dizzying blur? Those were the days, in the 1960s, when it was possible for an outsider, without any connections in the film industry, to get into the movies. Film-makers made the effort to 'discover' talent outside their own homes, which is how Jatin

Khanna – who did not look anything like the tall, fair, handsome, strapping north Indian men ruling Hindi movies back then – even dared to dream of stardom.

The area of Mumbai he grew up in, Thakurdwar, was a densely populated Maharashtrian-dominated part of the old city, culturally rich with theatre and classical music, but far from the planet of films that was concentrated mostly in the suburbs. Perhaps that is why he acted on stage in school (where his classmate was a certain Ravi Kapoor, aka Jeetendra) and college, and got awards for his performances. The youngster, with bad skin, a wonderful smile, loads of confidence and optimism, was renamed Rajesh by an uncle, and entered the All-India Talent Contest, organized by United Producers and *Filmfare* magazine in 1965. Among the 10,000 hopefuls were Subhash Ghai and Dheeraj Kumar.

The ordinary-looking guy won; the prize: getting cast as the lead in films by the producers who were part of the consortium that had started the competition. The first three films he did were Chetan Anand's *Aakhri Khat* (1966), Ravindra Dave's *Raaz* (1967), and Nasir Hussain's *Baharon ke Sapne* (1967), in which he was appreciated, but the films did not do well enough at the box-office, though the first was India's entry for the Academy Awards that year. Film-makers were a bit reluctant to sign him; he looks like a Gorkha, they said behind his back.

There is another saying in the film industry: when destiny is on your side, nothing can stop you. Destiny rode in for Rajesh Khanna in the form of Shakti Samanta's *Aradhana* (1969). The music of S.D. Burman, the voice of Kishore Kumar, and the man cheekily wearing a Nepali cap rode in a jeep alongside a train singing '*Mere sapnon ki rani kab aayegi tu*' to a blushing Sharmila Tagore pretending to read and peeking at him from the window.

How could she not fall in love with that crinkly-eyed smile, the adoring gaze, the teasing voice, as if there was no other woman in the world for him? Millions of young women who saw him on screen felt he was looking at them, singing and smiling just for them. He did not need to get into fisticuffs or macho posturing to impress the girls. All he needed to do was smile, blink, make that subtle come-hither gesture by tilting his neck … and sing. Most importantly, he was a complete original – he created his own style and mannerisms, without imitating anyone.

Today, stardom means how many Instagram followers a star has, how many people gather outside their houses on their birthday, or how many photographers wait hours outside airports to take their photos in trendy travel gear. Even minor actors are mobbed, because they are seen so often in public. But back then stars were elusive and unattainable – too gorgeous, too sophisticated, too distinguished. Women secretly sighed over Dilip Kumar, Dev Anand, and Raj Kapoor; men fantasized about Suraiya and Madhubala. Rajesh Khanna looked pleasant, neighbourly, unthreatening. But the frenzy that accompanied the initial years of his stardom was so unprecedented that a new word had to be coined for him: superstar.

His rise also coincided with the boom in gossip magazines in India. *Stardust*, *Cine Blitz*, and the like, by their sheer cheeky irreverence, either built up a few stars, or brought others down a notch or two. If readers could see what their idols wore on their day off (Khanna was often clicked in decadent silk lungi-kurtas in bright colours), where they holidayed, where they dined, whom they dated, it felt as if they were not so distant after all. Now there is television, internet, and social media to build fandom; in the past, there was the ubiquity of film magazines, found in barber shops, salons, and doctors' waiting rooms, if not in homes.

Rajesh Khanna did not even have that dazzling glamour expected of stars. He was short at just a little over 5 feet 6 inches, had spotty skin, an ungainly body that required the invention of the guru kurta that became his trademark, and the mercifully short-lived trend of belt worn over an untucked shirt. He had one clumsy signature dance move, like he was shooing a bird over his head and an animal running behind him, but he danced like nobody was watching. His lack of perfection was probably what caused his fans to go crazy. It may be just Bollywood lore, but women apparently left kiss marks on his car (a flashy Impala), wrote him letters in blood, and married his photograph. Fans collected the dust from under his car tyres like benediction from the gods. It is impossible to imagine this level of hysteria. He could hardly step out without fans throwing themselves in his path.

His record of fifteen solo hits in a row in just two years remains unbeaten, including four blockbusters, or what the industry called super-duper hits: *Aradhana*, Raj Khosla's *Do Raaste* (1969), Manmohan Desai's *Sachaa Jhutha* (1970), and M.A. Thirumugam's *Haathi Mere Saathi* (1971, written by Salim–Javed, who were soon to become marquee screenwriters). And they were entertaining, sentimental, audience-pleasing films that looked like they were made just for him, in keeping with his image as a romantic charmer. The he-man action stuff was left to Dharmendra.

Then there were the wonderful leading ladies he was paired with – Babita, Mumtaz, Tanuja, Sharmila Tagore, Nanda, Asha Parekh, Hema Malini, Zeenat Aman, Raakhee – women who could and did perk up any film. And the songs (R.D. Burman, Anand Bakshi, and Kishore Kumar at their best, but other composers of the time contributed to his stardom too): '*Roop tera mastana*' (that one-take lovemaking song, bold for the time), '*Chhup gaye saare nazare*', '*Yeh jo mohabbat hai*', '*Zindagi ek safar hai suhana*', '*Achha to hum chalte hain*', '*Gulabi aankhen*', '*Vaada tera vaada*', '*Kuchh to log kahenge*', '*Duniya mein logon ko*', '*Zindagi kaisi hai paheli*', '*Jai jai Shiv Shankar*'. All gems, all played on top of the charts on radio programmes, all adding to the appeal of the star who could just not make a wrong move in those days.

Apart from the blockbusters, there were films like *Bandhan*, *Khamoshi*, *Safar*, *Ittefaq* (this one had no songs), *Kati Patang*, *The Train*, *Sachaa Jhutha*, *Aan Milo Sajana*, *Mehboob ki Mehndi*, *Andaz*, *Maryada*, *Anand*, *Dushman*, *Amar Prem*, *Apna Desh*, *Raja Rani*, *Aap ki Kasam*, *Bawarchi* – at least a few classics in there. He worked with directors like Shakti Samanta, Hrishikesh Mukherjee, and J. Om Prakash, who gave him great roles and knew how to maximize his potential.

He had those set mannerisms and vocal quirks, but he also had range, within his romantic oeuvre – the heartbroken lover from *Khamoshi* was not the same as the unconditional supporter of *Amar Prem* or the flamboyant suitor of *Aan Milo Sajna*. He did try to break the mould by doing *Bawarchi*, in which he did not have a romantic interest; an 'art' film like *Aavishkar*, he even played a psychopath in *Red Rose*, but clearly for audiences of the time, evil did not suit him. The acceptance of the antihero came much later. Still this spirit of experimentation also made sure that he was not interchangeable – there are films in which one simply cannot imagine another leading man playing the part he played.

When films were not made to formula, his roles were unique and inimitable: the devastated jilted lover in *Khamoshi* (1969); the dying artist in *Safar* (1970); the convict sentenced to look after the family whose breadwinner he had killed in *Dushman* (1971); the poetic, platonic admirer of a courtesan in *Amar Prem* (1972); and in one of the high points of his career, *Anand* (1971), as a man suffering from a terminal illness, laughing at death, with the immortal line, '*Zindagi badi honi chahiye, lambi nahin*' (Life should be big, not long). He played the kind of sensitive, vulnerable man whom everybody wanted to protect from harm. In fact, in those days, it was said in jest, that the film in which Rajesh Khanna dies turns out to be a superhit!

Back then, stars worked multiple shifts and had several releases a year, unlike today when they do one or two films a year and spend more time promoting them than shooting them. So there was always a film coming up to feed the fan craze. The magazines – which familiarly addressed him by his pet name, Kaka, and a catty gossip columnist openly declared her passion for him – kept the pipeline of snippets flowing.

It was symbolic in a way that in 1969, he bought the sea-facing bungalow, Dimple – from Rajendra Kumar, who had been labelled Jubilee Kumar because of his past record of hits – and renamed it Aashirwad. For years it was a landmark in the area (like Mannat and Galaxy Apartments in the same vicinity are today). Fans knew he had been dating Anju Mahendru, whom he had snatched from the side of cricketing legend Gary Sobers, and suddenly one day, in March 1973, he married a much younger Dimple Kapadia, whose first film *Bobby* was yet to be released. It is said – and there may be some degree of exaggeration there – that a few broken-hearted young women attempted suicide and some wore the white of mourning.

It is very difficult to stay down to earth or humble after achieving that level of success, to be loved and worshipped by a country of movie fans. There was no support system to help him cope – a fifteen-year-old bride was not equipped for this role – just as there was no safety net when he started falling. Nobody could have been prepared for such drastic vagaries of fame, and Khanna said later, he certainly was not. He acquired delusions of grandeur, referring to himself by his name, in the third person. He could treat a person with cold hauteur one day, and the next day overwhelm them with his generous Punjabi hospitality. The same media that adored him also started reporting that he had become arrogant and eccentric. He arrived late to the sets, drunk, as his irritated co-stars waited. He surrounded himself with a bunch of sycophants, who flattered him and shielded him from his growing unpopularity with producers, if not the public, till that point.

Film-making then wasn't the smooth, corporatized affair it is today; it was chaotic and run by small family-run companies. A star not turning up to shoot or letting a film get shelved could ruin a producer financially. Film-makers grew wary of approaching Khanna. The offers he got started dwindling because no self-respecting director wanted to work with an egotistical, temperamental, disrespectful actor. They would put up with his tantrums and interference till he could guarantee hits. Once the decline started, they dropped him too. Another industry saying comes up now, '*Duniya chadhte sooraj ko salaam karti hai*' (The world salutes the rising sun). He had flown too close to the sun. It was time for him to experience what hubris felt like.

All too soon, the golden period was over. The line-up of flops grew – *Humshakal*, *Prem Kahani*, *Mehbooba*, *Bundalbaaz*, *Tyaag*,

Karm, *Chalta Purza*, *Palkon ki Chhaon Mein*, *Aashiq Hoon Baharon Ka* – interspersed with an average grosser or two. It seems he had lost that magic ability to pick winners, or maybe the winners did not want to throw in their lot with a fading star. Like that line in *Anand*, his superstardom was brief but meteoric.

The romantic heart-throb roles that he used to play went to the younger, cuter Rishi Kapoor, fresh out of the success of the teen love story, *Bobby*. At thirty-one, Rajesh Khanna was too old to compete for those roles. Besides, he had put on weight, and his styling was not in keeping with the latest fashions. The family weepies he specialized in had gone out of favour too.

Looking back, it is possible to pinpoint the exact moment the industry fell out of love with Rajesh Khanna. It happened when a film called *Namak Haraam* was released in 1973. It had, as his co-star, Amitabh Bachchan, who was a supporting actor in *Anand*, but a parallel lead in *Namak Haraam* (both films were directed by Hrishikesh Mukherjee). Bachchan had delivered a hit, *Zanjeer*, a few months earlier and established himself as the Angry Young Man. Khanna felt the writers were crazy to attempt a film like that, where the hero did not even have a song. He had misjudged the taste of the new generation of audience.

Post-Emergency, the mood of the nation had changed. The Rajesh Khanna fans had lived through the dark days imposed by then Prime Minister Indira Gandhi and had grown up almost overnight. The age of innocence was over. Now they wanted their hero to be a fighter, a rebel. Salim–Javed created Vijay, the brooding leading man of *Zanjeer* (1973), *Sholay* (1975), *Trishul* (1978), and *Deewaar* (1975). Those films were meant for Amitabh Bachchan, with his intense demeanour, baritone voice, and loping walk.

In *Namak Haraam*, audiences could see that Amitabh Bachchan had depth and range. Rajesh Khanna had remained stuck in his image, unable to reinvent himself, probably because the chamchas prevented him from reading the writing on the wall.

The new movie trend was for action movies and revenge stories. Producers also hedged their bets by making multi-starrers and

Rajesh Khanna did not want to do them. So Dharmendra, Vinod Khanna, Shashi Kapoor, Rishi Kapoor paired up with Bachchan and saved their careers in an era when a one-man battering ram was knocking down the competition and, as the media wrote then, was number 1–9.

As far as the industry was concerned, here was a star-actor who was talented and disciplined, so punctual that you could tell the time by his entry in the studio. The crown of 'superstar' was easily passed on to Amitabh Bachchan. The fanzines gave him labels like Big B, megastar, supremo and shifted their loyalty to the star who was professional, cordial, sober, and always dignified.

It's not as if Rajesh Khanna's career ended – among the row of flops, there was a sporadic hit like *Daag* (1973), *Aap ki Kasam* (1974), and *Roti* (1974) – but he could never regain that magical three-year period of back-to-back hits. The directors who had roles written for him moved on to other stars. Sadly, Rajesh Khanna became a parody of himself, speaking his dialogues in the same old style, unable to do either action or romance too convincingly, and could not compete with Bachchan, Dharmendra, Sunil Dutt, Vinod Khanna, Shashi Kapoor, Jeetendra, Shatrughan Sinha, Sanjeev Kumar, and Rishi Kapoor. Khanna had edged out Shammi Kapoor, Rajendra Kumar and Manoj Kumar. It was his turn to get off the pedestal.

After a few years of a clearly mismatched marriage and the birth of two daughters (Twinkle and Rinke), Rajesh Khanna and Dimple separated. They never divorced, but she walked out after he took up with Tina Munim (his sharing-a-toothbrush quote was widely mocked by the gossip press). During the making of *Souten* (1983), a publicity stunt was arranged by releasing photographs of Khanna's wedding with Tina, which was later revealed to be a scene from the Sawan Kumar Tak film. It did turn out to be a big hit, along with Mohan Kumar's *Avtaar* in the same year, in which he played an Angry Old Man who takes on his selfish sons for mistreating him and his wife (Shabana Azmi).

The success of these two films and the echoes of his past hits gave him second wind. There was a spurt of offers, but mostly mediocre films, and not many with A-list directors. Hrishikesh Mukherjee never worked with him after *Naukri* (1978), Manmohan Desai after *Roti*. Ramesh Sippy just did *Andaz* (1971) with him. Prakash Mehra never worked with him. Only Shakti Samanta did *Alag Alag* (which Khanna produced) and *Awaaz* with Khanna in the mid-1980s. Yash Chopra cast him in the multi-starrer *Vijay* (1988), which flopped. Still, in 1985, Khanna had an astonishing twelve releases, and a few hits, but hardly a memorable film among them. In a burst of petulance, he insisted on doing a political film, *Aaj ka M.L.A. Ram Avatar* (1984), because his rival Amitabh Bachchan was doing one too at the same time, *Inquilaab*. The press had a field day playing it up. Both were flops, but *Aaj ka M.L.A.* was a bigger bomb.

By this time, colour TV, the VCR, and the home entertainment revolution had brought the industry to a brink of crisis, and film-makers were scrambling to find ways of bringing the audience back into the theatres. The parallel cinema movement had created its own pantheon of stars. The only 'art' film Khanna did was *Aavishkar* (1974) with Basu Bhattacharya and audiences caught glimpses of the Rajesh Khanna of the past. Maybe, if he did not have the reputation of being difficult to work with, the new bunch of trendsetting directors would have signed him.

A younger lot of actors had arrived – Mithun Chakraborty, Sanjay Dutt, Govinda, Anil Kapoor, Jackie Shroff, Sunny Deol, and Salman Khan, co-starring with Sridevi, Tina Munim, Madhuri Dixit, Meenakshi Seshadri, Rati Agnihotri, Poonam Dhillon, and Amrita Singh. His off-screen relationship with Tina Munim made their pairing work on-screen too, but when he was cast with other young actresses, he just looked desperate, with his henna-ed hair and unstylish costumes. It is also possible that the nature of fandom changed and became less worshipful, less accepting of flaws.

His last two big hits were Sikander Bharti's *Ghar ka Chirag* (1989) and David Dhawan's *Swarg* (1991). By this time he had moved on to playing senior roles, but retained his style of acting that did not quite sit well on the characters he played. From 1991 to 2014, he had fourteen flops in a row, and it was clear that it was time to make an exit.

He tried his luck in politics, standing for elections as a Congress candidate, losing by a narrow margin to L.K. Advani and then beating Shatrughan Sinha in a by-election, to be a Member of Parliament from 1992 to 1996. He made no waves there.

The film offers had already dried up. His health was deteriorating. His last film release, *Riyasat* (2014), was posthumous. He died of pancreatic cancer on 18 July 2012. His family (including son-in-law Akshay Kumar) were there at the end, and the public, probably going through a collective guilt of having abandoned him, turned up in full force to bid him farewell. Even after his death, there was an unpleasant controversy when a live-in lady friend, Anita Advani, turned up. Later, that iconic bungalow was sold to a businessman.

Those who did not live through the Rajesh Khanna era cannot even imagine what it was like. Today stars can be seen in people's homes on the screen, appear on the smartphones in their hands, but they cannot achieve that godlike stature Rajesh Khanna did; maybe that kind of fandom exists in the south, but not in Mumbai any longer. Shah Rukh Khan and Salman Khan have legions of fans, Amitabh Bachchan still has people gathering for a glimpse outside his bungalow, but the madness of the Rajesh Khanna devotee has never been seen again in the Hindi film industry.

The tumultuous seventies saw political upheavals, a major war in 1971, Hindi cinema going through tectonic shifts, and amidst it all, a lesson in the fickleness of fame. A life so eventful that several books tried to explain the Rajesh Khanna phenomenon. A biopic is reportedly being planned. But nothing can fully capture the spirit of that charismatic superstar who used to be surrounded by screaming fans just wanting a glimpse of him, a touch of his magic, who ended his days having phantom meetings in an empty office and waiting for the phone to ring.

Dharmendra

He-Man and Master of the Universe

Roshmila Bhattacharya

I've watched Hrishikesh Mukherjee's *Guddi* (1971) innumerable times even though the first time I fell asleep halfway through. I guess I can be forgiven because I was just five years old at the time and tired out from watching three films, back-to-back, which my parents' friends had dragged us to that eventful Sunday. I can't even remember the names of the other two films, but the 9 p.m. show of *Guddi* has stayed on in my mind perhaps because its schoolgirl protagonist was wearing a uniform in the first few scenes and having just got admitted to a 'big school', Loreto Convent, I was impatiently waiting to try out on mine.

Growing up, the coming-of-age drama became my window to the Hindi film industry which I came to understand better over a career spanning three decades as an entertainment journalist. It starred Dharmendra, playing himself, a matinee idol whom Jaya Bhaduri's teenage Guddi is besotted with, who takes it upon himself to 'expose' his illusionary world by showing her that his on-screen herogiri is just playacting. Talking about the film years later, we agreed that it remains a textbook lesson for starry-eyed fans who believe the reel to be real. But when I applauded him for humanizing the demigod at the risk of his own image, Dharmendra surprised me by admitting that he had been apprehensive before the film's release, wondering if he would be accepted as a hero again.

To his surprise, *Guddi* made him a bigger hero. He believes it was the sequence in which he is playing badminton with Samit Bhanja's Navin and deliberately loses the game so Guddi will be impressed that won everyone's heart. 'Schoolgirls would troop up and hold out their palms or dupattas, asking for my autographs,' he reminisced with that bashful smile which had endeared him to generations of moviegoers since the sixties, during an interview for rediff.com in October 2021.

In 2023, Dharmendra and his Guddi returned to the theatres. Of course, I had to watch *Rocky Aur Rani Kii Prem Kahaani* (2023) even though he had sweetly pointed out that while Jaya would always remain his Guddi, she was no longer a shy newbie but a far more mature actress than him. The auditorium was packed, the seats uncomfortable because we had grabbed the last few, but I was as excited as the five-year-old child I had once been to watch the duo again. This time they were playing an elderly couple caught in a loveless marriage, he penning romantic verses for his fantasy woman, she running the family mithai business with a hard head and a cold heart. There was no sweetness in this relationship. The wide-eyed naivety which has kept *Guddi* dewy fresh for over half-a-century had turned into world-weary disillusionment. I normally enjoy Karan Johar's family dramas with their grandiose canvas, flood of emotions and colourful song and dance, but this time, when I returned home, I hunted out Hrishikesh Mukherjee's *Guddi* on YouTube, and despite the late hour, replayed some of my favourite scenes to banish the image of an embittered, sour-faced Jaya and a wheelchair-bound Dharmendra from my mind. Call me sentimental if you will, but I don't like to see my childhood idols growing old.

Manoj Kumar had once narrated how when he was nine years old, he had accompanied his uncle to Delhi's Ritz theatre to watch his first film, *Jugnu* (1947), which was in its forty-ninth week. He returned home in tears because Dilip Kumar and Noor Jehan's love story ended tragically. However, soon after, he spotted *Jugnu*'s dashing hero, Suraj, on a poster of *Shaheed* (1948). Delighted that he was still alive, but somewhat baffled too, young Manoj Kumar, who was called Harikrishna Goswami or more fondly Ghulu then, coaxed his uncle to take him for this patriotic drama too.

Five minutes into the film, he was reassured it was undoubtedly Suraj. And even though he was answering to the name Ram and romancing a different woman, Kamini Kaushal's Sheela, Ghulu was happy. But his happiness was short-lived. As the film progresses, Ram is drawn into India's struggle for independence against British imperialism. Arrested and tried as a terrorist, he is sentenced to death and hanged. The little boy once again returned home crying, wondering how a man could die twice.

It was his beeji who while putting him to sleep decoded the mystery for him. She pointed out that while mere mortals lived and died only once, farishtas live forever. That night, Manoj Kumar decided he wanted to be a farishta too. As he grew older, he understood that a man can only be resurrected on screen, but in his adoring eyes Dilip Kumar remained a farishta forever. Ditto Dharmendra for me.

Dharmendra, or Dharmender as he was called then, was the son of a schoolteacher in Punjab who had scant respect for the talking pictures. So, it was only when he was in the eighth standard that the lad went to the movie hall for the first time. Coincidentally, the film he saw was Dilip Kumar's *Shaheed*, and like Manoj Kumar, he returned home teary-eyed because Ram had died a martyr. However, once he moved from their village, Sahnewal, to Phagwara for higher studies and started watching more movies, young Dharam happily discovered that his idol was still alive even though the Tragedy King 'died' many more times on screen.

Later, working as an assistant driller for an American tubewell sinking company, Dharmendra would dream of seeing his face on film posters, and waking up, would ask his mirror image, '*Main Dilip Kumar ban sakta hun kya*?' (Can I become a Dilip Kumar too?) For someone who had no filmi background, it seemed like an impossible dream. But he stubbornly clung on to it and even thought of running away to Bombay. His mother, Satwant Kaur, begged him to be reasonable and chase the rainbow rationally by filling in an arzi like you did for a job. So, when he came across an announcement in *Filmfare* magazine inviting entries for the United Producers Talent Hunt contest which promised the winner roles in Guru Dutt and Bimal Roy's films, Dharmendra immediately applied and mailed it with some recent pictures.

To his delight, the handsome Jat was shortlisted and sent a train ticket to Bombay. Dharmendra sailed through the many auditions and eventually won the contest. However, to his dismay, the promised offers did not materialize immediately, and after several fruitless weeks, he returned home disappointed. Three months later, he had to rush back following a telegram from Bimal Roy Productions, and in 1958, he signed his first film. But *Bandini* (1963), opposite Nutan, released only five years later, so the daily rounds for work continued, this time with two other struggling actors, Manoj Kumar and Shashi Kapoor.

Makers showed little interest in casting him, and with a wife and a son back home, Dharmendra realized he couldn't stay jobless in the City of Dreams forever. He was all set to board the Frontier Mail to Punjab, but was persuaded by Manoj Kumar to wait another two months before he gave up. He gave in to the entreaties of his friend. On the third day, he landed Filmistan's *Picnic* (1966), but then lost the film when he contracted jaundice and grew too thin. Manoj Kumar eventually played Vinod in this Shahid Lateef directorial many years later. Dharmender (that's how his name was spelt in the credits) was launched by Arjun Hingorani in *Dil Bhi Tera Hum Bhi Tere* (1960). The dental surgeon turned director, whom he had met during his first visit to Bombay, had promised to make him a star, but Balraj Sahni, as Dharmender's conman friend, outshone him in the film.

However, the following year, *Shola Aur Shabnam* (1961), which he had bagged on Dev Anand's recommendation, became a hit. But life didn't get any easier even though the offers were now coming. During an interview in Screen in 2006, Dharmendra recounted how it had taken Mohan Kumar five hours to shoot a 200-foot scene for *Anpadh* (1962) because he kept bungling his lines much to the exasperation of his heroine, Mala Sinha, who had to leave for a function. At one point, producer Mohan Segal even suggested that they sew the scene together with cuts and close-ups, but not wanting to dent his hero's confidence, the director refused to compromise. 'We kept going, from 11 a.m., finally wrapping up the scene around 4 p.m. I'll always be grateful to Mohan-ji for his show of confidence,' he admitted, his relief evident even after almost half-a-century.

Anpadh, a social drama emphasizing the importance of education, was widely appreciated. *Ayee Milan Ki Bela* (1964), *Haqeeqat* (1964) and *Kaajal* (1965) also did well commercially. The wheel of fortune was turning when *Phool Aur Patthar* (1966), opposite Meena Kumari, opened. During the shoot, Dharmendra had almost lost his life when he got caught in a fire on the sets with Baby Farida in his arms. After its release, the film ignited the box-office and went on to celebrate a diamond-jubilee run. Dharmender Singh Deol, now simply Dharmendra, was finally a star, his chivalrous gesture in the film which left him bare chested making him the nation's heart-throb.

By the seventies, Dilip Kumar's stardom was fading while Dharmendra was a household name. Yet, he never forgot the man who had brought him to wonderland. He would drop by the thespian's Pali Hill bungalow, invariably on his birthday, to wish him, till age crept up and Dilip Kumar failed to recognize him. That was heart-breaking! 'In my innocence, or maybe my immaturity, I had believed that film stars never grow old, that they remain young and famous forever,' Dharmendra rued emotionally. Watching *Rocky Aur Rani Ki Prem Kahani,* I understood what he had meant. I too didn't want my childhood idol to grow old. I too wanted Dharmendra to remain an ageless farishta.

A seventies poll listed him amongst the ten most handsome men in the world. He was to my adoring eyes a Greek God and Roman general rolled in one. I remember him in *Dharam Veer* (1977), in a kilt-like costume which ended above his knees. On any other actor it would have looked ridiculous, but when Dharmendra wore it, the sleeveless vest underlined his bulging biceps and Herculean chest, and the short skirt the muscles rippling in his manly legs. After watching the film, his mentor, Mohan Kumar, had told him that his parents had to be complimented for producing such a fine specimen of a human being.

Dharmendra, who was born on 8 December 1935, was over forty at the time. Forty years later, he still cuts a dashing figure when posing for the paparazzi in a sharply cut suit or lounging around his Lonavala farm in casual denims and a cowboy hat. He's the evergreen 'He-Man'. The sexy 'Garam Dharam'. But surprising, he doesn't like either of these macho tags which have been appended to his name for years. Instead, he has coined an adage of his own, 'Darling D', explaining that he didn't become an actor to be fawned upon. Nor to buy houses and cars. Not even for name, fame and money. 'Acting is my beloved. It's the only way I know to stay on in the hearts of the people,' he has reiterated in almost every interview, adding with the poetic flourish of a shayar, '*Shaurat nasha hai, chadhta hai toh utar bhi jata hai, par mohabbat woh jazbaa hai jo dil mein ghar bana leta hai*' (Fame is like alcohol, once the hangover goes, so does the intoxication, but love is an emotion that builds a home in your heart).

Dharmendra entered Hindi cinema when the triumvirate of Raj Kapoor, Dilip Kumar and Dev Anand was still ruling. He was in every sense the son of the soil who with nothing but good looks, which he attributes to good genes, and an innate talent, which was unpolished, carved a niche for himself in the competitive world of show business. In the sixties, he stood up to a 'Junglee' Shammi Kapoor and withstood the charisma of 'Jubilee' star Rajendra Kumar.

When 'The Phenomenon', Rajesh Khanna, exploded on the scene with *Aradhana* (1969) and *Do Raast*e (1969), sweeping aside all competition with fifteen consecutive hits between 1969 and

1974, Dharmendra quietly but staunchly defended his citadel with blockbusters like *Aya Sawan Jhoom Ke* (1969), *Sharafat* (1970), *Jeevan Mrityu* (1970), *Mera Gaon Mera Desh* (1971), *Seeta Aur Geeta* (1972), *Raja Jani* (1972), *Yaadon Ki Baaraat* (1973), *Jugnu* (1973), *Dost* (1974), *Sholay* (1975), *Chupke Chupke* (1975) and *Pratigya* (1975). In fact, he pulled off a rare feat in 1973. Even as Rajesh Khanna continued his triumphant run, Bobby rocked the nation, and Amitabh Bachchan hit the big time with *Zanjeer* and *Namak Haraam*, Dharmendra delivered two blockbusters, *Yaadon Ki Baaraat* and *Jugnu*; two superhits, *Loafer* and *Kahani Kismat Ki*; two hits, *Jheel Ke Us Paar* and *Keemat*; and one average grosser, Jwaar Bhata.

In the mid-seventies, Rajesh Khanna was dethroned by Amitabh Bachchan. The 'Angry Young Man' reigned for the next two decades. But Dharmendra continued to create box-office history with *Sholay*, *Dharam Veer* (1977), *Ram Balram* (1980) and *Katilon Ke Kaatil* (1981).

In an industry where destinies change every Friday, he has continued his love affair with the camera for over six decades. Yet, for all his popularity and longevity, Dharmendra remains a largely unsung and underrated hero. He believes it's because he's not a businessman – that he is ruled by his heart rather than his head and has never promoted himself. He could be right because though journalists have always loved him, few have written that after Dharmendra became an overnight star with O.P. Ralhan's romantic drama *Phool Aur Patthar* (1966), Ramanand Sagar's 'small' spy thriller *Ankhen* (1968) suddenly became a coveted project. The film-maker ended up with a bigger budget, an A-list heroine in Mala Sinha, and could fly off to exotic locations like Tehran, Tokyo and Beirut all because of his hero.

According to his cousin Guddu Dhanoa, when there was talk of Dharmendra quitting *Sholay* because he didn't have dates to spare, the price per territory of the Ramesh Sippy curry western reportedly fell by half, from Rs 25 lakh to Rs 12 lakh.

However, unlike Amitabh Bachchan, his buddy Jai from *Sholay*, Dharmendra was never a true-blue professional.

His love for the bottle, along with his indiscriminate choice of films, brought on many career lows. Between 1984 and 1986, he featured in seventeen films, but only J.P. Dutta's *Ghulami* (1985) is remembered. The Tsunami of forgettable flops continued well into the nineties because he didn't know how to plot, plan and strategize, but accepted whatever work came his way, some of it to buy his farm in Lonavala where he would always feel at home. These films, many of whose titles even he doesn't remember, left him with a legacy of memes. '*Kuttey*', '*Kaminey*', '*Main tera khoon pe jaoonga*' – we mimic his distinctive snarl and laugh over these threats punctuated with a volley of blows. What we don't always remember is the poet-lover of *Anupama* (1966) who gave a tongue-tied, motherless girl the strength to stand up to tyranny, the wronged Shankar of *Devar* (1966) whose life hinges on a widow's haan or naa, and the idealistic engineer of *Satyakam* (1969) who marries a girl who has been violated and left pregnant. Hrishikesh Mukherjee picked out Satyakam as his best performance.

Dharmendra himself had once sighed that while *Loha*, one of the seven hits he delivered in 1987 which was packed with a dozen releases, worked because it was true to his He-Man image, another action-thriller, *Krodhi* (1981), didn't run because his fans couldn't accept his transformation from an avenging don to a healing sadhu. It's ironical that an actor who has carried off maar dhaad and drama, romance and comedy, even a '*Main Jat Yamla Pagla Deewana*' or a '*Rafta Rafta*' kind of a jig with wild abandon, would be caged by his own action image.

However, what sets Padma Bhushan Dharmendra apart is that every time he has been written off, or forced into retirement, he has risen from the ashes like the proverbial Phoenix and staged a triumphant comeback. '*Kabhi kabhi meri mehbooba mujh se rooth jaati hai, lekin phir main usse mana leta hoon*' (Sometimes my beloved sulks with me, but I always manage to woo her back), she can never be angry with me for too long,' he says with heart-melting simplicity, admitting frankly that whenever he's been away for too long, he has missed the camera. It's his elixir. It keeps him young at heart. And in the hearts of the people.

Besides this blessing of love, cinema has also given him something more. Years ago, whenever Dharmendra would watch another matinee idol, Raj Kapoor, his father Prithviraj Kapoor, his brothers Shammi and Shashi on screen, a thought would flit through his mind, 'I want to make my sons heroes too.' At the time, it seemed so preposterous a notion that he didn't dare voice it aloud. '*Bhagwan ne shayad meri baat bhi sun li*' (Maybe God heard my unspoken words) he points out.

His elder son, Ajay Singh Deol, popular as Sunny Deol, made a smashing box-office debut with *Betaab* (1983). He is still going strong with his now-legendary *dhai kilo ka haath* pounding the bad guys into pulp. Younger son, Vijay Singh Deol or Bobby Deol, made a 30-second special appearance, wielding a hammer as the young Dharam in *Dharam Veer* (1977), before debuting as a leading man in *Barsaat* (1995). Bobby too has exhibited the staying power of his father and brother.

Dharmendra's two daughters, Vijeyta and Ajeeta, are happily married, and even Aahna was not lured by the arc lights, but Esha created some *Dhoom* (2004) on screen. Even his nephew, Abhay Deol, has carved a distinct niche for himself. Now, a third generation of Deols, Sunny's sons Karan and Rajveer, have followed their grandfather into show business. Chances are that Bobby's sons, Aryaman and Dharam (named after his grandfather), will also be continuing the family legacy. While Dharmendra is happy to see successive generations of Deols take his dream forward, he's in no hurry to abdicate the throne. To borrow his own lines…

Mohabbat aapki na deti roshni agar mere naam ko,
Kaise banta Dharam main aap ka, pahunchta kaise iss mukaam ko.
Koi muskura deta hai, main haath badha deta hoon,
Koi haath badha deta hai, main seene se laga leta hoon,

Koi seene se laga leta hai, main dil mein basaa leta hoon.
Mohabbat hai Khuda, aur Khuda hai mohabbat
Khuda ke mohabbat ka ek farmaan hoon main,
Duniya sari bann jaaye ek kunba,
Ekta ki hasraton ka armaan hoon mein.
Pyaar, mohabbat, duayein aapki,
Seenchti hai jazbaaton ko mere
Issi liye aaj bhi jawan hoon main.

Which 1977 Vinod Khanna starrer was a remake of Akira Kurosawa's *High and Low* (1963)?

Answer: *Inkaar*

The first time the word 'computer' was mentioned in a Hindi movie was in 1978. Identify the movie.

Answer: *Trishul*

R.D. Burman, 1970s

The Master of Masala Excess as Global Musician

Kaushik Bhaumik

This essay on R.D. Burman is a rough map of sorts, a map of a certain body and aspect of his music. It is a loose cartography because we have thought too little about it and therefore know too little. The territory of his music that I seek to merely define the outlines of is conceptually and artistically very exciting, one with political and historic significance as well. My only hope is that what I have staked out here interests thinking about Burman's music in the future.

The Territory of Revolution

R.D. Burman (RD hereon) is the first political figure of Hindi film music composition. Of course, there is a politics to every artist's work, but with RD it is an explicit one. Explicit in two senses. Firstly, RD is perhaps the only music director in Bombay film music history, apart from A.R. Rahman, who invented his own brand of music and imposed it on the industry. Secondly, this music had strong political overtones in keeping with the history of his time, at least in that magnificent period between 1971 and 1975. RD's music also has the advantage of being seen as a composite piece of historical challenge and revolution in Hindi film sound because on its surface itself it is full of trumpet blasts and thrilling percussion beats that explicitly say, 'I am here to break down things forcibly.' And in that sense it is political already – a clarion call of the youth breaking down the walls of an older order.

Needless to say, this music was collaboratively carried out by a number of players, including RD himself but also film-makers, film writers, producers, lyricists, and, one would also say, actors. Magic of this kind starts and then some excited people come together to make up a band that shakes up the system. RD would not be possible without a Dev Anand, a Shammi Kapoor, a Nasir Hussain, a Ramesh Behl, a Gulzar, a Shakti Samanta, or a Rajesh Khanna, a Ramesh Sippy, an Amjad Khan, and of course Salim–Javed, amongst many others. RD is probably the only music director in Bombay cinema history who developed a 'scene' around him. The period 1971–75 saw the 'scene' cook up a storm of funky youthful energy around Bombay cinema never seen before and never experienced after.

I have laid out the specific territory of RD's music that my piece is about: the jazzy and funky hyper-percussive music in the soundtrack of films such as *Hare Rama Hare Krishna* (1971), *Yaadon ki Baaraat* (1973), *Jawani Diwani* (1972), or *Sholay* (1975). I am also interested in discussing this music specifically because I have noticed that discussions around his music tend to favour the more 'classical' meditative part of his music, one where writers can highlight the 'raga' base of his music, its classicism, and its continuity with 'tradition', the pre-RD Hindi film music. At most we get into jazz in S.D. Burman and Shankar–Jaikishan then, and RD now. But we don't get into the fact that the jazz RD uses in *Yaadon ki Baaraat* (henceforth *YKB*) is more the funk-phase rocked-up trumpet blasts of Miles Davis's album *In a Silent Way* (1969) to the *Bitches Brew* (1970) and beyond. And for a political reason.

Gone are the standard ballads in Davis's music, gone are the bourgeois gents suits; out comes the rock guitar of a Jimi Hendrix, the funk soul of James Brown and Sly and the Family Stone, moving on to disco with all the street kitsch sartorial splendour that Afro bodies so magnificently wear as emperors of glorious trash. It is this jazz trumpet that we hear in '*Lekar hum deewana dil*' and not SD and S–J's trumpet that have been Miles Davis trained at Juilliard. At least I enjoy (and even understand) Davis's amazingly zany jazz Dada of *On the Corner* (1972) well only because I enjoyed Pancham's music, music that a lot of people would find hard to listen to beyond the first few seconds. I understand the music and the politics, as a global conversation on Third World politics of the 1970s.

And once we have caught this subtle shift away within the category 'jazz' itself in Hindi film music, we shall understand two things. One, that the rocking youth of an earlier time – from the Navketan nightclub days, right up to S–J's *An Evening in Paris*'s (1967) smoky score – is as far away from the youth and excitement of RD's funky groove circa 1973 as the moon is from the sun. Two, we realize that the very politics that made Davis go funk – to connect the radical street politics of the hippie countercultural Black youth of the late 1960s to the early 1970s, away from old-style liberal genteel Afro-Americanism following Martin Luther King, and moving on to the borders of the Black Panther and Nation of Islam movements (Nation of Islam would birth hip-hop in the mid-1970s) – is also the reason RD moves away from even the radically disruptive rock 'n' roll of a *Teesri Manzil* to the more frenetic soundscape of a *YKB* (interestingly from one Nasir Hussain film to another, one in 1966 and the other in 1973, either side of that fateful year 1968).

RD wanted to express, for reasons personal and for reasons of changing film trends, a new energy to Hindi film music – that of the countercultural young in India of the early 1970s. *YKB* is a few supersonic knots ahead of even the psychedelic sensuous mayhem of 1971's *Hare Rama Hare Krishna*, for the simple reason that the hippie-scene-driven film was about White music, while in the Nasir Hussain film it moves into the hypnotic groove of Afro funk. In short, like Davis, RD was asking Hindi film to give up its tuxedo and don the Afro rag of street-smartese and funky youth groove that expressed both the 'freedom in the air' ethos of the times as well as an aggressive opposition to the establishment.

In the Global Village

That this move was not solely due to box-office demand but RD's personal commitment to a certain phase of his music, and in that sense political because the phase was countercultural, can be seen in his 1982 album *Pantera* cut in the US (released in India in 1987). Driven by a mix of Hispanic and Afro grooves of the percussionists Jose Flores and the legendary Babatunde Olatunji, *Pantera* was very much in the arc of fusion music straddling Afro-Latino jazz fusions, from Santana to Miles Davis, taking in the path-breaking Weather Report bang in the centre of things. Olatunji had played for Santana and funk guru Quincey Jones, amongst others. Bill Ortiz on trumpet became a regular member of the Santana band. Patrick Gleeson on synthesizer was a pioneering figure following on Trans Moog synth legend Wendy Carlos's avant-garde experiments and had gone on to play on Miles Davis's pianist Herbie Hancock's early albums. Gleeson was one of the first to pioneer the use of the Moog as a live instrument.

Much of jazz and fusion history thus flows between the Miles Davis trumpet blasts in '*Lekar hum deewana dil*' and Pancham's actual working with musicians who had worked on the scene that had inspired him in the early 1970s. By playing with Santana musicians, RD looped back through percussive echoes to the foundational event of the countercultural sixties, Woodstock, marked by a mesmerizing performance of '*Soul sacrifice*' by Santana.

Thus, *Pantera* was a project that was launched in the early years of the 1970s, a project celebrating a Third World street radicalism coursing through Brazil, Mexico, Ghana, Goa, Tokyo, Manila, Munich, Prague, San Francisco, and many other locations. It was a celebration of the 'thug' ethos – street-smart dropouts, wheeling-dealing dope-pushing tricksters, seeking sexual adventures in shady alleys and exemplifying radical rebel politics of the common person against the establishment. A world where swagger, funky music, and street fashion became political since their sight or sound would make the establishment cry 'the end of the world', projecting these as 'the work of the devil'. A global ethos of such politics at a time when the idea of the 'global' itself was being formed.

And, indeed, Pancham was the first global musical star of India of a certain reputation. Of course, Ravi Shankar was an icon of global music as well, but he was an inspiration for that music; RD was actually composing it. If there was anyone in India who understood the tension underlying Marshall McLuhan's term 'global village', describing the seismic cultural and historical changes happening the world over at that point in time, it was RD. His music lived up to McLuhan's description of the language of communication of this super-modern space-age global village as being of the order of radio signals of African drums rallying the neo-tribes of the world around the sound.

Pancham's Afro percussion grooves to a haunting floating jazzy flute in '*Jaane jaan*' in *Jawani Diwani* was literally doing so – rallying a group of erotic beautiful youth around its sound, egging them on to groove to a global village version of a nocturnal raas orgy. Or for that matter the legendary '*Mehbooba*' in *Sholay*. All this would culminate in that surreal excess of the luscious score for Nasir Hussain's *Hum Kisise Kum Naheen* (1975) where disco and jazz fusion descended from the Davis bands would mix effortlessly with his own flute improvisations in *Sholay*. Nestled inside the global village was a Third World political dialogue between India, Latin America, Africa, and Afro-America.

The Procession of Memories

But let us rewind from Nasir Hussain 1977 to Nasir Hussain 1973. *YKB*, a true classic of cinema, probably the first and the only truly great masala film Bombay has made. During a conversation, Javed Akhtar was very approving of the fact that I kept emphasizing *YKB* as the most interesting film they (he and Salim Khan) wrote. It followed up from Yash Chopra's *Waqt* (1965) with the theme of three lost brothers, a formula to be repeated again in *Amar Akbar Anthony* (1977). RD was working with Hussain who had produced his first great pop score in *Teesri Manzil*. The song '*Lekar hum*' was shot in the style of '*Hothon pe aisi baat*' in Vijay Anand's *Jewel Thief* (1967); Anand had directed *Teesri Manzil* the year before. The music here of course is by S.D. Burman (although RD was contributing substantially to Burman Dada's composing and recordings; his '*Dum maro dum*' guitarist Bhupinder Singh would provide the male vocals for this song). The similarity of the songs lies in the choreography of shots matching a series of mysterious action lines in the plot which happen simultaneously during the song. The song provides the 'cover', as it were, for the 'thriller' action to unfold in its shadows, or rather inside its folds.

In the 1967 song, the lead couple are dancing in a very complex group while a jewel heist attempt is underway even as the police are encircling the palace inside which all of this is happening. Percussion woven in with 'supernatural' Tibetan folk chants leads the thrills of the song. A blast of a Tibetan horn kick-starts the song. In the 1973 song, we see the lead couple on a rock music stage – the man with a guitar, the woman as dancer and singer performing with backing vocalists arranged in a simple linear formation quite like the Motown song format, but more Phil Spector Wall of Sound Motown than earlier avatars. Here, too, the song provides the cover for a series of background plotline thrills – a murder is committed, the hotel where the musical is staged is actually owned by a smuggler, and a man is leaping across the Taj Mahal hotel in Bombay on the way to stealing a Nataraja statue. The percussive music provides the heartbeat to the thrill of the moment. And, of course, the Miles Davis horns.

The RD-Nasir Hussain-Vijay Anand gharana of multi-layered song picturization (it was Vijay Anand who had recommended Pancham to Nasir Hussain for *Teesri Manzil*) as tradition? Yes, indeed. But also, not so substantially. Shammi Kapoor, who was central to *Teesri Manzil* and who gave RD the chance to make some memorable music for *Manoranjan* (1974), his directorial debut, released *Pantera* at the Bombay Hotel Sea Rock in 1987. Rocky's percussive beats on drums at the Park Hotel in Mussoorie to Santana's at the Sea Rock in Bombay. Tradition, yes, but much has changed as well.

What has changed? Let us put it like this: if '*Hothon pe aisi baat*' is framed charmingly by an equivalent of an autotune meme in the devilish Tibetan Vajrayana Tantra folk occult music world in Sikkim, '*Lekar hum*' is framed in the African *voudou* roots of jazz in the full heightened faux-stereo visceral immediacy of the sweat and grime, bump and grind of that music, jumping out of the screen to devour the spectator into an orgy of danger and sex. In the 1967 film, the devil is comic-book charming; in 1973, he has become graphic-novel noir. Caricature, yes, but with shades of real dread in postmodern irony.

The Onomatopoeia of Flesh of Masala Exploitation

RD's 'scene' was an experimental lab for a few who understood the radical charge of what he was doing. No one else could do this thing – this thing about the early 1970s – youth, hormones, skin, desire of money and bling, crime oozing out of that. In short, the young living on the edge, on the run from homes and the police but having dangerous fun in city fleshpots. RD's music in '*Lekar hum*' is in some senses the onomatopoeic sound of the desirous flesh bordering on the pornographic. But not pornography as a genre, but the edge of it, something that came to be called exploitation cinema. He uses Asha Bhosle's husky moans to heighten the erotic charge viscerally, driving music as close as possible to the sexual act. He will use percussion to convey the heightened beat of the body in sexual excitement or copulation in ways as explicit as possible. Nobody would dare to be so explicit after him, even when one expected things to move forward more radically in generations that became freer in desire.

Similarly, RD's experiments with catching speeding cars and trains onomatopoeically, the dread and tension of running feet chased by the police, or using vehicles' screeching to a halt as sound effect within a song sought to capture the body's actual physics of tension and desire directly rather than allusively as mudra, which used to be the rule earlier. '*Lekar hum*' is a monumental achievement of cinematic craft by any standards because it manages to catch death and sex in the same erotic code of the excited body. The body propelled by danger, gold to be stolen, and the sight of the body to be had sex with have the same percussive time-code, as well as the space-code – Bombay's Fort district. At night.

Neetu Singh crawls on her back backwards across the stage, the camera catching her movement with as explicitly pornographic an angle as possible, leaving us in no doubt as to what her body desires. Throughout the song the director presents Singh with a drugged-out look, eyes heavy with vague but explicit desires. An aroused pythoness snakes her way across the stage. The snake metaphor caught explicitly by the camera, literalized by the body visually, is apt for the song's Afro occult musical ethos of a *voudou* ceremony-type moment.

Or take '*Jab andhera hota hai…*' (*Raja Rani*, 1973), with a young boy fleeing a crowd and the police, through the streets of Bombay, after he has committed a theft, to the percussive beats of RD's memorable score for the song. The chorus, whispering '*chor chor*', is no longer the Greek tragedy chorus, but a chorus excited by the promise of excitement that the times and Bombay at night hold out. Such are the sublimely enjoyable corruptions of the decay of history and civilization into the masti of a new India, desiring destruction in submission not to the Vaisnava love of Radha or the mehboob but to the sexual urgency of the funk and disco woman.

What makes RD's music explicitly political is the way he catches the pop culture truth of the times, a collective consciousness of the Indian masses who are entering the world of shiny postmodern consumerism from Gandhian austerity of decades and being confused by that moment. One rushes towards the gold and naked body one has been denied for too long and one becomes one's own police, scared when faced with this excess. Mass pop culture can never be explicitly political, it can only give us a sense of the 'ground' of sensory feelings and drives in which politics works. And RD's music would capture the excitement of corruption of the Indian flesh by waves of erotic desire thrashing against the rocks on the Bombay seafront – gold lands, furtive boats in the middle of the night, as well as bikini-clad women emerging from the waves like a late redux of Botticelli's Venus dancing sinuously to Afro-funk erotica. A pop-culture perception caught, say, in pulp fiction of the times or the pages of tabloids like *Blitz* which ran a page for a bikini model and reported salaciously on the murders, corrupt doings of politicians, tales of smuggling, and sex scandals with great glee.

Generically, all RD did in a song like '*Lekar hum*' is set this whole narrative of McLuhan's global village of counterculture sensual excesses to Afro percussion beats. But above all, he made music that told the audience explicitly: I know the sounds of your desirous flesh, the sounds of the fantasy aroused by the dry print of the tabloid's bikini picture, to the point of being able to reproduce it in flesh in my music; let's play that music together and have a ball. A devil's pact if there was one.

Thus, RD's greatest political achievement, and indeed one of the great Indian political achievements as such, is that he is the only artist of the 1970s who could get away with articulating the global youth mantra of 'sex is revolution' so publicly in his music in film after film, in a language which was not allusive or titillating, but explicit and global. Not only was the music radical but it was a politics that succeeded at a mass scale, comparable only to the scale of the anti-Indira Gandhi uprising.

For the Future ... to Better Understand
'*Lekar hum*'

RD's music is the music of the body of the masala film's spectator, the one who enjoys it thoroughly, given to us as directly possible as onomatopoeia. But there are a few things to this music of the body that future thinkers of R.D. Burman might benefit from pondering about. One is the explicit loop between Bombay masala cinema like *YKB* with a B-cinema exploitation genre of the times, the Blaxploitation film which carried funky scores (of the kind inspiring Miles Davis and RD at the same moment in history to give middle-class propriety a kick up its pants by throwing some *Bitches Brew* at it) by legends like Curtis Mayfield and Isaac Hayes, to name two giants, and which pushed the envelope of sexual explicitness of cinema beyond the erotic into the actual coital via the framing music. If the famous Afro metaphor of 'let's make some sweet music together, baby' for sex was to be made visually demonstrable in a classroom, we would need to show a Blaxploitation film.

Blaxploitation was about cheap, sweaty street bodies, but voluptuous, provocative, not-White, and more openly desirous as well as more well-hung swaggered. Its politics was as much about Afro identities as it was about drawing the enemy, the White, into the arms of the pleasures that racism was denying them. In short, the dudes were pimping themselves to the Whites as erotically superior beings – scary to touch, destructive if touched since the White skin would not be able to contain the charge of the Afro voluptuous. But above all, this sexual excess is also the charge of a revolutionary movement like the Black Panthers.

Secondly, for the Indian context it would be interesting to see the connections between RD's jazzy music and Indian Tantra of death and sex, its darker hues, which RD, coming from Bengal, would be more openly at ease using. Of course, Tantra is a huge thing in Indian dance and music; even kathak is in the last instance a reworking through centuries of Tantric *Pancaratra* midnight orgy dances of the raas in the Mathura region. But RD is using Tantra at its more radical, revolutionary, disruptive origins as a music of ghouls arising from crematoria from which the first great Untouchable Dom Tantra masters came and who practised exotic sexual rituals with the radically powerful Tantra female Dombini masters to defeat brahmanical repression as well as throw this radical porn exploitation stuff on the face of the cowering weakly brahman as a superior and more content way of life.

Which is to say (finally), RD's funky music, coming via Africa and America, is used to catch a landscape of the ambiguity of the desires of the flesh, filled with dread of death and destruction and forbidden pleasures, one haunted by whispers and echoes of voices of danger and ambiguity – the ghoulish. A vast landscape that encapsulates many radical events in India at that moment, say the Naxalbari movement set in the heart of Vajrayana occult Tantra in north Bengal and with its Kali cult associations, a connect that Q's *Gandu* (2010) catches beautifully in a sequence where mother root Bengali lingo, the famous *caryapada*s of high Buddhist Tantra are recited in the Naxalbari site. As I have pointed out earlier, pop culture cannot be politically exact. It catches a wide landscape of general mass desires, even contradictory ones, which in this case might include a Naxal revolutionary in Bengal and the Angry Young Man of Bombay cinema through the swinging doors of a liminal figure such as Rahul Dev Burman.

More politically, we must think through what it is that makes great masters like RD or Miles Davis decide to destroy the civilizational by publicly broadcasting the decadent, untouchable matter of radically obscene pop culture material, not as a titillation Dada Kondke, but as coitus, as a serious bodily experience, as a revolutionary convulsion in orgasm. In both cases, an occult 'base' music of sorts, the untouchable, is used to upend the classical, the shastric, by masters who know the upper elite tonalities only too well. There is anger but a lot of humour and love here. The desire to get out of class boundaries and play in the mud as a savage (like those beautiful mud-bathing scenes at Woodstock).

Just as in Michelangelo Antonioni's *Zabriskie Point* (1970), the energy of 'fucking' is also to dissolve into the calm flow of the sand in which the orgy scene in Death Valley happens. (And why would Antonioni suddenly become so explicit in 1970, strip Italian classicism of its classical porn veneer and go full American explicit? I am sure at least to throw at Hollywood's and/or European classicism's repressed face the pleasures of counterculture sex. The film ends with the voluptuously sexual body of the girl destroying an American pleasure resort by merely staring at it, like Indic ascetics could. Pornography, with angry revolution as its flipside, is something that RD and Blaxploitation make explicit continuously.)

But above all, we must tarry and wonder hard about a music that celebrates becoming corrupt and decadent, to make a final point about RD's revolution – decadence to the point of self-destruction. *YKB* is magnificent as the first true masala film from Bombay, but also as the only blockbuster A-list Indian film which celebrates this descent into decadence as a good exploitation film must. But it does something slightly more. In '*Lekar hum*', in its framing sex vis-à-vis crime and violence, sex is not merely another face of revolution; it is ardent enough, especially through the drugged urgency of Neetu Singh's performance, that the bodies are willing to die in an orgasmic embrace.

What then is this politics that goes beyond the common-sense connection between sex and violence to the point of self-destruction? What is that trance space she wants to submit to in an almost spiritual sexual act? The fatigue of desperation of a young girl that her voluptuous body is being preyed upon by a corrupt world, as well as ardent sexual desire which cannot stop itself from the very gestures that porn cinema wants to kidnap her for into sex slavery and degradation. She cannot help but want her pleasures that also spell her doom. And such an in-between visual space cannot but be obscene – the true eye of the times.

Indeed, therefore, what then is the politics of pushing the sexual into the visceral immediate in public cinema through the radical aesthetics of colour, movement, and sound – something that Indian cinema does more explicitly and provocatively than most other cinema? There is also something more going on here beyond merely showing sex explicitly. A politics of the obscene? I refuse to accept this as exploitation for the sake of cheap money. In *YKB* it is a political thing driven first and foremost by RD's music. RD's greatness lies in his ability to celebrate the obscene as a revolutionary force – the only artist ever in the history of art who was able to do so in a public sphere of millions of people. It also is an indication of how the obscene functions very differently in the unconscious of the Indic public. Is Tantra a tradition that makes this possible in the collective unconscious of the Indic, in an India of very explicit brahmanical, folk, or Sufi erotics, all of which reach a radical intensity in Tantra? We do need to understand that 'excess' of public erotica standards in India are different from the repressed Western gaze.

Finally, one needs to ask the RD question more directly: How much did Burman's music as music manage to continue a radical tradition of the public politics of the obscene in its most radically provocative energy – the point where the orgasmic is viscerally made public? Maybe such a thing is not possible without music. And again we need to connect up with Blaxploitation, the ability of Black cinema earlier to make the public display of the slow build of sexual pleasure to climax possible without the need to become an underground porn genre. But here again a song like '*Lekar hum*' is more radical than anything else, whereas Blaxploitation – while it did similar things – was still ghetto cinema, never censored as hard as mainstream cinema, just as B-cinema in America could get away with a lot of extreme stuff because the censors knew this would not be playing on Main Street. '*Lekar hum*', by contrast, is mainstream *national* cinema of India. An India defined by different genealogies of bodies, aesthetics, and the public gaze. Just as in Japanese Roman Porno of the 1970s, one could show actual copulation on screen but the female vagina had to be blurred out. There are no universal standards for the civilizational.

I chose '*Lekar hum*' because in this song RD does something more than his reputation as a music director of masti and disco and groove warrants, helped along by the brilliance of *YKB* as a film written by Salim–Javed at their radical best. More radical than *Deewaar* or *Zanjeer* and probably even more than *Sholay*. Here, Pancham pushes sexual desire and violence towards an enigmatic space of self-destruction (he does this more subtly in '*Jaane jaan*' where youth bodies are seen as lost, depressed, sexually maximally aroused, and suicidal – all at once; as signified by the rag doll that Jaya Bhaduri carries and that flute score). It is more along the ethos of Nagisa Ōshima's legendary *In the Realm of the Senses* (1976). The philosopher Georges Bataille had something to say about this but not enough, not Tantric enough. But that is for us to work out in the future.

My own starting point would be that ludicrous piece of RD genius – the scream of a man being strangled to death (in RD's own voice) that kick-starts the sexual orgy/youth revolution of '*Lekar hum*'. The camera pans down as if the dead man descends into a place and what he sees are the orange fires of hell become cool red disco lights and a spectacle of the most gorgeous sex played by two characters who seem to be trapped in a spider's web as well as in the mesh created by the flashing of strobe lights. Is this heaven or is this hell? One can't tell. And that probably is the great philosophical question RD is asking of the 1970s as his most profoundly political contribution to India's history, a contribution to be taken as seriously as any other philosopher's, politician's, or historian's. Especially for our strange India in strange times these days.

Coda: RD, the Master of Our '*Besharam rang*'

Only by confronting the true political intent of the radical edge of RD's sound in our times can we truly understand why a certain 'bolder' show of groin bordering on the explicit sexual act on Deepika Padukone in '*Besharam rang*' becomes the recapitulation of a certain radical Indic national tradition of aesthetic politics, the tradition that only RD exemplified in the history of Indian cinema and Indian music. The Sufi spiritual song rendered in tones of sexual arousal claims that the saffron colour of her bikini is about a *besharam* tradition that publicly flaunts the sexual pleasures of a man and a woman entwined in passion – a political act in difficult political times, in times of chaos and apocalypse. Saffron is revolutionary fire and this saffron is sexual ecstasy.

Of course, it is also the greatness of the Bombay film music tradition that the song is not participatorily sexual; it is iconic, it is a representation, not a sharing as RD's music was – clever politics for difficult times when we can merely hint at the right kind of politics and not say things explicitly. The genius of a wily, well-honed tradition built by dissenting rogues since working in cinema was always an edgy act in staid Indian society. A band of tricksters who want to have the right kind of fun apt for the modern times but can only do so cleverly against the fascist censorial attitude that brahmanical modern Indian society is. '*Besharam rang*' is a wonderful creation of that trickster tradition.

Once the point is recognized, we wonder how it was possible to share this radical tradition between screen and spectatorial body in the 1970s and is no longer possible now. Answering that question, we intuitively know that the single-screen cinemas have disappeared to keep out the public mature enough to enjoy '*Lekar hum*' as a radical apocalyptic tradition of a certain Indic syncretism and why the public in multiplexes now need to be reminded of that tradition in a more distant, representational form and not in a commons of sharing. The public left out now actually watches explicit porn in cinemas like the Imperial in Bombay that was momentously important in creating cinema fury amongst the public for imported action cinema in the silent era, a fury that then went on to found the Indian film industry in Bombay. Losses everywhere – a middle class ignorant of India's history and a working class criminalized by destroying the tradition that RD's radical sound of '*Lekar hum*' came from.

In our difficult times the spirit of RD is back to tell twenty-first-century Indians that there was a man who had excavated like an archaeologist a great radical tradition of Indian aesthetics and gifted it to us. For which single-screen cinemas expanded to thousand seaters, just to listen to '*Mehbooba mehbooba*' on a scale that was apt for public revolution in the 1970s that would sweep Indira Gandhi away in 1977. More importantly, his sound was so clever that all classes came to watch the same film under the same roof. All classes shared the same angst that a song like '*Lekar hum*' conveyed in a participatory way. Ergo, all classes came together to vote against the political power that they thought was causing them to suffer in such ways. It takes a lot to pitch a difficult cultural sound – the obscene – in a way that the classes and the masses partake in the radical politics of screening the obscene publicly, without things going overboard, without one class feeling uncomfortable about the edgy.

That Pancham could do so is the true mark of his genius. That Salim–Javed wrote such a moment is their genius. That Nasir Hussain shot the sequence as he did is his genius. That Neetu Singh could play that song at the perfect pitch of the obscene edge is her genius. That all of these people came together to do such a difficult public act is the genius of the Indic unconscious, the genius of its political sense. But in the final instance, the film and the song is a product of the 'RD scene' in a profound way.

That was the true power of the 1970s Bombay film song under the wand of RD, the spirit of '*Lekar hum*', where the Miles Davis trumpet asks the hall to become bigger in sync with the scale of its revolutionary power. For it contains the death scream of exploited labour strangled by capital which goes underground and returns to vote in 1977. If this is not political, nothing is. Again, I cannot emphasize enough the importance of understanding the global dimension of this sound in the dialogue between RD and Black funk to get the real meaning of RD's music as a radical political force. The working class strangled is a global working class between Detroit and Bombay both of which find redemption in a particular radical funk sound emphasizing sexuality explicitly in public.

We need to remember India is a democratic republic, a *ganatantra*. It is run by the techniques (*tantra*) of the *gana*s, Shiva's ghoulish companions, whose favourite chant is '*Dum maro dum*', a metaphor for manual labour that smoked cannabis to endure enslavement. The essential spirit of Tantra. RD was the Wagner who composed their music in spectacular scale, pushing sound into stereo in *Sholay*, pushing it towards Dolby, the scale of a civilization revolting for which cinema halls needed to get bigger and bigger. This is the ganatantra that '*Besharam rang*' hints at in order to remind us that we need to retain that ganatantra for that Indian and Bombay cinema as the politics for our times. It is also an apocalyptic time when sex needs to be made explicit as a radical political act in public, to challenge the public's complacency, and also point out where the real human organic–existential problem of the India of today lies. Eros is withdrawing from the entire landscape of our country and is being replaced by Thanatos in a perilous way. RD taught us that when dangers are such, the counter-push to those dangers needs to be dangerous as well. We have to play Eros on the edge of Thanatos, in the line that is called obscene.

Anubhav (1971) was the swan song of one of India's finest playback singers. Who was the singer?

Answer: Geeta Dutt

Which Rajesh Khanna movie was a remake of a 1970 Kannada movie, titled *Baalu Belagithu*, which was also remade into MGR's *Oorukku Uzhaippavan* (1976)) in Tamil?

Answer: *Humshakal*

Gulzar

A Poet in Cinema

Shantanu Ray Chaudhuri

Ek mood, ek kaifiyat geet ka chehra hota hai – it is uncanny how one remembers the exact moment associated with certain epiphanies. A typical summer day in Delhi … my final-year BCom exams over, the results awaited. I had just completed a week-long summer job for the princely sum of Rs 500! Thrilled with my first income, I returned home with a cassette of songs by Gulzar, accompanied by his commentary: *Fursat Ke Raat Din*. Settling down to a cup of tea, tired from the week-long exertion under the unforgiving Delhi sun, I put the tape into the recorder. A voice floated in as if from some distant mountainscape aeons in the past, enveloping me in its misty cool folds…

Ek mood, ek kaifiyat, geet ka chehra hota hai
Kuch sahi se lafz jadh do
Mauzu se dhun ki lakeerein kheench do
Toh nagma saans lene lagta hai
Zinda ho jaata hai
Bas itni si jaan hoti hai ek gaane ki

Ek lamhe ki jitni
Haan kuch lamhe barson zinda rehte hain
Geet boodhe nahin hotey
Unke chehre pe jhurriyan nahin girti
Woh palte rehte hain, chalte rehte hain
Sunne walon ki umr badal jaati hai toh kehte hai,
Haan … woh uss pahar ka tila
Jab badalon se dhak jata tha
Toh ek awaaz sunayi diya karti thi…'

As the voice faded out, segueing to the plangent strains of Asha Bhosle's '*Phir se aaiyo badra bidesi*' (*Namkeen*), something within me shifted. The weariness seeped out, replaced by a wistful longing for something unnameable.

I have always been sceptical of people saying that a moment can alter the course of one's life. Surely, life is too unfathomable for one episode to usher in such tectonic changes. Yet, looking back, I cannot deny the transformation that moment wrought in me. And why not? Even Gulzar-ji has been on record about how one episode altered the course of his life. In the days preceding independence, he used to be an avid reader of pulp fiction and jasoosi novels, finishing one every night. Running out of books in the genre, the exasperated owner of the 'lending library' handed him a copy of Rabindranath Tagore's collection of poems *The Gardener*, thus facilitating the metamorphosis of a young boy's literary pursuit.

Of course, my experience has not led me to any such heights as Gulzar-ji has scaled. It, however, set me on course for a lifelong quest, an enduring love affair, for want of a better expression – one that continues. (I carry the frayed cover of that cassette in my purse even today!) Over the next couple of years, going through the motions of MCom and ICWA, I immersed myself in the songs and films of Gulzar-ji. I bought every cassette I could lay my hands on. I watched every film I could on the VCR, four of which left an indelible impression: *Mausam*, *Aandhi*, *Namkeen* and *Ijaazat*.

I have never understood why the sense of loss that permeated his work fascinated me so. It was as if relationships were made beautiful only in their unfulfilled longings. He made loss and separation in love appear more attractive than a lifetime together. If parting could be so luminous, who needed a happy ending? Thanks to Gulzar-ji, never again would I be able to fall in love without a part of me fervently wishing for a bittersweet farewell, so that years later I would come across my loved one to the strains of '*Dil dhoondta hai phir wahi fursat ke raat din*' in the background. Thanks to Gulzar-ji, at the age of twenty-three I was visualizing myself in grey hair and sideburns!

Then came *Lekin* (1991). Recovering from a long bout of illness, I could not watch the film in the theatres. My folks did and narrated the story to me. Something came over me and I composed a 'poem' on the theme. Sourcing his address from an 'India who's who' address book at the college library, I posted the poem with a letter. And to my utter astonishment, Gulzar-ji replied. Commending my effort in encapsulating the film in a poem, he wondered if, as my name suggested, I was a Bengali! For a while, I became a 'celebrity' among my college mates!

By this time, I had begun to translate his non-film poems into English and kept sending them to him, along with my own poems. He responded once in a while, always encouraging. Then, one day, Rupa announced the publication of his book of poems translated by Rina Singh, *Silences*. Gulzar-ji was to come to Delhi for the launch. And needless to say I was in the audience. For the longest time I kept looking at him from a distance, playing out introductory words in my mind. Then I walked up to him. 'Gulzar-ji, I am Shantanu Ray Chaudhuri.' He turned to me and said, '*Haan, Shantanu, aapke khat, nazm aur tarjume milte rahte hain*.' (I keep receiving your letters, poems and translations.) The rest of the evening remains a blur.

Those were the first words I exchanged with him. Over the next thirty years, I have spoken to him at length and yet even today I often find myself at a loss for words in his presence. Over a decade at HarperCollins, I was privileged to work closely with him on books that remain my most prized achievements, including his translation of Tagore and his first novel *Do Log/Two*. The Tagore translation was a long-time dream of his and it felt good to be part of putting it together. For the translation of *Do Log*, I remember spending ten day at his residence, from 10 a.m. to 6 p.m., working away. Then, there was A Poem a Day, a collection of 365 poems from India and the subcontinent that he translated into Hindustani. I worked on curating the book with him for seven long years before I left HarperCollins. Fittingly enough, my last book with him at Harper was his daughter Meghna's biography of him, *Because He Is* – fittingly because, whatever I am, whatever I was at Harper, is because he is.

Interestingly enough, I never published anything with him on his cinema. By the time I started working with him, he had left his film-making days well behind. Our conversations have traversed a wide spectrum, including films. For one, I realized how disdainful he is about nostalgia and our tendency to look at the past – particularly when it comes to films and songs – with melancholic sepia-tinted glasses. He never tires of saying, 'Surely, a girl and boy today will not court each other with "*main Ganga ki mauj, tu Jamna ki dhara*". In an era of high-rises, the heroine cannot sing "*Main tulsi teray angaan ki*" – where's the tulsi or the courtyard? One can lament the loss of purity of language, but language is not static, and popular culture has to reflect that. The gangster in *Satya*, unwinding with country hooch at the end of a day during which he has probably shot dead a few people, cannot sing "*Dil-e-naadan tujhe hua kya hai*".' No wonder then that Gulzar-ji has made '*Goli maar bheje mein*' and '*aankhen personal se sawaal karti hai*' fashionable in film lyrics!

Among the abiding memories of working with him are the conversations we have had in the course of editing the books, being privy to the stories *behind* the poems and the stories. And invariably at the end of every conversation would emerge a new book idea! A number of these took place on the phone, me on my way to office at 8 a.m., his first question of the day being: 'Have you crossed the river?' – a reference to the Yamuna which I had to cross every day to go to work.

And so it was that I discovered how Vishal (Bhardwaj) and he took off in a car, jumping lights, oblivious to the traffic – and how that gave birth to a poem. Or became aware, over a marathon ten-day session of translating and editing *Two*, of the real-life people and events that inspired large parts of his novel, narrated with all his film-making and screenplay-writing skills on display. Of his heartbreaking meeting with a couple in Delhi who were convinced he was the son they had lost during the migration of 1947. The pathos of his visit to his birthplace, Dina, seventy years after he had left it. Then there were the moments when he would drop everything to recite a poem he was composing at the time and work on it – even its translation. Sitting across from him in his study overflowing with books, his voice reciting Tagore in the original and then his own translation of the poem … Or a ride down Shanti Path on the way to the airport, looking at the row of Amaltas trees bending over in full yellow bloom, and hearing him compose the first lines of a poem…

These interactions also gave me an insight into his impish sense of humour, his almost childlike engagement with the ordinary joys of life, his ability to connect with children and his indefatigable energy. For all his tryst with poetry and distance from films, audiences at lit fests and book events invariably come up with questions on his films and songs. 'Once upon a time you wrote words like "*Teray bina zindegi se*" – *kitne shareef lafz thay* … what makes you write things like "*Beedi jalayi le*" and "*Kajrare*" now?' If that came as a wholly unexpected non-sequitur after a brilliant session of Tagore's poems and Gulzar-ji's translations, he betrayed no discomfiture as he deadpanned: '*Aap se kisne kaha ki main shareef hoon* – why do you assume I was ever the decent sort?'

Or the time I had his song '*Is modh se jaate hain*' (*Aandhi*) as my caller tune and he told me: 'Bachhu, that's a nice song you have – the guy used to write good stuff once upon a time, didn't he?' And my favourite: at the Delhi airport, a man approaching him as we made our way to the baggage claim. 'Sir, are you…' (He is unsure if this is indeed *the* Gulzar.) Gulzar-ji shook his head, 'No, no, I am not.' (The man is reassured.) 'Yes, I just thought you are … but it can't be, though you…' Looking at him, Gulzar-ji said with a straight face, 'I know … people tell me I look like him – but I am not … I am only a translation.'

A dinner in his room at a five-star hotel in Kolkata stands out in memory. As he talked about his early days in cinema, Shantanu Moitra and I lost all track of time. It was well past three o'clock. Suddenly hungry, Gulzar-ji wanted that quintessential everyday Bengali fare: *daal-bhaat-shorsher tel-dim sheddo-kacha lonka* (rice and lentils with mustard oil, boiled egg and green chilli). Try telling that to a five-star pantry at three in the night. Thanks to Shantanu's organizational skills, however, it was arranged – the tastiest of dinners I have had, definitely the simplest I have had in a five-star hotel!

That day thirty years ago triggered, among other things, a longing to be in the presence of this most luminous of men. That desire has still not been satiated. It will never be. Thirty years later, as I reflect on that hot summer day, I wonder what it was about that moment that made it so special. Was it just momentary exhaustion from a tedious week-long job? Was it the uncertainty of what I wanted to do – saddled as I was with a career in commerce and accounts? For some unknown reason, that voice, those lines, followed by the song soothed me then, and have enthralled me ever since, stood by me in my darkest hours. Every time I have felt down and out, I have gone back to his words, his songs … to that moment, as if living his song from *Seema*, '*Jab bhi yeh dil udaas hota hai, jaane kaun aas paas hota hai*'.

At a particularly low point in my life, it was his voice over the phone that lifted me as he said: 'Maybe there's something at the bottom of the whirlpool, why not leave the false security of the surface? And if that frightens you, hold on to the hand of this old man … he will dive as deep with you as you want to.'

W.B. Yeats's immortal lines come to mind: 'Had I the heavens' embroidered clothes.../ I would spread the cloths under your feet / But I being poor have only my dreams...' Had I the words, were I a poet, I would have composed a poem for him as tribute for his contribution to cinema and to my life. But I am not, and I have only prayers in gratitude for what I have been blessed with. I would rather let Buddhadev Bose's homage to Tagore do the work for me: 'Your words have I received within me / and so I am not afraid, and know that life will win.'

Women in the Cinema of Gulzar

> '*Mera shohar banne ki koshish mat karo. Biwi ho, biwi ki tarah raho.*'
> (Don't try to become my husband. You are the wife, behave as one.)
>
> – JK to Aarti, *Aandhi* (1975)

> '*Meera, ghar ki bahu ki tarah maryada mein raho.*'
> (Meera, conduct yourself with the decorum becoming of a daughter-in-law.'
>
> – Raja Bhojraj to Meera, *Meera* (1979)

Though separated by close to five centuries, it is possible to see a real-life medieval king, Bhojraj (played by Vinod Khanna in *Meera*), and a fictional hotel manager, JK (essayed by Sanjeev Kumar in *Aandhi*), as part of a continuum, almost mirror images of each other in the way they are pitted against women of substance, in their essentially patriarchal outlook (though they are not monstrous chauvinists in any way) and in the way they come to realize that their spouses are more than only that. In the lines quoted above, Gulzar proffers an insight into the 'default' mindset of even the best of men – one that was true as much in the era of Meera in the late 1400s, as it was during the Emergency in 1975 and as it is today.

The depiction and representation of women in Hindi cinema have been 'problematic', to put it mildly. Interestingly enough, the 1930s were marked by a progressive attitude to women in Hindi cinema – with stalwarts like Devika Rani, Durga Khote and Mary Ann Evans aka Fearless Nadia and films like *Duniya Na Mane* (1937) and *Achhyut Kanya* (1936). However, it was not long before women were relegated to mere appendages for the most part. The portrayal of women too languished, with Shyam Benegal memorably describing it as, 'Her virtue [lies] in being the good mother, wife, sister—a set of essential roles a woman has to play—which is a terrible kind of oppression; a glorification not allowing the woman any choice.' Even in the 1950s, a decade of enlightened film-makers, iconic women characters in some of the most talked-about films of the era – *Mother India* (1957), *Pyaasa* (1957), *Mr and Mrs 55* (1955) – adhered to these constructs, the all-sacrificing mother, the courtesan with a golden heart who needs the man to provide her dignity, or the free-spirit/tomboy who has to be taught to be feminine enough (*The Taming of the Shrew* being a favourite film trope for most of the 1960s and '70s).

Gulzar broke through this clutter. Eleven of the seventeen films he has directed feature a woman as the primary protagonist. The rest, barring possibly *Kitaab* (1977) and *Angoor* (1982), have women in pivotal roles. That says a lot about a film-maker operating in what were possibly the worst decades in Hindi cinema vis-à-vis the representation of women. As does the fact that glamorous mainstream stars like Jaya Bhaduri (*Parichay*, *Koshish*, both 1972), Hema Malini (*Khushboo*, 1975; *Kinara*, 1977; *Meera*, 1979), Sharmila Tagore (*Khushboo*; *Mausam*, 1977; *Namkeen*, 1982), Rekha (*Ghar*, 1978; *Ijaazat*, 1987), Dimple Kapadia (*Lekin*, 1990) and Tabu (*Maachis*, 1996; *Hu Tu Tu*, 1999) had their finest roles in films he has been involved with.

Gulzar's breakthrough in cinema – as a lyricist in *Bandini* (1963) – came about with a song that's a triumph when it comes to conveying feminine desire. Couched in the tradition of a Vaishnav bhajan, '*Mora gora ang lai le*' is as much a metaphor for a young women's sexual awakening, the first frisson of being in love. There is probably no other song that merges the corporeal with the metaphysical as seamlessly. A young girl on a secret tryst to meet her beloved, seeking the night's cover of darkness, as also a comment on a devotee's desire to become one with God, in this instance the dark-skinned Shyam. For a culture that values 'fair skin' above everything else, it is quite extraordinary how the song articulates a woman's desire to embrace 'Shyam-rang' for the sake of love.

At the same time, when called upon to articulate the raw eroticism of desire, Gulzar could be as explicit as he is in Basu Bhattacharya's *Aastha* (1991):

Labon se choom lo aankhon se thaam lo mujhko
Tumhi se janmoon toh shaayad mujhe panaah miley…

Main aarzoo ki tapish mein pighal rahi thi kahin
Tumhaare jism se hokar nikal rahi thi kahin
Badey haseen thay jo raah mein mein gunaah miley…

This understanding of the feminine psyche is also evident in the sensual and playful songs that he wrote for *Anubhav* (1971) – '*Koi chupke se aake*', '*Mera dil jo mera hota*' and '*Mujhe ja na kaho*'. Or for that matter '*Pehchan toh thi*' in *Griha Pravesh* (1979), a rare sensitive take, in Hindi cinema, on adultery that he also wrote. Then there's *Rudaali* (1990), where the impossibility of Shanichari's yearning finds a most evocative outlet in '*Dil hum hum kare*'. The film, written by Gulzar, based on a short story by Mahasweta Devi, is a landmark in the representation of women in Hindi mainstream cinema, highlighting gender inequality and patriarchy against the backdrop of class and caste divides, with scholar Priya Kapoor calling it 'a feminist treatise on solidarity against caste ostracization and the plight of the subaltern woman at the hands of landowning classes'.

Right from his debut as director, *Mere Apne* (1971), Gulzar's films have featured an array of memorable female characters, drawn with empathy. Though *Mere Apne* is more remembered today as one of Meena Kumari's final outings, one character who has escaped attention is Niranjan (Deven Verma), her husband. It is a rather interesting androgynous take on the persona. Even as Anandi (Meena Kumari) rues that, with their trousers and short hair, the 'modern' woman is no longer distinguishable from a man, the director cuts to Niranjan dressing up as a woman (he is part of a theatre troupe). There is something charmingly feminine in Niranjan's demeanour that adds a quaint dimension to the character.

Aandhi of course boasts one of Hindi cinema's most memorable female characters, Aarti Devi, played by Suchitra Sen. Here is an unapologetic look at a woman who marries for love and discovers that she is not cut out for domesticity. Unlike most other women in films of the era, she prioritizes her own needs, her career, over her husband, even her child. And her choice of profession too says a lot – a politician, an arena that has for the longest time been a male preserve. It is fascinating that Aarti is, literally, the only woman in the film – and yet she is the pivot around whom the narrative revolves. The other exceptional woman in politics in a Gulzar film is Maltibai (Suhasini Mulay) in *Hu Tu Tu*, again an interesting exposition of a woman's tryst with power and its corrupting influence.

If Aarti is a political worker in *Aandhi*, Kajli (Sharmila Tagore) in *Mausam* is a worker too. If Aarti does not regret her choice of career, there is none of that in Kajli either, even though she is a sex worker. It's a no-holds-barred portrayal that steers clear of the cliches that characterized leading stars playing women of disrepute in Hindi cinema. Of course, there's the element of change that comes over her with her growing affection for the elderly doctor, but that is never overtly underscored. The man here is not on a mission to uplift her. And if *Lamhe* was seen as ahead of its time, even in 1991, in the way it depicted a woman's feelings for a man who was her mother's lover, it is worth considering that *Mausam* did this as early as in 1975.

The other Gulzar film in 1975 (a remarkable year for the film-maker) that went against the grain in the way it framed its woman protagonist is *Khushboo*. Feminists may have a problem with the basic narrative where the woman, Kusum (Hema Malini), seems to be doing nothing but pining for the love of a man, Brindaban (Jeetendra), who has not treated her very well, though he too is a victim of the ways of destiny. In Gulzar's vision, however, Kusum emerges as a woman with dignity, one who is self-assertive and refuses to be taken for granted.

This comes across most memorably in her exchange with Brindaban's mother (Durga Khote). '*Chhodi hui ladki ko koi wapas le le, is se bada maan kya milega usey*? (What greater respect for a girl who has been forsaken than being offered marriage),' she tells Brindaban. But Kusum brings up the very important aspect of her desire and consent. As she tells her friend, '*Koi raaste par thodi baithi hoon, jab jee chahega chhod jayenge…meri marzi kuch nahin*? (Isn't my opinion important? I am not some destitute you take home or abandon as you please).' And in the definitive act of self-assertion, she returns the bangles that the mother patronizingly gives her as a token of her impending marriage to Brindaban. She, however, does this without in any way humiliating the mother. She affords her the respect that her age deserves.

Gulzar's choice of Hema Malini in the lead also demonstrates his ability to cast against type. The actor was at the time the superstar of Hindi cinema, the 'dream girl' who epitomized the glamour and kitsch that were the hallmarks of Hindi film heroines of the era. Like he did with Sharmila Tagore (another glamourous star) in films like *Mausam* and *Namkeen*, Gulzar gave Hema Malini a makeover in the three films that are considered her finest: *Khushboo*, *Kinara* and *Meera*. As the star herself said, 'I was too young to realise what kind of a strong character I was playing in that film (*Khushboo*), but this changed my image. I didn't have to wear bell-bottoms and fancy wigs or run around trees.'

Of these three films, *Meera* best articulates the director's political and feminist stance. Gulzar's triumph in *Meera* lies primarily in the way he strips the highly mythologized religious character of overt mysticism so that she becomes contemporary, timeless. Gulzar's Meera is a woman with a mind of her own, through whom the director addresses the hypocrisy of religious institutions and dogma as also aspects of secularism and statecraft.

Most of these arguments come across in the debates Meera has with the head priest (played by Om Shivpuri). He pontificates about the importance of Karwa Chauth (a regressive tradition that seems to have become more and more entrenched in our society in recent times) and says, '*Pati hi tumhara Parmeshwar hai* (Your husband is your God).' She responds, '*Parmeshwar hi mera pati hain* (Yes, God is my husband).' The exchange turns on its head Hindi cinema's fixation with the concept of 'pati-parmeshwar' while also driving home the point that Meera, the devotee, considered herself betrothed to Lord Krishna.

There is also a strong political awareness that Gulzar imbues Meera with. She dresses Krishna as a Rajput, reasoning '*Jaisa desh waisa bhesh*' (when in Rome do as the Romans do). She addresses the subject of caste in her relationship with poet-saint Raidas (A.K. Hangal). She even engages with Emperor Akbar (Amjad Khan), chiding him for keeping Tansen 'bound' to the court. (Akbar's articulation of his Hindustani roots gives the film a contemporary urgency too at a time when the Mughal kings are being increasingly viewed as religious invaders.) Gulzar's Meera actually provides the last word on shallow nationalism and the boundaries that separate nations when she tells the head priest: '*Aap apna desh bas wahin tak maante hai jahan tak aapka raajpaat chalta hai. Aapka desh kabhi ghat jaata hai, kabhi badh jaata hai. Main aapki seema ko apne desh ki seema nahin maanti.*' (Your notion of a country is confined to the land you govern. It waxes and wanes according to the territory you control. I am not bound to the boundaries you set for your state.)

And when she is finally put on trial for failing in her duties as a chaste woman, failing to do what her family and society expects of her as a wife, she provides the most eloquent statement of her identity as a woman: '*Main atman hoon, sharir nahin, main bhavna hoon, kisi samaj ka vichar nahin, main premi hoon, premika hoon, kewal prem naam ki jogan, kisi sambandh ki kadi nahin, kisi parivaar ki khuti se bandhi nahin.*' (I am the soul, not the body. I am an emotion, not a social construct. I am a lover, a mendicant of love, not a link to a relationship. I am not bound to the peg of a family.)

Films like *Namkeen* and *Ijaazat* are remarkable for the variety and depth of women characters they offer. In Amma, Nimki, Mithu and Chinki and their cloistered ramshackle world, *Namkeen* is an almost Chekhovian take on women. Maya in *Ijaazat* is unlike any woman in Hindi cinema of the era – impetuous, a free spirit who loves fiercely and without condition, who lives life on her own terms, offering a contrast to the other woman in the narrative, Sudha. As Saba Bashir observes in her book, *I Swallowed the Moon*, 'The film explores an extramarital relationship without either woman being projected either as conniving or as a victim.' Though the male protagonist, Mahender (Naseeruddin Shah), is the one in a relationship with both at different times in his life, it is Maya and Sudha who, even if they never meet, share a special bond with each other. It is a camaraderie born out of being women.

In *Lekin*, a woman who 'travels across lifetimes in search of salvation' becomes the conduit for the man's exploration and understanding of his own self. And of *Libaas*, the unreleased film, based on a short story, 'Seema', written by Gulzar himself, Saba Bashir writes, here's 'a woman seeking not only happiness in a marriage but also stability and fulfilment in relationships'. There's also *Ghar*, a film that addresses the subject of rape with a sensitivity that is astounding for its time. Though Manik Chatterjee is credited as its director, it is well known that he suffered an accident during the making. It is Gulzar who completed the film and the final product bears the master's unmistakable stamp.

Almost all these women stand out for their fortitude, their independence and dignity (despite straitened circumstances) and their empathy. But what sets apart Gulzar's unerring eye for the feminine is that even when the women are less than perfect – for example, the selfish relative in *Mere Apne*, the unfaithful wife in *Achanak* (1971), the sister-in-law in *Meera* and the manipulative politician in *Hu Tu Tu* – there is no value judgement being made. They are characters of flesh and blood, never caricatures.

And with humour being an integral part of Gulzar's cinematic oeuvre, what better homage to the power of women than this song from *Swayamvar* (1980) which not many might associate with the legend:

Naari kuch aisan aage nikal rahi hai
Mardan ke paon taley dharti phisal rahi hai

Woh din gaye ki ghar ke chulhe ma sar khapaya
Ek pair ab zami par ek chand par jamaya
Badli hai jab se aurat duniya badal rahi hai…

Mardan ko de ke pension ladti hai ab election
Kahte thay jisko sister ab hui gai minister
Mardan ki mombatti tap-tap pighal rahi hai…

Mardan ke paon taley dharti phisal rahi hai.

The Comic Genius of Gulzar

I have made a reference to Gulzar's response to a man who mistook him for, well, Gulzar, at the airport. In my long association with him, this is just one of the many moments that brought to light the impish and often whacky sense of humour that is so integral a part of his persona, and indeed his work in cinema. People are so enamoured of his 'serious' songs and films that one tends to overlook his contribution as one of the finest writers in the Hindi film industry when it comes to comedy. It also says a lot about the way we view humour in our arts as something less reverential that barring '*Kajrare*' none of his comic output as a writer and director has won any award.

As he never tired of underlining – the words you write must reflect the times you write them in, the vocabulary of the era. In an era devoid when WhatsApp and texting have redefined the way we communicate, when 'Hinglish' is the de facto mode of communication, your language has to reflect that to stay relevant. At the same time, a film song must adhere to the demands of the situation and the character. As I have mentioned, after a violent day's work, a gangster will not wind down with '*Dil-e-naadan tujhe hua kya* hai'; he is more likely to go '*Goli maar bheje mein*'.

In her well-received book on the poetry of Gulzar, *I Swallowed the Moon*, Saba Bashir writes, 'Gulzar believes in changing with the times. This is reflected in the conscious effort he makes in his films to portray generational changes in the use of language. For instance, in the film *Namkeen*, Amma, the mother, uses the word *beghairat*. Her daughter asks her, "*Yeh kaun sa shabd hai*?" To which the mother replies, "*Shabd kya hota hai, lafz bolo*."'

So, here is a look at some of the poet's more 'un-shareefana' contribution to films and film songs. I use the word in the same spirit as Gulzar-ji described himself as far from being shareef, because some of these constitute literature of the highest form and are consistently underpinned by a philosophical take on our life and times. This is by no means a definitive list. The works of Gulzar go beyond the limitations of a newspaper feature.

The Songs

It is true that most songs Gulzar penned in the films he has directed speak of the intricacies of relationships. Love, loss and longing permeate these songs. Songs like '*Dil dhoondta hai*' *Mausam*, 1975), '*Is mod se jaate hai*' (*Aandhi*, 1975), '*Koi hota jisko apna*' (*Mere Apne*, 1971), '*Yaara seeli seeli*' (*Lekin*, 1991) and '*Chhod aaye hum*' (*Maachis*, 1996) form the bedrock of his reputation as one of the finest lyricists in Indian cinema.

His own films have not often explored the sunny side of the lyricist. Barring probably '*Master-ji ki aa gayi chitthi*' (remember

'VIP underwear banyan'?) and '*Dhanno ki aakhon mein*' (the original 'item number' before the term was invented) in *Kitaab* (1977) and '*Aaki chali*' (only Gulzar can probably make '*panta bhaate tatka begun pora*' feel so intrinsic a part of a Hindi film song) in *Namkeen* (1982). However, when it comes to songs for other filmmakers, he has some of the most lovable songs that are sure to have you rolling with laughter.

'*Mummy o mummy*' (*Khatta Meetha*, 1978): Loosely based on the 1968 Hollywood film *Yours Mine and Ours*, Basu Chatterjee's 1978 well-loved family entertainer is one of the few Hindi films that put Parsis centre stage. Gulzar wrote the film's very popular songs, which include the side-splitting '*Mummy o mummy*', pictured on Deven Verma (who grabbed a *Filmfare* nomination for his role as a young man desperate to marry), imploring his mother (played by Piloo Wadia) to get him hitched.

'*Gol maal hai bhai*' and '*Ek din sapne mein*' (Gol Maal, 1979): Armchair discussions on Gulzar's contribution as a lyricist in Hrishikesh Mukherjee's evergreen laugh riot has largely been limited to '*Aane wala pal*' whose luminous brilliance has overshadowed two hilarious numbers that demonstrate the poet's ability to tickle the funny bone. Note the way the title song, '*Gol maal hai bhai*', takes on the theme of money and how one needs money in the first place to be able to earn some, and then line-by-line expands on the circularity: if you can't beg for money, better sweat for it; but if you sweat, you will need a handkerchief; well, you would need cloth for that; you can tear up a shirt to make one, or someone might just lend you the cloth for a shirt; but getting it stitched will again need money... And so round and round it goes.

Paisa kamane ke liye bhi paisa chahiye
Maange se na mile toh pasina bahaiye
Bahta hai jab pasina to rumaal chahiye

Rumaal bann gaya bhi gar kameez phaad kar
Kameez ke liye bhi toh phir kapda chahiye

Are kapda kisi ne daan hi me de diya chalo
Darzi ke paas ja ke woh pahale silaiye

Bin sili kameez pe toh kuchh nahi liya
Sili huyi kameez pe silaai chahiye
Silaai dene ke liye phir paisaa chahiye
Paisa kamane ke liye bhi paisa chahiye

The other song, '*Ek din sapne mein*', brings forth his genius at wordplay and conjuring bizarre scenarios in keeping with the demands of the situation. The hero (Amol Palekar) and his pals are at a picnic, daydreaming and singing about becoming celebrities.

Ek din sapne mein dekha sapna
Woh jo hain na Amitabh apna
Market se out hua, logo ko doubt hua
Meree vajah se woh gaya gaya gaya gaya
Kismat toh badalee kya kahu really
Mai Amitabh ho gaya

In the next stanza, it's football legend Pele who gets the treatment. Given the unreal world of a dream, Gulzar seamlessly merges football with cricket.

Ek din sapne me dekha sapna
Arre woh jo hai naa Mister Pele apna
Kehte khiladi hai bada anari hai
Meray saath match ho gaya gaya gaya gaya gaya

Arre mara jo chhakka toh catch ho gaya

It is in the final stanza that he outdoes himself, coining the term 'sapni' to rhyme with 'apni'. Again, what would be unacceptable in a poetic world becomes perfectly legitimate because it's a dream he is describing.

Ek din chhoti si dekhi sapni
Woh jo hai naa Lata apni
Lata ga rahi thi main tablay pe tha
Woh mukhde pe thi mai antre pe tha

'*Saare niyam tod do*' and '*Qayda qayda*' (*Khubsoorat*, 1980): In this film that marked a turning point for Rekha, Gulzar has two songs that underlined the theme of the film: a light-hearted takedown of regimentation and too much order. It's possible to view *Khubsoorat* as a parable about the Emergency the country had witnessed only a few years before, with the stern matriarch (played by Dina Pathak) standing in for Indira Gandhi. These songs in effect can thus be seen as protesting the dictatorial rules the Emergency engendered, albeit done tongue firmly in cheek.

'*Saare niyam tod do*' is a fun call to break all rules and have some fun. '*Qayda qayda*' paints the picture of a world where the sun and the moon and nature itself decide to abandon a strict adherence to order. From rivers of milk flowing on the moon to grass made of faluda (if only we could eat the moon, one spoon at a time, goes a line) to crops of toffee, trees laden with sweets and taps overflowing with coffee, the song is almost Lewis Carroll-ish in its imagery:

Achha socho suraj ka rang neela hota
Aur pedo ka rang lal
Panchhi hote paani mein
Aur machhi gagan vishal

'*Dil toh bachcha hai ji*' (*Ishqiya*, 2010): If Mallika Pukhraj had her '*Abhi toh main jawan hoon*' (written by Hafeez Jalandhari), Gulzar has '*Dil toh bachcha hain ji*', a wistful lament for lost youth that's pensive and funny in the same breath. The vision might be failing, the teeth no longer strong enough, the glow has gone missing from one's demeanour, yet, the poet asserts, the heart is still young and longs for that passion of youth. Gulzar is sublime in this take on the wayward ways of the heart at an age when it should know better, when it should have learnt to be quiet.

The Films: As Writer and Director

A film being primarily a director's medium, one tends to overlook what others may have contributed in ensuring its place in posterity. Take *Chupke Chupke* (1975), for example, one of the great comedies of Hindi cinema. Though a Hrishikesh Mukherjee film, its screenplay and dialogues were written by Gulzar, based on the Bengali original *Chhadmabeshi* by Upendranath Ganguly. Much of the joy in this funfest lies in the situations he creates and his terrific sense of wordplay. From *lohpath gami agnirath* to the funniest lesson in botany (corolla/karela) you are ever likely to come across, the writer's contribution to this classic comedy is immeasurable. Not to mention that in a year in which Amitabh Bachchan singed the box office with his smouldering performances in *Deewaar* and *Sholay*, this film had him in oversized glasses mumbling, trying to differentiate between '*gende ka phool*' and '*gobhi ka phool*'. A number of Hrishikesh Mukherjee films owe their quintessential flavour to Gulzar's pen – be it *Guddi* or *Bawarchi*. Even a four-hanky tearjerker like *Anand* has its droll moments in the character device of Murarilal (Johnny Walker as Issabhai Suratwala), leavening the inherent tragedy of the film.

Kamal Haasan's *Mrs Doubtfire* remake *Chachi 420* (1996) also benefits immensely from Gulzar's keen eye for the humorous, particularly in the way he fleshes out the character of Banwarilal Pandit, the secretary with a glad eye, played brilliantly by Om Puri. *Chachi 420* also offers a wonderful bouquet of zany songs written by him, including the alliterative '*Chupdi chupdi chachi*', '*Dowda bhaga sa*' and '*Jaago gori*' (a line in the song goes '*Saiyyan hamare hai Matahari*').

Given his many forays into the comic realm as a writer and lyricist, it is somewhat surprising that Gulzar has just one comedy to his name as a director. But that film has stood the test of time as one of the greatest in Hindi cinema. Based on Shakespeare's *A Comedy of Errors*, it is interesting that Gulzar had a hand (as lyricist) in an earlier version of the film, *Do Dooni Char* (1966), starring Kishore Kumar and Asit Sen. His 1982 remake, *Angoor*, is a laugh riot like no other, a mad medley of mistaken identities that benefits from the filmmaker's innate sense of timing and two (or should that be four?) great performances by Sanjeev Kumar (both named Ashok) and Deven Verma (both named Bahadur) in double roles. Both were nominated for the Filmfare Awards for Best Actor and Best Comedian, with Deven Verma – whom Gulzar has described as 'a humourist who excelled at comedy' – taking the trophy home.

In a film that literally bursts at the seams with laugh-out-loud moments – one of the Bahadurs looking for a rope to hang himself and bargaining over its price, one of the Ashoks as a detective pulp-fiction addict, another Bahadur lip-syncing to '*Preetam aan milo*' – it is impossible to zero-in on one. But my personal favourites come towards the end. Both reveal the film-maker's ability to ratchet up the laughter.

In one, set in the jewellery shop where a few of the film's key sequences play out, the harried artisan Mansoor Miyan (Yunus Parvez in a hilarious turn) tries to convince one of the Ashoks that he had indeed delivered the necklace, ending with this classic exchange, a triumph of comic writing:

Mansoor: ...aur maine haar aapki zaano pe rakkha...

Ashok: Kahan? Kahan rakkha tha?

Mansoor: Zaano pe ... mera matlab ghutno par...

Ashok: Jo aadmi ghutno ko zaano kah sakta hai, woh Ashok Kumar ko Kishore Kumar bhi kah sakta hai...

Mansoor: Askok sahab, Urdu mein ghutno ko zaano hi kahte hai

Ashok: Achha, toh phir, Urdu mein Ashok ko kya kehte hain?

Mansoor, stumped, mumbles to himself while his employer Chhedilal (C.S. Dubey) eggs him on: Batao batao, jawab do…

Mansoo (by now totally flummoxed): Lekin haar se Ashok ka kya taalluq?

Ashok: Lijiye, ab haar se hamara koi talluq hi nahin!

Chhedilal: Mansoor miyan, tumhe kya ho gaya hai. Haar ka talluq Ashok babu se nahin toh kis se hai

Mansoor: Lahoul bila quwat! Main kya bol raha hoon

In the other sequence, after the two Ashoks and two Bahadurs come face to face for the first time, the former have an exchange that is a fond send-off of the hoary Hindi film cliché of long-lost brothers/twins who have similar birthmarks on their bodies or some-such script contrivance that will prove their genealogical connection.

Ashok 1: Tumhara naam Ashok hain?

Ashok 2: Haan

Ashok 1: Mera bhi … Tum Raj Tilak ji ke bete ho?

Ashok 2: Haan

Ashok 1: Main bhi … Achha, yeh bataon … tumhare daaye kandhe mein til hil hai?

Ashok 2: Nahin…

Ashok 1: Mera bhi nahin hai … phir toh hum dono bhai huye…

Gulzar for the Dance Floor

For someone whose songs have defined and redefined the best of Hindi film music, it is only in the twilight phase of his career that Gulzar probably transcended the elite divide and became a balladeer of the masses. And he did so without compromising on the basic integrity of his art and craft. A new generation of composers led by A.R. Rahman, Shankar-Ehsaan-Loy and Vishal Bhardwaj created what would become bona fide dance-floor sizzlers, 'item numbers' with a difference, with class and style.

It probably began with '*Chhaiyyan chhaiyyan*' (*Dil Se*) and '*Goli maar bheje mein*' (*Satya*), both releasing in 1998. Using two diametrically opposite idioms – the purity of chaste Urdu (only Gulzar can make you shake a leg to esoteric lines like '*Woh yaar hai jo khushboo ki taraah/ Jis ki zubaan Urdu ki taraah*') and the streetwise slang of Mumbai's underworld – Gulzar rewrote the rules of film-song writing for a new era.

He carried the experimentation with form and words further with '*Banda yeh bindaas hai*' (*Aks*, 2001) before delivering what is arguably his biggest chartbuster as a lyricist with '*Kajrare*' (*Bunty Aur Babli*, 2005). At the age of seventy, he had the youthfulness to conjure a song that had teenagers swaying in pubs and discotheques and autorickshaws blaring it from their stereos. Shaad Ali and Shankar-Ehsaan-Loy would return nine years later with *Kill Dil* that had Gulzar penning the whacky title song:

Tar-coal ki ek sadak par do saaye hain
Andhere ki najaayaz aulaad hain shayad

Taara… dekh taara
Aasmaan pe latka hai bechaara
Yeh zameen gardish mein thi
Ghoom, ghoom, ghoom ke maara yaara

Mehangi hai ye zindagi
Koi chhota sauda nahi
Oonchi khajuri hai ye
Gamle ka paudha nahi

Some of his finest songs of this fecund phase as a lyricist have come in collaboration with Vishal Bhardwaj who, in chartbusters like '*Beedi jalaile*' (*Omkara*, 2006) and '*Darling*' (*7 Khoon Maaf*, 2011), to name only two, seems to have the uncanny ability to get his mentor to raise the bar every time. It is with Vishal as a composer that Gulzar broke free of the constraints of film lyrics, experimenting freely with Hinglish, English and Urdu, absurdist imagery and quirky wordplay. Who would have thought that the quintessential Hindi film action music signifying tension and excitement, 'dhantanan', would be reincarnated as the floor scorcher '*Dhan-te-nan*' (*Kaminey*, 2009). Rajesh Khanna used the word in *Bawarchi*, in the scene where he brings tea to the family patriarch – no prizes for guessing who wrote the film.

The situations that Vishal creates in his films seem to have inspired and emboldened Gulzar to more and more freaky experimentations. Consider, '*Oye boy Charlie*' in *Matru Ki Bijli Ka Mandola* (2013):

Nazar me tu hi tu hai
Tu meri Timbuktu hai
Oye boy oye boy Charlie
Tuney dil ki baazi maar li

And it gets zanier with every line, almost like a nonsense limerick:

Tere scent-vent ki khushboo mein
Main khoyi khoyi si rehti hoon

Oye my baby baby
Tera chakkar chala jalebi

Main dor tu patang udti jaa
Kahin atak-vatak naa jaana tu

Main dheel toh deta rehta hoon
Kahin bhatak-vatak na jaana tu

Or the inspired lunacy that informs two songs in *Rangoon* (2017), '*Bloody Hell*' (the infectious energy of '*Main chakkar kha gayi tezi mein/Ishq kiya angrezi mein/Khullam khulla do hothon ka/Jaam piya angrezi mein*') and '*Meray miyan gaye England*' (taking off from the classic C. Ramchandra–Shamshad Begum song written by Rajendra Krishan, and ingeniously incorporating Hitler and Churchill into the lyrics):

Meray miyan gaye England
Baja ke band
Na jaane kahaan karenge land
Ke Hitler chaunke na / Ke Churchill chauke na

Posterity will decide how these experimentations with form and language stack up vis-à-vis his more celebrated classics. There is however no doubting the virtuosity of someone who pens a '*Humne dekhi hai*' with as much felicity as a '*Kajrare*', who can have you double up with laughter in *Angoor* as easily as he can bring a lump to your throat in *Namkeen*, both in the same year.

The Political Gulzar

Paani paani kuwa sambhal
Jiska maati uska maal...

Jiski kheti uski zameen hai
Jiska ganna uske gander

Hum beej na denge
Hum byaaj na denge
Re kal ka karza aaj naa denge

Sun raja lootnewale mhare raja
O teri tanashahi, nahi chalne denge
Re apna morcha, nahi talne denge
– '*Lootnewale*' (*Matru Ki Bijlee Ka Mandola*, 2013)

Among the many delights of Vishal Bhardwaj's underrated and criminally overlooked satire on land grabbing and the exploitation of farmers is this exquisite song. Almost a decade later, as farmers staged a heroic year-long struggle against the government, its words – *hum beej na denge / hum byaaj na denge … / apna morcha nahi talne denge* – came back to me with a force all its own. And with a fresh realization of the 'political' firebrand in Gulzar, the eternal romantic.

Though more celebrated for his lyrical compositions and explorations of relationships, Gulzar is among the few film-makers in Hindi cinema who have addressed political realities facing the nation with a rare understanding and sensitivity. His work in the genre of political cinema may not possess the irreverence or hard-hitting nature of a Vijay Tendulkar and a Govind Nihalani – he approaches the subject more as a poet than a strident social/political commentator – or may not even be as quotable as Sahir Ludhianvi's '*Jinhe naaz hai Hind par woh kahan hai*' or '*Chin-o-Arab hamara*'. There is no doubt, however, of the importance of his political writing in the idiom of the cinema of which he has been a part.

For a film-maker/lyricist known more for the lyricism of '*Woh shaam kuchh ajeeb thi*' and '*Musafir hoon yaaron*', for pensive human dramas like *Mausam* (1975) and *Ijaazat* (1987), it is interesting that he not only debuted with a film with strong political overtones (*Mere Apne*, 1971), his last two films as director too (*Maachis*, 1996; *Hu Tu Tu*, 1999) were firmly rooted in the political space.

Bobby Sing, well-known commentator on music, cinema and culture, opines, 'An artist or poet's political expression can take two forms. As readers or viewers, we tend to be more drawn to or influenced by the first kind – the fiery, aggressive, provocative depiction that doesn't shy away from incorporating anger and bloodshed. In the second, the poet or the visualizer/director chooses the path of calm and subtle expressions with a touch of sarcasm. At times it also becomes comic (satire), intelligently commenting upon the political development without resorting to pamphleteering. Coming to Gulzar, I strongly feel that he started off belonging to the second category both in his poetry and films.'

Mere Apne: More than fifty years after the film was made, it is uncanny how contemporary the film and its observations on political chicanery remain. Of course, the timeless '*Haal chaal theek thaak hai*', a pungent commentary on the state of the nation, is the icing on the cake. It says something about the prescience of the song that as late as 2018, the NSSO reported that India has not seen a job crisis as severe since 1973 (the year NSSO conducted its first job survey, two years after *Mere Apne* released).

Haal chaal theek thaak hai
Sab kuch theek thaak hai
BA kiya hain MA kiya
Lagta hai sab kuch aiwayan kiya
Kaam nahin hain varna yahan
Aap ki dua se sab theek thaak hai

Aab-o-hawa desh ka bahot saaf hain
Qaida hain kanoon hai insaaf hai

But the song apart, one that bristles with contempt for the way things are and the people responsible for it, the politician – *roj ki meeting/roj ke bhashan/bhashan pe ration nahin hain yahan* – the film has some trademark Gulzar asides on the political class. Early in the film a group of young unemployed people whiling time over tea and adda discuss a weathercock. The reference to the political class is unmissable. '*Hawa ke saath rukh badalta rahta hai – bhurji wahi hai murge ka munh badal gaya*. Even the most communal and selfish parties use socialism to suit their purposes. *Karna dharna kuchh nahin sirf bhashan dena, naare lagana*.' Or the satire inherent in the scene where frustrated students vandalize college property while '*Saare jahan se achha*' plays in the background. It's possible to argue that the politicians in the film – played by Asit Sen and Mehmood – are crafted more as caricatures, and that somehow undermines the film, but it is also true that the only way one can survive our politicians is by looking at them as bungling fools.

Aandhi: Like *Mere Apne*, which couched its political strand in the bond between the old woman Anandi (Meena Kumari) and the young members of the two gangs at war, *Aandhi* too is primarily a film concerned more with the dynamics of a relationship between a couple. It is just that one of them – the wife, Aarti (Suchitra Sen) – happens to be a politician. That allows the director to comment on the shenanigans of this class. Primarily through the characters of Lallu Lal (Om Prakash in a delightful turn), Aarti Devi's veteran campaign manager who knows the tricks of the trade inside-out (witness the way he cajoles another candidate, played by Manmohan, to enter the fray so that the anti-Aarti votes get divided) and Chandrasen (Om Shivpuri), Aarti's rival candidate who is not averse to raking up a possible 'scandal' pertaining to his opponent's personal life.

With three Kishore Kumar-Lata Mangeshkar gems that have defined the R.D. Burman–Gulzar partnership, it is not surprising that the other song, '*Salaam kijiye*', sort of languishes in the shadows. It remains one of the most biting criticisms of political opportunism in Hindi cinema, and the film's strongest political statement.

Salaam kijiye aali janab aaye hain
Yeh paanch saalon ka dene hisaab aaye hain...

Hamare vote kharidenge humk ann dekar
Yeh nange jism chhupa detey hain kafan dekar
Yeh jaadugar hain chutki mein kaam karte hain
Yeh bhook pyaas ko baton se ram karte hain...

And in the lines '*Haan ye vote denge magar abke yun nahin denge/Chunao aane do hum aap se nipat lenge*' lie the most telling articulation of the power at the common man's disposal.

Maachis: This is Gulzar at his most political in what is arguably his most 'violent' film too. Which is not surprising given that it deals with one of the darkest chapters of post-independence Indian history, the insurgency in Punjab. As Bobby Sing says, 'Post the 1980s, the dark phase witnessed by Punjab as well as Delhi and other parts of the country led to a change in Gulzar-ji's expressions towards a more direct indictment of the system. A man strongly believing in one's roots, he related to the changing scenario as someone who was born Sikh. The anger seeped in along with frustration, and that's what resulted in films like *Maachis* and *Hu Tu Tu*, openly dealing with terrorism, a corrupt system, bloodshed and vengeance.'

The film derives its strength from the economy of expression with which Gulzar sets the context. He uses three newspaper clippings – the storming of the Golden Temple (Operation Bluestar), the assassination of Indira Gandhi and the pogrom against the Sikhs – to provide a background to and make sense of what made a whole generation of 'boys' take to terrorism. There is no doubt where his sympathies lie – none of the young men taking to arms in this film are hardcore militants. Each is a victim of state oppression and police brutality. As Sanatan (Om Puri), the group's mentor, says, '*Aatankvaadi kya khet mein ugte hai*?' Sanatan then becomes the voice of the writer/director as he declaims on the reasons for organized violence against the state. 'When someone has been subjected to injustice time and again... He looks for others like himself... Regardless of whom he's fighting, it's a response to that injustice.'

The film contains some of Gulzar's most bitter writing against the system, exploding the myth of our non-violent struggle for freedom. The anger and the pain are palpable when Sanatan says that half his family perished in 1947, the rest in 1984, both cataclysms the handiwork of politicians. Of what use is a democracy that cannot provide the basics of food, clothing, medicine and shelter to 60 per cent of the population even fifty years after independence? he asks. And then comes the punchline, the call for a revolution: *Seeli tiliyon se koi inquilab nahin bhadakta – maachis chiragh bhi jalati aur chitayen bhi.*

His softer poetic sensibilities have not deserted him though, and *Maachis* boasts one of the finest soundtracks in the history of Hindi cinema, not to mention being Vishal Bhardwaj's breakthrough album. However, at the risk of sounding blasphemous, I do feel that songs like '*Paani paani re*' and '*Tum gaye sab gaya*' – despite their brilliance – do dilute the narrative considerably. A few unfortunate script contrivances towards the end – in particular the 'surprise' return of Tabu to the narrative as a missile launcher – undermines the power of what has gone before.

Hu Tu Tu: From *Maachis* to *Hu Tu Tu* was a natural progression for Gulzar, the film-maker and writer. More ambitious than *Maachis*, in the sense that it is not limited to a specific history and encompasses the stink that pervades the entire system, *Hu Tu Tu* could have been his magnum opus political tract. If only his producers had allowed him a free hand with the narrative. Its original story pertained primarily to a schoolteacher-turned-politician, Malti Devi (Suhasini Mulay), who is not averse to using any means – fair or foul – in her quest for power. Unfortunately, the interference from the producers, which led to the focus shifting to the stars Suneil Shetty and Tabu, left this very interesting angle half-baked. It eventually led the film-maker to give up in exasperation and never direct another film again.

However, flashes of what the original could have been remain, particularly in the character of Bhau (Nana Patekar), the local balladeer. What Sanatan is to *Maachis*, Bhau is to *Hu Tu Tu* – the agency through which the writer speaks his mind.

In *Maachis*, Sanatan says, '*Azadi kaise mili? Khoon kharabe se … Azadi kisne laakar di? Arre koi ek admi tha jo gaya aur jakar azadi uthakar le aaya aur lakar hamein de di, ke lo tumhare liye laaye hain – lo baant lo.*' In *Hu Tu Tu*, Bhau observes, '*Pichle pachaas saalo mein hamare desh ne sirf mantri aur minister paida kiye hai … ek neta paida nahi kiya.*' Gulzar is relentless in his criticism of politicians, as Bhau says, 'Politicians are a strange breed – barely able to walk on their own, they are entrusted with running the country … every profession has a retirement age, barring politics. A politician never retires – unless he dies or is killed.'

In a telling sequence, a teacher looks at a photograph of Netaji Subhash Bose and says that if only India had become free following his path, we would have inherited a different nation. In another, at the funeral meet of Malti Devi's mentor, the political struggle to take on his mantle has already begun. As Malti consolidates her position, her mentor's lackeys try and convince his widow to jump into the fray. She demurs saying she knows nothing of politics, but suggests that her son, barely a teenager, could take over because he has always wanted to be in politics!

The film also contains another of his celebrated political songs, '*Ghapla hai*', that talks of the many scams that plague the nation – from oil and railways to fodder, defence and godmen:

Sadhu sant ki dadhi munchh ka ghapla hai
Aate mein ghapla hai
Baate mein ghapla hai…

Rail mein ghapla ji tel mein ghapla
LIC mein bank mein ghapla
Jeep mein ghapla tank mein ghapla

Faujo ke booton se lekar
Banduko mein ghapla hai
Teen crore ke note bhare in
Sanduko mein ghapla hai

The Screenplays: *Namak Haraam* (1973) and *New Delhi Times* (1986)

Apart from the four films that he directed, a couple of screenplays also stand testimony to his skill in narrating a political story. One of these is *Namak Haraam* (1973), an intelligent adaptation of the 1964 Peter Glenville classic *Becket*, starring Richard Burton and Peter O'Toole. Gulzar's screenplay takes on the story of the tumultuous friendship between Henry II of England and his friend-turned-bishop Thomas Becket and places it against the backdrop of a debate on capitalism which then allows him to explore labour relations in the turbulent seventies which was marked by conflicts between the capitalist class and workers' unions across the country.

The other, more potent, screenplay is Ramesh Sharma's 1986 thriller *New Delhi Times*, one of the finest of its genre in Hindi cinema. Few films in Hindi have explored the nexus between politics, business and media in the way this one does. Well ahead of its time – the 1980s were anything but a decade known for good, intelligent films of this variety, a songless one at that – *New Delhi Times* remains as relevant nearly forty years later. And that owes itself in no mean manner to Gulzar's writing. When Vikas Pande (Shashi Kapoor in arguably his finest performance) says that the distance between his small hometown Ghazipur and the capital is symptomatic of that between the ruler and the ruled, he could be talking any time in independent India. And in one of the film's most powerful sequences, the writer lays bare the anatomy of a riot and its political origins. Divide and rule, a character says, isn't an invention of the British – it is a prerequisite of those in power to stay in power. Things are no different as we have seen in riots flaring up in different parts of the country in recent times.

Poetry and Non-film Writing

It is however in his poetry and non-film writing that Gulzar explores the political with a freedom that cinema as a medium does not allow. Be it his novel *Do Log/Two* (which covers the span from 1947 to 1984 and to the Kargil War to reveal how little we have learned from history) or his collection of poems titled *Suspected Poems* (the title itself a play on the fact that if you are political, you are naturally a suspect in the eyes of the powers-that-be) or his huge body of work around Partition (including an anthology *Footprints on Zero Line*), it is here that one finds a mirror to India's political reality as it has unfolded in the last few decades.

Here, he is engaging and taking forward a storeyed tradition in Urdu literature. As author, literary critic and translator Rakhshanda Jalil observes, 'The political stream has always been vibrant, very robust in Urdu poetry. The slogan Inquilab Zindabad was coined by the eminent Urdu poet Iqbal and used as a rallying cry in a trade union rally in Calcutta in 1925 by another well-loved Urdu poet Hasrat Mohani. Some of the most prominent Urdu poets who have written overtly political poetry are Sahir Ludhianvi, Faiz Ahmad Faiz, Kaifi Azmi, Sardar Jafri and in modern times Javed Akhtar, Rahat Indori, Gauhar Raza. Gulzar Sahab's film and non-film poetry has many flashes of the political. Outside films, he has over the years been adding to the haiku-like series of 'Murari Lal ke maathe pe bal nahi padte'. Then there are the poems he wrote during the migrant exodus in the first and second wave of the pandemic. What is unique to his politics is the concern for the small man... "Murari Lal" is the literary equivalent of R.K. Laxman's Common Man. The series talks about price rise, budgets, elections, MLAs likened to chicken in a coop, etc.'

His non-film work around politics is too vast to recount here. It calls for a whole separate feature of its own. There is the deliciously wicked 'Nayi Dilli Mein Waise Toh Naya Kuch Bhi Nahin Hai', except that a new government comes in every five years to convert old issues to new schemes. Or the satirical '26

January', about a polio-afflicted boy trying to sell the tricolour at a traffic light, which gets a new urgency in the recent drive of 'har ghar tiranga'. There's a lament for M.M. Kalburgi and the cheeky 'Sultana Daku Ka Akhri Khat – Bete Ke Naam' where a professional robber warns his infant child to never mess with politicians. There's the delectable 'Jalsa' which likens an unending political speech to the G.T. Road and brings to life the drudgery of a political rally and a politician's speech with pithy insights of man hired to be part of the crowd. Or this, 'Tattoo', among the most acerbic of his poems, one that, in five lines, says everything about what blights our nation – a man escaping being lynched thanks to an image of a cow tattooed on his shoulder:

Usne jaane kyon apne daayen kandhe par
Nilgai ka ek tattoo gundhwaya tha
Mar jaata kal dango me
Achhe log thay –
Gaaye dekh ke chhor diya

No Child's Play: Writing for Children

'Writing for children is as easy as describing the history of the Byzantium in three words,' said Mo Willems, American writer, animator, voice actor, and author of children's books. It's a thought that Gulzar will endorse wholeheartedly. Gulzar says, 'It's while trying to teach children that one realizes what all we have to learn from them. Only when you read these books with children will you understand who the teacher is and who the student.'

It's nothing short of a national shame that a country as vast as India, with an aeons-old tradition of storytelling, has little to show when it comes to writing for children. Popular culture, barring Bengali, is almost bereft of this genre. Generations have grown up on imported fairytales – 'Snow White', 'Little Red Riding Hood', 'Cinderella', *The Jungle Book.* Films and songs for children can literally be counted on one's fingertips (and what is there is preachy and aimed at educating children to be better human beings, reminding one of what author Beverly Cleary said: 'As a child, I disliked books in which children learned to be better children').

The one exception in this arid landscape, someone who has ploughed a lonely furrow in this genre is Gulzar. Time and again he has created a magical world for children, through his films, songs and other non-film writing. A world that children can relate to, that does not talk down to them, that makes them laugh and look at the world with the wonder of their imagination. In this he has found willing collaborators like R.D. Burman and Vishal Bhardwaj, who share his vision and almost childlike glee and innocence in crafting these young worlds.

'I feel it is important for a writer to observe children, love them and indulge them,' Gulzar says. 'Only then can you write about or for children. The books we have for children are not suitable for them. They tend to be preachy. That is the greatness of Sukumar Ray and his *Abol Tabol*. In India there are only three languages at this stage which has worthwhile writers for children – Bangla, Marathi and Malayalam. There are no good original writers for children in Urdu, Hindi or Punjabi. You have the same translations of the Mahabharata and the Ramayana. But there is hardly any contemporary writing. And few filmmakers in Hindi cinema get the world of children right.'

'*Humko mann ki shakti dena*', *Guddi* (1971): A film song that became a school hymn across the country, this is typical of what Gulzar brings to the table. For one, it is a prayer song that dispenses with a god entity altogether. Instead, it calls for developing confidence in one's own self ('*khud pe hausla rahein*') and contemplation – the line '*Doosron ki jai se pahle khud ko jai karein*' is a mantra that we could all adhere to. And much before 'inclusiveness' and 'tolerance' became such maligned buzzwords, the song spoke of these virtues simply and eloquently. What makes the song resonate is the impish humour that marks it filming. As Gulzar says, 'It's a prayer song, so the words could not be frivolous. Hrishi-da (Hrishikesh Mukherjee), however, had a great sense of humour, and you see it in the way it is shot.' Apparent in the expressions the children – including Guddi (Jaya Bachchan), who is as usual late to the assembly – make, so typical of children who are often bored with these assembly routines. And given that Guddi is a die-hard Dharmendra fan, the line '*Saath de to dharam ka, chale toh dharam par*' is Gulzar at his meta-best.

'*Sa re ke sa re ga ma ko le kar*', *Parichay* (1972): A shining example of the poet's mastery over the medium, this is Gulzar giving us the seven notes of music in words, with everyday motifs – Sa (savera, morning), Re (reshmi kirnein), Dha (dhoop). But there are also aspects of the story playing in this song. Consider, for example: '*Papa nahin hain dhaani si didi, didi ke saath hain saare.*' Those who know their music will latch on to 'pa', 'dha' and 'ni' as part of the seven notes. But the line also implies that the children here don't have a father (*papa nahin hain*), and it is their 'dhaani si' sister who is with them. The word 'dhaani' is open to interpretation here. It could refer to the light-green sari Jaya Bachchan is wearing in the first part of the song. It could also mean, a very Bengali connotation, someone of a short stature (Jaya Bachchan), and/or, given her character's snappy attitude towards the new teacher in the early parts of the film, short-tempered. R.D. Burman's innate understanding of music that will appeal to children enhances the overall experience of the song.

'*Masterji ki aa gayi chitthi*', *Kitaab* (1977): Based on a story by Samaresh Basu, this is a rare Hindi film for children and adolescents that speaks to them in their language, without condescension. Nothing epitomizes this better than this almost anthemic song. No child growing up in the 1980s will ever forget the refrain 'VIP underwear banyan' – so typical of what children pick up from the world around them. Gulzar says, 'Have you ever seen a class when the teacher is absent? That's what I have tried to replicate here.

And thanks to Pancham's (R.D. Burman) genius, using desks to get the rhythm the children create, it comes alive. Pancham's sense of humour and his understanding of a child's world were amazing. He was a child at heart and that shows in his compositions for children with me.'

A great admirer of Sukumar Ray and his nonsense verses, Gulzar's words in this song are classic examples of this genre, with cats eating *zarda-paan*, mosquitoes with moustaches, and blushing cheetahs in *ghunghats*, all emerging from a letter. Then there's the delightful play of words between *agar-batti* and *magar-batti*, which segues into another inspired line: '*Agarbatti kachhua chap, aag pe baitha paani taap*'. Or '*English bolay matlab Hindi / If agar is hain but par what matlab kya / English mein algebra chhan*'. Just read that line closely: if (agar), is (hain), but (par), what (kya), and you get an inkling of the writer's understanding of a child's psyche. All of this made delightful with the musical refrain 'dhin-taka-taka-dhin' and the reference to the ad, 'VIP underwear banyan'.

'*Lakdi ki kaathi*', *Masoom* (1983): A perennial classic which takes off from a child's earliest plaything, a wooden horse. 'Children going *tak-bak-tak-bak, chal meray ghorey, chal chal chal* is something all of us have seen. When they do that, they actually imagine a horse but at the same time they know that it is not real. They are aware of that. Every child plays a role of a doctor and a teacher in some point of their life,' says Gulzar.

'*Lakdi ki kaathi*' is a triumphant amalgamation of nonsense verse with imaginative wordplay. 'You must remember that children have a vivid imagination, an infinite capacity to create their own language, and as a writer you have to take that into account,' says Gulzar. 'You have to give them images they can relate to, that are fun to imagine. You can see a child reacting to "*ghore ki dum pe jo maara hat*hora".'

That is what this song does with words like '*Ghoda pahuncha chowk mein, chowk mein tha naayi, ghode ji ki naayi ne hazamat jo banayi*'. Try translating that for meaning. But when you enter a child's mind-space, it makes complete sense. There's also Gulzar drawing upon his memories of Delhi with '*Ghoda tha ghamandi, pahuncha Sabzi Mandi*' and '*Chalta hai Mehrauli mein, ghoda apna Arbi hain*'. However, the references are not just a lyricist's whimsy. They flow organically from the screenplay, the fact that the film is set in Delhi.

The Vishal Bhardwaj Collaborations

If there's been one partnership after Gulzar–R.D. Burman that has yielded a treasure trove of content for children, it is the one between Gulzar and Vishal Bhardwaj. Interestingly enough, a majority of these originated in the television space, in what are Hindi dubbed versions of English and other-language series that aired on Doordarshan.

Vishal says, 'Gulzar Sa'ab was part of a creative committee at the Children's Film Society when Jaya Bachchan was chairperson. The CFS was importing a lot of content at the time. I had very little work in films, and there were no options other than Doordarshan. We used to sit down every fortnight to record a song. It was quite an enjoyable experience. The visuals were given. We had to create around that. They could not be re-edited. We could only redub. I used to watch the visuals, muting the sound, latched on to the tempo and put it on the metronome. It was a challenge to create an original song in the same tempo for existing visuals.'

These TV gigs include the alliterative '*Tap tap topi topi*' with phrases like '*ulat-palat galat-salat taain*' and '*ghugli jhinak jhaain*' in *Alice in Wonderland* (Vishal would use the refrain again in the song '*Tippa*' in *Rangoon*). Or the title song of *Sindbad Jahaazi*, '*Agar magar doley naiyya*', the title song of *Guchhe* ('*Kahani le lo*') and the cute dinosaur in *Dana Danasur*, recreated from *Denver: The Last Dinosaur*, with Gulzar giving the dinosaur a lovable spin of his own as 'Danasur', '*chhipkali ka naana, chhipkali ka sasur*', likening its shape to musical instruments, a tanpura and a manjira.

Vishal agrees with Gulzar-ji, that 'as a society we are insensitive towards our kids. The programmes telecast on television are usually dubbed from foreign languages. We don't make original content. It's a sad state of affairs. Only a handful of people, like Gulzar Sa'ab, devote themselves to creating for children. He has kept the child in him alive. It is such a beautiful thing. He is so evolved and at the same time so young at heart. It is remarkable how the three dimensions – the past, present and future – run parallel in him. He speaks in their language.'

'*Jungle jungle baat chali hain*' (*The Jungle Book*): Among the first of the Gulzar–Vishal collaborations, this is also probably the most enduring of them all when it comes to their work for children. Only Gulzar could have conjured up the 'chaddi' in a song and make it so evocative. He confides that officials in the Children Film Society had some issues with the word in a song for children and suggested he replace it with something like a lungi till Jaya Bhaduri put her put down. Thirty years later, the very idea of a lungi seems preposterous. 'The song also became part of the Republic Day parade in some state, Madhya Pradesh, if I am not mistaken,' says Vishal. 'Even now, I keep coming across people in their forties who say how much the song was part of their childhood.'

He continues, 'Somebody else was supposed to do the song. But the composer did not have the time. The song had to be recorded in two days. I had worked with Gulzar Sa'ab on the TV series *Daane Anaar Ke* (the title track '*Kissa hai kahani hai paheli hai*'). There were no mobile phone those days. I had an arrangement with a STD communication centre which would keep a log of any calls that came for me. I checked with him three-four times a day. One day, he told me that there was a call from Gulzar Sa'ab. I still remember the number – 6461500. I called him and he asked me over to his house. There was a song that we had to work on and record the day-after. I went over. He asked me play him a tune. I had composed almost all his poems in a book. One poem had the words "Gussa gussa gussa" – he had personified anger in it.

There was another that personified sorrow. I hummed the one I had composed for "Gussa". And he loved it. In thirty minutes we had cracked "*Chaddi pehen ke*".' The rest is history.

The funniest story to emerge from the song also comes from Vishal. And it has to do with poet Bashir Badr narrating how he had come across the RSS playing the song at one of its shakha parades. Somebody had obviously mistaken the chaddi and the flower for the organization's khakee shorts and the lotus, respectively, and appropriated the song!

'*O papa*', (*Billu Aur Pillu*): This was the Hindi version of *Tom and Jerry*, not the TV series, but *Tom and Jerry: The Film*, directed by Phil Roman, the first theatrical feature-length animated film starring the cat-and-mouse pair, who were given dialogues and songs. The story traces the adventures of an eight-year-old girl who is looking for her father. Pavan Jha, a veritable encyclopaedia on Gulzar who also hosts a dedicated website on the poet, says, 'The film had songs like "*Ek sikandar pahle tha*", "*Hum to pakke gubday hain*" and the title song "*Bil bil billu ki pillu se ladaai*".' But the one that both Vishal and Gulzar bring my attention to is '*O Papa*'. Vishal says, 'Normally, children's songs tend to have a maternal connect. But here the situation provided Gulzar Sa'ab the opportunity to come up with a heartfelt song that speaks about a daughter missing her father.' The imagery is vintage Gulzar:

O papa, tum pukaro
Main tumhare paas hoon
Papa, aaj main bahot udaas hoon

Papa, hum rainbow pe jhumenge
Papa, aaj hum chand choomenge

O Daddy, tum pukaro
Main tumhare paas hoon
Daddy, aaj main bahot udaas hoon

Baarishon mein Papa yaad aate hain
Bijliya dikhate hain, darate hain
Papa, tum badey kharab ho

Laal book mein aapki hidayate
Neeli copy mein meri shikayate
Papa, aao ab hisaab do

'*Panga*' and '*Chhutii*' (*Makdee*, 2002): For his debut directorial venture – something that too came about following Gulzar's advice that if he wanted to make his kind of music in the industry, he had to make his kind of films – Vishal chose a film for children. Gulzar wrote the songs. In '*Panga*', he nails the world of the feisty young protagonist with words that others may not even imagine in a song for children: '*O paapad wale, panga na le / thappad bajega / Ungli daba ke angutha bana dungi / chakle pe belu toh papad bana doongi*'. There are also philosophical insights to life coming from a character who lives by her wits and knows he way around: '*asli bhi, nakli bhi, farzi bhi / thenga se, malik hu marzi ki / thode shi shidhi, thodi si ghunni…*'

Like R.D. Burman, Vishal too brings his own sensibilities to his compositions for children. Gulzar says, 'If in "*Lakdi ki kaathi*", the phrase "tak-bak tak-bak" is quintessentially Pancham and his Bangla roots, with Vishal, it is the same. Look at how he incorporates "taun taun" in "*Panga*". It comes from his lived experience.'

Vishal laughs at the memory. 'One thing I have realized working with Gulzar Sa'ab is that, apart from keeping your inner child alive, for something to work for children there has to be something out-of-the-box compositionally too, some hook, something almost nonsensical, for want of a better word. The "taun-taun" that Gulzar Sa'ab mentions is something I created from my memory – how as kids we would tease our friends using that phrase. And he caught on to that and led from it. Similarly, for "*Chhutti*", you might remember wedding bands playing a certain tune (*hums the tune*) – I hummed it to him with the phrase "*Kisi pipdi mein kela bandmaster*". It was very catchy and it became the refrain around which he draped the words "*Hain kitabon se kutti, chhuti hain*". You have to find the connect with children. It is not something you can design, it comes spontaneously.'

This idiosyncratic element is apparent in the way *Makdee* is shot and the children are portrayed. It led Vishal to part ways with the Children's Film Society which was initially supposed to produce the film. Refusing to spoon-feed children like most films of the Society do, he decided to produce the film himself, becoming only the second composer in the industry after Salil Chowdhury to produce films. 'I refuse to treats kids like idiots. In *Makdee*, children are treated as mature people,' he said in an interview at the time of the film's release. No wonder that in Gulzar he found his soulmate.

The other song in the film, '*Chhutti*', celebrates the joy of a holiday, throwing away books, and a school-going child's perennial wish for a day off. Gulzar's words capture the world of a child finding any reason to stay away from school. Note how he brings the entire week into the child's ambit, culminating with the impish line '*Monday ko Sunday ki chhutti hai*':

'*Asmani chhatri*' and '*Tesoo*' (*The Blue Umbrella*, 2005): Vishal returned to the genre and the world of children with his adaptation of Ruskin Bond's story. '*Asmani chhatri*' is a child's loving ode to her beautiful blue umbrella – notice how ingeniously Gulzar describes it: '*ambar ka tukda toda, lakdi ka hatta joda, haath mein apna asmaan hai*, slicing off a piece of the sky, sticking a wedge of wood to it, carrying a fragment of the heaven in her hand, likening the umbrella to a *udan khatola*, its swaying in the breeze to a *hindola*, a swing. Speaking to me, Gulzar underlines the word 'hatta': 'It is a very culture-specific word. A lathi or danda would not do here.' Close your eyes and listen to the words. You can't help marvel at the personification of an umbrella. Vishal's compositional acumen – the refrain 'kukuri kukiri ku' –adds to the song's hummability quotient.

In the film's other song, '*Tesoo*', the poet and the composer bring to life a childhood memory, providing, in the words of Pavan Jha, a bridge between the old and the new. The Tesoo-Jhanjhi legend from the Mahabharata is popular in parts of north India, particularly the region stretching from Braj to Bundelkhand. Not so long ago, during the five-day period leading from Dussehra to Sharad Purnima, children went around collecting donations with a Tesoo-Jhanjhi effigy, singing the lines: '*Tesoo agar kare, Tesoo magar kare, Tesoo leke hi tarey, Tesoo mera yahin khada, mange rahi hain dahi vadaa / dahi badey mein banni, laao seth athanni.*'

Gulzar and Vishal introduce the ritual to a new generation, taking off from the words traditionally used during the festivities: '*Mera Tesoo yahin ada, khane ko maange dahi vada.*' And in a fashion we have come to expect of Gulzar, he goes on to create a string of surreal images, reminiscent of Sukumar Ray: '*Mendhak bole khari khari, naayi ki muchhe hari hari, gaay ki puchh pe dhaan uga, gaay ne kisi ki muchh chari, abhi muchh badi ki naayi bada*'. Again, try to translate this for sense. But seen through the eyes of a child, the imagery is irresistible.

The Lost Gems – '*Ek dafa ek jungle mein*' (*Sadma*, 1983); '*Dum kata*' (*Dum Kata*, 2007); '*Asmaan ke paar*' (*Rockford*, 1999): His many creations for children in films include the Kamal Haasan-Ilayaraja song '*Ek dafa ek jungle mein*' from *Sadma*, where the actor is narrating the tale of the blue jackal to a childlike Sridevi. As the words unfold, you can almost imagine the presence of a master raconteur sitting by a fireside, mesmerizing children with his stories.

Of a different hue is the song from *Rockford*, whose words highlight another aspect of writing for children that Gulzar articulates. 'Their language evolves with age, till they become adults. When you write for a five-year-old, the language is different from when you write for a nine-year-old.' And in '*Asmaan ke paar*',

Gulzar evokes the twilight zone of the teenage years, with their uncertainties, their hopes, with the world beyond the heavens calling out to them.

A special mention needs to be made of the song 'Dum kata' from the eponymous children's film, directed by Amol Palekar. The film was a major box-office disaster, which buried in its wake a gem by Gulzar, a song that is a personal favourite with him too. As he says, 'There is no aspect of a tail that I have not addressed in the song.' This is Gulzar at his whackiest, eulogizing a variety of tails:

Patang udey toh patang ke pichhe
Lambi latke poonch
Cycle par mushkil hai bhaiyya
Chain mein atke poonch

Gori Aishwarya ke sar pe
Chunri laage poonch...

Shero jaise chalna, oonchi karke poonch
Mome laga ke rakhna, seedhi karke poonch...

Itrati hain dekh gilhari
Gole ghumake poonch ko
Pahalwan ungli se jaise
Bal deta hain moonch ko...

This is only a small sample of Gulzar's work for children. There's a whole world of his books – written for his daughter, Meghna, his grandson Samay, translations of Tagore's poetry for children, translations of world and Indian classics like Pinocchio, Aladdin, Alibaba and Goopy Gyne Bagha Byne, his work for the special children's NGO Arushi and many others. But these deserve a separate feature of their own, vast as they are.

There's one test that any writing for children has to pass. 'Apart from the fact that it is important for a child to be able to relate to it, it is paramount that writing for kids must appeal to adults as well. That has to happen. It is only then that a child will relate to it,' says Gulzar. Needless to say, the works of India's very own Peter Pan hold up to this, appealing to the entire spectrum from age four to eighty and more.[1]

What is Tariq's character's name in the 1973 super-hit *Yaadon Ki Baaraat*?

Answer: Monty

The Asha Bhosle solo, '*Gum sum kyun ho sanam*' (*Bhala Manus*, 1979) composed by R.D. Burman has the unique distinction of appearing in the long play record of one movie but used in another. Identify the movie it was recorded for.

Answer: *Kasme Vaade* (1978)

[1] I would like to thank Anupama Chopra of *Film Companion*, where the introductory part of this essay first appeared, and Sumit Dasgupta for permission to reproduce parts of the essay from a fourt-part series of essays that were published in The *Telegraph*.

Raakhee

Beauty Unparalleled, Actor Nonpareil

Shantanu Ray Chaudhuri

In the almost schizophrenic world that was Hindi cinema of the seventies, Raakhee occupied a special place. A major star who was cast opposite all the mega heroes of the era, she was unique in many ways. There were Shabana Azmi and Smita Patil at one end of the spectrum. At the other end we had Hema Malini, Zeenat Aman and Parveen Babi. Firmly ensconced in the centre was Jaya Bhaduri (supported by directors like Hrishikesh Mukherjee and Gulzar who gave her author-backed roles). Raakhee made it big commercially despite neither being an arthouse favourite like Shabana Azmi nor possessing the Western chutzpah of Zeenat Aman (in fact, for a leading mainstream heroine of the era, Raakhee came across as distinctly gauche in the couple of sequences that come to mind in *Muqaddar Ka Sikandar* and *Kasme Vaade* in which she sported a Western outfit). For that matter she wasn't as nimble on her feet like Hema Malini (she never played a dancer) neither did she have big directors backing her like they did Jaya Bhaduri at the beginning of her career.

The Early Years

Raakhee gave early glimpses of her abilities in small but significant roles in *Reshma Aur Shera* and *Lal Pathar*, while delivering a knockout of a performance with two distinctly different characters in only her second film, *Sharmilee* – all in 1971. In *Reshma Aur Shera*, the sequence where she learns of the death of her husband is remarkable for what she brings to it so early in her career. A Filmfare nomination for *Ankhon Ankhon Mein* (1972), she is delightful in the 'come hither' song '*Ankhon ankhon mein baat honay do*' and a Best Supporting Actress win in *Daag* (1973), setting up a classic clash with Sharmila Tagore, followed by a National Award Special Souvenir for *27 Down*, all within three years of her debut in *Jeevan Mrityu*, provided a portent of things to come.

27 Down (1974)

Ramesh Bakshi's Hindi novel *Athara Sooraj Ke Paudhe* becomes Awtar Kaul's heartfelt existential meditation, and remains, even fifty years later, as striking a film as it was pioneering in 1974. Though A.K. Bir's handheld cinematography and the film's overall aesthetics, including its background score, are justly celebrated, Raakhee's nuanced take on an independent working woman who has more steel in her than the film's flawed protagonist – truly a break from the synthetic women in films of the era – deserves special mention. In a year that gave us two more memorable women characters in Hindi cinema who continue to be discussed – Lakshmi (Shabana Azmi, *Ankur*) and Deepa (Vidya Sinha, *Rajnigandha*) – Raakhee's Shalini in *27 Down* cries out to be rediscovered.

Women of Substance: *Tapasya* (1976), *Doosra Aadmi* (1977), *Baseraa* (1981)

It didn't get bigger than Yash Chopra for a Hindi film heroine of the era, and *Kabhi Kabhie* in 1976 cemented Raakhee's place in the industry. That she lost out on the Filmfare Best Actress award for *Kabhi Kabhie* speaks volumes of her performance in Anil Ganguly's tearjerker *Tapasya*, based on Ashapurna Devi's story. What sets Indrani Sinha apart from the many martyred women of Hindi cinema of the time is the amazing restraint and conviction she brings to her character and the risk she takes in essaying a mature, middle-aged woman so early in her career.

With *Doosra Aadmi*, Raakhee takes her penchant for experimentation even further. She plays Nisha, an executive in an ad agency, who falls in love with a married younger man who reminds her of her deceased lover. It was by every reckoning a gamble in an industry that put a premium on chaste heroines in sanctified relationships, and Raakhee makes it special.

In *Baseraa*, Raakhee, by now a bona fide star of major blockbusters, returns to the all-sacrificing mode of *Tapasya*. In one of her most acclaimed roles, she plays a woman returning to her family after being confined to a mental asylum for fourteen years. The plausibility or otherwise of the narrative becomes inconsequential in the face of her superb portrayal that puts to the shade even an actor like Rekha, then at the top of her game. This is, probably, the only film where the actress lip-synced to a song penned by her husband, Gulzar: the sublime '*Jahan pe savera ho*'.

Making it Count with Amitabh Bachchan

While Amitabh Bachchan's onscreen partnerships with Rekha, Zeenat Aman, Jaya Bhaduri, and even Parveen Babi are discussed quite often, the actor he co-starred with in the maximum number of films does not quite figure in conversations. Raakhee and Amitabh Bachchan acted together in as many as thirteen films. Even if one were to discount three – *Reshma Aur Shera*, *Shaan* and *Shakti* – in which they weren't cast opposite each other, that still leaves her with more films as Bachchan's leading lady than any other.

But more than the numbers, what is important is that she was a Bachchan heroine like no other. There was a gravitas about her in these films that few Bachchan heroines possessed. One reason for this might be that Bachchan was never cast as a lumpen element opposite her – barring *Kasme Vaade* (1978, in which too the ruffian was offset by the professor; interestingly enough it is Rekha who executes a mujra here) and *Muqaddar Ka Sikandar* (1978, where the Bachchan character though born low rises in life).

Kabhi Kabhie is probably her most discussed work with Bachchan. However, I have never been a fan of the film's schmaltzy tone, though there is no doubt that Raakhee is a vision and backs it with a strong performance. It is in films like *Trishul* (1978) and *Kaala Pathhar* (1979) that she offers a strong and mature counterpoint to Bachchan's overpowering presence, not to mention what she brings to offbeat films like *Jurmana* (1979) and as Bachchan's 'sakhi' in *Bemisaal* (1982). She was the woman the Bachchan hero could never be frivolous with. The dignity she brought to these characters set her apart from a lot of other heroines paired opposite the megastar.

Remarkably unmindful of being typecast and relegated to character roles, even while she was playing the lover/heroine opposite him in *Bemisaal* and *Anusandhan* (1981), she was essaying his elderly bhabhi in *Shaan* (1980), and more remarkably, his mother in a dynamic performance in *Shakti* (1982) with as much elegance. She was all of thirty-five at the time!

The New Bollywood Mother

Unfortunately for Hindi cinema, Raakhee moved to elderly roles early. Possibly because she realized there was little of substance on offer as the lead. She took to these as a fish to water, giving life to some legendary screen mothers. In *Shakti*, which must rank among her finest, she not only held her own against two legends, but was also instrumental in giving the film much of its emotional heft, devoid of which it would have remained a mere re-tread of countless other Hindi films. It speaks volumes of the conviction she brings to the role that she is as credible as

Bachchan's mother here as she was as his lover in other films at the time.

Ram Lakhan (1989) and *Karan Arjun* (1995) established her avatar as Mother Bollywood. Decades after she lip-synced to '*Meray do anmol ratan*' and uttered the iconic words '*Aayenge, meray Karan Arjun aayenge*', they remain the inspiration for countless memes. She brought a rare fire to her characters in these films, as also in *Baazigar* and *Anari*, unleashing a version of the Hindi film mother unique to her: a wronged woman who suffers unspeakable humiliation at the hands of the antagonists.

Sharda in *Ram Lakhan* is branded a thief, dragged by her hair and thrown out of her haveli, before her husband is killed in front of her. His blood spattered on her face and clothes as she cremates her, before donning black and swearing vengeance constitute the film's most dramatic moments. *Karan Arjun* revisits a similar fate on her as she watches her sons being butchered and waits for them to be reincarnated and avenge her. As she had prophesied in the presence of Goddess Kali with the much imitated reference to '*Karan Arjun aayenge*' which is now part of our pop culture.

Rahul Rawail's *Dacait* (1987) is the most disturbing of these roles. In an unsettling sequence of great impact, one of the most disquieting in mainstream Hindi cinema ever shot, her hair is cut off and she is forced to dance to the beats of a dhol. She goes insane and the way the film-maker uses this horror in subsequent sequences that feature her makes them almost unbearable to sit through. Her vacant eyes and uncomprehending demeanour tellingly convey the casual violence that women are subjected to by men as a means of exerting control.

The Bengali Outings: *Paroma* (1984) and *Shubho Mahurat* (2003)

Ironically for someone who started out in Bengali cinema, Raakhee made a splash in her native language only late in her career.

Chameli Memsaheb, the 1977 Bengali version of the Assamese classic, was an unfortunate misfire, while Shakti Samanta's 1981 smasher *Anusandhan* was more a gimmicky bilingual that rode on the novelty of being Bachchan's first appearance in a Bengali film.

She could not have chosen a better vehicle than Aparna Sen's *Paroma*: a powerhouse performance in what is probably her most sensual role in a film that challenged gender stereotypes and broke new ground in the way it portrayed feminine desire through a tempestuous extramarital affair that liberates the woman even as her steady and humdrum family life unravels. Witness her, soaked in torrential rain, with her lover, tossing her high-heeled sandals away – Raakhee has never been this ravishing.

Nineteen years after *Paroma* scandalized the middle-class, Raakhee returned virtually unrecognizable from the beauty of her halcyon days as the matronly, paan-chewing, film-gossip-loving spinster, Ranga pishima, an impish version of Agatha Christie's Miss Marple, in Rituparno Ghosh's *Shubho Mahurat*. Her effortless performance as she solves a murder without stepping out of home won her a National Award for best supporting actress. A particular attraction here is her delightful relationship with her niece, Mili (Nandita Das), who plays a journalist for a local magazine covering the film muhurat at which the murder takes place. This remains her last film appearance in twenty years.[1]

Vijay Anand plays a debauched landlord, Thakur Rajnath Singh Chauhan, in this acclaimed 1978 movie, also starring Deb Mukherjee among others. Identify the film.

Answer: *Main Tulsi Tere Aangan Ki*

[1] I would like to thank Sumit Dasgupta for permission to reproduce this essay which was first published in *The Telegraph* on 15 August 2023.

The Girl Next Door and Other Divas

Women in Hindi Cinema of the Seventies

Ratnottama Sengupta

Jaya Bhaduri was a schoolgirl when she breezed into the life of cinegoers – especially in Bengal – as Bani in *Mahanagar* (1963). On her first day on the sets of the film that won Satyajit Ray the top honours at Berlin, all he asked her to do was to keep wearing the specs she normally wore while reading. She had no dialogue. So, with no burden to 'act', she only had to be her usual chirpy self, comfortable in her skin, not daunted by the world. Instead she was free to interpret a scene and react to the emotion of the other characters. The entire unit indulged her like a little girl. It was like being out on a picnic!

Little did the petite girl with long dark tresses and trusting eyes, then studying in a conservative convent in Bhopal, know that this 'girl next door' identity would become her calling card in the years ahead, storming even the boulevards of tinsel-town.

Her Characters

The image was concretized with *Guddi* (1971). Hrishikesh Mukherjee gave Jaya Bhaduri a full canvas to emerge as an actor as the same bubbly girl matures into a woman who can differentiate between love and infatuation. An effervescent schoolgirl with a crush on the macho superstar Dharmendra, she epitomized what every teenaged girl felt in the years when Indira Gandhi was gearing up to show her gritty face to the world that was yet to mark a day annually for women. This was also the spirit of two other films which released that very year: Sudhendu Roy's *Uphaar* and Arabinda Mukherjee's Bengali laugh riot *Dhanni Meye*. One was based on Tagore's story '*Samapti*', tackled by Ray in *Teen Kanya*; the other had Uttam Kumar as a football fanatic. Both mapped the emotional graph of a free-spirited girl who evolves into a loving, responsible wife.

In two other Hrishikesh films, Jaya Bhaduri is a vivacious, friendly lass, spreading happiness wherever she goes. In *Bawarchi* (1972) she knits together a dysfunctional family that is reformed by an angelic 'cook'. In *Mili* (1975) she transforms an alcoholic misanthrope with her vivacity and ebullience. Before that, she had acted in Basu Chatterjee's *Piya Ka Ghar* (1972) which portrayed the predicament of newly-weds in Bombay's chawls, long before bank loans for 1-BHK started coming into phones every day. On one hand was the need for privacy; on the other was the bonding between members of a joint family that was the norm then. That same year came Gulzar's *Parichay* (1972) where a quiet young girl nurses bitterness against her guardian and affection for her orphaned siblings, offering Jaya the scope to traverse a gamut of emotions.

Then successively the screen glowed with her triumphant forays in *Koshish* (1972), *Abhimaan* (1973), *Kora Kagaz* (1974), *Sholay* (1975). These 'slice-of-life' storylines (other than the blockbuster *Sholay* in which she played a young widow) had her coming to terms with marital life and all its complications. *Koshish* gave viewers an empathetic insight into the hardships of the hearing impaired. *Abhimaan* tackled the delicate issue of ego marring happiness when wives outdo husbands professionally, while *Kora Kagaz* spotlighted the problem of ruptured marriage when the wife's class-afflicted mother keeps interfering. *Sholay* had the animated girl turn into stone following the tragic death of her husband.

Through all this, the girl next door grew up – and grew bigger than the 70mm screen. Club these roles to see why this unlikely 'heroine' of the silver screen became the rage of the 1970s and a role model for an entire generation of actors who would follow. Indeed, she proved the most influential leading lady of the decade, impacting young girls (simply watch her in the musical hit *Jawani Diwani*, a far cry from her other heavy-duty roles) as much as Hindi cinema through the decade. Because? Had she not played an insignificant *chakku chhuriyaan tez karaalo* girl, *Zanjeer* (1973) would not have taken off, and we would not have a certain tall, dark and brooding presence striding screens – big, small, Bollywood, Hollywood – for half a century and more.

It wasn't as if the suave actor did not have the breadth to laugh at human follies. *Chupke Chupke* (1975), for example: this lighthearted dig at obsession centred on a botany professor disguised as a chauffeur built upon mistaken identities to unleash laughter whenever it is screened. It opened the genre of comic roles for both Dharmendra and Amitabh. In particular, the so-far angry and brooding young man – the image reinforced by his tragic end in *Deewaar* and *Sholay* – would go on to patent the comic interludes that turned potboilers like *Coolie* (1983), *Shahenshah* (1986), *Bade Miyan Chote Miyan* (1998) into super hits. But Jaya, now Bachchan, seasoned in handling fractured marriage so well that *Silsila* (1981) had her facing, fighting, coming out unscathed by infidelity – rumours of which were shadowing the Bachchans.

Before long the girl was to grow into serious motherhood. *Hazaar Chaurasi Ki Maa* (1998) was a natural, character-driven protagonist: the mother of a Naxalite resting in a morgue, finally gets to know the stranger who came of her womb but had turned into a 'dangerous' rebel. Even in *Kabhi Khushi Kabhie Gham* (2001) where Gen X actresses like Kajol and Kareena Kapoor claim the screen, she steals the show as the submissive mother who asserts to her arrogant patriarchal husband, 'You were right on many counts but wrong when you separated a mother from a son.' In her latest outing, *Rocky Aur Rani Ki Prem Kahani* (2023), she does not hesitate to be that ogre, a domineering mother-in-law who doesn't want any other woman in her household to be empowered.

Koshish had helped Jaya understand the physically challenged, and she started working for the rehabilitation of the handicapped, training children, extending support, giving scholarships. Those were the first steps towards becoming a Big Girl, now known as 'Jaya Di'. For ten years she headed the Children's Film Society, where she got professionals to make films for young adults. When she became bigger than the organization, she stepped into Parliament.

Professional dignity came naturally to the instinctive actor trained in other methods of expressing emotion at the Film and Television Institute of India (1966–70). Initially the no *nakhra*, no mannerism, no melodrama performances were relegated to 'character' roles. Probably no one believed that a heroine could look and live like her screen self once she stepped out of the sets. Jaya Bhaduri was never over-the-top. Never dazzled with jewellery. Never seen in skimpy clothes or with tons of melting paint on her face. And she was never predictable. If she was Sanjeev Kumar's wife in *Koshish*, she was his daughter in *Parichay*, and daughter-in-law in *Sholay*. In Rituparno Ghosh's *Sunglass* (2013) she even played a psychiatrist with aplomb.

Age sits well on her, because she did not live a camouflaged life behind dark glasses. Nothing to hide. Almost every major photo-op has seen her in a sari: cotton, silk, chiffon, beige, white, ivory. She married, had two children, devoted herself to home and husband. She nursed him when he was fighting for every breath in Jaslok Hospital following that nasty accident on the sets of *Coolie*. She campaigned for him in Allahabad when he stood for the 1984 elections. And she stood by him when he was accused in the Bofors bribery scandal. She pulled no punches when she took on the powers that be. She struck out on her own, in public life, in heading offices, and finally in Rajya Sabha. Nowhere did she mince words, she spoke with confidence everywhere. A picture of determination, always.

Before Her: The Divas

Before Jaya came on the screen, there were a host of much admired, loved, even adored leading ladies. Many of those who set the screen afire in the 1960s continued to rule over their fan base in the next decade. Sharmila Tagore, another favourite find of Satyajit Ray, had gone from success to success with *Kashmir ki Kali* (1963), *Waqt* (1964), *Anupama* (1966), *An Evening in Paris* (1967), *Aradhana* (1969), *Safar* (1970), *Amar Prem* (1972), *Daag* (1973), *Avishkar* (1974), *Mausam* (1975), *Chupke Chupke* (1975), *Anand Ashram* (1977), *Griha Pravesh* (1979). Alongside, after her debut in Satyajit Ray's *Apur Sansar* (1959), she continued to rivet in the maestro's *Devi* (1960), *Nayak* (1966), *Aranyer Din Ratri* (1970) and *Seemabaddha* (1971).

Her swimsuit, pretty bold for those times, made people sit up. Her bouffant became her signature perhaps because she was conscious of her short height, especially when she was teamed with Shammi Kapoor or Dharmendra. Her eloquent eyes, her pronounced dimples, her *alhad* intonation of Hindi, claimed more than one Tiger-heart. Her interreligious marriage raised storms in teacups. Her popularity did not decline with motherhood but her shift to Delhi did reflect in reduced releases. However, the intermittent releases raised her stock as an actor.

Arthouse, crossover, mainstream – nothing was outside her ken. She even rose to be an acclaimed chairperson of the Central Board of Film Certification for the long, successful stretch from October 2004 to March 2011. As the years rolled on, advertisements needed her evermore. Her son, her daughter-in-law, her daughters – they all shine in her glory. If in her younger days she was a 'sex symbol', she oozes grace and exudes elegance with advanced years. Add to that her illustrious families; not one or two but three; counting the Tagore name, the Baruas of Assam, and the Begums of Bhopal.

Easy to see why the lofty Padma Bhushan, the French Order of the Arts and Letters, the Cannes Jury, the UNICEF Goodwill Ambassador, the honorary doctorate of Edinburgh University, the National Awards and Lifetime Achievements sit so pretty on her shoulders.

Mumtaz had debuted a year before Sharmila Tagore with *Sone Ki Chidiya* (1958). Coming from the disadvantaged background of a broken family, her father having abandoned them after her birth, in her preteens she played 'sidies', progressing to lead roles only in wrestler Dara Singh's films because of her height. Those films proved so successful that she did sixteen of them, including *Faulad* (1963), *Sikander-e-Azam* (1965), *Tarzan Comes to Delhi* (1965), *Daku Mangal Singh* (1966). But in these very roles she caught the fancy of filmgoers. 'To watch Mumtaz we'd go for repeat viewing of these movies,' celebrated painter-film-maker M.F. Husain once told me.

This feisty actor escaped her stunt film roots once she was cast against Dilip Kumar (*Ram Aur Shyam*, 1967), Dharmendra (*Mere Humdum Mere Dost*, 1968), and Shammi Kapoor (*Brahmachari*, 1968). With *Do Raaste* (1969) she came into her own as a diva. The popularity of Mumtaz–Rajesh Khanna pair proved second only to Rajesh-Sharmila's. *Bandhan* (1969), *Aadmi Aur Insaan* (1970), *Saccha Jhootha* (1970) – alongside these came *Khilona* (1970) where she paired with Sanjeev Kumar. Dev Anand cast her in *Tere Mere Sapne* (1971) and again in *Hare Rama Hare Krishna*. *Loafer* (1973) and *Jheel Ke Uss Paar* (1973) pitted her against the most sought-after Dharmendra. Even as she was garnering accolades for serious characterization in *Aap Ki Kasam* (1974), *Prem Kahani* (1975), and *Aaina*, in 1977, the year her last film released, the yet-to-be thirty Mumtaz bid goodbye to stardom and married a businessman from Uganda. She tried to make a comeback in Pahlaj Nihalani's *Andhiyan* with Shatrughan Sinha in 1990, but critics panned it, cruelly labelling the film 'Buddhiyan'.

Tanuja started as a child actor in *Hamari Beti* (1950). She peaked in the 1960s with *Bhoot Bangla* (1965), *Baharein Phir Bhi Aayegi* (1966), *Jewel Thief* (1967), *Izzat* (1968), *Jeene Ki Raah* and *Paisa Ya Pyar* (1969). Dev Anand, Dharmendra and Jeetendra gave way to Rajesh Khanna, the rage at the onset of 1970s, and *Haathi Mere Saathi* (1971) was a bigger hit than her previous ones. Loved for her flair for comedy, her appearances thinned but she kept growing with *Door Ka Rahi* (1971), *Anubhav* (1971), *Do Chor* (1972), *Yaarana* (1981) and *Masoom* (1983).

By now she was also a major presence in Bengal. Cast with Uttam Kumar and Soumitra Chatterjee, the biggest names then, her *Deya Neya* (1963), *Anthony Firinghee* (1967), *Teen Bhuvaner Paarey* (1969), *Pratham Kadam Phool* (1969) and *Rajkumari* (1970) proved all-time favourites. Marriage into Bollywood's legendary Mukherjee family and motherhood of two daughters did not rob her of charm or her love for cinema. The end of her marriage saw her back to playing 'sister' and 'mother' in *Khuddar* and *Prem Rog* (1982) and *Pitruroon* (2015) in Marathi.

Dancing diva Waheeda Rehman was the rage of the 1960s with *Chaudhavin Ka Chand, Sahab Bibi Aur Ghulam*, *Khamoshi*, *Neel Kamal*, *Guide* and *Teesri Kasam*. She glided into the next decade with *Reshma aur Shera* but by the end of it her fortunes had waned, with only a *Kabhi Kabhie* (1976), *Trishul* (1979) or *Namkeen* (1982) to showcase her compelling prowess.

Twinkle toe Vyjayanthimala started even earlier as a child in the 1940s and commanded the 1950s with *Devdas*, *Madhumati*, *Naya Daur*, and *Paigham*. She expended her grip in the 1960s with *Gunga Jumna*, *Suraj*, *Sangam*, *Amrapali* and *Jewel Thief*. Unlike Sadhana who rocked the 1960s with *Woh Kaun Thi*, *Mera Saya*, *Waqt*, *Mere Mehboob*, but failed to make the transition to the next decade, Saira Banu and Asha Parekh continued to be active through the 1970s – with *Gopi* (1970), *Victoria No 203* (1971), *Sagina* (1974) here, or *Mera Gaon Mera Desh* (1971), *Caravan* (1971), *Kati Patang* (1970), *Main Tulsi Tere Aangan Ki* (1978) there. But they were not making waves: the decade was marching ahead with new faces and newer ways.

However, one yesteryear's prima donna who stormed the Hindi screen during that decade was Suchitra Sen. One can't go past the 1970s without doffing our hats to *Aandhi* (1975). Tracing the arc of a middle-aged politician's life, her underplayed unfolding of emotional memory seeps deep inside viewers of every age. Twenty years after *Devdas* (1955) and a decade after *Mamta* (1966), she proved that age does not wither a diva. A fact that was established by Meena Kumari a year before she passed away, in *Mere Apne* (1971). Grappling with the social exploitation of widows, the film cast her as an old woman with no children who finds a family with unemployed youths who are being politically exploited. And Meena Kumari had – like Suchitra Sen – proved a trailblazer for the likes of Jaya Bachchan, carrying films on their shoulders playing senior citizens. Meena saved her best for her last: *Pakeezah* (1972) is rated among the decade's most memorable performances by a leading lady in Hindi cinema.

The dancing queen to arrive in this landscape was Hema Malini. And joining her to hold aloft the tradition of heroines from the south was Rekha. Both of them were here to stay, they proved.

Dream Girl Hema Malini, despite the pronounced southern tinge in her Hindi, had the ageing Raj Kapoor gushing over her in her debut vehicle *Sapnon Ka Saudagar* (1968). This was followed by a series of blockbusters featuring her with the biggest male actors of the time. Shammi Kapoor and Rajesh Khanna (*Andaz*, 1971), Sanjeev Kumar and Dharmendra (*Seeta Aur Geeta*, 1971), Dev Anand (*Johnny Mera Naam*, 1970), Shashi Kapoor (*Abhinetri*), Raaj Kumar (*Lal Patthar*, 1971), Jeetendra (*Khushboo*, 1975; *Kinara*, 1976), Vinod Khanna (*Meera*, 1979), Amitabh Bachchan (Kasauti, 1974, followed by a string of blockbusters in the 1980s). With Dharmendra she did no less than twenty-eight films including resounding hits like *Sharafat* (1969), *Raja Jani* (1971), *Naya Zamana* (1971), and *Pratiggya* (1975), *Charas* (1976), among others.

Sholay remains this pair's crowning glory. Basanti, talking nineteen to a dozen, and Veeru, willing to commit 'soocide' for her, will forever stay in our hearts as a couple. Did they gel because of the real-life chemistry that led to their unconventional marriage? She from the south of Vindhyas, he a Punjabi Jat; she a tradition-bound Bharatnatyam dancer; he, married with four kids. He gave Esha and Ahana their surname, Deol, but she raised the daughters under a separate roof. She was perhaps the Radha to his Krishna but, with dignity and without ruffling feathers, she rejected her overbearing mother; allowed her daughters their own space in life; directed *Dil Aashna Hai* (1993) and *Tell Me O Kkhuda* (2011).

Crossing hurdles with grace, Hema surprised with her mettle as she won elections and energetically nurtured her constituency, Mathura. Dancer, actor, mother, director, parliamentarian – Hema Malini has proved that dream girls do not fade away once reality catches up.

Rekha, the evergreen diva of Bollywood too has lived life on her own terms. But she always made a splash, being unabashedly vocal with her opinions. Unafraid of breaking expected – read, stereotypical – norms. Be it in her own life or on the silver screen. With flesh-and-blood characters like Sunita Devi (*Do Anjaane*, 1976), Arati Chandra (*Ghar*, 1978), Zohrabai (*Muqaddar Ka Sikandar*, 1978), Purnima Kohli (*Basera*, 1981), Manju Dayal (*Khubsoorat*, 1980), Chandni (*Silsila*, 1981)...

When I first saw Rekha, inside a studio, she was perhaps, like me, in her mid-teens. But she was in a dark, body-hugging gown, hair tied high up, eyes dramatically outlined, poised on her stilettos with a sensuous tilt to her head. Pardon me for saying this but she was a picture of everything I never wanted to be. To put it differently: she was the opposite of the girl-next-door personality I've nurtured through life. And then, she was doing *Sawan Bhadon* (1970), *Kahani Kismat Ki* (1972), *Pran Jaay Par Vachan Na Jaay* (1973) ... Films that succeeded at the box office but totally overlooked histrionic ability. Then came the ambitious actress in Dulal Guha's *Do Anjane*, the rape victim in Manik Chatterjee's *Ghar*, and the second wife in Ramesh Talwar's *Basera*. These amassed for her the sympathy of viewers, and the attention critics were unwilling to give so far.

Rekha, an out-of-wedlock daughter of the southern superhero Gemini Ganesan with Pushpavali, seized upon this opportunity to reinvent herself. Now her make-up was suave. Her dress sense turned classy. Her carriage had poise. She had less of 'Madrasi' accent and more of 'Lakhnawi' finesse. The duckling had transformed into a swan. Grace personified. Her characters would be the envy of any actress.

Khubsoorat marked the turning point, followed soon after by *Umrao Jaan* (1981). Well, I debated then and still do, whether the courtesan poet *Umrao Jaan* merited the Silver Lotus more than the Anglo-Indian teacher Ms Violet Stoneham of *36 Chowringhee Lane*. But the National Film Award brought on a platter the opportunity to showcase Rekha in Benegal's *Kalyug* (1981), the adulteress Rekha in Yash Chopra's *Silsila*, Rekha in Girish Karnad's *Utsav* (1984), Gulzar's *Ijaazat* (1987), and as the avenging angel of *Khoon Bhari Maang* (1988). The 1980s firmly belonged to Bhanu Rekha Ganesan.

Entering Bollywood in the 1970s with a challenging double role in *Sharmilee* (1971), her second release a year after her debut in *Jeevan Mrityu* (1970), Raakhee stood her ground midway between Sharmila Tagore and Jaya Bhaduri. She was neither the girl-next-door nor was she a begum. She had neither a Manik-da nor a Hrishi Kaku to see her through her toddler days in the industry. What she had was her captivating looks and her chutzpah. These kept her from being boxed in a stereotype.

No one expected her to hold her own against Shabana Azmi and Smita Patil. No one wished to see her waltzing with the West-inclined Zeenat Aman or Parveen Babi. Yet, she pitted her presence against Waheeda Rehman as a widowed bride early in her career (*Reshma Aur Shera*, 1971). And against Sharmila Tagore as Rajesh Khanna's second wife (*Daag*, 1973). She aced Hema Malini as the wife of Raaj Kumar (*Lal Patthar*). She had surprised as the notorious sister of the heroine in *Sharmilee*. Middle-of-the-path cinema? Yes, we could say that, had she not been the cynosure of Amitabh Bachchan's eyes in the blockbuster *Kabhi Kabhie* (1976). In *Tapasya* (1976), too, she had proved her mettle as the self-sacrificing sister. As the stylish modern woman, a recluse who is reminded by a young man of her dead boyfriend (*Doosra Aadmi*, 1977). As the wife who unexpectedly returns from a mental asylum (*Basera*). But prior to all this, she had surprised one and all as the not-to-be-subjugated working woman in *27 Down* (1974).

That she was confident of her position showed in the fact that while she played Bachchan's love interest in umpteen films like *Kasme Vaade*, *Trishul* and *Muqaddar Ka Sikandar* in 1978, *Jurmana* and *Kaala Patthar* in 1979, *Barsaat Ki Raat* (1981) and *Bemisaal* (1982); she also played his mother in these very years in *Lawaris* (1981, albeit in a flashback) and in *Shakti* (1982). Before transitioning to iconic mother roles in *Ram Lakhan* (1989) and *Karan Arjun* (1995).

Indeed, her self-confidence was also reflected in the long gaps between her meaty projects in Bengali films: as Parama in Aparna Sen's 1984 film of the same name she earns the ire of the whole family by stepping out of the housewife's 'laxman rekha'. As Pishima she solves a murder mystery without stepping out of her house in Rituparno Ghosh's *Shubho Mahurat* (2003). And in 2020, Goutam Haldar's *Nirban* finds her as an orthodox woman whose salvation lies in embracing a child from a different religion.

In her outings through commercial Hindi cinema, Raakhee is seldom a gritty woman who determines her own course in life. In reality, she has lived life on her own terms. Full throated laughter, books – more so in Bengali – and cooking: whenever she can, for as many people in her life as she can, friends, family, unit members, staff … happy to eat from roadside dhabas too, despite the multitudes: that's Raakhee!

In the Mould of Jaya Bhaduri

> 'I was completely enchanted by Jaya Bhaduri after watching a diploma film, *Suman*. It was unlike any other performance I had seen. I marvelled at that. I thought to myself, "If by going to FTII I can achieve that, I want to do that…"'
>
> – Shabana Azmi

Shabana Azmi had acting in her genes. Her mother Shaukat Azmi and father Kaifi Azmi, committed members of the left ideology, were both deeply connected with theatre, acting in plays, writing, hosting performers. Yet Shabana schooled herself at the FTII to emote as per the demands of a character, a situation, a script. And even this exemplary actress who has the highest number of Golden Lotuses – five National Awards – in her kitty, was inspired by Jaya Bhaduri to make it big in cinema.

Arthouse, parallel, new wave, formulaic, Hindi, English, Indian, international – you name it, she's done it. Correction: she's *doing* it. Fifty years after opening the account with Shyam Benegal's cult creation *Ankur* (1974) she's doing it all. A liplock with Dharmendra in *Rocky Aur Rani Ki Prem Kahani*. An ad for Winkies Swiss Roll, '*Katega toh sab mein batega*', shadowing her *Godmother*. Theatre, notably Feroz Abbas Khan's *Tumhari Amita*; M.S. Sathyu's *Safed Kundali*; Rifco's *Happy Birthday Sunita*...

Small wonder, though; for Satyajit Ray had summed her debut in these fulsome words: '...in two high-pitched scenes she pulls out all her stops and firmly establishes herself as one of our finest dramatic actresses.'

With looks that did not match the classic definition of a screen goddess, she came armed with poise and presence. And she crafted her signature with realistic portrayal of serious, progressive social content upholding human values. She came to be identified with reformist content. Partly because in real life too she took up cudgels for, voiced her objection against, and came down on the streets to register protest.

Activism was soon her middle name. For women's rights. For the homeless. For migrants. For the AIDS afflicted. Against obscurantist mindset. Of communal, exploitative forces of religion. Standing with Swami Agnivesh. Standing up to those who called for a fatwa against A.R. Rahman. Goodwill Ambassador of the UN Population Fund is just one recognition under her belt; Padma decorations and nomination to the Rajya Sabha honour the actor who has set benchmarks in delivering powerhouse performances.

Viewers would wait for her unpredictable next. What will she be? A prostitute? A killer? A lesbian? A deaf and dumb woman married to a tree? A pregnant woman crossing the river? A septuagenarian kissing on the screen? Directors wrote characters with her in mind. Not only maestros Satyajit Ray (*Shatranj Ke Khilari*), Mrinal Sen (*Khandhar*), Shyam Benegal (*Mandi*), John Schlesinger (*Madame Sousatzka*), and auteurs Aparna Sen (*Sati*), Goutam Ghose (*Paar*), Sai Paranjpye (*Sparsh*), Deepa Mehta

(*Fire*), Meera Nair (*The Reluctant Fundamentalist*), Shekhar Kapur (*Masoom*), Mahesh Bhatt (*Arth*), Vinay Shukla (*Godmother*), but also box-office majors Manmohan Desai (*Amar Akbar Anthony*), Prakash Mehra (*Jwalamukhi*), Karan Johar (*Rocky Aur Rani Ki Prem Kahani*).

Smita Patil, coming after Shabana following in the footsteps of Jaya Bhaduri, was the Woman Who Could Be Me. She was captivating in an unconventional way. She was darker than the *gehua*, wheatish brown that is coveted by Indian mothers for their daughters. She grew up speaking Marathi with her classmates in a Pune school but went to the elite Elphinstone College and St Xavier's in Mumbai.

Pune had a robust theatre scene, dominated by Vijay Tendulkar, P.L. Deshpande, Mahesh Elkunchwar, Satish Alekar, Jabbar Patel … Pune was the home of the FTII, the cradle of the New Wave Cinema that washed the Hindi screen in the 1970s. These factors, as much as her political activist parents, disciplined her to view the arts as a mirror to reflect the reality in society. So when she took to anchoring news on Doordarshan, she became The Girl in Every Home. In less than eight years she shored up six times that many titles. In so many languages: Hindi, Marathi, Gujarati, Bengali, Kannada, English. All this transpired because, like Jaya Bhaduri, Shabana Azmi and Deepti Naval, Smita was more committed to the arts than to signing up photos for fans.

That could be the reason why she chose scripts that explored a woman's position in an exploitative social order. Her characters sought to advance their plight. Sometimes they challenged the pecking order assigned by society. Often they projected a collected soul who could chose her own path. Perhaps that is why Smita would choose her own costume or, at times, delve into production design. The sheer range of emotions she could bring into play in a single scene was repeatedly tapped by Satyajit Ray, Mrinal Sen,

Benegal, Aravindan, Govind Nihalani, Jabbar Patel, Ketan Mehta, Muzaffar Ali, Sagar Sarhadi, Robin Dharmaraj.

Smita started with arthouse, against avowed antiheroes like Om Puri and Naseeruddin Shah. She captured mainstream with macho men like Raj Babbar and angry young men like Amitabh Bachchan. And the characters she made her own? They were complex. She was Bindu who takes a lead in the White Revolution of *Manthan* (1976). In *Bhumika* (1977), she mirrored Hansa Wadkar, the exploited diva of Marathi screen. She became Nagi, the tribal who is raped and killed to frame her husband (*Aakrosh*, 1980). She was Roma (*Shakti*, 1982), living in sin with a caring criminal. Dukhi Chamar's wife in *Sadgati* (1981). In *Arth* (1982) she's the other woman breaking under the burden of wrecking a home. Sonbai of *Mirch Masala* (1987) turns the ubiquitous chilli flakes into a killer weapon against the all-powerful tax collector.

Beginning with *Nishant* (1975) she continued with the much-lauded *Jait Re Jait* (1977), *Gaman* (1978), *Kondura* (1978), *Akaler Sandhane* (1980), *Chakra* (1981), *Umbartha* (1982), *Charandas Chor* (1982), *Baazar* (1982), *Ardh Satya* (1983), *Giddh* (1984), and *Chidambaram* (1985). Where would the Other Cinema of India be had Smita Patil not taken to reading news on Doordarshan?

She broke the 'good girl' stereotype of Indian heroines, yet she kindled empathy, concern, love among her viewers. And when she breathed her last, leaving behind a baby she had mothered only in her womb, Smita had not succumbed to the need to enter into any marriage with the already married father of her son. Did we talk about breaking stereotypes?

They Too Made It Big

Neetu Singh, born Harneet Kaur, was barely an eight-year-old when, following her father's death, she debuted in the super-hit *Suraj* (1966). Soon Baby Sonia, as she was then called, carved a place for herself playing the twins central to *Do Kaliyaan* (1968). By the time she was in her teens, she was cast in lead roles by directors like Nasir Husain and Yash Chopra, in *Yaadon Ki Baaraat* (1973) and *Deewaar* (1975) respectively. With *Khel Khel Mein* (1975) began the winning onscreen combination with Rishi Kapoor. *Kabhi Kabhie* (1976), *Amar Akbar Antony* (1977), *Dharamveer* (1977), *Adalat* (1977), *Kasme Vaade* (1978), *Kaala Patthar* (1979), *The Burning Train* (1980) and *Yaarana* (1981) make a wonderful roster of some of the era's biggest hits. Note the diversity in these films: from horror to disaster to thriller to fantasy to masala to musical to crime to romantic to social drama!

Vidya Sinha is synonymous with Basu Chatterjee and Amol Palekar. Think *Rajnigandha* and *Chhoti Si Baat*. She was the thinking man's women of the era. If Amol Palekar was Everyman, Vidya Sinha, probably more than anyone else, epitomized its feminine avatar. She figured in *Pati Patni Aur Woh* with Sanjeev Kumar and Ranjeeta. None of these had the trappings of a 'star' heroine although the lady was much into modelling before her screen career that spelt a mere thirty films in ten years. And despite commercial success and the acclaim of *Kitaab* and *Meera*, of *Josh* and *Love Story*, she opted for a hiatus since her first husband was ailing.

Reena Roy, born Saira Ali, was first seen in *Zaroorat* (1972). *Jaise Ko Taisa* (1973) and *Zakhmee* (1975) got her wider recognition. She became a star with the film that gave Shatrughan Sinha an image makeover, *Kalicharan*, which along with *Nagin* became the biggest grossers of 1976 at the box office. She rose to be the highest paid actress of her times. Her tryst with commercial success continued unabated through the decade and in the 1980s too with *Jaani Dushman* (1979), Aa*sha* (1981), *Naseeb* (1981) or *Sanam Teri Kasam* (1982). She won a Filmfare award for *Apnapan* (1977), but declined it as she believed her role was not that of 'Supporting Actress'.

Ranjeeta also trained at the FTII in the art of emoting, had a promising start opposite Rishi Kapoor in *Laila Majnu* (1976). In 1978, she tasted success with Sanjeev Kumar in *Pati Patni Aur Woh* and with Sachin in the box-office hit *Ankhiyon Ke Jharokhon Se.* Cast in nearly fifty movies in about fifteen years, her best teaming was in a string of films with Mithun Chakravarty, the most well-known of which is the super-hit *Surakshaa* (1979) and the love story *Tarana* (1979). She played Amitabh Bachchan's love interest in *Satte Pe Satta* (1982), but her career benefitted little from that.

Parveen Babi appeared out of nowhere, or so it seemed when B.R. Ishara's *Charitra* (1973) released. By then Zeenat Aman had already consolidated her position as a glamour queen in the Western mould that was ridiculed in *Purab Aur Paschim. Hare Rama Hare Krishna* (1971) had of course decried the ganja-pot addicted, 'carefree' lifestyle that had no need to touch the feet of elders, no need to cover themselves in dupattas, no compunction in sporting bell-bots and T-s. Yet, the dawn of the decade that had seen the girl-next-door rise to glory also saw the rise of Zeenat Aman and Parveen Babi to the extent that *Time* magazine, no less, sported them on the cover. Babi was the first Indian actor to be thus crowned.

Initially making her mark as a model, Babi rose rapidly to lead the cast with Amitabh Bachchan, first in *Majboor*, then in *Deewaar*, and then in *Amar Akbar Anthony.* She got top billing in *Suhaag* (1979), *Kaala Patthar* (1979), and in the 1980s in films like *Kaalia*, *Khuddar*, *The Burning Train*, *Shaan* and *Namak Halaal*, even displaying rare comic talent in Hrishikesh Mukherjee's *Rang*

Birangi. Even when an ensemble cast featured Hema Malini or Rekha, Babi was seldom relegated to a 'supporting' or 'sister' role. And, true to her image as a social rebel, she had no desire to hide her relationships with men, often married, such as Kabir Bedi, Danny Denzongpa and Mahesh Bhatt.

Babi disappeared from the scene while she was still lapping up the adulation. In a sad ending to a short but shining career, she accused her co-star of trying to eliminate her. She had by then lost trust – in everything, from the food she ate to the water she drank and the men she loved. For film aficionados, her final legacy are the Hindi films that spun their fabric from the story of her life, notably *Arth* (1982) and *Woh Lamhe* (2006), both written by Mahesh Bhatt.

One leading lady who raised a storm at the onset of 1970s and then was not seen until the 1980s is Dimple Kapadia. Born to wealthy parents, launched by Raj Kapoor with his son Rishi, Dimple was everyone's heart-throb when *Bobby* released in 1973. Her knotted shirts and miniskirts set the silver screen on fire. But even as the film became a phenomenon, out of the blue she got married to The Phenomenon, Rajesh Khanna. Only after they separated did Dimple return, to deliver a series of hits. In films like *Saagar*, *Lekin*, *Rudaali*, *Antareen* and *Drishti*, she reminded us what a loss it was for Hindi cinema of the era that she went missing in action between 1973 and 1985.

Tina Munim, crowned Femina Miss India in 1975, entered the industry with a bang in Dev Anand's *Des Pardes* (1978). She made a mark when she was cast as a desi Eliza Doolittle against Dev Sa'ab's Prof Higgins in *Man Pasand* (1979). She is best remembered for Basu Chatterjee's *Baton Baton Mein* with Amol

Palekar, and for *Karz* with Rishi Kapoor. Another hit in her career, *Souten* (1982), teamed her with Rajesh Khanna, a pairing that would be repeated in over ten films. Once she got married into the wealthy industrial family of the Ambanis, she turned away from the camera but not from the limelight. Supporting artists through workshops and exhibitions, holding art auctions, presiding on the administrative bodies of ICCR Delhi, NGMA Mumbai, NID Ahmedabad, Peabody Essex Museum in Massachusetts, she was active in rehabilitation of street children, providing healthcare for senior citizens, and restoration of the heritage Elephanta Caves.

Interestingly, Tina Ambani did not return to acting after 1991 even though her husband, Anil Ambani, acquired majority stake in Adlabs which had interest in production, processing and exhibition of films. In fact, Reliance Mediaworks went global and even contributed to the making of Steven Spielberg films, notably, *Lincoln*. Their marriage, which initially faced family resistance from his family as she was from the glamour-oriented world of fashion and films, has proved pretty stable by most accounts.

I am underscoring this to drive home an observation about the leading ladies of 1970s. Unlike the generation preceding them, most of these stars went to school, often convents; went for higher education; were groomed for careers, in fashion or beyond; married on their own terms; most of them had high-profile marriages; gave up their screen careers to raise families; then returned to face the camera again. Not out of necessity but for a second innings in life.

Acting, occasionally, cohabited with performances for the small screen, in other languages, or on stage. Hema Malini took to directing, and later featured in advertisements. Years ago Dimple Kapadia indulged in a business of creating scented candles. Significantly, this generation of actors paved the way for their millennial colleagues to take the entrepreneurial plunge. Setting up their own production house was the most logical step. Juhi Chawla partnered Shah Rukh Khan in setting up Red Chillies Entertainment and, going beyond that, in ownership of the Kolkata Knight Riders. Many former leading ladies have set up fashion labels, beauty brands, jewellery and perfumes. Line of handbags is another successful area of business. Home decor ideas, skincare, fitness products, ownership or investment in the Indian Premier League, authoring books, writing regular columns. So many avenues!

More importantly, these leading ladies took to playing more significant roles in public life. They headed institutions. They plunged into philanthropic activities. Education, especially of underprivileged children, healthcare, care of senior citizens, of the differently abled, women empowerment, animal rights activists. They have been nominated to Parliament, and they have not taken their seats for granted. Some of them have actively joined political parties and stood for elections. This is something the previous generation of actors, for example, Meena Kumari, Madhubala, Nutan, who continue to rule millions of hearts decades after their passing, never contemplated.

Ajay Chandra, the protagonist of this 1979 middle-of-the-road Basu Chatterjee movie, dreams big. He wishes to become an entrepreneur and start a galvanometer business – the only film to use this electromechanical instrument in the main plot! The film was a remake of a cult Bengali film. Identify the original, the Hindi remake and the actor who essayed the role of Ajay Chandra.

Answer: *Manzil* (1979), a remake of Mrinal Sen's *Akash Kusum*; Amitabh Bachchan

The story of which 1979 Basu Chatterjee movie has characters solely from the Christian community in Bandra, Bombay?

Answer: *Baaton Baaton Mein* (1979)

Anand Bakshi

The Common Man's Poet and Philosopher

Shantanu Ray Chaudhuri

With over 6000 songs in more than 300 films, Anand Bakshi is arguably the most prolific songwriter in the history of Hindi films. Right through the seventies, 'Lyrics by Anand Bakshi' was as ubiquitous in the opening credits as was 'Sound by Mangesh Desai'. With such a voluminous output, it is a given that quality will vary. And Anand Bakshi has his share of mediocre songs like many other lyricists who have much lesser numbers to contend with. Purists may crib, but Anand Bakshi made the Hindi film song democratic, hummable, relatable to everyday concerns. At the same time, when the milieu allowed him, he could better the best of poets with a treasure of 'philosophical' songs that were the envy of the best of lyricists.

'*Achha toh hum chalte hain*' ... '*Bye-bye miss good night kal phir milenge*' ... '*Ilu ilu*' ... the list goes on ... Arguably, no other lyricist in Hindi cinema can boast of as many songs that have become everyday catchphrases. But then Anand Bakshi was no ordinary songwriter. He was a master of the anthem, the connoisseur of the quotidian. If '*Yeh dosti hum nahin todenge*' (*Sholay*, 1975) became the quintessential song celebrating friendship, '*Meray sapnon ki rani*' (*Aradhana*, 1969) was the song with which to serenade your lover, '*Dum maro dum*' (*Hare Rama Hare Krishna*, 1970) caught the zeitgeist of an impatient generation with its nihilist undertones, few songs probably capture the yearning for the motherland as evocatively as '*Chitthi aayi hai*' (Naam, 1986) does.

Then there is his mastery of the love song – the heartbreak in '*Wo tere pyar ka gham*' (*My Love*, 1970), the wistfulness that informs '*Pyar diwana hota hai*' (*Kati Patang*, 1970), the mischief or impishness of '*Aaj mausam bada, beimaan hai bada*' (*Loafer*, 1973), the joy of '*Dafli waley*' (*Sargam*, 1979) or the sheer agony/ecstasy of '*Yeh dil, diwana*' (*Pardes*, 1997). And each of them in a language that is easy to understand and sing along with. No wonder then that Anand Bakshi was the go-to lyricist for all teenage/youthful love stories, in particular those heralding a new star pair: from *Bobby* (1973) to *Ek Duje ke Liye* and *Love Story* (both 1981) to *Hero* (1983), his songs played the biggest role in the colossal hits these film became. No one probably articulates the playfulness of young lovers like he does with '*Mujhe kuch kehna hai*' (*Bobby*), or the heartbreak of first love as well as he does with '*Solah baras ki baali umar ko salaam*' in *Ek Duje ke Liye*. And if he was the voice of the times in the 1970s, with *Jawani Diwani* (1972), he was no less so as we approached the new millennium with '*Tujhe dekha toh ye jaana sanam*' in *Dilwale Dulhania Le Jayenge* (1995).

No one could hold a torch to him when it came to the chartbusting item number either – '*Dum maro dum*', '*My name is Anthony Gonzalvez*' (*Amar Akbar Anthony*, 1977), '*Om shanti om*' (*Karz*, 1980), '*Jumma chumma de de*' (*Hum*, 1991) and '*Choli pe pichhe kya hai*' (*Khalnayak*, 1993), to name just a few. Though the last couple of songs copped some criticism for lapse in taste, it has to be borne in mind that, one, here is someone with over 3300 songs in 600+ films in a career spanning close to five decades, and, two, someone who is purely a songwriter (one who does not have the luxury of directing the film or writing it, like some of his eminent contemporaries have) asked to deliver a song as per the situation conceived by the director and/or writer.

In all the hosannas heaped on him for his ability to churn out chartbusters and all the barbs directed at him for his 'simple' verse, there's a whole segment of Anand Bakshi songs that advocate a certain philosophical take on life that are not recognized as such. Many a Hindi film lyricist's songs have been quoted in the context of the 'metaphysical' statement they make – and it is true that the Hindi film song at its best does speak of the highest philosophical thoughts of the poet and the character in the film. However, though these Anand Bakshi songs figure among the finest in Hindi cinema, not much has been said about how beautifully each one conveys an attitude, an approach to life. Maybe it's because these words speak of life's truth in the simplest of language, one that is accessible to everyone. Above all, though all of these are set to certain specific situations in a film, take them out of their cinematic contexts and they still ring true. And in these can be found the true measure of Anand Bakshi, the everyday poet.

'*Yahan main ajnabi hoon*', *Jab Jab Phool Khile* (1965)

Though this one belongs to be the decade before the seventies, it is important in the evolution of the lyricist. This is the film that launched Anand Bakshi into the big league, with each song a chartbuster. I remember watching it at a theatre in the mid-1980s when a number of old hits were rereleased in the absence of new films. One moment still stands out in memory: the whole hall bursting out in applause as Shashi Kapoor lip-synced to the lines, in Mohammad Rafi's tremulous timbre: '*Main kaise bhool jaun / main hoon Hindustani*'. In the lines '*main jo hoon bas wahi hoon*' you have the last word in being comfortable in your own skin. I am reminded of the universality of the line in the context of Popeye's well-known statement: 'I am what I am.' The poet's son, Rakesh Anand Bakshi, says: 'The song was not written for the film, but the situation fit the film, so he added verses to suit the story. He wrote it from the humiliating experiences he had in Bombay during his first visit in 1950. He had felt like an alien and unwanted soul. He went back to the army and returned in 1956 to make it as a songwriter.'

'*Maajhi chal, o maajhi chal*', *Aaya Sawan Jhoom Ke* (1969)

The boatman has always been a philosopher in our music, particularly in the east, in Bengal, with the boat, the river and its currents standing for life, the body and soul, and our own motivations. Rakesh remembers, 'He would say, the mind is the oarsman, the body is the boat; the mind leads the body like the oars leads the boat … the oarsman, the boat and the changing currents together make life what it is.' In wonderful imagery, Anand Bakshi likens life to the flowing river, the body the boat, the mind the rudder that runs it. Like many boatman's songs, this one too calls for hope and fighting despair. Like the river, life will flow on. And in a masterstroke, he exhorts us to leave even today behind – this day is gone too … what lies ahead is tomorrow: *aaj toh peeche rah gaya hai, samne hai kal.*

'*Dum maro dum*', *Hare Rama Hare Krishna* (1971)

Just four lines, and yet what impactful ones they are. '*Duniya ne humko diya kya / duniya se hamne liya kya / ham sabki parwah karein kyon / sabne hamara kiya kya.*' Even taken out of the drug-induced haze of the film's protagonists, the lines speak of an attitude to life that everyone who has ever been young will vouch for. In what stands testimony to the astounding versatility of the poet, the very next year, Anand Bakshi would have another song espousing a similar thought but in words infused with lyricism of a different kind: '*Kuch toh log kahenge / logon ka kaam hai kehna / chhodo bekaar ki baton mein…*'.

'Chingari koi bhadke', *Amar Prem* (1972)

The existential agonies of Anand Babu found the most appropriate expression in the immortal words of Anand Bakshi, in two songs that I consider not only the finest in his extraordinary repertoire but among the best in Hindi films ever. As his son says, it was 'Anand Bakshi's favourite song. Interestingly enough, it was not written for the film. Shakti-da heard it, wanted it for the film and created the situation to fit it in.' Much has been written about it but even fifty years later '*Humse mat poochho kaise mandir toota sapnon ka*' evokes the despair of unrealized dreams like few other lines in Hindi films. The helplessness articulated in being undone by the entity one hoped would lead to one's salvation, is conveyed in similes and metaphors, each better than the other: the garden laid to waste in spring, a wound inflicted by a loved one, a thirst accentuated by the very drink that's supposed to quench it. And of course '*Saawan jo agan lagaye…*' has become proverbial.

'Kuch toh log kahenge', *Amar Prem* (1972)

Another of Bakshi saab's songs whose mukhda has become idiomatic. How many of us have actually used the words in our daily lives, exasperated with the thought of what people might say. In the words of Rakesh, 'This was inspired from the Ram Leela plays he acted in as a teenager. He wrote his own verses for the play and would compose them to his own tunes and sing them on stage.' He also recollects a legendary writer and lyricist drawing inspiration from this song at a difficult crossroad in his life when he was in a dilemma about ending his marriage and beginning a new relationship. It was this song that helped him take the decision without worrying about the consequences. With what simplicity he puts across ideas that are eternal: '*har ek subah ki shaam hui*' and '*Sita bhi yahan badnam hui*'.

'Yeh jeevan hai is jeevan ka', *Piya ka Ghar* (1972)

Even before concepts like yin and yang became fashionable for faith healers, this song speaks of the philosophy. The song has worked like a medicine for me in the toughest of times. A lesson in dealing with the vicissitudes of life, it gently cajoles you into accepting what the world has to offer us with grace. '*Yeh ye na socho is mein apni haar hai ki jeet hai / Usey apna lo jo bhi jeevan ki reet hai*' is a philosophy to die for … or maybe to live with. His son offers Bakshi saab's insights: 'He would say, *life main aisa koi kaam nahi jis men har saal* Diwali bonus *miley*. Some years you will not receive a bonus, some years you will. That's life, just like there is sweet there is bitter, dawn and dusk, opposites are a part of life … happiness and sorrow are two sides of a coin.' And what better lines than '*Dhan se na duniya se, ghar se na dwar se*' to convey what in the end really matters in life.

'Gadi bula rahi hai', *Dost* (1974)

The boatman and the itinerant singer have often voiced a poet's take on life in our films. In this song, Anand Bakshi uses the journey of a train to convey a whole spectrum of philosophies. Unfettered by the necessity of having the song lip-synced, the poet gives free rein to his imagination in the many stanzas of the song that play at relevant passages in the narrative. There's an appeal against taking one's life that seems ever so relevant:

Gadi kaa naam
naa kar badnaam,
patari pe rakh ke sar ko
himmat na haar
kar intazaar
aa laut jaae ghar ko
ye raat jaa rahi hai
wo subah aa rahi hai

There's also an exhortation that echoes Swami Vivekananda's 'Arise awake and stop not till the goal is reached', overcoming all obstacles with hope and determination:

Sun ye paigam
ye hai sangram
jeevan nahi hai sapna
dariyaa ko faand
parvat ko chir
kaam hai ye uskaa apna
neendein udaa rahi hai
jaago jaga rahi hai

'*Aadmi musafir hai aata hai jata hai*', *Apnapan* (1977)

The itinerant fakir with the humble peti or ektara has been the fount of many a philosophical musing. In this song that won him the Filmfare Award, Anand Bakshi speaks of Man as the eternal traveller, creating memories on the way … *dil bhool jaata hai jab kisi ko, wo bhool kar bhi yaad aata hai*, how the heart tends to remember even when we think we have forgotten. Despite the general upbeat tenor of the song, there's an underlying pathos to it, like a moment that's just out of reach, that's gone, leaving behind something ephemeral. The words are also laced with a rare understanding of the essential loneliness of man: *melay mein rah jaaye jo akela, phir wo akela hi rah jata hai.*

'*Zindagi ke safar mein guzar jaate hain jo makaam*', *Aap Ki Kasam* (1977)

There are probably few songs in Hindi films that convey with such eloquence and poignancy the finality of times that are gone. Lines that hold true even when taken out of the context of the film and its characters, giving the song a timeless, universal feel, reminding me of Charles Lamb's poem 'The Old Familiar Faces': 'So might we talk of the old familiar faces /How some they have died, and some they have left me / And some are taken from me; all are departed; All, all are gone, the old familiar faces.' Friends who have left us never to return howsoever much we pine for one last glimpse, seasons we have left behind … and in six most telling lines the relentless journey of a whole lifetime: *subah aati hai / shaam jati hai / waqt chalta hi rahta hai rukta nahin / ik pal mein yeh aage nikal jaata hai / aadmi theek se dekh pata nahin / aur parde pe manzar badal jaata hain / ek baar chale jaate hai jo din-raat subah-shaam*… Rakesh says, 'He wrote this from the experience of a friend whose marriage suffered due to the husband being suspicious. When the director narrated the story, he remembered his friend's experience. Javed saab [Javed Akhtar] asked Dad for the pen he wrote this song with. He gifted him another pen the next day. Javed saab once said that if the world were to leave him on an island, he would like to have this song to spend the rest of his days with.'

'*Seesha ho ya dil ho aakhir toot jata hai*', *Aasha* (1980)

Bakshi saab's songs that have acquired idiomatic status are legion, and this is another one in the long list. And in the words of his son, this too emerged from mundane everyday experiences. 'When a glass vessel or expensive cutlery at home broke and my mom would stress or worry, he would say calmly, sheesha ho ya…' And in an exquisite turn to the English phrase 'many a slip between the cup and the lip', he says: *Lab tak aate aate haathon se, saagar chhoot jaata hai.* The song, structured quite intricately and differently from the standard mukhda-antra Hindi film song format in vogue at the time, abounds in such aphorisms. In six lines of great depth and utter simplicity, he lays out the way our desires and longings play out: *Kaafi bas armaan nahin / Kuch milna aasaan nahin / Duniya ki majboori hai / Phir taqdeer zaroori hai / Yeh jo dushman hai aise / Donon raazi ho kaise / Ek ko manao to duja rooth jaata hai.*

It is impossible to do justice to the work of this remarkable lyricist whose songs carried films to box-office glory and played the definitive role in the stardom of so many actors of the decade in an essay. Just a potted roster of the films for which he composed songs will be enough to give an idea of his contribution to the decade: *Humjoli*, *Jeevan Mrityu*, *Sharafat*, *Aap Aaye Bahar Aayi*, *Dushman*, *Mehboob Ki Mehndi*, *Mera Gaon Mera Desh*, *Raja Jani*, *Julie*, *Pati Patni Aur Woh*, *Mr Natwarlal*, *The Train*, *Apna Desh*, *Seeta Aur Geeta*, *Heera Panna* ... Here is a lyricist who could write a rambunctious '*Duniya mein logon ko*' with as much aplomb as a sensuous '*Bhool gaya sab kuch*' or give us the sheer rapture of '*Yeh shaam mastani*'. No other lyricist in the seventies had this range to offer.[1]

What is the name of the company in which Amol Palekar's character, Arun Pradeep, works as a line supervisor in the 1976 film, *Chhoti Si Baat*?

Jackson Tolaram Pvt Limited

In the Gulzar classic, *Aandhi* (1975), starring Suchitra Sen and Sanjeev Kumar, Om Shivpuri plays a rival politician. What is the name of his character?

Answer: Chandersen

[1] I would like to thank Sumant Batra and Cinemaazi, where the essay was first published, for permission to use this in the volume.

Laxmikant–Pyarelal

Mass Music, Class Act

Deepa Buty

Towards the fag end of the 1940s, a ten-year-old boy playing the mandolin in a Lata Mangeshkar concert held at the Radio Club, Colaba, Bombay, caught the singer's attention. It was learnt that the boy was in a poor financial condition and needed help. Lata Mangeshkar recommended him to some of the stalwarts of the music industry. He started getting opportunities to play the mandolin under several music directors. Barely ten years old, with no academic education, the boy worked shift after shift, recording after recording, to make ends meet. After one such recording he saw several boys of his age playing cricket and joined them. It was here that he met another boy of almost the same age. The two soon became friends and started to spend time together. They had a lot in common. If he was a phenomenal mandolin player, his friend was as good a violinist. Both came from a poor financial background and both had a zest for music and life. They had already started dreaming of making music together. Little did they know that their dream would not just come true one day but they would be acknowledged as one of the greatest music director duos in Indian cinema: Laxmikant–Pyarelal.

As a musician, Laxmikant played the mandolin under several masters of the game – C. Ramchandra, O.P. Nayyar, Shankar–Jaikishan, Hemant Kumar, Roshan, Ravi and S.D. Burman – while Pyarelal played the violin under Bulo C. Rani, Madan Mohan, Naushad, C. Ramchandra, Chitragupt, Khayyam and S.D. Burman. It was as teenagers, during their days at Sureela Kala Kendra, an academy started by Lata Mangeshkar for upcoming artists, that their friendship grew. Sureela Kala Kendra had fifteen to twenty boys including Laxmikant, his brother Shashikant, Pyarelal and his brothers Gorakh and Ganesh, Hridaynath Mangeshkar. They were occasionally joined by Meena and Usha Mangeshkar.

Chalking out their future together as music directors, they worked round the clock as music assistants, arrangers and musicians. They always revered Shankar–Jaikishan and later Kalyanji–Anandji as music directors. Before becoming the brand LP and acquiring a distinctive sound of their own, their music showed a lot of resemblance to that of Shankar–Jaikishan. They were fond of huge orchestration. They carved a niche for themselves with R.D. Burman (*Chhote Nawab*), Usha Khanna, Ramlal and Kalyanji–Anandji (*Satta Bazar*, *Chhaliya*, *Bluffmaster*, *Poornima*, *Mehndi Lagi Mere Haath*). They were associate music directors for Kalyanji–Anandji in *Jab Jab Phool Khile* and *Juari*.

Becoming independent music directors wasn't a cakewalk. This was an era when the Hindi film music landscape had a number of stalwarts, one bigger than the other, and the competition was tough. Though LP got their break in *Parasmani* (1963), before that three of their films remained in the can, among them Kalpataru's *Tumse Pyar Ho Gaya*. They signed *Chhaila Babu*, which got delayed and eventually *Parasmani* became their first film. With *Parasmani*, they got the recognition they needed as music directors. But the struggle was still on and they continued working as music assistants and musicians. Their last film as assistants was *Bahu Begum* (1967). The Filmfare Award for the best music director for *Dosti* (1964) consolidated their place in the industry but it was only after *Milan* (1967) that they truly arrived, never to look back.

The film industry was going through a lot of change in the seventies. Music especially became more physical. The era saw the rise of R.D. Burman and Laxmikant–Pyarelal. In the period between 1970 and 1979, Laxmikant–Pyarelal scored the music for 166 films, which is not only a massive number but a record of sorts. Despite this, their versatility remained intact. That they were hugely inspired by the Shankar–Jaikishan school of music when it came to arrangement and composing was apparent. Laxmikant was the Jaikishan follower to the extent that he adopted Jaikishan's style of wearing the watch too while Pyarelal emulated Shankar's style of composing. However, in the seventies, they steadily began to become brand LP. Even if their orchestration remained extravagant, like SJ, they slowly weaned off from the SJ style and set their own. Pyarelal came to be known for his expertise in conducting an orchestra.

Few composers could compose the kind of massy music that they could – earthy, connected to Indian roots, inspired by folk music or classical ragas. Their orchestration was dominated by the dholak, violin, sitar and tabla. *Aan Milo Sajna*, *Humjoli*, *Aap Aaye Bahar Aayi*, *Mehboob ki Mehndi*, *Bobby*, *Roti Kapada aur Makaan*, *Prem Kahani*, *Amar Akbar Anthony*, *Anurodh*, *Dharam Veer*, *Satyam Shivam Sundaram* are some of the films that make up the LP hit parade for the decade, films that owed their success to their music in no mean manner and that are remembered as much for their music.

However, it is interesting to discuss some of their work beyond the parameter of hit or flop. *Abhinetri* (1970) was their second film with Hema Malini, the first being *Sharafat* (1970). A box-office hit produced by Subodh Mukherjee, *Abhinetri* is still recalled for its music. The album is dominated by Lata Mangeshkar's solos. Of these, '*O ghata sanwari*' needs a mention when it comes to Lata solos. A rain song which begins with the santoor and Lata's aalap, it has minimal orchestration and impresses with its melody. The African harp, glockenspiel, flute and mandolin create the rain effect in the song which is all about falling in love or beginning to feel love. Lata Mangeshkar provides the required quiver of first love with a slight flutter in her voice. Lyricist Majrooh Sultanpuri provides the apt lines: '*Aawaz kal thii yahi, phir bhi aise lehekati na dekhi.*' Drums playing with brushes provide the required subtle rhythm while the use of angklung, an Indonesian instrument made of bamboo, gives the required bubble effect in the song.

If Subodh Mukherjee's banner was a known one, Kishore Sahu's was a little less known. *Pushpanjali* (1970), produced by his banner, was one of the earliest of the 302 films in which Anand Bakshi and Laxmikant–Pyarelal collaborated. Though the album is not impressive enough as a whole, its duet by Lata Mangeshkar and Manna Dey, '*Shaam dhale Jamuna kinare*', is a show stealer. Based on Raag Khamaj, the song is dedicated to Bhagwan Krishna and Radha. Picturized in the scenic backwaters of Kerala, it has character actor Moolchand and actress Naina Sahu (Kishore Sahu's daughter) lip syncing the words. Here too the music by LP is subtle. With vibraphone, temple bells, flute, pakhawaj, cellos, violins and tambourine they give a devotional touch to the song. The song speaks a lot about their arranging and composing skills. Since it is a boat song, they conjure the rowing effect by simply passing the grains (jowar or sorghum) from one winnowing basket to the other. The overlapping chorus and the aalaps make this song a worthwhile listen.

The seventies also brought in a lot of masala films, from multi-starrer family dramas to violent dacoit films. In the year that V. Shantaram's *Jal Bin Machhali Nritya Bin Bijli* (1971) became the first film to record all its songs in stereophonic sound, LP had another huge box-office success: *Mera Gaon Mera Desh*. This was another successful partnership of the Anand Bakshi–LP team and another album dominated by Lata Mangeshkar. Let us talk about the typical mela song, one of the many chartbusters by LP in that year. The instruments used create quite a frenzy while the police search for Jabbar Singh in the crowd and Laxmi Chhaya, in the iconic role of Munni Bai, hints at his whereabouts. LP used the traditional ravanhattha, flutes, clarinets, tambourine and ghungroos. The rhythm section for this song was a large one: eight dholaks, duffs, tablas, matka tablas and big dhols. All these instruments create the frenzy of the feverish search. The chaos is well depicted and the instruments heighten the edginess of the situation. The beats and instrumentation are geared to make the pulse quicken, with Anand Bakshi adding a Punjabi touch to the song with lines like '*tey akkhaan mastaniyan*' and '*tey kare beimaaniyan*'.

Talking about the LP repertoire from the seventies, we cannot overlook Manoj Kumar's *Shor* (1972). The film depicts an emotional journey of a mute son and his father. '*Ek pyar ka nagma hai*' is an anthem, a tale, of a close-knit family trying to face the troubles in life with a smile. A solo violin played by Jerry Fernandes in the opening is noteworthy. The rest of the instrumentation is soft and matches the harmonies of the violins. A constant pace in the rhythm is achieved with congos, bongos, electric banjo, cellos, flutes and guitar which is played by Pyarelal's brother Gorakh. The entire song weaves a delicate bonding of a family, with Santosh Anand's lyrics a particular standout:

Kuch paakar khona hai, kuch khokar paana hai
Jeevan ka matlab toh, aana aur jaana hai
Do pal ke jeevan se, ek umr churani hai
Zindagi aur kuch bhi nahin, teri meri kahani hai.

This was the era when R.D. Burman was also on top with his innovative and creative sound experiments. His repertoire boasts of songs where sound is the real hero. LP were no exception when it came to creating something new. Take, for example, the song from Ravi Tandon's *Anhonee* (1973), '*Hungama ho gaya*', picturized on Bindu, which boasts Asha Bhosle at her electrifying best. The prelude to the song has a typical robotic '*wa wa wa*' sound. An extra gadget was introduced to create this sound with electric guitar and keyboards. It was called the Wah-Wah pedal. It alters the timbre of the electric guitar completely. This Wah-Wah sound is peppered throughout the song. It is tough musical arrangement done under the guidance of Pyarelal Sharma with the help of his brother Gorakh Sharma. Though the film credits mention Charanjit Singh on the bass guitar, Pyarelal Sharma says it was his brother Gorakh. Shashikant, Laxmikant's brother, was the music assistant while Manohari Singh played the saxophone. A powerful bass effect, congos, bongos, alto and tenor saxophone harmonizing with the female chorus voice, the song is an example of perfection on multiple levels. A masterpiece which is remixed and enjoyed over years after its creation. A hungama in a true sense.

Laxmikant–Pyarelal had a great association with Kishore Kumar over the years. The singer affectionately calling them 'Laxmikatam Pyarelalam' says everything about their rapport. From *Mr. X in Bombay* (1964) to *Mr. India* (1987), Kishore Kumar has rendered as many as 402 songs for the composer duo. His solos with LP are noteworthy, my personal favourite being '*Yeh jeevan hai*' from *Piya ka Ghar* (1974). Made under the illustrious banner of Rajshri Productions, the film was directed by Basu Chatterjee. The song was also the first Kishore Kumar number for a Basu Chatterjee film, a mellow, background song where the singer almost whispers into the lonely night. The song has been used as the music phrase throughout the film. Rhythm guitars, bass guitars, keyboards form the main body of the song but the whistling along with Kishore Kumar's voice give the song its soul.

A number of big banners or banners launched by stars opted for Laxmikant–Pyarelal as music directors. Rajshri Productions, Raj Khosla, J. Om Prakash, Manmohan Desai, Subhash Ghai, Boney Kapoor, Manoj Kumar, Mohan Sehgal, N.N. Sippy, H.S. Rawail are some of the banners who made big-budget films and chose LP as their music directors. When Yash Chopra started his production house with *Daag* (1973), he too opted for Laxmikant–Pyarelal. Producer and financier/distributor Gulshan Rai helped

Yash Chopra with the finances but had his doubts about the film's ending. He didn't want to take any chances and hence went for a small opening (in nine theatres only) in Bombay. The film, through its music, soon gained a lot of popularity and became a blockbuster. LP's music once again became the winning factor. The Kishore solo, '*Mere dil mein aaj kya hai*', became an anthem for lovers. An evocative song written by Sahir Ludhianvi, it has the keyboards played by Vipin Reshammiya. One can also hear the Iranian santoor, electric mandolin, vibraphone, dholak, and organ. *Daag* was the highest grosser of the year, with LP and Kishore Kumar being nominated for the year's Filmfare awards.

Adept at every genre of music, LP worked with almost all the lyricists of their times. If their partnership with Anand Bakshi is widely known, their songs with Majrooh Sultanpuri have been much appreciated. Whether the song was philosophical, sombre, romantic, comic, the collaboration has been applauded most of the time. LP navigated Majrooh's brilliant words wonderfully. *Imtihan* (1974) is just one example. During one of her interviews, Lata Mangeshkar said that LP, just like SJ, loved to compose songs for her that were high pitched. 'They would really push my limits!' But Lata being Lata mastered every song like a pro, even if it was an unconventional song like '*Roz shaam aati thii*'. The song is an apt example of how LP and Majrooh worked as a team. Starting with the chirping of birds followed by the flugelhorn, acoustic guitar, Iranian santoor and the tabla tarang, the song brings out the evening atmosphere and its aura even without the visuals. Lata Mangeshkar's voice, though soft, scales some high-pitches which only she could do. The Iranian santoor by Pandit Shiv Kumar Sharma is another delightful element of the song, in complete sync with Lata's voice. Those small pauses give you the feel of climbing and reaching somewhere high. A peerless and surreal evening on the mountain top.

Just like Lata Mangeshkar, Mohammed Rafi was associated with Laxmikant–Pyarelal from their debut itself. Rafi's solos with the duo have a special place. One of their most-loved songs happens to be from *Jaani Dushman* (1979). Produced and directed by Rajkumar Kohli, the film was a multi-starrer in the truest sense and narrates the story of brides who go missing soon after their marraiage. '*Chalo re doli uthao kahaar*', a solo by Rafi, is a bidaai-geet. This particular song does not have any prelude which is an exception since LP were known to have long preludes. It starts with the chorus humming, typical of palanquin bearers. It creates pace and rhythm in the song. The humming is accompanied by dholaks, shehnai and violins. While Rafi sings, the background music is almost negligible except a few tinkling sounds giving the song the much-needed sublime effect and making it drastically different other LP numbers. The higher pitch in the song emphasizes the pathos of a bride leaving her parents' home and also the fear of the unknown abductor of the newly wed brides.

Music lovers might raise an eyebrow if someone mentions LP and Gulzar in the same sentence. It is such an unorthodox combination clearly because they have altogether different temperaments when it comes to films and songs. Yet they collaborated for three films, beginning with *Palkon ki Chhaon Mein* (1977), and following up with *Gehrayee* (1980) and *Ghulami* (1985). *Palkon ki Chhaon Mein* was the directorial debut of Meraj who was otherwise an assistant with Gulzar. Apart from '*Daakiya daak laya*' by Kishore Kumar, none of the other songs finds much mention in discussions on music. But there is a hidden gem by Lata Mangeshkar, picturized on Hema Malini. '*Koi mere maathe ki bindiya sajaa de re*', which brings to life a bride's emotion, her desire, her rapture, her ecstasy. With some very expressive guitar notes, there's shehnai, tabla, dholak, swarmandal, violins and piano. It conveys a gust of emotion, with the prelude, the sign line, interludes and the stanzas following each other without any pauses.

It is impossible to do justice to LP's repertoire from the seventies in one essay. They built a mountain of music with a large number of hits and an equal number of flops but somewhere between that their music was a winner. In one of the interviews, Pyarelal Sharma said, 'It requires not only years of ceaseless study and application but a continuous exercising of your artistry to do justice to the craft of composing. Music is an art as well as science. You can never learn enough of it.' In this perhaps lies the secret of their success.[1]

What is the symbol of Aarti Devi's party in *Aandhi* (1975)?
Answer: Panchhi / Bird

Who acted as Sheela, Seeta's uncle's daughter, in the Ramesh Sippy classic, *Seeta aur Geeta* (1972)?
Answer: Honey Irani

[1] I would like to thank Ajay Poundarik (*Laxmikant Pyarelal: Music Forever*), Joy Christie, and RJ Anirudh Chawla (*Tere Sur aur Mere Geet*).

'Kahaan Hai Re Doosra?'

Amitabh's Jodidaars in Films of the Seventies and Eighties

Nirupama Kotru

'*Achha, toh yeh hai Thakur ka fauji. Sambha, Kaaliya toh kehta tha do hain? Yeh doosra kahaan hai? Kahaan hai re doosra? Ay Fauji, tera jodidaar kahaan hai, bataa*?'(So this is Thakur's soldier? Sambha, Kaaliya said there were two, where's the second one? Hey soldier, where's your partner?)

Thus spoke the notorious Gabbar Singh in the famous Holi scene from *Sholay* (1975). In this scene, Gabbar corners a defenceless Jai (Amitabh) and asks him to give up his partner Veeru (Dharmendra), who is hiding at that point. Veeru eventually comes out of hiding, and together the friends manage to drive away Gabbar and his men, as if to emphasize that it took two heroes to save the village. Another famous *Sholay* dialogue pertains to the pre-Holi scene between Gabbar Singh and his men, who have returned empty-handed from Ramgarh village after their latest round of banditry, having been thrashed by Jai and Veeru. It goes as follows:

Gabbar: *Kitne aadmi thay*? (How many men did you have to confront?)
Henchman: *Do, sardaar* (There were two of them, chief.)

These memorable dialogues of *Sholay* can be seen as suggesting that two heroes were better than one when it came to ensuring box-office success. This trend, of directors casting two saleable heroes in a film, peaked in the seventies, and coincided with the rise of Amitabh Bachchan. It may have had its beginnings, though, in the hero-driven films of the 1950s when the holy trinity of Dilip Kumar–Dev Anand–Raj Kapoor ruled the Hindi film industry.

One of my favourite two-hero films from the fifties, possibly among the first few films in Hindi cinema which had two leading actors pitted against each other in a love triangle, is Mehboob Khan's *Andaz* (1955), in which real-life friends and neighbours Dilip Kumar and Raj Kapoor vie for the hand of leading lady Nargis. Although their contemporary Dev Anand had charted his own solitary, flamboyant path, he did act in one film with Dilip Kumar (*Insaniyat*, 1955). In most of their films, these three heroes were paired with sidekicks like Rashid Khan and Johnny Walker, rather than with another lead male actor.

The sixties was an era of romance, and lone heroes like Raj Kapoor's younger brother Shammi Kapoor danced their way into the audience's hearts in films of Vijay Anand (*Teesri Manzil*, 1966) and Shakti Samanta (*An Evening in Paris*, 1967). Shammi's younger brother Shashi followed in his footsteps with musicals like *Jab Jab Phool Khile* (1965), *Pyar Kiye Jaa* (1966) and *Pyar Ka Mausam* (1969). A comedian such as Rajendra Nath or Mehmood provided comic relief in these films. Raj Kapoor brought in Rajendra Kumar to complete the love triangle in his blockbuster colour home production *Sangam* (1964). Actor Raaj Kumar was often part of love triangles which also had heroes such as Rajendra Kumar (*Dil Ek Mandir*, 1963), Dharmendra (*Kaajal*, 1965) and Jeetendra (*Mere Huzoor*, 1968).

Where the films of the seventies differed from earlier decades was that the two heroes were no longer fighting over the heroine; they now had bigger problems. More often than not, they joined forces to defeat evil men who had wronged their loved ones.

The turn of the decade saw Rajesh Khanna become the first male superstar with fifteen back-to-back super hits starting with *Aradhana* (1969). These were mostly romantic films with the occasional thriller like *The Train* (1970). Kaka's hit films did not often have second male leads, except for *Safar* (1970) which had Feroz Khan. But he made an exception for Hrishkesh Mukherjee. A certain tall and lanky hero was signed up to play Dr Bhaskar Banerjee in *Anand* (1970). By the time *Namak Haraam* was released in November 1973, the tables had turned. Khanna's films had started flopping. *Mere Jeevan Saathi* had bombed in 1972, followed by *Maalik* in the same year. Amitabh's stars were on the rise with *Zanjeer* having been released in May 1973. The careful viewer will find a significant difference in Amitabh's body language in *Anand* and *Namak Haraam*; the confident, suave businessman Vikram/Vicky of *Namak Haraam* is a far cry from the diffident, gawky Doctor Bhaskar/Babu Moshai of *Anand*. By the late 1970s, Bachchan had some solid hits under his belt, and by the early eighties he was clearly numero uno at the box office.

Ramesh Sippy's *Sholay* (1975) proved to be a game changer as far as dual-hero films were concerned. The winning combination of Amitabh and Dharmendra set the box office on fire. '*Yeh dosti hum nahi todenge*', written by Anand Bakshi and composed by R.D. Burman, is perhaps the friendship song with top recall as far as Indians are concerned. Incidentally, Dharmendra, Sanjeev Kumar and Hema Malini got top billing in *Sholay*. Amitabh's name came at fourth position in the opening credits. The casting was brilliant; Dharmendra's effortless comic timing made his portrayal of the effervescent Veeru delightful, while Amitabh brought gravitas to the portrayal of Jai, Veeru's brooding, introverted other half. Some critics say the film hints at homoeroticism.

The two actors also acted in Hrishikesh Mukherjee's comedy *Chupke Chupke* which was released in the same year as *Sholay*. *Chupke Chupke* had Dharmendra in the lead as botany professor Parimal Tripathi, with Amitabh playing his friend Sukumar Sinha, a professor of English literature. Amitabh clearly played second fiddle to Dharmendra in these two films. By the time their next film, *Ram Balram* (1980), was released in 1980, Amitabh's stock had soared. He had acted in a variety of films, and had delivered several hits in the previous two years. Dharmendra had only *Kartavya* in 1979, an average grosser. And yet they got equal billing in Vijay Anand's *Ram Balram*, a nod to Dharmendra's loyal fan base.

If Jai and Veeru represented the epitome of bromance, Ravi and Vijay became synonymous with blood brothers. Shashi Kapoor first played righteous younger brother Ravi to Amitabh's angsty older brother in Yash Chopra's *Deewaar* (1975). His straight-as-an-arrow, dedicated police officer was a perfect foil to Amitabh's rebel-turned-gangster. To date their exchange remains gold standard for dialogues between estranged brothers.

Deewaar was inspired by Dilip Kumar starrer *Gunga Jumna* (1961) in which Kumar played the outlaw, while his real-life younger brother Nasir Khan played his younger brother, an honest police inspector. Despite Dilip Kumar's virtuoso performance, it is Amitabh and Shashi's Vijay and Ravi team which has become the most iconic brotherhood in Hindi cinema. Yash Chopra's *Kabhi Kabhie* (1976) saw both the heroes play older characters. Shashi Kapoor's character, architect Vijay Khanna, marries poet Amit's (Amitabh) college sweetheart Pooja, played by Raakhee. Vijay is an affectionate man, an extrovert. Amitabh plays the introvert who nurses grudges against all and sundry, and sulks constantly. In one memorable scene, the film's highlight, Vijay chides Amit for being part of the tribe of narrow-minded men who judge their wives for having been in a relationship before marriage, while thinking nothing of their own shenanigans.

After tasting box-office failure in the badly made *Immaan Dharam* (1977), Shashi and Amitabh bounced back in style, returning as stepbrothers in Yash Chopra's *Trishul* (1978). *Kaala Patthar* (1979) had Shashi play sympathetic, pro-worker engineer to Amitabh's naval officer-turned-coal miner. Manmohan Desai's quickie *Suhaag* (1979) saw them play bosom buddies once again. In 1980 they played brothers in Chopra's *Silsila*, Shashi now the older brother. The boisterous banter between the two on-screen brothers in *Silsila* is indeed memorable, especially their reminiscence about the neighborhood hottie which recalls a hit song from yesteryears: '*Neeche paan ki dukaan, oopar gori ka makaan.*' Ramesh Sippy's *Shaan*, also released in 1980, saw them play brothers on the same (wrong) side of the law. Sunil Dutt plays their older, policeman brother, who disapproves of their thieving ways. The two actors also played rival crooks in *Do aur Do Paanch* (1980), a laugh riot in which the two constantly try to upstage each other.

Manmohan Desai and Prakash Mehra, who had a golden run during this decade, with Amitabh the winning horse they primarily bet on, often added Vinod Khanna to the mix, possibly to increase their chances of box-office success. Vinod had started out as villain opposite heroes such as Rajesh Khanna in *Sachaa Jhutha* and *Aan Milo Sajna* (both released in 1970) and Dharmendra in *Mera Gaon Mera Desh* (1971), in which his Jabbar Singh was a forerunner of *Sholay*'s dreaded dacoit. He continued to act in two-hero films like *Qurbani* (1980) with Feroz Khan and Dharmendra in *The Burning Train* (1980). However, it was with Amitabh that Vinod delivered the biggest box-office hits of his career.

Vinod and Amitabh's first big hit together was Prakash Mehra's *Hera Pheri* (1976). The two heroes play crooks who cook up elaborate schemes to hoodwink gullible rich folk. The satirical number '*Waqt ki hera pheri hai*' shows their perfect comic timing to great effect. Next came the box-office bonanza, Manmohan Desai's *Amar Akbar Anthony* (1977) in which they play brothers separated in childhood. Vinod grows up into police inspector Amar Khanna while Amitabh plays small-time goon Anthony Gonsalves. Their first major encounter in *Amar Akbar Anthony*, or *AAA*, where

Anthony gets bashed up by Amar, is truly whistle worthy. Kader Khan's dialogues add tremendous value to this sequence.

Manmohan Desai *Parvarish* (1977) came next, another hugely successful film in which Amitabh plays Vinod Khanna's foster brother. They were pitted against each other in Rakesh Kumar's *Khoon Pasina* (1977), in which they play childhood friends-turned-rivals, who team up in the climax to fight crime. Prakash Mehra's *Muqaddar ka Sikandar* (1978) was their last big film together. Mehra's interpretation of the widely adapted Bengali novel *Devdas* had Amitabh's character Sikandar yearning for his Paro-like childhood sweetheart, the unattainable Memsahib played by Raakhee. Rekha plays courtesan Zohrabai (a take-off on Chandramukhi) who loves Sikandar. Vinod plays Raakhee's fiancé. Vinod also did a special appearance in *Zameer* (1975) in which Amitabh played the lead. *Zameer* wasn't Vinod's first special appearance in a Bachchan film though; he had done one earlier, in Sunil Dutt's 1971 film *Reshma Aur Shera* in which Amitabh plays Shera's (Dutt) mute brother Chhotu.

In each of these films starring them together, Vinod Khanna gave Amitabh Bachchan a tough run for his money, and indeed ended up overshadowing Amitabh, most notably in *Hera Pheri*, *Parvarish* and *Khoon Pasina*. Amitabh Bachchan was ambitious and continued working hard, delivering hit after hit. Owing to the fickle ways of filmdom, by 1982, Vinod experienced an existential crisis, quit films, and sought refuge in Osho Rajneesh's ashram in Pune, and later in Oregon, USA.

Like Vinod Khanna, Shatrughan 'shotgun' Sinha started out with small roles as the villain in films like *Mere Apne* (1971), *Rampur Ka Lakshman* (1972) and *Blackmail* (1973), among others. He broke through as the hero in Subhash Ghai's *Kalicharan* (1976), in which he played a double role. As was the trend in the seventies, despite his stock going up, Shatrughan continued doing two-hero films.

In 1972, Shatrughan played antagonist to Amitabh Bachchan's hero in Mehmood's home production *Bombay to Goa*. In 1979, he was once again pitted against Bachchan in Yash Chopra's *Kaala Patthar*. Amitabh plays Vijay, a former naval officer who has been disgraced and court-martialled, following a maritime disaster that takes place on his watch, and seeks a life of anonymity as a coal miner. Shatrughan plays Mangal Singh, an escaped convict hiding from the police by working in the same mine as Bachchan. Both these hot-headed miners aspire to become the alpha male of the mining community, and their face-off over something as trivial as a cup of tea in a roadside shack makes for one of the great cinematic action scenes of the seventies. Common consensus holds that Shatrughan Sinha scored over Amitabh Bachchan, though it must be said that the former had the more flamboyant role and audience-pleasing dialogues. The two actors did more films in the eighties where they played good friends, such as Ramesh Sippy's *Shaan* (1980), Raj Khosla's *Dostana* (1980), where Shatrughan Sinha gave Bachchan tough competition once again, and Manmohan Desai's *Naseeb* (1981).

By the late 1980s, both Shatrughan Sinha and Dharmendra had aged considerably. Thanks to the demand for action films in smaller cities and towns, these two actors found themselves in the running once again. They acted in some B-grade action films together such as *Loha*, *Insaniyat Ke Dushman, Aag Hi Aag* (all 1987) and *Zalzala* (1988). Soon they were both relegated to playing older characters and returned to the silver screen once in a while. After his five-year spiritual sojourn, the charismatic star Vinod Khanna returned to films with a couple of action thrillers in 1987, namely *Insaaf* and *Satyamev Jayate*. But he could never replicate the magic of the seventies when he was seen as a challenger to Bachchan. His last notable role, before his demise in 2017, was as Salman Khan's father in *Dabanng* and *Dabanng 2* (2010, 2012).

The seventies may have been an era of angst and violence, but the chocolatey, fresh-faced Kapoor boy Rishi held his own, acting in romantic films such as *Bobby* (1973) and *Rafoo Chakkar* (1975), with the odd thriller like *Khel Khel Mein* (1975) thrown in for good measure. Rishi Kapoor had a successful pairing with Amitabh during this decade, which continued well into the eighties. Their age difference of ten years worked in favour of these films. Amitabh and Rishi first shared screen space in *Kabhi Kabhie* (1976). *Kabhi Kabhie*'s story, written by Yash Chopra's wife Pamela, with a screenplay by Sagar Sarhadi, showed some interesting relationships between its leading characters. Vijay and Pooja's son Vicky (Rishi Kapoor) is in love with Pinky (Neetu Singh), who is the illegitimate daughter of Amit's wife Anjali (Waheeda Rehman) from her premarital relationship with another man. In other words, Rishi Kapoor plays Amitabh's stepson-in-law in this film. Like his screen father Shashi, Rishi Kapoor played a flamboyant, lovable character in this film; a complete contrast to Amitabh's brooding, retired poet character.

Rishi went on to play Amitabh's younger brother in three super-hit films, all directed by Manmohan Desai: *Amar Akbar Anthony* (1977), *Naseeb* (1981) and *Coolie* (1983), though in the last film he was more of a foster brother. In *AAA*, Anthony (Amitabh) is the big brother figure in qawwaal Akbar Illahabadi's (Rishi Kapoor) life who supports both his musical career and his romantic relationships. In *Naseeb*, Johnny (Amitabh) works hard as a waiter so that his younger brother Sunny (Rishi) can get a good education. Heartbroken after a failed love affair, Johnny hits the bottle and takes to the streets. Sunny, the doting younger brother, begs his brother to come home, even offering to carry him on his back, singing '*Chal mere bhai tere haath jodta hoon*', a number that rocked the charts. Rishi played the quintessential Tinguji to Bachchan's Lambuji in Manmohan Desai's *Coolie* (1981), and a song from this film '*Lambooji, lambooji, bolo tinguji*' immortalized their relationship. Shashi Kapoor directed Amitabh and Rishi in his 1991 film *Ajooba* in which the two actors played buddies Ali and Hassan. Rishi and Amitabh were reunited after twenty-seven years in the 2018 comedy drama *102 Not Out*, in which Rishi plays a cranky, seventy-five-year-old man and Amitabh plays his happy-go-lucky, one-hundred-and-two-year-old father.

Coming back to Bachchan's peers, both Rajesh Khanna and his arch-rival Amitabh joined the Indian National Congress in the

1980s. Even as they were taking baby steps in politics, Amitabh and Rajesh Khanna were acting in controversial films which depicted politicians as a scourge on humanity: Amitabh gunned down the entire cabinet of ministers in the climax of *Inquilaab* (1984), while Rajesh Khanna exposed corrupt and hypocritical politicians in *Aaj kaa M.L.A. Ram Avtar*, also released in 1984. While Amitabh quit politics in 1987 in the wake of the Bofors scandal, famously calling politics a cesspool, Rajesh Khanna continued to serve the party actively until his demise in 2012. Vinod, Dharmendra and Shatrughan had two things in common – they made a comeback with action films in the late 1980s, and they had a second successful career as politicians, joining the Bharatiya Janata Party (BJP). While Vinod Khanna joined the BJP in 1997, Shatrughan Sinha followed in the early noughties. Both Shatrughan and Vinod became cabinet ministers in Atal Bihari Vajpayee's cabinet. Dharmendra followed them, becoming a BJP MP from 2004 to 2009.

The Kapoor scion Shashi Kapoor stayed away from politics, turning, towards the end of the seventies, to promoting theatre through the revival of Prithvi Theatre which had been established by his father Prithviraj Kapoor. He also started producing and distributing some excellent films under his Filmvalas banner, such as *Junoon* (1979), *36 Chowringhee Lane* (1981), *Kalyug* (1981), *Vijeta* (1982) and *Utsav* (1984). Shashi directed a fantasy superhero film *Ajooba* (1990), which tanked at the box office, despite Amitabh Bachchan headlining the cast (Amitabh is reported to have acted gratis in the film, as a favour to his friend and colleague Shashi).

Lambuji, as Bachchan was once referred to in the seventies and the eighties, turned out to be a true *lambi race ka ghoda*, who continues to act in mainstream films in meaty roles specifically written for him, while his contemporaries and jodidaars have long retired or passed on.

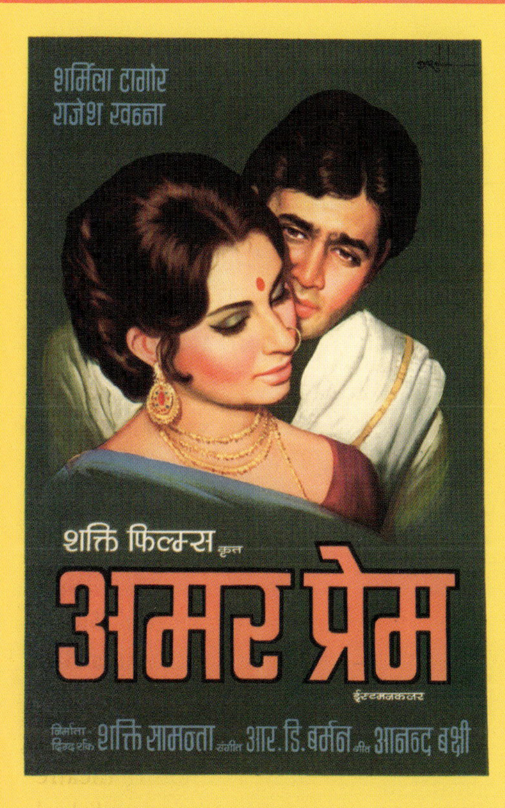

Rajesh Khanna was by all accounts the biggest star of the seventies, with films like *Amar Prem* striking gold at the box office, leading him to be called the first superstar of Hindi cinema
(Picture courtesy: National Film Archives of India)

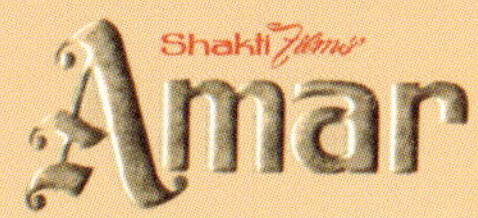

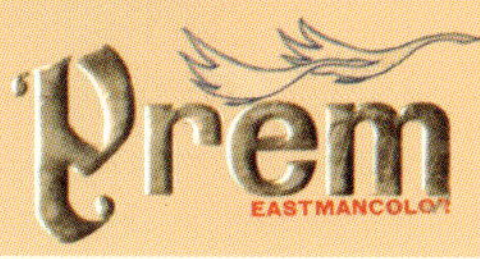

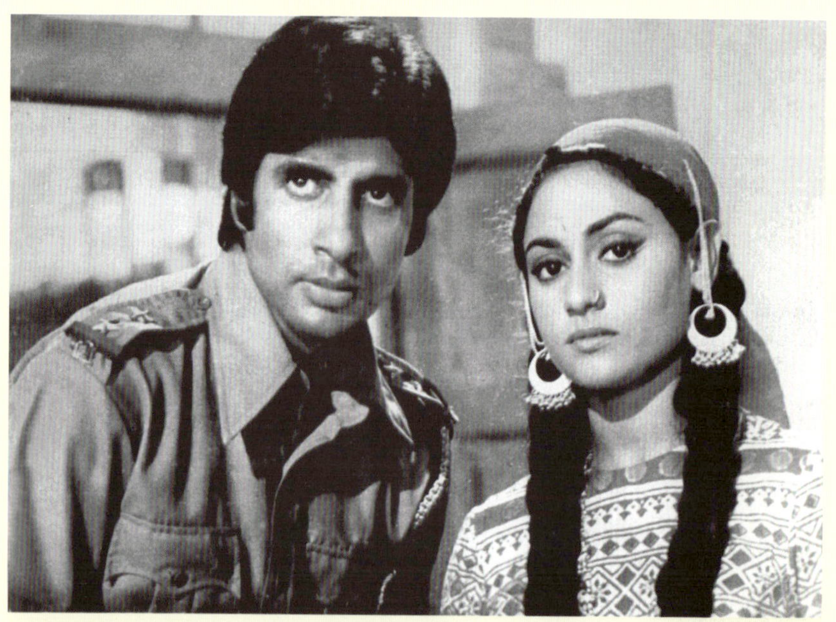

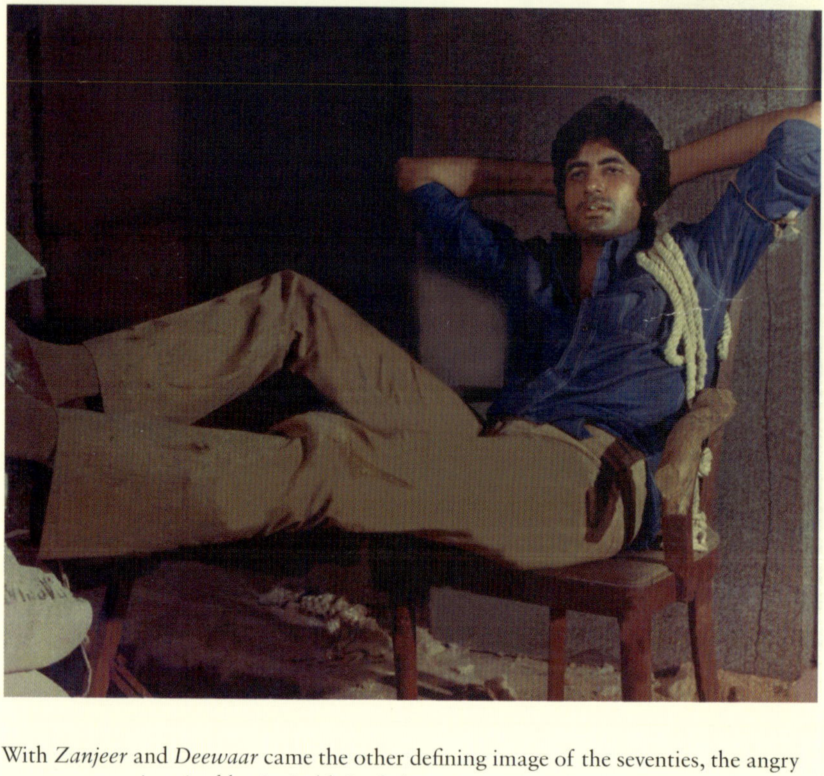

With *Zanjeer* and *Deewaar* came the other defining image of the seventies, the angry young man, epitomized by Amitabh Bachchan
(Picture courtesy: National Film Archives of India)

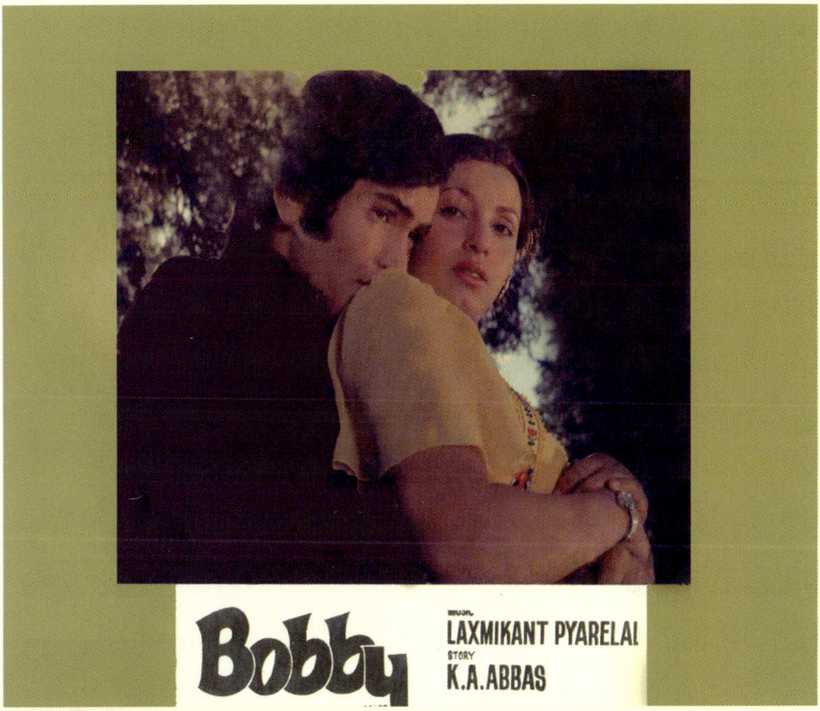

Bobby

LAXMIKANT PYARELAL

STORY

K.A.ABBAS

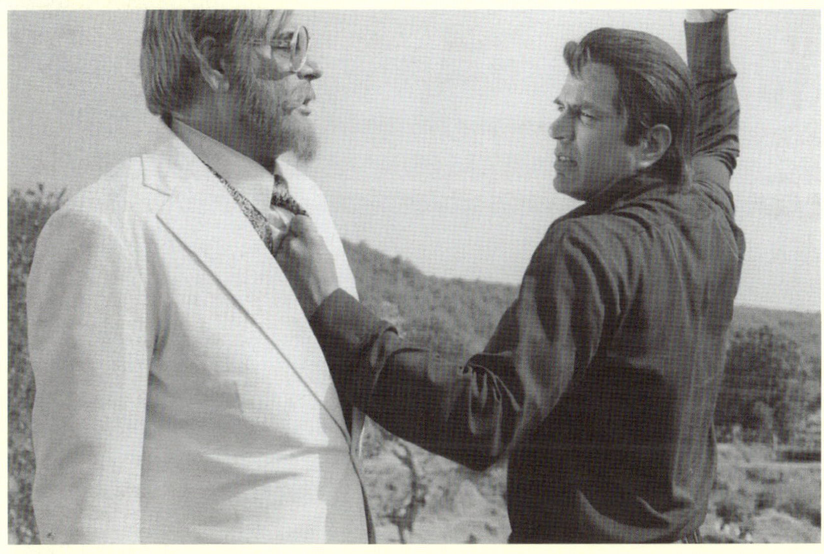

The year 1973 was a watershed, with *Zanjeer* giving us a new star, while *Bobby* and *Yaadon Ki Baaraat* marked two opposite spectrums, the teenybopper romance and the violent revenge drama

(Picture courtesy: National Film Archives of India)

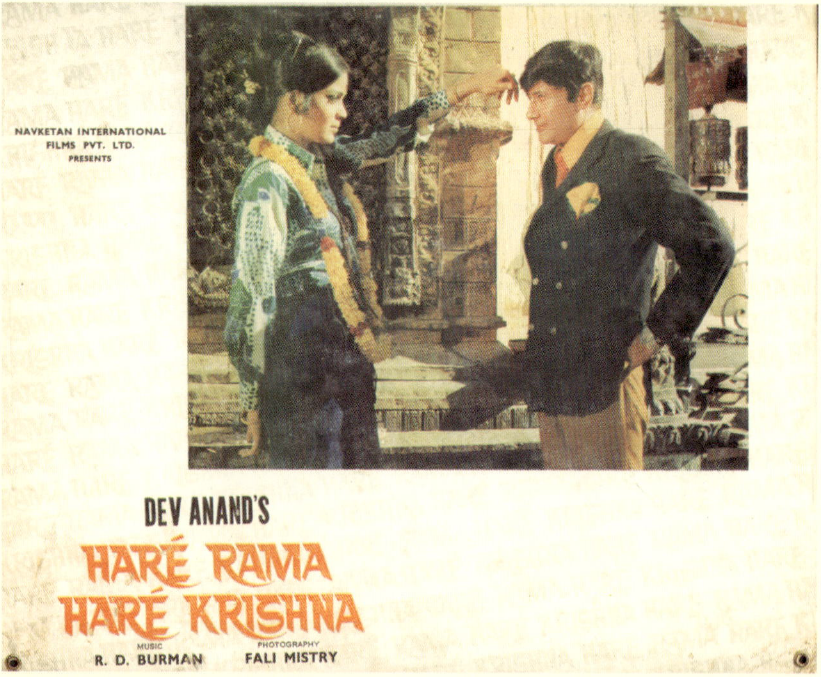

NAVKETAN INTERNATIONAL
FILMS PVT. LTD.
PRESENTS

DEV ANAND'S

HARÉ RAMA
HARÉ KRISHNA

MUSIC
R. D. BURMAN

PHOTOGRAPHY
FALI MISTRY

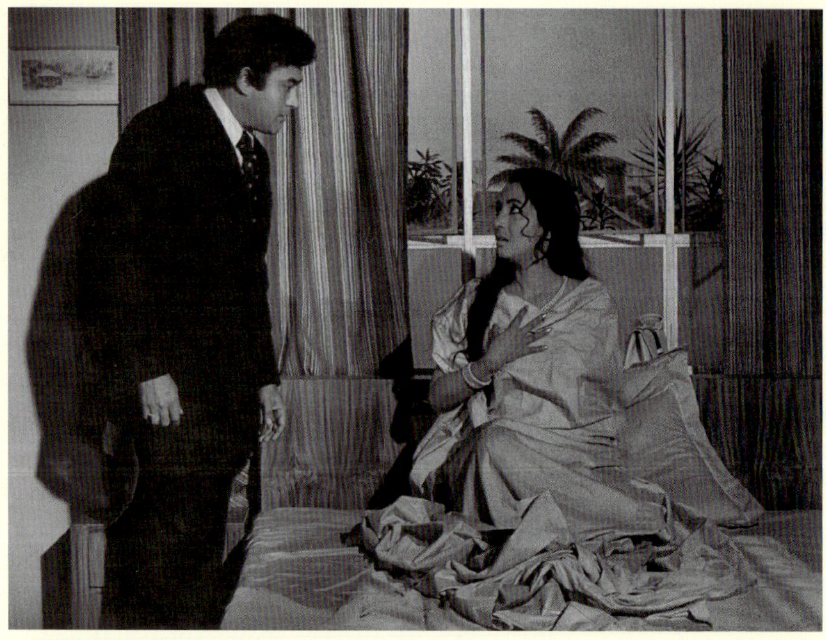

The music of R.D. Burman defined the era, with *Aandhi* and *Hare Rama Hare Krishna* demonstrating the range he was capable of
(Picture courtesy: National Film Archives of India)

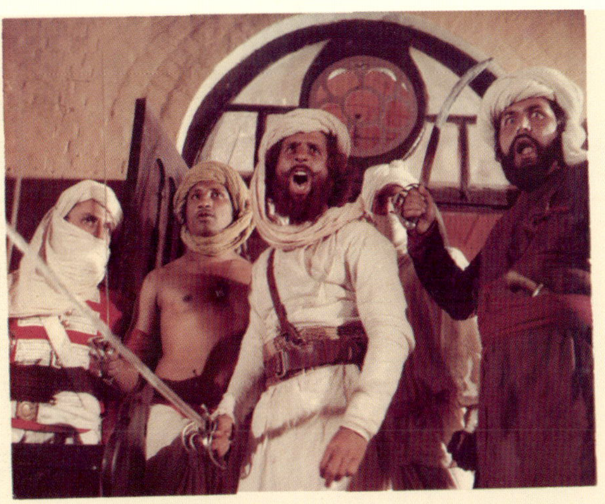

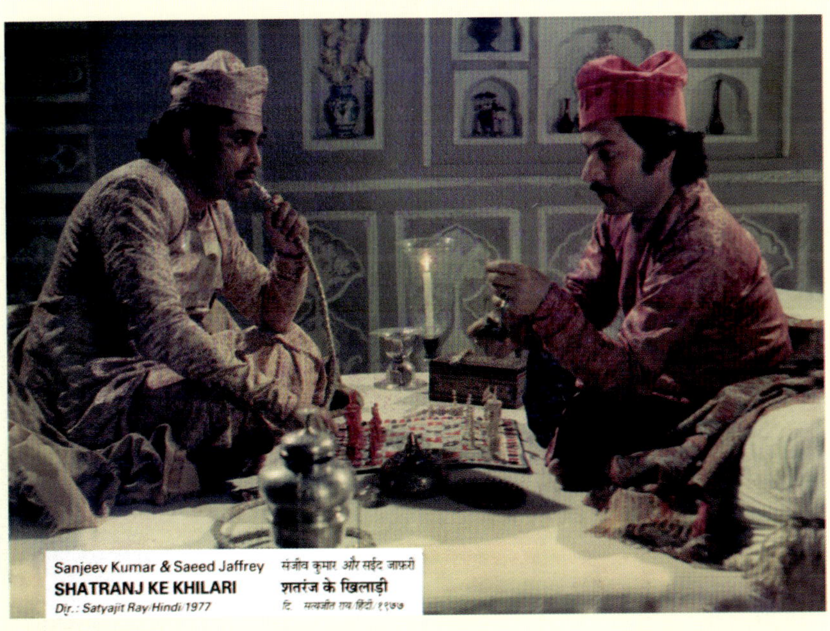

Interestingly, in the late seventies, both Shyam Benegal and Satyajit Ray made films based on stories set during the First Indian War of Independence, 1857: *Junoon* and *Shatranj Ke Khilari*
(Picture courtesy: National Film Archives of India)

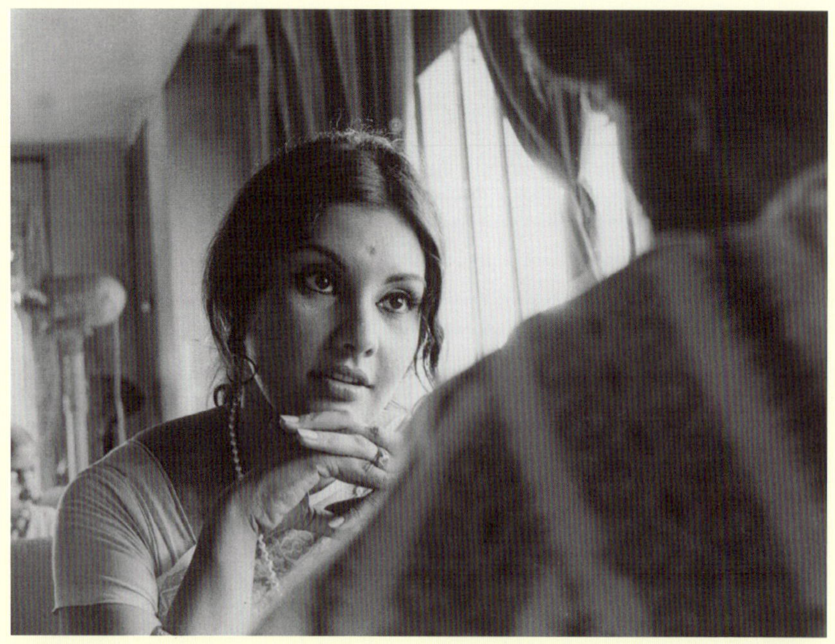

Rajnigandha

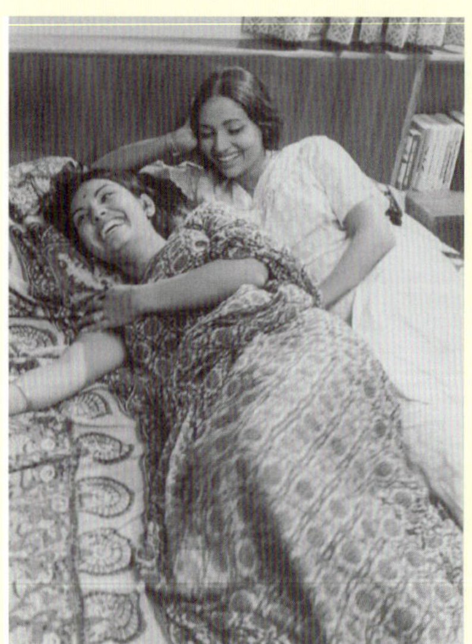

Rajnigandha

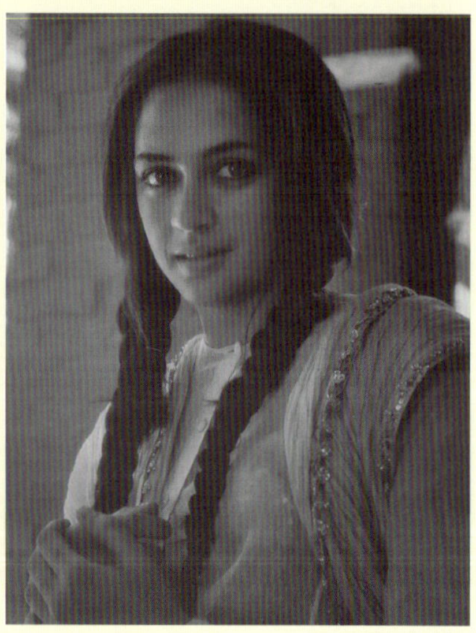

Junoon

The many faces of Eve in the seventies
(Picture courtesy: National Film Archives of India)

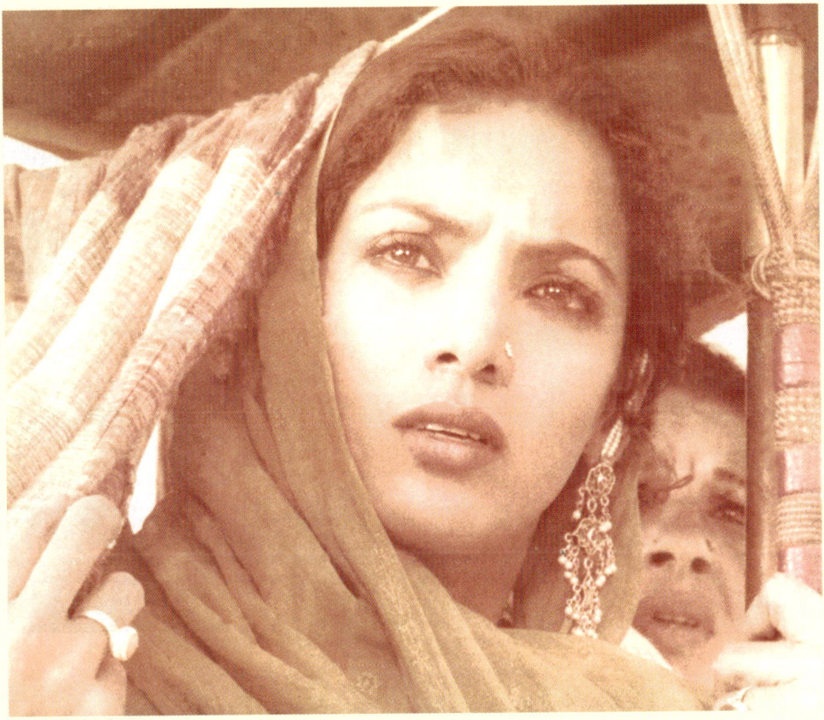

Junoon

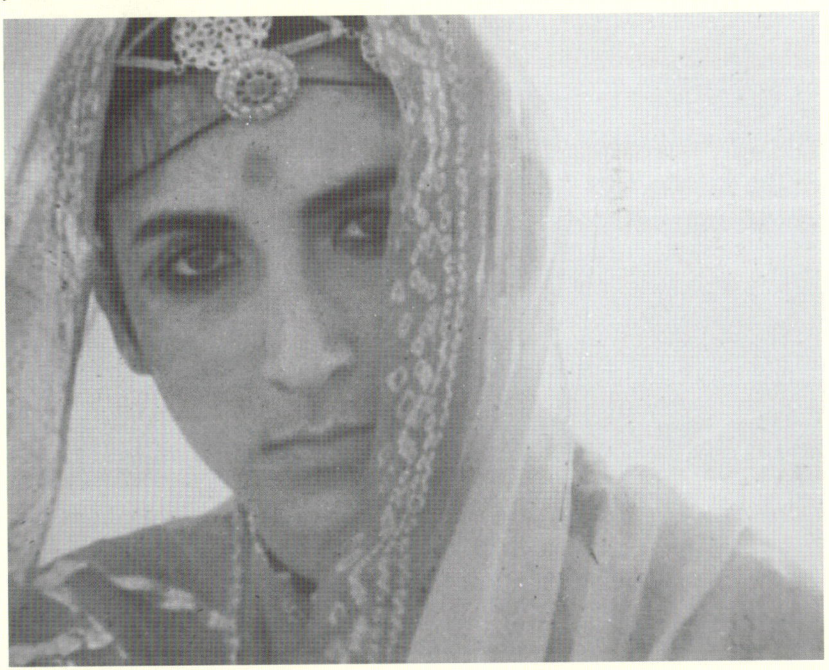

Duvidha

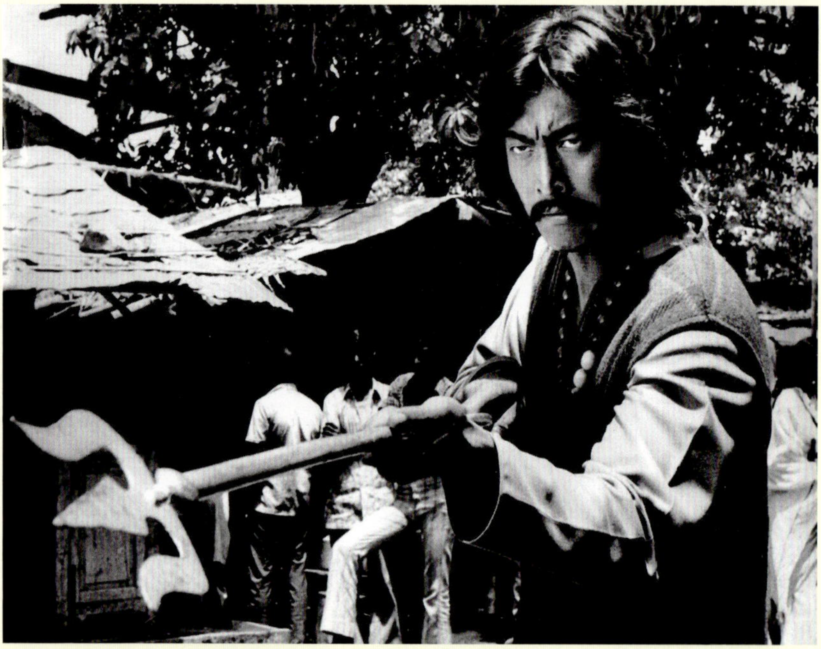

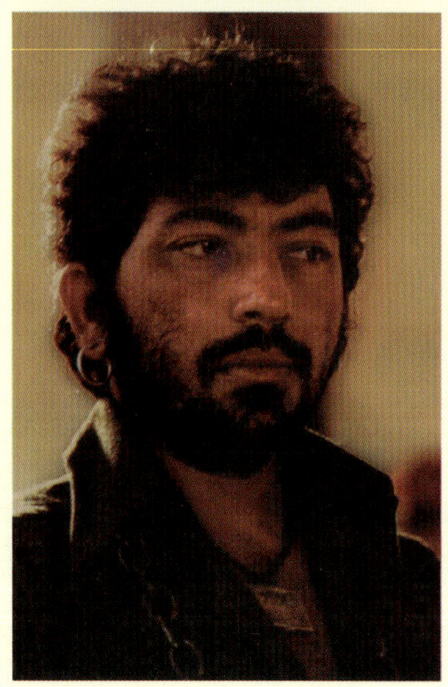

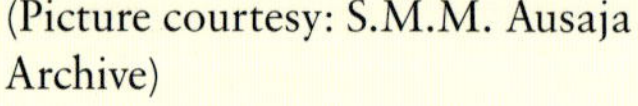

(Picture courtesy: S.M.M. Ausaja Archive)

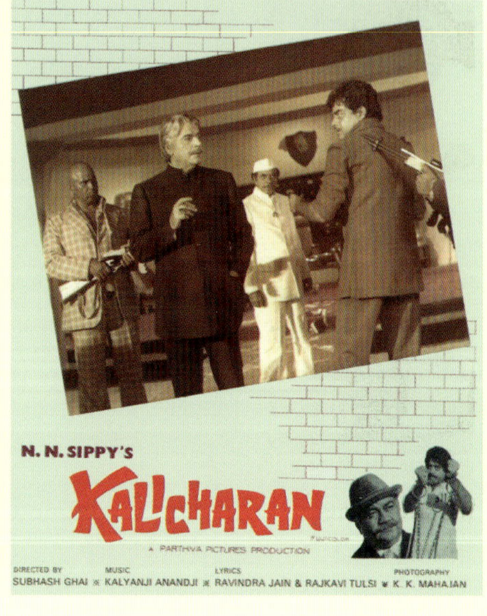

(Picture courtesy: National Film Archives of India)

A few bad men of the decade – interestingly, Shatrughan Sinha started out as a villain before transitioning to play the hero with *Kalicharan*

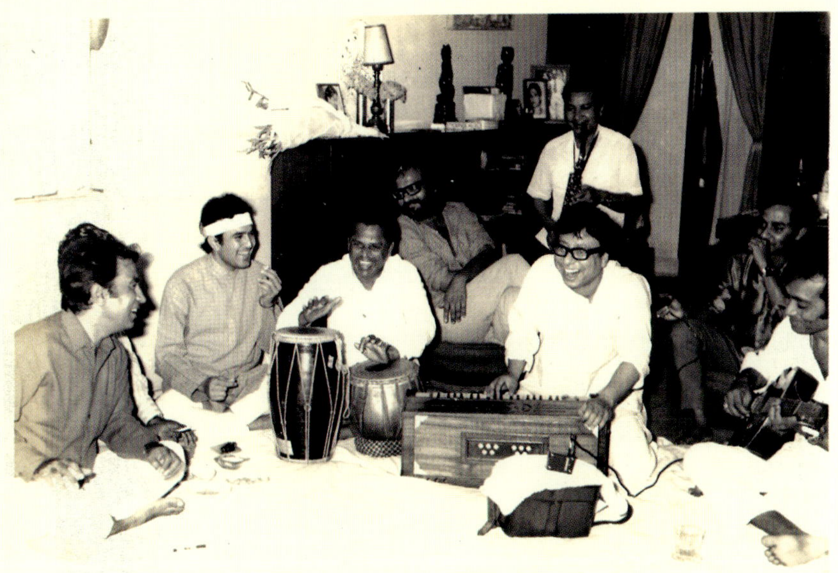

(Picture courtesy: Anirudha Bhattacharjee)

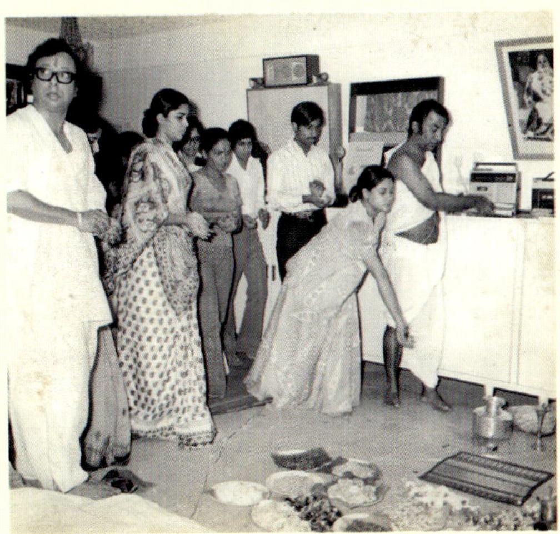

(Picture courtesy: Anirudha Bhattacharjee)

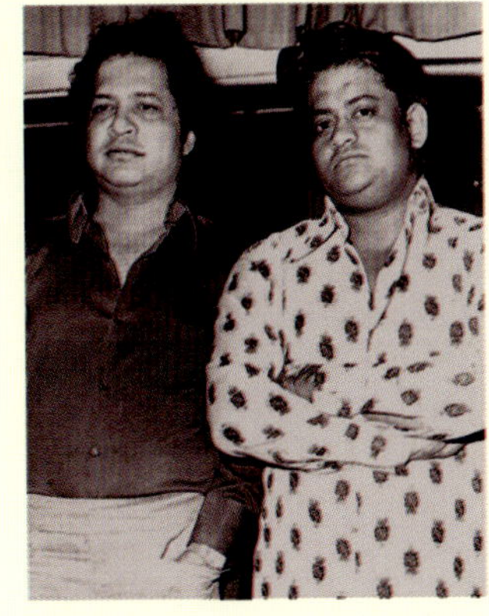

(Picture courtesy: S.M.M. Ausaja Archive)

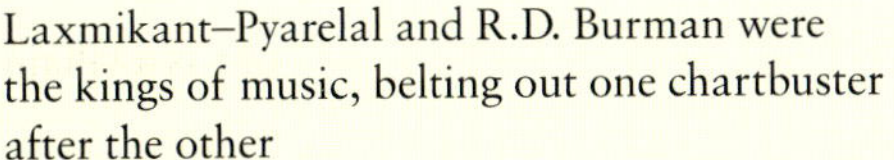

Laxmikant–Pyarelal and R.D. Burman were the kings of music, belting out one chartbuster after the other

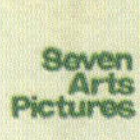

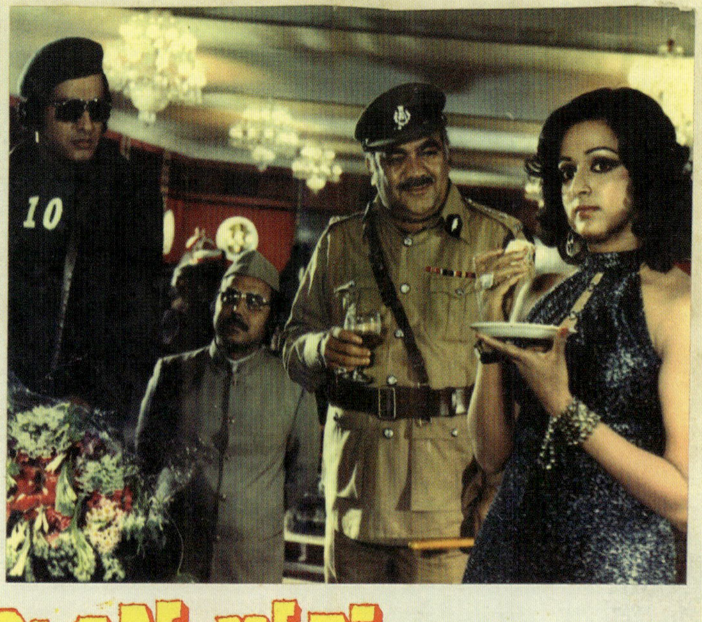

(Picture courtesy: National Film Archives of India)

(Picture courtesy: S.M.M. Ausaja Archive)

Manoj Kumar was one of the most successful directors and actors of the era

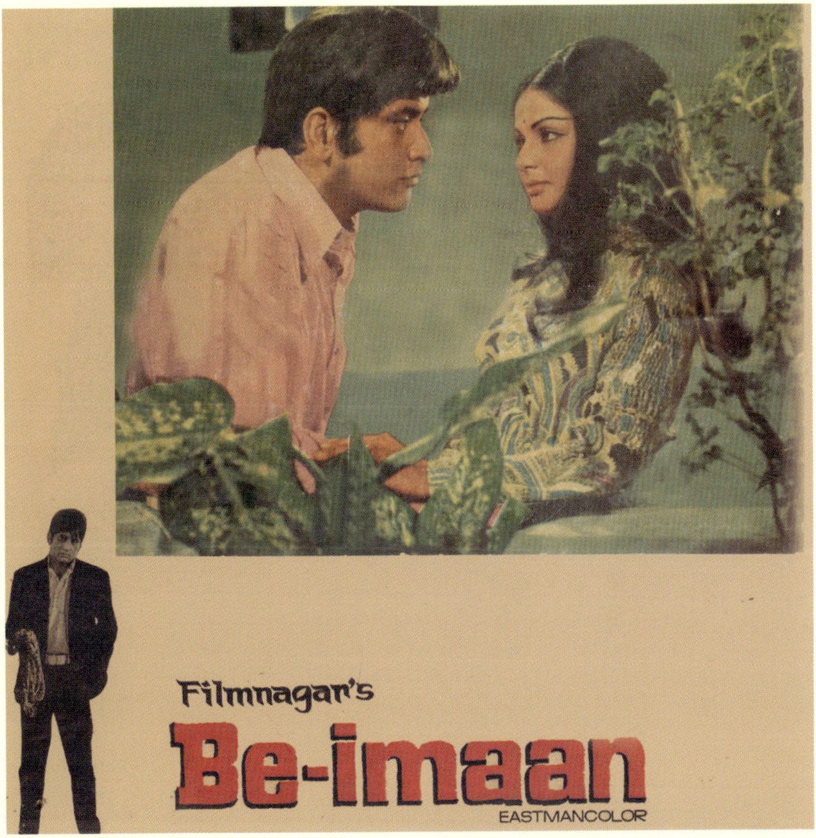

(Picture courtesy: National Film Archives of India)

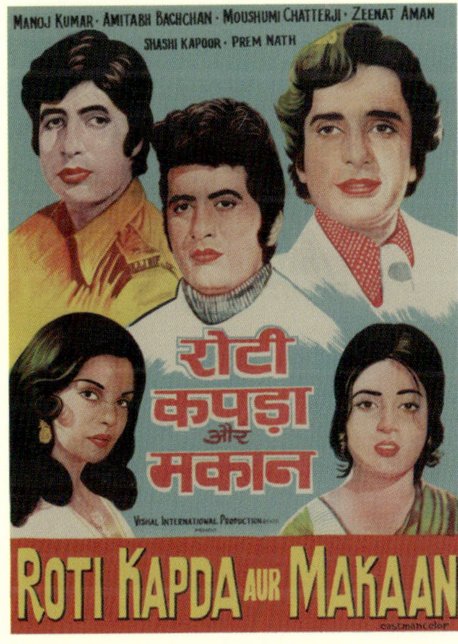

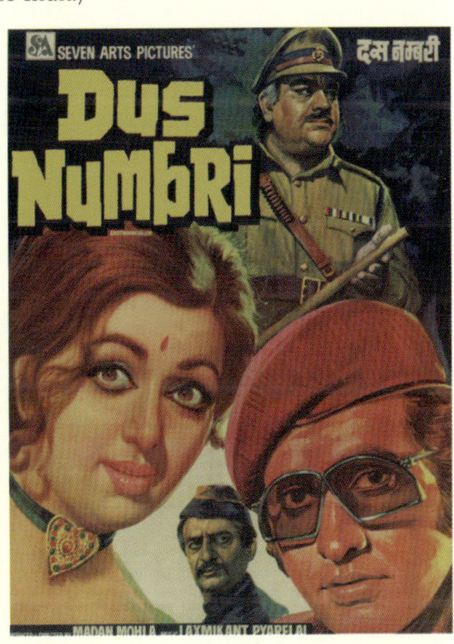

(Picture courtesy: National Film Archives of India)

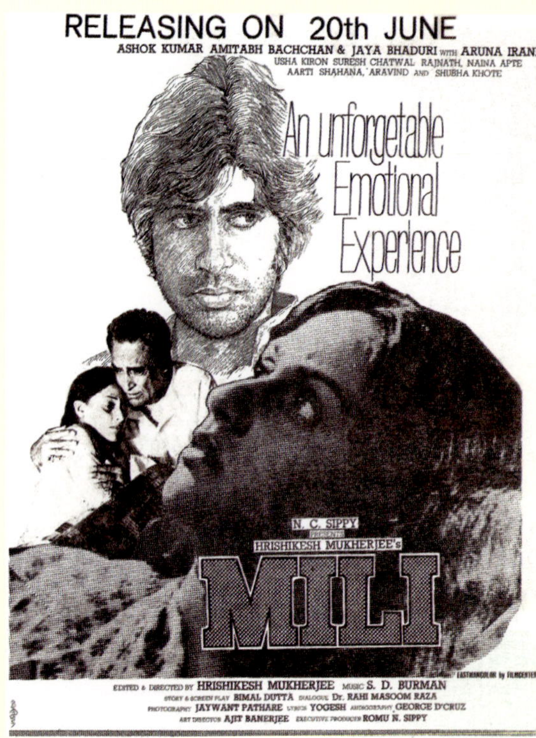

(Picture courtesy: S.M.M. Ausaja Archive)

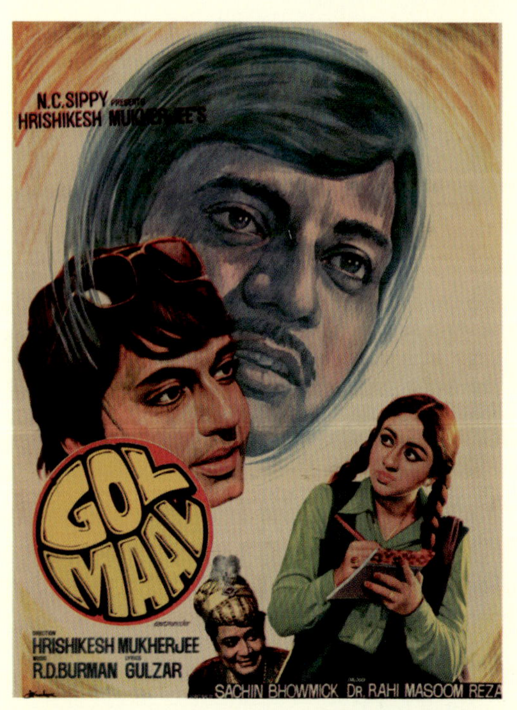

What made the seventies special was the coexistence of the mainstream blockbuster with the arthouse while directors like Hrishikesh Mukherjee, Gulzar and Basu Chatterjee blazed a new trail with their middle-of-the-road cinema

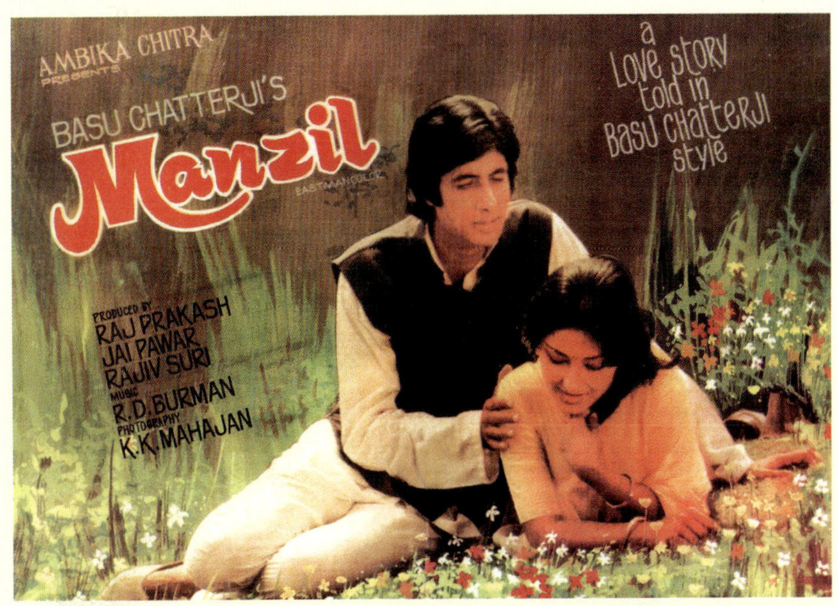

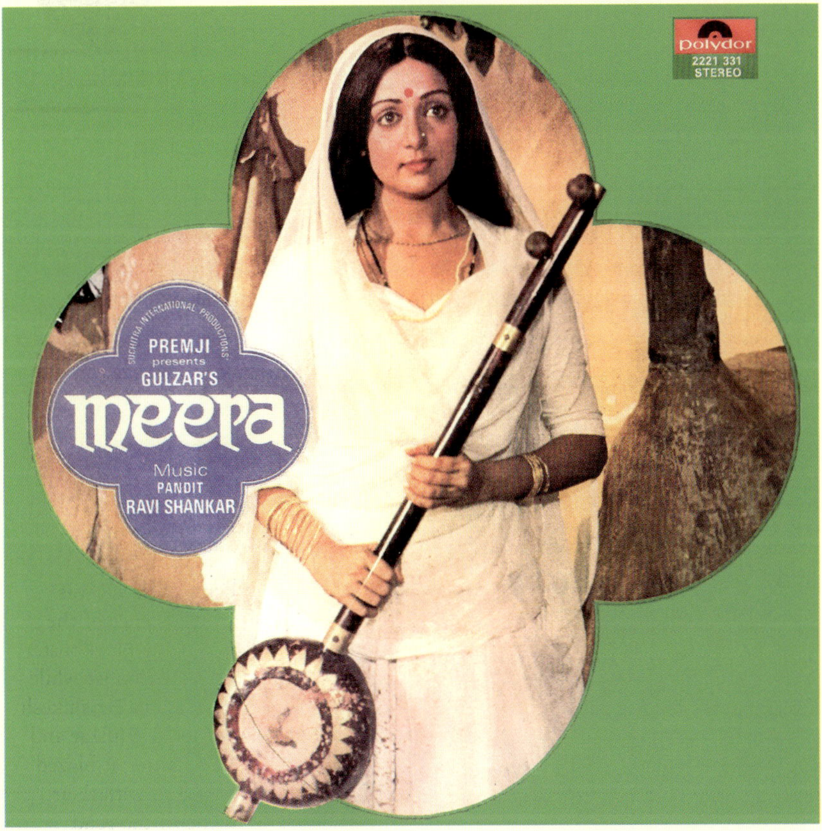

(Picture courtesy: National Film Archives of India)

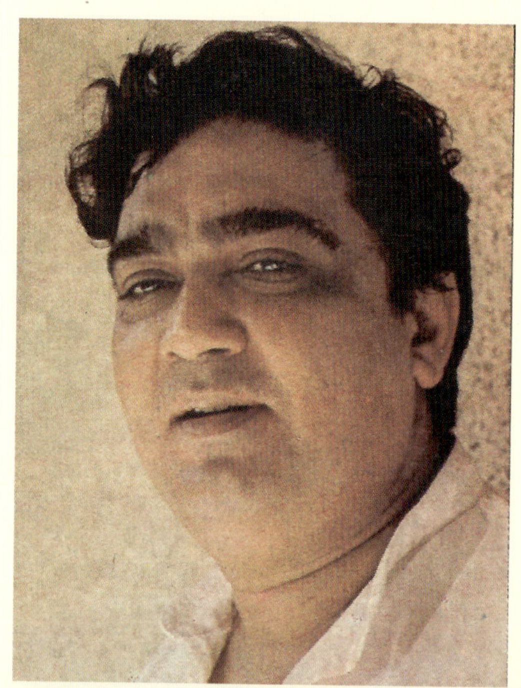

The big four film-makers of the seventies

(Picture courtesy: S.M.M. Ausaja Archive)

Prakash Mehra

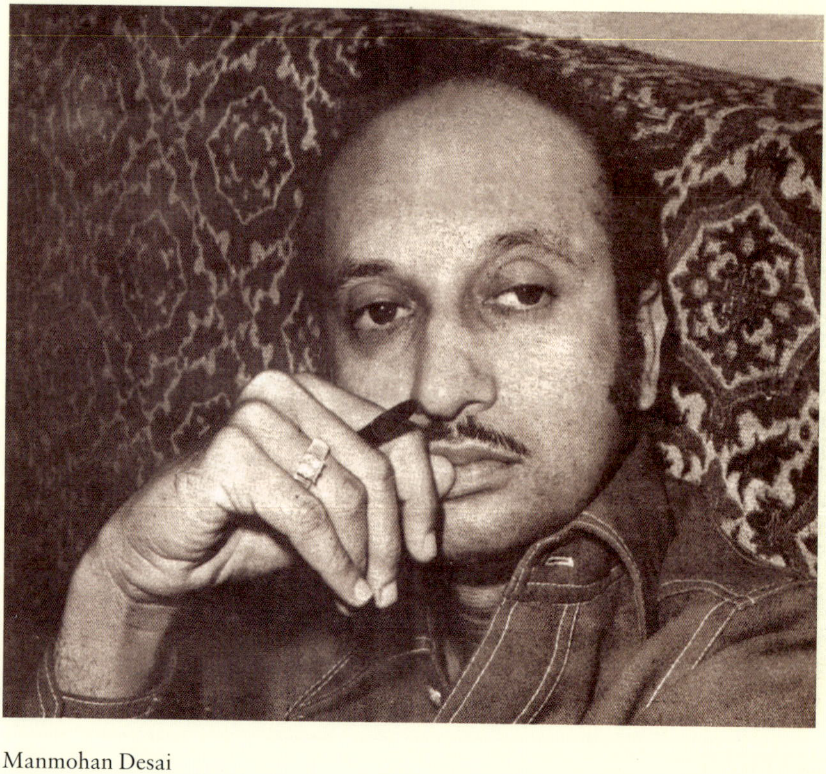

Manmohan Desai

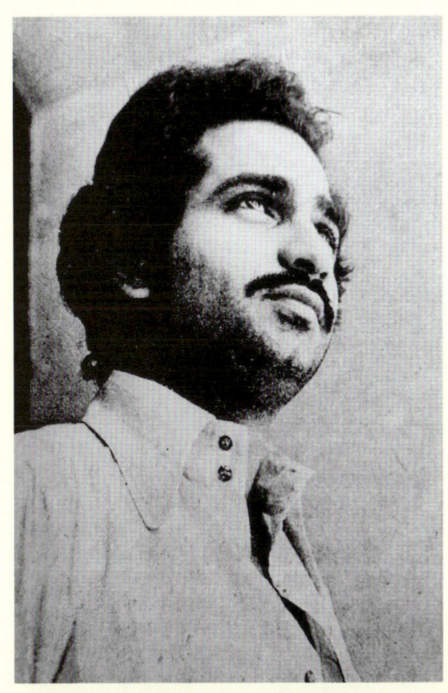

Ramesh Sippy

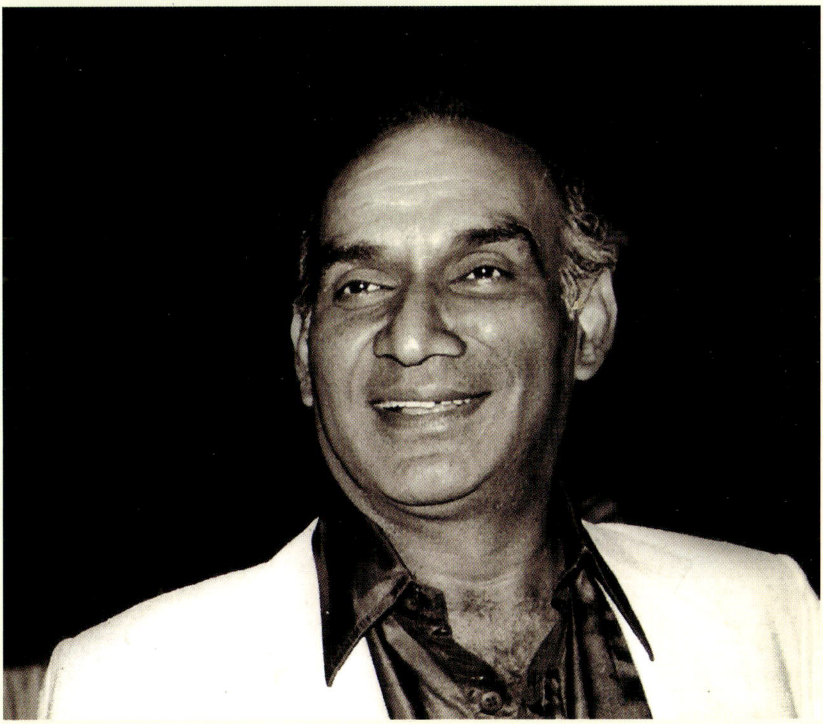

Yash Chopra

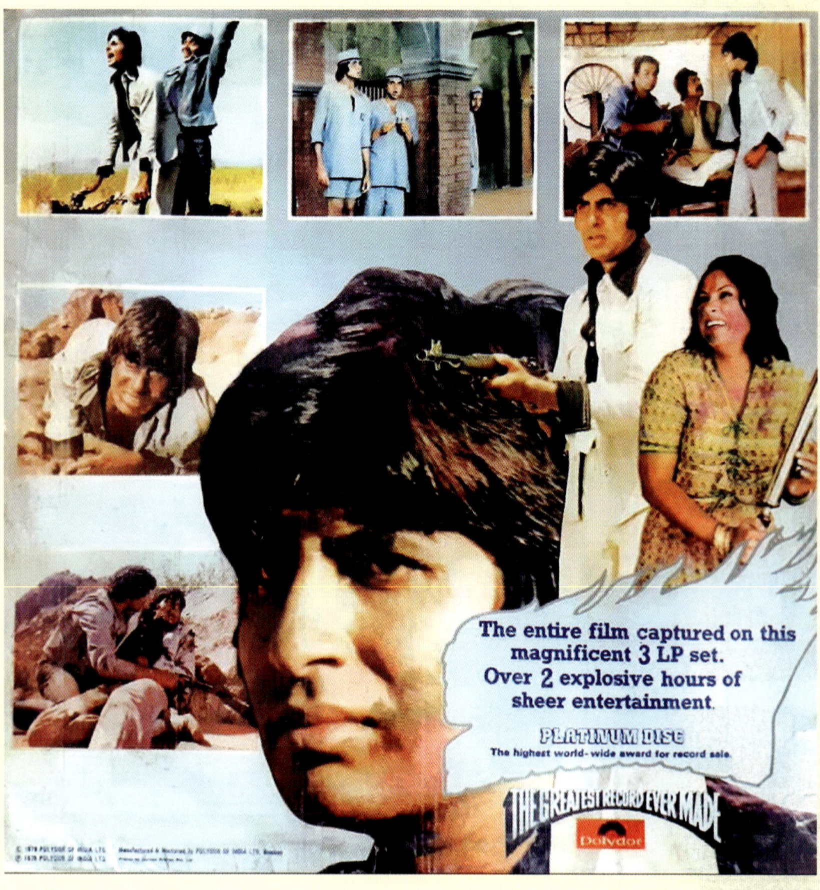

Sholay was not only the biggest blockbuster of the decade, it also revolutionized the sale of vinyl, with Polydor releasing different dialogues' EP records of famous scenes from the film, carrying interesting quotes like 'The merry marriage proposal leading to the "Sooside" act'. It also released a three-LP set of complete dialogues and songs from the film, with a duration of almost three hours, with an inviting three-fold artwork, a first for the Hindi film industry
(Picture courtesy: Bobby Sing)

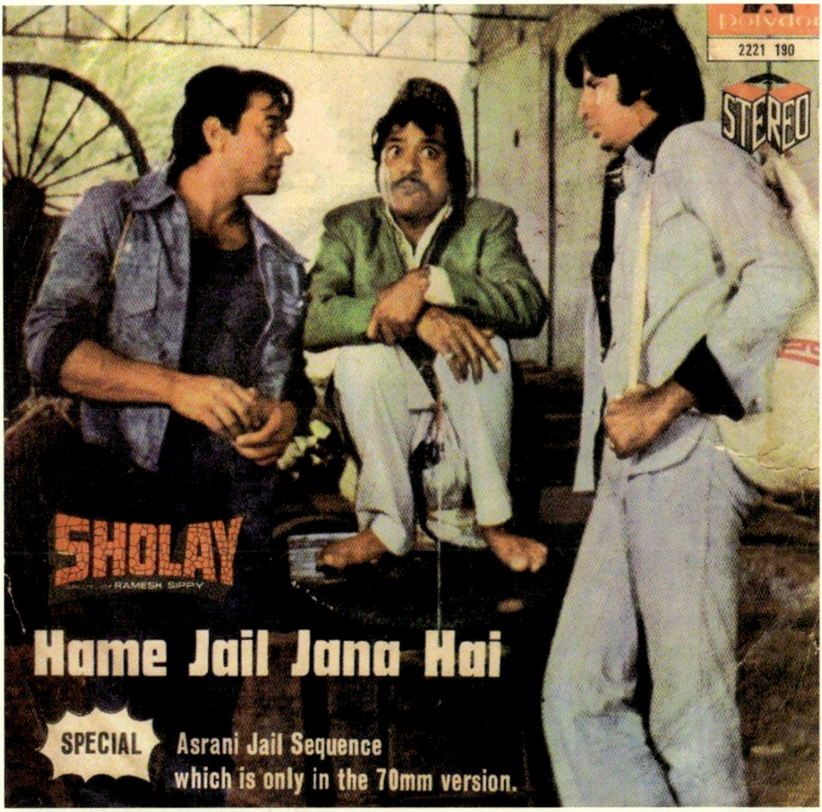

polydor
2221 190
STEREO
SHOLAY
RAMESH SIPPY
Hame Jail Jana Hai
SPECIAL
Asrani Jail Sequence
which is only in the 70mm version.

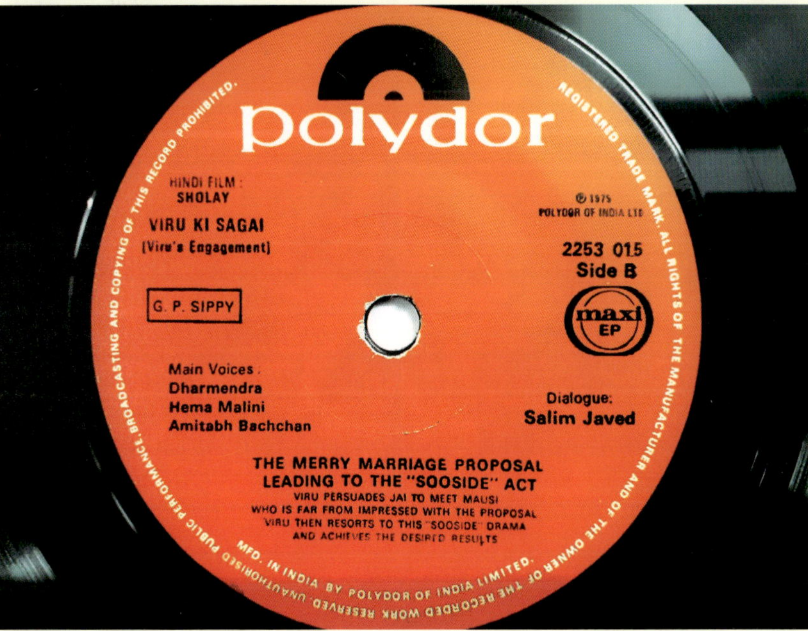

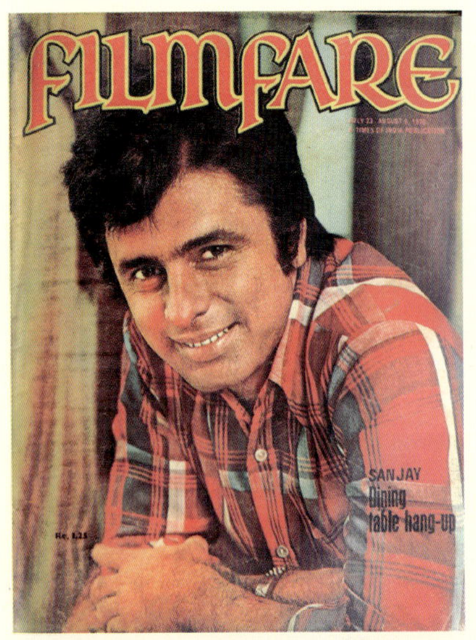

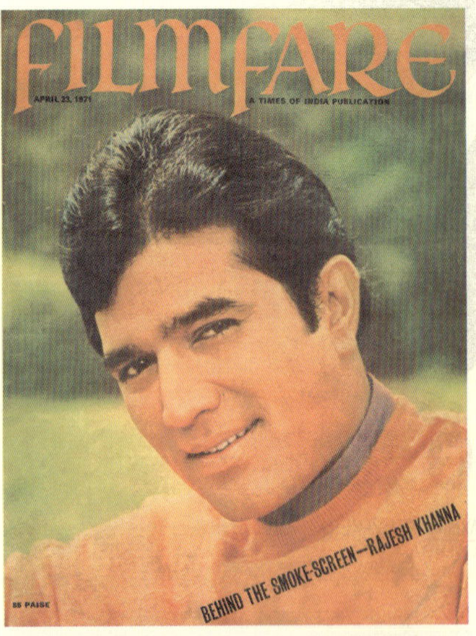

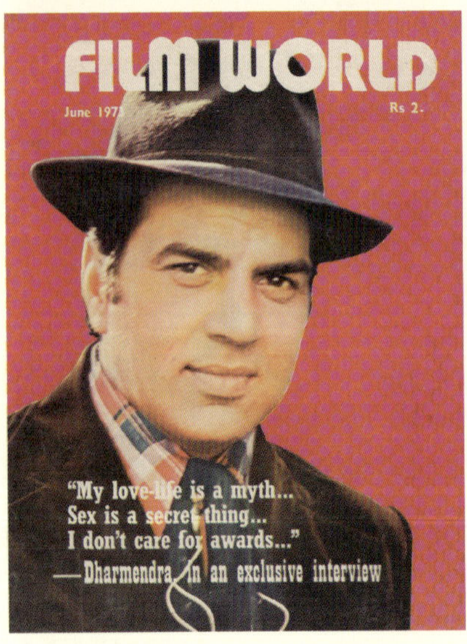

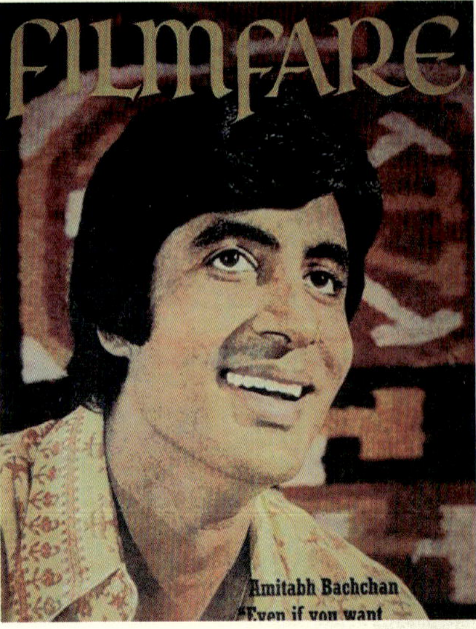

The seventies revolutionized film journalism too
(Picture courtesy: S.M.M. Ausaja Archive)

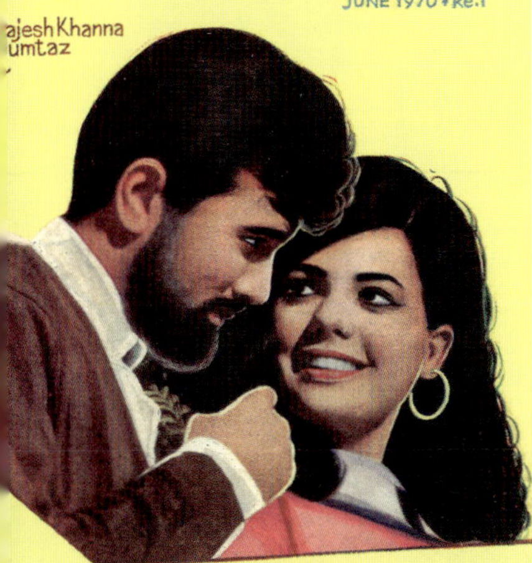
PICTURPOST
JUNE 1970 • Re.1
ajesh Khanna
umtaz
in Raj Khosla's
DO RAASTE
EASTMANCOLOR
MUSIC: LAXMIKANT PYARELAL • LYRICS: ANAND BAKSHI
THE FILM THAT HOLDS THE ALL-INDIA RECORD OF 25 HOUSE-FULL WEEKS!

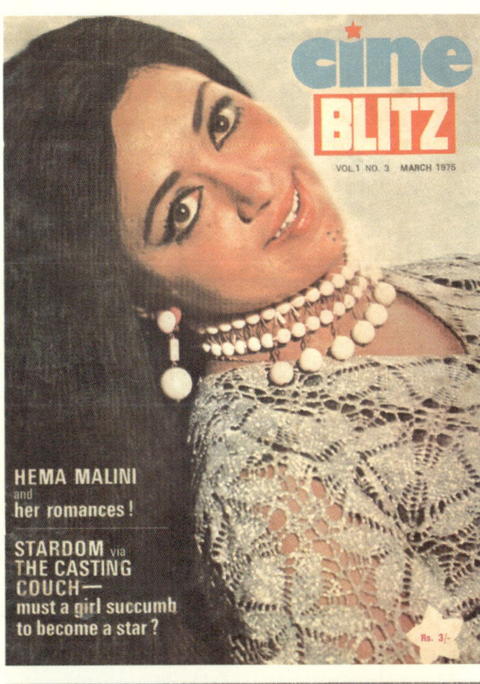
cine BLITZ
VOL.1 NO. 3 MARCH 1975
HEMA MALINI and her romances!
STARDOM via THE CASTING COUCH— must a girl succumb to become a star?
Rs. 3/-

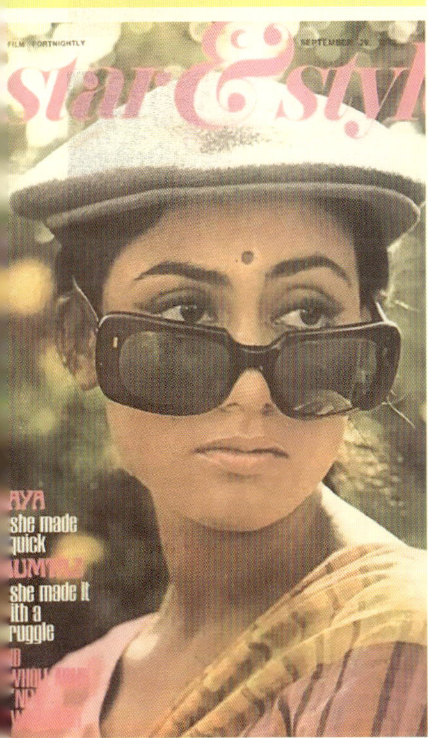
FILM FORTNIGHTLY
she made
quick
she made it
ith a
ruggle

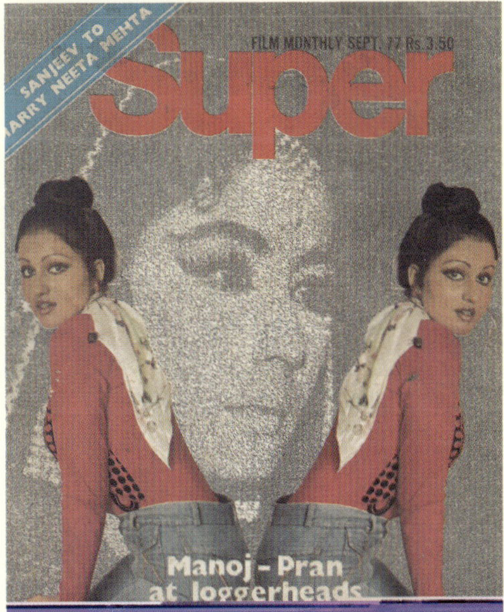
SANJEEV TO
ARRY NEETA MEHTA
FILM MONTHLY SEPT. 77 Rs. 3.50
Super
Manoj - Pran at loggerheads
From Meena to Reena
Devi exposes them all

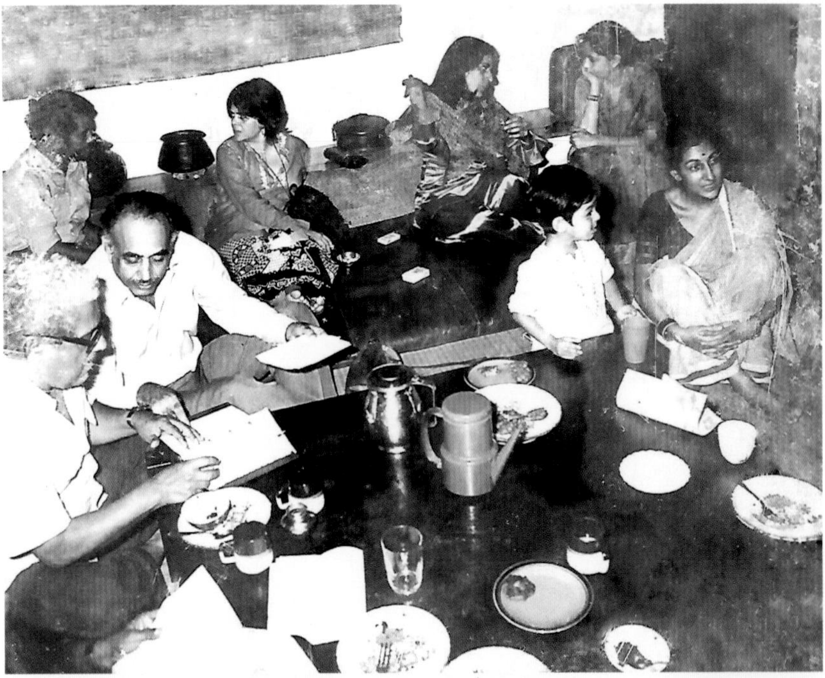

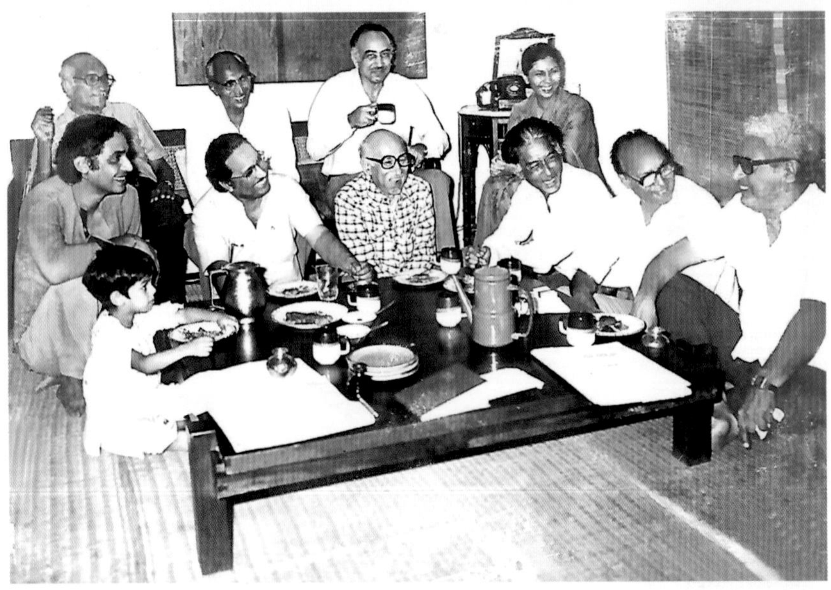

Film-makers in the parallel stream got together in 1977 to form MUKT, the Marketing Union of Kine Technicians, to work as a pressure group to propel the FFC into action to not just fund but also release non-formulaic films. The founders were Muzaffar Ali and Kantilal Rathod whose films *Gaman* and *Kanku* were lying in the cans (Picture courtesy: Rinki Bhattacharya)

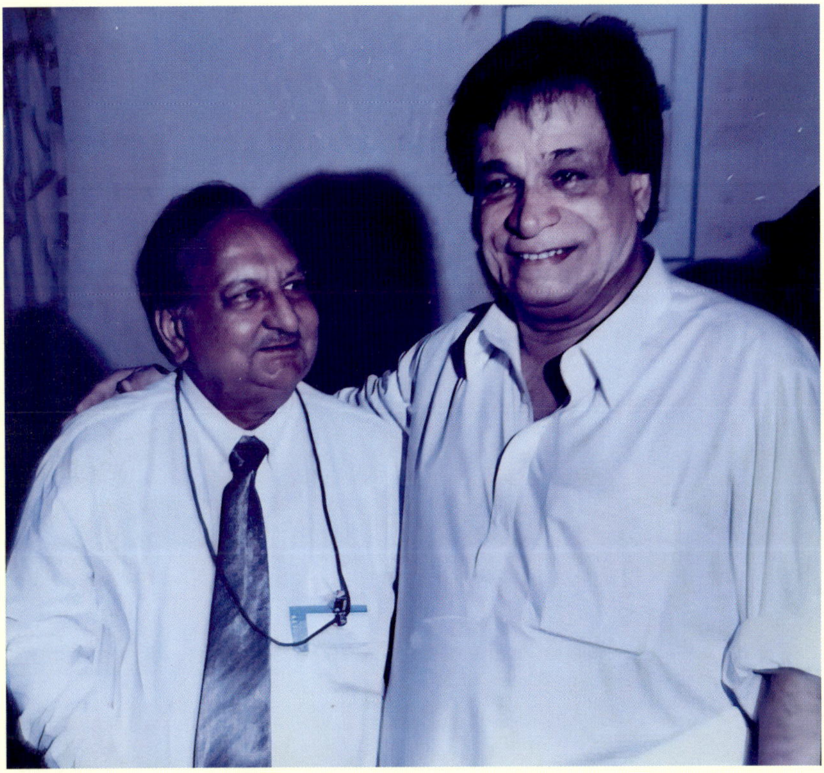

Prayag Raaj and Kader Khan

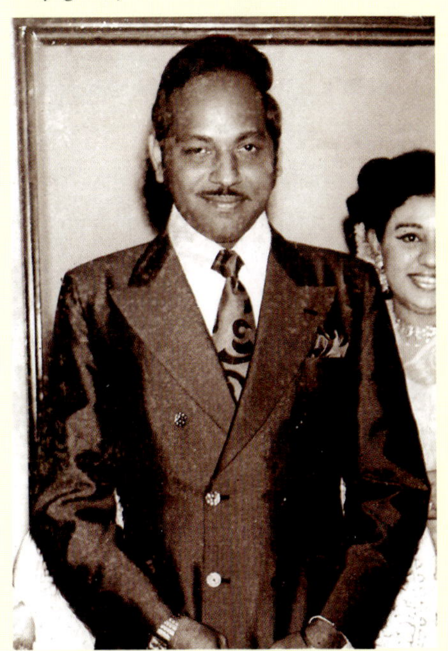

Though Salim–Javed were the acknowledged kings of scriptwriters in the decade, K.K. Shukla, Prayag Raaj and Kader Khan delivered some of the era's biggest hits, particularly in association with Manmohan Desai (Picture courtesy: S.M.M. Ausaja Archive)

K.K. Shukla

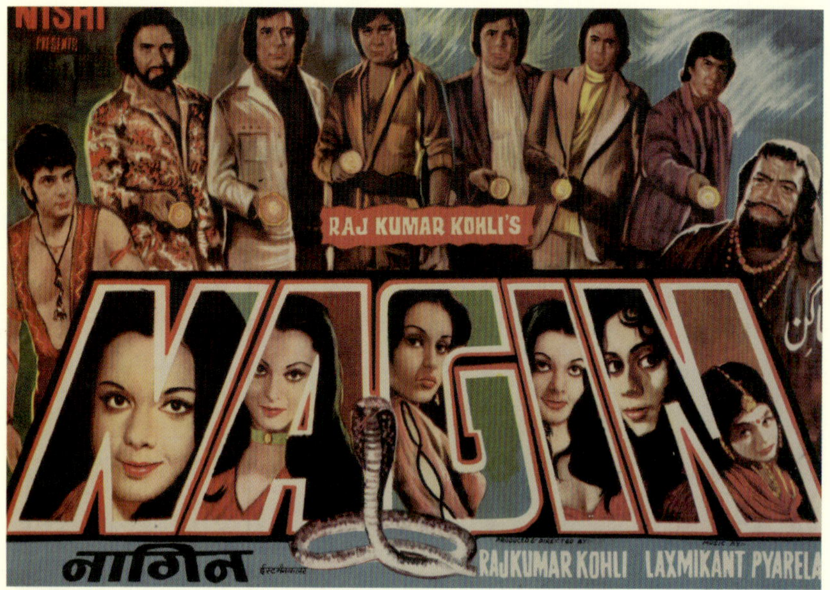

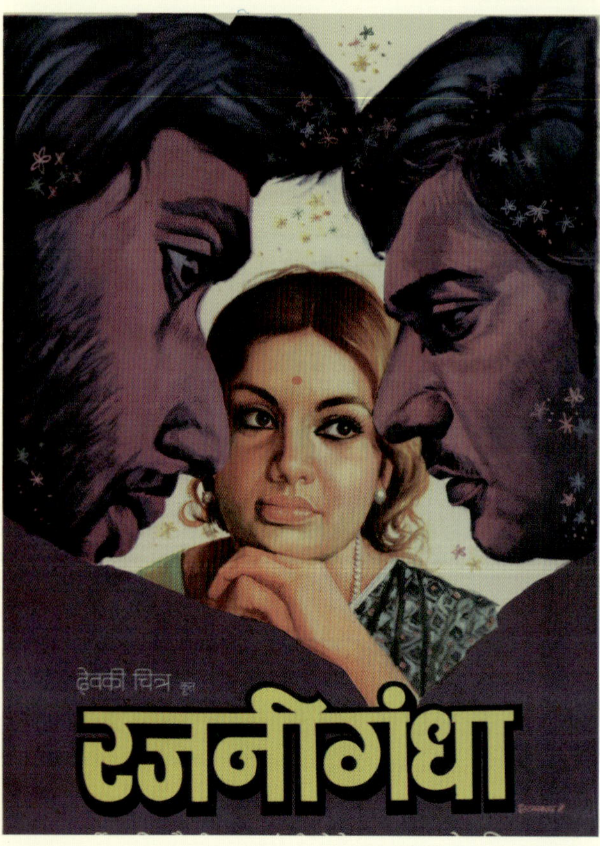

(Picture courtesy: National Film Archives of India)

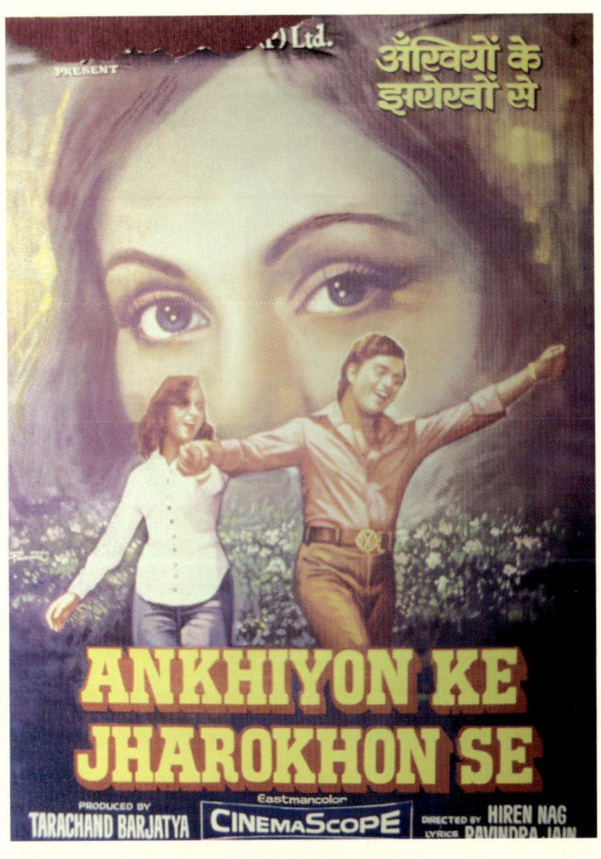

Arguably, no other decade of Hindi cinema offered the variety that the seventies did: from *Zanjeer*'s Angry Young Man to the Rajshri Productions' tearjerker *Ankhiyon Ke Jharokon Se*, to Basu Chatterjee's heartwarming offbeat dramas *Chitchor* (again produced by Rajshri Productions) and *Rajnigandha*, to blockbusters like *Nagin* (directed by Rajkumar Kohli, who specialized in bombastic multi-starrers featuring the who's who of the industry)

(Picture courtesy: National Film Archives of India)

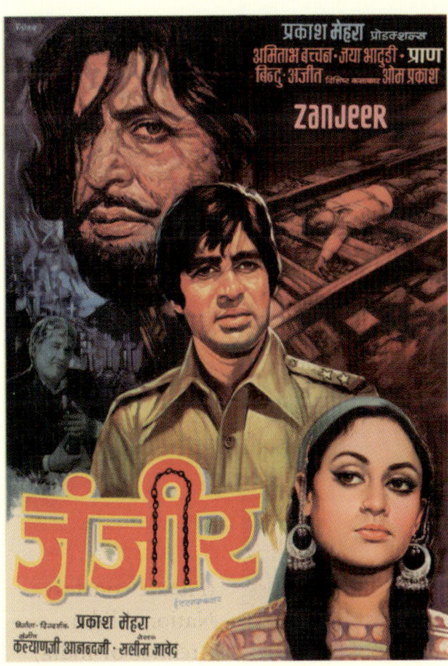

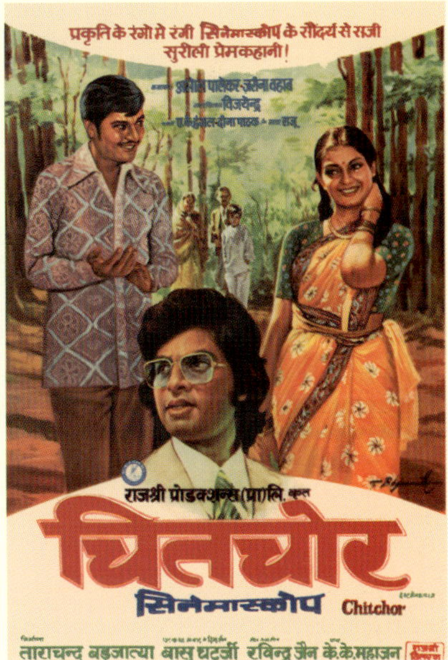

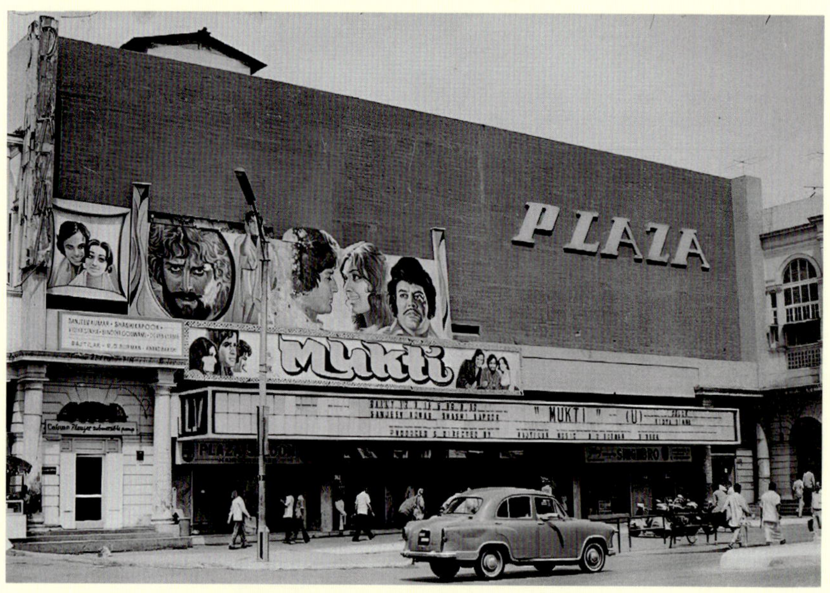

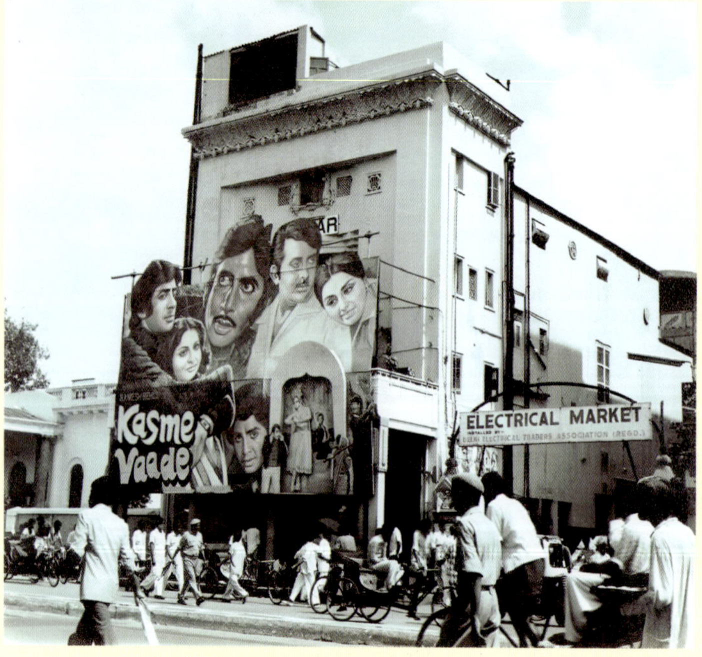

The single-screen theatre with serpentine queues remains an abiding memory of the cinema of the seventies
(Picture courtesy: Bobby Sing)

Section III

Themes and Tropes

Dharmendra and Sanjeev Kumar acted in six movies together. In one of the six movies, during casting, Dharmendra expressed his interest in the role that was eventually played by Sanjeev Kumar; and Sanjeev Kumar wished to play the role of the antagonist, which was then essayed on screen by a rank newcomer. Identify the movie.

Answer: *Sholay* (1975)

It is said that the ailing S.D. Burman went into a coma after rehearsing this famous Kishore Kumar song. Identify the song and movie.

Answer: *Badi sooni sooni hai* (*Mili*, 1975)

A Tale of Two Vijays

Violence in Hindi Cinema of the 1970s
From Salim–Javed to Vijay Tendulkar

Amborish Roychoudhury

> 'There is more violence in places with fewer theatres. How can we say cinema is spreading violence in society?'
>
> —JAVED AKHTAR

> 'The spirit of aggression is something that the human being is born with … Without violence, man would have turned into a vegetable.'
>
> —VIJAY TENDULKAR

It was 1971. Almost a quarter of a century after India's independence from the oppressive British regime. The naïve dream of a utopian state seemed to have been shattered. Rampant corruption existed at every level, a 'Licence Raj' stifled industries, and unemployment ran amok. Organized crime had grown by leaps and bounds. During these turbulent times emerged three writers whose work responded to this disillusionment. The writing team of Salim Khan and Javed Akhtar burst onto the scene with *Haathi Mere Saathi*

(1971) while the Marathi film *Shantata! Court Chalu Aahe* (1971) introduced Vijay Tendulkar to the world.

Unlike Salim and Javed, Vijay Tendulkar was already a known name in the Marathi literary circuit. As a playwright, he had begun to make his presence felt by tackling hitherto untouchable and unpalatable issues. His plays had much to say and were already making people uncomfortable. The duo of Salim–Javed, on the other hand, had started working together with *Adhikar* (1971) but the first time they were credited jointly as a team was in *Haathi Mere Saathi*. But they were biding their time. At this point, the Hindi film hero existed in a vacuum. He had no connection with the real India and its ground realities. These characters were cut out of cardboard, devoid of agency or opinion. Salim Khan said in an interview, '*Uss waqt ka jo hero tha, woh itna submissive thha, itna passive thha … woh rota hi rehta tha.*' (Those days, the hero was so submissive, so passive … he used to cry all the time.)[1]

And thence came the brooding Angry Young Man who seldom laughed or cracked jokes, and never sang or danced. He had a single-minded objective: to fight the system. The 'system' in the case of *Zanjeer* (1973), this hero figure's first outing, was personified in a gangster called Teja who inhabited the upper echelons of society. Our hero fights through various rungs of the ladder till he reaches Teja. All this violence is intensely physical, further amplified by the brooding screen persona of Amitabh Bachchan. The actual fight scenes are not numerous, but his seething rage makes it seem as if there's absolute mayhem on screen.

As the young Salim and Javed laid the foundations of this violent archetype, Vijay Tendulkar was examining violence in his own way. Unlike the writer duo, Tendulkar's intent was not to entertain. Far from it. He wasn't interested in giving the audience 'a good time'. As a point of fact, it was the exact opposite. His writing was designed to make people uncomfortable and cause

---

[1] *The Boss Dialogues with Indu Mirani*, source: https://www.youtube.com/watch?v=h3mxTWGxSKM

them to shift in their seats. About a year before *Zanjeer* came out, Tendulkar's seminal play *Sakharam Binder* was staged for the first time. It is one of the most violent pieces of work ever created in the Indian subcontinent. Its brutality is unrelenting. One doesn't have to watch it; even reading the play fifty years later is enough to make one wince. Sakharam, a bookbinder by profession, brings home abandoned women. They can stay or leave at will, but if they choose to stay, they must do his bidding. They must feed him and look after his needs, or else ... Sakharam believes he has a higher moral ground than husbands who marry their wives and tie them down. In his case, the women are free to leave whenever they wish. If they don't listen to him, however, he is not averse to a little domestic violence. There are scenes which make chills run down your spine. But while giving Sakharam his comeuppance for his deeds in the play, Tendulkar avoids delivering summary judgements on him. He explained in an interview, 'An individual is profoundly impacted by the environment in which they grow up, and it is not possible that that impact renders them non-violent ... I actually like Sakharam. The aggression of human beings under very specific circumstances—it's my favourite theme.'[2]

Some would say Salim–Javed's trademark violence reached its zenith in *Deewaar* (1975). The film's protagonist Vijay beats up a gang of hoodlums within an inch of their lives in a celebrated scene which unfolds inside a warehouse. It is not the stylized action that Bollywood developed from this grain and continued to propagate throughout the 1980s and 1990s. There is a near-perverse brutality in *Deewaar*'s Vijay, like his namesake from *Zanjeer*. He doesn't pull his punches. In the aforesaid scene, once he has accomplished his task, he has to extinguish the rage seething within him by placing his head under a flowing tap. The 'anger' is palpable. But what's interesting about *Deewaar* is that most of the aggression it is known for is more projected than actual. Apart from the warehouse

---

[2] *Tendulkar aani Hinsa* (Tendulkar and Violence), https://www.youtube.com/watch?v=rTqj3GVs6bM

showdown and the climax, the hero doesn't lift so much as a finger to hurt anyone. The 'violence' that one perceives in the film comes from the intensity emanating from the lead character, a rebellious coolie from the docks who rises the ranks to be a dreaded gangster. In his book *Written by Salim–Javed*, Diptakirti Chaudhuri writes:

> *Deewaar* had just this one fight scene but the film always comes across as exceedingly violent because, in the viewers' minds, Vijay starts getting beaten up the day the disgruntled workers tattoo '*Mera baap chor hai*' (My father is a thief) on his arm. It is only now that he is able to give it back and begin the process of finding some sort of closure … This was a common pattern in Salim–Javed's scripts: the action scene would be announced much in advance and the tension kept simmering till it exploded into the actual fight.[3]

The first Hindi film that Vijay Tendulkar wrote a screenplay for was also the one that introduced Naseeruddin Shah. *Nishant* (1975) explored violence in unexpected ways. A zamindar's (Amrish Puri) wayward brother Vishwam (Naseer) lusts after Sushila (Shabana Azmi), the schoolmaster's wife. One evening, Vishwam's brothers kidnap her and take her to their house. There are witnesses but no one opens their mouth. At the house, Sushila finds herself hostage and having to deal with Rukmini (Smita Patil), Vishwam's wife. For a brief period, these women find kindred souls in each other, till Sushila sees that the only way to liberation is through usurping the position of being 'the woman' in an all-male household. Gradually, she develops a relationship with Vishwam and uses that to wield power.

Outside the house, Sushila's husband (Girish Karnad) bands with the temple priest (Satyadev Dubey) and accumulates a large

---

[3] Diptakirti Chaudhuri, *Written by Salim-Javed: The Story of Hindi Cinema's Greatest Screenwriters* (New Delhi: Penguin, 2015), pp. 222

group of villagers to rescue Sushila. The consequence is gory and exceedingly violent. In her book *Smita Patil: A Brief Incandescence*, Maithili Rao narrates:

> Anna is all dressed up in a formal dhoti and angavastram to offer obeisance to the deity outside the main door. The teacher attacks him just when he is about to receive the aarti plate. As if waiting for this spark, the crowd turns into a mob and pours into the haveli. Once anger is let loose and the mob unleashed, there is no safety. Not for innocent Rukmini who may be part of the feudal household but not part of their criminal misdeeds. Rukmini is the witness to a revolution unleashed by a feudal family's relentless tyranny and becomes its victim too. Her husband has been a passive aggressor and so she must pay the price. Revolutions need the blood of innocents.[4]

Violence occurs on many levels in *Nishant* – the obvious violence of the kidnapping brothers, the beneath-the-surface violence between the two women, and the sanguineous end.

Nishant heralded a new kind of cinema that refused to turn away from the ugliness in our everyday lives. Simultaneously, a starkly different cinematic revolution was taking place with *Sholay* (1975). It was more than three hours' worth of gratuitous violence, one in which almost no blood was spilt on-screen until the climax. *Sholay* contains one of the most violent acts humans can conceive of – killing a child. But it doesn't happen on screen. As all members of the Thakur's (Sanjeev Kumar) family are gunned down, Master Alankar is left staring at Gabbar. The following gunshot is heard, not seen, and the next thing on the screen is the kid's body wrapped in a white sheet. The most dastardly acts of savagery in *Sholay* happen off-screen. Whether it's chopping Thakur's arms off

---

[4] Maithili Rao, *Smita Patil: A Brief Incandescence* (Noida: HarperCollins, 2015), pp. 52

or killing Ahmed (Sachin), none of it is shown. As Chaudhuri writes, 'Each one of these scenes is unimaginably violent without focusing on the actual act of violence.'[5]

But *Sholay* does give the impression of being a violent film, and it is undeniably violent. Compared to *Zanjeer* or *Deewaar*, *Sholay* does feature more frequent action set pieces. Gunfights, shootouts and fistfights are all front and centre. The audience took their time to grasp what they were witnessing. The critics were not kind. Veteran critic Krishnanand Amladi of *Hindustan Times* called it a 'gravely failed attempt'. He explained, 'The leading exponents of the current screen cult of bloody reprisals are scriptwriters Salim and Javed, whose none-too-original scenarios only succeed in stating the obvious: That the defence against violence must always be more violence … *Sholay* manages to raise screen violence to almost unimaginable heights.'[6] But how *Sholay* went on to capture the public imagination and broke all box office records is now part of popular movie lore.

If Amitabh Bachchan was Salim–Javed's quintessential Angry Young Man, Vijay Tendulkar's subversive angry man was Om Puri. This was manifested in two distinct films: *Aakrosh* (1980) and *Ardh Satya* (1983). Both Tendulkar and Salim–Javed's protagonists sprung from (and were symptomatic of) the same injustice, corruption, and a general breakdown of the moral fibre that was witnessed in post-Independence India. They are met with violence and they react to it with violence. But the similarities pretty much end there. Salim–Javed's storytelling, while raising some potent questions here and there, aligns with the old adage 'cinema is entertainment'. Tendulkar's work is the opposite of entertainment. His stories are meant to be disturbing. They are supposed to discomfort the viewer, forcing them to introspect. Social scientist Ashis Nandy once wrote, 'Tendulkar never guarantees a good

---

[5] Chaudhuri, *Written by Salim-Javed*, p. 221

[6] 'The Big Fight: How Salim-Javed changed Hindi cinema', https://www.rediff.com/movies/special/the-big-fight-how-salim-javed-changed-hindi-cinema/20151130.htm

bedtime read … He never fails to make you feel that you have entered a dentist's chamber with an undiagnosed abscess in the molars.'[7]

Consider Bhiku Lahaniya (Om Puri), a daily wage labourer, who is constantly bullied by the contractor (Achyut Poddar), but refuses to cower down. To teach him a lesson, the contractor and his men rape his wife, murder her, and frame Bhiku for the crime. Lawyer Bhaskar Kulkarni (Naseeruddin Shah) is appointed to fight his case, while Bhaskar's mentor Dusane (Amrish Puri) stands on the other side. But Bhaskar is helpless as his client refuses to speak. To protect his father and sister (and ostensibly because he doesn't expect any semblance of justice from the 'system'), Bhiku has stopped speaking entirely. Bhaskar desperately wants to win the case and tries his best to uncover the truth. He is threatened and beaten up black and blue. In one of the most heartrending moments ever captured in Indian cinema, as Bhiku is brought in by the cops and unshackled so that he can complete his father's last rites, he picks an axe lying nearby and hacks his sister to death. She was the last member of his family, who they could take advantage of.

If Vijay Tendulkar's primary motive was to unsettle the audience, he was more than successful with *Aakrosh.* In the closing scene, Om Puri's character looks at the skies and lets out a primeval scream. Helplessness and frustration seep out of the screen and lodge in our heads. *Aakrosh* is the pinnacle of Tendulkar's meditation on violence. In Bhiku, this violence is personified. His eyes are like burning coal and you are scared to look into them. Before we get to Tendulkar's definitive ode to anger and righteous violence, we need to take a quick look at two other Salim–Javed films in which the Angry Young Man archetype finally came of age.

After watching *Trishul* (1978), legendary producer Sashadhar Mukherjee told Salim–Javed, 'I have seen this picture three times

---

[7] Ashis Nandy, 'Breakfast with Evil: Vijay Tendulkar on Violence', in *Breakfast with Evil and Other Risky Ventures: The Non-Essential Ashis Nandy* (New Delhi: Oxford University Press, 2021),

to try to see why it's successful, but I can tell you that if you had come to me with this script, I would not have taken it.'[8] He said it because this film's hero only wants one thing in life – to destroy his father. This was inconceivable in Hindi cinema back then. With *Trishul*, Salim–Javed were making a comeback to home territory. They had not made a film with 'Vijay' since *Deewaar*. In *Zanjeer* and *Deewaar*, the protagonists played by Amitabh Bachchan shared a common first name, Vijay, which became the writer duo's short hand for his Angry Young Man persona. Post-*Deewaar*, they took a break from Vijay. Both Jai from *Sholay* (1975) and Ahmed from *Immaan Dharam* (1977) were conmen who discover causes worth fighting for. With *Trishul*, Vijay was back in his element. This time, he had to avenge his mother, and the only way to do that was to destroy his father's business empire and the new life he had built. Vijay is able to accomplish this within a relatively short period of time. *Trishul* had some action scenes that bookended the film, but it resembled a family drama more than anything else. The 'angry' man was still pissed off but he had mellowed down to an extent. It was as if this Vijay had had a skirmish with his father and as soon as it is resolved, his agenda switches from revenge to getting his family together.

In *Kaala Patthar* (1979), Vijay has a new and unique villain: himself. This time, his conflicts are internal. The concept of a disgraced captain who abandoned his crew was borrowed from Joseph Conrad's classic novel *Lord Jim*. After his trial and humiliation, Jim takes refuge in a distant village, where he seeks redemption and acceptance. In Vijay's case, he hides out at a coal mine. The disaster shown in the film was based on a real-life incident at a mine in Dhanbad. It is the disaster that allows Vijay a chance at coming to terms with his past. Of all the collaborations between Yash Chopra and Salim–Javed, *Kaala Patthar* is probably one of the darkest. At least the hero in *Deewaar* allows himself a

[8] Quoted in Rachel Dwyer, *Yash Chopra: Fifty Years in Indian Cinema* (New Delhi: Roli Books, 2002), p. 109.

little indulgence when he is rich and has found himself a girl. *Kaala Patthar*'s Vijay is on penance. He is drawn to Sudha (Raakhee) but doesn't surrender to his urges. The only moments of levity are during his fights with Mangal Singh (Shatrughan Sinha), an ex-con and a rogue with a heart of gold.

Meanwhile, Vijay Tendulkar continued with his exploration of relentless psychological violence that finds a way into the physical. S.D. Panwalkar's short story *'Surya'* provided the germ of *Ardh Satya* (1983). The story didn't have a goon called Rama Shetty, nor did it have Anant Welankar's (Om Puri) incessant run-ins with the system. It is the story of a father and his son. Anant's father was a cop and is hell-bent on making his son join the force too. But that's the last thing on Anant's mind. He is in love with Jyotsna Gokhale from college. They play badminton together. He doesn't want to be a police officer but doesn't have the courage to stand up to his domineering father. He grew up watching him order his mother around and felt helpless. As he unwillingly dons the uniform, Anant drifts away from everyone. He indulges in smoking and drinking. Finally, one day when his father visits him, Anant unleashes all the pent-up rage and lets out a volley of insults. The story ends with him waking up to find his father sleeping on the floor. As the sun rises, Anant pulls a blanket over his father's face.

This poignant but rather tame story eventually morphed into the rage-filled saga called *Ardh Satya*. All the politics and violence that one sees in the film comes from the keen mind of Vijay Tendulkar. Tendulkar's body of work till then was characterized by either implicit or explicit violence. He infused *Ardh Satya* with both. It was Tendulkar who introduced Govind Nihalani to S.D. Panwalkar's collection of Marathi short stories called *Surya*. Nihalani read the translation, and the first story in the book, also called *'Surya'*, attracted his attention. As the decision to make a film on the idea took shape in his mind, Tendulkar built a superstructure around the basic storyline. Anant Welankar was placed in the turbulent Bombay of the early 1980s, with political violence, labour unrest, and corruption at their peak. The abusive father was present, but more fleshed out and more misogynistic. Jyotsna was a more etched-out and richer character, someone who gladly shows a mirror to Anant while being the only one in his life who understands his agony. And Rama Shetty walked in, straight out of oblivion.

Rama Shetty, a quintessential Vijay Tendulkar creation, is a product of the endemically corrupt political system. A smooth-talking goon, he works his way up the ranks as we progress through the film. From heading gambling dens to active politics, his rise is rapid and spectacular. It was a difficult role to cast back in 1983. Most 'villains' in Hindi films till then were cardboard characters, who inhabited a synthetic world created over the years. Rama Shetty belonged to the stark, real world of Bombay's underbelly that had hardly ever been seen in Indian cinema earlier. Govind needed a fresh face who could pull off the menace and dread of a real gangster without resorting to loud theatrics. Tendulkar once again came to the rescue. He told Govind about a Marathi play called *Hands Up*, in which the veteran Bhakti Barve was pitted against a new actor called Sadashiv Amrapurkar (Bhakti later starred in *Jaane Bhi Do Yaaro* as the ruthless journalist). Rama Shetty and the character Sadashiv played on stage that evening were poles apart. And yet, something convinced Govind Nihalani that this man could do justice to the role.

Legend has it that Amitabh Bachchan was considered for the part of Anant Welankar. Bachchan had, just ten years before this, created history by playing the brooding, angry cop Vijay Khanna in *Zanjeer*. Anant was similar to Vijay in many ways, but the differences were striking. Vijay Khanna carried his gloom around like a badge, and Anant Welankar sported the widest grin as soon as he set his eyes on Jyotsna. Vijay fought one man, Anant was fighting the system. Reportedly, Bachchan couldn't commit to the schedule and finally Om Puri was cast.

Puri had been around for quite some time but never really played the lead before. Managing to get this one shot, he gave it everything he had. At that point in time, nobody else in the world could have played Anant Welankar like Om Puri did. He played his greatest asset to maximum advantage: his face. Like Naseeruddin Shah (who himself glitters in a bit role as suspended officer Mike Lobo) once said, 'Om's face … is a landscape in itself.' Jyotsna Gokhale was played by Smita Patil, who could host a masterclass on how to deliver an unforgettable performance with so little screen time. She dazzles the most when she just sits and listens to Anant let it all out.

That moment when Anant Welankar enters Rama Shetty's lair and Shetty looks up and goes, '*Aao saab, aao*' is etched in cinematic history. Sadashiav Amrapurkar's eyes spell danger and make your blood curdle without him touching a gun or killing a soul. His voice, unlike the hero's, stays even and never goes up beyond a notch. Except in that last scene where his life is being squeezed out of him, Rama Shetty is calm as the Pacific. It is difficult to comprehend that Sadashiv Amrapurkar had never been in a film before (barring a Marathi film called *22 June 1897* where he played Bal Gangadhar Tilak but didn't have a lot of screen time). And nor did Sadashiv himself have any inkling of what was actually happening. He had around three to four days of shoot. He did his job and went back to his life in theatre. By the time *Ardh Satya* released, Sadashiv Amrapurkar had completely forgotten about the film and about Rama Shetty. It was the sheer impact of the film that made him realize what he had done and what had really happened.

Many moons later, Sadashiv asked Vijay Tendulkar, 'What made you conceive of me in that role?' Tendulkar replied nonchalantly, 'It's your eyes. You've got opportunist eyes.'

In sum, Salim Khan and Javed Akhtar didn't set out to bring about any social change. Akhtar's own upbringing in a communist environment might have informed the choice of characters, who always inhabited the fringes of society. But these influences are cursory and by all accounts, they just wanted to write thrilling, entertaining movies. It's only in retrospect that one sees how it allowed the discontented urban youth of India an outlet in the form of Vijay, Bachchan's angry, brooding persona. It's a curious irony that around the same time, another Vijay was venting his anger, but on paper. Unlike Salim–Javed, Vijay Tendulkar's meditations on violence had a social core. The frustrations, sorrows, and rage of the middle class found echoes in his scripts. He believed violence to be endemic to human nature, and his characters reflected that truth.[9]

Which Indian playback singer passed away while on tour in Detroit, Michigan, in 1976, leading his son, then a budding playback artist himself, to complete the rest of the tour?

Answer: Mukesh

[9] I thank Shri Bhagyesh Lad, who graciously helped me translate Vijay Tendulkar's Marathi interview from the documentary *Tendulkar aani Hinsa*.

You Sharrup! Sharrup You!

The Missus, The Moll and Everyone In-between

Nandini Ramnath

She resembles no other secretary of a housing complex's managing committee. She is wearing a low-cut black gown with sheer sleeves, an ochre sash and ochre jewellery.

If I knew you would be dressed like this, I would not have called you, says the man on whose complaint she has been summoned.

I designed the outfit myself, I call it provocation, she says with a sly grin. It's indecent, you look like a C-grade heroine, he snarls. And you look like nothing at all, she retorts.

Ms Provocation, or Runa Singh, is a minor character in Hrishikesh Mukherjee's *Mili* (1975), about the romance between the misanthropic Shekhar, who has a tragic backstory, and the bubbly Mili, who is suffering from an untreatable disease. *Mili* stars Amitabh Bachchan and Jaya Bhaduri as the leads and Ashok Kumar as Mili's father. Most of the scenes revolve around their characters. Why then is Aruna Irani's Runa Singh unforgettable?

Might this be because Runa's spunk so deftly deflates Shekhar's sexism? Or that, unlike the rich, unemployed and frequently sozzled Shekhar, Runa spends her time in gainful ways?

Unfulfilled passion simmers between Mili's brother and Runa, whose husband has abandoned her for another woman. It is Runa who nudges Shekhar towards redemption. Runa is outspoken, glam and wise, but she rules from the margins, like so many other women in the Hindi films of the 1970s.

The 1970s cinema seethed with superhuman heroes, virginal heroines and ghastly villains. There were clearly defined slots for good and evil. Punishment, banishment or worse awaited whoever didn't fit in. And yet, untamed feelings flourished at a time when post-Independence optimism had evaporated and the certainties of the Nehruvian era had been eroded. Writers and film-makers stuck to a template created several decades ago but tweaked it ever so often too.

Heroes traumatized by absent fathers, smugglers who lived high on the hog, cheeky vamps, broken families, premarital sex and post-marital flings, wild music, orgasmic singing, licentious lyrics, suggestive choreography, flamboyant clothing, screaming sets, cameras that abused the zoom function – the 1970s oozed elements that could not always be controlled. Some of the women were out of control too in ways that have survived the formulaic storytelling, lack of narrative finesse and stifling moralizing.

Film-makers and scriptwriters left enough room for restless women to exist, even if on the side of the frame or in the background. The singleton, the dance-floor diva, the underworld moll, the unhappy housewife and the woman in a one-sided relationship moved in sidewinder fashion among mummy-obsessed heroes. These women equally defined the 1970s, sometimes by design and sometimes by accident.

Sawan Kumar Tak's pulp classic *Hawas* (1974) has nearly everything that gives the 1970s its outré flavour, with an additional parodic tone to top off Usha Khanna's funk-heavy score. The lust of the title is exuded by Bindu, one of several actresses whose very mononym telegraphed notoriety. Bindu's Kamini pants for young men who are not her husband. Her keen eyes are encased in gigantic close-ups, while her open mouth – a vamp specialty – spouts carnality.

A criminal gang sends its member Anil (Anil Dhawan) to take advantage of Kamini's weakness for 'rangraliya' (a euphemism for sex). Kamini is a nymphomaniac, Anil's boss warns him, thereby enlightening him and innocent viewers of this very shocking and very tantalizing condition.

From the vagina-shaped entrance of the gangster's lair to the cigar puffed by Rekha in a guest song, *Hawas* takes its theme very seriously. Using her standard pick-up line – you resemble my dead lover – Kamini crawls all over Anil, who should be grateful but isn't. The manic cinematography includes a feverish colour palette and upside-down shots of Kamini cavorting with Anil. We are treated to copious imbibing, abominable behaviour in the bathtub, and at least one moment of sincere regret.

Kamini rips off her clothes in an attempt to frame the policeman Mehmood (played by Mehmood) for rape. Why did you bother? Mehmood asks. Fetch me some nightclothes and let's get on with it. He scoots as soon as Kamini leaves the room, but his rueful expression sums up *Hawas* and the decade itself.

Kamini was ahead of the curve that led to Usha, the actress from Shyam Benegal's *Bhumika* (1977). Usha, who has a controlling mother and an abusive husband, embarks on a series of relationships in her mission to gain control of her life. This singular exploration of a woman's desire, indelibly depicted by Smita Patil, includes a statement by Usha that doubles up as a feminist slogan for the 1970s: Henceforth, I will do as I please.

Bhumika was among the few films in the decade that resonated with events beyond the big screen. Women were stirring the pot far beyond the kitchen, entering workplaces and legislative councils in greater numbers than before. They were swelling the ranks of protests centred on land rights, domestic violence and unchecked inflation as well as revolutionary movements aimed at toppling the state.

You wouldn't know of this social ferment that influenced generations of Indians from such films as Gulzar's *Khushboo* (1975), in which Kusum tells her lover, why don't you use your authority over me to destroy my arrogance? In Raghunath Jalani's *Anamika* (1973), a self-declared misogynist shelters a woman suffering from memory loss. He calls her Anamika – the woman with no name and, as it turns out, barely a brain either.

Iconic Hollywood actress Bette Davis is supposed to have said, 'Some young Hollywood starlets remind me of my grandmother's old farmhouse – all painted up nice on the front side, a big swing on the backside, and nothing whatsoever in the attic.'

Also Bette Davis, cutting to the chase: 'I am just too much.'

Ravikant Nagaich's *Kaala Sona* (1975) sees Feroz Khan's Rakesh ordering an admirer to leap into a pool and stay there. She obeys. The film's heroine is named Durga, but she needs Rakesh to defend her virtue. The surprise package is no surprise at all.

Like *Mili*'s Aruna Irani, the movie star tag eluded Farida Jalal despite her natural effervescence. In *Kaala Sona*, Jalal's feisty Bela, who is Durga's sister, is a welcome alternative to Durga's vapidity.

Farida Jalal is also the soul of Hrishikesh Mukherjee's *Alaap* (1971). Amitabh Bachchan, as Alok, is paired with Rekha, but the real deal is Alok's platonic friend Sulakshana, played by Jalal. When Alok contracts tuberculosis and lies lachrymose on a hospital bed, Sulakshana will have none of it. Have you seen yourself in the mirror? How dare you behave like a martyr? So what if you have tuberculosis? You are coming with me!

The lass with sass was a philosophical counterpoint to the average girly-voiced heroine – like Asha Bhosle to Lata Mangeshkar. Free with her body and loose with her tongue, she defied the belief that women should be seen and not heard.

For every utterance associated with wilting women and their fragile honour – *Ofo daddy! Bachao! Chhod do mujhe! Main tumhare bachche ki maa banne wali hoon!* – there were gleeful exemplars of impolite company. In Desh Mukherjee's *Immaan Dharam* (1977),

Helen's Jenny demands 'Whisky, one whiskey', following it up with 'You sharrup! Sharrup you! Rascal! You scoundrel!'

If Helen ruled the dance floor, she was also bound by it – literally so in one of her most famous songs. In '*Piya tu ab toh aa jaa*' from Nasir Hussain's *Caravan* (1971), Helen's character Monica thrashes about with a giant cage in the vicinity before ending up inside the cage.

Caravan also features Aruna Irani as Nisha, a knife-wielding dancer with a travelling troupe. Irani's terpsichorean talent ensured her enrolment in the Department of Easy Virtue that was ruled by Helen and comprised cabaret dancers, gangster's molls and grifters. Nisha throbs for the driver Mohan (Jeetendra), who directs his attentions to the demure runaway Sunita (Asha Parekh). A stereotyped hussy, Nisha is treated shabbily by Mohan, who tries to pair her with a dimwitted troupe member. I can only love a woman who is educated and civilized, Mohan declares.

Remember me if only occasionally, Nisha pitifully says as she sacrifices herself for Mohan's happiness. We do, Nisha, we do, and not only occasionally.

Two of *Caravan*'s best songs belong to Nisha ('*Dilbar*') and Monica ('*Piya tu ab toh aa jaa*'). Some of Hindi cinema's finest music emerged in the 1970s. Many of the earworms are inextricably associated with nightclub dancers, and many of them were belted out by Asha Bhosle with wanton vigour.

Although Helen and her sisters were added to films as visual bait and sonic interruptions, to be discarded after they had served their purpose, they created a space for sexual desire often not available anywhere else in the movie. Their professionalism was matched by the libidinous imagination of film-makers, music composers, lyricists and singers. But the dancer nearly always paid a heavy price for her transgressions. Unrestrained at the club or in the boudoir, she was eventually reined in by lashes of the narrative whip.

Shakti Samanta's *Kati Patang* (1971) is the convoluted tale of Madhu (Asha Parekh), who rejects an arranged marriage match in order to be with her lover Kailash (Prem Chopra). Upon learning that Kailash is bedding down with the dancer Shabnam (Bindu), Madhu runs away, assumes the identity of a widow and then meets Kamal (Rajesh Khanna), who happens to be the man she had rejected in order to be with Kailash. It's a very small world ruled by contrivance and coincidence. Madhu inspires zero confidence, constantly getting into trouble so that she may be rescued by Kamal. As the moral obverse to the white sari-clad Madhu, Shabnam is literally colourful – and infinitely more interesting.

In the song '*Mera naam hai Shabnam*', Shabnam frenetically writhes in a glittering one-piece outfit studded with orange-and-black sequins. Shabnam's loaded threat to expose Madhu as well as her loyalty to the odious Kailash pave the way for a prison sentence.

At least Shabnam survives her ordeal, unlike Nisha from *Caravan* or Lily from *The Train* (1970). The crime thriller, starring Rajesh Khanna as a police inspector and Nanda as his girlfriend with a secret, includes Helen as Lily, a scheming dancer. When a woman decides to do something, she does it, Lily says, adding for good measure, I love life.

But life doesn't love her back. Lily perishes in the end.

Death frequently awaited these fall girls, who existed for the pleasure of men and the consternation of women. Apart from being the target of sententious rhetoric, they were leered at, groped and assaulted by the villain and his posse. They usually bowed out with a well-aimed bullet in the very belly that had been undulating furiously only a few scenes ago.

May no woman suffer as Tara from Vijay Anand's *Johny Mera Naam* (1970). Tara (Padma Khanna) performs a desperate striptease to free her lover from the villain's clutches. Tara begins the song '*Husn ke lakhon rang*' clothed. She is down to her lingerie by the end of it.

Rape follows. Death is a few more reels away.

The women weren't always left to burn in hellfire. At least some film-makers appear to have absorbed French philosopher

Simone Weil's observation that 'Every sin is an attempt to flee from emptiness'.

In Ravi Tandon's *Anhonee* (1973), Rita (Bindu) runs a gambling den, has a scene with a doctor and shows off her martial arts moves in the action-heavy climax. The song *'Hungama ho gaya'* proves just how sensational Rita is. Verma Malik's lyrics skewer the hypocrisy of armchair moralists in the 1970s and beyond. Everyone is drunk, but if I just so much as take a sip, it's a scandal, Rita sings as the inimitable Bindu takes charge of the dance floor. Everyone else behaves as they please, so why pick on me?

Rare is the woman who chooses her own sexual partner. Even rarer is the woman who flouts the one-man-only principle.

Awtar Krishna Kaul's *27 Down* (1974) stars Rakhee as a Life Insurance Corporation employee who falls for M.K. Raina's Indian Railways inspector. The psychodrama memorably crawls into the head of a diffident young man who flees rather than faces life's mysteries. Raakhee's Shalini is unusual in that she lives by herself and decides for herself when Sanjay retreats into a self-induced depression.

That Shalini has made a bad choice is evident when she first meets Sanjay in a crowded Bombay local train compartment. Sanjay inconsiderately remains seated while Shalini uncomfortably stands around. Shalini's decision to break up is a surprise only to Sanjay.

Sanjay's reaction to Shalini's choices reflects some of the disquiet over working women in this period. After all, who were the Ritas and Monicas but working women, trying to survive by shimmying through the netherworld?

Some of the women who crossed the domestic threshold faced the same workplace dangers as did dancers or sex workers. The boss's secretary was barely different from the sex worker – up for grabs, but for free.

In B.R. Chopra's sex comedy *Pati Patni Aur Woh* (1978), the paunchy Ranjeet (Sanjeev Kumar) seduces his secretary Nirmala (Ranjeeta Kaur) by giving her a fake sob story about a terminally ill wife. Nirmala's entry into Ranjeet's cabin is accompanied by the kind of jaw-dropping reserved for the cabaret artist. Just to be sure, the camera zooms in hard on Nirmala's cleavage.

In Basu Bhattacharya's marital trilogy *Anubhav* (1971), *Aavishkar* (1974) and *Griha Pravesh* (1979), secretaries and typists eagerly linger at the hero's desk to distract him from his vows. The films are unconventional in that they explore the emotional and sexual distance that sometimes grows after marriage, but most conventional in that their heroines are homebound and wait for their errant men to return from their wanderings.

In *Griha Pravesh*, Amar, who has a wife and son, is forced to share a cabin with Sapna (Sarika) – a prospect he welcomes. There was clearly a shortage of desirable men in 1979, going by Sapna's confession to Amar that his 'lack of desire' has provoked desire in her. Sapna astutely analyses Amar's predicament – you love your wife but lust for me – and yet hangs around, waiting to be rejected by him.

The fate of the high-ranking working woman is equally perilous. Ramesh Talwar's *Doosara Aadmi* (1977) sends out an early signal about its theme through Deven Verma's music teacher, who says that he wants only female pupils because they don't have brains (and then proceeds to paw them).

Nisha (Raakhee) transforms the fortunes of Karan's advertising company. Dressed in modish saris with sleeveless blouses, an open consumer of cigarettes and alcohol, and an advertising whiz, Nisha should be a role model. Alas, Karan reminds Nisha of her dead lover Shashi. (An in-joke, since Karan is played by Rishi Kapoor and Shashi by Kapoor's real-life uncle, Shashi Kapoor.) The possibility of Karan and Nisha getting together is as remote as a vamp and hero sashaying into the sunset.

A single mother governed India as prime minister in the same decade when a character inspired by her, upon meeting her estranged husband after years, proceeds to fix him a cup of tea.

Gulzar's *Aandhi* (1975) stars Suchitra Sen as a politician who shares the silver streak in her hair with Indira Gandhi. Sen's Aarti

Devi has been pushed into politics by her ambitious father, causing a rift in her marriage with the hotelier JK (Sanjeev Kumar).

Is Aarti ever her own woman? When she first meets JK, she is drunk (her drink has been spiked, of course) and passes out presumably unclothed in her bathtub in JK's presence. When they marry, JK prefers Aarti to be a housewife.

The so-called respectable women who purposefully clutched handbags and found love at work were like snowstorms in the summer. Some of them were to be found in Basu Chatterjee's films, which crystallized urban middle-class aspirations with humour and tenderness.

Prabha from *Chhoti Si Baat* (1976) and Nancy from *Baaton Baaton Mein* (1979) meet their prospectives because they are working women. Prabha runs into Arun at a bus stop and bonds with him because they work in the same office district. Nancy too encounters Tony while travelling on Mumbai's suburban railway network. The trudge to and from the workplace allows lovers to meet unsupervised and away from the prying eyes of family members.

Hrishikesh Mukherjee's *Abhimaan* (1973), about a popular singer's resentment when his wife becomes more successful than him, is as much a marital drama as it is an examination of the anxiety over working women. The sideshow to Subir and Uma's marriage is provided by Chitra (Bindu), Subir's 'friend' who 'expects nothing more than friendship' from him.

In her stoic acceptance that she is only fit to pass the time with, and in her observation that 'A sad song is the real note of life,' Chitra cuts deep to the film's melancholic core while being relegated to the sidelines.

A straight line runs from good-time secretary to sex work in B.R. Ishara's *Chetna* (1970). Opening scenes of Seema (Rehana Sultan) offering multi-faith prayers ease us into the film's voyeuristic handling of Seema's journey from modelling to prostitution. Salvation appears in the form of Anil (Anil Dhawan), who accepts Chetna's past and moves in with her. In a strange sequence by both

1970s and contemporary standards, Seema looks amorously at a bare-chested Anil while he is asleep – a reversal of the male gaze.

If words wound Seema, she too passes a judgement on her situation. Since 'A broken mirror cannot be put back together' and 'When my womb is full of poison, no medicine can cure me', Seema is doomed to failure and death.

Sex workers barely survived cinema's punitive tendencies. From the courtesans of such films as Kamal Amrohi's *Pakeezah* (1972) to the prostitute in Shakti Samanta's *Amar Prem* (1972), these designated fallen women suffered deeply and bled magnificently.

Sharmila Tagore, who starred in *Amar Prem*, also headlined Shakti Samanta's tellingly titled *Charitraheen* (1974). The film uses the device of the court case to pronounce a verdict on Rosy. Accused of aiding an embezzlement, Rosy's guilt is presumed since she is 'immoral and infamous', a 'public woman', a lawyer thunders.

Rosy has only been helping Inder, her former lover. I won't come in your way, the selfless Rosy tells the since-married Inder, I am going away. And she does, to that place in movie heaven where the whores and vamps and viragos and tarts and floozies and harridans and hussies are.

Twinkle Twinkle Little Stars

Flirting with Stardom

Avijit Ghosh

> Slip slidin' away
> Slip slidin' away
> You know the nearer your destination
> The more you're slip slidin' away
> —Paul Simon, US singer-songwriter

In the summer of 2007, cricketer Manoj Tiwary was hot and happening. Scoring runs in domestic first-class games seemed easier than drinking coffee to him. The ustaads couldn't stop praising his style and strokes. Then suddenly one day, Providence played the villain. Selected for a Bangladesh tour, Tiwary dived in the outfield on the eve of his debut international game. He dislocated his shoulder and was ruled out for the entire trip. 'I went back to the hotel room and cried,' he confessed in an interview many years later.

The injury pushed Tiwary back in the queue of cricketers aspiring to break into Team India. The moment and the momentum were gone. Eventually, Tiwary tasted a modicum of international success. His career never touched the expected heights, though at thirty-eight he was still good enough to play for Bengal. By the way, he is the state's sports minister too.

What happened to Tiwary isn't unique to cricket. Hard-luck stories abound in the world of entertainment too. Hindi cinema is riddled with careers that could have touched the stars but ended with a fistful of stardust. You can say the scripts let them down, or the big banners looked away, or perhaps, luck was not in love with them. Some even flirted with success. But then, like water running through fingers, stardom slipped away from their grasp.

The Men

Navin Nischol

Navin Nischol is Hero No. 1 in this class of little stars who twinkled briefly in Bombay cinema. The Lahore-born and FTII-trained actor arrived with *Sawan Bhadon* (1970). There was a messianic mania surrounding Rajesh Khanna those days. But both Nischol – he was Nischal then – and his movie held their own.

Sawan Bhadon was a notch above the staple matinee. Directed by the dependable Mohan Segal (*Saajan*), the movie's plot was as twisted as a cryptic crossword, but somehow everything seemed to fall in place. The dialogues (Ali Reza) were crisp and Sonik–Omi's boisterous melodies ('*Kaan mein jhumka, chaal mein thumka*') a perfect fit for the north-Indian hinterland the film was located in.

Nischol played a foreign-returned heir to a vast rural estate. Slender and fetching, he looked remarkably assured for a debutant, especially in scenes of confrontation with veterans: the wily stepmom (Shyama) and the delightfully devious maternal uncle (Krishan Dhawan). His voice, diction, and dialogue delivery underlined that the gold medal earned in Poona was well deserved. The film made Nischol an instant star and an accidental trendsetter. Suddenly, many more producers were willing to bet on freshers.

For a time, Nischol was cover-story material. He looked dapper serenading Yogeeta Bali in the song '*Yoon na sharma phaila de apni gori gori bahein*' from *Parwana* (1971), while second-fiddle Amitabh Bachchan enviously looked on. And he looked at home as the urbane Canada-educated owner of a forest in Deven Verma's *Nadaan* (1971). The character, we are told, studied plantation. In the film, he largely chopped trees.

Parwana bombed. *Nadaan* less so. But Nischol bloomed. He pranced and wooed the equally slender Saira Banu in Brij's crime comedy, *Victoria No. 203*, a runaway hit of 1972. But the past-master pair of Ashok Kumar and Pran offered laughs and walked away with the claps. In 1973, producer–director Chetan Anand's *Hanste Zakhm*, an unlikely love story between a cabbie and a sex worker, became a surprise box-office winner, with a clutch of divine Madan Mohan compositions playing their part. The same year, the actor reunited with his *Sawan Bhadon* co-star Rekha for producer S.K. Kapur's *Dharma* (1973), an innovatively scripted dacoit drama. The film roared to success but was more talked about for the performances of Pran and Ajit, and for one of the most *paisa-vasool* qawwalis ever, '*Raaz ki baat keh doon toh*' (written by

Kabir Bedi

Tall and devilishly attractive, Bedi failed miserably in Bombay cinema of the 1970s. Ironically, the urbane hero tasted success only as a rustic dacoit in Raj Khosla's *Kuchhe Dhaage* (1973). But Bedi went on to become India's most successful actor abroad in the super-hit Italian TV miniseries *Sandokan* (1976). He was mobbed across Europe. Bedi also acted in the Bond film *Octopussy* and the captivating TV serials, *Dynasty* and *The Bold and the Beautiful*. Later, he enjoyed a strong second innings in Hindi cinema as a character actor.

Verma Malik and composed by Sonik–Omi). Moral of the story: You might be part of a box-office winner, but the credit may not come to you.

At this stage, Nischol needed a solo hit to move up the ladder. He hooked up with mentor Mohan Segal in *Woh Main Nahin* (1974). The actor had a meaty double role, one of them of a heartless killer who changes professions and identities. In image-conscious Bombay cinema of the 1970s, few stars would have agreed to do the part. Balaji Vittal, author of *Pure Evil*, a book on the villains of Bollywood, says, 'Nischol's multi-dimensional performance including the different body language and dialect was not very far from Sanjeev Kumar's in *Naya Din Nayi Raat* (1974). Alas, this role does not get spoken about to the extent that it should.'[1] Much was expected from the film but it sank like a pebble in a pond. About twenty years later, Shah Rukh Khan would take a similar route to super success with *Baazigar* and *Darr*.

Now flops started chasing Nischol like a dark shadow. Social drama *Paise Ki Gudiya* (1974) and crime caper *Ek Se Badhkar Ek* (1976), both directed by the capable Brij, didn't work. By the mid-1970s, action was the big game. Nischol fiddled with adventure yarn *Zorro* (1975), action-driven *Aafat* (1976), and *Mere Sajna* (1975), a crime drama where he played a hired gun. All crashed.

Yet Nischol was seldom short of work. On the contrary, he played the lead in at least twenty films even in the early 1980s. But big banners ignored him, a multi-starrer like Manmohan Desai's *Desh Premee* (1982) being an exception.

Nischol earned praise for his moody and melancholic businessman act in Rajshri's tender love story *Ek Baar Kaho* (1980) – inspired by *Come September* (1961) – and lent a certain refinement to Ramsay's suspense-filled *Saboot* (1980) and horror

---

1 Avijit Ghosh, 'Teja, Gabbar, Loin: The 1970s saw the most exciting villains', interview with Balaji Vittal, *The Times of India*, 3 April 2022, https://timesofindia.indiatimes.com/blogs/Addictions/teja-gabbar-loin-the-1970s-saw-the-most-exciting-villains/?source=app&frmapp=yes

yarn *Hotel* (1981), both 'plus' projects. But there was no discernible profit to his career. Then bad luck struck again. He was reportedly considered and dumped for the role Kulbhushan Kharbanda performed in *Arth*.

By 1986, Nischol was playing father to Sunny Deol in Rahul Rawail's *Samundar*. Much of his work in the 1990s is unremarkable. Home audience loved him, though, in the zany sitcom, *Dekh Bhai Dekh* (1993–94). And he sucked satisfyingly on Rekha's resolute toe in director Basu Bhattacharya's *Aastha* (1997). The new millennium was forgettable too; the jholawala theatre artiste in Dibakar Banerjee's feel-good hit *Khosla Ka Ghosla* (2006) was his last remembered performance.

By now, the actor had made peace with his downgraded status. In an interview, Nischol confessed that he didn't mind getting into an auto rickshaw. 'I never fooled myself into believing that my stardom would last forever,' he said.[2]

In 2007, the actor was charged with abetting wife Geetanjali's suicide. He was acquitted later. Perhaps the case drained him out. Nischol died of a heart attack while travelling to Pune in 2011. 'Lower the car AC,' were his last words. It was the day after his sixty-fifth birthday.

Anil Dhawan

Like Nischol, Kanpur-born Anil Dhawan entered the industry with a box-office hit. Tall, fair, and handsome, the actor was also blessed with the finest mop of hair this side of the Sutlej. But his awkward smile was a big B minus.

The bank manager's son was introduced by FTII classmate and friend Shatrughan Sinha to director B.R. Ishara, who was looking for a fresh face for *Chetna* (1970). 'We went to Bombay Lab in Prabhadevi. I got down from the car, walked up to him, shook his hand and introduced myself. He just took the cigarette out of his

---

[2] Meena Iyer, '...And When Stars Fade', *The Times of India*, 2 November 2006.

mouth and said, "You are what I was looking for: a young man with an innocent face,"' Dhawan once recalled.[3]

Produced on a shoestring budget and shot over twenty-six days in Poona, *Chetna* was about a guileless young man who falls in love with a call girl and marries her. She finally dies by suicide. The film's poster had a voyeuristic camera ogling at a bare-legged Rehana Sultan, her legs spread like an upturned letter V. The shot is a pin-up moment of 1970s Hindi cinema. Dialogues such as '*Maine itne nange mard dekhe hain ki mujhe kapde pehne hue mardon se nafrat ho gayee hai*' (I have seen so many naked men that I have started hating them in clothes), scenes considered explicit in their time, and a provocative storyline helped the film become a sleeper hit. Sultan – she married Ishara later – was praised for her performance. But Dhawan gained more from the triumph.

The year 1971 was a mixed bag for Dhawan. Director Feroz Chinoy's *Do Raha* (1971), made on the lines of *Chetna*, was a modest success. Like Nischol, Dhawan also acted with a pre-*Zanjeer* Amitabh Bachchan in Raveekant Nagaich's *Pyar Ki Kahani* (1971). The *Times of India* (*TOI*) wrote, 'Anil Dhawan ... looks as wooden

Rakesh Pandey

The actor from the hills of Himachal Pradesh made a promising and successful debut as the introverted hero in director Basu Chatterjee's debut venture, *Sara Akash* (1969). He was preferred to Subhash Ghai for the role. Pandey played the lead in several movies in the early 1970s including Gemini's *Ek Gaon Ki Kahani* (1975). He is said to have been chosen over Amitabh Bachchan for *Andolan* (1975). Both failed. Pandey finally attained stardom in Bhojpuri films after *Balam Pardesiya* (1979).

[3] Avijit Ghosh, 'Film director Ishara dies at 77', *The Times of India*, 30 July 2012, https://timesofindia.indiatimes.com/india/film-director-ishara-dies-at-77/articleshow/15151742.cms.

as he did in *Chetna*.'[4] The producers either didn't read the review or simply didn't care. The same year, he signed seven films during the Diwali week.

When Basu Chatterjee's *Piya Ka Ghar* (1972) fared well both critically and commercially, Dhawan was declared a lucky star. Dhawan and fellow FTII-ian Jaya Bhaduri made a cosy couple whom you wanted to spend more time with. The film, which underlined Bombay's lack of private space for young couples, was enlivened by Chatterjee's lightness of touch.

In the next couple of years, Dhawan seemed to be in the capable hands of similar reputed Bengali directors. He was the unassuming do-gooder in Asit Sen's *Annadata* (1972), where he again had Bhaduri for celluloid company. In Ajoy Biswas's *Samjhauta* (1973), he was the naïve and sentimental country singer who arrives in Bombay to try his luck. *Honeymoon* (1973), directed by Hiren Nag, was a frothy romantic comedy from the house of Rajshri. But none of these gentle movies, including Sen's *Anokha Daan* (1972), fetched 'houseful' boards. Neither did N.N. Sippy's love triangle *Har Jeet* with Rehana Sultan and Radha Saluja, even though the film's story was written by K. Balachander, and Gulzar penned the screenplay, both future Dadasaheb Phalke winners. These films exposed his limitations as an actor. In 1972 and 1973, he had a combined thirteen releases; most flopped. Dhawan was no longer the hot new kid on the block. Box-office had deserted Dhawan like a lover determined not to return.

The actor tried to change his goody-goody image in Firoz Chinoy's *Shaitan* (1974), where he was a playboy, and Saawan Kumar's *Hawas* (1974), in which he played a slick willy trying to entrap a moneyed girl. Neither worked, but *Darwaza* (1978) did. However, as in any Ramsay Brothers horror movie, the monster was the real hero. By the 1980s, Dhawan too had moved to supporting roles. In the '90s, he was doing television, where the roles were meatier and cash flow regular. 'In the '80s, multi-

---

4 '"Pyar Ki Kahani" mediocre', *The Times of India*, 16 May 1971.

starrers and action movies started coming in. I was a total misfit … I started doing a lot of character roles. I made that transformation beautifully … An actor has to survive, too,' Dhawan confessed in 2018, underlining that he did not let ego get in the way of his survival.[5]

With the passage of time, his brother, director David, and nephew Varun, became the more famous Dhawans. The cameo of a yesteryear star in Sriram Raghavan's super-hit *Andhadhun* (2018) reminded him of the heady 1970s. 'Now, I can pack up,' he said.[6] But Anil Dhawan goes on and on like a tireless Duracell.

Vijay Arora

Like Navin Nischol, Vijay Arora too was an FTII gold medallist. Unlike Nischol, his debut film, B.R. Ishara's *Zaroorat* (1972), nosedived. Yet top directors reposed their faith in him. Hrishikesh Mukherjee checked him out with his boldest film, *Sabse Bada Sukh* (1972). Nasir Hussain employed him in *Yaadon Ki Baaraat* (1973). Satyen Bose, director of *Chalti Ka Naam Gaadi* and *Dosti*, cast him in *Mere Bhaiya* (1972). Even the Urdu literary great Rajinder Singh Bedi, fresh from his success of *Dastak*, teamed him with Jaya Bhaduri in the sensitive but ultimately unfulfilling *Phagun* (1973). Both Arora and Bhaduri earned praise for their performance.

Rajesh Khanna predicted that Arora could be his successor. The forecast went spectacularly wrong. But it looked a reasonable guess at a time when Arora was serenading the veteran Asha Parekh with '*Achhi nahi sanam dillagi diley bekarar se*' in *Rakhi Aur Hathkadi* (1972) and questioning Tanuja, '*Teri meri jodi kaisi lagti hai?*' in *Insaaf* (1973). And when Arora flung an acoustic guitar on

---

[5] Alaka Sahani, 'I am experiencing the same adulation that I did in the '70s: Anil Dhawan', *The Indian Express*, 18 October 2018, https://indianexpress.com/article/express-sunday-eye/anil-dhawan-interview-5409483/

[6] Patcy N., '*Andhadhun* made a forgotten star famous again', 27 November 2018, https://www.rediff.com/movies/report/andhadhun-made-a-forgotten-star-famous-again/20181127.htm.

his shoulder, nuzzled Zeenat Aman's freshly shampooed hair and bared his heart with the words, '*Chura liya hai tumne jo dil ko*', he looked debonair and destined-to-be. Even today, the actor with appealing eyes and Brylcreamed hair looks every inch in vogue and with-it in the groovy track. That song from the smash hit *Yaadon Ki Baaraat*, with Dharmendra in the central role, became his badge of identity. But like other members of his tribe, Arora needed a solo hit to improve his resumé and market value.

Two films were fundamental to his future: romantic drama *Natak* (1975) and family social *Jeevan Jyoti* (1976). *Natak* was directed by Sohanlal Kanwar, also maker of Manoj Kumar hits like *Beiman* (1972) and *Sanyasi* (1975). *Jeevan Jyoti* was produced by the respected south Indian banner AVM. Both were watchable films that few watched. Based on Amrita Pritam's bold literary novel, *Dharti, Sagar Te Sippiyan*, the experimental *Kadambari* (1976) could have added gravitas to Arora's oeuvre. But it hardly made it to the theatres. The sinking of these films seriously stalled Arora's career as a lead actor.

By the late 1970s, Arora was into supporting acts. One of his most memorable celluloid moments came in the 'special appearance' of a postman who sang the melancholic track, '*Ik ritu aaye, ik ritu jaaye*', with Shashi Kapoor riding pillion in Subhash Ghai's *Gautam Govinda* (1979). The small role underscored

Satish Kaul

The FTII graduate was Rehana Sultan's love interest in Ved Rahi's bold relationship drama, *Prem Parbat* (1973), and played the lead in *Mere Sartaj* (1975) and *Harfan Maula* (1976). He switched to character roles but found his true métier in Punjabi films where he became a huge star. His hits include *Sassi Punnu* and *Vehra Lambran Da*. Kaul went through hard times in his last years, including spending time alone in an old-age nursing home. The actor passed away in 2021. He was seventy-four.

that he could act and it was only a poverty of imagination that stopped directors from giving him challenging parts.

Throughout the 1980s, Arora was busy doing dozens of bread-and-butter roles. In Ravi Chopra's vigilante hit *Aaj Ki Awaz* (1984), the actor again showed that he could hold a scene when he shouted back at the cop (Shafi Inamdar) and refused to be bullied into becoming a witness. And, yes, in those monopoly days of Doordarshan, everybody recognized him as Indrajit/Meghnad in *Ramayan* (1987–88).

When stomach cancer claimed him in 2007, Arora was close to completing a century of films and TV shows. He was sixty-two. After watching his debut film, *Zaroorat*, many predicted a bright future for him. Nobody gave a second look to its inelegant heroine, who also made her debut. Arora fell through the cracks; she became a star: Reena Roy. For Vijay Arora, life remained an irony.[7]

Mahendra Sandhu

Whipping out pistols with panache and galloping with gusto on horses through rugged terrains, Mahendra Sandhu was custom-made for the slot of He-Man. It didn't matter that his dialogue delivery was a flat monotone and his face displayed fewer emotions than a saucepan. His unbuttoned shirt, self-confident swagger, and six-foot frame had *Stardust* swooning even before his first release. In its November 1972 issue, the film magazine wrote a gushing two-page article on him, titled 'Swinger Sandhu hits the town'.

An FTII graduate like many others in this essay, Sandhu kick-started his career in the unlikeliest of ways. Noted art director Sudhendu Roy, who had previously directed Rajshri's *Uphaar*, made him wear thick eyeglasses and teach Bertrand Russell to college students in the irritatingly verbose *Sweekar* (1973). But the

[7] Avijit Ghosh, 'Diamonds and Dust', *The Times of India*, 13 February 2007, https://timesofindia.indiatimes.com/edit-page/diamonds-and-dust/articleshow/1599164.cms.

Patiala-born actor displayed a flair for depicting emotions subtly and a *TOI* review hailed him as 'a promising discovery'.

The same year, producer F.C. Mehra shabbily repurposed Clint Eastwood's *Dirty Harry* into *Khoon Khoon* (1973). The original was riveting and scripted around two finely etched characters: a cop and a serial-killer. But in the remake, the script feels partial towards the maniac (Danny). Sandhu played it cool but ended up looking cold. *The Times of India* found him 'dull and listless'. The tilt neither helped the film's fate nor the leading man's future.

Ek Ladki Badnaam Si (1974), *Madhosh* (1974), and *Goonj* (1974) – all fizzled out like damp Diwali rockets, relegating the actor to lowbrow ventures with Joginder, the king of C-grade action yarns, in *Yaari Zindabad* (1976). In *Rangaa aur Raja* (1977) too, Joginder had the showier part of an avenger while Sandhu's cop lacked spark.

Everybody was surprised when the Rajshris, known for producing gentle love stories and kind-hearted family dramas, decided to make *Agent Vinod* (1977) and cast Sandhu in the title role. The reason, the actor recalled, was that Rajshri boss Tarachand Barjatya had seen Shibu Mitra's well-crafted *Khoon Ki Keemat* (1974), and was impressed by Sandhu's performance where he had displayed a flair for the funny. 'The Rajshris offered me *Alibaba* and *Zorro* but I refused those scripts. They were offended but still offered me *Agent Vinod* (1977). I took the script home, read it in two hours and agreed to do the film,' he said.[8]

Sandhu was first-rate as Agent Vinod. He visibly relished playing a desi Bond who is quick with the gun and rapid in reciting shers. The actor said, 'It ran for more than 40 weeks in Bangalore, notched up a silver jubilee in Surat and played to packed houses in Punjab.'[9] Unfortunately for him, there was no sequel to either *Agent Vinod* or this single silver jubilee of his career.

---

[8] Avijit Ghosh, 'My name is Sandhu', *The Times of India*, 18 March 2012, https://timesofindia.indiatimes.com/home/sunday-times/deep-focus/my-name-is-sandhu/articleshow/12312224.cms.

[9] Ibid.

Nonetheless, the hit produced some positive rub-offs. Sandhu acted alongside Vinod Khanna in Ratan Mohan's *Khoon Ka Badla Khoon* (1978), duelled with Mithun Chakraborty in Devar's *Main Aur Mera Haathi* (1981), and reaffirmed his penchant for action in Shibu Mitra's hit *Paanch Qaidi* (1981).

But he remained a hero of B-grade action movies in sweaty tin-roofed mofussil theatres of north India. Their names – *Guru Ho Jaa Shuru* (1979), *Khoon Ki Takkar* (1981), *Jawala Daaku* (1981), *Raakh Aur Chingari* (1982), *Mujhe Vachan Do* (1983) – give away their content. There was one exception, *Yahan Se Shehar Ko Dekho* (1983), which was based on Urdu litterateur Krishan Chander's great novel. Few, if any, saw the film.

Sandhu made a last bid for stardom producing and directing *Kis Main Kitna Hai Dum* (1992), where he played an enforcer cop. The film became another box-office lemon. A cameo in the new *Agent Vinod* (2012) didn't work out either. The actor, who came from a family of big landowners in Punjab, smartly switched channels to become a real-estate businessman.

The Women

In the 1970s, women-centric mainstream movies were rare in conservative Bombay film world. The logic proffered was that they didn't sell tickets. But there was also subtle patriarchy at work. Nonetheless, like Nischol and company, a small but distinct group of women tried to touch the stars but failed to grasp them.

Rehana Sultan

Allahabad-born Rehana Sultan stunned India in the '70s with her 'bold' roles in Rajinder Singh Bedi's *Dastak* (1970) and *Chetna* (1970). In *Dastak*, the debutant FTII graduate played a middle-class homemaker who moves into a flat previously resided by a sex worker. Sultan's performance earned her a National Film Award for Best Actress. In *Chetna*, she played an assertive sex worker, which again won her praise. *Dastak* was a mini success; *Chetna* a roaring hit. But in the image-conscious era, she was immediately typecast and ruled out of family socials and mainstream romances. Rehana continued to play the rebellious 'outsider' in films such as *Prem Parbat*, *Khote Sikkay*, and *Sajjo Rani*. But the A-list mainstream producers stayed away from her and she gradually gave up work after marrying B.R. Ishara, who had directed her in *Chetna*.

Zarina Wahab

Zarina hit tinsel town armed with an FTII degree and possessing a severe Jaya Bhaduri hangover, best evident in director Basu Chatterjee's super-hit family romance *Chitchor* (1976). Bhimsain's *Gharaonda* (1977) again paired her with Amol Palekar. The film was about a young couple's search for a house and the cold-hearted choice they make to own one. Slender and dusky, Zarina was approved by the critics but made no headway into the big league despite playing the lead in another winner, Rajshri's *Sawan Ko Aane Do* (1979). *Sitara* (1980), directed by Gulzar's former assistant Meraj, could have been her ticket to the big league. The film paired her with the rising star Mithun Chakraborty, but the story of a struggling singer flopped. After her marriage to fellow actor Aditya Pancholi, Zarina continued to act in films, TV serials, and ads. In *My Name Is Khan* (2010), Wahab played Shah Rukh Khan's mother.

Rameshwari

Rameshwari's sensitive performance as the dutiful bride who wins over the family's heart in Rajshri's jubilee hit *Dulhan Wohi Jo Piya Man Bhaaye* (1977) came for fulsome praise. But a freak eye accident during a film shooting set her career back. She was cast opposite Jeetendra in *Asha*, 1980's biggest hit, but Reena Roy had the meatier role. Like others, she continued to wade and stumble through the 1980s, *Sharda* (1981) being another box-office winner. But there were no second innings to her career.

Neeta Mehta

Tall, photogenic, and an FTII product, Neeta Mehta attracted attention as the glamour girl who gets married to a rustic Randhir Kapoor in *Ponga Pandit* (1975). The film, heavily publicized on Radio Ceylon, had the naughty chartbuster '*Jija-ji, jija-ji, meri didi hai anari*'. But the film sank. *Inspector Eagle*, a cinematic interpretation of the hit radio programme, got stuck and was finally released years later. Neeta got a second shot at prominence in the Raj Khosla hit *Main Tulsi Tere Aangan Ki* (1978). Vinod Khanna serenaded her with the track, '*Yeh khidki jo band rehti hai*'. The film became a runaway success, but her career remained mired in B-grade ventures. Later, Khanna temporarily quit films in search of salvation. Mehta has done the same. She can be seen preaching as Swami Nityanand Giri on YouTube.

Vidya Sinha

A former Miss Bombay, Vidya Sinha made swift inroads into middle-class hearts playing women who were half-confined, half-free in two Basu Chatterjee hits, *Rajnigandha* (1974) and *Chhoti Si Baat* (1976). At a time when heroines were typified by shimmery glamour and inviting pouts, Vidya briefly became the divergent other in middle-of-the-road movies. She also acted alongside Rajesh Khanna in B.R. Chopra's flop *Karm* (1977) and the same director's rambunctious hit, *Pati Patni Aur Woh* (1978). Sanjeev Kumar played her husband. But Vidya's career too never progressed beyond a point. She boldly took her chances in the 1980s, enacting a killer in Ramsay's *Saboot* and the evil exploiter of child beggars in Raj N. Sippy's *Josh* (1981). But by then she was also playing mother to Vijeta Pandit in *Love Story* (1981). Like Wahab, she continued to act in films, TV shows, and ads. The last decade of her private life was turbulent. Vidya passed away in 2019.

Bindiya Goswami

The story goes that she bore facial resemblance to Hema Malini which prompted a recommendation to her mother. In the mid-1970s, there was a buzz about Ms Goswami as the new happening girl in town who could fit into gentle urban comedies – *Khatta Meetha* (1978), *Golmaal* (1979) – as well as young romance like *College Girl* (1978), *Prem Vivaah* (1979), and action-dramas like *Dada* (1979). It seemed that she had made it to the A-grade when Ramesh Sippy cast her opposite Shashi Kapoor in *Shaan* (1980), but the film flopped, and while she continued to act in films for a few more years, the big moment was gone.

Summing Up

In October 1971, film journalist Mohan Bawa wrote about the dozens of actors, both men and women, who had suddenly emerged on the Hindi film scene. He spoke with Nischol who said, 'This influx of newcomers … occurs every 10 years. Many newcomers come but not all of them remain … Out of the current crop of newcomers I foresee only a handful remaining in the limelight 10 years from now…'[10]

The prophecy came true in an ironic way. By 1981, the limelight had shifted away from Nischol, Dhawan, Arora, and Sandhu. They were around but diminished in stature. One theory about their relative failure is that they were not suited to action which became the dominant genre from the mid-1970s. But that doesn't explain how 'a chocolate hero' like Rishi Kapoor survived and thrived during the same period. Vinod Mehra too did much better than them.

Stardom is a mysterious potion. No one knows its ingredients. Nischol, Dhawan, Arora, and Sandhu saw it from close range, tasted it, before it slipped away. To their credit, they were all self-

[10] Mohan Bawa, 'Freshers in Films', *The Times of India*, 24 October 1971.

made individuals. But perhaps they lacked the X-factor which endears an actor to the larger audience.

Many films that they acted in during the 1970s are now available on YouTube. And if the viewers' comments are to be believed, they are still loved and remembered. Among their fans, they also evoke a sense of lingering regret. Everybody knows they promised far more than they finally delivered.

Master Bobby plays the role of the young Nandu in the Rajesh Khanna–Sharmila Tagore movie, *Amar Prem* (1972). Which actor plays the grown-up, adult Nandu?

Answer: Vinod Mehra

Well Begun

Opening Credits in Seventies Hindi Cinema

Uday Bhatia

'Pay no attention to that man behind the curtain,' says the titular conman in *The Wizard of Oz* (1939). Three decades later, Hrishikesh Mukherjee might have chuckled over his audience being given no choice but to pay attention to the man – or rather, the man's voice – behind the ugly purple curtain. For the first two minutes of his 1972 comedy *Bawarchi*, rather than the names of cast and crew appearing onscreen, the opening credits are spoken by an offscreen Amitabh Bachchan. He identifies himself as well – it's still a year to go for *Zanjeer*.

In his book *The World of Hrishikesh Mukherjee* (2015), Jai Arjun Singh mentions the pointedly theatrical nature of *Bawarchi*'s opening. As with a lot of Mukherjee films, the play *is* the thing – but this is also just a bright, funny way to start a film. Mukherjee even slips in a silly joke, Bachchan saying '*peeche se awaaz*' (voice from behind), and then, correcting himself, '*parde ke peeche se awaaz*' (voice from behind the curtain). Hindi film audiences aren't always locked in, or even in their seats, from minute one, but those watching *Bawarchi* in 1972 must have felt their needs were being seen to from the first frame. (I have yet to see an Indian film with sung credits. This was done brilliantly by Italian composer Ennio Morricone for the 1966 Pier Paolo Pasolini comedy, *Hawks and Sparrows*.)

Saul Bass, the legendary American graphic designer, fought against the idea that opening credits and title sequences were an appendage, something within the film but not really of it. 'My idea is the first frame of the film is the first frame of the film and the film begins then,' he said. Try imagining *North by Northwest* (1959), *Anatomy of a Murder* (1959) or *Spartacus* (1960) without Bass's titles – it's like removing a crucial scene. And yet, so many Hindi releases of the 1970s had, as their opening sequences, rudimentary credits – often cast and crew names against a vague psychedelic background – that could easily be separated from the 'real film'. Many directors, even very good ones, saw credits as something you had to include but not get too cute with. The actual business started once they were out of the way.

Manmohan Desai, the quintessential '70s Hindi director, might have argued that he was entertaining enough in every other respect for audiences to care that he simply plastered titles in bright colours over freeze-frames (of a roti in *Roti*, 1974) or an unfolding scene (the blood in the IV flowing upwards in *Amar Akbar Anthony*, 1977). Thankfully, there were also directors who, like Bass, reckoned their films should be interesting and invested from the second they began. Their credits were thought through, not perfunctory – a smart bit of design or wordplay, a gag like in *Bawarchi*, anything to grab the viewer in those two or three minutes.

As assorted New Waves started cresting around the world in the '60s, Indian films reflected this excitement. You could see a desire to shake things up in the opening credits of the more ambitious films. Sometimes the idea was simple, like the uninterrupted shot of a moving tram cable that opens Satyajit

Ray's Bengali film *Mahanagar* (1963). Sometimes it was hugely elaborate, like Chetan Anand's *Aakhri Khat* (1966), in which the titles end some seven minutes after they start and encompass a car journey, a flashback and a lot of plot. As the decade drew to a close, credits became more frenetic. Mrinal Sen's *Bhuvan Shome* (1968) and Basu Chatterjee's *Sara Akash* (1969) had exhilarating starts: train tracks speeding past in the former, the streets of Agra zipping by in the latter.

Sen and Chatterjee's films were in the Middle/Parallel Cinema ballpark, but this wild energy could also be seen in some of the openings of commercial films of the time. The first minute of Subodh Mukherji's *Abhinetri* (1970) has Hema Malini performing an energetic dance recital on stage. Then, her image shrinks and the rest of the screen goes black. Credits start appearing, each title accompanied by a rectangle with a different part of Malini's body – eyes, legs, hands. Laxmikant-Pyarelal's Carnatic violin music rattles along, echoing the furious taans of *Bhuvan Shome* and *Sara Akash*. The sequence feels bracingly abstract for a mainstream comedy-drama. It's the kind of opening that would occur to someone who has been studying Saul Bass.

The start of *Abhinetri* is a smartly worked-out thing, syncing music, editing and graphic design. In a similar vein, though less sophisticated, is the opening of Brij's heist film *Victoria No. 203* (1972), which follows a horse carriage through the streets of Bombay, the screen splitting into four as the credits appear and a singer croons the title over and over, in English and Hindi. But you could even set your film's credits apart with little more than a distinctive font and a few simple frames. Mani Kaul's credits were a reflection of his films: artistic, spare, unhurried. *Uski Roti* (1969) has credits in Hindi against an inky black screen, *Ashad Ka Ek Din* (1971) against a still frame. He tried something more evocative for his desert film, *Duvidha* (1974), credits in rust red against a background like sandy parchment, Rajasthani folk music playing. The names are handwritten, with the straight lines on top of the Hindi letters unusually, artfully extended.

The best credit sequences gave you a sense of the film to come. The simple, effective opening of *Sholay* (1975) has panoramic shots that echo the classic Westerns of John Ford and Anthony Mann: an indication to the audience that were going to be watching something with scale and ambition (in a nice touch, when the protagonists pass through a village, the music becomes more typically 'Indian'). In *Garm Hawa* (1975), the titles are superimposed over images of freedom fighters, apt for a film that questions what the nation did with that freedom. *Kaala Patthar* (1979) has intriguingly downbeat credits – three minutes of coalminers going about their daily grind. Change a few details and these vignettes might have been from Barbara Kopple's *Harlan County, USA*, a landmark 1976 American documentary about a miner's strike. Bachchan, the star, doesn't turn up till the end of the sequence … and when he does he walks unassumingly into the frame. It's a worker's trudge, not a hero's entry – a fitting start to this uncommonly gritty look at the exploitation of miners by soulless corporations.

The opening credits in Merchant-Ivory's *Bombay Talkie* (1970) – set in the Hindi film industry of the time – play over a three-minute sequence so exquisite they hardly require a film after. We see a series of hand-painted movie billboards scattered across Bombay: in an empty green field, on a crowded sidewalk, on Marine Drive. These billboards have the likenesses and names of cast and crew, every single one, from stars Shashi Kapoor and Jennifer Kendall to script girl Janine Bharucha (the Taj Mahal Hotel gets a poster of its own). It's strangely moving to see these gorgeous posters at large, never to be used for anything but this sequence. Shankar-Jaikishan's score, a sitar melody with wordless humming, underlines the melancholy beauty of the sequence.

The otherworldliness of cinema mixing with the bustle of everyday life in Bombay also informs the opening of Krishna Shah's delightful documentary *Cinema Cinema* (1975), with its static shots of Edward Theatre from across the road. At first there's only a man sleeping on the pavement, but as the city comes to life, our view of the movie theatre is blocked by cyclists and cattle carts and

BEST buses. It's a quiet few minutes with the real city, at a slight remove from the noisy theatre where we will spend the rest of the film. Years later, Ram Gopal Varma's *Rangeela* (1995) offered yet another take on the idea of a cinematic city: a succession of stills of golden age stars overlaid with everyday street sounds. I wrote in my book, *Bullets Over Bombay: Satya and the Hindi Film Gangster* (2021): 'It's a stunningly effective way to begin a film that is set both in middle-class Bombay and the world of movie-making. In *Rangeela*, the city is a film set and everyone is always performing, as if some cosmic director had forgotten to call "cut".'

Not all effective credit sequences gave viewers an accurate idea of what was in store, though. In Mehmood's *Bombay To Goa* (1972), a woman is chased through the streets of Bombay at night as the credits unfold. She manages to jump onto a bus, which pulls away just in time, leaving behind a curious Amitabh Bachchan. If you went by this sequence alone, you might assume the film was a stylish noir thriller. But *Bombay To Goa* was a road movie and a comedy, with just a bit of suspense thrown in for seasoning. It's not hard to imagine Mehmood, concerned only with the audience's entertainment at any given moment, prioritizing gripping credits over more representative ones.

Then, as now, a large percentage of opening credits were a scene, or several short scenes, with multiple pauses for important cast and crew names or just one pause for the film's title – building to some dramatic point where the narrative could start again in earnest. This workmanlike approach came alive in the films of Basu Chatterjee, who was brilliant at letting scenes play out as the credits rolled. The credits in *Rajnigandha* (1974) unfold as Vidya Sinha stands outside a cinema hall, impatiently scanning her surroundings for Amol Palekar, who is running late. It's a neat bit of meta-commentary: she is waiting for a film to begin, and so are we. In Chatterjee's *Piya Ka Ghar* (1972), a priest takes a leisurely walk through a Bombay chawl. Everything in those crowded lanes seems to delight him: a little boy on a makeshift swing, a dog jumping through a hoop of fire. In the film proper, two minutes of dialogue-less, song-less action might have left audiences distracted. But this stretch of observational comedy is an ideal credit sequence.

For more obsessive fans, credits represent information to be parsed, puzzles to be solved. Why has this composer been partnered with that lyricist, this cinematographer with that art director? Watch enough films of a particular era and you will start to notice the same names pop up in 'below the line' jobs. While researching this piece, the name I encountered most frequently (with the exception of Lata Mangeshkar or Kishore Kumar) was Mangesh Desai, a sound recordist who worked on every kind of film imaginable (to give you some idea, he did *Alaap*, *Shatranj Ke Khiladi*, *Bhumika* and *Amar Akbar Anthony*, all in 1977).

Sometimes, written information was the crux of the credits. In Muzaffar Ali's *Gaman* (1978), the credits arrive around the half-hour mark, with Ghulam, the dreamy slacker played by Farooq Shaikh, on a train from his village to Bombay. Fittingly, the last 'acting' credit is 'Residents of Kotwara and the taxi drivers of Bombay' – the village they shot in, and Ghulam's brethren in the city. It recalls the lovely, succinct credit in Chetan Anand's location-shot 1954 film, *Taxi Driver*: 'And city of Bombay'. Shyam Benegal's 1976 film on the founding of the Amul milk cooperative begins with the line '500,000 farmers of Gujarat present … *Manthan*'. This unique top billing tells us right away that the film was crowdfunded, half a lakh farmers donating 2 rupees each.

Vidhu Vinod Chopra's student film *Murder at Monkey Hill* (1976) also hints at the circumstances of its creation, but more sardonically. In keeping with its metatextual tone, the credit sequence – a series of production stills with eerie music – dubs the whole enterprise 'an attempt at communication with the Bombay financier' (there is some irony in this, as Chopra later became one of the most successful producers in Hindi cinema). Not all credits were this oblique. The animated opening of *Do Jasoos* (1975) describes Raj Kapoor and Rajendra Kumar's co-star as '*Bobby* singer Shailendra Singh', and the leading lady as – rather uncomfortably – 'teenager Bhavna Bhatt'.

Finally, there were credits with a single good idea – nothing more, nothing less. *Chhupa Rustam* (1973), an uninterrupted shot from the point of view of someone standing at the back of a train, cast and crew names appearing on the tracks (it's the same idea as *Bhuvan Shome*, though not as dynamically executed). *Shaan* (1980), scenes from the film projected on a dancer's body. *Shatranj Ke Khiladi* (1977), a closeup of a chessboard, with the players' bejewelled hands entering the frame to move the pieces. *Aavishkar* (1974), soft-edged, billowing images of Rajesh Khanna and Sharmila Tagore in happier times, the daydream of a guilty conscience. Saul Bass wrote that he made titles 'to induce the theatre inhabitants to sit down and watch, because something is really happening on the screen'. The best opening credits in '70s Hindi films had this same ambition – not just a pit stop to quickly get the film back on the road, but a few minutes of invention and excitement: something really happening on the screen.

Of the six Hindi films that Uttam Kumar acted in, only one, directed by Shakti Samanta, and co-starring Sharmila Tagore, was a box-office success. Name the film.

Answer: *Amanush* (1975)

Good Flops, Bad Flops and *Shalimar*

The Anatomy of the Box Office

Nirupama Kotru

If the movie landscape of the 1970s were a beach, it would be littered with the flotsam and jetsam of films which failed at the box office – known in trade parlance as 'flops'.

Unlike today where the success of a film and actor is measured by where the film's gross lies in relation to the '100 crore club', in the '70s, a 'hit' was a film where the producer reportedly made a sizable profit over and above his/her investment. A 'super hit' was one which made a bigger profit than a hit, and a 'blockbuster' was typically a multi-starrer made on a lavish scale that made of lots of money for everyone who had invested in it. None of these terms was clearly quantified. Trade guides published box-office figures from major territories, but it is not clear whether smaller territories were fully accounted for or not; hence these papers usually carried disclaimers. These dodgy numbers also indicated sizeable concealment of taxes by everyone in the higher rungs of the ladder in the film industry: producers, financers, distributors, exhibitors and actors.

Obviously, the bigger budget a film had, the more tickets the exhibitor had to sell for everyone to make a profit. One must remember that the only money a film could make in the '70s came from selling seats in cinema theatres and from selling long-playing discs of music and/or dialogues. Today a film-maker can make a decent return on his/her film even before its theatrical release by selling music, satellite, OTT and other rights, and entering into brand partnerships.

Owing to this general opacity of data, we ended up with some mystifying successes like *Beimaan* – a mediocre, medium-budget 1972 film starring Manoj Kumar, Pran and Raakhee –which, as per trade papers, made more money at the box office than the Dev Anand–Mumtaz–Zeenat Aman starrer *Hare Rama Hare Krishna* or the Rajesh Khanna–Sharmila Tagore starrer *Amar Prem*, both of which were released in the same year.[1] *Beimaan* also won an incredible seven *Filmfare* awards.

My focus in this piece, however, is not outliers like *Beimaan*, but films that, it is generally agreed, were made at a substantial cost and failed to recover the same, and were hence designated as 'flops'. A rather harsh term, considering that it suggests that the film's (celluloid) cans were fit for the dustbin, despite all the efforts that had gone into making it.

The 1970s are a remarkable decade. Although big-budget cinema and superstars like Rajesh Khanna, Amitabh Bachchan, Hema Malini, Dharmendra dominated the decade, so did the art of storytelling. These stories were such that they could be followed by audiences in A, B and C distribution circles. There were some basic human values and emotions depicted in these films which appealed to a lot of Indians. And music was an extremely important part of the pan-Indian success of these films.

I believe that there are good flops and there are bad flops. An apt example of a bad flop would be *Immaan Dharam*, released in 1977. Despite having three top stars, Amitabh Bachchan, Shashi

[1] Box-office figures from www.muvyz.com

Kapoor and Sanjeev Kumar, the film, written by Salim–Javed, tanked at the box office, shaking the confidence of the industry for a while. In my opinion, *Immaan Dharam* was a mediocre film, badly written, directed and edited. Unlike other commercial disasters of that era such as *Mera Naam Joker* or *Shalimar* which have earned a cult status over the years, *Immaan Dharam* had no redeeming features which could merit a rediscovery. The only gain from the debacle of *Immaan Dharam* was that it prompted Aparna Sen to quit acting, and start writing and directing films – apparently during the shoot she had an epiphany that she was wasting her time waiting for the shot to be ready.[2]

The decade had begun with *Mera Naam Joker*, *Prem Pujari* and *Gopi* (all three films released in 1970), marking more or less the end of the reign for the holy triumvirate of Raj Kapoor, Dev Anand and Dilip Kumar respectively. *Mera Naam Joker* was criticized for its inordinate length (it was more than four hours long). Raj Kapoor's self-indulgent saga didn't resonate much with audiences. The lukewarm response to *Gopi* was followed by the box-office disaster *Dastaan* in1972, Dilip Kumar's first flop in six years. Unlike the super-hit *Ram Aur Shyaam* (1967), even two Dilip Kumars couldn't save *Dastaan*. The box-office debacle of Dev Anand's directorial venture for his own company Navketan Films, *Prem Pujari*, was followed by poor box-office collections of other Navketan productions such as *Ishk Ishk Ishk* (1974) and *Jaaneman* (1976), as well as those in which he acted for other production houses, such as Yash Chopra and Gulshan Rai's *Joshila* (1973).

Pakeezah, Meena Kumari's swan song, opened to a lukewarm response upon its release in 1972. Continuity issues marred an otherwise well-made film backed by excellent music, a moving story, beautiful sets, dances and costumes and above all, notable performances by all the lead actors including Meena Kumari, Raaj Kumar, Ashok Kumar and Veena. Kamal Amrohi had taken fifteen years to complete the film; during this time he had

---

[2] 'Aparna Sen: Fame by Frame', Deepa Gehlot, *Hindustan Times*, 31 July 2022

divorced Meena Kumari and she had started drinking heavily. Unfortunately, Meena Kumari succumbed to her illness soon after the film's release. It is widely believed that Meena's untimely death revived the fortunes of the film and it went on to become a huge commercial success and a landmark in Indian cinema.

However, Kamal Amrohi disagreed with this view.[3] In his interview to *Gulfaam* magazine published in April 1982, he said, 'Meena Kumari died on 31 March1972, fifty-five days after the release of the film. The fact that a big film continued to run in the theatres for that long alone signifies that it was doing well. Therefore, to insinuate that Meena Kumari's death was responsible for the success is not an astute observation. Instead, it was *Pakeezah* that immortalized Meena Kumari.'

Music was the mainstay of another box-office disaster of the time, *Mere Jeevan Saathi* (1972). In fact, so confident were the film-makers of the music of this Rajesh Khanna starrer they released it a couple of months before the film hit the theatres. The music did well, but the film bombed. *Prem Kahaani* (1975) also flopped in a similar fashion, despite it having Shashi Kapoor in addition to the hit pair of Rajesh Khanna and Mumtaz.

Which brings us to the biggest debacle of the decade – Krishna Shah's magnum opus *Shalimar*. *Shalimar* was a crossover film with a difference. Instead of Indians acting in a foreign film, *Shalimar* had Hollywood actors acting in an Indian film shot on Indian locations. Krishna Shah's audacious attempt at pulling off the impossible deserves to be appreciated.

Pulling off the Impossible

Shah's tryst with films started rather late in the day. At first he was associated with Broadway theatre of New York City in the 1960s, after which he moved to television. It was only after he did

---

3 '*Kitaab-e-zindagi se chand waraq*', published in *Gulfaam*, April 1982, as reproduced in Yasir Abbasi's, *Yeh Un Dinon Ki Baat Hai*

a film-making course at UCLA that he shifted bag and baggage to Hollywood. He started with two small films – *Rivals* and *The River Niger* (based on a Pulitzer-winning Broadway play) – both of which did rather badly in commercial terms. Undeterred, Shah went back to the storyboard to work on his grand project, *Shalimar*. The film was based on a script Shah had written called *Johannesburg Jigsaw*, which he originally meant to shoot in a Jamaican island or in South Africa. By mid-1976, Shah knew he wanted to set the film in India.

For *Shalimar*, Shah was adventurous enough to cast the double Tony Award winner and Academy/Golden Globe/BAFTA nominee several times over, Rex Harrison, in the role of Sir John Locksley. Harrison's films *My Fair Lady* (1964) and *Doctor Dolittle* (1967) had done very well in India, and hence Shah hoped getting the star as Sir John would appeal to Indian audiences.

It was a long and arduous journey that led Shah to Rex. In his book about the film, *The Shalimar Adventure*, Bunny Reuben recollects how the film was ridden with obstacles right from the beginning. At first, Amitabh Bachchan was finalized for the leading role, but Amitabh was under tremendous pressure from the Yash Chopra–Gulshan Rai–Salim–Javed camp. As a result, Amitabh had to withdraw the dates he had committed to Shah for *Shalimar*. This was obviously a painful experience for Shah, who felt that the bigwigs of the industry were ganging up against him, the quintessential outsider. Shah had the grace to request a face-to-face meeting with Amitabh in Yash Chopra's presence, at the end of which he is said to have remarked, 'Congrats, Yash. You have got a terrific actor,' thereby releasing Amitabh from the contract. Shah next asked Zeenat Aman, who had been recommended to him by Amitabh, if she still wanted to continue, now that Amitabh was no longer in the film. Zeenat graciously stood by him.

After the Amitabh fiasco, unknown to Shah, there was yet another casting catastrophe coming. Shah had planned a huge mahurat to be followed by a press conference in Taj Mahal Hotel,

Bombay, where he would announce Gina Lollobrigida as one of his leads, along with Dharmendra and Zeenat.

By 1977, Italian actress Gina Lollobrigida was fast losing her hold in Hollywood. Yet, as per Rueben, from day one Shah made Gina feel like a queen. He flew her first-class to Bombay and put her up at the Taj Hotel. His leading actors Dharmendra and Zeenat were very warm and hospitable to her, lavishing her with gifts and attention. Apparently all this went to her head.

The mahurat day saw one mishap after the other. Dilip Kumar had consented to be present, but had to make a quiet exit when neither of the leading ladies showed up even an hour after his arrival. Zeenat chose the same day to demonstrate to Gina who the prima donna in *Shalimar* was, by timing her own arrival only after that of Gina's. Finally, Gina gave the mahurat shot clap in which Dharmendra and Zeenat enacted a brief scene. After the mahurat, an executive from Egypt Air told Gina that Shah had reduced her to a clapper girl. Gina's insecurities led her to becoming unreasonable all of sudden. She demanded a much higher remuneration for doing the film. Being a man of principles, Krishna Shah was forced to show her the door.

Sadly, Shah had wasted a chunk of the film's budget on flying Gina to India in style and had paid through his nose for all her lavish expenses in India. The press conference that followed the mahurat was a complete washout because Gina was no longer in the film. *Shalimar* got plenty of bad press and seemed doomed to fail. Shah finally cast Oscar-nominated actress Sylvia Miles (of *Midnight Cowboy* fame, the 1969 film starring Dustin Hoffman and Jon Voight) in the role that Gina was to play.

The next star who had to be removed from the film because of date issues was Peter Ustinov. The only star who stayed by Shah's side was his good friend John Saxon, who had played Bruce Lee's rival-turned-friend Roper in the 1973 smash hit *Enter the Dragon*. And as if all these problems were not enough, Shah's personal life was getting affected. His wife Diane could not adjust to life in India and their son's schooling was suffering, hence his family moved back to LA. It seemed the whole universe was conspiring against *Shalimar*. As Rueben says, 'Whomsoever they talked to about making a film in India was still asking the inevitable questions, about dysentery, drinking water, cholera, the bureaucracy, and so forth.' The only person who stood by Krishna through thick and thin was his producer Suresh Shah.

After the Gina fiasco, distributors in LA were unwilling to touch *Shalimar*. 'I talked to other agents and even to some distributors but they all repeated what (agent and friend) Jerry Levy had said: I'd not get a big commercial release in America; it'd only be on the modest art- cinema circuits like the ones that occasionally screened Satyajit Ray's movies. Worse, they said, mine would be neither an art movie, nor a commercial movie, but some strange, in-between creature! They pointed out that Dev Anand had once associated himself with a movie called *The Evil Within*. It had been financed by 20th Century Fox and when I met one of the Fox representatives they told me that this movie had been a big joke wherever it had been screened! They could not even release it everywhere! It was a story about Vietnam and had Dev Anand and Zeenat Aman in it.'

Shah couldn't even bring himself to tell the distributors that he had cast the same lady, Zeenat. His Hollywood friends helped him narrow down the choice of leading man to Marlon Brando, Rex Harrison, Burt Lancaster and David Niven, in that order. For reasons of convenience as well as to save money, Shah shifted his office from New York to London and did the rest of the international casting from London. As it turned out, Brando was busy. With less than three months left for the shooting to begin (the schedule in Bangalore started from 15 September1977), after a nerve-racking, visa-less entry into Paris, Shah flew down to Nice where Rex Harrison stayed. He spent two days at Rex's lavish estate, convincing himself and the star that Rex was the perfect Sir John. Rex finally came on board.

But Rex's arrival in India was another fiasco which was the talk of the town for days to come. The customs officers at Bombay airport gave Rex Harrison such a harrowing time that he was ready to return by the next flight. It took all of Shah's Zen-like demeanour and persuasive powers to make Rex stay back, but the press conference to announce Rex in India had to be called off. Fortunately by then, Indian distributors had picked up the film for a good price on the sheer strength of the fabulous music composed by R.D. Burman and Anand Bakshi.

The shooting itself, much like what had gone before, was a tumultuous affair. Dharmendra, in his overenthusiasm, had concealed his painful back condition from everyone and eventually had to be given a spinal injection on the sly to save his back. Hema Malini stayed by his side during those critical days, and was treated by the unit like she was part of the film. It was indeed a miracle that the film was completed as per the tightly drawn schedule.

The Plot

The film starts in the fashion of a slick crime thriller of the 1970s, with a sniper trying to set up a shot from a busy overhead bridge in Bombay. Kumar (Dharmendra) is seen managing a club called Fergusons Dance Studio in which Aruna Irani is imparting cha-cha lessons to a motley crowd. Raja Bahadur Singh (Prem Nath), who is playing cards in the club, is shot at. Kumar saves Raja's life, but he is suspended from his job shortly after because his club is not making money. He steals an invite that he finds upon the person of the injured Bahadur Singh, and lands up at the Saint Dismus Island (said to be in the Indian ocean), pretending to be Bahadur Singh's son.

On the island, he runs into a bunch of interesting characters, all of whom have been invited by Sir John to the island to try their luck at stealing the famed ruby Shalimar which is in John's possession. These include 'Romeo' Iyengar (O.P. Ralhan), Countess Sylvia (Sylvia Miles), Colonel Columbus (John Saxon) and Dr Dubari (Shammi Kapoor). He also meets his estranged girlfriend Sheila (Zeenat Aman).

Thus the film starts on a very interesting note, with the thieves attempting to steal the gem one by one, set to some exciting background music composed by R.D. Burman. In fact, lovers of Hindi film music rate *Shalimar* as one of the most outstanding and fresh original soundtracks in Hindi films ever, with Polydor claiming to have sold 500,000 long-playing records (a still to this effect appears at the beginning of the Shemaroo Movies print of the film available on YouTube). The track for the countess ('*Countess caper*') is particularly noteworthy, as is the Bond theme–like title track, '*Mera pyaar, Shalimar*', the soulful '*Hum bewafa*' and the poignant '*Aaina wohi rehta hai*', among other tracks.

After some exciting twists and turns, Kumar ends up successfully stealing the gem and winning back Sheila. Had the film ended here, audiences would have perhaps been satisfied with the happy ending. Unfortunately towards the end, the film goes off-track and suddenly we have Dr Dubari leading a revolt of the tribals against their overlord Sir John, the trigger being the mysterious last moments of Columbus, when the tribals hear the mute Columbus cry out, upon which they promptly anoint him as their Naag Devta (serpent lord). Perhaps this track threw off the audience who had invested their time and money in a linear crime caper.

Extensively shot on locations across Karnataka (including Bangalore and Mysore), Maharashtra (Bombay) and Tamil Nadu (Mahabaleshwar), with superb shots of the iconic Mysore Palace, the film faltered in trying to mix too many exotic elements in one film. For instance, you have a Carnatic music recital in one scene, peppy modern music by R.D. Burman interspersed with some soulful numbers, tribal dances (there is a long dance sequence before the song '*Naag devta*'), mumbo-jumbo, white lords and brown slaves. You also have a condensed history lesson about a 3000-year-old, 1214-carat ruby worth Rs 135 crores which was once said to have been possessed by Chandragupta Maurya who won it from Alexander, and so on and so forth. This exotic, quasi-Indian cocktail was perhaps too heady for Indian audiences while Western audiences probably found it bizarre.

Cultural Appropriation

If *Shalimar* is viewed from a twenty-first-century lens of wokeism, one can argue that the film was guilty of cultural appropriation. For instance, costumes of the tribals in *Shalimar* were a mishmash of Roman and Greek costumes, and indigenous dresses of some tribes found in different regions of India. Krishna Shah could have researched the costumes better and ensured that they were representative of a tribe indigenous to India. Also the language these tribals spoke in was gibberish. As a result, the meaningless phrase 'Jhingalala hum',[4] invented by Team R.D. Burman who were fond of scatting and gibberish lyrics, which first appears in the song '*Hum bewafa*' and later in '*Naag devta*', has unfortunately come to be identified as a term used to disparagingly refer to tribal inhabitants of India. However, does this subsequent usage of the term indicate that the makers wanted to be disrespectful to tribal cultures of India? I think the film was silly in a lot of respects including the depiction of the inhabitants of the fictional island of Saint Dismas, but not disrespectful. In fact Shah tried to bring some balance to the film by showing the tribal subjects of Sir John not only rebelling against him, but actually killing him in the end.

Nothing Ventured, Nothing Gained

The trouble with *Shalimar* was perhaps that this was an attempt by a brown man to impress a white audience with Indian exoticism combined with Western production values. For one, Krishna Shah had no plans of shifting to India, given that he was trying to establish himself in Hollywood. His American distributors had warned him that Indian films were not taken seriously in the West. The Hindi film industry also perhaps did not extend him a warm

---

[4] Incidentally, the popularity of the phrase has endured for close to five decades, what with Tata Sky appropriating it for its campaign '*Isko laga dala toh life jhingalala*'. In this usage, *Jhingalala* seems to denote fun. Making this term the equivalent of *Hakuna matata* in *The Lion King* (1994).

welcome, despite the fact that most of his budget was spent in India, giving employment to a lot of Indians.

Shalimar is said to be the most expensive Indian film of its time. In an interview to *Trade Guide* in 1979, Shah expressed his gratitude to producer Suresh Shah for handing out Rs 4 crore at a stretch for the film.[5] The production cost of one single song ('*One two cha cha cha*') is said to be Rs 11 lakh, a big sum in those days.[6] The publicity of the film, which included the ill-fated press conference, was said to be an unprecedented Rs 11 lakh, a figure that Krishna Shah denied, while at the same time admitting that the publicity looked top-notch because the makers pulled out all stops – print advertisements in trade papers like *Screen*, television advertisements, radio (All India Radio) insertions, books (4 lakh copies sold by Vikas Publications in three languages), merchandise such as Shalimar Chess Sets, flasks and T-shirts, etc.[7] Shah did not cut corners as far as technique and technology are concerned. He blended sixty-seven tracks in six-stereophonic tracks. This resulted in superior sound effects.

At that kind of cost, it was near-impossible for *Shalimar* to make a profit. Remember, *Sholay* was made at a cost of Rs 3 crore during 1974–75.[8] *Shalimar* was a much riskier proposition from the very beginning, given its foreign cast and unique plot and story. Compared to *Shalimar*, *Sholay* seems to have followed a linear form of storytelling, with some good guys ganging up to kill a bad guy and bringing succour to a whole village terrorized by the bad guy. What is even more surprising is that despite the bad publicity at the mahurat-cum-press conference, *Shalimar* got a rather nice treatment at the hands of critics. Leading dailies

---

[5] 'The fact is that *Shalimar* is a diamond jubilee verdict,' says Krishna Shah, *Trade Guide*, 6 January 1979, Vol. 25, issue number 11

[6] 'Star capers', *Society and The Arts News*, 31 January 1978 (indiatoday.in)

[7] 'The fact is that *Shalimar* is a diamond jubilee verdict,' says Krishna Shah, *Trade Guide*, 6 January 1979, Vol. 25, Issue number 11

[8] '*Sholay*: How Ramesh Sippy managed to get Rs 3 crore from his dad for the film', 26 October 2016, hindustantimes.com/bollywood

in English, Hindi, Marathi and Urdu languages, namely, *Blitz, Screen, Navbharat Times, Daily Sakal, Janshakti, Maharashtra Times, Sunday Standard, Rasrang, Loksatta, Janmabhoomi, Hindi Blitz, Cine Advance, Sandhyakal, Poona Herald, Chitrapat, Inquilaab* and *Kay Tee Reports*, praised *Shalimar* for its technical excellence, sleek presentation and R.D. Burman's music. Cameraman Harvey Genkins got some well-deserved accolades.[9]

Shah also reportedly tried to bring some professionalism to the film scene in India that was completely missing at that time. The film was shot twice, first in English and then in Hindi, all in the space of three months. The entire film was insured in New York, which meant the stringent deadline had to be respected. The project was co-financed; Indian cast and crew were paid in India and the rest abroad. This meant that Indian actors received their cheques in time, a fact that was appreciated by Shammi Kapoor who was used to chaotic shooting schedules and erratic payment commitments.[10] Dharmendra was given rigorous English tuitions, and Sylvia Miles in Hindi. Kader Khan dubbed for Rex Harrison, and Nadira for Sylvia Miles. In fact, the 400-plus cast and crew learnt to coexist so well that everyone shed tears when it was time to say goodbye.

Shalimar's problem was that the film had some great ingredients but when you put them together, it made for an unpalatable dish. The film had everything going for it – a good-looking lead pair, some international stars, lots of action in a ruby heist, special effects and above all, one of the best soundtracks in the history of Hindi cinema. Perhaps Krishna Shah was too ambitious. He dreamt of conquering the hearts of both Indian and foreign audiences. Neither warmed up to the film.

The English version of the film called *Raiders of the Sacred Stone* has been cut quite differently from the Hindi version. It

---

[9] 'Critics' Verdict: Krishna Shah's *Shalimar* 70mm', *Trade Guide*, 6 January 1979, Vol. 25, Issue number 11

[10] 'Star capers', *Society and The Arts News*, 31 January 1978 (indiatoday.in)

starts with the scene where Dharmendra lands at Saint Dismas Island by boat. The length of the film was whittled down by about an hour. Sir Rex Harrison enunciated his dialogues in impeccable English, though Dharmendra's voice was dubbed by a voiceover artist. There was no playback singing. Unfortunately, the English version had few takers, but the Hindi version of the film went on to attain a cult status on the video circuit. Its campiness has been welcomed by audience across the world, especially those viewers who yearn to watch simple crime capers which were typical of the 1970s.

As Bunny Rueben says in the concluding paragraph of his book: 'In attempting, completing and releasing *Shalimar* in the same style and the same flamboyance with which Hollywood presents any of its major motion-pictures, these two men (Krishna Shah and Suresh Shah) have widened the horizons of commercial film-making in our country.'

The sheer audacity of the film-maker was mind-boggling. Not only did he successfully complete two versions of the same film, one in Hindi and one in English, with a cast and crew of over 400 people, against all odds – illnesses, fights, walkouts, rumours and bureaucratic nightmares – but he even took his film to Cannes, advertised it through a 'win a ruby contest' and made sure that Rex Harrison was the toast of Cannes1978.

'Because of that,' says Rueben, 'no matter what its eventual outcome at the box offices, *Shalimar* will always remain a landmark in the history of Indian cinema.'

I agree wholeheartedly.

What is the name of Dev Anand's character in *Hare Rama Hare Krishna* (1971) and in which city is his family based?

Answer: Prashant Jaiswal; Montreal

Looking Through the Keyhole!

Film Journalism in the 1970s

Sathya Saran

I am trawling through the web looking at film magazine covers. Film magazines, like all magazines, have become inconsequential to daily life. Newspaper supplements and YouTube videos and the other far-reaching arms of social media have taken magazines down from the main shelf to barely visible ones in dimly lit corners of the mind. But they exist. Barely breathing, but holding on to dear life.

So what did I find? Well, skin is in, and so are muscles. Depending on the gender of the icon on the cover. Eye contact remains sacrosanct. So far, nothing new. If you can't sell sex directly, sell it by lighting up the relevant portions of the brain for a vicarious high. But the titillation ends there. The stories selling the magazine are surprisingly tame. Sample this, circa 2022: 'Meet the latest sensation in show biz', reads the text that sits beside a trying-to-look-seductive Tiger Shroff. 'The Eye of the Tiger' is the catchphrase meant to draw your eye to meet his gaze. The text adds nothing by way of persuasion. The onus is on the photo. You like it, you pick up the copy.

Another example: A cover embellished with a picture of the actress who made it really big – Priyanka Chopra. The star who is simultaneously every starlet's role model and object of envy. The cover blurb reads, 'Super Power', followed by her hyphenated name. Did we need *Filmfare* to tell us that?

Are PR trainees being hired to write the cover lettering? Or are they a window to the new face of film magazine writing that is going the way of fashion writing? Safe, guarded, strictly aimed at ensuring good relations with their respective galaxies. *Filmfare* is not the only example of the taming of the scribes. Even as it sports a cleavage-showing Kangana Ranaut on its cover, *Stardust* asks its readers the rhetorical question: 'Has Bollywood's mindset really changed?' Tacked above this is the line: 'From running naked to opinionated heroines', and the catchphrase, 'Bohemian Rhapsody'. Hmm. Really? The photograph itself is a tame one, displaying none of the in-your-face attitude the actress is famous for.

Take, instead, a look at the issues of the same magazine, circa 2005. The covers screamed sensation from the rooftops. 'The child Aamir Khan abandoned', 'The Secret Dimple keeps from Rajesh', 'Hrithik–Kareena rekindle their love affair'. The promise was that if you picked up an issue, it would explode, spilling guilty secrets and hidden sins out of its pages. Wind back to the swinging seventies where it had been hotter still. That was the decade Rekha decided to 'bare it all' for *Stardust* fans. In 1997, Sunjay (sic) confessed on the *Stardust* cover, 'Yes, I'm marrying Rhea', even as the magazine wondered about 'Raveena Tandon's nervous breakdown' and whether 'Akshay would get wooed back'. While an August issue asked 'Will the Bachchan marriage survive inspite (sic) of Zeenat?'

If the swinging sixties were the years claimed by the Beat Generation, journalism ensured the seventies were given over to sensationalism; larger-than-life stories about celebrities with a sharp focus on the icons of filmdom became the norm. Suddenly gossip was in, and there was no shame in fixing one's eye to the keyhole and peeping into what, till then, had been the very private lives of film stars. Everything changed, going topsy-turvy in a way that delighted readers, fans, and moviegoers, ensuring the first step was taken to tattle-tale journalism becoming the norm.

So what happens in the seventies to make this sea change possible? What brought the stars of cinema, till then shining in an out-of-reach galaxy, within touching distance of every fan worth the name? For decades they had allowed only carefully composed, studied photographs, and sterilized write-ups about themselves to be printed by film magazines, creating an aura of leading perfect lives, always looking beautiful and radiant, happy at home even as they wept or sang or indulged in villainous acts onscreen.

Of course, there were occasional rents in the fabric. Especially when Devi the Dreaded decided to run her talons along the seams. Dressed in white organdie saris that billowed outwards from her ample frame, her nails painted to perfection, and eyes outlined in dramatic black, Devi was India's answer to Hollywood's much-feared film journalist Hedda Hopper. She was possibly the only intellectual successor to the scathing Hollywood columnist whose writing spared no icon of the silver screen. As she floated in and out of the *Star & Style* office, her voice carrying news of her arrival even before she entered, Devi was a film journo who blazed her own path. Using the privilege of her youth, commanding personality, and her claim to a vicarious lineage, Devi won the confidence of a selected pantheon of stars to become the star of *Star & Style*. The fact that Devi's father had worked with the Holkar royal family added its own heft.

Among her select band of friends was Vyjayanthimala whose career was at the top in the 1960s. The role Devi played in the star's affair with Raj Kapoor got her into the coveted RK camp and led to other producers pampering her and giving her access to their stars. In every way, with her column 'Frankly Speaking', which turned her spotlight on every star and laid bare many secrets, Devi ruled the roost. Hers was the single voice that could be heard in the surrounding PR din about current favourites, and though it evoked interest that fanned the reader's curiosity, it was the film industry that watched closely with a mix of satisfaction and fear about what Devi would dig up next.

If Devi herself sometimes felt the heat generated by her column, she could remain unscarred and smiling. Irked by her hints about his private life, when a somewhat tipsy Dharmendra made to attack her during a star rally at the Mahalakshmi Turf Club, Devi took to her heels. The actor followed in hot chase, shouting out her name and abuses, and when fellow journalist Krishna 'Leo' of *Cine Blitz* intervened to stop Dharam, he got a black eye for his chivalry. Leo took his revenge by writing two paragraphs with eloquent details which his editor ran in *Blitz*. And the film industry, taking note, had stalwarts like Raj Kapoor, Dev Anand, and Dilip Kumar speaking up against the 'shameful behaviour' of chasing journalists and demanding an apology. Even the Producer's Guild was alerted to take note. Post this event, it was as if Devi's reign was absolute as a feeling of live-and-let-her-write prevailed. It was a forerunner of things to come, for 'Frankly Speaking' was at the cusp of a new era of film journalism.

All art is a mirror to the world around it. Social change found reflection in the movies of the late sixties. The Chinese aggression had rudely snatched off the rose-tinted glasses that Indians wore when looking to the governance at the Centre. Dissenting voices, political and social, rose to counter what was seen as a betrayal of the populace by Nehru's shortsightedness about his Chinese counterparts and their intentions. Films like *Haqeeqat* (1964) by Chetan Anand, though dressed up with great music and a love story, showed the trauma of being victims of aggression.

The shift that had started in the sixties was by the early 1970s a wave. The 'yahoo' call of Shammi Kapoor had already not just cemented his star status, it had made him the symbol of a younger, effervescent India, seeking expression out of its moribund cultural taboos. Suddenly it seemed that the new stars were also more accessible, ready to shed their light on their fans, in real life too. And the new generation, in turn, was not prepared to adore from afar; it wanted more. Into this fertile space, ripe with possibility, wandered two people: one looking for adventure, the other for an escape from boredom. They would earn their place in journalistic history by being the first to reach out and pluck the stars from the sky and bring them down to ground level. And it happened almost by accident.

Businessman, maverick, ad-man, publisher – Nari Hira was nothing if not ambitious. He was already an established one-man industry but dreaming of new horizons to conquer. He was toying with the idea of a film magazine with a difference. A film magazine that would cock a snook at the established mandarins in the business. When his protégée Shobha Rajadhyaksha (Shobhaa De), who was then a copywriter, wafted into his cabin waving a resignation letter because she was fed up to the gills with writing copy, Hira told her to hold her horses. He would hand her the reins of his new venture, the film magazine *Stardust*.

Nari Hira had been steering the fledging magazine towards the youth, talking to them in short sentences, which were in sharp contrast to the poetic prose of the more serious film magazines. If the editors at *Filmfare* took pride in making tinsel town a place to spill their literary outpourings upon, Hira opened up the gates of chat, so even a twelve-year-old would understand the content. This tabloid format of text combined with bolder, racier photographs were diametrically opposed to what the public had been seeing till then. If the Diwali issue of *Filmfare* carried a full-length shot of Nanda standing prettily in a Navwari (a nine-yard traditional sari), with nose ring and other jewellery in place, Nari Hira offered up Helen in a shot from one of her film numbers, dressed scantily with cleavage on display. No guesses about which cover was picked off the stalls faster.

When *Hare Rama Hare Krishna* opened up a new licence on screen by way of subject and clothes, in 1972, *Stardust* grabbed the opportunity to entice the younger stars – Zeenat Aman, Neetu Singh, Parveen Babi, Kalpana Iyer, Yogita Bali, and Rekha – to dress daringly differently in tube tops and minis, and gave the photographs ample space. It was a win-win for both the publicity-thirsty stars and a circulation-hungry magazine.

Shobhaa, when she was handed the reins, picked up on Nari Hira's formula. She knew nothing of Hindi films, and for the moment the stars on the Indian firmament were below her notice. If there was one exception, it was the suave Shashi Kapoor whom she had watched in *The Householder* (1963). But that was not going to stop her. The fact that she did not feel the awe that Hindi film stars evoked in the normal film-going Indian gave her writing a dash of irreverence. Sitting at her desk, with pages to fill, she and her team dashed off imaginary interviews with the stars of the day, mostly hearsay, with a twist of familiarity that was both shocking and seductive to the reader. The articles would spend paragraphs on description, be personalized as if the author was the star's confidante and friend, and in keeping with the irreverence, the writing was conversational, almost signalling a take-it-or-leave-it tone.

Unlike the film journalists of the day, Shobhaa, despite being the editor of *Stardust*, 'never went to a premiere or film party; and had no face-to-face with the stars'. There was thus no fear of a reaction like the one Devi had faced, and the articles continued to feature on the pages with cheeky impunity.

There was a brief flirtation with walking the tried-and-tested path of offering film reviews. But the experiment proved a disaster. When a fledgling M.J. Akbar was asked to review Gulzar's *Mere Apne* (1971), he offered up a cerebral, social analysis of the film that readers confessed in a survey was quite beyond their understanding. The review idea was promptly dropped.

Within months of the magazine hitting the stands, Nari Hira's mandate of *Stardust* being the masala mix that Hedda Hopper and her ilk offered readers in Hollywood was established as a reality. If the other magazine editors were shocked by the unverified gossip and the dirty linen that the new kid on the block was dragging out of closets once thought untouchable, the public found a deep satisfaction in knowing that the larger-than-life denizens of the big screen were as human as they themselves were. Gossip, and loads of it, spoken tongue firmly in cheek, was the mainstay of *Stardust*.

As were full-page photographs. New blood coursed through the ranks of the staffers – unknown entities who were recruited for their ability to turn a quick phrase and cook up a likely story or shoot candid, frank photographs of the stars. Much later, from among them, Ingrid Alberqueque and Uma Rao would become editors in their own right, keeping the magazine exactly where Shobhaa and Nari Hira had wanted to place it – as a commercial, hot-selling proposition.

And the fact that unlike its competition, Nari Hira did not care about allowing film industry ads to bolster the bottom line of his products gave *Stardust* a rare freedom of expression. While other magazines would never dare to criticize a top star or their work because it would affect box-office returns and thus miff the advertiser, Shobhaa could proclaim gleefully that 'Jumping Jack Jeetu could not act to save his life'. In her inimitable words, 'We did not care a flying F who said what.'

If *Stardust* is held guilty of bringing slang into journalism, it was Hira who set the ball rolling. According to veteran film journo and National Award-winning scriptwriter Nina Arora, 'People picked up *Star & Style* for Devi's column. She often quoted the stars verbatim, the language bordering on the colloquial and with heady potions of slang. Hira decided he would "make all of *Stardust* sound like Devi's column".'

Shobhaa continued the trend, honing in on her own exposure to the voices that made Bombay the city it was. As she cocked her ear, '...listening to the dialects of the bhelpuri wala, the dhobis of Dhobi Talao, and the many voices that ring out in public transport ... that ... and my love of slang did the rest. I picked up phrases from the languages, it was fun. And it expressed so much more than the stiff-necked Queen's English could.'

At another level, Bombayia was also a contribution of the film industry. With scripts being based on characters, and dialogues being a bhelpuri of languages, a new ease of expression had entered a more informal-themed cinema. *Stardust* picked up from it, creating a unique Hinglish that every English-reading Bombay-wala, regardless of their roots, found easy to understand and chuckle over.

Stardust soon enough got the bigger stars too to take notice. The circulation numbers could not be ignored. It made good sense to be part of the best-selling magazine. When the stars started to reach out to give interviews, *Stardust* knew it had arrived. The interviews were very different from the tame, goody ones in other magazines till date; here stars outdid each other giving scoops on themselves or on competition or just people they did not like, hoping to catch space on the cover or get the lead story. Scoops became the order of the day; among them the red-hot story of Rajesh Khanna's secret marriage by his longstanding ex-flame Anju Mahendru's mother being a case in point.

Talking of the stories that almost burnt the pages they were printed on, Shobhaa says in retrospect, 'We never invented the gossip. We got a hint of the story, then through talking to people around the subject, built on it. Only those items we could not corroborate would go as blind items.'

As the issues came month after month to feed a slavering readership that had ballooned beyond expectation, the film industry found it had mounted a tiger it could not tame or jump off from. 'They grumbled and whined, but could not challenge the stories to risk more details being uncovered.' Of course, this success inevitably set off a trend. Imitators mushroomed. Even *Cine Blitz*, a magazine that had galloped along comfortably under Russi Karanjia's control, changed its spots. Nina Arora, who watched the changes happening, adds that 'it took four years for Karanjia to realize that film journalism as he had practised it, needed to abandon its coyness and start looking through keyholes'.

As imitators cropped up, including *Super*, helmed by Rauf Ahmed who was a writer of no mean talent, *Stardust* continued to laugh all the way to the bank. By now Shobhaa's wicked wit and poison-dipped pen which could destroy families and careers without a second thought had found favour with readers across the border. Of her own admission, 'Copies were being smuggled into Pakistan and sold in black.' The print run exceeded that of any magazine, matched perhaps only by the *Illustrated Weekly* that would claim a circulation of four lakh copies per week and was a household staple.

Not that the competitors did not fight for their place in the sun. If *Stardust* sold the sex-kitten image, *Cine Blitz* went one step further, inspiring the story of the irrepressible Protima Bedi streaking on Juhu beach. And at *Super*, Rauf Ahmed added his tongue-in-cheek humour with double entendre headlines like 'Kaul Girl' to hint at the rumour that the actress Rita Kaul was a call girl.

By the mid-seventies the face of film journalism wore a decidedly yellow hue. And no one cared a hoot. Starlets and newcomers, the FTII grads, the influx of youngsters from the small towns – all found space, their four-letter words and short dresses included. When Arora wrote an article in *Stardust* about the actress Asha Sachdev's many scandals in the industry, Uma Rao would give the piece an irresistible title that screamed, 'What makes Asha Sachdev the biggest bitch in the industry'. And no one, not even the actress minded. The other publications were not far behind. Everyone was having a field day with words thrown about with no thought of whether such language could be used in polite society.

Not much later, even the pink papers started peppering Hinglish and tiny gossip items on their pages. The impact of Nari Hira's new frontier was huge; journalism would never be the same again. The impact on the journalists themselves was equally dramatic. Shobhaa De airily admits that she spent not a single sleepless night worrying about the damage her pen might have caused in the life of her victims.

> I cared nothing about how my article would affect Hema and Dharam when I wrote about their marriage, they were adults taking decisions ... I had no stabs of conscience. Again, writing about the casting couch was something

> much needed. Every aspirant knows when they put a foot into the industry that it is a planet by itself, and the casting couch is a bed every one of them must inhabit at some point. It is about exploitation, but each one deals with it differently. Some retire hurt and do not come back, others jump at the chance. Writing about it was only holding a mirror to the fact of it.

Not all the editors who followed in Ms De's path had the same steel nerves. Many would find themselves shaken. Arora mentions an episode regarding Uma Rao, who, while on location, threw her weight around as the editor of the number one magazine. Shatrughan Sinha and Mithun Chakraborty were at the shoot, stars still to blaze their trail; and Rao, miffed by a bad joke cracked by Sinha, called him a Double Bore Shotgun. The name would stick, as many of those coined by film writers did. But Shatrughan, well read and FTII alumni that he was, did not miss the double meaning of the moniker. He took revenge by plundering the laundry basket and strewing Rao's clothes all over his bed and calling journos from other magazines to insinuate that she had shared his bed!

The constant pressure and the tensions of an undeclared war between *Stardust* editors digging for dirt and their powerful victims would, more often than expected, result in nervous breakdowns or frequent meltdowns by the editors, even as the star moved on to a new film, licking the wounds the magazine had delivered. The story goes about an editor who, being married to an industry person, found the stress of her job so intense that she tumbled into obsessive behaviour, washing her hands all the time, and going off food for long stretches and having to be force fed. And *Cine Blitz* had to cope with the suicide of one of its editors.

But no editors need to worry about such emotional dilemmas now. The broadsheets spew gossip, but just enough to start the eye pursuing the lines. Film magazines have, as we saw earlier, lost their bite. The bottom line rules. And *Stardust* too has abandoned its penchant for scooping up the dust, and instead lets the starlight shine through.

The seventies changed film journalism, making it more a common man's recipe, but the poison has leaked away; the bombs no longer fall. Only the smell of a near-forgotten smoke remains.

'*Zindagi to bewafa hai*' is the sad version of a happy song shot on Amitabh Bachchan. The sad version is sung by his co-star, Vinod Khanna, in the final scene of this famous Prakash Mehra movie. Identify the song and movie.

Answer: '*Rote hue aate hain sab*' (*Muqaddar ka Sikandar*, 1978)

'Kya Khoob Lagti Ho'

The Costumes and Style Statement of Seventies Hindi Cinema

Niyati Bhat

In Hindi cinema, the 1970s remains the decade of decadence, when changing notions of morality, modernity and desire frequently invaded the screens. This decade gave us the angry man, the original chocolate boy Rishi Kapoor, the heartthrob Shashi Kapoor, the poet Amitabh Bachchan of *Kabhi Kabhie*. It was also a decade that blurred the lines between the men at the margins and those in the middle-class. The decade, mired in the shadow of Emergency, produced some of the most diverse films – *Purab aur Paschim*, *Abhimaan*, *Bobby* and *Golmaal*, just to give you an idea of the diversity on offer.

In 2023, a couple recreated the song '*Rim Jhim Gire Saawan*' for their twenty-fifth wedding anniversary. Rekindling in our memories Amitabh Bachchan in a suit and tie, and Moushumi Chatterjee in an emerald-green sari roaming on the streets of Bombay in rain. Zeenat Aman made her Instagram debut and left everyone in awe of her knack for storytelling and sensitive insights into the world of film-making and anecdotes about various scenes and costumes that left an indelible mark on the cinemagoers of 1970s – bell-bottom pants and wide-collared shirts, Dimple Kapadia's polka-dotted white crop top in *Bobby*, the saris worn by Jaya Bhaduri, Rekha and Sharmila Tagore, the provocative saris and cholis donned by Zeenat Aman in *Satyam Shivam Sundaram* in stark contrast to the domestic white kurta and cotton saris worn by Rekha in *Ghar*.

Bell-bottoms, flared pants, palazzos, crop tops have all made a comeback in recent years, while saris and jeans have remained classic choices. The costume designers who gave us the iconic looks discussed in this essay relied heavily on the labour of garment-makers, tailors, darzees, whose work often went unrecognized. Over the years, a few stars have shared anecdotes about their time in the industry in their biographies and autobiographies, with an interesting anecdote or two about how the beloved iconic looks were created.

Catching Up With the 1970s

In an issue of the *Filmfare* magazine in 1970, an angry reader wrote a letter about his distaste for the film *Tum Haseen, Mai Jawaan*. The reader, a naval officer himself, had an issue with two things: a) the irregularity of the ranks as depicted in the naval uniforms worn in the film and b) scenes depicting the naval officers, played by Dharmendra and others, enjoying a cabaret performance and chasing a nurse in a hospital. He thought it unbecoming of someone who wore a

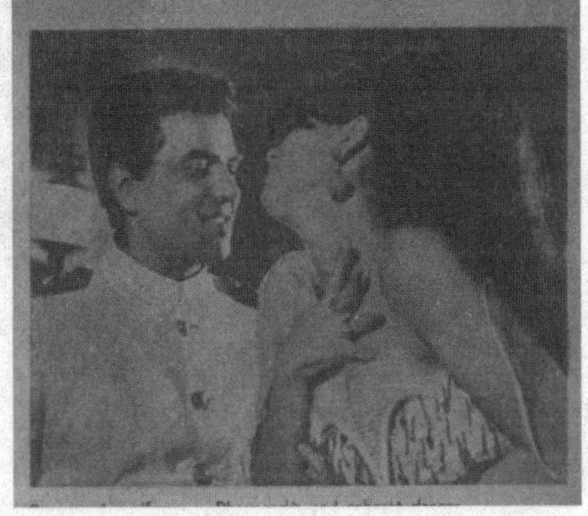

naval uniform and questioned how the film could have gone past the censor board. One wonders then about the many cabaret performances strewn across the landscape of Hindi cinema and made iconic by, among others, Helen. Would the gentleman have expressed his anger if Dharmendra were seen wearing civilian clothes? The song intending to titillate and accentuate the allure of the uniformed officer seemed to have hurt a naval officer's sentiment. *Filmfare*, however, quite cheekily dubbed the moment as 'Romance in uniform'.

In the same film, Hema Malini is seen wearing high buns, donning colourful eyeshadow in blues and greens – reminiscent of the previous decade of cut-crease eyeshadow and winged eyeliner, high hair buns as seen in films like *Do Raaste* (1969). Interestingly, the hair and makeup in 1960s Hindi cinema and early 1970s is also reminiscent of French actress Brigitte Bardot's style in Jean-Luc Godard's 1963 film, *Le Mépris* (*Contempt*).

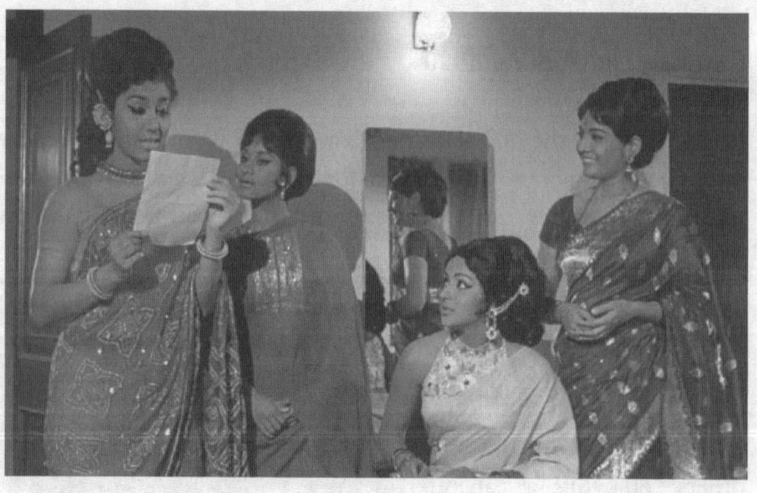

Hema Malini (second from left) in a still from *Tum Haseen, Mai Jawaan* (1970)

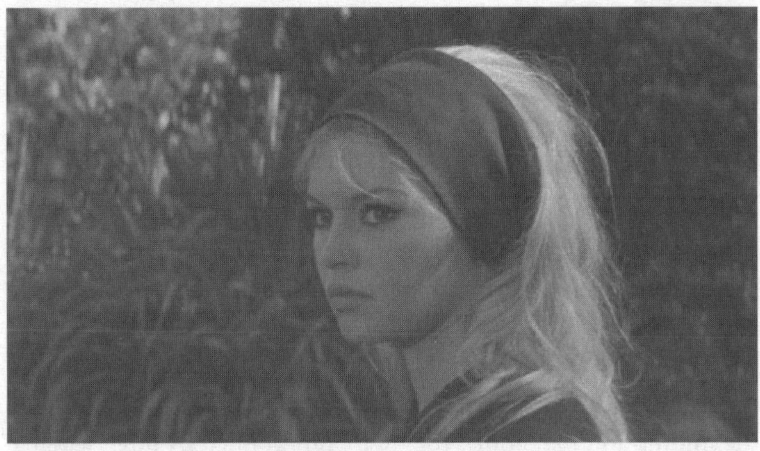

Brigitte Bardot in *Le Mépris* (*Contempt,* 1963).

Saira Banu's character Preeti in *Purab aur Paschim* quite literally embodies and channels Brigitte Bardot in terms of her appearance, mannerisms, and the way she holds a drink in one hand and a cigarette in another.

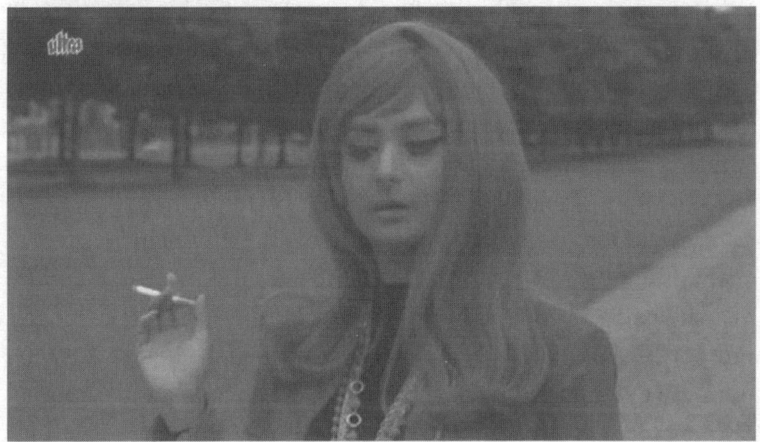

Saira Banu in *Purab aur Paschim* (1970).

A break away from the previous decades and their defining styles is seen in Zeenat Aman's filmography. Zeenat Aman's character in *Hare Rama Hare Krishna* (1971) brought the flower-power generation to our doorstep and along with it, the Woodstock fashion. Zeenat Aman defined the fashion of the 1970s and shifted the style of the leading women of Hindi cinema. Ranjani Mazumdar remarks on this moment and says, 'The emergence of the actress Zeenat Aman marked a distinct shift, since Zeenat naturalized the Western look (for example, in *Hare Rama Hare Krishna*, 1971, and *Yaadon Ki Baaraat*, 1974). Zeenat was never the vamp; she always played the heroine.'[1] Her hair was parted in the middle and flat, unlike the high buns donned by other leading ladies. Her makeup was understated and she moved through characters completely at ease in her sexuality. The outfits she wore in films like *Yaadon ki Baaraat* (1973), *Dharam Veer* (1977) and *Don* (1978), such as glimmering dresses, short midi with knee-length boots, the iconic white dress with silver hoops in '*Chura liya hai tumne jo dil ko*', were usually associated with vamps or cabaret acts in the films of the 1960s and '70s.

It is worth noting that cinemagoers may not know the names of costume designers of the '70s and '80s the way they are acquainted with contemporary fashion designers such as Manish Malhotra, Rohit Bal or Neeta Lulla, but they surely remember the iconic outfits created by the costume designers of the era such as Leena Daru, Mani J. Rabadi and Oscar winner Bhanu Athaiya.

Leena Daru, a graduate of JJ School of Art, was instrumental in solidifying the 'western look' that came to be associated with Zeenat Aman as Mazumdar mentions. In the 1960s, mid-length and pencil skirts were all the rage but women desired to have an alternative. Pants – as opined by Rajesh Khanna to pants-wearing Mumtaz in *Do Raaste* (1969) – made the women 'seem like men'. To circumvent these stereotypes, women started wearing

[1] Ranjani Mazumdar. 'Desiring Women'. *Bombay Cinema: An Archive of the City*, University of Minnesota Press, Minneapolis, MN, 2007.

'palazzos'. They are flared pants but the wide-length of palazzo pants remains even from waist to ankle. Palazzos did for women what bell-bottoms did for men. They became the staple of 1970s fashion, and even today, one cannot think of recreating a '70s look without bell-bottom or palazzo pants. In India, it was Leena Daru who introduced palazzos to the Indian market and Zeenat Aman made them popular in *Yaadon ki Baaraat*. Daru is also credited to have created knotted blouses, patterned scarves and iconic college-going mini-skirts and dress outfits for Neetu Singh in *Khel Khel Mein.*[2]

When Zeenat Aman played the village belle in *Satyam Shivan Sundaram* (1978), her outfits created an uproar. The outfits were designed by Bhanu Athaiya. The plain white sari sans a blouse or petticoat in the titular song, '*Satyam Shivan Sundaram*', left a lasting impression. Aman, self-confessed 'non dancer' when it came to classical dance sequences, felt immense pressure in choreographed sequences. It was Athiaya's costumes and fantastical and dreamy sets in the song, '*Chanchal sheetal nirmal komal*' that gave life to the song sequence. The outfits consisting of a two-piece blouse and skirt in sequins, glitter and vibrant colours became a significant character in constructing the imaginary sequence in which the protagonist Roopa imagines what it would be like to not have scars and be loved by Rajeev (played by Shashi Kapoor). In the song, she remains an enigma, a mirage being chased by Rajeev, and the costumes indicate that unattainable quality. Zeenat Aman, here, embodies desire itself – both the desire of wanting to be perfect and the desire to be loved. Her costumes do bring us closer to her intended desires. Let us look at other film costumes from the 1970s that display the significant shifts and present to us the cultural and socio-economic, religious, and political aspects of the decade.

---

[2] https://www.thequint.com/entertainment/celebrities/legendary-leena-daru-tribute-bollywood-costumes-madhuri-dixit-rekha-sridevi-neetu-kapoor#read-more

The Woman of the House in the 1970s

Bhanu Athaiya also designed Rekha's costumes throughout the decade for various dance sequences including those in *Do Anjaane* (1976) and *Karmayogi* (1978). But it was the role of Aarti in *Ghar* (1978) that allowed Rekha to venture into a non-glamorous role of the woman of the house. The film deals with a sensitive subject matter of sexual assault and how the traumatized woman copes with it. As the domesticated Aarti, Rekha wore cotton saris and dhoti-kurtas in light pink, beige, blue, red and muted colours along with long braids, sindoor, bindi, red bangles, mangalsutra and kohl-rimmed eyes – all representative of the married Indian woman of the time. Jaya Bachchan (nee Bhaduri) in *Abhimaan*, *Mili* and *Uphaar*, Sharmila Tagore in *Chupke Chupke* also carried these motifs that represented the 'woman of the house' in the 1970s. Athaiya, who is well-known for her work on period dramas and won the Academy award for *Gandhi*, created costumes for the Academy award-nominated *Lagaan* and the memorable *Swades*. She had her pulse on the attire of the aam aadmi (common man) and middle-class India for years before these films and expressed these costume designs first in *Ghar*.

Another costume designer of note in the 1970s was Mani J. Rabadi. She was instrumental in creating Dimple Kapadia and Rishi Kapoor's iconic outfits such as the polka-dotted crop top (for Kapadia) and a black leather jacket (for Kapoor).[3] Both Rabadi and Leena Daru contributed to the fashion that defined the college-going youth of 1970s. Rabadi, alongside costume designers Ramola Bachchan and V. Scharwachter, also worked on the costumes for *Don* and those costumes blurred the line between the hero and the villain. I will discuss this further in the later sections of this essay.

---

[3] https://www.cinemaazi.com/people/mani-j-rabadi

The Muslim Social of the 1970s

Ira Bhaskar and Richard Allen have written extensively about the Muslim social films, especially the contrasting films made in the genre in 1970s. On the one hand, there is *Pakeezah*, (1972) set in the never-never land of the classic Muslim social that invokes the nostalgia of an imagined nineteenth-century Lucknow and that does not delve into the economic struggles or social discrimination against Muslims.[4] On the other hand, there is *Garam Hawa* (1974) that addresses the aftermath of the Partition.[5] Ranjani Mazumdar writes, '[in popular Indian films] the picturization of a new kind of fashion has been able to find easy entry within a narrative structure that has historically allowed for a fluid movement into the world of fantasy'.[6] Furthermore, 'the song and dance sequences operated as display windows offering the spectator a range of clothing/costumes'.[7]

In *Pakeezah*'s opening sequence, wearing a white kathak costume (churidar, angarkha and dupatta),[8] Meena Kumari plays Nargis, a courtesan. She is not accepted by her lover Shahbuddin's family and dies a lonely death. Her daughter Sahibjaan (also Meena Kumari) continues her legacy as a courtesan trapped within the walls of a kotha. Raaj Kumar, the actor with a unique voice and style of dialogue delivery, plays Salim, Sahibjaan's love interest. Unbeknown to either of the characters, Salim is also her paternal cousin and Shahbuddin's nephew. Knowing the kind of fate that awaited a courtesan who chose to step out of the kotha, Sahibjaan rejects Salim's offer to marry her. Salim agrees to an arranged

---

[4] Ira Bhaskar and Richard Allen. 'Muslim Courtesan Films'. *Islamicate Cultures of Bombay Cinema*, Tulika Books, New Delhi, 2009, 92.

[5] Ibid, 93.

[6] Ranjani Mazumdar. 'Desiring Women'. *Bombay Cinema: An Archive of the City*, University of Minnesota Press, Minneapolis, MN, 2007, 95-96.

[7] Ibid, 96.

[8] Ira Bhaskar and Richard Allen. 'Muslim Courtesan Films'. *Islamicate Cultures of Bombay Cinema*, Tulika Books, New Delhi, 2009, 93.

marriage and invites Sahibjaan to perform at the wedding. In this climax, Sahibjaan invokes her mother's fate by wearing the same white kathak costume in a pivotal song, '*Teer-e-nazar dekhenge*' wherein she performs the song as a confrontation with Salim in front of her father's side of the family. Meena Kumari's costumes in *Pakeezah* made churidar salwar-kameez an eternal addition to the Indian wardrobe. She is said to have designed the costumes herself[9] (with Tanu Sakharam from the costume department of the film).[10]

Raaj Kumar, who played the protagonist Salim, had had a vibrant career in Hindi cinema but that popularity seemed to be feeble in comparison to the meaty roles offered to Amitabh Bachchan in the 1970s. Yet, according to a *Filmfare* profile on Raaj Kumar written during the shoot of *Pakeezah* in Mysore, his aura in leather jacket, riding boots and a hookah, remains unmissable. He maintained a mysterious air about himself according to the magazine and was not an easy man to read. The men he portrayed on screen, including Salim, also carried the traces of a nawabi past, a nostalgic legacy, and his role in *Pakeezah* further cemented him as a romantic hero of a bygone era with the lines 'don't put your feet on the ground' that Salim writes to Sahibjaan after seeing her feet decorated with aalta and a pair of anklets.

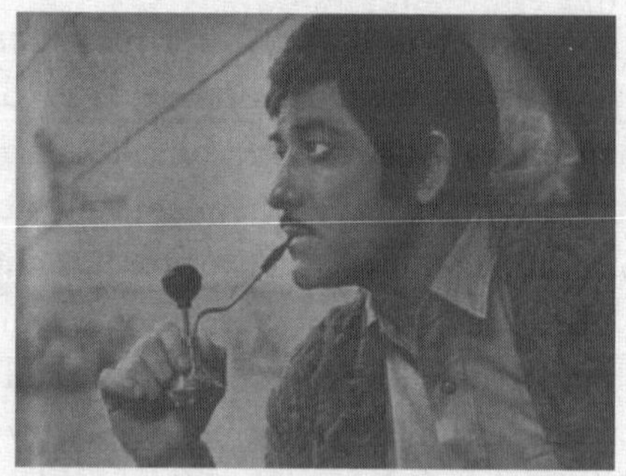

Raaj Kumar on the sets of *Pakeezah* in Mysore, *Filmfare* Magazine, 1970.

[9] https://www.unnatisilks.com/blogs/bollywood-barfi/paakeezah-making-immortal-classic

[10] https://www.cinemaazi.com/people/tanu-sakharam

The Common Man: *Dhoti, Kapda aur Makaan*

Basu Chatterjee's *Chhoti Si Baat* (1978) and *Rajnigandha* (1974), coupled with Hrishikesh Mukherjee's cinema also brought to the fore the common man's clothes through the characters played by actor Amol Palekar. In the early 1970s, Amol Palekar, who was employed at the Bank of India and worked part-time as an actor, was dubbed to be 'too simple-looking for a hero'[11] by Raj Kumar Barjatya. In *Chhoti Si Baat*, Asrani (Govardhan Asrani) plays Nagesh, a cosmopolitan, outgoing man in comparison to the meek protagonist Arun (Amol Palekar) who feels hesitant in social situations and dresses modestly. Their outfits present this picture more clearly. Nagesh shirts are always unbuttoned till his chest and carry bright coloured prints while Arun wears understated office shirts in light colours such as white and blue. Arun is in a constant tussle with Nagesh who owns a scooter (a status symbol of the time) to win over Prabha (their love interest played by Vidya Sinha). To overcome his shy personality, Arun seeks out Colonel Julius Nagendranath Wilfred Singh (Ashok Kumar) who is known to help many in overcoming their shortcomings and turn their lives around.

During his first meeting with the colonel, Amitabh Bachchan (in a cameo playing himself) walks into the room to seek his advice regarding a personal matter. Bachchan is dressed in his brown suede jacket from *Zameer* (1975) and remarks that he is visiting directly from a shooting location. It is an interesting moment in the film about the common man's aspirations. The ideal man as projected by 1970s mainstream cinema walks into the room and that becomes the desired measure of confidence that Arun seeks out for himself so he can win over his love interest – the 'heroine' of his life.

In another scene, Arun imagines himself and Prabha (Vidya Sinha) as protagonists in the beloved song '*Janeman, janeman*'

[11] Anirudha Bhattacharjee. 'The Common Man.' *Basu Chatterjee: And Middle-of-the-Road Cinema*, Vintage, Penguin Random House India, 2023.

replacing Dharmendra and Hema Malini. Both the couples are seen wearing understated outfits – shirts and pants for the men and everyday saris for the women. Chatterjee – using song, fantasy, and costume – replaced the 'hero' and 'heroine' with his own protagonists, the ones that every cinemagoer identified with. The film is about the Bombay of the salaried man. But Basu's common woman was uncommon for her time.[12] She was an officer worker with an interest in novels and she was friends with her male co-worker, Nagesh – an arc that one did not see often in Hindi cinema.

Vidya Sinha turned georgette and cotton saris into the working woman's attire in Basu Chatterjee's films. In *Rajnigandha*, she plays a Deepa, PhD scholar. She wears georgette or Swiss voile (a kind of woven cotton fabric) saris, her hair is in a braid, carries a white handbag and puts on large sunglasses as her outfit to a movie date with her love interest. In an interview, Nandita Thakur mentions, 'Basu-da wanted the characters to look natural.'[13] In both the above-mentioned films, Chatterjee created the character of the common man and woman using costumes and hairstyles that were natural, that the audience identified with. Hrishikesh Mukherjee's cinema was akin to the common man's cinema of Basu Chatterjee, and the costumes for *Anand* reflected the same – dhoti, kurta, plain shirts and trousers.

Heroes and Villains: Code Switching through Costumes

Bachchan was new on the horizon and experimenting with the kind of star he wanted to be. The film that cemented that stardom was *Zanjeer* that was released the same year as Rishi Kapoor's *Bobby*, in 1973. Clare M. Wilkinson-Weber remarks that it was in *Zanjeer* that denim pants and overalls first appeared as outfits worn by assailants even though jeans were as yet not commonly worn at all

[12] Ibid, 92.

[13] Ibid, 98.

either in films or in India as a whole.[14] The denims certainly left a lasting impression on filmgoers and the film fraternity as a whole. Amitabh Bachchan and Dharmendra, on the insistence of Ramesh Sippy, would go on to wear denim jackets and denim pants in *Sholay* (1975), which also revolutionized the villain in Indian cinema.

The costumes for the villain evolved over the decades from *Mother India*'s village moneylender and dacoits in dhotis to *Sholay*'s Gabbar. Having army fatigues for Gabbar was the director's stylistic choice. It is noteworthy because the villains in that era were known to have suave, stylish, and sparklingly clean outfits such as Ajit as Shakaal in *Yaadon ki Baaraat*. Or as Teja in *Zanjeer*. Or 'Loin' in *Kalicharan*. However, for *Sholay*'s Gabbar, Amjad Khan was dressed in used army fatigues reportedly bought at Chor Bazaar (Anupama Chopra 2000, 85).[15] Ranged against Gabbar, we had two urban outlaws, Jai and Veeru, with their denims and a BSA WM 500 motorcycle with a sidecar.

Bachchan, who played the tragi-romantic Jai in *Sholay* went on to play the outlaw, the underdog, the man against the system, and ultimately, with *Don*, he, too, embodied the role of the villain. The stark demarcations between the hero and the villain made clear in their differing outfits, mannerisms, intentions, and characteristics were completely swapped in the costumes designed by Mani J. Rabadi, Ramola Bachchan and V. Scharwachter.[16] It is said that Bachchan's look of the printed vest with a gamchha in the song '*Khaike paan Banaras wala*' was Rabadi's handiwork.[17] Wilkinson-Weber suggests that this swapping happens quite literally by the swapping of clothes by the hero, Vijay, and the villain Don (both lookalikes played by Amitabh Bachchan).[18]

---

[14] Clare M. Wilkinson-Weber. 'Shifty Villains.' *A Companion to Indian Cinema*, Wiley Blackwell, Hoboken, NJ, 2022, 109.

[15] Ibid, 114.

[16] https://www.cinemaazi.com/people/mani-j-rabadi

[17] Ibid.

[18] Clare M. Wilkinson-Weber. 'Shifty Villains.' *A Companion to Indian Cinema*, Wiley Blackwell, Hoboken, NJ, 2022, 106.

If one were to think of the impact of the clothes and outfits, costume departments, designers, tailors, material providers and the ultimate and lasting impact of the trendsetting decade on the common man and the retro vibe we keep referring to, one does not need to think of the present time in which this fashion has certainly made a comeback from flared pants to overall denims (they never quite left), polka-dots, winged eyeliner, timeless saris, palazzos. But we can find a film that summed up the impact of 1970s on the cinemagoers.

The year is 1979. The film is *Gol Maal* by Hrishikesh Mukherjee. The protagonist is Ramprasad Dashrathprasad Sharma, a chartered accountant played by Amol Palekar. And he is heading out for a job interview. At the last minute, on the advice of his uncle, he changes his attire from a modern-day office shirt and pants to a crisp dhoti-kurta. He adopts subtle mannerisms and learns of things that please his hiring manager and boss, Bhawani Shankar. This is essentially him bowing down to Shankar's traditional biases. In his interview he stresses on the importance of a moustache (that Shankar also dons) as a sign of a strong character. It works in his favour and he gets the job. Unemployment of the 1970s is subtly hinted at in this film released after the Emergency.

The 1970s was a time of push and pull between the traditional and the modern. The fact that youngsters replicated the outfits worn by their favourite stars in various films is satirized in *Gol Maal.* This conversation between the uncle and the nephew regarding what clothes say about a man signifies the cultural and socio-political context of the times. Outside the office life, Ramprasad continues to follow his love for Hindi cinema and wears his modern and flamboyant clothes. One day, Ramprasad is out with his friends at a hockey match, dressed in a patterned shirt with vibrant colours and sunglasses. His boss, Shankar, spots him at this match and is in disbelief at the transformation of his employee Ramprasad from a mild-mannered, dhoti-kurta and Nehru jacket-wearing man to this modern-day man who loves hockey and cinema. Shankar becomes suspicious of Ramprasad and the values that Ramprasad projected to land the job. Caught in a fix, afraid of being exposed as a liar and a fraud, and afraid of losing his job, Ramprasad pretends that it was his twin brother, Lucky, whom Shankar saw at the match. This leads to a comedy of disguise and errors as Ramprasad tries to keep up the charade of being both the moustached and traditional Ramprasad and clean-shaven and modern Lucky to win Shankar's confidence. Using costumes, Mukherjee depicted the way the nation was navigating how to sail in two boats, i.e., keeping traditions and history alive while trying to modernize its different aspects. It clearly depicted the impact that cinema and the stars of the time had had on cinemagoers.

Costumes are an invitation into the world of a film. They tell us who the heroes and villains are. They tell us who we look like, who we want to look like and how we want the people we fall in love with to look like. They leave behind trends that last for decades. The 1970s Hindi cinema gave us timeless characters (mostly named 'Vijay'), classic dialogues (*mere paas maa hai*/*Don ka intezar toh gyarah mulkon ki police kar rahi hai*/*Babumoshai, zindagi badi honi chahiye, lambi nahin*), songs that make us groove and make us melancholic. At the heart of these stories are the costumes they wear when they embody these characters. The fashion, costumes and clothes discussed in this essay contributed to making 1970s Hindi cinema memorable. And quite like Zeenat Aman, that fashion too is making a comeback.

The Seventies: Hindi Cinema's Defining Decade

Eloquence of Extremes, Rigour of Fresher Forms

Amrit Gangar

The 1970s was the decade that provided Hindi cinema with new defining moments in terms of its visuality (cinematography, lensing), aurality (sound recording and designing), mise-en-scene or how the narratives were woven together (editing), choices of stories (literature, screenwriting) which was radically different from the previous decades (loosely 1940–60) decorated as the Golden Age, largely due to lilting songs and grandness of stories and ways of mounting them/sets (economics). Most significantly, it was this decade that produced new dynamism of production and articulation of thoughts around cinema by practising film-makers themselves (filmosophy, criticality), which, I can claim, had never happened before in the history of Hindi cinema. In retrospect, the 1970s takes a definite turn on the historical timeline, a defining moment. In its sheer rigour and radicalism of production of thought, Bombay (later Mumbai) very much distinguishes itself from the rest of India, including Calcutta.

The impact of the establishment of training, financing, and conservation institutions such as the Film Institute of India (later Film and Television Institute of India), the Film Finance Corporation (later National Film Development Corporation), the National Film Archive of India (NFAI) in the 1960s had begun to impact the film-making practice and thinking in the decade that followed. The period between 1969 and 1972 was a significant time that inaugurated the decade with unprecedented cinematographic works, including Mrinal Sen's first Hindi film *Bhuvan Shome*, Mani Kaul's *Uski Roti*, Basu Chatterjee's *Sara Aakash* and Kumar Shahani's *Maya Darpan*, all debut feature films of the respective directors. Following the French Nouvelle Vague, journalists declared *Bhuvan Shome* heralding Indian cinema's New Wave. It was this decade that gave birth to a new, non-glamorous, non-idolatry *nayak* and *nayika* (hero, heroine) within the realm of Hindi cinema. It was during this decade film production began to witness its new ecosystem, both in terms of creation of forms ('cinematography' in the Bressonian sense)[1] and consumption of contents (market).

In this essay, my attempt would be to comprehend the *temporality* under its sprawling *spatial* shamiana to gauge how Bombay and its cinema (later acquiring the moniker of Bollywood) distinctly enriched the mind and matter perhaps in more ways than we had thought of, and it is the production of new 'thought' during the 1970s that I would like to begin with. The 1970s Bombay had a fascinating intellectual life that had its innovating intensity along with vibrant groups of cineastes and film-lovers. It was also the time when the film society movement was beginning to acquire a cerebral edge. Based on my reading and working experience, I think my articulation of such thought–practice mosaic that

[1] 'Cinematography' for Bresson has the special meaning of creative film-making which thoroughly exploits the nature of film as such. It should not be confused with the work of a cameraman.

occurred demonstratively in the 1970s might help film scholars in some way in comprehending the period at stake.

Incidentally, the decade situates itself almost midway on the historical timeline between *Bhakta Pundalik* (silent, 1912) and *Monica, O My Darling* (2022), the latter echoing the 1971 Hindi film *Caravan* and its song '*Piya tu ab to aaja/Monica, O my darling*'. The decadal positioning of the 1970s is crucial as it sandwiches itself between the sowing decade of the 1960s and the cropping decade of the 1980s, so to speak. So let me begin with the production of more dynamic and original thoughts that eventually led to the evolution of new aesthetics in thinking and making of cinematographic creations in the realm of Hindi cinema.

In this essay, though my focus is on Kumar Shahani and Mani Kaul, the two *filmosophers* (a new term to suggest the film-makers who comprehended film-making practice within the broad contours of *filmosophy*, or film + philosophy), the emerging contours would have wider ramifications on Indian film-making practice emanating from the 1970s. A new applied theory had come into being through the production of those very thoughts.

The Production of Thoughts, 1970s: New Aesthetics

Sound and silence

It was for the first time a practising film-maker (not the sound recordist or designer) who brought in new perceptions to sound and silence in cinema. Kumar Shahani's presentation of the paper *Notes for an Aesthetic of Cinema Sound* at a seminar in Delhi in 1978 was a marker. Tonalities and intonations of human speech (*dialogues* in Hindi cinema's common parlance) he had already practised in his debut film *Maya Darpan* (1972). In his practice, he strived to imbue cinematography with its own *being*, not dominated by the theatricality it was hitherto profusely plagued with. In retrospect, even in the time of digital technology and in the year 2023, what he said remains significant to the aesthetics of our cinematographic practice. In his paper, he said:

> As for incidental and atmospheric sounds in the cinema, they lie between.
> The organized sounds (music) drifting into entropy and
> Contextual sound (speech).
> The rest is silence.

Both the senses of sight and sound, he noted, 'arose out of the need to perceive movement; to locate an object and one's own relationship to it'. These were completely new thoughts the previous decades had never imagined or articulated. Something significant was happening under the skin of the *time*.

Montage and its relevance

While reflecting upon the relevance of Eisensteinian 'montage' then, Shahani drew parallels with the principles of composition; the reference here is to his paper presented at a 1978 seminar in Calcutta. As if his words pulled Brahma (creator) and Shiva (destroyer) together when he thought, '(…) that we construct as compulsively as we destroy. If, in the process, we do not discover something that takes us by surprise, it is hardly worth presenting it back to nature or society.'[2]

The decade carried a certain emotional-intellectual restlessness to confront reality, 'Usually, the surprise is painful, the contact electrifying the limits of reason stretched and expanded to a tear, if one wants to approach a reality that one lives through with every gesture, word, movement, hiding and revealing it through composition.'[3]

---

[2] Kumar Shahani, *The Relevance of Montage Today*, paper presented at a seminar in Calcutta, 1978

[3] Ibid.

Four years earlier in the 1970s, a new thought on montage…

Four years preceding the above-mentioned thoughts on montage, Mani Kaul had drawn 'a strange parallel between the discovery of Eisenstein of some major elements of montage and the division of consciousness of the universe perceived in the *Bhagavad Gita*'. Kaul wrote:

> In Chapter XIII, shloka 15, it speaks of three categories which are permeated by the *purusha*. They are away and near, immobile and mobile, interior and exterior. In Eisenstein they have been almost replaced by his vision of montage or the cinematic totality as close shots and long shots, pieces of graphically varied directions; pieces resolved in volume with pieces resolved in area, pieces of darkness and pieces of lightness. (Cf. 'Cinematographic principle and the ideogram' in Sergei Eisenstein's book *Film Form*).
>
> It is Eisenstein again who credits the oriental mind with 'monism' of ensemble, where the elements do not accompany each other but are brought into function as elements of equal significance whose balanced juxtaposition must lead us into that precious experience of the undifferentiated mass of consciousness.[4]

A decade later, Shahani, again on montage, in Calcutta… 'No escape from montage!'

It is interesting to note that exactly a decade later again in Calcutta, speaking at the Rita Ray Memorial Lecture hosted by Chitrabani, Shahani said, 'There is no escape from montage.'

---

[4] Mani Kaul, 'Explorations in New Film Techniques', *Indian Film Culture*, Autumn 1974.

It is a known fact that in their film-making practice, both Shahani and Kaul followed a different path vis-à-vis 'montage', yet both remained close to Ritwik Ghatak whose faith in Eisensteinian theory was intact.

Colour and Image-Relationships

Maya Darpan is the first film in the history of Indian cinema that established new radical relationships between colours and inner–outer equations in a cinematographic image. In *Maya Darpan*, I suppose, Shahani innovates a montage *bhava* between them. *Maya Darpan* works with the red-yellow-blue oppositions of the colour cycle; the warm colours (orange, red, magenta) were woven into the narrative which was radically a new thought-in-practice that significantly manifested in the decade of 1970s that we cannot just ignore.

On the other hand, Mani Kaul's 1973 film *Duvidha* provides yet another significant example of film-making practice from this decade, but the *thought* would precede. *Duvidha* was to bring about what really belonged to the interrelationship of colours unlike what Shahani had done in *Maya Darpan*. Kaul argued:

> Since we know of contrary and complementary colours, imbalance and balance can be controlled – in other words, a structure can be built. Even the proportions have been already worked out by great masters. If green is suddenly introduced after an excessive use of red and in twice the quantity of red, a kind of 'settling' would be effected. But if the film abstains from using green and goes to part of the green (which is yellow + blue; as red is posited against the other two primary colours combined into green), let us say a yellow inclined towards orange rather than green, the shift would cause a whiter tonality and a mildly warm feeling.[5]

[5] Ibid.

Kaul constructs a completely newer figurative relationship between colours which would not be loaded with meanings nor with the conventional sensuous–intellectual equation.

> Colours would neither become meanings nor represent meanings, for in both these cases the use is figurative rather than actual. While on the other hand, whenever the subject matter of the film rises to be the meaning, it will also be total and complete: the colour, in such a situation is 'absent'; its assertive quality is absent. When the form and the object behind it, which are actually one, appear separated in expression they should in that separation acquire total and independent existences. For only then the true experience which neither belongs to the sensuous nature of the form nor to the intellectual quality of the meaning, (but to both) and is yet intangible and beyond analysis which the materialists mistake for 'mystical' or the 'metaphysical' – but which is actual and real is born.[6]

Optics/Lensing Philosophy

To my mind, Mani Kaul's debut film *Uski Roti* (1970) was the first Indian film that had consciously explored the camera lenses' optic properties. This could be an interesting study for students of cinematography in the current digital age after over half a century since 1970. I personally call two film-makers in India, Ritwik Ghatak and Mani Kaul, the 'lensing philosophers'. Even as film-makers, individually they were very aware about the camera lenses and their employment towards achieving cinematographic enrichment. Shot by the visionary cinematographer K.K. Mahajan, *Uski Roti* employs two lenses: 28 mm wide angle deep focus and 135 mm telephoto, which were

[6] Kaul, 'Explorations in New Film Techniques'.

deeply integral to the film's narrative. This was unprecedented in the history of Hindi cinema.

Explorations in New Film Techniques

In his 1974 essay, Kaul founds several new theoretical propositions as a practising film-maker, not as a critic or theoretician. To reiterate, I call both Shahani and Kaul *filmosophers*, the gift from the 1970s, significantly from Hindi cinema, if you will, and Bombay.

How could one define the newness of a work? Kaul had already thought about it, 'The newness of a work refers to the subjective originality of the filmmaker and tradition to a more collective acceptance of certain norms. Their relationship embraces a legitimate contradiction which all valid attempts in art forms must seek to resolve.' By contradiction, Kaul refers to those works that remain enamoured with the more superficial aspects of the folk culture. 'An inversion of the stated position can also reach an absurd point when the strictly traditional begins to use half-scientific truths to induce a modern sensibility in the orthodox area, when, in actual fact, it is in need of no such justification.'[7]

Kaul was perhaps sighting the 'middle-roader' cinema on the horizon. The decade was grappling with finding ways of engagement with the ticket-buying audiences. It had already embarked upon its existential battle! A film journal had asked some film-makers about the difference between the 'art' film and the 'commercial' film. Among many varying responses, Kaul's was, as I try to recall, 'Art film is the one that takes the maximum risk in its making while the commercial film is the one that makes the maximum profit.' And this will perhaps provoke us to see what lay on this decade's mosaic, as also why and how.

---

[7] Ibid.

Eloquence of the Extremes and Towards Exploration of the Middle

Within this decadal parenthesis, I would like to place the following five films on the 'risk' end of the axis: *Uski Roti* (1970), *Ashad ka Ek Din* (1971), *Maya Darpan* (1972), *Duvidha* (1973), and *Ghashiram Kotwal* (1976). Though the last one was in Marathi, it was jointly made by several FTII alumni, none of whom was Marathi-speaking or a Maharashtrian. They had formed the Yukt Film Co-operative to produce the film *Ghashiram Kotwal* and later in 1978 *Arvind Desai ki Ajeeb Dastaan*, directed by Saeed Mirza. I will talk about these films soon.

Financed by the FFC and based on Mohan Rakesh's Hindi story of the same name, *Uski Roti* is considered to be the first consistently formal experiment in Indian cinema. Since it charted intensely new, non-theatrical cinematographic path, many found it *durbodh* or inaccessible. Hence, it was violently attacked by the popular press but was strongly defended by India's aesthetically sensitive cineastes, indicating the mood of the time and the preparedness of the governmental support for risk-taking propositions, the credit for which should go to Indira Gandhi, the then Union Minister of Information and Broadcasting. She was also associated with the film society movement which was headed by Satyajit Ray. Also, there still existed a sense of resistance to complete surrendering to populist pressures. About *Uski Roti*, I have already referred to its formal optic engagements.

Soon Kaul went a step further in his risk-taking rigorous formal exploration in *Ashad ka Ek Din* which he had adapted from Mohan Rakesh's 1958 Hindi play of the same name; it featured the legendary Sanskrit playwright Kalidasa. In this film, Kaul experimented with the interrelationship of theatre and cinema. The whole play was prerecorded after its division into sound cycles (of measured rhythm) and played back at the location. Other variations of acoustic change were also used from areas that would reproduce dead-flat sound to the echo quality, finding a state in between. Let me emphasize, for Kaul techniques were not just gimmicks, nor were they any special effects jugglery, which is a staple of the films in the digital era now. Kaul writes, 'The techniques are not gimmicks inasmuch as they do not involve any disrespect for historical development: all that we used was an extension of what had been used for naturalistic purposes – and all naturalistic methods employ varying techniques as an accompaniment to create an ensemble.'[8]

Completely non-theatrical, even the sparse realism that we find in *Uski Roti* is replaced in *Ashad ka Ek Din* by K.K. Mahajan's sensuously shot landscapes and languid camera movements, minutely registering light changes within the frame, at times slowly shutting the aperture.

The intensity of formal rigour continues in Kumar Shahani's *Maya Darpan*, also shot by K.K. Mahajan with his intuitive sense of rhythm and illumination. Adapting Nirmal Verma's short story of the same name, Shahani turns it into a dialectical ensemble of colours (as already referred to earlier) that creates its own opera-like musicality and a Marxian, materialist cinematographic rendition. This was an extraordinary contribution to Hindi cinema from the decade under study.

Back to Mani Kaul and his prolific production of thoughts as well as films. *Duvidha*, adapted from Vijaydan Detha's short story, was not financed by the FFC like the previous two films, *Uski Roti* and *Ashad ka Ek Din*; instead, it was made with the help of the painter Akbar Padamsee's Workshop (which was part of the Jawaharlal Nehru Fellowship Scheme) and Rupayan Sansthan of Borunda in Rajasthan. Incidentally, Kaul also belonged to Jodhpur in Rajasthan and was therefore familiar with the landscape and milieu of the region. The 1970s were, in a way, battling against the hegemony of 'capital' and 'market'.

The discipline in this film acquired a much more comprehensive meaning. Folk material, as stated above or elsewhere, provides a schematic design, apart from the chronological order of events that it follows.

---

[8] Ibid.

> In the schematic design, the representation of an event is reducible by graphic or oral means to such a generalised degree that a common denominator is finally discovered as the basic norm from where all particularities spring. The combination of such as interior/exterior not only remains at a graphic level which is quantitative, but extends itself to the qualitative aspect of the film.[9]

Kaul explains the key scene from the film very succinctly thus:

> A ghost enters into the room of the girl, a child is conceived (is in the womb), the actual husband returns and questions the ghost's impersonation of the husband. The child is born (comes out of the womb). The villagers take the ghost and the husband outside the village where a shepherd, through a kind of fundamental genius, puts the ghost into or inside the drinking leather bag. The bag is dumped into a well. The husband and the villagers re-enter the village. The husband re-enters the bride's room. And here the tragic quality of the bride, who was in love with a ghost, or with the impersonation of her own husband, emerges. This feeling is due mainly to the cessation of the exterior/interior relationship with the actual husband.[10]

Just to reiterate, in *Duvidha*, Kaul breaks down the colour-conventionalities, e.g., the colour is made to belong to its fact of physical condition, which, as Kaul clarifies, should not be confused with the idea of the setting being realistic in the contemporary sense. In fact, the film belongs to a period. Also, the film does away with any rigid or absolute interpretation of colours. Red, for instance, may not suggest violence all the time; it may often mean

[9] Ibid.

[10] Ibid.

joy. To my mind, until 1972–73, colours in films were just props for beauty or novelty to attract audiences.

In this conceptuality, I would like to include the Marathi film *Ghashiram Kotwal*, collectively directed by K. Hariharan, Mani Kaul, Kamal Swaroop, and Saeed Mirza. This 104-minute colour film was shot by Binod Pradhan, Rajesh Joshi, Manmohan Sigh, and Virendra Saini, all FTII alumni. Music composer Bhaskar Chandavarkar taught at the FTII. Based on Vijay Tendulkar's play, the film uses Maharashtrian folk forms such as Gondhal and Keertan in their choreographic elaborations. The film features Nanasaheb Phadanavis, the powerful prime minister of Peshwa Madhavrao II (1774–95). Tendulkar's play was allegorical about the draconian emergency imposed around that time.

The film's main significance resides in the way it adapts theatre to investigate its cinematographic relationship. Yukt Co-operative was India's earliest formal cooperative body which had borrowed money from Dena Bank in Mumbai. For Screen Unit, the film club I was privileged to head then, I had, after great persuasion, succeeded in obtaining the prints of the film from the bank for our screening. Perhaps Screen Unit was the only film club in India that had screened *Ghashiram Kotwal* through fresh positive prints of the film, straight from the bank's vaults.

Yukt also produced yet another film in 1978 – Saeed Mirza's debut *Arvind Desai ki Ajeeb Dastaan*. It was again the most experimental Hindi feature film that had attempted to elaborate its own construction, politically. Some critics could see Michelangelo Antonioni and Ben Barka's influences on the film. After producing Mirza's film, Yukt Co-operative wound up. All these films stay on the extreme end of my conceptualized axis on Hindi cinema's timeline – the charismatic 1970s.

A Belated Caesura

The 'defining decade' was witness to the narrative and the non-narrative rigours of the Khayal (Shahani), of Dhrupad (Kaul), and of Sugam Sangeet[11] (Benegal), but it stood at its *vilambit* liminality that had perhaps subconsciously awaited the *drut*[12] of the digital, of the horrendous times of the dismantling of institutions that had nurtured (Vishnu) both modernity and tradition in the 1970s. Winds of the neoliberal economy had begun to blow that Premchand's chess players were not ready to heed. In those times of the 1970s, the Bengali maestro Satyajit Ray's first entry into the realm of Hindi/Hindustani cinema had created a storm soon after the national Emergency imposed by Prime Minister Indira Gandhi in 1975. *Shatranj ke Khilari* (1977) was a gift from the 1970s. And from somewhere afar, the whistle of *27 Down* (Awtar Krishna Kaul, 1974) blew into the darkness, rushing. Pure blood oozed from *Pakeezah*'s feet during this decade, the blood that still rings through the caesura while we are busy fighting over the temporal residue.

The liminal 1970s were also luminous with rich textural looks made possible by the ace cinematographers of Hindi cinema – Fali Mistry, Joseph Wirsching, Radhu Karmakar, Jaywant Pathare, N. Satyen, Peter Pereira, and Kay Gee – while K.K. Mahajan, Govind Nihalani, K. Vaikunth, and A.K. Bir orchestrated the hues of the formal cinematographic rigour on the octave of *time*. The 'defining decade' gave us the vocabulary of the 'parallel', a stream that flowed with the 'main' in its multivalent sonority as we heard the *ghungroo*[13] in the mirror and saw the *ghost* in the *mashk*.

---

[11] A form of classical vocal music incorporating more of words with a different rhythm and style, generally, the more audible the words, the less classical the musical form. I have used the term suggesting the middle path between two extremes, often branded as the 'middle-roader' cinema.

[12] Also called *drut laya*, generally meaning fast tempo, it is the concluding section of the performance of a raga in Hindustani classical music (u in *drut* pronounced as in *brut*).

[13] One of many metallic bells stung together to form *ghungroo*s, a musical anklet tied to the feet of classical Indian dancers. My reference is to the films *Pakeezah* and *Shatranj ke Khilari* and the dance form kathak. Big mirrors are generally placed on the walls in the kathak dance rooms.

Looking the Star in the Eye

The Everyman Avatar of Superstars

Gautam Chintamani

For Hindi cinema the 1970s were marked by epoch-making moments that would go on to define the zeitgeist and create templates that would last for a long time. Much like the world that it operated within, Hindi cinema of the 1970s, too, was a product of its past. It was a point in history that took from the past, chose to experiment liberally, at times failing more gloriously than succeeding, but refused to be shackled by it. In the bargain it created – while it didn't follow the thirty-year cycle – the theory that posits that popular culture adheres itself to a discernible pattern wherein styles and motifs of the past resurface every three decades.

The 1970s are believed to have truly started with the arrival of the Angry Young Man circa 1973 with *Zanjeer*, further cemented in its truest form with *Namak Haraam*. However, the seeds seem to have been sown earlier. One can see the origins of the Angry Young Man in Gulzar's *Mere Apne* (1971), a remake of Tapan Sinha's *Apanjan* (1968), and even earlier, in O.P. Ralhan's *Phool*

Aur Patthar (1966). The Meena Kumari–Dharmendra starrer laid the foundation of a new kind of leading man, someone who was a throwback to the kind that first emerged in the 1940s with Ashok Kumar in *Kismet* and later Dev Anand in the 1950s' neo-noir.

Decades do not have a definite beginning or end when it comes to popular culture, and so the 1970s for all practical purposes began in 1969 – a year that marked the coming of the superstar in a new avatar with Shakti Samanta's *Aradhana*; the true forerunner to the 'angry young man' in Yash Chopra's *Aadmi Aur Insaan*; and the release of three films that ushered in Indian arthouse, Mani Kaul's *Uski Roti*, Basu Chatterjee's *Sara Aakash* and Mrinal Sen's *Bhuvan Shome.* On a side note, all three were shot by K.K. Mahajan, a trailblazer and pioneer who revolutionized the visual language of Hindi cinema. These films redefined the leading man and woman, showcased how the next decade would experiment with the texture and context of this singular element in terms of pushing the envelope and, most importantly, isolated the 1970s from its past and future.

There is little doubt in the minds of observers, commentators, fans and aficionados that cinema in the 1970s was a period of great change. In the West, Hollywood broke with the past as the old auteurs (Alfred Hitchcock, Howard Hawks, John Houston, John Ford, et al.) petered out, leaving studios to make a beeline for the wunderkids (Francis Ford Coppola, William Friedkin, Martin Scorsese, Brian De Palma, Steven Spielberg, George Lucas, to name a few). British cinema witnessed a resurgence with the New Wave of the 1960s marked by the richly rewarding works of Nicolas Roeg and Anthony Simmons. Ingmar Bergman delivered three of his greatest works – *Cries and Whispers*, *Scenes from a Marriage* and *Autumn Sonata*. In the East, Japanese cinema witnessed the young and some not-so-young masters confront outdated notions, and Hong Kong saw a flurry of films with radical ideas that challenged traditional values.

It's hardly surprising then that Hindi cinema too reacted to its surroundings. Coming out of the broken Nehruvian stupor that had failed to deliver fully on the promises made at the time of India's independence, Hindi cinema was looking for new heroes. It never really settled for the second wave of leading men, the likes of Shammi Kapoor, Sunil Dutt, Rajendra Kumar, and Manoj Kumar, who more or less mirrored their idols Dev Anand, Raj Kapoor, and Dilip Kumar.

The younger lot was led by Dharmendra, the perfect mix of the genteel hero and muscles. Dharmendra stood apart from the ilk, balancing the demands of the Bimal Roys, O.P. Ralhans, Arjun Hingoranis and Ramanand Sagars. He could play the ideal beta, the doting bhai, and the loving devar. He could save the family or the nation, depending on the call. There was Jeetendra, jumping his way into stardom. Asha Parekh broke away from the past and was filling the shoes discarded by the like of Nargis, Meena Kumari and Madhubala. However, it was Rajesh Khanna who managed to race past the others. Khanna took a little from the heroes who had gone before – enough to evoke a sense of familiarity – but made it all his own to stand out.

Close on the heels of the runaway success of *Aradhana*, which made him an overnight star after three years of misfires, Khanna delivered two performances where he experimented with the template of the leading man in *Ittefaq* and *Do Raaste*. Both released in 1969 and set the mood for the 1970s – the star experimentation, even if within the realm of popular Hindi cinema. Before the 1970s, stars famously struggled to crack the code, and once they did, they ensured that they wouldn't change a thing if someone was buying the tickets or paying for them to don the greasepaint.

What truly made the 1970s a departure from the norm was that the bigger a star became, the more they sought to do something off the beaten path. It was a throwback to the time when they were not encumbered by the dynamics of the game. Often, they went back to the film-makers who helped create their onscreen persona and then asked them to break it, even if just a little. Khanna would do this often with Samanta; once in *Amar Prem* (1971) when he got to know that his busy schedule had stopped the film-maker from offering the film to him and then in *Anuraag* (1972) where Khanna torpedoed his way to be cast in a guest appearance. He would again, in the 1980s, merrily feature in an extended cameo in J. Om Prakash's *Aakhir Kyon?* (1985). In Bachchan's case, too, the actor would feature as the second lead in Hrishikesh Mukherjee's *Mili* (1975) or *Chupke Chupke* (1975) only because such challenges rekindled the fire.

This desire to see themselves in avatars that were different from their usual ones was a common phenomenon throughout the decade. Dev Anand, one of the few stars from the 1940s and '50s who continued to remain significant through the 1970s, officially started his innings as a director with *Hare Rama Hare Krishna* (1971) where he cast the more glamorous actress among the two in the film as his sister, with a definite whiff of incest in the relationship. He would later experiment on similar lines in *Heera Panna* (1973) and *Prem Shastra* (1974). The former has the 'heroine' sacrificing her life to save the 'hero' as she doesn't see a reason to live after she realizes he is her dead sister's fiancé, while the latter has the leading man (Dev Anand) falling in love with a much younger woman (Zeenat Aman) who could well be his stepdaughter. Today, Dev Anand's films might not be taken seriously and even mocked, but these films, showing darker shades of love, make you realize how significant they are in the annals of Hindi cinema.

Rajesh Khanna went on to try something exciting at every opportunity he got and sometimes he created them when none were on the horizon. He refused to throw his stardom at Samanta and sway the director to tilt the scales ever so lightly while playing second fiddle to the women in *Kati Patang* and *Amar Prem*; worked for pittance in Hrishikesh Mukherjee's *Bawarchi* (1972); and took a solid pay cut to feature in Basu Chatterjee's *Avishkaar* (1974), a film that was shot in the film-maker's apartment, and where his co-star, Sharmila Tagore, wore the film-maker's wife Rinki's saris. He felt that his character, Kamal, in *Aap Ki Kasam* (1974) was the villain but it gave him some of his best moments onscreen.

He featured in Shammi Kapoor's box-office let-down *Bundalbaaz* (1975), a fantasy comedy that later found a cult following, nearly got cast in *Manoranjan* (1974), the remake of *Irma La Douce* (1963), but had to leave the project as Kapoor was wooing Salim–Javed to write, and they wouldn't agree to work with him.

The 1970s was the period when the writer finally got his due and, in some cases, such as Salim Khan and Javed Akhtar, they got much more. A product of the Sippy Films Story Department, operated at that time by a gentleman called Satish Bhatnagar, a writer who was associated with the BBC in London and was asked by Guru Dutt to write for him, a dream that never materialized, Salim–Javed practically rewrote the history of Indian cinema across the scripts they furnished between *Haathi Mere Saathi* (1971) and *Mr. India* (1987). They wielded enough power to get the likes of Yash Chopra and Gulshan Rai to brush away Rajesh Khanna from projects, one of them *Deewaar* (1975); nearly changed the course of Amjad Khan's career when they suggested dubbing his voice in *Sholay*; and almost launched Kanwaljit Singh to take on Bachchan (legend has it that both writers who enjoyed their drink did not turn up in time for the grand launch of the film, and later the stars never really aligned); and demanded and got more money than any of the stars featured in their films.

Salim–Javed dominated the landscape unlike any other writer but it's not like the era did not have others. This was also the phase where Kader Khan penned iconic lines for Bachchan in *Amar Akbar Anthony* (1977), *Khoon Pasina* (1977), *Muqaddar Ka Sikandar* (1978), and *Suhaag* (1979); Sachin Bhowmick continued his streak with *Caravan* (1971), *Be-Imaan* (1972), *Dost* (1974), *Khel Khel Mein* (1975), *Hum Kisise Kum Naheen* (1977) and *Gol Maal* (1979). But what is truly intriguing is how many of them, while penning blockbusters for a bunch of stars, often failed to give them that one role which would satiate the actor within.

The runaway success of *Zanjeer* made Bachchan the first port of call for A-List projects, at least the ones that featured Salim–Javed. As Salim–Javed continued to imagine Bachchan as the embodiment of their Angry Young Man, Bachchan took on projects that harked back to the days of *Parwana* (1971), *Anand*, and *Namak Haraam* that had initially cemented his reputation. These include *Saudagar* (1973), still considered one of his finest acts, and *Manzil* (1979), which came at the peak of his stardom. Based on a story by Narendranath Mitra, *Saudagar* was helmed by Sudhendu Roy, who also wrote the screenplay, while P.L. Santoshi wrote the dialogues. *Manzil* was loosely inspired by Mrinal Sen's Bengali film *Akash Kusum* (1965) and was jointly written by Ashish Burman and director Basu Chatterjee. These films saw Bachchan in a different avatar but none of these inspired either Salim–Javed or Prakash Mehra, Manmohan Desai, Ramesh Sippy or Yash Chopra to look beyond the template that they had created for Bachchan. Although Chopra did give him *Kabhi Kabhie* (1976), a slight departure from the kind of fare Bachchan had come to be associated with.

Contrary to the popular conception of Hrishikesh Mukherjee getting stars of the day to play Everyman, Chatterjee gave some of the biggest names of the decade exceptional opportunities to shed their larger-than-life image. Chatterjee's decision to cast Dharmendra as a Sanskrit professor in *Dillagi* (1978) opposite Hema Malini, who played a chemistry lecturer, remains one of the brightest spots in the actor's oeuvre. The film might not be as readily referenced as *Chupke Chupke* but many, including this writer, find it a more nuanced performance. Based on the novel *Kalidas O Chemistry* by Bimal Kar, Chatterjee also wrote the film. Some sequences such as the one where after getting soaked in rain, Dharmendra borrows Malini's sari to cover himself and both quietly sip tea show how underutilized the former remained when it came to romance and comedy.

In the same light, Hema Malini, the first bona fide woman superstar of the 1970s, enjoyed a rare anti-heroine outing in *Lal Pathar* (1971), a kind of role that none of her contemporaries or even the ones that followed suit in the 1980s and to a large extent in the 1990s could have dared to accept. A remake of a Bengali film by the same name and written by Prasanta Chowdhary with Vrajendra Gaur penning the dialogues, *Lal Pathar* had Malini playing the mistress of an aristocrat (Raaj Kumar), who would go to any lengths to maintain her status after he marries a much younger woman (Raakhee). This was after *Johny Mera Naam* (1970) established Malini as the new superstar, a status that was cemented with *Seeta Aur Geeta* (1972), Salim–Javed's reworking of *Ram Aur Shyam* (1967), where stars like Dharmendra and Sanjeev Kumar featured in extended cameos. It wouldn't be till the mid and late 1980s that Malini would revisit such experimentation with *Ek Chadar Maili Si* (1986) and *Rihaee* (1988).

What set the 1970s apart from the decades before was the immediacy that informed its cinema. Feroz Khan's remake of *The Godfather* (1972), *Dharmatma* (1975) best exemplified this, when the film-maker refused to employ the likes of Salim–Javed or Kader Khan to write; Kaushal Bharti, a former Army man, wrote this fascinating adaptation that took one of the most underrated characters from Mario Puzo's book – the Don's son-in-law – and made him the chief villain.

The imposition of a national Emergency by Prime Minister Indira Gandhi in June 1975 changed how popular Hindi cinema approached subjects and themes – see the difference between the films that released before 1975 and those that came 1976 onwards and you will see how escapism became the mainstay. Who in their right minds would have liked to take the government machinery head-on? The arthouse films of the early 1980s from Saeed Akhtar Mirza, Govind Nihalani and Sai Paranjpye would largely do what mainstream Hindi cinema had done in the 1970s, in more 'realistic' milieus. By the time the 1970s came to end, and *Ardh Satya* in 1983 fetched Om Puri the best actor award over the Bachchans, Khans, Khannas, Sinha and Kapoors, the 'star' was no longer the same. Those who earlier shone on the silver screen were now available on videocassettes, forever changing the equation. No more would you look up to see a star; you could look them in the eye in your living room.

The Bards of Bombay

Songwriters of the Seventies

Mira Hashmi

Perhaps unsurprisingly, one running thread throughout the days and months (years?) of the COVID-19 pandemic has been a collective, overwhelming sense of nostalgia – the urge to 'look back' at our halcyon days. On Netflix, the 1980s muscled their way back into our consciousness, with *Stranger Things* and *Cobra Kai* skyrocketing to new heights of popularity. On YouTube, this manifested in seemingly unending, desperate searches, in the millions, for older TV episodes, films, and music. A curious genre of 'reaction videos' also erupted on the ubiquitous web purveyor of videos, in which young people from different corners of the world 'react' to old music and movies, while (older) commenters on said videos go into nostalgia-fuelled paroxysms.

Of course, one had to remind oneself that like all retreads of good times gone by, this communal memory binge was also overwhelmingly pleasant because it separated the proverbial wheat from the chaff. Those rose-tinted glasses we tend to put on when exploring our cultural past mask a lot of banal, mediocre offerings that we conveniently forget ever existed. I learned this the hard way when I decided to watch old 1970s episodes of the now-long-defunct British pop music chart show *Top of the Pops* on YouTube (that decade is, after all, considered to be the zenith of all things arty in the twentieth century). I discovered to my dismay that for every David Bowie or Blondie or Led Zeppelin or Donna Summer on the British charts, there were about twenty disturbingly awful acts whose names and output have thankfully been consigned to the garbage bin of history. A glance-over at movie lists produced the same result. From an intellectual standpoint, it made sense; from an emotional perspective, it still stings to realize that this rosy view of the past is basically curated by our brains in an effort to coddle and comfort our delicate sensibilities. What we don't remember can't hurt us.

It was with this in mind (and thankful for it) that I approached the daunting but welcome task of looking at the 1970s in Hindi cinema. Again, with the flotsam and jetsam largely erased from memory, this is an era that for Hindi movie aficionados of a certain vintage represents the best of worlds – when the elder statesmen of celluloid graciously made way for the young Turks, when 'masala' and 'middle-of-the-road' and 'parallel' gingerly found ways to coexist. The prism of time and venerational reminiscence is even kinder to Hindi film music, quieting the din of lesser fare and leaving only the lustre of the big guns that are seen as the benchmark for all that has followed. From this vantage point, Hindi film music, already a hugely popular subgenre, in the 1970s evolved in hitherto unseen directions of East–West fusion, becoming a gargantuan industry in its own right that often eclipsed (and outsold and outlasted) its visual partner.

Hindi film music of the 1970s has of course been written about extensively in the ensuing decades. In particular, the late R.D. Burman has been hailed, almost unanimously, as the uncrowned melody-maker of the decade (no argument from me there). But what of the other, oft-overlooked aspect of the Hindi film song, i.e., the lyrics? Granted, it's the melody and rhythm which elicit the initial, visceral response in a listener, but the quality of the words certainly aids and abets the song's staying power to a significant degree. And Hindi cinema has had the good fortune of having some truly remarkable film poets on its roster through the decades, such as Shailendra, Shakeel Badayuni, Sahir Ludhianvi, Hasrat Jaipuri, to name just a few.

If one were to try and distill the one quality of a great film lyricist (other than mastery of the language) that is common to all those acknowledged as filmdom's best, it is probably this: the ability to understand and practise the notion that poetry written for film songs is inherently separate and different from that written at the poet's discretion for their pleasure and as an expression of their individual artistry, which is either published in book form and/or recited at mushairas. The film lyricist's biggest challenge is to adapt and mould their style to an often wildly varied range of plot situations as well as characters, and Hindi cinema's greatest wordsmiths are able to pull this off seemingly without effort.

And so it was, for example, that Sahir could write the comical '*Sar jo tera chakraye*' for Johnny Walker's Sattar, the seductive '*Jaane kya tu ne kahi*' for Waheeda Rehman's Gulabo, and the tragic '*Yeh duniya agar mil bhi jaaye to kya hai*' for Guru Dutt's Vijay, in the same film, *Pyaasa* (1957). Or Shailendra weaving with enviable ease between the Bhojpuri-inflected playfulness of '*Paan khaaye saiyyan hamaro*' (*Teesri Kasam*, 1966), the romantic longing of '*Tere mere sapne ab ek rang hain*' (*Guide*, 1965), and the quiet, simmering anger of '*Dost dost na raha*' (*Sangam*, 1964). In addition, the lyricist had to be mindful that even for the most complex of thoughts, the language and turns of phrase used had to be comprehensible to a broad audience comprising people from varying ethnic, linguistic, educational, and economic backgrounds.

Given the colossus that is the genre of Hindi film music, trying to do an overview of all the great songwriters of the 1970s would be an exercise in futility, so I offer instead an amuse-bouche, as it were, i.e., a cherry-picked list of five of the decade's best lyricists and my favourite one of their songs. The premise is of course somewhat laughable, but, like most listicles, it is an excuse to listen to the greats, and to remind oneself of the incredible, unmatched richness of words and music that Hindi cinema had to offer once upon a time.

Yogesh

Looking back at Yogesh's lyrical output of the 1970s, one is suddenly reminded how inextricably one's memories and affection for some of the most celebrated middle cinema films of the decade are wedded to the songs written by this man from Lucknow. His work for Basu Chatterjee was particularly prolific and has aged remarkably well. That is to say, it has a timeless quality which is borne out by its continued popularity and what is referred to as 'recall value'. It is also worth noting that the deceptive simplicity of his word choices conceals the dexterity with which he rises to a variety of challenges. For example, in '*Na bole tum na maine kuch kaha*' (*Baaton Baaton Mein*, 1979), Yogesh takes the notion of the unspoken to create a verse that is deeply sensual, erotic even, but with the way he goes about it, playing with words that tiptoe around the subject, the listening audience is none the wiser:

Ghuli si aaj saanson mein kisi ki saans hai
Yeh kaun aaj dil ke mere aas-paas hai
Yeh dheere-dheere ho raha hai pyaar ka nasha

Needless to say, it is difficult to choose just one song from Yogesh's oeuvre as one's purported 'favourite' but, to sustain the premise of this piece, I shall do so, and my choice is '*Kahin duur jab din dhal jaaye*', from Hrishikesh Mukherjee's superlative classic *Anand* (1971). Admittedly, this choice is fairly safe, but surely an obvious one, for amongst a lineup of many dazzling songs, this one shines especially bright. In tandem with Salil Chowdhury's achingly beautiful music, Yogesh's words capture the melancholic longing that the titular character momentarily allows himself to express, albeit only in solitude (or so he believes). Anand (Rajesh

Khanna), the poster boy for cracking jokes in the face of adversity, finds himself alone and finally lifts his veil of levity, revealing a soul struggling to keep despair at bay, even as he is haunted by both lost love and the spectre of his mortality:

Kabhi yunhi jab hui bojhal saansein
Bhar aayi baithe baithe jab yunhi aankhen
Kabhi machal ke, pyar se chal ke
Chhuye koi mujhe par nazar na aaye

And he at last also acknowledges the terrible weight of choosing not to share his pain with those who love him, instead taking on their troubles as his own:

Hai meethi uljhan, bairi apna mann
Apna hi hoke sahe dard paraye

This plaintive bitter-sweetness of the song, so poignantly expressed by Yogesh's lyrics, has given it an enduring resonance that extends to generations born well after it was first recorded.

Majrooh Sultanpuri

While some might argue that by the 1970s Majrooh's best work was behind him – with his contributions to classics like *Aar-Paar* (1954), *Mr. & Mrs. 55* (1955), *Kala Pani* (1958), *Sujata* (1959), *Jewel Thief* (1967), etc. – a quick glance at the list of songs from the decade that bears his credit suggests otherwise. In fact, it is nothing short of remarkable (though hardly surprising, given his prominent position among the literary avant-garde of his time) how smoothly Majrooh adapted his style to suit the requirements of the new Hindi cinema aesthetic, especially in the case of the work he did for producer Nasir Hussain, an association that is an important landmark in Hindi film history. It is plain to see that the partnership yielded a smorgasbord of musical gems, even more so when R.D. Burman entered the fray as the third angle of the holy trinity *Teesri Manzil* (1966) onwards. Majrooh's snappy, infectious lyrics provided the perfect conduit for the younger Burman's modernist, fusion-heavy musical stylings. One need only look at (or listen to, rather) the brilliantly cheeky '*Aap ke kamre mein koi rehta hai*' from *Yaadon ki Baaraat* (1973), or the glorious '*Yeh ladka haaye Allah kaisa hai deewana*' from *Hum Kisise Kum Naheen* (1977), to realize not only how well the composer and the wordsmith complemented each other, but also how deftly the latter fulfilled the demands of every kind of song situation cooked up by Nasir Hussain's dream factory.

Like other greats of Hindi cinema, Majrooh could seemingly write something of beauty and substance for every occasion, whether it be a love duet ('*Kitna pyara vaada hai*'), bitter lamentation ('*Kya hua tera vaada*'), sultry seduction ('*Dilbar dil se pyaare*'), or a frenzied cabaret ('*Piya tu ab to aaja*'). But my pick for Majrooh's top film song of the '70s would have to be the title qawwali from *Hum Kisise Kum Naheen*. Though most closely associated with the Sufi poetry traditions of India (and as first brought into prominence by Amir Khusro), the qawwali in its filmi avatar was an unlikely crowd-pleaser in Hindi cinema. Forgoing its religious/spiritual roots in favour of using it as an atypical expression of your typical cinematic romance, film-makers chose to employ the qawwali as a showstopper, with glittering sets and costumes, and playback singers challenged to up their game faced as they were with a combination of complex rhythm structures and the demanding vocal requirements of Indian classical singing. It was no less a challenge for lyricists, who had to eschew the conventional structures of nazm and ghazal in order to write for a form heavily dependent on beat and (varying) tempo (as expressed in the all-important 'taali' accompaniment). And of course, like other film songs, the qawwalis were more often than not situation- and/or character-specific.

Framed as the hero's (Rishi Kapoor) open challenge to his paramour (Zeenat Aman) to defy those who would keep them apart, Majrooh's '*Hum kisise kum naheen*' dispenses with the customary qawwali preamble and jumps headlong into a daringly brief mukhda that immediately throws down the gauntlet:

Hai agar dushman (dushman)
Zamana gham naheen (gham naheen)
Koi aaye (koi aaye)
Koi aaye (koi)
Hum kisi se kam naheen, kam naheen!

But it is in the antaras that Majrooh really ratchets up the rebellious mood of the song, not only with his words but also with his deviation from the accepted Hindi film song verse structure. Instead of using the usual four–five phrase grouping before returning to the main chorus, the poet (to more closely approximate the composition of a qawwali) pens two *consecutive* verses comprising a whopping eight phrases *each*, and then circles back to the mukhda. The powerful imagery conjured up by his words brings home the mutinous spirit of the hero:

Kya karein dil ki jalan ko
Iss mohabbat ke chalan ko
Jo bhi ho jaaye ke ab to
Sar se baandha hai kafan ko
Hum to deewane diljale
Zulm ke saaye mein pale
Daal kar aankhon ko tere rukhsaron pe
Roz hi chalte hain hum to angaron pe
Aaj hum jaise jigar waale kahan
Zakhm khaya hai tab huye hain jawan
Teer ban jaaye doston ki nazar
Ya bane khanjar dushmanon ki zubaan
Baithe hain tere dar pe
To kuchh kar ke uthenge
Ya tujhko hi le jaayenge
Ya mar ke uthenge

The madness of the prem deewana in song has rarely been bettered.

Anjaan

There have been many instances in the history of recorded music where an artist has created a work so transcendent, so immediately recognizable, that it wouldn't be an exaggeration to posit that had they not produced anything other than that one work, their place in the history books would still be secure. Think of the solitary, mysterious note that is struck at the beginning of the theme from the *Pink Panther* (Henry Mancini, 1963), or the drum solo that forms the backbone of 'Wipe Out' (The Surfaris), or the velvety vocals of Nazia Hassan in '*Aap jaisa koi meri zindagi mein aaye*' (*Qurbani*, 1980).

Similarly, one can contend inarguably that if lyricist Anjaan had never written any other song before or after '*Khaike paan Banaras wala*' (*Don*, 1978), his name would still resonate through Hindi film history. Such is the continuing and gargantuan popularity of the song, over forty-five years after its release, that it has almost eclipsed all the other songs that Anjaan penned in his nearly fifty-year career as a lyricist, which include gems like '*O saathi re*' and '*Rote huey aate hai sab*' (*Muqaddar Ka Sikandar*, 1978) and '*Chhookar meray mann ko*' (*Yaarana*, 1981).

Even so, this success must have felt particularly sweet to the writer, coming as it did in the middle of a golden streak after his early years of steady work but few big hits, not to mention that in it he also got to display his affinity for and mastery over the *khari boli* dialect of his home state Uttar Pradesh. Ironically, the song which surely contributed immensely to the box-office success of *Don* (and is possibly Kishore Kumar and Amitabh Bachchan's most beloved number) had been written and composed five years earlier for an entirely different film: the Dev Anand-starrer *Banarsi Babu*. One can only wonder if that paan would have had the same impact that it did if it had ended up in Dev saheb's mouth instead of AB's as originally intended.

That kind of conjecture aside, Anjaan's role in making '*Khaike paan Banaras wala*' the song that it became cannot be emphasized enough, for his lyrics give it that sly, irreverent character that makes it so infectious. Consider just the preamble to the mukhda:

Arrey bhang kaa rang
Jamaa ho chakaachak
Phir lo paan chabaay
Arrey aisaa jhatka lage jiya pe
Punar janam hoi jaay

Had there ever been as gleeful an ode to getting high in Hindi cinema before this? And then the mukhda itself, extolling the virtues of Banarasi paan and the tenacity of the street-smart Banarasi lad:

O khaike paan Banaras wala
Khul jaaye band akal ka taala
Phir to aisa kare dhamaal
Seedhi kar de sabki chaal
O chhora Ganga kinaare wala

The antara expertly conveys the 'fish out of water' situation that the main character Vijay, a roadside entertainer, is stuck in as the suave titular criminal's lookalike:

Arrey Ram duhaai
Kaise chakkar mein pad gaya haay
Kahaan jaan phansaai
Main to sooli pe chadh gaya haay
Kaisaa seedha saada
Main kaisa bhola bhaala
Jaane kaun ghadi mein pad gaya
Padhe-likhon se paala
Meethi chhurri se hua halaal
Chhora Ganga kinaare wala

Though Anjaan would go on to write other hits, including wildly popular songs in *Laawaris* (1981), *Namak Halaal* (1982), and *Disco Dancer* (1982), '*Khaike...*' remains his calling card, the one this Banarasi *chhora* will be remembered for, for posterity.

Neeraj

When one considers that Gopaldas Neeraj's career as a lyricist in Hindi films lasted barely a decade, it is all the more impressive that those ten years yielded some of the loveliest songs of the era. And yet, strange are the ways of fate, for although Neeraj's lyrical output could never be faulted on its literary quality, and nor did his songs want for popularity, most of the big films he wrote for either did average business or came completely undone at the box-office. With the industry's penchant for apportioning the blame for failure to any and all players involved, it is likely more than mere conjecture that Neeraj too came under friendly fire, and saw his Bollywood sojourn start to falter. This, coupled with the poet's focus on his work outside of films, as well as his disenchantment with the film world after the loss of close collaborators Jaikishan and S.D. Burman, led to Neeraj saying goodbye to a profession with which his relationship had increasingly been more courteous than passionate. But the songs he left behind (from fewer than two dozen films) formed a lasting legacy whose value cannot be discounted. And he did so despite bucking the established trend of using Urdu as Hindi film songs' lingua franca.

Neeraj, having been influenced in his youth by poets like Harivansh Rai Bachchan, instead opted to employ Hindi as his medium of expression, albeit a conversational style of it rather than too heavily Sanskritized a version, which ensured that the lyricist could work within his preferred zone while also remaining accessible to a broad audience. His collaborations with S.D. Burman in particular yielded an array of gems that are rightly considered classics, from films such as *Tere Mere Sapne* ('*Jeevan ki bagiya mehke gi*', '*Jaise Radha ne mala japi*'), *Sharmeelee* ('*Megha chhaaye aadhi raat*', '*Khilte hain gul yahan*', '*Aaj madhosh hua jaaye re*'), and *Gambler* ('*Choodi nahi yeh mera dil hai*', '*Dil aaj shayar hai*') – all in 1971.

But it is their partnership on Dev Anand's ambitious flop *Prem Pujari* (1970) that resulted in some of Neeraj's most sublime and fondly remembered songs: '*Shokhiyon mein ghola jaaye*', '*Phoolon ke rang se*', and '*Rangeela re*'. Any of the three songs could qualify as my Neeraj favourite but I will go with the last one, if only for the way that the song revels unflinchingly in its pathos even as it spits fiery words of reproach to a cruel, unfeeling lover:

Rangeela re tere rang mein
yoon ranga hai mera mann
Chhaliya re na bujhe hai
kisi jal se yeh jalan

In the verses Neeraj conjures up powerfully plaintive imagery:

Dukh mera dulha hai, birha hai doli
Aansu ki saari hai, aahon ki choli
Aag main piyoon re jaise ho paani
Naari deewaani hoon, peeda ki rani
Manwa yeh jale hai, jag saara chhale hai
Saans kyoon chale hai piya
Waah re pyaar, waah re waah

No wonder that Dev Anand, despite the fact that *Prem Pujari* was a commercial disappointment, reportedly called '*Rangeela re*' his favourite song from the annals of Navketan, a roster overflowing with timeless classics.

Anand Bakshi

Where does one even begin? For nearly fifty years, Anand Bakshi was filmdom's most prolific lyricist, penning hit after hit. From film to film and from composer to composer, the poet from Punjab switched gears effortlessly, rummaging in his bottomless bag of words to produce lyrics so infectious (and deceptively simple) that once heard became near-instant earworms. Consider just a cursory sampling of films with superhit music he wrote the lyrics for in the 1970s: *Bobby* (1973), *Amar Akbar Anthony* (1977), *Satyam Shivam Sundaram* (1978), *Julie* (1975), *Kati Patang* (1971), *Hare Rama Hare Krishna* (1971), *Sholay* (1975) – Bakshi, it seems, could write for any assortment of characters, situations, and emotions. He captured the first blush of teenage love in '*Mujhe kuch kehna hai*' (*Bobby*), the depths of despair in '*Na koi umang hai*' (*Kati Patang*), spiritual longing in '*Satyam shivam sundaram*', sensual ecstasy in '*Dil kya kare*' (*Julie*), and the spirit of hippie rebellion in '*Dum maaro dum*' (*Hare Rama Hare Krishna*). In a song like '*Jab tak hai jaan*' (*Sholay*), he demonstrated his absolute mastery over matching phonetic cadence with musical rhythm.

Bakshi's most celebrated soundtrack of the 1970s, though, has to be the utterly flawless *Amar Prem* (1972), one of those rare instances where not a single song is dispensable or even middling, a tour de force from beginning to end. That R.D. Burman did not win the Filmfare Award for Best Music Director for *Amar Prem* that year (losing to Shankar–Jaikishen for the decidedly forgettable *Be-Imaan*) is of course an infamous episode of Bollywood lore. That Bakshi came a cropper for Best Lyricist for '*Chingari koi bhadke*' was as monumental a travesty, especially when you weigh the song's scorching, enduring intensity against the catchy but banal winner '*Jai bolo be-imaan ki*'.

Other songs from *Amar Prem* are equally beautiful, such as the sonorous '*Raina beeti jaaye*', and the soothing '*Kuch to log kahenge*', so choosing '*Chingari koi bhadke*' is like drawing from a set of long straws – you have a winner no matter which one you pick. I don't think it's going out on a limb to state that this Burman–Bakshi collaboration is probably among the top ten greatest of Hindi film songs. While the composer creates an impossibly arresting melody, the poet embellishes it with his inimitable literary artistry to express the feelings of a man wounded by love and life:

Humse mat puchho kaise
mandir toota sapno ka
Logon ki baat nahi hai
ye kissa hai apnon ka
Koi dushman thhes lagaaye
to meet jiya behlaaye
Mann meet jo ghaav lagaaye
use kaun mitaaye

Any further words that one could use to try and wax eloquent about the indomitable Mr Bakshi would doubtless feel futile, feeble, so it is better to end with his final stanza from '*Chingari*':

Maana toofaan ke aage
nahi chalta zor kisi ka
Maujon ka doshh nahi hai
ye doshh hai aur kisi ka
Majhdhaar mein naiyaa dole
to maajhi paar lagaaye
maajhi jo naav duboye
use kaun bachaaye.

What is the name of Jaya Bhaduri's character in the Hrishikesh Mukherjee classic, *Chupke Chupke* (1975)?
Answer: Vasudha

Fat Lady

Feminism and Desire in Hindi Cinema of the Seventies

Maitreyee B. Chowdhury

1977: *Taxi Taxie* – Mother of nine children
1978: *Satyam Shivam Sundaram* – Fat lady
1978: *Ankhiyon Ke Jharokhon Se* – Fat lady in the theatre
1979: *Baton Baton Mein* – Imaginary Nancy's mother

These are Wikipedia entries for character actor Tun Tun's roles in various films through the seventies. It gives a fair idea of the status of women, who were different from the common understanding of femininity in Indian society – slim, fair, young – while also providing an insight into the way sexuality was perceived in Hindi cinema.

Tun Tun's entry into the film industry was through the circuitous route of a playback singer, before she switched careers to make people laugh with her comic timing and body size. The long history of Hindi films has close to no comediennes, unless you choose to count the rare occasions when actresses like Bindu,

Aruna Irani, and later, Juhi Chawla, dabbled in a few comic roles. While it might be safe to presume that no film-maker thought of presenting Tun Tun as a sexy heroine, both Bindu and Aruna Irani did venture into that precarious zone where funny is sexy.

Speaking of desire, one can hardly not talk about beauty in Hindi films because both these words were interchangeable as far as our films were concerned. Fair and slim women were object of desire for respectable wealthy men driving fancy cars and living in palatial homes. The sultriness of a Smita Patil or a Shabana Azmi was not only slow to be realized but also mostly served the purpose of being showcased as 'dark-skinned' rural women attracting notorious kinds of men, different from the sophisticated, well-educated city types.

One must take note that the swinging seventies pioneered the introduction of sex and sexiness to Hindi films. Take, for example, the case of *Chetna*. Released in 1970, directed by B.R. Ishara, *Chetna*'s obvious hints at sex is anything but coincidental. In retrospect, was the director really such a badass guy who came up with one of the most scandalous posters to ever rock the film industry, or did he just think it was quirky? Either way, with its poster involving the heroine's legs spread wide apart (which was in sync with the A certificate the censor board awarded it), the film made headlines. Those bare legs were, however, probably the only piece of bare flesh that the film showcased.

Or consider *Dastak* (1970), a film by Rajinder Singh Bedi that was hailed by critics for its sensitive handling and nuanced storytelling, but which probably carried one of the first nude scenes in Hindi cinema. Salma, the heroine, feeling trapped in her own house, and suspected to be a prostitute by her neighbours, strips naked as a form of protest, and lies down on the floor while singing. Probably one of the strongest and most effective ways of incorporating nudity into a scene that justified the storytelling, *Dastak* showcased sexuality in Hindi cinema with sensitivity.

A woman's space in Hindi films, barring the niche parallel cinema, has traditionally been limited to being a prop. And strangely enough, showcasing a prostitute seems to be the favourite window to sexuality. B.R. Ishara, in a famous interview, had once apparently said that 'every prostitute is a woman' – a thought that we often see repeated in many Hindi films where themes of sexuality, especially when it comes to unabashed un-genteel sexuality, is shown through the 'defiled' body of a prostitute.

When sexuality is in the air, can titillation be far behind? The seventies were all about free love, experimentation, LSD, and rock 'n' roll in India – imports from the West which had gone through these in the 1960s. How could Indian films be far behind? This was also a time when the reign of India's first superstars had arrived. Cinema saw a tremendous resurgence, and stars lived flashy, bold and colourful lives, now more than ever, which somehow came to be reflected in the films that were being made too.

On the prowl was Hindi cinema's biggest movie Mughal Raj Kapoor, and his obsession with women in white. Turning women's sexuality into an art was something he had mastered. He worked towards making nudity acceptable as an art form in cinema. Whether he was ahead of his times or just someone who took a leap of faith, changing the depiction of sex from a juvenile escapade into the land of adulthood, Raj Kapoor was savvy enough to cash in on the commercial viability of showcasing sexuality in an artistic manner in his films. Kapoor had famously said, 'Let them come to see Zeenat's tits, they will go out forgetting her body and remember the film', and indeed catapulted the 'modern heroine' Zeenat Aman into a new realm of stardom with his film *Satyam Shivam Sundaram* (1978). Others like Parveen Babi followed suit.

While Sharmila Tagore had already pushed the envelope with her bikini shot for a film magazine in the 1960s, it was the heroines in the seventies and the experiments that film-makers seemed to be intent on making that gave the era a kind of unprecedented sexy edginess. A slew of films followed, which took risks and went into domains so far considered taboo. Of course, liberal feminist thoughts were on the rise throughout the world, and the world of Hindi cinema wasn't to be left behind.

Refreshingly though, the seventies stayed away from confusing sexy as feminist. Something that a lot of contemporary films seem to do nowadays. In the year 2015 when Kangana Ranaut's character Tanuja sashays through her Kanpur home in a skimpy towel to participate in a family gathering in the film *Tanu Weds Manu Returns*, we had a band of cheerleaders immediately branding the film as a feminist one, without questions being asked about why a woman needs to be walking around in a towel to assert her independence.

Interestingly enough, a very similar scene to that of Ranaut's was first played out by Mumtaz in the 1972 film *Dhadkan*. Mumtaz was shown receiving a phone call while taking a bath. The difference between both films though is in the attitude of the heroine. Mumtaz's towel-clad character isn't bothered to explain or quantify the reason for her being in a towel, and the scene is seen as a sexually pronounced subtle act of titillation and left at that.

Looking back, it is easy to see why the seventies are regarded as interesting, and refreshingly sexy. And because sexiness rarely confines itself to shedding of clothes, one must delve into other forms of sexiness that this era was all about. Take, for instance, the risk-taking capabilities of film-makers from this time that give us a fair understanding of why this era was so special.

Anyone who lived in Bombay in the seventies knows that it was experimental, exhilarating, amoral, and a city that allowed new things to happen. In some ways perhaps it was fractured too, as some would call it, and yet, it was never dull. In many ways, the seventies' Hindi films scenario was perhaps comparable to the experimentation and flamboyance of any film city. There was a strange scent of unparalleled excess. People, film directors, and actors were experimenting, doing whatever they wanted. Eventually some of them would lose their minds, become bankrupt, but one could never accuse them of not having tried. Disillusionment, poverty, unrest, confusion – all of it became a loaded time bomb, ready to explode through the infinite realm of experimentation, finding one's way through this labyrinth.

Let's rewind and go back to a beautiful and luscious Zeenat Aman sizzling in the rain, wooing Manoj Kumar in *Roti Kapada aur Makaan* (1974), or Meena Kumari in *Pakeezah* (1972) inhabiting the life of a tawaif, dealing with unprovoked desire. Or films like *Aandhi* and *Julie*, both in 1975, talking about the lives of two very different kind of women. If *Julie* addresses the issues faced by Christian woman who is considered too modern for a conservative Indian society, *Aandhi* is the story of how society perceives a powerful woman who has chosen to lead a public life as a politician, and the effect such a move has on her personal life.

In an interview, director Goutam Ghosh had once spoken about Shabana Azmi: 'She had come to know that I was casting for *Paar* (1984). I had Smita in my mind for that role, but for some reason, it hadn't worked out, also Smita was reluctant to shoot in the water. Shabana came to meet me, not only prepared for the role, but also convinced me that she could swim! I was flabbergasted and delighted by her dedication and drive for good work.'

These were actresses who had the courage and the conviction to break barriers, and in their own ways they were risk takers. One often heard of the term 'free-spirited' to describe such women, as if it were a crime to want to do different kinds of roles, face different challenges. But thanks to the work of feisty actresses such as Smita Patil, Shabana Azmi, Zeenat Aman, and Deepti Naval, to name a few, Hindi cinema had begun to and continued to showcase stories related to women who defined their life by choices they had made for themselves, instead of what was expected of them.

In this regard, one remembers films like *Nishant* (1975), *Manthan* (1976) and *Bhumika* (1977) that showcased the most intriguing female characters who were not only rebellious but often chose to carry the story on their delicate shoulders. These were actors who also owned their sexuality and weren't afraid to flaunt it. In *Shatranj ke Khilari* (1977), when Shabana Azmi orders her Nawab husband to pay attention to her and then proceeds to sit atop him, she bends the gender game, and how! Whether one admits to it or not, many a times the undertones of the sexuality of the roles inhabited by these characters also underwent remarkable modifications because of who was playing it. This, in turn, made way for unpredictable narratives that often defied the way stories and their characters were supposed to unfold in Hindi cinema.

One of the more delightful ways in which Hindi cinema added sexiness to the narrative was the invention of the luscious vamp. Rather matter-of-fact in their ways, open about their sexiness and not caring two hoots about what society thought of them, the vamp is mostly considered the antithesis of a film heroine, a contrast to, and an extreme departure from the traditional Indian girl who would never deviate from her good-girl image. Names such as Helen, Aruna Irani, Bindu, and Kalpana Iyer were favourites for such roles. Most often, the vamp was a licentious female with a predominantly westernized sense of dressing and mannerisms considered too modern for the era. And even though the vamp was mostly part of the story through song and dance sequences, sidelined from the main storyline, one rarely forgot her.

With the passage of time though, the representation of sexuality and feminism changed in Hindi films. More and more stories took inspiration from those who could portray the earthy sexuality of middle-class life, as opposed to only glamorous ones.

And while we talk about sexuality, how can one not be reminded of reality? At this juncture, Hindi films saw the emergence of a category of actors (both men and women) who transcended the crop of traditionally good-looking actors such as Dharmendra, Hema Malini, and Shashi Kapoor. A rare mix of intellect, sexuality, and a stimulating earthiness crept into our screens. These faces and their body language, coming together, giving rise to new trends. And here began a merging of commercial and parallel cinema, with stars like Zeenat Aman and Amitabh Bachchan sharing screen space with the likes of Naseeruddin Shah and Smita Patil.

Now if that ain't sexy, nothing really is!

If we take a deeper look into the sexuality inherent in these films from the seventies, we see a certain trend of flirtatiousness, even desperateness, that seems almost brazen given the context of a still traditional Indian society. Scenes especially filmed on actors such as Shabana Azmi or Smita Patil brought out the suggestiveness of a woman's sexuality and a sort of hunger evident in their glances and body language. Smita Patil, especially, in many of her films portrayed this rather deliciously, making her an obvious choice for stories that showcased a more sensual portrayal of the thinking woman. In many of these films, we see her flirting or expressing sexual desire, either with her eyes, subtle body movements, or even with a mere touch of the fingers – a clear departure from heroines like Parveen Babi or Zeenat Aman with their open sexuality and sartorial choices.

This subtle twist to Hindi films was a sharp contrast to that prevalent tendency of a very black-and-white portrayal of women thus far. Both the demure Indian woman and the sexual predator-like westernized vamp were replaced by a more realistic portrayal of the woman we saw in our homes on a daily basis. Perhaps this transition drove home the interesting and brave middle road to cinema better than any other aspect, and actually changed not only the way women were portrayed in Hindi films but also how people perceived cinema as a medium and its changing dimensions in the years to come.

In that sense and more, the seventies were an era that brought in the maximum social and cultural changes in Hindi films which began to be reflected within the country too. It was suddenly alright for women to talk about their own desires. It was also the beginning of the trend of wonderful stories, because the most beautiful stories are the ones that are real. In that the country probably owes it to the seventies to show the path that made us all sit up and take notice of these stories that had begun telling a different tale.

A Few Bad Men

Villains in Hindi Cinema of the Seventies

Balaji Vittal

When it comes to the arts, a decade does not exist in isolation. It feeds off what has gone before and into what is to come. The 1970s were no exception.

The films of the 1960s usually had a dream world of well-to-do people who would depart to exotic locales like Kashmir, Shimla, Tokyo, or Paris at the first opportunity the story conspired to provide. There was delectable music in the meadows by the day and in cosy clubs in the evenings, with a comedian thrown in to lace the pudding with laughter. Nothing could go too wrong in that world and a 'happy ending' was guaranteed. This 'guarantee' made almost everything about the film predictable. It also extricated the venom from the villain's teeth as his villainy could not be of the extreme variety lest it be out of step with the overall geniality of the film.

Let us study the villain Shyam (Pran) in *Mere Sanam* (1965). Shyam is a dishonest employee who converts his employer Mr Mehra's (Nazir Hussain) bungalow in Kashmir into a hotel without his permission. And once Shyam discovers that Nina

(Asha Parekh), one of the young boarders at the hotel, is the long-lost daughter of the wealthy Mr Mehra, he charms Nina's elderly mother for championing his candidature as a worthy groom for Nina and, just to be doubly sure, fabricates lies about Nina's chocolate-faced boyfriend Kumar (Biswajeet). Shyam has a keep called Kammo (Mumtaz) who threatens to rat on Shyam's evil designs to Mr Mehra. And Shyam has her taken care of.

Shyam is a greedy manipulator, a forger, a devious conspirator, and a two-faced liar, but an individual operator, with no more than a couple of flunkeys in tow. His is not an organization, and he is an enemy of the *individual* (an enemy of the hero Kumar and Mr Mehra) and not of the *society*, unlike the zamindar and the moneylender in the films of the 1950s. Neither is Shyam an enemy of the *nation*, unlike a smuggler or a spy of a foreign intelligence agency in films that would follow later in the decade and in the seventies.

Enter a very different flavour of villains in the 1970s like Rai Sahab Bhupendra Singh (Premnath) in *Johny Mera Naam* (1970). Based in Nepal, he heads a network of loyal accomplices across Bombay, Calcutta, and Kathmandu that smuggles stolen diamonds from India across the border and exports contraband drugs hidden inside cargoes containing musical instruments to America via Calcutta. This is in addition to stealing idols from temples and selling them to overseas buyers with remittances preferred in foreign currencies.

Bhupendra Singh has built a faithful team and has the skills to keep the multi-location operational structure functioning smoothly. He is finance savvy and has the spunk to play in the Big Boys' league rather than staying contented as the knife-wielding street-corner thug. By the way, Bhupendra Singh's activities are in sync with the truth of India's precious gems and invaluable artefacts becoming a soft target for smugglers in the 1970s to pilfer away abroad. The Antiques and Art Treasures Act came into existence no earlier than 1972, and even that act has seen tardy implementation, according to senior journalist and editor Neeta

Lal in her story 'Smuggling India's Antiques' in the September 2015 edition of *The Diplomat.*[1]

It is not surprising that a silk-smooth conniver like Shakaal (Ajit) in *Yaadon ki Baaraat* (1973) feels encouraged to engineer the theft of a valuable Nataraja idol from a museum. Shakaal owns a swank hotel which he uses as one of the fronts to conduct his smuggling activities. The hotel business gives the smugglers' illegal activities a handy quasi-legitimacy, as the smugglers can hide behind the respectable nomenclature of 'businessmen'. The dacoits of the 1950s and '60s, for instance, could not call themselves anything else. These hotels also serve another purpose – that of a captive venue in which to entertain their overseas buyers with liquor and women.

Coming back to Shakaal in *Yaadon ki Baaraat*, this act of an hotelier stealing the Nataraja idol and selling it to someone abroad was probably inspired by the notorious real-life theft of six metal antique idols including that of a Nataraja from the Sivapuram temple in Tamil Nadu's Thanjavur district. These changed various hands before ending up with one Manohar Lal (Manu) Narang in Bombay, who sold the Nataraja idol for a few lakhs of rupees to New York-based art dealer Ben Heller. Film-maker Chandra Barot (of *Don* fame) shared that Manu had purchased Hotel Ambassador in Bombay. And that completed the profile of Shakaal, the hotelier-smuggler. Shakaal runs a multilayered organization with himself as the unquestioned boss. He leaves the job of eliminating insubordinate former employees (and garroting to death redundant current ones too) to his men. His starched, full-sleeved shirts throughout are symbolic – Shakaal never dirties his hands.

The smuggler-villain was thus the first urban, 'corporatized' villain in Hindi cinema. Like successful corporate climbers, he knew that the ascent would require him to sometimes use as a rung

---

[1] Neeta Lal, 'Smuggling India's Antiques', *The Diplomat*, 16 September 2015, https://thediplomat.com/2015/09/smuggling-indian-antiquities/.

the very people who trusted him. Teja (Ajit) in *Zanjeer* (1973), a manufacturer and distributor of spurious liquor, kills his boss and mentor Patil early on in his career because there could be only one boss. And Bhupendra Singh in *Johny Mera Naam* is an imposter whose real name is Ranjit Singh. He has incarcerated his brother, the real Bhupendra Singh, and taken on his identity.

Being businessmen, the smugglers are material agnostic and steal whatever fetches them money. *Kartavya* (1979) is about poachers headed by Dewan Dhanpat Rai (Utpal Dutt) in Madhuban jungle who sells elephant tusks, tiger skin, rhino's teeth, and sandalwood illegally abroad. To add more variety, Vikram (Danny Denzongpa) in *Aashiq Hoon Baharon Ka* (1977) smuggles out uranium from a laboratory.

Smuggling was also about bringing goods inside the country. The 1960s and 1970s, with their 'License Raj', saw prohibitively high import tariffs in India and a lack of enough top-quality goods available locally for the consumers. This gave an incentive for smugglers like Arun Gawli (played by Arjun Rampal) in *Daddy* (2017, a biopic of Gawli set in the 1970s) to beat the tariff barrier and service the domestic demand by smuggling foreign-made perfumes, VHS players, and transistor radios into the country. Gawli describes these activities as 'import-export'. True, but sans the government duties.

Didn't smugglers and gangsters exist in Hindi films prior to the 1970s? They did – in *Marine Drive* (1956), *Jaali Note* (1960), *Passport* (1961), *CID 909* (1967), *Night in London* (1967), *Teesra Kaun* (1965), *Smuggler* (1966), and *Jewel Thief* (1967). What did we miss in these? Firstly, black-and-white is a good medium for capturing emotions in close-ups, but films involving smugglers include rollicking action sequences that demand panoramic and landscape shots. As also exotic, foreign locations. Nothing less than colour would do. Secondly, a smuggler is a wealthy social star whose parties people aspire to get invited to. His expensive personal accessories, ornate furniture, plush workplaces, designer apparel, chauffeur-driven left-hand drive cars, and perquisites like fine dining with finer women define him. And therefore, production values, cinematography, editing, and other technicalities that optically place the smuggler-villain at the epicentre of these trappings to establish him as the face of consumerism and a connoisseur of good life are critical. Apart from *Jewel Thief*, the other named films missed out on one or both these counts. Film historian Kaushik Bhaumik underlined the difference, 'With *Yaadon ki Baaraat* we see a very direct depiction of this world of greed and violence. The camera moves closer to the body and the zooms take over ... also the décor of films becomes gaudy and kitschy to project a world of greed.'

This world of illegal wealth looked worryingly far easier to achieve in *Deewaar* (1975). While it took the whole of his youth for Shakaal get to where he did, in *Deewaar* the young coolie Vijay, still in his grimy dockyard uniform, is richer by a wad of banknotes within an hour of meeting the smuggler Daavur (Iftekhar). And he is only in his late twenties—maybe the same age as Shakaal's son Rupesh (Imtiaz Khan). Soon after joining Daavur's gang, Vijay moves into a bungalow and is seen drinking in a bar in Bombay's Sheraton Hotel with a gorgeous stranger. The bill at the bar for Vijay and the woman's drinks is comparable to the monthly salary of Vijay's policeman brother Ravi. (Of course, nothing explains how a coolie could turn suave so easily.)

With the 1970s arrived another giant basilisk that hypnotized youngsters and led them to their slow annihilation: drugs. *Hare Rama Hare Krishna* (1971), about ganja-addicted hippies in Kathmandu, established itself as a landmark film in this category. Interestingly, the other smuggler villain in the film, Dronacharya, is a part-comical character, maybe by design, to show the contrast between him and the more insidious villain of the story – the invisible drug mafia that claims victims like young Jasbir/Janice (Zeenat Aman) and her friends.

Both Reena (Nanda) in *Naya Nasha* (1973) and Roshi (Jyoti Bakshi) in *Bullet* (1976) get addicted to LSD, while Nimmu (Aruna Irani) in *Charas* (1976) is trafficked to Malta, force-addicted to charas, and made to dance at a nightclub to entertain its guests. Ajit was back again as the unruffled, uber-cool Kalicharan in *Charas*, who by this time had 'graduated' from antiques to narcotics, agreeing to supply charas worth five crore rupees to Sheikh Abdul Sattar (Sujit Kumar), who intends to make a tenfold profit. Big money in drugs lay in the overseas market and scriptwriters in Bombay recognized this.

Meanwhile in 1972, Francis Ford Coppola's *The Godfather* had released and the production of two Hindi films commenced as soon as the concerned people had a chance to watch Coppola's classic: *Dharmatma* (1975) and the much-delayed *Don* (1978).

Dharmatma was a watershed movie for a few key reasons. Firstly, Dharamdas (Vito Corleone's counterpart played by Premnath) has diverse businesses like gambling, matka (betting and lottery), offering protection to antisocial elements and criminals, and influencing trade unions. Secondly, unlike villains in Hindi cinema up to this time, who had always been enemies of the system, Dharamdas makes friends with the establishment to convince the governor to grant reprieve to a man sentenced to the gallows. Historically, scriptwriters had chosen to blur the space between the bad man's morality and his criminality. A bad man had to be bad in every respect. But for Dharamdas, the family is at the core of his life (like Vito Corleone's). He is a loving father, a devoted husband, and a devout Hindu. This lends the character additional dimensions and, hence, credibility.

In the post-*Dharmatma* world, the don's family comes into view prominently. For example, in *Vidhaata* (1982), Sobhraj (Dilip Kumar), who heads the underworld group Mizya, values his grandson Kunal (Sanjay Dutt) more than anything else in the world and begs the other members of the Mizya group to spare his dear grandson's life just the way Vito Corleone enters a truce with the other Sicilian families over Michael Corleone's safe return to America.

Thirdly, both Vito Corleone and Dharamdas care for the waters they fish in and stay away from the drugs business as it would alienate the establishment. Moreover, drugs would ruin the next generation. So, somewhere they still have a streak of morality intact. Dharamdas is a philanthropist too. This is not to even remotely suggest that Dharamdas is a Robin Hood. His 'generosity' is partly to launder his black money and partly to garner public goodwill with a view to becoming part of the establishment by turning into a politician.

Don (1978), however, is a very different film. Don works for a gang that smuggles gold and drugs in several countries, and he is the one that Interpol is very keen to capture. Unlike Bhupendra Singh, Dharamdas, Shakaal, Teja, Kalicharan, or Seth Durgadas (in *Victoria No. 203*), who were like football coaches directing their players from the sidelines, Don (Amitabh Bachchan in all his elegance) in *Don* is the star striker of his team, front-ending dangerous rendezvous with stunning self-confidence. The Big Dog of the gang is Vardaan (Om Shivpuri) but the gang leans on young Don for his incredible charm, his daring, his ability to deliver results, his 'X-ray' ability to spot and eliminate police informers who infiltrate the gang, and his proverbial nine lives, giving the police the slip every time in the face of imminent arrest. As Don brags cockily, '*Don ko pakadna mushkil hi nahi, namumkin hai*' (It is impossible to capture Don).

While these gangsters made merry, what happened to those enemies of the individuals like Shyam of *Mere Sanam*?

When youngsters discovered that buttering the future mother-in-law would not impress the girl anymore, they resorted to more violent methods. Take the case of a young man with the screen name Kundan in a 1971 film. His girlfriend Kamini (Raakhee) ditches him for another man, Ajit (Shashi Kapoor). After an unsuccessful attempt to dissuade her from marrying Ajit, Kundan tries blackmailing her and then finally resorts to raw physical force that includes pinning Kamini down on the grass and landing heavy slaps on her face. This visceral sequence was a landmark of sorts for its depiction of the use sexual dominance to win over the lady by force when all else failed. The film was *Sharmeelee*, and the actor playing Kundan was Gopal Bedi, better known as Ranjeet. With his loathsome on-screen personality and a lewd look in his eyes, he became the quintessential rapist-villain.

That Ranjeet made a difference as the rapist-villain is evident in *Uljhan* (1975), in which he plays Brij, the playboy who has in his possession the love letters written to him by his ex-girlfriend Kamla (Farida Jalal) and who demands that the now-married Kamla sleep with him one last time as a price for those letters.[2] The overconfident snigger pasted on Brij's face is like an obscene graffiti on the walls of a whorehouse. Raw lust oozes from Brij's eyes on meeting Karuna (Kamla's friend who comes to meet him to negotiate on her behalf) in his hotel room, even as his state of being underdressed in a nightgown is a clear non-verbal signal to Karuna. When Karuna refutes his advances, Brij employs that familiar physical force in his attempt to fulfil his vile agenda.

The decade also witnessed other immoral characters at an individual level. In *Dastaan* (1972) and *Achanak* (1973), the leading ladies enter into a consensual physical relationship with their husbands' best friends. The chasm between these wives and those in the 1960s was Grand Canyonic. Meena (Mala Sinha) in *Gumrah* (1963) sacrifices her love interest Rajendra (Sunil Dutt) for the sake of her deceased sister's children and marries her brother-in-law. But Meena and Rajendra run into each other again and the romance rekindles. For all her selfless sacrifice, the script reprimands Meena for transgressing the 'Lakshman rekha' and meeting another man. The seventies were more accepting, if not forgiving.

A few famous wives of the 1970s went a step further. In *Ek Naari Do Roop* (1972), the sexy Lolita (Rashmi) convinces her boyfriend Vishal to murder her wealthy but quadriplegic husband so that Lolita and Vishal may live off her inheritance. But why didn't divorce with a financial settlement as an exit option cross the

---

[2] *Uljhan* was a remake of *Kangan* (1959) with Iftekhar playing Ramesh, the equivalent of Brij.

minds of the second wives like Mrs Rai Bahadur Singh (Kamini Kaushal) in *Anhonee* (1973) and the nymphomaniac Kamini Singh (Bindu) in *Hawas* (1974)? The 1970s was a time when wives in Hindi cinema had shed the '*bharatiya nari*' image of the 1950s-'60s but hadn't embraced the pragmatism of legal separation yet. So that left these women helpless. They had to kill their husbands.

The morality among men had descended several notches too. While the intruders in *Dastaan* and *Achanak* have no qualms in sleeping with the wives of their buddies, Ranjit Mullick (Prem Chopra) in *Do Anjaane* (1976) gets his friend Amit drunk and pushes him out of a speeding train so that he may carry on his relationship with Amit's ambitious wife Rekha whom Mullick entices with the promise of a career in acting.

And finally, what happened to those dacoits on horsebacks that ruled the ravines of Chambal in the 1960s in *Jis Desh Mein Ganga Behti Hai* (1960), *Gunga Jumna* (1961), and *Mujhe Jeene Do* (1963)? They discovered that the noisy metropolis with crisscrossing cars and scurrying people was now the stock backdrop of the 1970s, and yet managed to carve out a share of showtime for their ilk. How? For one, the urbanite heroes like Feroze Khan, Dharmendra, and Sunil Dutt saw the dacoit genre as a means of infusing variety into their hero image. And so they temporarily got out of their western clothes and donned the dhoti, playing the good-hearted dacoits rather successfully in *Mela* (1971), *Samadhi* (1972), *Patthar aur Payal* (1974), *Heera* (1973), and *Pran Jaye par Vachan na Jaye* (1974). And there were biopics like *Sultana Daku* (1972) and *Pultibai* (1972) too. Secondly, even the prominent villain actors kept dabbling with dacoity with Pran playing the titular *Dharma* (1973) and Ajit playing Mangal in *Mera Vachan Geeta ki Qasam* (1977).

But the most impactful dacoit in the pre-1975 era was Daku Jabbar Singh in *Mera Gaon Mera Desh* (1971), a cold-hearted demon who shoots to death a six-year-old child and the child's father. Jabbar was played brilliantly by Vinod Khanna who once again grabbed audience attention playing the bad dacoit Sarju in *Patthar aur Payal* (1974). Bombay filmdom somehow felt it inappropriate to waste such a manly, handsome man as a villain and, thus, Vinod Khanna was whisked away to playing hero roles. And amidst all this, there emerged a new variant of these outlaws in the 1970s.

In the early 1960s, the rugged cowboy heroes in Hollywood westerns like *The Magnificent Seven* (1960) and Sergio Leone's Dollars trilogy emerged as one of the most popular characters internationally. These cowboys on their horses with their rifles, the chewed cigar hanging from the lips, and their embedded machoism were tailor-made for our desi dacoit sagas to be served with Mexican hot sauce. And thus came *Khote Sikkay* (1974) with a merry band of outlaws, the swagger, the cape, and the shootouts borrowed heavily from the Spaghetti Western. The opening scene with Feroze Khan as the lonely rider, with the sun in the background, resembled the silhouetted horse rider in the opening credit roll of *A Fistful of Dollars* (1964). And there is the bad dacoit Janga (played by Ajit) who murders the judge who had sentenced him to life imprisonment.

A year later, with *Sholay* came arguably the mightiest villain ever, Gabbar Singh – undeniably 'Cowboy Western' in spirit.

Gabbar Singh, based on the real-life dacoit Gabra, is pure evil. Gabbar terrorizes people, loots villagers, has fun killing his colleagues in cavalier fashion, and wipes out an entire family without any remorse. He dresses in army fatigues, speaks in an Awadhi-flavoured Hindi, wears a week-long stubble, and chews tobacco – a character Javed Akhtar hailed as belonging to a place somewhere between Mexico and Uttar Pradesh. Gabbar walks as if he owns the earth. His men are bound to him by sheer fear, as failure usually results in death.[3] To this day, *Sholay* remains a passionate subject of research for film critics and authors who have analysed and traced back various sequences of the film to

[3] A case of plagiarism was filed against *Sholay*'s director Ramesh Sippy by Joginder Shelly who alleged that Sippy had copied the character Ranga Daku (played by Shelly himself) from Shelly's film *Bindiya aur Bandook* (1972).

their Hollywood origins. But nobody denies that *Sholay* split Hindi cinema into two eras – Before *Sholay* and After *Sholay*. It revolutionized the box office, film budgets had new baselines, a villain that could surpass Gabbar would take some re-imagination, and Ramesh Sippy would be doomed to live in the shadow of his own glory ever after.

Nonetheless, the 1970s had a few clean alcoves. The police weren't corrupt, for one. The politicians in *Aandhi* (1975) and *Mere Apne* (1971) were opportunists but not criminals, the doctors were still godlike, the media persons were upright, and terror financing had not entered the lexicon yet.

And then came the 1980s.

He was the lead actor in many notable middle-of-the-road movies in the 1970s, like *Piya Ka Ghar* (1971), *Annadata* (1972), *Honeymoon* (1973) and *Hawas* (1974). He also happens to be the elder brother of David Dhawan and uncle to Varun Dhawan. Name the hero.

Answer: Anil Dhawan

Conjuring a Different Beat

Parallel Cinema's High Noon

Maithili Rao

The seventies swung both ways. Unequally perhaps. With hedonistic abandon to the call of *dum maro dum* juxtaposed with the brooding young man whose bursts of anger were punctuation marks of the decade. At the other end of the spectrum was the awaited dawn of independent cinema: with hope and not dread of a besmirched light of *yeh daagh daagh ujala* that left Faiz Ahmed Faiz disillusioned in '*Subh-e-Azadi*', his anthem of despair. Dawns are ushered with trepidation. Uncertainty and excitement are uneasy bedfellows. Our New Wave washed our shores like rippling wavelets, not a tsunami that swept away the old. It learnt to live with, not under, the shadow of the behemoth that was mainstream Hindi cinema – and still is.

This challenging dawn came before 1970 and its high noon arrived bang in the middle of Amitabh Bachchan in his iconic avatar. And of course the many dated blockbusters that have only limited recall value – nostalgia for the most part and a lot of curiosity about what made them so massively popular.

Cusp years are always intriguing: promising yet difficult to relate to for an audience weaned on formulaic narrative tradition. Parallel cinema's aesthetics were new, so were its thematic preoccupations that were often challenging to the audience. In 1969, Mani Kaul's first film *Uski Roti* was confined to the festival circuit and film society cineastes. Kumar Shahani's *Maya Darpan* followed in 1972. Hailed by film aesthetes as radical departures, even a curious but non-cine-educated viewer was left puzzled by the non-linear, deliberately undramatic experiments in film language. Mani Kaul and Kumar Shahani, joined like Siamese twins as torchbearers of pure cinema, are very different but share the same commitment to film as art as defined by their sensibility.

Shahani the scholar–film-maker sought to fuse Ritwick Ghatak's epic resonance with Robert Bresson's austerity. More appreciated as a teacher than film-maker, his more accessible epic canvas of *Tarang* and the mesmerizing definitive documentary *Bhavantarana* on Kelucharan Mahapatra came in the 1980s. Mani Kaul is master of the image that has a certain purity of line and a layered sensuousness suggested by the stillness of a camera's unblinking eye. His films have an intrinsic musicality, like the unfolding of a raga exploring its nuanced structure. Mani the musician imbued the image with subtle resonances. *Duvidha*, made in 1973, revealed an artist gifted with an exquisite sense of colour and texture along with the eloquence of silent faces. It felt organic unlike the schematic colour code that is obvious.

An important point to remember. With the advantage of hindsight, we should be allowed the luxury of taking an entire body of work – never mind the timespan – to evaluate an important film-maker's contribution. An auteur is not confined to the calendar, be it just a couple of years or a decade. Auteurs, of arthouse, middle-of-the-road or mainstream cinema, transcend decades with the ease of a long jumper and sometimes the stamina of a marathoner. This holds true of most film-makers with a significant body of work.

It was a film society cineaste who made *Sara Aakash* in the same year as *Uski Roti* that was rooted in middle-class reality. But

Basu Chatterjee quickly abandoned the stark realism of shooting in the author's own house to film Rajendra Yadav's well-known story. The little gem did not find an audience. Out of disappointment or driven by the survival instinct, he used his talent for storytelling to become the darling of an educated middle class that wanted something more intelligent and relatable yet not too alien in its narrative style. Popular for his romantic comedies-cum-gentle satire, Chatterjee along with Gulzar, Hrishikesh Mukherjee and Basu Bhattacharya were exponents of what came to be called middle cinema.

Bhuvan Shome, again dated 1969, is officially crowned the harbinger of the New Wave produced by the FFC (Film Financial Corporation that later morphed into the National Film Development Corporation). Mrinal Sen, ever adventurous, stepped out of Bengal to the charms of rural Gujarat for the engaging encounter between a crusty bureaucrat set in his ways and a winsome rustic lass, intelligent where it matters and refreshingly free of respectful obedience to city bigwigs. *Bhuvan Shome* did not only spawn other well-crafted 'different' films that won prestigious awards but also had a decent run in chosen theatres. Mrinal Sen began the trend of choosing Amitabh Bachchan's baritone (before he stamped his larger-than-life persona as the iconic rebel with a cause) to voice the commentary that introduces the film. Satyajit Ray put the final seal of authority on Bachchan's mastery of the spoken word in *Shatranj Ke Khilar*i (1977). It is a masterclass of using inflections to suggest a range of comments on the unfolding history of British encounter with Nawabi India. This also proved that the giants of Indian cinema had no reservation about using a megastar from Bombay if he was the best for the film. For the truly great, divisive labels did not matter.

Parallel cinema needed a master communicator to bring together all these inchoate yearnings (of the audience yet to be discovered) and film-makers waiting in the wings to follow the lead of a man with a clear vision of what he was setting out to do. Shyam Benegal is the trendsetting auteur who created a niche audience that was waiting for something different from the mainstream formula but didn't exactly know what they wanted. Benegal is a multifaceted genius. A creative artist who explored the many layers of feudalism bequeathed to a society on the threshold of modernity. Tradition coping with change is a constant in any society at any age. That's a given. Benegal brought humanity to those we would damn as oppressors.

One striking example is enough to explain this important aspect of his oeuvre. In *Ankur*, Anant Nag, the overbearing landlord's son, is dispatched to the village to look after the land since he is an academic failure in the city anyway. A coward taking the easy way out, he starts the affair with the winsome and willing Laxmi – Shabana's unforgettable debut in a landmark film, a sapling that grew into a banyan tree. Anant Nag's vulnerability is as much a part of him as cowardice. Benegal makes us understand him. One of the many keys the director gives us without artifice and obvious effort, to read his characters (with all their weaknesses and strengths) and the layered narrative.

His background in advertising gave him the acumen to not depend on government funding to make the films he wanted in the way he wanted. He is the most successful auteur who could crowdfund his third film of the loose rural trilogy. *Manthan* was made with contributions from the dairy farmers of Gujarat (some gave just 2 rupees) to tell the inspirational tale of the White Revolution that transformed their lives. Benegal's casting and engaging narrative brings to life the fiery Bindu (Smita Patil) and the simmering attraction between Dr Rao (Girsih Karnad) and her. He is the catalyst from the city who has come to start a milk cooperative in the face of a hostile dairy owner and suspicious villagers. Naseeruddin Shah's accusing glare as the cynical Bhola is almost a visual punctuation mark, of changing attitudes from mistrust to support.

An interesting sidelight to the making of *Manthan* not many know. In an interview decades ago, Vijay Tendulkar told me how ironical it was that his national award for best script was for

Manthan. Benegal wanted Tendulkar to be on location with the crew but since the writer could not make it, Karnad and Benegal improvised the required changes. Kaifi Azmi's dialogue is a delight of satirical humour and it accommodated Gujarati patois for aural authenticity.

Shyam Benegal is the true pioneer. He found a steadfast producer who backed his neo-realist classics. He had the discerning eye to see potential in a dusky Marathi TV newsreader and the versatile thespian in a savvy Xaverite with an impeccable artistic lineage. Thus were born iconic stars Smita Patil and Shabana Azmi who won their first National Award for Best Actress in *Bhumika* and *Ankur* respectively. He recognized the burning intensity of repressed anger in Naseeruddin Shah who went on to be the thinking person's angry young man. Om Puri came a little later and this star actor for all seasons was the first to make an international career against all odds. This quartet became icons who shone bright and steady in a parallel universe. Smita and Shabana were the stars whose light was borrowed by dyed-in-the-wool mainstream directors to add the cachet of seriousness, looking for a certain artistic élan to differentiate their films from the routine, overexposed glamour of the reigning female stars. The men of this quartet had to wait longer, for *Sparsh* and *Ardh Satya*, to be accepted by the mainstream.

Benegal is also the first director to establish a repertory of actors who emerged as talented actors on their own – Neena Gupta and Anant Nag are prime examples of success – and a pool of dependable actors, many from theatre and overlooked bit players who found recognition in a series of films made by Benegal. His films introduced and defined what ensemble excellence means. Benegal also introduced us to the delights of Dakhni, its rustic rhythms and democratic dispensing with hierarchical forms of addressing social superiors. Hitherto we had Punjabified Hindi, bastardised Bambayya and elegant Urdu of courtly courtesies and nawabi andaaz. Benegal married the dialect to its milieu. Something that resurfaced in the new millennium when Hindi cinema went in search of different habitations and its localized idiom.

Along with his repertory, Benegal built up his informal but influential school of film-making with a chosen crew: writers Shama Zaidi, Atul Tiwari and Satyadev Dubey on occasion, Govind Nihalani the cinematographer till he turned independent auteur, Bhanudas Diwakar the editor and maestro Vanraj Bhatia for his distinctive score. There was discipline and democracy in the film-making process. Actors multitasked when needed. Smita is credited with costume design for *Kondura/Anugraham* (his only Telugu film) for she took over when Nira Benegal had to leave the film. In spite of such improvisations, Benegal's films look organically complete, with no rough edges.

Nishant demands special mention for the complexity of ideas that are embedded in the narrative. A place that is a large village that's almost a small town is the setting for the ruthless regime of the local landlord. The new schoolmaster's wife can be abducted with impunity and be the mistress of the youngest brother. The relationship between the new bride and the mistress who seems to succumb to the Stockholm Syndrome is a shifting power game, yet with an undertone of sisterhood because they are both prisoners of patriarchy. The narrative suggests that when the educated middle class (the teacher) and religion (the disillusioned priest) join forces, they can trigger a bloody revolution that goes out of hand. Innocents are killed along with the oppressors. A foreboding cautionary tale from 1975.

A star was born on the shoot of *Nishant*. Both the still photographer Krishna Basrur and cinematographer Nihalani could not stop raving about Smita Patil's arresting screen presence, recalled Benegal when I was talking to him for my book on Smita Patil. That's when she became Benegal's muse for *Manthan* and *Bhumika*, two seminal films where the woman is both the focus and filter, the emotional centre and metaphor for wider meaning. She was courted by mainstream directors and the eighties were a mixed bag – the acme of achievement in an epic *Mirch Masala* and the pits of *Galiyon Ka Badshah*.

Shabana made wiser choices and had it easier. She straddled both streams of cinema with poise, because of Kaifi Azmi and brother Baba Azmi's association with popular Hindi cinema. She has the gift of being in sur with the film. As a trained actor, she is in tune with the general tone – the narrative, other actors and the director's overall sensibility. Smita on the other hand seemed out of touch with the rest of the cast and gave all her intensity to a role and story that did not demand or deserve it.

An ironic aside. Parallel cinema made big strides to reach its zenith in the eighties with other directors swelling the ranks. Benegal explored more ambitious and complex films like *Junoon*, *Trikal* and *Suraj ka Satwan Ghoda*. In contrast, mainstream Hindi cinema hit the doldrums with B-graders catering to the lowest common denominator.

While Benegal basked in critical acclaim, sniping came from acolytes of the Mani Kaul–Kumar Shahani school dedicated to 'pure cinema' and adherence to personal aesthetics. These disdainful loyalists dubbed Benegal and his cohorts as makers of 'arthouse films with commercial edge' and did not give credence to their exploration of serious gender/social issues. They preferred the unpretentious masala film. I met quite a few such lost students looking for a cause and a break,

The seventies were a tumultuous decade politically. The Emergency and its aftermath were uncertain times for Hindi cinema. Paradoxically, Indira Gandhi allowed an overt and covert anti-establishment stance that was intrinsic to many New Wave films. Even earlier, as the Minister for Information and Broadcasting, she was approachable, and looked kindly (if not benignly) upon the woes of struggling film-makers. This did not extend to creating the infrastructure for the distribution of arthouse films. In an era where protest was very much in the air, film-makers in the parallel stream got together in 1977 to form MUKT, short for Marketing Union of Kine Technicians. The founders were Muzaffar Ali who had made *Gaman* and Kantilal Rathod whose film *Kanku* was lying in the cans. Rinki Bhattacharya's detailed report of MUKT's purpose and the frustration of unreleased films brought in practically all parallel film-makers to actively participate and work as a pressure group to propel the FFC into action. It is not enough to fund non-formulaic films but also release them. Finally, *Gaman* was released.

The much-maligned FFC produced a classic that will be a classic forever. In 1974, *Garm Hawa* singed the conscience of a nation. M.S. Sathyu's remarkable first film reminded people of the tragedy of Partition and the price a Muslim family of Agra paid. Sathyu was from the Indian People's Theatre Association (IPTA) and cast a comrade in the central role. If anyone was born to play Salim Mirza, it was the incomparable Balraj Sahni. Sathyu later on admitted that he deliberately staged the scene of a shocked father's first sight of his beloved daughter lying dead, her slit wrists staining the white sheet, to force the actor to remember his own daughter's suicide. Heartless but a wrenching moment of cinema, the price extracted from a sensitive actor. *Garm Hawa* should be shown every five years, if not every year, to warn us where we are headed as a divided country torn by hatred of the Other.

Another forgotten page from history. The genius from Calcutta made his first foray into Hindi with *Shatranj Ke Khiladi* in 1977. A most accomplished film that centred the mania of two blissfully oblivious Lucknow nawabs and their addiction to chess to encompass the larger imperial game of swallowing vulnerable Indian states one by one. Sophisticated and witty, the mise en scène is a masterclass in design and perfect casting. The rave reviews in Bombay (shown in just one theatre) alarmed Mughals of Hindi cinema. Satyajit Ray venturing into Hindi (actually it was in Urdu with a sprinkling of Awadhi) was a threat to their fortress. He could remain in Calcutta and win as many awards as he could abroad. Rumours were rife that the Bombay film mafia sabotaged the run of the film and Ray swore off making another Hindi/Urdu film. An unsavoury chapter that does no credit to the biggest film industry in India. In spite of all the superhits and a brand-new superstar to reign unopposed, does this betray the industry's vulnerability? They could deal with Benegal's growing reputation and start borrowing his actors. They ceded ground to Benegal and then Nihalani who heralded the eighties with the anguished cry of *Aakrosh*. They could also bend the dramaturgy of this neo-realist school and water it down it to suit their larger-than-life myths.

The comeuppance was waiting to ambush this collective arrogance in the eighties, a lost decade for Hindi cinema. The seventies are a strange mix of paradoxes. Arthouse and mainstream coexisted with grudging regard for each other but dared not impinge on strictly marked territories. Coexistence but not cohabitation. Respect with undertones of rancour, perhaps? Or do we tend to see the past through glasses misted with nostalgia?

Gulzar spotted him when he essayed the role of Naseer in an Indo-Iranian film named *Subah-o-Shaam* (1972) and signed him for his next film. They were to work together in more than five films over the next ten years. Identify the actor.

Answer: Sanjeev Kumar

From Gungi Gudiya to Maa Durga

The Evolution of Indian Cinema in the 1970s – A Cultural Tapestry of Revolution and Renaissance

Vinta Nanda

Every era of Indian cinema serves as a window into the societal shifts of its time. The 1970s was a period of profound transformation. This essay aims to explore the multifaceted landscape of Hindi cinema during the 1970s, examining its socio-political context, thematic evolution, portrayal of women, impact of globalization, and the changing dynamics of the film industry.

While this decade was famous for bell-bottoms and the rise of the influence of Western music in Hindi cinema, it was also an era of economic struggle, cultural change, and technological innovation. It was marked by a series of socio-political upheavals both in India and around the world. In the West, movements for women's rights, gay rights, and environmental activism collided with political scandals such as the Watergate scandal, energy crises, and the Vietnam War. Similarly, India grappled with its own set of challenges including the Indo-Pak War, inflation, student protests, and the Emergency of 1975–77.

Amidst these turbulent times, cinema emerged as a powerful medium for social commentary and cultural reflection. Film-makers responded to the changing zeitgeist by incorporating relevant themes and narratives into their works, providing audiences with a lens through which to interpret and understand the world around them.

The themes explored in Hindi cinema during the 1970s reflected the social, political, and economic realities of the time. While commercial blockbusters dominated the industry, a parallel cinema movement emerged, spearheaded by film-makers like Mrinal Sen, Shyam Benegal and Mani Kaul. These film-makers sought to break away from the conventions of mainstream cinema and address pressing social issues with a greater degree of realism and authenticity. Films like *Ankur* (1974), *Garm Hava* (1974), and *Bhumika* (1977) tackled themes such as caste discrimination, rural poverty, and gender inequality, offering audiences a more nuanced and introspective view of Indian society. These films were characterized by their gritty realism, complex characters, and socially relevant narratives, marking a departure from the escapist fantasies of mainstream cinema.

Politically speaking, the first spell of power for the iconic Indian woman of post-Independence India, Indira Gandhi, who became prime minister of the country in 1966, was quite unremarkable. She was surrounded by a heavyweight cabinet in which she was less than an equal and even heavier-weight regional satraps who commanded her to listen to them. They symbolized her by the contemptuous phrase used by the socialist leader Ram Manohar Lohia when they dismissed her as a 'gungi gudiya' – literally, a dumb doll. However, 1971, the beginning of a powerful but tumultuous decade for India, was her finest hour: triumph in a general election, and an astounding feat of diplomatic–military skill by which Bangladesh was liberated. And then, Atal Bihari Vajpayee described her as Maa Durga.

It was from the 'gungi gudiya' to 'Maa Durga' that the portrayal of the Indian woman, too, evolved in the cinema of the

1970s. Storytelling, overall, both commercial and art, reflected the empowerment of the Indian woman. Traditionally relegated to secondary roles as love interests or damsels in distress, women began to take centre stage in films of this era, portraying characters with agency, depth, and complexity. Moreover, parallel cinema offered a platform for female film-makers and actors to explore themes of female empowerment, identity, and liberation. Actresses like Smita Patil, Shabana Azmi, and Deepti Naval emerged as trailblazers, challenging societal norms and redefining the role of women in Indian cinema.

Raj Kapoor's cinematic journey from the 1960s to the 1970s, as exemplified by films like *Sangam* (1964), *Mera Naam Joker* (1970), *Bobby* (1973), and *Satyam Shivam Sundaram* (1978), reflects his evolving perspective as a male storyteller. While some view this phase of Kapoor's career as voyeuristic, I interpret it differently. He portrayed the male gaze as the curiosity of a young man, placing female protagonists at the forefront of his narratives. Kapoor transcended the traditional male gaze by celebrating and acknowledging the worth of women, portraying their sensuality in empowering ways. Characters like Mary (Simi Garewal), Meena (Padmini), and Marina (Kseniya Ryabinkina) in *Mera Naam Joker* were depicted with depth and complexity. In *Bobby*, Kapoor acknowledged Dimple Kapadia's agency, while in *Satyam Shivam Sundaram*, he captured Zeenat Aman's allure without objectifying her. Through his films, Kapoor critiqued societal attitudes towards women, accusing the male gaze rather than the women themselves.

Mera Naam Joker, though not a blockbuster, nuanced an important societal shift towards capitalism. *Bobby* explored the dynamics of love across class boundaries, while *Satyam Shivam Sundaram* delved into beauty, disfigurement, highlighting the treatment of women in 1970s India.

The 1970s also witnessed the impact of globalization on Indian cinema, as film-makers began to incorporate Western influences and aesthetics into their works. Films like *Purab Aur Paschim* (1970) and *Hare Rama Hare Krishna* (1971) explored themes of cultural identity, tradition, and modernity, highlighting the tension between western values and Indian traditions. Furthermore, the proliferation of international film festivals provided Indian film-makers with greater exposure to global audiences and perspectives. This exposure led to a cross-pollination of ideas and styles, resulting in a more diverse and eclectic range of cinematic expressions.

Purab aur Paschim emerged from the creative vision of actor, director, screenwriter, editor, and producer Manoj Kumar. This blockbuster grappled with the clash between western ideals and Indian values, portraying traditionalists resisting the inevitable march of progress. Set during the British rule in India, the plot revolves around Harnam's betrayal of a freedom fighter, leading to tragic consequences. Years later, his son Bharat travels to Britain for education, only to discover that many Indian expatriates there have distanced themselves from their homeland. Determined to bridge this cultural gap, Bharat embarks on a mission to challenge their perceptions. The introduction of a blonde heroine of Indian origin, portrayed by Saira Banu, symbolizes the westernized Indian woman within the broader narrative of Indian cinema.

Similarly, Dev Anand's *Hare Rama Hare Krishna* shed light on the complexities of the modern Indian family struggling amidst India's rapid transformation. Set against the backdrop of the burgeoning Hare Krishna movement, the film depicts a Montreal-based family grappling with the breakdown of their marriage. Divorce, a taboo subject in India at the time, adds layers of tension to the narrative as the couple's children are separated. The clash between western and Indian cultures is palpable throughout the story, enriched by the film's evocative music. Zeenat Aman's compelling performance solidified her status as a symbol of the modern Indian woman.

During the 1970s, cinemas served as the primary source of mass entertainment in the country, remaining undeterred by the tumultuous political climate. Amidst the chaos, film-makers continued to produce a diverse array of films ranging from formulaic blockbusters to gritty realism simultaneously. This era witnessed the emergence of three distinct trends that shaped the landscape of Indian cinema.

Firstly, there was the rise of the low-budget 'new wave' films, characterized by their experimental narratives and unconventional storytelling techniques. These films challenged traditional norms and pushed the boundaries of cinematic expression, garnering attention for their artistic merit and thought-provoking content.

Secondly, middle-of-the-road cinema gained prominence, catering primarily to urban audiences with its relatable themes and nuanced characterizations. These films struck a balance between artistic integrity and commercial viability, appealing to a wide spectrum of viewers while addressing contemporary social issues.

Lastly, the era saw the emergence of epic multi-starrer extravaganzas, characterized by their grand scale, star-studded casts, and larger-than-life narratives. These films aimed to captivate audiences with their spectacle and entertainment value, often overshadowing their smaller-budget counterparts in terms of box-office success.

Despite their disparate business models, mainstream cinema driven by commercial objectives and low-budget 'art cinema' competed for audience attention, each offering a unique cinematic experience. This dynamic landscape made impressionism pervasive within Indian cinema, reflecting the diverse tastes and preferences of audiences across the country.

At the dawn of the 1970s, Hindi cinema found itself in a state of thematic stagnation until the arrival of the dynamic screenwriter duo, Salim–Javed, who breathed new life into the industry. With ground-breaking works like *Zanjeer* (1973) and *Deewaar* (1975), they pioneered the gritty, violent genre of Bombay underworld crime films, offering a raw portrayal of urban life in 1970s India. Drawing inspiration from rural classics like *Mother India* and *Gunga Jumna*, Salim–Javed reinterpreted these themes within urban contexts, capturing the growing discontent and disillusionment of the masses amidst unprecedented urbanization and the proliferation of slums.

Their collaboration introduced audiences to Amitabh Bachchan, the iconic Angry Young Man, whose thundering voice resonated with the struggles of the urban poor, becoming a symbol of defiance against societal injustices.

As the decade progressed, Hindi cinema underwent a paradigm shift, moving away from traditional themes of nationalism, idealism, religiosity, and mythology. Instead, a new wave of storytelling emerged, characterized by a focus on individual narratives and unorthodox themes.

Films like *Guddi* (1971) and *Anand* (1971) exemplified this shift, offering fresh perspectives on arranged marriages and terminal illness, respectively. *Guddi* followed the story of a teenage girl who rebels against her family's attempts to arrange her marriage, choosing instead to pursue her passion for cinema and idolize the heart-throb actor Dharmendra. This narrative challenged societal norms surrounding arranged marriages and highlighted the dreams and aspirations of young girls, while also making a comment on the Indian public's love for cinema.

On the other hand, *Anand* presented a poignant tale of a terminally ill man who seeks to embrace life to the fullest before his inevitable demise. Through its narrative, the film not only entertained audiences but also introduced the concept of Entertainment Education (EE), using compelling storytelling to inform mass audiences about contemporary medical science.

Mrinal Sen's *Bhuvan Shome*, hailed as the best feature film at the National Film Awards in 1970, served as a catalyst for the emergence of the new wave movement in Indian cinema. Following in Sen's pioneering footsteps, film-makers like Shyam Benegal, Girish Karnad, and Mani Kaul continued to push the boundaries of cinematic expression.

The new wave cinema of this era presented audiences with intense and immersive narratives, shedding light on the harsh realities faced by rural and impoverished communities. Films like *Ankur*, *Garm Hava*, *Nishant*, and *Bhumika* sparked conversations about social injustice and inequality.

Ankur depicted the struggles of lower-caste individuals like Lakshmi, portrayed by Shabana Azmi, and her deaf-mute husband Kishtayya, played by Sadhu Meher, as they navigate the complexities of feudal society. Lakshmi's journey, marked by exploitation and injustice, highlighted the pervasive casteism and discrimination faced by marginalized communities. Despite her circumstances, Lakshmi's defiance and resilience portrayed her as a woman who takes ownership of her sexuality while maintaining a strong moral stance against societal injustice.

Through its powerful narrative and gut-wrenching portrayal of caste-based oppression, *Ankur* challenged societal norms and provided a platform for marginalized voices to be heard. In doing so, it paved the way for a new wave of socially conscious cinema that sought to address pressing issues facing Indian society.

Nishant, crafted from an original screenplay by Vijay Tendulkar and enriched by the poignant dialogues of Satyadev Dubey, boasts a stellar ensemble cast of parallel cinema luminaries including Girish Karnad, Amrish Puri, Shabana Azmi, Mohan Agashe, Anant Nag, Sadhu Meher, Smita Patil, and Naseeruddin Shah. The film delves into the dynamics of power within feudal rural elites, shedding light on the pervasive issue of sexual exploitation faced by women in such contexts.

On the other hand, *Bhumika* offers a distinct narrative rooted in the Marathi-language memoir *Sangtye Aika* of the renowned actress from the 1940s, Hansa Wadkar. This cinematic exploration of individual identity and self-fulfilment sees Smita Patil delivering a tour de force performance, seamlessly transitioning from a vivacious teenager to a wise yet deeply wounded middle-aged woman.

Meanwhile, *Garm Hava*, helmed by M.S. Sathyu and featuring Balraj Sahni in a compelling lead role, emerged from the pens of esteemed writers Kaifi Azmi and Shama Zaidi. Drawing inspiration from an unpublished short story by Urdu writer Ismat Chughtai, the film unfolds against the backdrop of post-Partition India, particularly focusing on the plight of a north Indian Muslim businessman and his family in the city of Agra. As the protagonist, Salim Mirza, grapples with the profound dilemma of whether to migrate to Pakistan or remain in India, *Garm Hava* stands as one of the rare cinematic depictions of the struggles faced by Muslims in the aftermath of Partition, offering a sobering glimpse into their post-Independence reality.

Mainstream cinema thrived, offering a plethora of narratives to Indian audiences, transcending geographical and socio-economic barriers. It entertained audiences from all walks of life, bridging the gap between rural and urban demographics. In theatres, patrons from the upper stalls to the balconies and dress circles experienced the same cinematic marvels, albeit at different price points.

Films like *Amar Prem* (1972) depicted the journey of an abandoned woman forced into prostitution, while *Bawarchi* (1972) portrayed the transformation of a dysfunctional middle-class family through the intervention of a multi-talented household help. *Koshish* (1972) followed the struggles of a speech-and-hearing-impaired couple as they navigated societal prejudices to gain acceptance. In *Abhimaan* (1973), a popular singer's conflicting emotions towards his wife's success in show business reflected themes of jealousy and insecurity.

Mega blockbusters such as *Deewaar* explored the vulnerability of the oppressed to crime, while *Sholay* subtly introduced the idea of widow remarriage into collective consciousness. *Amar Akbar Anthony* (1977) celebrated brotherhood and harmony among the three major religions of Hinduism, Islam, and Christianity, symbolizing India's secular ethos. Indian cinema had matured, recognizing its potential as a tool of soft power. It presented a secular, pluralistic India on screen, inviting diverse populations to engage with its stories and serving as a cultural ambassador on the global stage.

The act of watching movies underwent a significant transformation, evolving from a passive experience to an interactive cultural phenomenon. Theatres buzzed with activity as audiences engaged in lively behaviours such as hooting, whistling, and even coin-flinging during screenings. Vendors circulated through the crowds, peddling cold drinks, chai, paan, and samosas, while black-market traders exchanged tickets for coveted 'first day, first show' slots. Inside the cavernous auditoriums, often filled beyond capacity, viewers were swept up in the emotional rollercoaster of the film, dancing in the aisles amidst the rhythmic hum of the projector.

Since the establishment of the first single-screen theatre in Calcutta (now Kolkata) in 1907, this insatiable appetite for cinema had grown into a cultural revolution of unparalleled magnitude. Indian cinema earned its distinction as the world's largest film factory during this period. Over the decade, a staggering 4,945 full-length films, averaging 494.5 films annually, graced the screens of the nation's 10,000 cinema halls, captivating millions of viewers. Film production surged from 398 films in 1970 to a staggering 680 in 1979, representing nearly two films completed every single day.

The cinematic landscape between parallel/art cinema and mainstream blockbusters, which dominated Hindi cinema, was enriched by the contributions of illustrious film-makers like Hrishikesh Mukherjee, Gulzar, Basu Chatterjee, and Basu Bhattacharya. These visionaries consistently delivered award-winning films, showcasing mature storytelling across various genres.

Rajnigandha (1974), adapted from the short story 'Yahi Sach Hai' by Hindi writer Mannu Bhandari, offered a realistic portrayal of urban middle-class life, featuring stellar performances by Amol Palekar, Vidya Sinha, and Dinesh Thakur. *Aandhi* (1975), a political drama starring Sanjeev Kumar and Suchitra Sen, purportedly drew inspiration from the life of then-Prime Minister Indira Gandhi and her relationship with her estranged husband. Despite being banned during the Emergency, the film sparked nationwide debates and was eventually premiered on state-run television after Gandhi's defeat in the 1977 general elections.

Gulzar's *Mausam* (1975), featuring Sanjeev Kumar and Sharmila Tagore, and Hrishikesh Mukherjee's *Chupke Chupke*

(1975), boasting an ensemble cast including Dharmendra, Amitabh Bachchan, Sharmila Tagore, Jaya Bhaduri, Om Prakash, Usha Kiran, David, Asrani, and Keshto Mukherjee, emerged as landmark films of the decade. Basu Bhattacharya's National Award-winning *Anubhav* (1971), starring Sanjeev Kumar, Tanuja, and Dinesh Thakur, formed a part of an introspective trilogy on marital discord in an urban setting, alongside critically acclaimed films like *Avishkaar* (1974), starring Rajesh Khanna and Sharmila Tagore, and *Griha Pravesh* (1979). The review of *Avishkaar* by the Hindu stated:

> Here you can see Khanna inhabiting a disillusioned husband with all the details. There is nothing trademark about Kaka here as you only see Amar with all his frailties come alive on screen. It must have been challenging for the raging star to pick a role where he was not the hero in the conventional sense. The film was a box office hit. Khanna waived 70 % of his remuneration to star in this project.

As much as the entertainment industry flourished in this decade, the essence of cinema began to wane in the next. The advent of television in the 1980s marked a turning point, as the once-powerful medium of cinema, which had served as a mirror reflecting society's complexities through diverse storytelling, gradually lost its prominence. The emergence of television, initially under government control but later dominated by media Mughals during the satellite TV boom of the 1990s, transformed storytelling into mere 'content'. Gatekeepers within the industry now dictated the narrative, reshaping stories to align with commercial interests. Unlike the 1970s, when storytellers drove the market, the dynamics had shifted, with commercial imperatives now dictating the direction of storytelling.

The 1970s was a transformative period in Indian cinema, characterized by its bold experimentation. Film-makers of this era dared to push the boundaries of storytelling, challenging societal norms and conventions while reflecting the hopes, aspirations, and struggles of a nation in transition.

The legacy of 1970s Hindi cinema continues to resonate today, as film-makers and audiences alike draw inspiration from its themes, characters, and narratives. While the industry has undergone significant changes since then, the spirit of innovation and creativity that defined this era remains a guiding force for future generations of film-makers and storytellers.

In essence, the cinema of the 1970s serves as a testament to the power of storytelling to inspire, provoke, and illuminate, transcending boundaries of time, culture, and geography. As we look back on this pivotal period in Indian cinema, we are reminded of the enduring impact of art and the enduring legacy of those who dared to dream.

Which music composer duo composed '*Kaan mein jhumka*' (*Sawan Bhaadon*, 1970) picturized on Navin Nischol and Rekha?

Answer: Sonik-Omi

SECTION IV

Insiders' Insights

Languages, Learning, Theatre and Films

A Conversation

Mohan Agashe

This interview was recorded at Dr Agashe's residence in Pune on 3 December 2022. Dr Agashe was shooting for the film *Outhouse*, in which Sharmila Tagore plays his love interest. *Outhouse* is the last script written by Sumitra Bhave, and the film is directed by Sunil Sukthankar, her co-director from films like *Astu* and *Kaasav*.

Over lunch and two cups of tea, Dr Agashe spoke to Nirupama Kotru about progressive Marathi cinema, influx of Pune theatre stalwarts into the Bombay film industry, and also camps within the elite parallel cinema club. Through this interview, readers can get valuable insights into one of the brilliant minds who came into the limelight thanks to parallel cinema of the 1970s. Surely the stimulating atmosphere in the industry during that decade must be given due credit for encouraging professionals such as Dr Agashe to pursue their creative passion; often this entailed their crossing over from theatre into cinema.

Nirupama Kotru: Sir, thanks for taking time to speak to me despite your busy shooting schedule.

Mohan Agashe: No problem, but first, tell me, how much do you know about Sumitra Bhave?

Nirupama Kotru: I know she was a brilliant director; I met her in NFAI.

Mohan Agashe: Before I talk to you about films of the 1970s, let me tell you something about Sumitra. Sumitra met a lady in a conference and they became friends. They were doing a project on problems of women in slums, on their survival issues. After collecting their data, they were supposed to collate it and report it. But during the process of research, they realized that most of these women could not read or write. So the conventional tools of research were third rate and useless for them. That's how she thought why not make a film to tell a story, and give the scientific information about their problems of survival.

With the help of her cinematographer friend she was able to write a small script and make a film. The film was called *Bai* (1985). They took a projector to the slums and screened the film. The whole purpose of research was served much better. At the same time, Sumitra was approached by an NGO to make a film on water problems of Adivasi women who had to walk 10 to 15 miles to fetch water. She made a film called *Paani* (1987). Both these films were invited to so many festivals, and she was asked to talk about these issues. She made up her mind to use film to deliver what she wanted to say. Film uses two languages, not only the language of cognition but the language of emotion. She and Sandip went on to direct many films together. After *Dithee* (2019), this (*Outhouse*) will be the only film directed by Sandip alone. She is the only film director in the world who has made engaging films about six high-stigma medical conditions – HIV, schizophrenia, Alzheimer's, leucoderma, depression and suicide. And superstitions.

Nirupama Kotru: That's wonderful, sir. Mental health issues don't get enough attention in our society.

Mohan Agashe: So what's your book about?

Nirupama Kotru: It is about Hindi-language films of the 1970s.

Mohan Agashe: Let me stop you right there. When we speak of films, and we say Hindi-language films, Marathi-language films, you are unconsciously admitting that the language of words is the most important language of communication, ignoring that film speaks two other rich languages, which are primary languages of emotion and communication; and that is seeing and listening.

This is almost amounting to intellectual terrorism. When we say Marathi-language film, do we say Marathi-language music, Marathi-language painting? First of all, you don't know anything about languages and you have already eliminated people who know language that is sensitive but not cognitive, and you are dominating them and exploiting them, because there are better artists in that community than in your community. What I am very much against now is intellectual terrorism, and formal education is completely dominated by intellectual terrorism. We develop thinking and no sensory recall.

Earlier, after six years, only when all sensory systems are developed, you went to school. Now your formal education begins at the age of one or two, thereby promoting cognition, demonstrating Mark Twain's famous quotation, 'I didn't let school interfere with my education.' These intelligent people have devised a term: extracurricular activities; all sensory skills are clubbed under that and they are considered inferior to intellectual skills. And you know that most of our world-famous artists have not even completed school. By looking down upon such people, what they are promoting is the worst exhibition of egos.

My first statement is, when you say Hindi-language films, you are not at all understanding language. At the most, you can say I am limiting myself to films where the spoken language is Hindi, not the language of film. If you reconstruct your opening sentence, I will proceed further.

Nirupama Kotru (*laughs*): Consider it done, sir. I wanted to start by asking you, having had a highly successful and fulfilling career as a psychiatrist, what inspired you to join the arts? What or who were early inspirations? How did you finally take the plunge in the 1970s, starting as per my knowledge, with Sai Paranjpye's Marathi play for children? Please tell us at length about your debut.

Mohan Agashe: See, before Sai went to Delhi for the National School of Drama, she ran a wonderful theatre for children with Arun Joglekar, called Children's Theatre. And she wrote excellent plays for children – *Satyanagari, Conference of Birds, Nirupama aur Pari Rani* in which I played Pinocchio. And obviously I was fond of acting, a fact recognized more than me by my teachers. When I went to school, they asked me about it. And so, on my own, I went to meet Sai Paranjpye at home. I told her, 'Why don't you take me in Bal Udyan (theatre for children in Pune).' This began in school. You also must have acted in school. Which child hasn't acted for his or her parents? Their first audience. And then they give up.

But, in (my) school, there used to be serious theatre activity. We had good directors. My primary activities were acting, elocution and playing. And also 'soot katayi' (spinning of cotton thread). My father said I don't have money for summer activities, so do whatever is free. Acting (class) was free, and soot-katayi was free. I used to do those classes and I got some awards in school competitions. Then I did BSc. The real crucial time is when you get admitted to professional college, not even when you go to arts, or commerce or BSc, etc. Engineering or medicine puts a lot of pressure on you; you have to focus on your career. And I joined medical college. Jabbar Patel was the first one among us to join medical college. Very gifted actor. Theatre took over all other activities in our college.

Nirupama Kotru: Jabbar Patel was in your college?

Mohan Agashe: Jabbar is four years senior to me, Dr Shriram Lagoo is twenty years senior to me. We're all from the same college – Behramjee Jeejubai Medical College, Pune. All of us are Sangeet Natak awardees, all of us are Padma Shri awardees.

To be very honest, in a middle-class, white-collar, educated family, children were very protected. So forget about themselves, they didn't know anything about the world. Decisions were made for you by your parents at that time, because we didn't have enough information about anything. So if you were good in academics, first choice you had after matric (class ten) was engineering, and then medical. Those are the two most favourite careers, not even law. So I went to medical.

I went to Purushottam, a prominent and reputed inter-collegiate theatre competition in Pune. Many of us have come from there, including Vikram Gokhale, Jabbar Patel and myself. So I continued theatre in college. As I told you, I was sent to medical college; even admission was taken by my father. I didn't know how to take admission. During those five years, I started thinking on my own, at the end of which I decided, now that I have become a doctor, if I at all I have to practise, I have to do post-graduation and I will do psychiatry or I will do general practice. I wanted no other specialization. And one of the reasons that I think was behind my choice was that both literature and theatre, as well as psychiatry, deal with human emotions, unlike any other profession. And in fact both are rich source of information about human emotion.

So I took psychiatry but all (my) formal education was based on cognitive logic. Human life is full of emotions. You may get information from a book, but you will truly understand that information if you know literature, cinema or if you have experience of life, because human logic is not cognitive logic. Human logic is combined, cognitive and emotional, and that is why there, in that logic, three and three is not necessarily six, it can be anything but six.

After all, what is literature, what is theatre, what is poetry? All this is product of the mind. Whatever you want to do comes from your mind – whether you want to run away or want to fight (when you see danger). Your mind works first, and then your limbs. So the whole charger is mind; unconscious and subconscious are projected more in literature because it is not possible to project them in real life as you grow old. As a child you express emotions as they come to your mind – if you feel angry you will be angry, if tears come you will cry. As we grow older, especially in our culture, we are taught not to express our emotions. If you can conceal your emotions, that is called maturity, emotional maturity. In his book, *Inner World*, psychologist Sudhir Kakar talks about ego development, and says that in our culture, sacrifice is considered the greatest virtue. It is an achievement to sacrifice, which is not considered so in American culture at all. It (American culture) is achievement-oriented, their concept is to look after oneself first: swarth karo, phir parmarth karo (look after yourself before you seek greater good). But in our culture, your priorities shift from self to children. So if you don't achieve your ambitions, your children should.

So in my case, my connection with theatre was both curricular and non-curricular. In fact I would like to say that cognitively I am not intelligent. I find it difficult to understand by reading; if the same thing was taught by my teachers, I understood better. Reading those medical books, I understood I was meant for physical exercise rather than this reading. I was scared … how will I finish reading these books? And unlike current times, there was no respect for intellectually challenged or autistic persons. I would say at home … *mujhe samjhta nahi hai* (I don't understand). *Pehle hota tha, thappad khao aur padho* (get slapped and get down to studying).

So I found my own solution, because I realized that my reading doesn't help but a teacher explaining it helps me to understand better. So I went to the library. There was a side advantage to that – a myth developed that I was very studious, because I visited the library every day. What I did is, I chose one corner of the library, took a book and from there I watched my friends who were enjoying reading their books. If you could diagnose from their non-verbal behaviour, most studious students were using highlighter and ruler to mark important portions. While reading a student would smile, indicating he has understood. For about forty-five minutes or one hour, he would concentrate. After forty-five minutes, his position would change. That was the time I would get up and go to that student and say, '*Chai peene chalein*?' The poor chap was hesitating to take a break. He wanted to wait for that moment when someone would ask him, because he would otherwise feel guilty. So what I did was controlled provocation. Over a cup of tea I would ask him what he had learnt. In this process I made friends with a lot of seniors. That's how I did my medical studies.

During this time I continued doing theatre. Now there were advantages and disadvantages to doing theatre – some teachers liked it, some disliked it. Secondly, one had to remove the stigma attached to failure. And it was revealed to me in medical college that failure actually meant you were a good student. I was therefore one of the best students. Because medical studies were so tough, once you have faced failure there, you would never be afraid of anything in your life.

First important experience of life is that you have faced failure and learnt to cope with it ... then life is full of success.

Nirupama Kotru: It's like the first scratch in your car!

Mohan Agashe: Yes! Jabbar Patel and a group of people joined a theatre group and we liked to do plays for state productions.

Nirupama Kotru: You did *Ghasiram Kotwal* (one of Vijay Tendulkar's acclaimed plays) in the 1970s?

Mohan Agashe: It was in 1972. Originally it was an amateur theatre production. And there was a big controversy. Big means very big.

Nirupama Kotru: Some people in Pune objected to the portrayal of Nana?

Mohan Agashe: Arrey, you don't know? There were two kind of controversies. First the play was performed for an amateur-level competition; it didn't win any award. Then, when it was being performed for a state-level competition, the president of the association came and told us that this play is said to be anti-Brahmin, so it can't be performed. You have to stop the shows. So we left en bloc – sixteen of us – and we formed our own group. Then there was another production, there they went to court. Finally Balasaheb Thackeray supported the play, and it could be showed.

The second, much bigger controversy was in 1980, when the play had to travel to Berlin. Vasant Sathe, the then I&B minister, said that the play is a distortion of historical events and shouldn't be allowed to go abroad. Well, that gave us publicity that we could have never dreamt of.

Nirupama Kotru: Really? I thought Sathe had a reputation as an amenable and liberal-minded person.

Mohan Agashe: He was. It was all the ministers, people around him, who conveniently had or had not watched the play, but wanted it to be banned anyway.

Nirupama Kotru: When did you first meet Shyam Benegal and start doing films?

Mohan Agashe: There are many struggling actors but I didn't have to struggle. My first film was also with Sai Paranjpye. She wrote a play on which a Marathi film for children was based, called *Nirupama aur Pari Rani*. Nirupama is a little girl with polio, and is home bound, and makes friends with all the characters in the book who actually come into her life – Peter Pan, Pinocchio, Cinderella. That was my first film, and it was made in Kolhapur.

After *Ghasiram Kotwal* in Pune, there wasn't a single theatre or film person who hadn't seen the play, from Satyajit Ray to the Bengalis … Shekhar Chatterjee, Ajitesh Banerjee, Utpal Dutt … and Shyam Benegal.

After *Ankur* (1974), Tendulkar was writing a screenplay for Shyam, for *Nishant* (1975). There are four brothers (in the film) … all of us were doing theatre Amrish Puri, Anant Nag, Naseer and I. Actually, have you seen the film *Hello Dolly*?

Nirupama Kotru: No, who acted in it?

Mohan Agashe: Barbara Streisand. So, even Barbara Streisand had to audition before she was selected. You see, I hadn't suffered enough (*smiles*). But I got the role because of theatre. Anyway, I was happy doing one film a year, as I was working in a hospital and I liked the work.

Once you are born in Pune, generally your education is in Pune. And once you are born in art-cinema orbit, or parallel-cinema orbit, you move only in that orbit – from Shyam Benegal to Govind Nihalani, to Jabbar Patel to Goutam Ghose to Satyajit Ray (*laughs*). And any new film-maker who doesn't want to pay good money, (but) who wants good people.

So I kept on doing that for a few years, with occasional appearances in minor roles in Bollywood films. My break came with *Trimurti* (1995), as the main villain, and my biggest fortune was that it was the first flop of Subhash Ghai (*laughs loudly*). And I was saved from becoming Sadashiv Amrapurkaṛ or Amrish Puri. Otherwise I would be doing only that (villain's roles in commercial films).

This way, I could continue with my medical profession and my acting. Because I was doing these kind of films in the seventies and eighties, festivals became normal for me, film festivals. Seminars became normal for me because of my 50 per cent thinking ability, when teaching. But the real benefit came when I realized how films can be used for better teaching, particularly teaching psychiatry. And not only films, theatre too. One of my playwright friends, Satish Aher, wrote two phenomenal plays, one is called *Mahanirvan*, a black comedy about death, and the second, *Begum Barle*. This has become my admission test. Anyone wants to do psychology-psychiatry has to know these.

So with Shyam Benegal I did *Nishant*, I did *Manthan*. Then he dropped me like a hot potato.

Nirupama Kotru: Why is that?

Mohan Agashe: I still argue with him about this. Because I didn't belong to the Bombay camp, Satyadev Dubey camp. And he actually replaced me with Amol Palekar; Amol stole my role.

Nirupama Kotru: Which film?

Mohan Agashe: *Bhumika* (1977). Amol was not part of his camp, he was Basu Chatterjee camp, but because of Dubey, Amol entered Shyam Benegal camp and I was thrown out. So anyway, by then, Goutam (Ghose) had cast me, then Satyajit Ray ... (*laughs*). So I was happy.

Nirupama Kotru: You did *Sadgati* (1981)...

Mohan Agashe: Yes, and meanwhile I made some foreign friends. In 1979, I did a small role in Andrew Victor McLaglen film, *The Sea Wolves*, in which Gregory Peck, Roger Moore and David Niven acted. I had one scene with Trevor Howard.[1] Then I did *Mississippi Masala* (1991) with Mira Nair. And then, interestingly enough, a Malaysian man of Chinese origin, living in Canada, making a film on an Indian widower set in Montreal, cast me in the role of an Indian widower running a hotel. It was called *Seducing Maarya* (2000). With Nandana Sen. This film will not be shown

1 *The Sea Wolves* was a World War II film released in 1980, based on the fictionalized adventures of Calcutta Light Horse, a regiment of the British Indian army. Mohan Agashe plays a brothel keeper.

in India, because it has all taboos – it has incest, it has father-in-law–daughter-in-law relations, gay relationships (*laughs*). Very interesting film. His (director's) name was Hunt Hoe.

Meanwhile, fortunately again, the Marathi film industry became very rich. For about fifteen years, it survived only because of Sumitra Bhave. Because Jabbar Patel and Amol Palekar vanished from Marathi films. So it was only Dada Kondke on one side and Sumitra Bhave on the other. Consistently making films. Sumitra Bhave trained all these film-makers doing well – Umesh Kulkarni, Sachin Kundalkar, Mangesh Joshi, Varun Dawalekar. Especially rural people like Nagaraj Manjule and Makarand Mane; they are making such good films now. So I came back to Marathi, and I did films with them. Especially this film *Astu* (2013).

Nirupama Kotru: That phase was required in cinema, because if you didn't have parallel films, cinema would have gone down a completely different path.

Mohan Agashe: Those ten years (the seventies), all over India, both in theatre – Habib Tanvir, Vijay Tendulkar, Girish Karnad – and in films – Shyam Benegal, Mrinal Sen, Girish Karnad, B.V. Karanth – they came with low-budget, parallel films, which, till TV came, was a good substitute for the awful cinema we had. And once TV came, it became very difficult for this cinema to get an interested audience. So all of them turned to television – Ray, Mrinal, Goutam – everybody made TV serials. So, the whole crowd of parallel filmwalas came to television.

And then when digital came, the whole face of audio-visual medium changed. So those ten glorious years, the world was small, everybody knew everybody else.

Nirupama Kotru: Theatre–film linkage was strong.

Mohan Agashe: Film festivals were great because everybody knew everybody.

Nirupama Kotru: It must be an interesting community, of people who read literature.

Mohan Agashe: It was a manageable community ... '*Chhota parivar, sukhi parivar*' (small family, happy family).[2]

Nirupama Kotru: Vijay Tendulkar was quite a dominant force in that decade.

Mohan Agashe: No doubt, all film-makers for whom scripts were written by Tendulkar became big – Jabbar Patel, Ketan Mehta, Shyam Benegal, Govind Nihalani. So many of their films were written by Tendulkar – *Nishant*, *Manthan*, *Ardh Satya*, *Sardar*.

At one point, Tendulkar was hired by Ray for writing exclusive scripts for Ray's films. They met, they talked, and both of them decided that it would be better if they wrote their own scripts. I'll show you a letter written by Ray, requesting me to act in *Sadgati*. All these people who send me twenty-page contracts, I show them this letter and say, 'Your twenty pages don't cover what he said in one.' Now these are slavery contracts (idea for which) came from hiring slaves in Africa or China.

---

[2] Also a family planning slogan of the 1970s.

SATYAJIT RAY

1-1 Bishop Lefroy Road, Calcutta 700020 7 July 81

Shri Mohan Agashe
1212 Shukarwar Peth
Subhas Nagar, Lane 4
Pune.

Dear Mohan Agashe:

I have been making enquiries about you, and was grieved to learn that you were in hospital with a spinal complaint. I do hope you have fully recovered by now.

The reason for my enquiry was that I would be very happy if you could play one of the two leading parts in my one-hour Hindi film of Premchand's story SADGATI which I am making for Doordarshan. For you it will involve about ten day's shooting in a village in Chhattisgarh, plus a day in the studio in Calcutta. The shooting will be done in the first fortnight of September. If it comes to that, I could come down to Bombay some time in August for a more detailed discussion. In any case, I shall send you the script as soon as possible provided you are in a position to accept my offer.

Please let me have your reaction as soon as possible.

With best regards.

Yours sincerely,

Satyajit Ray

SATYAJIT RAY

1/1 Bishop Lefroy Road. Calcutta 20. 15th Aug 81

Dr Mohan Agashe

Dear Dr Agashe

Here is a copy of the English version of the script. It will give you an idea of what you are supposed to do. You will play Ghasiram the Brahmin.

The Hindi translation will be ready around the 24th/25th, when I will send it along to you.

It would be most convenient if you could arrive in Raipur on the 1st of September. One of our representatives in Bombay will go to Poona & see you. He will arrange for your train ticket. Please keep yourself free for at least a fortnight.

I'm off to Raipur this evening to pick the locations & will be back on the 20th. If there is anything you are not clear about, please let me know.

Yrs sincerely

Satyajit Ray

P.S. I hope you're completely cured of your ailment.

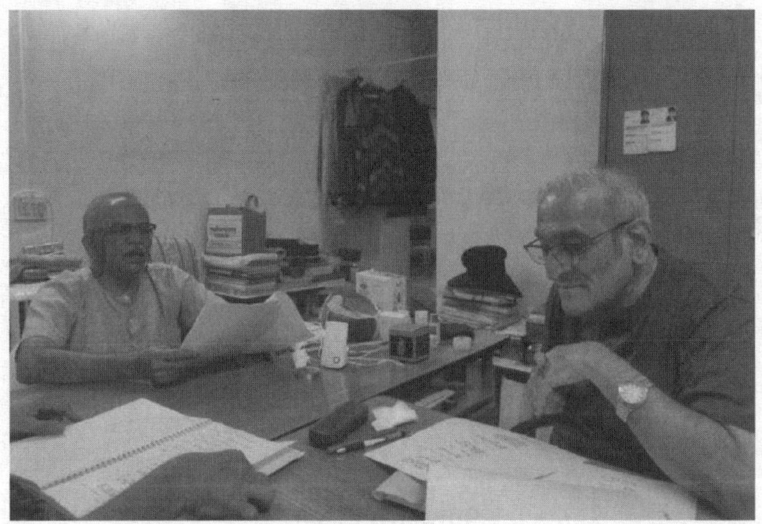

(Mohan Agashe rehearsing a scene of *Outhouse* with a co-actor)

Nirupama Kotru: With Ray you did *Kissa Kathmandu Mein* as well.

Mohan Agashe: Yes, first I did *Sadgati* and *tarpore* (Bengali for 'after that') he turned to television. He wrote *Satyajit Ray Presents* – thirteen beautiful short stories – and *Kissa Kathmandu Mein* (1986–87). And then he wrote a film for his son Sandip, which Sandip shot after Ray passed away, called *Target* (1995). Like Sumitra's last script, I acted in Ray's last script. Om Puri and me, and Bangladeshi actor Shampa Islam.

Nirupama Kotru: In the early days Doordarshan had good quality, they had not joined the commercial bandwagon. Later it completely deteriorated.

Mohan Agashe: Yeah, yeah. But now thanks to (smart) televisions, we can watch more films (on OTT). My shot is ready. Now let's resume the shoot (of *Outhouse*).

Storyteller Extraordinaire

A Conversation

Subhash Ghai

This is a transcript of an interview with Subhash Ghai conducted at Whistling Woods, Mumbai. Over the course of an hour and a half, Subhash-ji reminisced about his childhood, his love for telling stories, and his journey from the FTII to the film industry. Subhash-ji spoke at length about the art and craft of film-making in the 1970s.

Nirupama Kotru: Subhash-ji, let's start at the beginning. How did you come into films? How did you choose this career?

Subhash Ghai: My father was a dental surgeon in Delhi. After partition he came to Delhi, to Chandni Chowk. I was born in Nagpur, I studied there up to fourth standard. My parents brought me to Delhi in fifth standard; around that time, I started taking interest in stories. My mother used to tell me to read the Bhagavadgita. I wouldn't read the complete Bhagavadgita but I would read its stories. I would come straight to the moral of the story. That's how my interest was born in story writing.

After studying in Sanatan Dharm High School, Delhi, up to eleventh standard, I went to Vaish College, Rohtak, and I graduated in commerce.

My father wanted me to do chartered accountancy but I did not tell him I wasn't interested. Those days we were under pressure, we couldn't tell our parents what we really wanted to do. But when I went to hostel in Vaish College, I had the freedom to pursue my interests. I joined theatre and other activities of the cultural club, whatever was offered, dance, drama, music, etc. I used to write, direct and act; I took part in every kind of cultural programme. My father allowed me to participate in these activities and I brought a lot of trophies home.

After I finished B.Com I came to Delhi. My college principal met my father at a party in Delhi and told him that your son is brilliant in arts; send him to Bombay. My father was shocked, 'How can he do movies! I had sent him for doing B.Com!' The principal said, 'No, no, forget it, his heart is in the arts.'

Then my father called me and said, 'If you want to go to films, go through proper training, since you don't know anyone in Bombay.' So he sent me to the FTII in Pune. I was quite thrilled. I thought, let's enter the field and see what develops. They offered me the acting course. Throughout my two years there, I was more interested in watching other departments like sound department. I enjoyed watching world cinema, other cinema. I learned in FTII that there is more to cinema than Raj Kapoor. I knew only about Hindi films earlier; there I came to know about different styles of films, but my core was always storytelling.

Nirupama Kotru: You have written a lot of films for yourself, as well as for others. For example, you wrote *Khan Dost* for Dulal Guha…

Subhash Ghai: I'm coming to that. So I came to the film industry after FTII in 1965, through the Filmfare Talent Contest with Rajesh Khanna.

Nirupama Kotru: Rajesh Khanna was with you?

Subhash Ghai: No, he was not in FTII, but he was in the same contest. He got the films, I didn't (*smiles*). My struggle started. But I had an inner power, my best friend was Dale Carnegie. So I tried to be a likeable boy everywhere, tried to get connected to senior people. I got a few roles in films like *Aradhana* (1969) and *Umang* (1970), small roles.

Nirupama Kotru: *Umang* was not a small role, you were one of the lead actors in an ensemble cast, weren't you?

Subhash Ghai: Yes. I did 5-6 films as a hero but I never enjoyed them. While acting I felt that the dialogues are someone else's, the story belongs to someone else, the singer is another person, I am only lip-syncing to the song. What am I doing, other than being in front of the camera, and speaking the dialogues sincerely? I don't own any part of this creation. It is then that I understood the reality of film-making – the star gets the credit for what is not his.

I was not happy. Also I did not get good directors at that time. So I started talking to people – this is how the story should be. One of my co-actors, Mr Bhalla, he knew many producers. He told one producer, 'Subhash narrated a story idea yesterday.' The name of this producer–director was Prakash Mehra, a very famous name in the 1970s. He called me and said, 'I want to hear from you the full story, the idea of which your friend has shared with me.' I narrated the whole film to him. He loved it and said, 'This story is mine. I won't hire your services as an actor, I have many stars, but I will take your story.' It was a story called *Aakhri Daaku*, released in 1978. He took Vinod Khanna and Randhir Kapoor as lead actors. He gave me a very good price at that time for the story, the equivalent of Rs 1 crore of today! That felt good. I needed the money and I discovered that I was a good storyteller, I could tell stories.

Many directors started calling me – Dulal Guha also called me. It was Shatrughan Sinha's production. I narrated the story, it was called *Khan Dost* (1976). Dulal Guha liked the story so much, he took Rs 500 from his pocket, gave it to me and said, 'Don't narrate this story to anybody else, please.' I felt happy and I wrote six scripts for various directors including Feroz Khan, Harmesh Malhotra and others. Within a year and a half, I could sell six of my scripts to various directors. But then I felt no one could make the film the way I had narrated it.

The seventh script I wrote was *Kalicharan*. When N.C. Sippy called me, I said, 'I don't have a story, but I will tell you after one week'. After one week I told him, 'I have a story but everyone has rejected it, including Shatrughan Sinha.' Sippy said, 'Narrate it to me.' After hearing the narration, he said, 'It's a very good story.' After hearing the story for the second time, he said, 'Why don't you direct it?' I had never even been assistant director before.

Nirupama Kotru: You had never assisted another director, ever?

Subhash Ghai: No, never, but when I was telling a story, I was telling the visuals of the story, right? I would tell everything including lighting – there's a difference between normal lighting and film lighting. My narration was strong, so I told myself, 'This is good stuff.' Then I told the technicians, 'Listen, I have not directed a film before, I don't know technicalities but when I narrate the story to you, you will understand what I want.' I talked to the cinematographer, the sound recordist, I told them what I wanted. The first song I recorded was '*Ja re ja o harjai*'.

Nirupama Kotru: That song remains popular after all these years.

Subhash Ghai (*smiles*): The picture became a big hit with a lot of compliments from the critics. I wanted that whatever I do should be excellent. I couldn't do mediocre work. My colleagues with whom I had trained at the FTII were John Abraham, Adoor…

Nirupama Kotru: Adoor Gopalakrishnan was your batchmate?

Subhash Ghai: Yes, Adoor, Mani Kaul, Kumar Shahani were my batchmates. We used to watch videos, all of us used to discuss cinema, I used to listen to them but my bent of mine was always commercial cinema, mainstream cinema. I belong to the masses. I couldn't understand their language, how they were going to reach viewers. I was always fascinated by mainstream cinema; I wanted to excel technically even in mainstream cinema. I thought, 'How do we take mainstream cinema and raise its standard technically?' Because I was a student of cinema, I made some films in which I could do what I wanted. *Vishwanath* (1978) came next, then *Gautam Govinda* (1979). In 1978, I entered into production of films. I launched my banner Mukta Arts, our first film was *Karz* (1980). *Karz* gave me a lot of boost, and after that there was no looking back.

The major change came in 2000, when I went corporate. I had ten to twelve hits by then, and I wanted to establish my studio. I got money through the IPO. With the money I got, I made Whistling Woods, India's first film training institute in the private sector.

Nirupama Kotru: Apart from these changes you tried to bring in, like raising the standard of commercial cinema, bringing fresh techniques and technologies, etc., one of the things that stand out in your films is that the negative character, the antihero, the villain, is very powerful. Whether it is *Kalicharan*, or right up to *Khalnayak*…

Subhash Ghai: Indians are lovers of epics, we are born and brought up in an atmosphere where epics like the Ramayana and the Mahabharata are heard everywhere in our homes. There are always very good heroes, like Rama is the much-loved hero. But if you have noticed, our epics always had very powerful antiheroes, to make the hero look like god. If the night isn't dark, how will the light of the lamp shine bright? Being fond of epics and stories from childhood, I understood this.

The only person who can make your story interesting is a villain. That is why you have to spend time creating that character.

My strength and natural talent lay in storytelling rather than in characterization. Because of my ability to tell stories, I worked very hard on the characterization. I would spend ten to fifteen days building a character. Sometimes I would take up to fifty days just to create my main characters. I would sketch them, paint them, think about their personal lives, their traits, their likes and dislikes, their thinking, their backstory. Even if these things are not shown on the screen, as a director I must know my characters thoroughly. That this person has a backstory; this is his backstory, this is his philosophy, this is how he was raised.

I developed my own faculties. I was trained as an actor, I had a backup that gave me confidence. Till today, I devote more time to telling the story. Storytelling is more important than the story. We have the same stories – same Mahabharata, same Ramayana, we have heard the stories many times, 36,000 stories, but essentially the same. The human being is the same. Human life is clichéd … same jealousy, same emotions, same Nava Rasa. There is a child, he grows up, becomes a youth, becomes old, dies. This is repeated. If you read *Natya Shastra* it says the same things.

I was a very good reader. I would visit Delhi Public Library. I would read *Chandrakanta*. Children are attracted to their interests. I was interested in storytelling, so I read a lot. Technologies are changing … cameras changed, now you have digital cameras. My focus is always on writing, conceiving stories, conceiving characters. Cameras will change fifty times, main thing is what story you are telling.

Nirupama Kotru: I heard you say in an interview, in the context of *Pardes*, that you never wrote a character keeping a star in mind, rather you chose an actor who fits your character. You convinced Shah Rukh, 'You are a romantic character, you will be a matchmaker, but you will not get to romance the girl till the end.'

Subhash Ghai: Yes, Shah Rukh was very uncomfortable, fresh from success of *DDLJ*.

Nirupama Kotru: But what a lovable character that was … Arjun. One of Shah Rukh's best.

Subhash Ghai: Yes, because I was firm (*smiles*).

Nirupama Kotru: For *Kalicharan*, I believe the producer wanted Rajesh Khanna.

Subhash Ghai: I told the producer there is Shatrughan, but he hasn't liked the story.

Nirupama Kotru: He was your batchmate from FTII.

Subhash Ghai: Yes, but he didn't want to do the film. These things happen. One must understand how a star is born. Stars don't drop from the heavens. You make a character, people find that character lovable, and a star is made.

Nirupama Kotru: You made Shatrughan a star with *Kalicharan*, but I also remember *Hero* (1983) – what it did for the career of Jackie Shroff. That was huge. The way he burst upon the screen.

Subhash Ghai: Also *Khalnayak* (1993)

Nirupama Kotru: Yes, the way you brought fact into fiction, what Sanjay Dutt was going through at that time. You also spoke about reforming the prisoner, what V. Shantaram had said in *Do Aankhen Barah Haath*. I remember that song, '*Aye maa, tujhe salaam, apne bacche tujhko pyare, Ravan ho ya Ram*'. That every antihero deserves a chance.

Subhash Ghai: A mother sees her son as a hero.

Nirupama Kotru: Yes, you really touched a chord with Indian audiences, the mother–son bond is something we have seen celebrated in our culture from Yashoda–Krishna to present times. The other thing that I find striking about your films is the villain. Such iconic characters and dialogues, like Ajit in *Kalicharan – Sara shahar mujhe Loin ke naam se jaanta hai*. You wrote these?

Subhash Ghai: Yes, the characters, the dialogues are all written by me. Also *Vishwanath … Jali ko aag kehte hain, bujhi ko raakh kehte hain…*

Nirupama Kotru: And Ranjeet's dialogue in *Vishwanath*: Once in a blue moon, kabhi-kabhi!

Subhash Ghai (*laughs*): Whenever Ranjeet meets me, he says I have done 800-850 films but your dialogues are what people remember even today, after all these years.

Nirupama Kotru: Then there is 'Bad Man' (nickname of a character from *Ram Lakhan*, 1989)

Subhash Ghai: Gulshan Grover is called Bad Man even today (*smiles*).

Nirupama Kotru: Does this come naturally to you? This sort of writing?

Subhash Ghai: (It's) because you are into it, no? You must know the grammar of writing. It's one thing to just write, but knowing grammar helps. What's the difference between an engineer and a foreman? Both are going to press a button to start a machine, why do you pay the engineer more? He knows more…

Nirupama Kotru: The emotional connect a director establishes with the audience in commercial cinema, can one ever achieve that in parallel cinema? You were talking about your batchmates…

Subhash Ghai: Art cinema is a thought. It's the mindset of the film-maker that he conveys. Fair enough. In commercial cinema, emotions are very important. Emotions connect the film to a poor labourer as well. '*Har karam apna karenge*' (a popular song from *Karma*, 1986) … it reaches the common man. Art cinema is intellectual. It conveys thoughts, maybe debatable thoughts. It's the point of view and perspective of the film-maker about the world, which is why it is respected by the elite. It's like literature. What's the difference between literature and bestsellers? There's a lot of difference between James Hadley Chase and *Wuthering Heights*. Sumitranandan Pant is different from Anand Bakshi or Salim–Javed. Expression is different, story is same – Munshi Premchand, Saratchandra. Many film-makers made Saratchandra's *Devdas* – Bimal Roy made it differently. Sanjay Leela Bhansali gave it a bigger canvas. Bimal Roy's version was internalized, lot was unsaid. Bhansali externalized the thoughts and emotions of characters. Bimal Roy I find mainstream, still artistic.

Nirupama Kotru: Among Indian film makers who influenced you the most? Was it Raj Kapoor? I remember you were called The Great Showman at one time, like Raj Kapoor.

Subhash Ghai: That was because of the canvas, the scale of my films. Plus the parties, the social life. I loved many film-makers. Mehboob Khan was a great film-maker, a great storyteller, he made *Mother India* (1957). It's still a textbook for me, a complete film. Raj Kapoor's was one kind of cinema – innocent boy, man on the street. Raju had his own niche. But look at the range of Mehboob Khan – he made *Andaz* (1949) and *Aan* (1952) also. I liked Satyajit Ray also, I liked Bimal Roy. I like Vijay Anand … he gave a lot of dignity to commercial cinema. What I liked about these film-makers is that they could never be vulgar.

Nirupama Kotru: Let's talk about the seventies, the decade in which you started a flourishing career as a director. What do you think about the films of that decade?

Subhash Ghai: In the 1970s there was an invasion of the mass audience. People came to their sense after euphoria of independence was over, they saw bureaucracy for what is was. People saw great disparity of wealth. The anger of the poor came to the surface – the country got freedom twenty-five years ago, but what did we get? Anti-establishment films started coming.

Films of the 1960s were about families, the 1970s brought action, angry young man, Amitabh Bachchan the star was born. A young boy grows up watching injustice all around, he abuses the government, opens fire inside parliament, opposes politicians … all the anger was expressed through cinema. The mood changed in the 1980s, people like Yash Chopra cooled down the audience, they brought poetic films to the screen. But thanks to FTII, parallel cinema thrived.

In the 1950s, when *Pyaasa* (1957) worked, the audience was more educated. They understood literature and poetry. Otherwise films like *Pyaasa*, *Neecha Nagar*, *Do Bigha Zamin* would not have worked. People who made films were educated, people like Bimal Roy were educated.

By the seventies, those who thought about the masses, not the classes, started making films. Prakash Mehra, Manmohan Desai, Salim–Javed – these guys gave birth to the anti-establishment child. The upper classes used to sit in the balcony, masses in lower and middle stall used to enjoy whistling. The educated audience in the balcony would visit the cinema theatre to watch the people in the lower stall – how they threw coins at the screen, how they whistled … (*laughs*) Then Shyam Benegal, Mrinal Sen brought good cinema. Because we were from FTII, we knew these films were good.

Nirupama Kotru: K.K. Mahajan (renowned cinematographer known for his work in the Indian parallel cinema) worked with you?

Subhash Ghai: Yes, he worked with me in *Kalicharan*. *Ardh Satya* came. Middle-of-the-road cinema. Film-makers who were from the Bimal Roy school of cinema – Hrishikesh Mukherjee, Basu Chatterjee, but the dominant cinema was cinema of violence, action, emotion, anger. In the 1980s love stories came back – *Hero*, *Maine Pyaar Kiya* (1989), *Love Story* (1981), *Betaab* (1983) … Yash Chopra brought mature romantic stories.

Nirupama Kotru: One thing I noticed about the seventies was the star system. How did you resist it? How were you able to make films on your own terms?

Subhash Ghai: My films didn't get a great opening. They did not do the biggest box office. My films survived for thirty years. Those who delivered blockbusters went away in six months to a year. Even today, *Karz* and *Kalicharan* are premium titles in my library. My films had longevity. My films didn't do that big current business. For example, *Qurbani* came along with *Karz* in 1980 and was a blockbuster. If we did Rs 30–40 business, *Qurbani* did Rs 100. But do you remember (much of) *Qurbani*? You remember *Karz* – it lasted longer, its songs and scenes stayed with people longer.

Because of my artistic taste and my being a student of cinema, I always tried to keep a balance, of my expression of cinematic language, as well as connecting with mass audience. You could say that I made films that would appeal to the masses as well as the classes.

Nirupama Kotru: Did this cause problems for you? Did you find financiers easily? Especially in initial times when industry was unorganized, there were lot of 'fly-by-night' operators, who were not really interested in films.

Subhash Ghai: This corporatizing of films has its own plus points and minus points. Like these corporate people who have come into the industry, they are handling cinema, they don't know cinema. TV series and web series are also coming. When corporate executives start choosing your subjects … I am not demeaning them … but it's not your job.

Nirupama Kotru: I agree, it would be a disaster. I remember the time when self-styled management guru Arindam Choudhuri conducted a market survey and thought he had hit upon the formula and ingredients for making a hit film. His film *Rok Sako Toh Rok Lo* (2004) was a disaster. It showed that doing an MBA and market research doesn't mean you can make a film.

Subhash Ghai: No research work can tell you whether a film will work or not.

Nirupama Kotru: There have been phases – creative side and financial side – the industry worked in a very haphazard manner in the seventies...

Subhash Ghai: It was an unorganized sector. The rate of interest was 36 per cent per year, for raising money.

Nirupama Kotru: My god, it must have been very difficult to convince someone to invest in your film, especially when you were not well established?

Subhash Ghai: I took funds for *Karz* at 36 per cent to begin with. Your film should have the potential to do well, then it was worth raising the money.

Nirupama Kotru: Did you have to convince distributors to take your film?

Subhash Ghai: If the distributors liked your previous film, they would buy the current one.

Nirupama Kotru: Did they have a say in the film? Did they interfere in the making of the film?

Subhash Ghai: Never. No distributor or financier could interfere with my film.

Nirupama Kotru: They never told you, add a song here, change the ending?

Subhash Ghai: Never. That is why I am no longer making films (*smiles*). I know two people will hit my film – one is the star, and one is the studio. These two are running the industry. I never got along well with either. (*Lots of laughter all around*) I told both, stay away from me, let me make my films. Both of them permitted me to make films for 25–30 years. Now they don't permit me (*smiles*).

Nirupama Kotru: It has been a tough path for you, but you have stuck to your path.

Subhash Ghai: Yes, take my recent film – *36 Farmhouse* (2022). My first condition to the studio was: you will not send your creative team. I will make a pocket play, drawing-room drama. The film was a hit. I took an ensemble cast, no star.

Nirupama Kotru: So are you planning to direct some more films?

Subhash Ghai: Let us see, I may, if I get a conducive atmosphere, but I will not make films on their (studio's) terms.

Nirupama Kotru: What about these web series?

Subhash Ghai: Now it is a new era, my company has to do something about it.

Nirupama Kotru: Looking back, you must be really proud that you created your own space.

Subhash Ghai: It's very satisfying. I never ran after money, never. I only ran after quality in my film. My mainstream cinema should be good. I never pretended that I was making award-winning films; I never made films for festivals. I never made films for awards or rewards; if they won awards, I welcomed it, like *Iqbal* (2005, directed by Nagesh Kukunoor) won a National Award. I was clear – my film should make money for those who invested in it.

Nirupama Kotru: Yes, critics should understand this aspect of making films – that they need to earn a return. I want to touch upon one more aspect of your craft – song picturization. How did you develop this faculty?

Subhash Ghai: I was very interested in music from my childhood, I love music. During the pandemic I wrote 30–40 songs, I composed music for them, I kept busy.

Nirupama Kotru: You had an ear for music, it was obvious to me as a viewer.

Subhash Ghai: Again, it's our epics, our culture. See, the Ram Lila is narrated through song. *Ram ko banwas, toh gaana, Sita se bichhadna, toh gaana, Ravan aaya, toh gaana* ... a song for every occasion in the Ramayana. Music is part of who we are as Indians.

Nirupama Kotru: How much did you influence your music directors? Did you have sittings for every film?

Subhash Ghai: Of course.

Nirupama Kotru: What did you enjoy working on? *Karz* was so popular, then came *Ram Lakhan*, *Hero* and others.

Subhash Ghai: I had a great rapport with all my music directors. I add music to my script – a violin will be played here, a guitar there, this guy will play folk music, this guy will bring element of bravery through music, this guy will bring empathy, etc. And then I share this with my music director. I have always created music through collaboration.

Nirupama Kotru: Whom did you enjoy collaborating with the most?

Subhash Ghai: I loved working with everyone, especially Laxmikant Pyarelal (LP) and Rahman. I learnt a lot from LP, I had a good tuning with A.R. Rahman, like in the film *Taal*.

Nirupama Kotru: You made Aishwarya (Rai) a star with *Taal*.

Subhash Ghai: I wanted to do my job, it's how you present your character, that's how stars are made. Not just *Hero* and Jackie, there were also Madhuri (Dixit), Manisha (Koirala), Meenakshi (Seshadri), Mahima (Chaudhry), Kareena (Kapoor), Katrina (Kaif) – all have done so well.

Nirupama Kotru: When it came to song picturization, were you inspired by anyone?

Subhash Ghai: When you yourself conceive a song, the picturization is decided at conception stage itself. Then the director conveys his vision to the lyricist and composer. Then it is easy for them to create the music. Like '*I Love My India*' (*Pardes*).

Nirupama Kotru: What do you think explains the pan-Indian appeal of films of the 1970s and of film-makers like you who were quintessential storytellers?

Subhash Ghai: If you know the people of India, if you have grown up with them, everyone will like your films, whether that person is from Bengal or south India or any other part of the country. What is your book about – people of cinema, craft of cinema or evolution of cinema?

Nirupama Kotru: It's about how the seventies was an important decade for growth of Hindi cinema.

Subhash Ghai: Intellectually the fifties was the best decade of Hindi cinema. The seventies was about cinema of violence – think of *Sholay* – it was a high-energy cinema.

Nirupama Kotru: Yes, I think violence was a recurring theme. Thank you, it was very fulfilling experience for me to talk to you about cinema.

Subhash Ghai: Good. I am happy to learn about your book. Writing is a good habit, it's a meditative habit. Keep writing.

'I Came to the Industry Because of Gulzar Sa'ab'

Memories of Cinema of the Seventies

Vishal Bhardwaj

Nirupama Kotru: Speaking about Hindi cinema of the 1970s, I was talking to Subhash Ghai and he was telling me about how directors in parallel cinema used to look down upon commercial cinema (his batchmates at the FTII were Adoor Gopalakrishnan, Mani Kaul and Kumar Shahani). Subhash Ghai made his own path. I remember Guru Dutt used to say, 'You can be self-indulgent and make a film for yourself. But what is the point? Neither did the audience enjoy, nor did the financier recover his money. That is one viewpoint we should respect.' Coming to middle-of-the-road cinema, its flagbearers in the seventies were Hrishikesh Mukherjee, Basu Chatterjee and Gulzar Sa'ab. I think you came in the industry because of people like Gulzar Sa'ab. Is that correct?

Vishal Bhardwaj: Yes, I came because of Gulzar Sa'ab.

Nirupama Kotru: Were you interested in music?

Vishal Bhardwaj: My father was a poet. He was in government service. He was a sugar (licence) inspector. But at heart he was a poet. He kept coming to Bombay. And started working with people like Laxmikant–Pyarelal, Usha Khanna, etc. As kids we used to come with him to Mumbai during our summer vacations. I think I was in Class 5 or 6 then.

Nirupama Kotru: You must have been fascinated by films. What year was this?

Vishal Bhardwaj: Yes. I think it was 1976 or 1978. I was eleven or twelve years old. My father had friends who were directors, like Mr Chand – he made films like *Shankar Shambhu* and *Dafa 300*. My father wrote songs for *Khoon ka Badla Khoon* and *Heera Moti*. The latter film was composed by O.P. Nayyar Sa'ab. So we met Nayyar Sa'ab as children. We attended the recording also. So I had that inspiration; I wanted to be a creator.

As for music, I could play any instrument I picked up. I had a banjo and my brother had a mandolin. In Class 5, for the first time, I played the banjo in a school programme. The tune I played was a song from *Purab aur Paschim*: '*Purva suhani aayi re*'. I remember this film. I had watched it in a theatre. Manoj Kumar was a friend of my father's.

Nirupama Kotru: Yes, his *Roti Kapada aur Makaan* and *Beimaan* were the biggest box-office hits of their respective years, 1976 and 1978.

Vishal Bhardwaj: *Purab aur Paschim* was released in 1970. I was very young but I remember watching the film. I was only five years old.

Nirupama Kotru: It was remarkable year. Vijay Anand directed *Johny Mera Naam*, Chetan Anand had *Heer Ranjha*, and Dev Anand had *Prem Pujari*.

Vishal Bhardwaj: Yes, I remember. I was so young. I have watched both *Johny Mera Naam* and *Prem Pujari* in the theatre. *Heer Ranjha* had beautiful, brilliant music.

Nirupama Kotru: The music must have attracted you. Songs usually go deep into our psyche.

Vishal Bhardwaj: There was a time before college when I was confused about what I wanted to do with my life. When I decided to become a composer, the music scene had become very bad. The 1980s. *Himmatwala*, etc. It was a time of crass music, perversion of music. One day a friend of mine came home and said, 'If Gulzar Sa'ab can survive in this industry, in such times, there is hope for people like you.' That stayed with me. Gulzar Sa'ab kept himself insulated from that atmosphere. He kept himself pure. And he kept himself relevant.

I remember Gulzar Sa'ab's film *Meri Apne*, which released in 1972. And the dialogues? I remember in Meerut, reciting the dialogues was common. '*Shyam se kehna Chhenu aaya tha.*' '*Meri kisi bhi ladke ko hath lagaya, toh mohalle ka mohalla jala kar raakh kar doonga.*' I remember these dialogues even today. The kind of gangs they showed in *Mere Apne* existed in Meerut.

After that came *Parichay* and *Koshish*. I remember some cousins of mine watched *Koshish*. And they came and described this scene to me. There is a dialogue. Both boy and girl are deaf-mute. Someone asks the boy, 'What is your name?' He picks up a green chilli. And puts it at the feet of the person asking. That person figures out that the boy is called Hari Charan (green + feet). I remember this dialogue, it's difficult to forget.

Around this time, Gulzar Sa'ab started coming inside the system. *Unka jo cinema tha, middle-of-the-road cinema tha*. I loved all kinds of films, though. I loved *Amar Akbar Anthony*. I really enjoyed *Kalicharan*. When we were young, there was no distinction. We just enjoyed everything. All kinds of cinema. When *Vishwanath* was released, a friend of mine came and told me, 'You know, the next film of Subhash Ghai is going to be called *Gavaskar*.' He was convinced that all films of Ghai were named after cricketers! We all believed him. Seriously, Alvin Kalicharan and Gundappa Viswanath were heroes for us cricketers. We watched *Vishwanath* in Eves Theatre, Meerut.

For me, seventies cinema is more about Gulzar Sa'ab: *Khushboo, Kinara, Aandhi*. He made a lot of films in that decade, one film every year. Jeetendra got a different image in *Khushboo, Kinara, Parichay*.

Nirupama Kotru: It was a big change for us to see Jeetendra with glasses, etc. Before that, he was famous for dancing. He was called Jumping Jack, if you remember.

Vishal Bhardwaj: I remember the songs of his films. What lovely songs of Gulzar films. Like '*Ek hi khwab*' from *Kinara*.

Nirupama Kotru: During that time, Gulzar Sa'ab wrote beautiful songs for other film-makers as well, like for Basu Bhattacharya's 'marriage trilogy'. There's this lovely song by Bhupendra and Sulakshana Pandit in *Griha Pravesh*: '*Boliye, surili boliyan*'. *Anubhav* songs are also brilliant, all written by Gulzar Sa'ab. Which other films did you enjoy during childhood?

Vishal Bhardwaj: *Amar Akbar Anthony* was such a good film. I remember it clearly. *Sholay* also I remember. I was ten years old. I remember one thing. When it was released, it didn't do well. The craze increased gradually. I remember Menaka Theatre of Meerut, that's where it was released. And Amitabh Bachchan's dance in that film became popular with the youth of that time. His movement, raising his arm and dancing, became very famous. Also, my father brought the HMV LP record home. It had dialogues of *Sholay*.

Other films like *Roti Kapada aur Makaan, Shor* I remember. *Roti Kapada aur Makaan* had this scene where the heroine brings a roti hidden in a cap. Probably it is that song '*Mehangai mar gaye*e'.

I also remember Jaya Bachchan in *Shor* – the song was '*Zara sa usko*'. And that scene and song where they are riding a cycle non-stop. The song was '*Jeevan chalne ka naam*'. Very inspiring. '*Ek pyar ka nagma hai*' from *Shor* had a sad and emotional connect. Also I distinctly remember that scene in *Shor*, in which the noise of the city disturbs the hero, he finds it deafening. It left a deep impact on me. Let me demonstrate. (*Vishal opens the window. And you can clearly hear the noises from the street. It's very noisy and windy.*) I had to install soundproof glass in this window. So I remember *Shor* distinctly. His son cannot hear, Manoj Kumar also cannot hear.

Nirupama Kotru: People like Manoj Kumar understand how audience will relate to a scene or song. Look at '*Main na bhoolunga*', the emotional connect is so strong that I watched it recently and couldn't help the tears. Such drama!

Vishal Bhardwaj: Look at these scenes, how good they are. Would you consider *Shor* a commercial film? I think because of the songs, and the casting, it is treated as commercial. Otherwise, it was an artistic film. Similarly, Gulzar Sa'ab's cinema. He used mainstream actors. That helps reach the audience.

Nirupama Kotru: Hrishikesh Mukherjee also used stars.

Vishal Bhardwaj: Amitabh Bachchan did only one film in the eighties which was an art film, *Main Azaad Hoon*. At least you remembered his effort. But I feel Amitabh Bachchan was the one really responsible for new wave cinema not flourishing. Commercial cinema took a turn for the worse in the eighties. Had he wanted, he could have stopped the deterioration of cinema, he could have changed the course of cinema. The way music was affected as well was sad.

Nirupama Kotru: The book on R.D. Burman (Anirudha Bhattacharjee and Balaji Vittal) talked about this. I also wrote an article about it, 'RD Burman and the horrible '80s' (*Vishal laughs heartily*). Amitabh Bachchan finished music.

Vishal Bhardwaj: His films were more about action. Melody was finished. Yes, I think the seventies was a golden period for music, for films. Because so many different kinds of films were made, which I really enjoyed. Whether it was *Amar Akbar Anthony*. Or *Shor*. Or Gulzar Sa'ab films. *Achanak* was also made in the seventies. There was one more film. Yash Chopra's film with Rajesh Khanna. Rajesh Khanna plays a criminal, a murderer. I think it was called *Ittefaq*. A songless film (*Ittefaq* released in 1969).

Nirupama Kotru: Sunil Dutt had made *Yaadein* in the sixties, he is the one and only character in the film.

Vishal Bhardwaj: There was a film called *36 Ghante*, directed by Raj Tilak in 1974. It was a remake of an American film, *The Desperate Hours*. We used to steal a lot of films. Because we didn't know that one day, people would come to know the truth (*laughs*). We can call it inspiration, but it's actually chori. For example, take the Amitabh Bachchan starrer *Benaam* (1974). It picked up the plot from a Hitchcock film, *The Man Who Knew Too Much*. Another film, *Imtihan* (1974), was a remake of a Tamil film which was a copy of *To Sir With Love*.

Nirupama Kotru: Do you remember B.R. Ishara and Rehana Sultan? They made a number of films.

Vishal Bhardwaj: Rehana started with *Dastak*. *Chetna* was an adult film. I remember the poster; her nude image became a talking point. It was also a big thing those days. I think we have regressed since.

Nirupama Kotru: Actually that (in)famous poster only showed her bare legs.

Vishal Bhardwaj: Really?

Nirupama Kotru: Yes, *Chetna* was actually a sentimental love story. The protagonist, a professional hooker, says to the hero that I'm a bad person, don't try to change me ... I drink, I smoke. The hero (Anil Dhawan) accepts her as she is, doesn't leave her hand till the end. There's such a beautiful song by Mukesh, '*Main to har mod par*'. The film was actually narrating a woman's perspective. She wants to be left alone and doesn't want to be domesticated.

Vishal Bhardwaj: I didn't remember the story, such a different and bold subject for its time. Very nice subject. Progressive. We have regressed since then. I think the change came in the year 2000 again. Post late 1990s, the change started. *Maachis* came in 1996. Anurag Kashyap and others followed. In fact, with *Mission Kashmir*, Vidhu Vinod Chopra went down a different path. Parallel cinema started coming back. That was good. When I look back, the seventies was actually a golden period, after that we regressed quite a bit. And we again became progressive in our choice of subjects in the late 1990s and 2000.

Nirupama Kotru: I was telling Subhash Ghai that he brought back the antihero with *Kalicharan*.

Vishal Bhardwaj: Correct. After Dev Anand who would play a black marketer, etc., in the fifties, the sixties became romantic with Shammi Kapoor and Rajesh Khanna. In the seventies, interesting characters came back. Of course, there was Amitabh Bachchan with his 'angry young man' image. But also characters played by Shatrughan Sinha. That was interesting. We had more shades of grey in the seventies.

Nirupama Kotru: The seventies were interesting because you had bad boys, bad girls. Good boys, good girls, all kinds.

Vishal Bhardwaj: There used to be a character called the vamp. Has this word come from vampire? (*Laughter all around*)

Nirupama Kotru: I think it's in Indian concept. Otherwise, it used to be called a gangster's moll. But these 'Mona darling' kind of characters are unique to our films of the seventies.

Vishal Bhardwaj: There was always a seduction song. Like '*Raat akeli hai*'. When the heroine started doing this songs, the vamps went away.

Nirupama Kotru: The change came from *Tridev* (1989). I wrote about it in a piece called *'Dancing Divas'*. When Madhuri Dixit, Sangeeta Bijlani and Sonu Walia danced to '*Gajar ne kiya hai ishara*', performed item songs in the climax of that film, the vamp was buried forever.

Vishal Bhardwaj: Bindu and Aruna Irani were quite popular.

Nirupama Kotru: Bindu played many different, interesting characters in the seventies. Like in *Abhimaan*. She's a friend to Amitabh Bachchan, makes his drink.

Vishal Bhardwaj: I remember Bindu in *Imtihan*. Because of that song '*Ruk jana nahin*'. It's nice to go down memory lane. And remember these films I watched in my childhood. The problem with seventies' cinema is that 50 per cent of the films were lifted from Western films. Film festivals were not easily accessible those days. It wasn't easy for everyone to go there. So film-makers used to attend these festivals, copy the plots and make films. *Majboor*, a very popular Amitabh Bachchan film, was inspired by two English films, *Zigzag* and *Cold Sweat*. *Dharmatma* was based on *Godfather*.

By the 1980s it became more blatant. People used to pick up videocassettes and just copy the entire film, scene-by-scene. At least in the seventies it was not that blatant. Luckily, art cinema or parallel cinema was on a different level altogether. Films like *Ankur*, *Nishant* or *Ardh Satya* which came a bit later in 1983. *Albert Pinto Ko Gussa Kyon Aata Hai* released in 1980. Saeed Mirza, Shyam Benegal, Govind Nihalani. But commercial cinema lifted hugely from Hollywood. The audience would never come to know at that time. They weren't bothered if it was original or not. There was no other entertainment, if you remember. Cricket also … there was no way of watching matches. We didn't have TV. So obviously we craved entertainment.

Bobby is also from the seventies. I remember it vividly. What music! I believe if *Mera Naam Joker* had not flopped, commercial cinema in India would have been something completely different. After *Mera Naam Joker*, Raj Kapoor never made that standard of artistic film again. Khwaja Ahmed Abbas wrote his story and screenplay. *Bobby* was very enjoyable. But the failure of *Mera Naam Joker* was a big, big setback for commercial films. I think Raj Kapoor was so badly wounded that after that, everyone went into making formula films. Nobody wanted to experiment.

Bobby was so popular that we had the Bobby motorcycle and Bobby T shirts. Bobby motorcycle was a big hit. It's a very small motorcycle. My friends had it, and it was nice to roam around college on that bike. What a trendsetter it was.

Nirupama Kotru: Raj Kapoor shot in Kashmir for *Bobby*. The hut in the song '*Hum tum ik kamre mein band ho*' in Gulmarg is to date called 'Bobby Hut'. Kapoor came back to Lolab Valley, Kashmir, to shoot parts of *Ram Teri Ganga Maili*. *Bobby* was a craze in Kashmir. There was a singer called Kailash Mehra Sadhu, a very popular Kashmiri singer, part of the Holy Trinity of Kashmiri music along with Shamima Dev Azad and Raj Begum. Raj Kapoor almost gave Kailash Mehra Sadhu a break. Unfortunately, she couldn't take the opportunity to go to Bombay at that time due to family reasons.

Vishal Bhardwaj: Wow! How many nice things we finally talked about today.

Nirupama Kotru: If there is one film of Gulzar Sa'ab you would like to talk about, which one would you pick?

Vishal Bhardwaj: *Aandhi*.

Nirupama Kotru: Before you start, can I tell you an anecdote which Gulzar Sa'ab shared with me?

Vishal Bhardwaj: Please do.

Nirupama Kotru: (In Gulzar sahib's own words) ... I had taken dates from Suchitra Sen and was under pressure to finish writing the script. I had about ten to fifteen days to finish it. So I booked myself a room in Akbar Hotel, Delhi (now an office of the Ministry of External Affairs), and started writing. I would write for hours, non-stop. This young waiter would watch me write. He was a sweet boy and served me with love and affection. On the last day he finally asked me, 'Sir, what do you keep writing all day with a bolster on your lap? I told him it was the script of my upcoming film. He was very happy. I told him, 'Beta, you have served me with such love and affection, what's your name?' I wanted to do something so that I would always remember his dedication to his job. He said his name was JK. And that's how Sanjeev Kumar came to be named JK in the film.

Vishal Bhardwaj: Nice. *Gulzar ki Aandhi* – that's how trade papers and film magazines announced the film. The film, Gulzar Sa'ab's boldest film. For someone like me, this was unimaginable and gave me tremendous courage to express myself through cinema. The day I watched *Aandhi*, I made Gulzar Sa'ab my guru. I felt that only someone of his stature could pull off such a sensitive subject.

There was tremendous speculation about the title. Some thought it was meant to rhyme with the surname of the PM whose election had been declared null and void by a brave judge of the Allahabad High Court.

What left a deep impression upon me was that Gulzar Sa'ab tone was never judgemental at any point in the film. Nor did he try to hide the unpleasant realities of life in politics. Neither Aarti nor JK is depicted as being at fault for their marriage breaking up; instead, it is circumstances that drive them apart. Aarti's adversaries ogle at her; at one point an opponent (Manmohan) suggests that he would concede to her if she agreed to sleep with him. In fact this infuriates JK and he rushes to bash up the guy. Despite his distaste for politics, JK respects Aarti's choice of career and bids her a warm farewell in the end.

The music of *Aandhi*, created by Gulzar Sa'ab's friend Pancham, is so beautiful that it is difficult to emulate their high standards. Simply outstanding. Gulzar Sa'ab shot many portions of the songs in beautiful locations of Kashmir like the Pari Mahal, Cheshmashahi in Srinagar as well as the ruins of Martand temple and Avantipora. I revisited some of these locations such as Martand temple in *Haider*, but I shot the film mostly in Chillai Kalan as the film needed a stark landscape.

I have tried to emulate my guru by depicting the reality of relationships, especially between men and women, with sensitivity. Another speciality of Gulzar Sa'ab is how he draws the best out of children. Remember Master Raju in *Kitaab* (1977), *Khushboo* (1975) and *Parichay* (1972)? I have tried to treat children with the respect they deserve, in my films like *Makdee* (2002) and *The Blue Umbrella* (2005).

Somewhere, perhaps at a subconscious level, I must have absorbed a lot of Gulzar Sa'ab's ideas of film-making. I feel blessed that I continue to have his guidance in every film that I make, from my breakthrough film as a composer, *Maachis*, to my latest film as director, *Khufiya* (2023). Every creative collaboration with him leaves me enriched.

Duvidha

Mani's Dilemma

Rajat Kapoor

At twenty-eight, I had been out of the film school for a year.

It had been a good year. I had assisted a film-maker that I had wanted to learn from. There was a long way to go; I had not even started out, so to speak. But in my mind, I was already an accomplished and much acclaimed film-maker, travelling to international film festivals, collecting awards.

One stupid thing came into my head one day: The film that I would make perhaps in another five years … would I want to remake it twenty years later? Just daydreaming…

At that point in time, I didn't even know if I was going to ever make a film. And yet I was already contemplating doing a remake. Why not? Hitchcock made *The Man Who Knew Too Much* twice, and Ozu remade his *Floating Weeds*. So, in all fairness it was a valid fantasy.

I was in the front seat of a cab, going from Altamount Road to the NFDC office in Worli. I think that is where we were going. This was my second stint as an assistant – after Kumar Shahani's *Khayalgatha,* I was lucky enough to be working as an assistant on

Mani's *Nazar*. Mani Kaul was in the back seat when I was busy with this inane fantasy.

I turned around and with absolute impunity that only a twenty-eight-year-old can have, asked Mani, 'Mani, if you were to remake one of your films, which one would it be?'

'Why, why do you ask me that?'

'No ... just...'

Mani was quiet for some time.

I turned away and looked at the sea on my left, feeling that I might have pissed him off.

After a while, he said, '*Duvidha*.'

He did not elaborate.

I did not ask him any more questions either.

Why did he say *Duvidha*?

How did he want to reimagine it then; some sixteen–seventeen years after he had made the film?

What would he have changed?

Why *Duvidha*?

It's almost the most perfect Mani Kaul film.

संयोग की बात कि उस खेजड़ी में एक भूत का निवास था।
(As it happens, a ghost resided in that tree.)

Pretty early in the film, we see frozen moments.

Stills.

There is movement of the camera in the film, precise and articulated.

But the overall feeling is of stillness. Her stillness.

Once she gets to the haveli after her marriage, her destiny is fulfilled. This is it.

Nowhere to go now ... nothing to look forward to.

विवाह के खर्च का सारा हिसाब सँभलाकर ठीक तीज के दिन मुझे
व्यापार के लिए दिसावर जाना है। ऐसा शुभ मुहूर्त फिर सात बरस
तक नहीं है। पर गँवार दुल्हन को इस शुभमुहूर्त की बात
सुनकर रत्तीभर भी खुशी नहीं हुई।

(After wrapping up accounts of the wedding ceremony,
on the day of Teej festival, I have to leave for the foreign
land on business. Such an auspicious date won't come
again in the next seven years. The boorish bride was not
in the least bit pleased to hear about the auspicious date.)

Within three days of their marriage, the husband decides to leave for business for five years.

What takes over her life is the white walls of the haveli that is her home now.

The camera celebrates those white walls.

The many shades of white, and the stillness all evoke the summer heat of this village in Rajasthan.

It smells of the desert land.

Nothing moves.

Till there is a storm.

मैंने तो भूत होकर भी कोई बात नहीं छिपाई।

(I didn't hide anything at all, despite being a ghost.)

The storm in her life is the ghost, the 'bhoot', who fell in love with her at first sight, who takes the shape of her husband – and while the husband is gone on the business trip, the impersonator takes his place at home.

He has achieved what he wished for.

But the honest ghost has a dilemma.

He cannot bring himself to fulfil his desire without letting her know the truth.

He tells her everything – how he fainted after getting a glimpse of her face, fell in love with her, how he met her husband, deceived the boy's parents and is here now.

He passes his '*duvidha*' on to her.

She is not sure what would have been better – to know this truth, or to not have known it.

She doesn't say anything.

अभी तक यह बात मेरी समझ में नहीं आई कि यह भेद प्रकट होने
से ठीक रहा या प्रकट न होने से ठीक रहता। कभी पहली बात
ठीक लगती है और कभी दूसरी!

(I am yet to understand whether things are better now,
since the truth has been revealed, or were they better
earlier? Sometimes the former feels right,
and sometimes, the latter!)

And then, in a most stunning sequence of shots – when the camera moves down from the white walls to their faces – both looking away from each other, struggling with the storm of possibilities within. Sometimes in mid-shots, sometimes in extreme close-ups.

No one says anything.

There is nothing to be said.

Finally she moves to him and sits next to him. We see the back of her head, covered in the pallu.

Then she puts a hand on his shoulder.

After a few seconds, he puts a hand on her arm.

Then the camera goes slowly towards her. Her head is bent, and then she looks up at him.

The camera sees her eyes in extreme close.

Stillness? What stillness?

The stillness is external – but it takes you into the characters' souls, and nothing is at rest there.

You feel the thunderstorm that is going on within.

It is because of the stillness outside, the lack of movement, lack of gesture, lack of expression (and performance), that lets us witness real movement – the delirium in their souls.

We are supposed to be in the business of moving pictures

Yes, pictures move, we know that, we have spent over a century trying to make that point.

The camera could be performing all kinds of acrobatic acts, and the actors could jump up and down till they turn blue in the face, but is that the proof of the pudding? Oy! Yeah, look at us – we move!

But do the pictures move you? That is the real test. That is what cinema should be doing.

Moving its audience by illuminating them through an experience.

This scene in *Duvidha* moved me like very few things I have seen on screen.

Sometimes one experiences that feeling in films, when confronted with landscape – shots of nature.

After the acute suffering and trauma and the extreme pain of characters' lives, sometimes a film-maker cuts to a shot of the mountains, or a river, and suddenly it gives a perspective to human suffering, and I find that very moving.

Here, the faces of these two actors serve as that landscape.

We are able to witness directly, the tumult and joy of the human soul.

There is no stillness there.

भला, मैं दूसरा कैसे हुआ?
(How am I the 'other' man?)

And the performance of the lead actor, Ravi Menon, is one of the best in any of Mani's films.

Very often his actors get confused by this diktat to not act, and it might result in a seemingly wooden performance, a flat delivery of lines – which of course Mani encouraged.

But if those words are without a spirit, they really fall dead.

Ravi is alive in each of his steps – there is no planning there, no method, but a sense of being which is authentic and palpable.

Both as the husband and the ghost, Ravi Menon has so much truth in each one of gestures.

And he just knows how to work in tandem with Mani and Navroze's (Contractor) camera – when to turn and walk back, where to stop and look into the camera.

Nothing seems practised, prepared.

It is as truthful and as free flowing as the film itself.

सहेलियों का झुंड, भाई–भतीजे, तालाब का किनारा, गीत, गुड्डा–गुड्डी का
खेल, झुरनी, आँख–मिचौनी, धमा–चौकड़ी ये तमाम सुख छिटका कर
इस पति का हाथ थामा।

(My gaggle of girlfriends, brothers and nephews, songs,
playing with dolls, hide-'n'-seek, boisterous play – I left
behind all these pleasures to accept my husband's
hand in marriage.)

And then there is the sound design.

I watched the film again recently – some fifty years after it was made, and I marvelled at the sound.

It blows in and out like a breeze.

The celebratory folk songs, actors' words, night cricket, footsteps – every little sound enhances the magical space.

This is our world, the world that we are very familiar with – and yet it has an otherwordly aura.

The everyday sounds of this village seem to come from very far, as if they are covering the distance created by memory.

How did he even manage that sound mix, when there were just two magnetic tapes to bring the whole soundscape together?

पर तुम इस क़दर परेशानी में क्यूँ पड़ गई? जन्म देने वाले माँ–बाप
भी जब नहीं पहचान सके तो भला तुम कैसे पहचानती?
इसमें तुम्हारी कुछ भी गलती नहीं है।
(But why are you so worried? When biological parents
couldn't recognize their own son, how could you have?
You are not to blame at all.)

Of all the film-makers of the Indian New Wave, and later, Mani aligned himself to literature more than anybody else, which seems almost counterintuitive.

Mani who was the most rebellious, he needed a something of a start; something from which he could move away, so to speak.

Mohan Rakesh's *Uski Roti* and *Ashadh ka Ek Din*, Vijaydan Dheta's *Duvidha*, Muktibodh's poems, Dostoevsky's *A Gentle Creature* (remade as *Nazar/The Gaze*) and *The Idiot*, Vinod Kumar Shukla's *Naukar ki Kameez* (*The Servant's Shirt*)

These were not adaptations for the screen, rather his improvised response to the text.

But he was always seeking the essence of the original, which got him excited in the first place.

And finally, there is another personal anecdote about this film.

Those days, National Award–winning films were shown at Vigyan Bhavan.

Our father, being the film buff that he was, would go and watch these films.

He took us along, me and my brother, to watch *Duvidha*.

This was 1974. I was thirteen years old, my brother was twelve.

Who takes their kids to watch a Mani Kaul film at that age?

Our father was not a film scholar; he was a regular guy who ran a printing press.

And still he got Mani's films.

Why was there (still is) such resistance to Mani Kaul's films?

Are we so used to a singular kind of narrative that we are thrown off by anything departing from that path? Anything that is even a step out of the well-established way of telling tales is labelled 'arty'?

Really?

No wonder we as a people have become so opposed to the very idea of diversity.

Everyone must sound the same, look the same and buy the same brand.

The familiar makes us feel safe.

Guilty Pleasures

The Masala Entertainers of the Seventies

Sriram Raghavan

Blood-red dripping titles set to a pulsating Kalyanji-Anandji score … a boxing match followed by a murder and then another. A smuggler in lock-up befriends a convict planning an escape. And a midnight prison break … all in the first ten minutes. Much before I drank my first beer, I had tasted Vijay Anand's heady cocktail of thrills, music and cinematic cool. I walked out of Vasant Talkies, screening *Johny Mera Naam* (1970), like a happy drunk walks out of a bar.

I grew up in Pune, when it was called Poona. Though my parents were film buffs, as kids we weren't allowed to watch too many films. But the magic of cinema was everywhere … radio ads, newspapers, hoardings and of course the single-sheet posters…

All directors, sometimes humbly, insist that they are still students of cinema … and will keep learning for as long as we are making films … but where did all that film education begin? For me it was on the way to school. At strategic crossroads, there would be posters and billboards. NOW SHOWING. NEXT CHANGE. COMING SOON. The hand-painted graphic posters with a buffet of bewitching images were portals though which one could escape into different universes.

Alankar, Rahul, Alpana, Victory, Mangala, Neelayam, Apsara, Sonmarg, Ratan, Shreenath, Minerva, Empire, Westend … every cinema was within cycling distance. And of course, Apollo, which was closest home and my temple. A highlight of Apollo was the attached Irani café which could be accessed by regular customers and cinema audiences who came out at the interval. From a strategic seat at Café Apollo one could listen to the soundtrack of the film playing inside. And when the crowd rushed out during the interval for their samosas one could already see the fate of the film on their faces. Though those days we were generous viewers. Those who lived in Rastapeth, Poona, will also remember the Interval Bhel House.

I remember waiting nervously for my dad to finish his shave so I could get my report card signed, as Ameen Sayani's voice boomed on the radio. '*Yaadon ki zanjeer mein lipta hua inteqam ka shola*.' It was the radio spot for *Zanjeer* and I mentally booked tickets as my dad was scolding me. My classmate Hormuz sang '*Yeh laal rang kab mujhe chhodega*' when he saw his report card. The tuck shop near my school had a mirror at the washbasin which said '*Rajesh Khanna, kangi na karna*'.

Do Gaz Zameen ke Neeche, The Cheat, Jugnu, Bond 303, Gehri Chaal, Chhupa Rustam, Bandhe Haath, Loafer, Pocket Maar, Bindiya aur Bandook, Raakhi aur Hathkadi, 36 Ghante, Kaala Sona, Dhund, Warrant, Gambler, International Crook, Beimaan, Dus Numbri, Apradh, Anhonee, The Great Gambler, Memsaab, Double Cross … I better stop before I sound like the Anand Bakshi song in *Ek Duje Ke Liye*.

There are at least a hundred definitive mainstream films from the 1970s and luckily there are books and theses on them. But there are a whole lot of films that won't make any top ten lists, and yet magically transport you to a time, an era, a memory. And when, occasionally, you find another person who loves that obscure film as much, you feel you've made a new friend. Just yesterday, I made a couple of innocents enjoy L-Ps funky brilliance in '*Ae hero, chal aage badh*' from the Dharmendra starrer *Keemat*, directed by Raveekant Nagaich, one of my unsung heroes.

I read comments on YouTube closely and marvel at how septuagenarians come alive describing which hall they saw which movie at what age. I often forget everything about a movie I watched last week but the films I watched in my childhood are permanently archived in my mind. And good prints too.

The single-screen cinemas with their crowded cycle stands, garlanded houseful boards and black-marketing aunties who would pull out tightly folded tickets from one bosom and stuff your money in the other, are a thing of the past. With every cinema hall going, so many of our memories get destroyed … Please check your longings before leaving the cinema.

The French auteur Jean Pierre Melville, who has made some fantastic crime thrillers, said, 'I take care my films are never realistic.' The mainstream Hindi film-makers of the seventies would have heartily agreed.

The seventies began with some defining films. *Johny Mera Naam* was the blockbuster followed by Manmohan Desai's *Sachaa Jhutha*, which again cast a magical spell on me. Imagine … a poor trumpeter arrives in Bombay to eke out a living and has his suitcase stolen the same day. Barefoot and bewildered, he lugs the trumpet, looking for a place to spend the night when suddenly the traffic stops and he is welcomed to a huge fancy-dress party and treated like royalty. And even as he is taking it all in, he is tapped by a Zorro lookalike. Among the film's many highlights is a sequence where the undercover cop Mumtaz spikes Rajesh's drink on a boat. The sheer joy I get when the boat lurches and the drinks get exchanged … The film has many other items including a mad jewel heist with people freezing when they sip spiked Coca-Cola. And if I ever build a mansion, I will definitely include a fridge which opens into a passage leading to my basement den.

Manmohan Desai repeated the hit Rajesh Khanna–Mumtaz jodi in his next, *Roti*, which had nothing to do with Mehboob

Khan's hard-hitting 1942 film. This *Roti* was apparently inspired by two newspaper items Mr Desai read on the same day. One was about a man who killed another for a single roti. The other was about how a death-row convict in Mexico was rescued from the gallows by a chopper attack on the jail. It's a sheer marvel how these disparate items were strung into a compelling action adventure musical romance comedy ending with unexpected pathos and tragedy.

Why do I love *Dharam Veer* in spite of the atrocious shot of the horse jumping over the castle wall? Or do I love it because of shots like that. If you don't like *Dharam Veer*, I suggest you check your pulse. *Dharam Veer* was Dharmendra's father's favourite film. Mr Desai is probably the only film-maker in the world who had four blockbusters releasing in the same year (1977). I remember his interview before the release of *Naseeb*, where he said, 'Story *zara* weak *hai*, but my film is full of happy things…'

Shetty, an icon of the seventies, waits at the door of a speeding train … It's dark but you notice the bloody knife in his teeth … He jumps into a river and swims ashore to a waiting car. The train reaches Bombay Central and a sweeper knocks twice, then opens a first-class coupe … There's a dead man inside. Titles … Animated, designed by Bhim Sain who later directed *Gharonda*.

The Train (1970) will confound you with its simplistic plotting but you will not even realize it till the film is over. The murder mystery is replete with masks and disguises and the investigation has an Enid Blyton quality. But it doesn't matter … it's got '*Meri jaan maine kaha*', one of the greatest R.D. Burman scores ever, and displays the director's gleeful approach to storytelling.

Ravi Nagaich is unknown to audiences today. And yet he worked with the biggest stars and created some too. A cinematographer, he turned director with *Farz*, a spy drama that catapulted Jeetendra to fame. He repeated the character Agent 116 in *Keemat*, which had Dharmendra busting an international human-trafficking ring. And a few years later created another snazzy spy Gun Master G 9 in *Surakksha* starring Mithun

Chakraborty as the spy. Its success spawned a sequel *Wardat* when such things were unheard of.

Nagaich dabbled in various genres including horror and children's films. He shot his own films and his style comprised jazzy jump cuts and graphic, surreal frames. He also made his stars run for their money. Literally. Stars just keep running during the songs. Check out '*Gulabi aankhen*' from *The Train* or '*Phool hain baharon ka*' from *Farz*.

A few days back, by sheer chance I bumped into Deepak Bahry, the director of the original *Agent Vinod*. Both Saif and I had loved the film and we decided to borrow the title and reinvent the character. The original had all the Bond tropes including gadgets and girls. My favourite gadgets were a golden gun that fired in reverse, killing the shooter. And a coat which fires from the armpits when the owner is asked to 'Hands Up'! I loved those things but didn't dare go there. Maybe I should have.

Three spy films I loved as a kid and still do in varying degrees are *Humsaya*, *Shatranj* and *Prem Pujari*. All three flopped at the box office and are alive today only because of their music. So many average or rank-bad films are alive purely because of the songs. And watchable thanks to the combo of deliciously imaginative choreography, costumes and sets. And the stars. We fought over our favourites. *Apna Desh*, directed by Jambu, is one of the seventeen consecutive hits of Rajesh Khanna and is a romp if you can sit it out. Mumtaz plays a coconut vendor in the first half and a sexy blonde post interval.

Raj Khosla has made some seriously good films including family sagas, fine noirs and dacoit dramas. But my guilty pleasure is *Shareef Badmaash*. I still remember the poster. Dev Anand stepping out of a jail. The tagline said: Was he a gangster in the garb of a good man or a good man in the garb of a gangster? The opening is maddeningly convoluted as a bunch of thugs chase an elusive jailbreak artist. Dev Anand is Rocky, the expert prison breaker or is he? As a Dev Anand lover, I didn't care then that the film is nowhere near the great *Johny Mera Naam* with the same lead pair.

James Hadley Chase was essential reading for schoolkids who had finished with the Enid Blytons and Hardy Boys. It was also essential reading for the film writers of the time. I totally enjoyed the unknown director Madhusudan's *Ek Nari Do Roop*, based on *The Wary Transgressor*. Shatrughan Sinha played the classic Chase hero, hurtling to his doom, and the femme fatale was Rashmi Dhawan, another FTII graduate. The film failed. Interestingly, Yash Chopra's *Joshila* too borrowed heavily from the novel and also flopped.

Firoze Chinoy was an FTII graduate who adapted Chase's *Tiger by the Tail* as *Kashmakash*, with Feroz Khan, Rekha, Shatrughan Sinha and I.S. Johar. The cringe factor wins over the thrills but there are minor rewards to seek in the sets and décor. Salim–Javed adapted *Come Easy Go Easy* into *Aakhri Dao* about a safe cracker who wants to go straight and almost succeeds, till the baddies catch up and there's a Dharam Sankat in the climax, inspired by an O. Henry short story. The Jeetendra–Saira Banu starrer was one of their lesser successes. A Chase novel was like a movie you could watch in your head, whilst reading it. I often wonder why his stories didn't work when they were adapted into movies.

Firoze Chinoy's serial-killer film *Shaitaan* again starred Shatrughan Sinha, this time with Anil Dhawan, also known as Pramod Sinha circa 2018. *Andhadhun* had a scene where Pramod Sinha, played by Anil Dhawan, watches *Shaitaan*, where he is at a club watching '*Dil to mane na*'. Bindu dances as RD's pulsating 'tribal' beats crash into big-band jazz.

The hero is trapped in a nightclub and he knows it. The cabaret dancer possibly reads his mind and sings the breathless '*Bachke kahan jaoge*'. *Yakeen* (1969) is a Bond-inspired caper with a *Face-Off / MI* kind of premise with Dharmendra being replaced by a lookalike Hindi-speaking foreigner named Garson. The director Brij was another director whose films I used to look forward to,

Brij's breakout success was *Victoria No 203*, where the key in the wig is more important than the key in Hitchcock's *Notorious* or *Dial M for Murder*. Inspired by a similar device in Chase's *There's a Hippie on the Highway*, Brij fashions a zany caper with two lovable ex-cons, Ashok Kumar and Pran, and Saira Banu sporting a moustache for a large part of the film. The first twenty minutes introduce an array of villains out to double cross each other. The writer K.A. Narayan was quite a master at these plots. Also responsible for *Chori Mera Kaam*, which is near impossible to narrate. The MacGuffin here is a book named *Chori Mera Kaam*, the autobiography of a master thief that the villains are trying to get their hands on, so they can imitate the crimes. Once again, a potpourri of grand dens, outrageously obvious disguises and mad song situations. My favourite is when the Commissioner of Police (Pran) disguises himself as a notorious hitman and disarms the crooks as he promises to unmask the policeman in the gang, which is himself. If that makes any sense at all.

Where there's Pran, there's life. That was the tagline on the poster of director Chand's *Dharma*. The actor plays a wanted dacoit who moves to the city and assumes the guise of a Nawab and befriends his neighbour, the police commissioner played by Ajit whose life mission is to nab Dharma. The cat-and-mouse games between the two kept us hooked. The qawwali '*Raaz ki baat keh doon toh*' ensured a jubilee for the film.

Where there's Pran, there's disguise would be an equally apt tagline for *Jangal Mein Mangal* whose USP was Pran in a triple role. An elderly college professor, a hippy student in his class and an elderly spinster who sings too! Needless to say it took immense perseverance and persuasion to convince my parents that I needed to watch these films very badly.

I wonder what my father thought about me when I dragged him on a Sunday to Bhanuvilas cinema to watch *Badhti Ka Naam Dadhi* (1974). An eccentric millionaire wills his wealth to the man with the longest beard. Kishore Kumar, the actor, producer and director played several roles in the film and also appears before the titles to warn viewers that this may not be their cup of tea. Was this venture made as a tax write-off, or was it Kishore Kumar satirizing the films of his time? As an adorer of Kishore Kumar, I loved the film and recommend it highly. Unfortunately only a bad copy exists on YouTube.

Nagin, *Apradh*, *Gaddaar*, *Buddha Mil Gaya* and so many more including one disaster film, which I love, that a haloed reviewer panned as 'The Turning Brain'. I often watch excerpts and songs from these and occasionally find nuggets. Like Basu Chatterjee controlling the traffic as Amitabh and Moushumi cavort in the Bombay rains during '*Rim jhim gire sawan*'. I recently discovered that Iftikhar's office in *Deewaar* overlooking Marine Drive was Madan Puri's office in *Jab Andhera Hota Hai*. And promptly added it to my collection of cheap thrills. By the way, which whodunit had the director's credit as Murdered by Hrishikesh Mukherjee?

My movie-loving uncle Padmanabhan was a professor of chemistry and watched every film that released. And when I asked him what he thought about the movie, his answer was the same. '*TERRIBLE*!' And yet he went the next week, often taking us along too.

So why did we like these movies?

I think because there's so much joy, colour and sheer happiness in them. They move from sensations to sensations. They don't worry logic as long as the emotion is strong. Of course, many of them are nonsensical and over the top, but they are also sincere and passionate. The outré set designs, the inspired costume choices and hairstyles cast their own spell. So do the villains, vamps, their getups, lairs and inventive torture chambers. Title sequences, interval points … they embrace me in a *yaadon ki baaraat*. Or maybe I am just stuck on the tracks like Shakaal in the same film.

I am guilty of taking money from my dad to purchase the same well-preserved notebook again and again to finance a movie ticket, but I definitely don't remember feeling guilty about slipping out of the tuition class and into one of the cycling-distance cinema halls.

Post Credit: A Guilty Pleasure in a Poona Cinema Hall

He was a student from Mauritius and a huge fan of Dev Anand which is why we became friends. One Friday morning he excitedly told me that *Solva Saal* was showing in Shri Krishna Talkies noon show.

I'd already seen the 1958 Raj Khosla directed romantic thriller, set in one night. I gave him directions to Shri Krishna Talkies and warned him that it's a shady cinema in the red-light district of the city. Mostly frequented by the working girls from the area.

Distance or a decrepit hall cannot stop a Dev Anand fan. My friend got a balcony seat and looked around. Yes, there were some garish ladies all around. Just as the newsreel got over and the theatre went dark, he saw a pretty woman enter the hall. She entered his row… and sat down right next to him. He got a whiff of her perfume. The movie began…

'*Hai apna dil toh awara*' – Dev Anand singing in a local train. (R.D. Burman played the mouthorgan for the Hemant Kumar number.) My friend was hooked on the film but equally distracted by the young woman sitting next to him. Their elbows touched on the armrest. She removed her hand first.

A dramatic scene with a b/w Waheeda Rehman. And then *suddenly* he felt her hand on his thigh. He very casually glanced at her but her eyes were focused on the screen. And then she started moving her hand up his thigh. Hell, she was feeling him up. Or was it heaven? His mind was a whirl and the movie a blur as she slowly settled her hand on his crotch. He sat frozen. Should he reciprocate? Would she demand money later?

Interval. The lights came on. He looked at her. She was beautiful. And then without even a glance at him she got up and out.

But her hand was still on his crotch.

And then he looked down.

There was a large rat sleeping on his corduroy trousers.

A Turning Point

The Beginning of a New Wave

Ketan Mehta

The 1970s marked a turning point in Indian polity, and cinema as a mirror to the society reflected this change.

By the beginning of the 1970s, the euphoria of Indian independence had faded, the idealism attached to freedom struggle had dissipated, the challenges and contradictions of a new democracy had surfaced, and widespread poverty and economic disparity were generating resentment and protests.

The golden age of Indian cinema helmed by the likes of Satyajit Ray, Ritwik Ghatak, K. Asif, Mehboob Khan, V. Shantaram, Chetan Anand, Raj Kapoor, Guru Dutt, Bimal Roy, etc., had also lost its mojo, and crass commercial concerns had taken hold of Hindi mainstream cinema.

Simultaneously, some of the national liberal arts institutions established during the Nehru era, like the National School of Drama, National Institute of Design and the FTII, had started churning out students who were trained with a global mindset and exposed to the best practices in their respective fields. Around the same time the National Film Finance Corporation was also created to give a boost to the more global creative urges of film-makers. Film societies were becoming popular in university campuses. The International Film Festival of India was making it possible for film enthusiasts from across the country to enjoy a wide variety of films in various genres and languages from all across the globe, not just Hollywood blockbusters. The institution of national and regional film awards was supporting the new trends in Indian cinema and film criticism was emerging to engage a growing discerning film audience.

It was a time of great churn when I joined the FTII immediately after my graduation in the early 1970s with a belief that cinema was the most powerful medium of expression ever created, with the largest possible reach and the power to become a catalyst in social/political change.

With Mrinal Sen's *Bhuvan Shome*, Mani Kaul's *Uski Roti* and *Ashadh Ka Ek Din*, Kumar Shahani's *Maya Darpan*, M.S. Sathyu's *Garam Hawa* and Shyam Benegal's *Ankur*, a new kind of cinema was emerging from the shadows of the mainstream commercial cinema. This cinema was more attuned to seeing cinema as a medium of creative, artistic expression and reflecting a social conscience.

Mainstream Hindi cinema full of melodrama and colourful romances was also going through a major change with films like *Zanjeer* and *Deewaar* and Amitabh Bachchan emerging as the angry young man of Indian cinema, reflecting the mood of the nation. And then there was the middle-of-the-road cinema of Hrishikesh Mukherjee, Basu Bhattacharya, Basu Chatterjee, Sai Paranjpye, etc., catering to the middle-class family audiences.

Major contributors to these changes were film directors, artists and technicians coming out of the film institutes. Actors like Jaya Bhaduri, Shatrughan Sinha, Shabana Azmi and others were having an impact, and trained technicians from film institutes were finding acceptance in the film industry. While earlier the only way to join the film industry was to become an apprentice to established film-makers and production houses, the new breed of artists and technicians were professionally trained in the art and craft, technique and technology of film-making and were exposed to cinema from all over the world, familiar with the work of great international film-makers like Stanley Kubrick, Vittorio De Sica, Godard, Resnais, Antonioni, Fellini, Tarkovsky.

The political scenario also was going through a dramatic change with imposition of the Emergency, stifling of independent voices and the resultant turbulence in the political and economic sphere. Multi-starrer extravaganzas like *Sholay* and *Amar Akbar Anthony* monopolized the popular cinematic universe.

While the pioneers of the so-called 'parallel' cinema continued with their oeuvre, with films like *Duvidha*, *Tarang*, *Nishant*, *Bhumika*, etc., the new energy in Indian film-making was also becoming visible in other parts of the country. Film-makers like Mrinal Sen in Bengal, Adoor Gopalakrishnan, John Abraham and Aravindan in Kerala, Girish Karnad and B.V. Karanth in Karnataka, were making films deeply rooted in their cultural ethos and socio-economic conditions of their respective regions.

With the lifting of the Emergency and holding of democratic elections, a new vigour and vitality also emerged in Indian cinema. Towards the end of the 1970s, with nearly a decade of the transformations sweeping through Indian cinema, a whole new generation of film-makers burst on to the scene with youthful energy. Film-makers like Govind Nihalani, Saeed Mirza, Kundan Shah, Vinod Chopra, Sudhir Mishra and immodestly myself – 'The New Wave of Indian cinema' had truly arrived. Along with a new breed of young, modern actors like Naseeruddin Shah, Om Puri, Farooq Shaikh, Smita Patil, Deepti Naval and others they changed the landscape of Indian cinema through innovative form and content, experimenting with new techniques and technology conjuring up new ideas and images.

And this new spirit was not only limited to Hindi cinema. Regional films and film-makers like Buddhadev Dasgupta,

Goutam Ghose in Bengal, Jahnu Barua in Assam, Nirad and Manmohan Mahapatra in Odisha, Girish Kasaravalli in Karnataka, Shashidharan, K.C. George in Kerala, Jabbar Patel in Maharashtra – these totally diverse and uniquely Indian films were consolidating into the 'New Wave' of Indian cinema over the next decade.

II

My journey into cinema also started in this period of churn. Graduating from the FTII in 1975, with a mindful of dreams, youthful zest and a desire to participate in changing the world through my medium of choice – cinema.

Fortunately for me, at that time, a unique experiment in communication called 'SITE' (Satellite Instructional Television Experiment) was being launched by ISRO (Indian Space Research Organization) to directly beam 'science education' and 'social awareness' television programmes into rural areas via satellite, bypassing the need for the infrastructure-heavy terrestrial network. For a largely rural and illiterate country this was a truly transformative use of new, emerging technology. So immediately after my passing out of the film institute, I got an opportunity to work in this path-breaking initiative and started working as a content producer for ISRO at Ahmedabad in Gujarat.

The new and emerging video technology was also breaking out of the studio mode with its requirement of heavy cameras and equipment. Lightweight, mobile cameras made it possible to go out and shoot in remote areas with agility.

With this freedom started my real learning, the exploration of real India. Travelling to remote villages, making content on real issues faced by real people. Bonded labour, caste atrocities, female infanticide, superstition, feudal attitudes, became the subjects of the television programmes, with scripts evolving with the involvement of the villagers, on subjects immediately relevant to them, with the villagers participating as actors, and the output being telecast directly to rural households. It was a heady experience, intense, exciting, disturbing.

And out of these experiences emerged the ideas for my first three films, *Bhavni Bhavai*, *Holi* and *Mirch Masala*.

My first film *Bhavni Bhavai* (in Gujarati), also titled *Andher Nagari* in Hindi, was based on a Gujarati folk tale called 'Achhoot no vesh' or 'the garb of the untouchable'. The story revolved around a humiliating dress untouchables had to wear during ancient times to be instantly identified at a distance, and how finally it was discarded. It was a most blatant example of caste discrimination and exploitation. The script evolved using the vibrant folk theatre form of Gujarat called Bhavai, mixing it with the 'epic theatre' form of the German playwright Bertolt Brecht and iconic 'Asterix' comic books created by French artists Uderzo and Goscini. It was a musical costume drama with humour and action and with a large cast.

But who would fund such a project by a first-time director, on such a controversial subject? Undeterred, along with some film institute technicians, we formed a film cooperative society, and applied for a loan from the Film Finance Corporation, which later became the National Film Development Corporation, and managed a funding of rupees three and a half lakhs.

Wow, the journey had begun! The next step was to rope in actors. Friends from the film institute days – Naseeruddin Shah, Om Puri, Smita Patil, Mohan Gokhale, Benjamin Gilani, Suhasini Mulay – were approached to work in the film for free. They all willingly agreed for the love of good cinema. What an incredible ensemble of amazing actors!

And so we began filming, on remote locations, with minimum facilities, smallest possible crew, working round the clock, testing limits of endurance. Can you imagine all these actors, in intense summer heat, sleeping under the sky, on mattresses lined up on a terrace, using common toilets, eating local food from a common kitchen, without any make-up vans or personal assistants, helping each other to make this crazy film possible?

To top it, on the first day of shooting on location, in a Harijan basti, even before a single shot had been filmed, I, the director of the film, was bitten by a rabid dog. But the show must go on. So, for the next fourteen days I was visiting the local government hospital, first thing in the morning, to get a 'rabies shot' on my stomach, before embarking for the shooting. And so Om Puri started a joke. 'Why does Ketan Mehta make a film? Because he is bitten by a mad dog.'

Soon the money ran out, we begged and borrowed, robbed friends and family to complete the shooting in thirty days.

Fortunately, the film won many national and international awards, received a lot of critical acclaim and was showcased at numerous international film festivals across the world. And so, my journey in cinema started.

It was during the editing of the film at the film institute that the idea for my second film, *Holi*, emerged. Mohan Gokhale, the actor, read out a Marathi play *Holi* written by Mahesh Elkunchwar, about unintended violence on a college campus, reflecting the angst of the youth, suffering under an outdated, autocratic and corrupt education system in post-independence India.

During my ISRO days, while travelling in tribal areas, witnessing tribal dances which happened all around, I often wondered how cinema could break out of the two-dimensional screen and become an immersive experience. The new technology of silent, lightweight, 16mm film cameras just being introduced in India offered a unique possibility. As compared to the old 35mm cameras with their 400-foot film magazines which could shoot for only 4 minutes on one load, the new 16mm cameras could film for over ten minutes at a stretch. Since *Holi* was a play with limited number of scenes, in a single location, the idea of a new film form emerged. What if we could shoot each scene of around ten minutes in a single continuous shot? If we could choreograph the action and the camera in constantly moving action with large number of students going all around the camera, we could also generate an immersive experience, creating the illusion of the audience being an active participant instead of a static, passive spectator. It was crazy, audacious, verging on madness.

When some students at the institute heard of the idea, they proposed that we do it as a workshop with the students and so it was decided to shoot the film at the institute. We selected actual college students, with no previous experience of film, as actors, did a week-long workshop with them. It was a complex, extremely challenging shoot, and Jehangir Choudhary, an ace cinematographer from the institute, took up the challenge. And the entire feature film of nearly two hours was designed in eighteen shots. With so much of camera movement and so many characters in every shot, doing sync shooting was also extremely challenging. It was unheard of. Naseeruddin Shah, Om Puri, Deepti Naval, Dr Shriram Lagoo, Mohan Gokhale, Paresh Rawal, etc., lent their support by agreeing to participate in guest appearances in this crazy experiment.

Each shot was carefully choreographed and rehearsed with the camera. And in twenty days we completed the entire shooting, including a song which was also sung and shot in sync with the actors. Many of the young actors like Ashutosh Gowarikar, Aamir Khan, Amole Gupte, Neeraj Vohra, etc., went on to have long, successful careers in cinema.

The third film, *Mirch Masala*, though made in the mid-eighties, was conceived earlier and made in the same spirit. Though Smita Patil, Naseeruddin Shah, Om Puri, Deepti Naval, Raj Babbar, Suresh Oberoi, etc., were already well established, busy stars in mainstream Hindi cinema, they readily agreed to do the low-budget NFDC production. The story set in pre-independence India in a small village in Gujarat was about a feudal lord arriving in a village to collect taxes, getting attracted by a woman, Sonbai, played by Smita Patil, and demanding her submission, polarizing the entire village with some in favour of the woman being handed over to the lord, and a few resisting it. How the women of the village react to the situation and eventually unite to defy the exploitation formed the basic narrative.

Red chillies formed a crucial element in the film. When I went for location scouting, I realized that the chillies season was coming to an end and if we did not start shooting the film within a month, we would have to wait for a whole year. I rushed back to Bombay, dreading the prospects. But sometimes in life miracles happen. All these busy stars adjusted their commitments and accommodated their dates to do the film. The shooting was tough, with heat, dust and red chillies powder all around, but everyone cooperated enthusiastically to make the film happen. The film went on to win many national and international awards and was one of the first films to cross over and get wide international release.

III

It was a very exciting phase in Indian cinema, with a wide variety of themes, and experimentation with cinematic form. A whole new generation of brilliant actors and technicians and film-makers with courage and vision. It was truly a brave new wave of Indian cinema.

Since then the Indian cinema and media–entertainment industry as a whole has gone through many waves of transformations. The first was the arrival of colour television in India in the mid-eighties, with Doordarshan, the only television channel at that time, attracting many talented film-makers migrating to the new medium. Then with economic liberalization in the early nineties, the focus of film-makers shifted to the NRI audiences living outside India. At the turn of the century, with the recognition of film production as an industry, arrival of multiplexes, and entry of the Hollywood studios into India, the entire structure of film production and distribution got overhauled, drastically increasing the costs, changing the content and the entire process of film-making, and recently with new technology enabling streaming platforms, not only the content but also the film-viewing habit is changing dramatically.

Change is imperative and necessary but the only thing that is constant is the human desire to tell and share stories. So cinema will live on. These stories we see and share, influence us, unite us, inspire us, define us. They really make us who we are – humans.

SECTION V

End-credits

Twenty-Twenty

The Ones that Made It

Nirupama Kotru

Making lists is a futile task; brickbats invariably follow. There are bound to be a few gasps of shock, and the odd expressions of delight. In the immortal words of Anand Bakshi, whose film *Amar Prem* we finally included after a lot of debate (the film may not have been Shakti Samanta's biggest hit but it did make Pancham a star composer): *Kucch toh log kahenge, logon ka kaam hai kehna* (You can't prevent people from talking, so why bother?)

But my co-editor, Shantanu, is an inveterate list-maker, having in fact coaxed two of our contributors, Balaji and Anirudha, to write a book of the best fifty Hindi film songs. It does not get more dangerous and difficult than selecting fifty songs out of a bank of a lakh and more. In a country like India where everyone has a list of her own best fifty songs. Compared to that exercise, compiling this list was a breeze, though we did go back and forth a number of times. You can imagine how hard it was to arrive at the final list from one example: Shantanu considers *Anand* overrated and feels *Namak Haraam* deserves to be in the list more than *Anand*. I felt that the writing and music of *Anand* made it an obvious choice. So, *Anand* it was. Also, we started with ten films on Shantanu's insistence as he thought that twenty would lead to a few undeserving ones creeping in. However, he soon agreed with me that ten would be too restrictive for a decade that produced such an astonishing variety of Hindi films.

So, here goes. Our list of top twenty films from the decade, in chronological order of the year of release. These films represent different genres and different schools of film-making. We have tried to take a sample of work of well-established as well as upcoming directors of the era. Superstars as well as the girl/boy next door have been represented. Hopefully the reader will find something to her taste in our list. Feedback is welcome.

1. *Johny Mera Naam* (1970)

The year 1970 saw multiple releases by the talented Anand brothers. Dev Anand presented his directorial debut *Prem Pujari* and Chetan Anand released *Heer Ranjha* the same year. But it was brother Vijay Anand who wrote and delivered the biggest hit of the year, *Johny Mera Naam*, starring Dev Anand, Hema Malini, Pran, Prem Nath, Jeevan and others. The film was an entertaining crime thriller with a chartbusting soundtrack by Kalyanji–Anandji and Indeevar, which included Kishore Kumar's all-time hits '*Pal bhar ke liye*' and '*Nafrat karne walon ke*'. Dev Anand and Pran play brothers separated at birth who are united in the tearful climax, where they are forced to watch silently as their mother (played by Sulochana) is thrashed by the villain's henchmen. Highlights include mixed identities (Dev claiming '*Johny mera naam nahin*!' with some 'bishooms!' thrown in for good effect), a pretty thief with a conscience (Hema singing '*Mosey mora Shyam rootha*'), a seduction song (Padma Khanna in '*Husn ke lakhon rang*'), and I.S. Johar's hilarious triple act as Pehle Ram, Dooja Ram and Teeje Ram, for which he won a Filmfare award. The film has inspired many film-makers including Sriram Raghavan, whose debut film was called *Johnny Gaddar*.

2. *Anand* (1971)

Rajesh Khanna may have achieved stardom with Shakti Samanta's *Aradhana* (1969), but it was Hrishikesh Mukherjee who made the superstar immortal. *Anand* is recognized as one of the finest performances of Rajesh Khanna, who did complete justice to an author-backed role of a dying man who is determined to spread cheer all round, despite his failing health. Amitabh Bachchan held his own in the role of Dr Bhaskar (Babu Moshai). It is a well-known fact that Hrishikesh Mukerjee had modelled the happy-go-lucky character of Anand after his dear friend, actor–director Raj Kapoor, who had earlier acted as leading man in Mukherjee's 1960 hit, *Anari*. Gulzar's dialogues, including the B.R. Ambedkar inspired '*Zindagi lambi nahi, badi honi chahiye*' (a good life should be meaningful, rather than merely being long), have attained cult status. In a departure from his usual playback singer Kishore Kumar, Rajesh Khanna lip-synced to Manna Dey ('*Zindagi, kaisi hai paheli*') and Mukesh ('*Maine tere liye hi*' and '*Kahin door jab din dhal jaaye*'). Lyrics for this beloved Salil Chowdhury soundtrack were written by Gulzar and Yogesh.

3. *Hare Rame Hare Krishna* (1971)

Hare Rama Hare Krishna was Dev Anand's first topical film; he went on to make many more, such as *Des Pardes* (1978) about illegal immigration, *Hum Naujawan* (1985) about crime in college campuses, *Sachche ka Bol-bala* (1989) about corruption and the media, etc. *HRHK* portrayed hippies as good-for-nothing junkies, even vilifying them by suggesting that they were involved in crimes like smuggling of idols from temples. The world was not so close-knit those days as it is now, hence American 'flower culture' of the 1960s took nearly a decade to reach our shores, along with other global trends and trendsetters like the Bee Gees, the Beatles, ABBA and Boney M, all of whom influenced Hindi film tracks in the 1970s. Zeenat Aman made a sensational debut as Janice, the hippie avatar of a young girl called Jasbeer, who is the younger sister of the hero, a pilot with Air India (played by Dev Anand himself). Mumtaz plays a local Nepali girl and his love interest. The film was one of the first mainstream Indian films to be shot on location in and around the magnificent Swayambhunath Temple complex in Kathmandu. The viewer is hooked right from the opening shots of the city taken from the air quite imaginatively (picturized on Dev and his co-pilot who fly low over the city before landing, to the delight of locals). R.D. Burman delivered a magnificent score that captured the zeitgeist of the era, with Kishore Kumar's evergreen hits like '*Phoolon ka taaron ka*', '*Kaanchi re kaanchi re*' (a duet with Lata) and '*Dekho o deewano*', and Asha Bhosle at her delightful best in '*Dum Maaro Dum*' and '*I love you*' (both songs with Usha Uthup).

4. *Pakeezah* (1972)

Kamal Amrohi's magnum opus took fourteen years to complete, leading to serious continuity issues. He and Meena Kumari had separated during this time, and the 'tragedy queen' had taken to drinking heavily. *Pakeezah* opened to a lukewarm response; perhaps the visible ageing of the leading lady put off critics and audiences. It is widely believed that the sudden demise of Meena Kumari, plus word-of-mouth publicity, brought audiences flocking back to the theatres. However, Kamal Amrohi has disputed this account. As per his piece in *Gulfaam* magazine, April 1982, titled '*Kitaab-e-zindagi se chand waraq*', he said, '*Pakeezah* was released on 4 February 1972, and it was immediately received with a lot of enthusiasm … Meena Kumari died on 31 March 1972, fifty-five days after the release of the film. The fact that a big film continued to run in the theatres for that long alone signifies that it was doing well. Therefore, to insinuate that Meena Kumari's death was responsible for the success is not an astute observation. Instead, it was *Pakeezah* that immortalized Meena Kumari.'[1]

Whatever be the reason, *Pakeezah* was declared a super hit by all leading trade papers. The film had a brilliant soundtrack by composer Ghulam Mohammed, with background score by Naushad. Meena Kumari herself headed the costume department. The brilliant sets, costumes, music, dances by Lachhoo Maharaj and cinematography by Josef Wirsching helped re-create the lost world of tawaifs, one which has been copied by film-makers repeatedly since. Raaj Kumar's dialogue '*Aap ke paanv dekhe, bahut haseen hain*...' (I saw your beautiful feet...) became hugely popular. This is probably the most un-1970s like film of the decade, harking back to the sensibilities of the fifties. That it worked so brilliantly is testimony to the power of Meena Kumari's performance and the film's superlative music.

5. *Amar Prem* (1972)

Shakti Samanta was a master of storytelling. He was also one of the first Hindi film directors to successfully use colour film. *Amar Prem* was a remake of *Nishi Padma* (1970), starring Uttam Kumar and Sabitri Chatterjee, based on Bibhutibhushan Bandopadhyay's short story *Hinger Kochuri*. The eternal love in the title of the film goes beyond the usual love story tropes popular during the era; it denotes the love of a mother for her (adopted) child. Lata Mangeshkar delivered some of her most exquisite melodies for the film, such as '*Raina beeti jaye*' in Raag Todi and Khamaj and '*Bada natkhat hai re*', a recurring track in the film that reminds viewers of the immortal love between Yashoda and Lord Krishna. Some of Kishore Kumar's career best hits are from the film, including '*Kuchh to log kahenge*', '*Yeh kya hua*' and '*Chingari koyi bhadke*'. This film was the turning point in R.D. Burman's career and it is said

---

[1] Reproduced in Yasir Abbasi's *Yeh Un Dino Ki Baat Hai: Urdu Memoirs of Cinema Legends*.

that with this film S.D. Burman was finally satisfied that Pancham was a worthy heir. Samanta's favourite heroine Sharmila Tagore was delectable as the virtuous courtesan who is hungry for love and finds succour in nurturing a neglected child who lives down the street. Rajesh Khanna was her perfect foil as the lonely, rich man who sought companionship outside an unhappy marriage.

6. *Bobby* (1973)

After Raj Kapoor's introspective and poignant *Mera Naam Joke* (1970) bombed at the box office, he made a startling U-turn and delivered what was arguably the first mainstream Hindi film about a young couple defying social mores and trying to cross the class divide by attempting elopement. It laid the foundation for the teenybopper romance in Hindi cinema, with *Love Story* (1981), *Betaab* (1983), *Qayamat Se Qayamat Tak* (1988) and *Maine Pyaar Kiya* (1989) successfully taking the theme forward. *Bobby* was refreshing and different, and it struck a chord with the audiences. Raj Kapoor's long-time collaborator Khwaja Ahmed Abbas, wrote the story and screenplay. Both Rishi Kapoor (in his first role as an adult) and Dimple Kapadia, made stunning debuts. The film launched a thousand dreams, with the Bobby polka-dot top and mini-skirt becoming all the rage. The Bobby motorcycle was another trend the film launched. Pran was perfect as the rich, obdurate father who is completely out of touch with his son's feelings; in fact it would not be far-fetched to suggest that the film had shades of *The Graduate* with Aruna Irani briefly playing Mrs Robinson. Prem Nath delighted audiences as the whiskey-swigging, badass Catholic fisherman father who loves his daughter to death. Prem Chopra's dialogue '*Prem naam hai mera, Prem Chopra*' (credited to Jainendra Jain) continues to resonate with audiences even over fifty years later. The soundtrack counts among Laxmikant-Pyarelal and Anand Bakshi's finest with one memorable track after another. With '*Main shayar to nahin*', Shailendra, debuting as a playback singer, came to be identified as the voice of Rishi Kapoor until Kishore Kumar took over with *Khel Khel Mein*. The hut in Gulmarg, Kashmir, where '*Hum tum ik kamre men band ho*' was shot, is even today known as the 'Bobby Hut'.

7. *Zanjeer* (1973)

Did you know that the role which gave Amitabh Bachchan the 'Angry Young Man' image was offered to several heroes by scriptwriters Salim–Javed? Javed Akhtar has revealed in an interview that he and Salim Khan first sold the script to Dharmendra, but he wasn't interested. Director Prakash Mehra now had a script but no actor. Mehra also approached Dev Anand, who apparently refused it as the hero had no songs. Thespian Dilip Kumar turned it down because he found the role too one-dimensional. He later told Salim Khan that this was one role he regretted turning down.[2] According to Akhtar, Mehra had a tough time signing a hero, as Rajesh Khanna was the reigning superstar and musical romances were in. '(In *Zanjeer*) from the first frame to the last frame, the hero was supposed to be a very grim, serious, bitter person. This was never seen that time on the screen so obviously it was so different that everybody refused,' he said.[3] Raaj Kumar, who had worked as a sub-inspector in Mumbai Police, told Mehra that the film reminded him of his own career as a cop. However, he too turned it down. Finally, Mehra selected Amitabh after Pran suggested that he watch the young hero's performance in *Bombay to Goa*. Mehra's son Puneet remembers everyone thinking his father had gone senile when he signed Bachchan in the lead role.[4] The name 'Vijay' came to be identified strongly with Amitabh from *Zanjeer* onwards.

---

[2] https://www.news18.com/movies/did-you-know-amitabh-bachchan-was-planning-to-leave-bollywood-after-11-flops-7241761.html

[3] https://indianexpress.com/article/entertainment/bollywood/javed-akhtar-reveals-prakash-mehra-was-scared-before-zanjeer-release-as-amitabh-bachchan-films-flopped-8438286/

[4] https://www.hindustantimes.com/entertainment/bollywood/after-he-cast-amitabh-bachchan-in-zanjeer-people-said-prakash-mehra-had-gone-senile-says-director-s-son-101653823736226.html

Ajit played a perfect nemesis, Teja, to the hero, with Bindu playing the eponymous 'Mona Darling' of the Ajit joke universe. Pran shone as Sher Khan, the goonda with a conscience who becomes best buddies with the tough cop Vijay. The film birthed a new superstar and shaped the Hindi film industry not only during the decade but beyond.

8. *Yaadon ki Baaraat* (1973)

One of Nasir Hussain's biggest hits, this multi-starrer owed its success chiefly to two factors: Dharmendra at his peak who ruled the marquee even without a leading lady by his side, and R.D. Burman's scintillating music. Dharmendra's spectacular entry scene, where he (or rather, his double) jumps off a bridge onto a moving goods train, makes you whistle in appreciation even half a century after the film's release. Zeenat Aman shone on the silver screen in each and every song she appeared in. Vijay Arora and Tariq scored the biggest hits of their lives. Several authors and film critics including Kaushik Bhaumik and Diptakirti Chaudhuri (both of whom have contributed to this anthology) have called the film the first quintessential 'masala' film of Bollywood, which combined elements from action, drama, romance, musical, crime and thriller genres. With this film, *Hare Rama Hare Krishna* (1971) and *Jawani Diwani* (1972), R.D. Burman changed the sound of Hindi film music.

9. *Ankur* (1974)

Ankur was part of the opening act of the golden age of parallel cinema in Hindi movies, which lasted for over a decade. Its creative team included most of those worthies who would come to be regarded as the usual suspects in parallel cinema to come – director Shyam Benegal, cinematographer Govind Nihalani, also actors Anant Nag and (debutante) Shabana Azmi. *Ankur*, which explores themes of feudalism, casteism, relationships and sexuality, was set in a Deccan village and scripted in Dakhani. None of these topics were new to Hindi cinema, but these had hitherto not been dealt with at this level of authenticity. This style of film-making probably set the pattern for even grittier realist Hindi arthouse cinema to come, such as *Aakrosh* and *Ardh Satya*. The movie ends on a note of menace, just a hint on the subaltern rebellion that could come, and probably inspired Benegal to go for bolder endings in his future creations such as *Nishant* (1975).

10. *Garm Hava* (1974)

Based on Ismat Chughtai's short story, this film, written by Kaifi Azmi and Shama Zaidi, and directed by M.S. Sathyu, is one of the most important Hindi films ever made on the subject of the partition of India in 1947. Salim Mirza, the head of a Muslim family based in Uttar Pradesh, must take the most important decision of his life – whether his family should stay back in India, or move to Pakistan in search of better prospects, along with other Muslim friends and family members. Balraj Sahni played the patriarch in one of his career-defining roles. Few films since *Garm Hava* have tackled this subject as sensitively – about what it means to see one's status in society being eroded overnight; having to deal with the fear of being treated as a second-class citizen in the land of one's birth. The film was India's official entry for Best Foreign Film award at the Academy Awards (Oscars) and was also one of the few Indian films ever to be nominated for the Palme d'Or (Golden Palm award) in the 'in-competition' section of the Cannes Film Festival. The film features one of the most exquisite qawwalis to adorn the silver screen, '*Maula Salim Chishti*', picturized on location at the saint's mausoleum in Fatehpur Sikri, near Agra. The qawwali was sung by Aziz Ahmed Khan Warsi, with Kaifi Azmi providing the lyrics, and Bahadur Khan composing the melody.

11. *Rajnigandha* (1974)

The Nayi Kahani movement in Hindi literature of the fifties and the sixties did not leave Hindi films untouched. In 1969, Basu Chatterjee, one of the finest screenplay writers of Hindi cinema, had adapted Rajendra Yadav's magnificent Hindi novel *Sara Akash* for the silver screen. In 1974, he turned to Mannu Bhandari's short story '*Yehi Sach Hai*' and adapted it for the screen as *Rajnigandha*. His deep and abiding friendship with Mannu Bhandari ensured smooth sailing, which was not the case with films like *Aap Ka Bunty* which was based on her novel by the same name. Basu and Bhandari collaborated on the screenplay of his film *Swami* (1977), as well as the TV serial *Rajani* (1985).

The result of their collaboration on '*Yehi Sach Hai*' was a refreshing story of a young girl who is on the horns of a dilemma – she must choose between taking up a job in a different city where there is a danger of her being thrown into the arms of her ex-boyfriend, and staying put in her current city where her ever-dependable, supportive fiancé waits in anticipation of marriage. It's a lovely film, with Vidya Sinha putting in a charming performance in her first major role as leading lady. Amol Palekar and the late Dinesh Thakur were memorable as the fiancé and ex-boyfriend, respectively. The film is among the few Hindi films where two or more women have speaking parts and they discuss something other than the men in their lives (this was earlier called the Bechdel Test which is now considered reductive, and therefore redundant). Salil Chowdhury and Yogesh crafted evergreen gems such as '*Kayi baar yun bhi dekha hai*', sung by Mukesh, and '*Rajnigandha phool tumhare*', sung by Lata Mangeshkar.

12. *Sholay* (1975)

As per IMDB, *Sholay* holds the all-time record for highest number of footfalls in a theatre in India, 18.25 crore, way ahead of *Bahubali-2: The Conclusion*, 2017 (10.77 crore), *Mother India*,

1957 (10 crore), *Mughal-e-Azam*, 1960 (9.25 crore) and *Hum Aapke Hain Kaun*, 1994 (7.79 crore).[5] *Sholay* was declared 'Film of the Millennium' by BBC India in 1999, featured in *Time Magazine*'s Best of Bollywood list (2010), and was number 1 on the British Film Institute's 'Top 10 Indian Films' of all time (2022 poll). Ramesh Sippy's most successful film was inspired by *The Seven Samurai* as well as numerous classic Westerns of Hollywood. *Sholay* broke new ground by using latest techniques and technologies. The film was shot in 70 mm and the screen had to be stretched to fit the image in. Stereophonic sound came to theatres with *Sholay*; to spread the sound and to match it with the larger-than-normal 70 mm screen, Ramesh Sippy used a six-track stereophonic sound. The sound recording was done in London; also the stuntmen and fight choreographers were British. The length of the film was 198 minutes during the first run. Such was the craze for the film among audiences, who returned to the theatres again and again with their whole families, that the director added extra tracks, such as the extended one of Thakur Baldev Singh (Sanjeev Kumar) meeting a young Radha (Jaya Bhaduri) on the day of Holi. It's a rare film where all the characters – not just the lead characters of Jai, Veeru, Basanti, Thakur and Gabbar – became household names: the jailor played by Asrani, a character inspired by Chaplin's caricature of Adolf Hitler in *The Great Dictator* (1940); Soorma Bhopali, the local raconteur, a character said to be based on a relative of Salim Khan's; not to mention Kaalia, Sambha, Maulvi sa'ab, even Hariram Nai, and the horse, Dhanno. R.D. Burman's magnificent background score added a whole dimension to the film. *Sholay* was also the first Hindi film to release a set of two LP records, one of which (a red-coloured disc) contained only dialogues and background music; a tribute to Salim-Javed's scripting and dialogue writing skills. And Amjad Khan's Gabbar Singh remains the benchmark for the villain in Hindi cinema (so popular was the character that it was even used

---

[5] https://m.imdb.com/list/ls047470041/

for a Parle-G biscuit commercial, a first for a villainous character endorsing a product).

13. *Jai Santoshi Ma* (1975)

The mother of all devotional films, this film rocked the box office in a year which saw one of the biggest multi-starrer blockbusters to ever hit the silver screen in India (*Sholay*). Made on a small budget which was a fraction of what its competition cost, this film held its own against the multi-starrer tsunamis that swept through the year, including *Deewaar*, proving once again that religion is indeed the opiate of the masses. As per *Screen* magazine,[6] the film which was made at a cost of Rs 25 lakh, earned Rs 5 crore at the box office. On the other hand, *Sholay*, which is said to have made Rs 35 crore from domestic sales, was made at a cost of Rs 3 crore.

Anita Guha, a popular actress from the fifties and sixties saw her career get a shot in the arm with her appearance as the eponymous Goddess in this film, while Kanan Kaushal, a hitherto lesser-known actor, became a household name after the release of the film. Kaushal played a damsel-in-distress whose evil sisters-in-law starve her till she is forced to beg for food. The Goddess intervenes and the evil ones get their just deserts. This divine retribution saga became a prototype for TV serials to come, the kind of which are popular even in this day and age, where the dutiful wife's life is wrecked by evil sisters-in-law or the husband's mistress/a female ghost, until some deus ex machina sets things right. The songs sung by Usha Mangeshkar and lyricist Kavi Pradeep himself, and set to music by C. Arjun, became immensely popular, and remain the touchstone in the genre of devotional music. The film single-handedly ushered in the solah-shukrwar (sixteen Fridays) tradition of the worship of the Goddess, with women all over the country dutifully observing the ritual.

---

[6] Screen magazine, archived online at https://web.archive.org/web/20031022065526/http://www.screenindia.com/20010622/f1975.html

14. *Deewaar* (1975)

The seventies was truly Salim–Javed's decade. Their storytelling skills and powerful dialogues gave at least four film-makers some of the most successful films of their careers: Manmohan Desai's *Chacha Bhatija*, Prakash Mehra's *Zanjeer*, Ramesh Sippy's *Sholay* and last but not the least, Yash Chopra's *Deewaar*. *Deewaar* not only consolidated Yash Chopra's position as a successful film director, but gave Amitabh Bachchan some of the best dialogues of his career that have become gold standard for aspiring film actors who joined the industry after Bachchan. *Zanjeer* and *Namak Haraam* gave birth to and consolidated Amitabh Bachchan's Angry Young Man image, but it is *Deewaar* that remains the defining film with that character. A treasure trove of memorable dialogues, with '*Mere paas ma hai*' continuing to inspire meme makers to date, the film boasted some of the most brilliant scenes in Hindi cinema that have been endlessly imitated but seldom equalled.

15. *Aandhi* (1975)

There was something about 1975 if one looks at the variety of films that released in the year. This was also the year an internal emergency was proclaimed throughout India. The period immediately after the declaration (25 June 1975) saw frenzied censorship of films critical of the establishment. Obviously, *Aandhi* took a hit; however, the decision to ban it came after the film had had a run of twenty weeks. Though the film had parallels with the life of Indira Gandhi, the then prime minister of India, the film-makers denied that it was modelled on her. The film was released on national television by the government, well after the emergency was lifted in March 1977, and the Janata Party had come to power following the general elections of 1977. This was Suchitra Sen's finest moment in a fledgling Hindi film career. The film is a sensitive take on the sacrifices and compromises made by a couple in the journey of life, and a rare Hindi film of the time that gave its woman lead an agency. At no point in the film are viewers encouraged to judge either the ambitious woman who has no time for the finer things of life such as spending a quiet day with her husband, or the husband who refuses to adjust to his wife's lifestyle, preferring to go his separate way instead. A timeless soundtrack created by Gulzar and R.D. Burman includes some of the best duets of Lata Mangeshkar and Kishore Kumar.

16. *Amar Akbar Anthony* (1977)

As Shantanu says, others invented it before him, Manmohan Desai made an epidemic of it. If anyone wants proof that no one quite used the lost-and-found formula in film better than Manmohan Desai, look no further. The story may sound ridiculous to some on paper – three brothers who are separated in childhood, being raised by people of different faiths, and coming together in the climax to teach the bad guys a lesson – but Desai makes it work. Helped by the delightful screenplay by K.K. Shukla and Prayag Raaj, with Kader Khan's dialogues ushering in a new language to Hindi cinema. The dialogues spoken by Amitabh Bachchan in the film were in a unique 'Bambaiyya', or tapori-speak, another first in a mainstream Hindi film. With one outlandish set piece after another, *Amar Akbar Anthony* was an out-and-out entertainer, the kind of film that Indian audiences are fond of calling 'paisa vasool' (perfect value for money). It helped that three leading male stars of the day played the brothers – Amitabh and Vinod Khanna were at the zenith of their careers. Legendary poet and satirist Akbar Allahabadi lent his name to the character of Akbar the qawwaal played by Rishi Kapoor. Amitabh's character's name was a tribute to music director Laxmikant's Goan musician guru, Anthony Gonsalves, and LP made his name familiar to audiences across India with the song '*My name is Anthony Gonsalves*' which had a bit of British ex-Prime Minister Benjamin Disraeli's memorable speech in the British Parliament thrown in for good effect: 'You are a sophisticated rhetorician intoxicated by the exuberance of your own verbosity' (Disraeli used 'inebriated' instead of 'intoxicated').

17. *Shatranj Ke Khilari* (1977)

The only full-length feature film made by Satyajit Ray in Hindi (he also made *Sadgati* for Doordarshan), the film was a collaborative effort between Ray, producer Suresh Jindal, dialogue writers Shama Zaidi and Javed Siddiqui, Kathak maestro Birju Maharaj and many others. It can safely be said that unlike Munshi Premchand, whose story the film is based upon, Ray was far kinder to the king of Awadh, Wajid Ali Shah, who was beautifully portrayed on screen by Amjad Khan. Besides the decadent noblemen /chess enthusiasts Mirza Sajjad Ali and Mir Roshan Ali played by Sanjeev Kumar and Saeed Jaffrey respectively, the film also had Sir Richard Attenborough as General Outram, and Tom Alter as his aide-de-camp. Other actors in the exceptional ensemble cast include Victor Banerjee, Veena, Shabana Azmi, Farida Jalal and Farooq Shaikh. Pandit Birju Maharaj composed and sang the enchanting thumri '*Kanha main tosey haari*', which was performed by Saswati Sen, Birju Maharaj's disciple. The attention to detail such as production and costume design, paid off, and the film continues to enthral viewers decades after its release. Its successful opening in theatres unnerved the industry Mughals who allegedly sabotaged its theatrical run – also resulting in an ugly running down of the film by the makers of *Junoon*, which came the following year, and covered the same period.[7]

18. *Junoon* (1978)

Shashi Kapoor set up his own production house Film-Valas in 1978, and the first film he produced, *Junoon*, was based on Ruskin Bond's novel *A Flight of Pigeons*. The film was directed by Shyam Benegal.

[7] Shashi Kapoor called the film a 'disaster' in an interview to *India Today*, issue dated 31 October 1978.

The duo also made *Kalyug* (1981), which was loosely based on the epic Mahabharata. The Kapoor–Benegal films would perhaps classify more as middle-of-the-road cinema rather than hard-core arthouse, in terms of content and form. Benegal's other films like *Nishant* and *Ankur* were inspired by neo-realistic cinema of Europe which had earlier influenced Satyajit Ray and Ritwik Ghatak in Bengal, and Mrinal Sen, Basu Chatterjee and Mani Kaul's Hindi films in 1969. Production values and budgets of Film-Valas studio were better, and the cast usually included stars such as Rekha and Shashi Kapoor, leading some critics to wonder if 'Shyam Benegal had succumbed to the siren call of commercialism'.[8]

Junoon recounted the story of the mutiny of 1857 from three points of view. The first perspective is that of the wives, mothers and daughters of British officers who were grateful for the kindness shown by locals to them during a period of great strife. The second one is the Indian nobles who were kind to such English families. The third perspective is that of rebels and commoners who detested their colonial masters. The film starts with the depiction of the incident of burning of the church by the rebels (the real-life incident occurred in Bareilly, in 1857, in which forty British subjects were killed). Shashi Kapoor plays Javed Khan, a feudal chieftain who gives shelter to an Englishwoman (played by Jennifer Kendall Kapoor) following this incident, and finds himself irresistibly attracted to her young daughter Ruth, played by debutant Nafisa Ali. The Englishwoman throws a challenge at him: *Dilli aapki toh Ruth bhi aapki* (if the rebels capture Delhi, you can have Ruth's hand in marriage). The inevitable ending, where the ill-prepared and ill-equipped Indian rebels are crushed by the British army, has Naseeruddin Shah who plays Sarfaraz Khan, Javed's rebellious brother-in-law, lamenting while angrily setting free the pigeons lovingly reared by Javed, '*Humare inhi junoonon ki wajah se humari maat ho gayi. Hum Dilli haar gaye*' (Our foolish passions are the reason for our downfall. We have lost Delhi). He is alluding, of course, to Javed's obsession with Ruth.

[8] *India Today*, 31 October 1978.

19. *Ankhiyon Ke Jharokhon Se* (1978)

Rajshri Productions was started by Tarachand Barjatya in 1947, with a clear objective of providing clean and wholesome entertainment for family audiences. To their credit, scions of the House of Rajshri have never budged from their stated objective for over seven decades. The production house released several successful low-budget musicals in the 1970s which made a decent profit .These included *Geet Gaata Chal* (1975), *Tapasya* (1976), *Chitchor* (1976), *Dulhan Wahi Jo Piya Mann Bhaaye* (1977), *Sawan Ko Aane Do* and *Tarana*, both in 1979. These films were directed by Hiren Nag, Anil Ganguly, Basu Chatterjee, Lekh Tandon, Kanak Mishra and Deepak Bahry respectively The Rajshris reprised *Chitchor* rather unsuccessfully in 2003, with the Hrithik Roshan–Kareena Kapoor–Abhishek Bachchan starrer *Main Prem Ki Diwani Hoon*, which inspired a whole meme fest.

The Hollywood blockbuster *Love Story* (1970), based on the novel by Erich Segal and starring Ryan O'Neal and Ali Mcgraw in the most famous roles of their careers, was the inspiration behind *Ankhiyon Ke Jharokhon Se.* A young couple meets and falls in love; the boy is heartbroken when they discover that the girl is suffering from cancer. The much-dreaded disease was widely considered incurable during that time. Hrishikesh Mukherjee had previously used a similar theme in *Anand* (1971). Unlike *Anand*, though, this was a story of doomed young lovers, and it hit the mark. Audiences shed copious tears, just like they had in *Love Story*. Ravindra Jain, who gave his best tunes for most Rajshri films of the 1970s, composed some memorable tunes for the songs in this film too, including the title song. The film, made at a modest budget of Rs 48 lakh, collected Rs 2.2 crore worldwide, making it a super hit.[9] In a year dominated by the superstar Amitabh Bachchan with

---

[9] https://ksboxoffice.com/ankhiyon-ke-jharokhon-se-1978-movie-box-office-collection-budget-and-facts/movies-facts/

five big releases, including *Muqaddar Ka Sikandar*, *Trishul*, *Don*, *Ganga Ki Saugandh* and *Kasme Vaade*, *Ankhiyon*… came as a breath of fresh air.

20. *Gol Maal* (1979)

Hrishikesh Mukherjee hit a sixer with *Gol Maal*, which is universally recognized as one of the best comedies in the history of Hindi cinema. Amol Palekar plays Ramprasad Sharma who curries favour with his boss Bhawani Shankar (Utpal Dutt) right from the interview stage, by pretending to be a conservative, god-fearing family man. At the suggestion of his best friend Deven Verma (who plays himself), he starts playing a second character, that of his fictional twin brother Laxman Prasad Sharma ('Lucky') who woos Dutt's daughter Urmila (Bindiya Goswami) while giving her music tuitions. The dialogues of the film, written by Dr Rahi Masoom Raza, never fail to bring a smile to the lips, even forty-five years after the film's release. Dina Pathak plays the fictional, deeply religious mother of the twin brothers, and also her party-hopping twin sister Kamala Srivastava. Gulzar's lyrics in the picnic song '*Ek din sapne main dekhi sapna*', as also the title track sung by music director R.D. Burman himself, '*Gol maal hai bhai sab gol maal hai*' – set the tone of the 'mad hatter tea party' right at the beginning of the film. Dutt's absurdist and obstinate take on everything in his life, from his employee's whiskers ('A man's character can be judged by his moustache') to his daughter's life partner ('*Tumhari shaadi us sey nahi hogi jis se tum prem karti ho, tumhari shaadi us sey hogi jis se main prem karta hoon* / You cannot marry the man you love, you will have to marry the man I love) is quirky and delightful.

Notes on Contributors

Alaka Sahani is a National Award-winning film critic. She works with *The Indian Express*, Mumbai.

Amborish Roychoudhury is a Mumbai-based writer, biographer and film historian. His book *In a Cult of Their Own: Bollywood Beyond Box Office* (2018) won a Special Mention at the 66th National Film Awards, 2019. He is also the author of *Sridevi: The South Years* (2024). He has written for *Outlook*, *Firstpost*, *Filmfare*, *Huffpost*, *MUBI Notebook* and the *Free Press Journal*, among others. For the past couple of years, Amborish has been working on the official biography of Raj Khosla.

Amitava Kumar is the author of several books of non-fiction and also four novels. His book, *A Time Outside This Time*, was described by *The New Yorker* magazine as 'a shimmering assault on the zeitgeist'. Kumar teaches literature and writing at Vassar College in upstate New York. Kumar's work has appeared in *Granta*, *The New York Times*, *Harper's*, and several other publications. He has been awarded a Guggenheim fellowship and residencies from Yaddo, MacDowell, and a Cullman Center Fellowship at the New York Public Library. His novel *Immigrant, Montana* was on the best of the year lists at *The New Yorker*, *The New York Times*, and President Obama's list of favourite books of 2018. His latest book is *My Beloved Life*. More at www.amitavakumar.com.

Amitava Nag is an independent film critic based in Kolkata, India, and editor of *Silhouette* magazine (www.silhouette-magazine.com). He writes extensively on cinema in Bengali and English and has authored ten books on cinema till date. His most recent book is *75 years 75 films: India's Cinematic Journey* published by Publications Division, Government of India. A poet and storyteller as well, Amitava can be reached at www.amitavanag.net.

Amrit Gangar is a Mumbai-based writer, film theorist, curator and a historian, who has been active almost for the past five decades. He is a bilingual (English and Gujarati) writer whose books on cinema in Gujarati have been awarded by the Gujarati Sahitya Akademi, Gandhinagar, and other institutions. Former consultant curator/content developer of the National Museum of Indian Cinema, he has also been the curator of film programmes at the Mumbai International Film Festival for Documentary, Short and Animation Films, the Kala Ghoda Artfest, the Kochi–Muziris Biennial, etc. He has presented his theory of *Cinema of Prayoga* at Pompidou Centre, Paris; Tate Modern, London; Danish Film Institute, Copenhagen; International Film School, Lodz, Poland as also at the Kala Bhavana, Santiniketan. His comprehensive Gujarati book on Satyajit Ray has been published by the Gujarat Sahitya Akademi, Gandhinagar.

Anirudha Bhattacharjee, an alumnus of IIT Kharagpur, is an SAP consultant by profession, a musician by passion, and a chronicler of music and cinema by avocation. *R.D. Burman: The Man, The Music*, his first book (HarperCollins, 2011, co-written with Balaji Vittal), won the National Award for best book on cinema in 2012. *Gaata Rahe Mera Dil* (HarperCollins, 2015, also co-written with Balaji Vittal) won the MAMI Award in its inaugural year, 2015. His other books include the critically acclaimed *S.D. Burman: The Prince-Musician* (Penguin, 2018, co-written with Balaji Vittal), the bestseller *Kishore Kumar: The Ultimate Biography* (HarperCollins, 2022, co-written with Parthiv Dhar), and *Basu Chatterji: And Middle-of-the-Road Cinema* (Penguin, 2023).

Aseem Chhabra is a film journalist and the festival director of the New York Indian Film Festival. He is the author of the biographies of Bollywood actors Shashi Kapoor, Irrfan Khan and Priyanka Chopra. He has been published in *The New York Times, The Boston Globe, The Philadelphia Inquirer, BBC.com, Mumbai Mirror, Rediff.com, The Hindu, The Hindustan Times*. Aseem is the voice of Shadow Puppet #1 in the acclaimed animated film, *Sita Sings the Blues*.

Avijit Ghosh is an associate editor with *The Times of India*, New Delhi. His books on films include *Cinema Bhojpuri*, *40 Retakes: Bollywood Classics You May Have Missed* and *When Ardh Satya Met Himmatwala: The Many Lives of Bombay Cinema of the 1980s*. He is also the author of two novels, *Bandicoots in the Moonlight* and *Up Campus, Down Campus*.

Balaji Vittal is an author of books like the National Award–winning *R.D. Burman: The Man, The Music*, the MAMI Award–winning *Gaata Rahe Mera Dil: 50 Classic Hindi Film Songs*, and the highly acclaimed *Pure Evil: The Bad Men of Bollywood*. Balaji is also a columnist contributing to *News18*, *Outlook* and *The New Indian Express*. He is also a TEDx speaker, a Bollywood commentator and an award-winning podcaster. He can be reached on X (formerly Twitter) at @vittalbalaji and his website is www.balajivittal.com.

Bobby Sing began his journey, exploring avenues as a stage artist, musician, poet, educationist and a graphic designer, and is now an experienced critic, creative-music consultant, and a prolific writer on cinema, active in the field since the late 1990s. Though his real name is Harpreet Singh, his lasting relationship with cinema began with the nickname Bobby, inspired from Raj Kapoor's cult film released in the early seventies. His passion for cinema flourished while working with music and home video companies, when the audio-VCD-DVD market was at its peak in India. As a columnist, he has been associated with reputed publications like *Indo-US Dialogue Magazine*, *Network 18*, *Free Press Journal* and more. He has also been active as a creative script and music consultant in Hindi and Punjabi cinema. As an author, his 'Did You Know' series of books (available in both English and Hindi) is specifically conceived for all young friends eager to know about classics of Hindi cinema and lesser-known stories related to their making. And for friends, wondering where the 'h' has gone from his last name 'Singh', it was an innovation tried in the early part of his career as a singer that continues till date with His Blessings. He can be reached at www.bobbytalkscinema.com and bobbysing@gmail.com.

Deepa Buty is the founder of *TheSongPedia.com*, an online music magazine. She has co-authored the books *Guide, The Film: Perspectives*, *Majrooh Sultanpuri: The Poet for All Reasons*, and a coffee-table book on Dev Anand, *Ke Dil Abhi Bhara Nahin*. She continues to be enthralled by the role music plays in one's life and has always been fascinated by Hindi film music. She has been writing music-related articles for the past eight years. Some of her articles have been translated into Hindi for News18 Hindi (Entertainment). She can be reached on deepabuty@gmail.com.

Deepa Gahlot is a critic, columnist, editor and author. She writes extensively on cinema, theatre, the arts, women's issues for several publications and websites including her own, deepagahlot.com. She has won the National Award for Best Film Criticism. She has edited several cinema journals, her work has appeared in anthologies on women's studies and cinema: *Bollywood Popular Indian Cinema*, *Behind the Scenes of Hindi Cinema: A Visual Journey through the Heart of Bollywood*, *Janani*, *Bollywood's Top 20: Superstars of Indian Cinema*, *Legends of Indian Silver Screen: The Winners of Dadasaheb Phalke Award (1992–2014)*, *The Oldest Love Story*. Her books include *The Prithviwallahs* (co-authored with Shashi Kapoor), and biographies of Shah Rukh Khan and Shammi Kapoor, *Take 2: 50 Films that Deserve a New Audience* and *Sheroes:*

25 Daring Women of Bollywood. She is currently consulting editor for *Mumbai Theatre Guide*.

Diptakirti Chaudhuri is into marketing by day and movies by night. His love for marketing has resulted in a twenty-five-year-old career in the corporate world. His passion for Hindi cinema has yielded innumerable social media posts, many articles, a few books and a nearly defunct blog. A big fan of Amitabh Bachchan and Salim–Javed, the seventies is his favourite Hindi movie decade. He lives in Bangalore with his wife, a son and a daughter. He can be found on social media as @diptakirti.

Gajra Kottary is the writer of cult and award-winning and record-breaking TV serials like *Astitva: Ek Prem Kahani* and *Balika Vadhu* among others. She is also a novelist and short-story writer. Her published works include the novels *Broken Melodies*, *Once Upon a Star* and *Girls Don't Cry*, and a collected volume of stories, *Autumn Blossoms*. She is also a contributor to the anthology *The Moving Finger: Writers on Writing*, published by Om Books International.

Gautam Chintamani is a film historian and the author of *Rajneeti* (Penguin-Random House, 2019), the first biography of Rajnath Singh. He is the author of the bestselling *Dark Star: The Loneliness of Being Rajesh Khanna* (HarperCollins, 2014), *Qayamat Se Qayamat Tak: The Film That Revived Hindi Cinema* (HarperCollins, 2016), *Pink: The Inside Story* (HarperCollins, 2017) and *The Midway Battle: Narendra Modi's Roller-Coaster Second Term* (Bloomsbury, 2020). He hails from a literary tradition that runs deep on both sides of his family – the late Telugu poet Arudra is his maternal grandfather and the liberal thinker Sir C.Y. Chintamani is his paternal great-grandfather. He was on the National Film Awards jury for Best Writing on Cinema in 2016. The British Film Institute included *Qayamat Se Qayamat Tak: The Film That Revived Hindi Cinema* in their library in 2016. In 2017, Gautam contributed an essay on the cinema of Franz Osten for The British Film Institute's restoration project of the film-maker's 1928 masterpiece *Shiraz*. In 2022, Gautam contributed to the content for the Pradhanmantri Sangrahalaya, New Delhi. The unique museum explores the history of India through the eyes of its prime ministers. Gautam Chintamani is currently working on *A Class Act: The Life of Vinod Khanna*. He and his wife, Amrita, along with their dog, Buddy, live in Gurgaon and in the hills of Himachal.

Harini Srinivasan is an author, editor and content management professional. She writes historical fiction and romantic comedies. Her works include *Shadows and Secrets: The Pataliputra Conspiracy* (2024), *The Ex Factor* (2023), *The Curse of Anuganga* (2019), and the novellas *Ek Confusing Love Story* (2019), and *Death at Arcade Emporia* (2022). A former civil servant, she is an aficionado of old Hindi cinema, dance and books. Harini Srinivasan lives in Gurgaon.

Jai Arjun Singh is an independent writer and critic. His books include *Jaane Bhi Do Yaaro: Seriously Funny Since 1983*, *The World of Hrishikesh Mukherjee*, which won the MAMI Cinema Writing Award, and *The Popcorn Essayists: What Movies Do to Writers*. His columns, reviews and essays have appeared in dozens of publications, and are available on his culture blog Jabberwock (http://jaiarjun.blogspot.com). He has taught a film-history course at O.P. Jindal Global University, as well as independent online courses about cinema and literature, on such subjects as the Mahabharata and the use of song sequences in Hindi films.

Kaushik Bhaumik is associate professor in cinema studies at Jawaharlal Nehru University, New Delhi, India. He has been deputy director of the Osian's Cinefan Festival of Asian and Arab Cinema. He is co-editor of *Visual Sense: A Cultural Reader*, *dates. sites: Project Cinema City* and *Project Cinema City*. He has also edited the *Marg* centennial issue on the 100 years of Indian cinema. He has written extensively on various aspects of Indian film history in international journals and anthologies. His monograph on early Bombay cinema is due to be out from Jadavpur University Press later in 2024.

Kaveree Bamzai is an independent journalist. She was the first, and so far, only woman editor of *India Today*, where she was employed till January 2019. She is the author of *The Three Khans and the Emergence of New India*, *No Regrets: The Guilt-Free Woman's Guide to a Good Life*, *Bollywood Today*, and three monographs in the Zubaan series on 'Women in Indian Film'. She is on several committees, among them the Women Exemplar Committee of CII, and is recognized as a change-maker by Save the Children charity.

Ketan Mehta is one of India's most internationally celebrated film directors. On his first film *Bhavni Bhavai* he was called 'the brightest talent of the new generation' by the legendary film-maker Satyajit Ray. He has been a leading light of the 'New Wave' of Indian cinema in the seventies and eighties. A graduate from St Stephens college, Delhi, he studied film-making at the Film and Television Institute of India. He has made many critically acclaimed and popular films including *Holi*, *Mirch Masala*, *Maya Memsaab*, *Sardar*, *Mangal Pandey: The Rising*, *Rang Rasiya* and *Manjhi: The Mountain Man*. He was honoured by the French government with The Officer of the Order of Arts and Literature.

Krishna Shastri Devulapalli is a humour writer, columnist, screenwriter, novelist, playwright and illustrator/cartoonist. His novels include *Ice Boys in Bell-bottoms*, a 1970s bildungsroman, *Jump Cut*, a seriocomic thriller set in the Tamil film industry, and the comic *The Sentimental Spy: The Family Bond*. His other works include a humorous epistolary play, *Dear Omana: Notes on How To Be a Literary Sensation*, with the backdrop of the Indian publishing industry, and a book of non-fiction, *How To*

Be A Literary Sensation. He has co-edited *Madras on My Mind: A City in Stories*, and writes regularly for *The Hindu*, *Deccan Chronicle* and *Scroll*, among other journals. He is currently at work on a detective series for the web, and a feature film. His essay on humour is part of the anthology *The Moving Finger: Writers on Writing*, published by Om Books International. His forthcoming books include *The Artful Dodger: How I Side-stepped Life with Movies, Books and Music* and a sequel to his first novel titled *Rally Days and Disco Nights*.

Maithili Rao drifted into subtitling and writing on cinema after a brief stint as lecturer of English. From hobby to passion for writing on films was a natural progression. Her book *The Millennial Woman in Bollywood. A New Brand?* was released in 2023. *Smita Patil: A Brief Incandescence* came out in 2015. She co-edited *The Oldest Love Story: A Motherhood Anthology* and *Films Through Women's Eyes*, in 2022. Rao contributed chapters to many books on cinema like *Stardom in Contemporary Hindi Cinema*, *Encyclopaedia of Hindi Cinema*, and a few more. She has written for many national and international publications. She has served on national and international juries, including those of the National Film Awards, MIFF, The International Children's Film Festival in Hyderabad, Fipresci at Sochi, and APSA (Asia Pacific Screen Awards). She was member of the script committee at the NFDC and CFS. She believes that besides aesthetics, films must have relevance to social and political reality.

Maitreyee B. Chowdhury is a poet and writer. She has four books to her credit – *The Hungryalists: The Story of a Poetry Revolution from Bengal and Bihar in the 1960s*, *One Dozen: Hasan Azizul Huq* (translation), *Uttam Kumar and Suchitra Sen: Bengali Cinema's First Couple* and *Where Even The Present Is Ancient: Benaras (Poetry from the gallis of Benaras)*. She is editor of *The Bangalore Review*, a literary journal. Maitreyee has written for journals like *Himal South Asian*, *Scroll*, *Outlook*, *National*

Geographic, *The Hindustan Times*, *Sunday Guardian*, amongst others. Her forthcoming work is centered around the eccentric genius poet Binoy Majumdar. She can be found at https://www.maitreyeechowdhury.com/

Mira Hashmi is a lifelong cinema fan, and has also taught undergraduate film studies for over twenty years. She is the author of *Gulzar's Ijaazat: Insights into the Film* (2019). Mira currently resides in the UK with her husband and children.

Mohan Agashe is a psychiatrist, theatre and film actor. He has been awarded the Padma Shri as well as the Sangeet Natak Akademi award. He has been honoured with the Order of Merit of the Federal Republic of Germany and the Goethe award.

Nandini Ramnath is a film journalist and critic with *Scroll.in*. She has worked with *Mint*, *Time Out Mumbai*, NDTV and *The Indian Express*.

Niyati Bhat is a writer, translator (Hindi and Kashmiri to English) and editor of Kashmiri Pandit origin from New Delhi, India. She is the 2024 recipient of the Creative Writing and Translation Fellowship' by Charles Wallace India Trust and Literature Across Frontiers-UWTSD. She is also a PhD candidate in cinema studies at Jawaharlal Nehru University. Her PhD dissertation engages with the cinematic imagination of the Sri Lankan civil war and its aftermath. Her MPhil thesis was on the cinematic, music and new media practices in Kashmir from 2000 to 2018. Her work has appeared in leading Indian and international publications such as the *A Map Called Home* (poetry anthology), *India Today*, *The Hindu*, *Scroll.in*, *Vogue India*, *Asymptote Journal*, *Summer Hill Journal* among others. You can read more about her work at http://niyatibhat.in/.

Raja Sen is a film critic who has written for various national and international publications. He has been writing an ongoing column on streaming television for *Mint Lounge* since 2016. He has written the children's book *The Best Baker in the World,* which is an illustrated all-ages adaptation of *The Godfather*. He is a full-time screenwriter, writing on films like *99*, *Go Goa Gone,* and, most recently, co-writing *Chup*, a film about the killing of film critics. He is currently creating a fantastical sitcom.

Rajat Kapoor is a film-maker and a theatre director, and sometimes also an actor.

Ratnottama Sengupta turned director with *And They Made Classics*..., a documentary on the unique bond between screenwriter Nabendu Ghosh and legendary director Bimal Roy. A journalist for forty-four years, she writes for newspapers and journals, participates in discussions on the electronic media, teaches film appreciation and mass communication students, writes for books on cinema and art, programs film festivals and curates art exhibitions. She has written on Hindi films for the *Encyclopaedia Britannica*; been a member of CBFC; of the NFDC Script Committee; served on the National Film Awards jury, and has won a National Award. She has been the editor of an entertainment website, *CineBengal.com*; and the former arts editor of *The Times of India*. Currently she has columns in *Borderless Journal*, *Silhouette* and *Kanjik*. She has contributed chapters/essays in *Films Through Women's Eyes: 17 Indian Directors*, published by Suchitra Film Society (on Aruna Raje); *Ashok Kumar: From Bombay Talkies to Bollywood* (for a volume on Phalke Winners); *Master of the Middle Path: Centenary Homage to Hrishikesh Mukherjee* for the 28th Kolkata International Film Festival brochure published by the Information and Culture Department, Government of West Bengal. She also features in *Monalisa Does Not Smile*, an anthology published by Om Books. Author of *Krishna's Cosmos* and several other volumes, she has edited *Dadamoni: The Life and Times of Ashok Kumar/2022, Mistress of Melodies/2020,*

That Bird Called Happiness/2018, Me And I/2017, Kadam Kadam/2016, Chuninda Kahaniyaan/2009.

Roshmila Bhattacharya is a senior journalist who, in a career spanning over three decades, has worked with *Filmfare, The Asian Age, Screen, Hindustan Times* and *Mumbai Mirror.* She also brainstormed with the late National Award-winning editor, Rauf Ahmed, on a monthly film magazine, *Zee Premiere.* She has contributed to *The Telegraph*, *National Herald*, *Deccan Herald*, *Free Press Journal* and *Rediff.Com*, breaking several stories on the national platform. She was a columnist for over fifteen years and continues to find enjoyment in journalism. In July 2019, she released her first book, *Bad Man*, a biography of Gulshan Grover, published by Penguin. Her second book, *Matinee Men: A Journey Through Bollywood*, was published by Rupa Publications in December 2020. It is listed amongst the 20 Best Bollywood Movie e-books of All Time by Book Authority, and *The Times of India* recommended it as one of the eight books every Bollywood lover should read. In July 2022, *Tera Chhalaava*, a crime anthology for which she has written four stories, released on Hungama Play and MX Player. She is also the author of *Spooked: Bollywood's Encounters with the Paranormal*, published by Om Books International in December 2023.

S.M.M. Ausaja is a film historian, author and archivist. He began his career with a stint in TV software production, joining Plus Channel in Mumbai under Amit Khanna and Mahesh Bhatt as a trainee on India's first English daily, *A Mouthful of Sky*, in 1996. He went on to produce several TV shows in the years to come. He has written extensively on cinema across media platforms. His stint with TV software production continued in companies like Integral Productions, HFCL Nine-Broadcasting and Gemini Studios where he executed various popular projects. He has also directed documentaries on Lata Mangeshkar, Amitabh

Bachchan, Shah Rukh Khan and Hema Malini which were telecast on prime-time television. He then ventured full-time into film archiving, documentation and auctions. Previously senior vice-president at Osians, then Fantico and now with Tuli Research Centre for India Studies, Ausaja is a specialist in documenting cinema heritage. His debut book, *Bollywood in Posters*, released in 2009, was nominated at the prestigious Vodafone-Crossword Book Awards under the Best Non-Fiction and Best Popular Book categories. He then co-authored *Bollywood: The Films, The Songs, The Stars* (DK Books, 2017). His third coffee-table book, *The Bachchans*, a pictorial tribute to the family, was released by Amitabh Bachchan in 2024.

Sathya Saran is best known for her long association with *Femina*, which she edited for twelve years. She is also the author of a number of books. *The Dark Side* reflects her love of the short story, while the critically acclaimed biographies, *Ten Years with Guru Dutt: Abrar Alvi's Journey*, *Sun Mere Bandhu Re: The Musical World of S.D. Burman* and *Baat Niklegi Toh Phir: The Life and Music of Jagjit Singh* bear testimony to her love of cinema and music. Sathya's latest books include biographies of Pt Hariprasad Chaurasia and Ritu Nanda. She is currently consulting editor with Penguin Random House. Sathya also teaches fashion journalism at NIFT Mumbai. She has been a stage actor with Veenapani Chawla. Passionate about writing, she has conceptualized and curated the first of its kind writers' conclave titled 'The Spaces between Words' the unfestival sponsored by JSW at Kaladham near Hampi, Ratnagiri, and Sholtu in Himachal Pradesh.

Shamya Dasgupta is a sports journalist, currently with ESPNcricinfo as a deputy editor. He enjoys writing, and that's grown into a bunch of books: *Bhiwani Junction* (2012, on Indian boxing), *Cricket Changed My Life* (2014, life lessons from the game), and *Don't Disturb the Dead* (2017, on the Ramsays, horror film-makers), and has translated Mahasweta Devi's *Laayl-e*

Aasmaner Aayna from Bangla to English, as *Mirror of the Darkest Night* (2019). He lives in Bengaluru with his wife, Ajitha, and their dog, Nimki.

Sriram Raghavan is a Mumbai-based film-maker and cinema lover. In a film career spanning two decades, he has made only half-a-dozen films: *Ek Hasina Thi*, *Johnny Gaddaar*, *Agent Vinod*, *Badlapur*, *Andhadhun* and *Merry Christmas*, a bilingual in Hindi and Tamil. A graduate of the Film and Television Institute of India, Sriram's films are largely about characters with flexible morality trapped in situations. He is credited with introducing the neo-noir genre in Hindi cinema, something he denies.

Subhash Ghai, a graduate of FTII, eminent director, producer, screenwriter, music composer and lyricist, is popularly known as the Showman of Indian Cinema. He holds an enviable record of making iconic blockbusters in mainstream cinema from 1975 to 2015 including films like *Kalicharan*, *Vishwanath*, *Karz*, *Vidhata*, *Hero*, *Meri Jung*, *Karma*, *Ram Lakhan*, *Saudagar*, *Khalnayak*, *Pardes*, *Taal*, *Yaadein*, *Kisna*, *Black and White* and *Iqbaal*. He has introduced and groomed many stars including Jackie Shroff, Madhuri Dixit, Anil Kapoor, Sanjay Dutt, Manisha Koirala and Mahima Chowdhary. In 2001, Subhash Ghai became the first producer in hundred years of Indian cinema to corporatize the film industry by making his film company, Mukta Arts Ltd., a public listed company. In 2006 he established a world-class film school of creative performing arts known as Whistling Woods International. He has been the chairman of CII Media and Entertainment from 2005 to 2007 and chairman, Skill Council of Media and Entertainment under the Ministry of Skill Development, Government of India, from 2019 to 2022 where he initiated a unique public movement called Vidyaadan, a Guru-Shishya platform for sharing knowledge and experiences.

Uday Bhatia is a film critic and journalist with *Mint Lounge* in Delhi. He is the author of the non-fiction book *Bullets Over Bombay: Satya and the Hindi Film Gangster*.

Varun Grover is a screenwriter (*Masaan*, *Sacred Games*, *Sandeep aur Pinky Faraar*), National Award–winning lyricist (*Gangs of Wasseypur*, *Dum Laga Ke Haisha*, *Ankhon Dekhi*, *Fan*, *Udta Punjab*), stand-up comedian, and writer (short-story collection *Paper Chor* and graphic novel *Biksu*) based in Mumbai. His debut short film *Kiss* (2022) has travelled to more than twenty film festivals and has won multiple awards. His debut feature film *All India Rank* released in early 2024.

Vinod Krishnan is a technology manager by profession and a quizzer by heart, both pursuits he has been following for over thirty years. He is an avid and eclectic reader and hopes to continue to retain much of what he reads! He works in Mumbai and commutes to Gurgaon a couple of times each month.

Vinta Nanda, former director, programming, at Zee Network, is the director of *#Shout* (2023), a documentary feature on feminism in India. She is the editor of *The Daily Eye*, an online media (www.thedailyeye.info). Vinta has produced, directed and written the long-running television series *Tara, Raahein, Raahat, Aur Phir Ek Din, Sansaar* and *Miilee* among others. Her critically acclaimed film, *White Noise* (2004), starring Rahul Bose and Koel Purie, screened at international film festivals including Karachi, Florence, Seattle and Pune. Her edutainment work includes the television serials *Sheila* and *Kasbah*, films *Anant*, *Aparajita*, and the documentary film *The Distant Thunder*. From 2013 to 2018, Vinta led The Third Eye program in partnership with Norman Lear Center's flagship program Hollywood Health and Society at USC Annenberg to build an edutainment model through intensive audience research for the Indian entertainment industry. It was funded by the Bill and Melinda Gates Foundation.

Presently, Vinta is working on a documentary film while writing her first book. She is a photographer, creates visual effects, motion graphics, and is a digital designer for theatre and film. In Nadira Zaheer Babbar's recent theatre production *Farida*, Vinta created the visual effects and graphics.

Vishal Bhardwaj is an Indian film director, screenwriter, producer, music composer and playback singer. He is known for his work in Hindi cinema, and is the recipient of eight National Film Awards and three prestigious international awards from the Cairo, Chicago and Rome Film Festival.

Acknowledgements

Nirupama Kotru

A wise man once told me that every book comes with its own destiny. I think that's true of any production, including a film. And just like a film cannot be made without the contributions of various departments, this anthology could not have been possible without the support of the following people, to whom I owe my gratitude:

To Soumitra Chatterjee, one of Shantanu's and my favourite actors, for acting as a catalyst in bringing this book to the world;

To Ajay Mago of Om Books and to Shantanu, my co-editor;

To Jai Arjun Singh and Vishal Bhardwaj for their unstinted support to the book from its inception to release;

To Gulzar sa'ab for his love, affection and patience;

To Ketan Mehta, Rajat Kapoor and Vidhu Vinod Chopra for always being there for me;

To Dr Mohan Agashe-ji, Subhash Ghai-ji for their valuable contributions to the book;

To Saeed Mirza sa'ab for his guidance;

To Balaji Vittal, Anirudha Bhattacharjee, Uday Bhatia, Avijit Ghosh, Yasser Usman and Yasir Abbasi for their precious suggestions;

To Sriram Raghavan and Varun Grover for making time for the book despite being busy with their own films;

To Raju Hirani and Shekhar Gupta-ji for their kind words and encouragement;

To all our contributors for their excellent essays, for being patient and for putting in the effort to redraft the essays until these were perfect;

To Jasbir Singh, manager, and Saba Sheikh, archivist, at the National Film Archive of India (NFAI), Pune, for helping me with my research and for granting me access to priceless film journals, magazines, posters and photographs from the seventies;

To Amitava Kumar for teaching me how to commit to writing and for delivering his essay in record time;

To my batchmates and friends from the civil services, school, college and university for always having my back;

To Sanjoy Roy and Jaipur Literature Festival for giving the book a befitting launch;

To my darling sisters Shailja and Anupama, for being the most dependable encyclopaedia of Hindi films and film music I have ever known; and also to my film crazy/reliable fact-checker cousins;

And above all, to Gautam, my Rock of Gibraltar, permanent editor-in-residence and ruthless warrior against run-on sentences and split infinitives.

Gratitude to my beloved parents and elders in the family, and to the Almighty, for all their blessings.

In Gratitude

Shantanu Ray Chaudhuri

To Namita Gokhale, for planting the seed of this idea in my mind sometime after I lost my job at PRH, which in the event proved a blessing in disguise.

To Ajay Mago for enabling the publication of this book and coming up with a suitably colourful cover idea.

To all the contributors for their essays, some of them stalwarts of the film industry battling their own productions and commitments, for bearing with the delay from the time the project was initiated in 2022 to its completion in 2024, some with great grace and patience, others with more than a little consternation.

This book would not have been possible without Nirupama Kotru, my co-editor. Right from the time I bounced the idea off her, she has supported this wholeheartedly, sometime in the face of my delays and often going MIA.

To Shiv Pandey for designing the text layout and Sheena Agarwal for the cover. To the NFAI for images in the inserts.

To S.M.M Ausaja for being so generous with his images in the photo inserts. Bobby Sing, thank you for the images of *Sholay*'s vinyls and of the theatres.

To my friends Krishna Shastri Devulapalli and Neha Tiwari Bhattacharyya, for their support at crucial times when things looked bleak and depressing. To Soujannya Das for keeping my perspective young and helping me with a lot of stuff and for some lovely times in Kolkata.

To Sumit Dasgupta, Ramona Sen (for making me part of her many gastronomical explorations) and Reshmi Sengupta for encouraging me to write for *The Telegraph* and for much else – no words are enough; to Vinta Nanda for her support during the bleak lockdown years and for giving me a space to write in *The Daily Eye*. And to Gajra Kottary – how does one thank you…

And to my Guru Maa, for blessings that enable me to overcome all odds…